Eighteenth-Century English Literary Studies:

A Bibliography

by
Waldo Sumner Glock

The Scarecrow Press, Inc.

Metuchen, N.J., and London

1984

Library of Congress Cataloging in Publication Data

Glock, Waldo Sumner, 1925-
    Eighteenth century English literary studies.

    Includes index.
    1. English literature--18th century--History and
criticism--Bibliography. I. Title. II. Title: 18th
century English literary studies.
Z2012.G56 1984 [PR441]   016.82'09'005   83-20057
ISBN 0-8108-1658-X

In memory of my mother,

Betty Wellman Glock

Acknowledgments

It is always a pleasure to acknowledge the gifts of friendship and assistance that have made possible the accomplishment of a task otherwise less likely to be realized. Much of the research involved in compiling and annotating this bibliography was supported by three research grants from the Research Center of New Mexico State University, and they helped to obtain the valuable assistance of Shirley Baca and Elizabeth Scheidegger, who devoted the better part of two years to drawing up the preliminary list of titles and to annotating a considerable number of them. Without the services of Interlibrary Loan, and especially without the cheerful and meticulous assistance of Vita M. Orme and Holly S. Reynolds, the completion of the work would have been all but impossible: the majority of the material had to be obtained from other libraries, and their knowledge and determination in searching out hard-to-find journals and little-known books were indeed invaluable.

Equally invaluable have been the interest and encouragement of friends who have shared both actually and vicariously the many hours of pain and pleasure that such a project inevitably entails: Col. Fred J. Frank, Miss Lynn Moncus, Dr. Eugene R. Cunnar, and Bob W. Williams, M.D., always ready with words of comfort and advice, always eager to make the course of labor less arduous and difficult; and especially Sue Ann Williams, who, in an extraordinary display of friendly interest, typed a large portion of the manuscript and freely and generously offered many hours of her time to bring the book to completion.

And above all, my deepest gratitude goes to my father, Dr. Waldo S. Glock, Sr., who has offered encouragement and assistance whenever they have been most needed, and to my wife, Sharlene, whose constant and devoted work on the bibliography has been an inspiration in time of discouragement. This work might never have come to fruition without my wife's painstaking collaboration, constant willingness to help and advise, and love that smoothed over small irritations and large mistakes. My gratitude to her is immense.

Table of Contents

The purpose of this book is to provide the undergraduate and grad-
uate student and the scholar, in a handy and convenient form, a
comprehensive but not exhaustive survey of the critical literature
on the most important writers of the eighteenth century. Other bib-
liographies exist--The Year's Work in English Studies, the MLA In-
ternational Bibliography, the MHRA Annual Bibliography, and especially the annual issues of Philological Quarterly (1926-1975) and its
successors, sponsored by the American Society for Eighteenth-
Century Studies, which have been devoted exclusively to literature
written between 1660-1800--but in every case they are either unan-
notated or the listings are scattered throughout so many volumes as
to make the search for items on a particular work both tedious and
frustrating. If, for example, one wanted to determine what significant work had been done on The Rape of the Lock, one would be
compelled to examine between 50 and 60 volumes of several of the
bibliographical series--a labor that the present volume is intended
to alleviate. Obviously, given the enormous amount of critical and
historical scholarship on the eighteenth century that has been produced during the past half century, it would be impossible for one
volume to include all significant books and articles on all writers
and subjects of interest to scholars of the period. A person desiring to know all the available scholarship on a specific subject would
inevitably have to examine, not one bibliographical tool but several,
for no bibliography can garner successfully every relevant item per-
taining to a particular topic. The present bibliography, therefore,
aims at a more modest and achievable goal than that of complete-
ness. Instead, it aims at providing the student and scholar with a
volume that may possibly serve all of his needs--very rarely does
one require every bit of information on a subject--and only occasionally will prove insufficient to the point that it will be essential to
proceed on to, for instance, the Philological Quarterly volumes (now
known as The Eighteenth Century: A Current Bibliography). It is
hoped that the present volume, though not attempting to be all things
to all readers, will nevertheless be a serviceable tool by which a
user may gain easily and quickly an overview of the main criticism
that has been done on a particular author or work.

The intention has been to concentrate primarily but not exclusively on books and articles that emphasize critical or interpretive aspects of eighteenth-century literature, or whose historical
scholarship serves to illuminate the meaning or significance of a
work. Biographical material has generally been omitted, except

when a biography has achieved classic stature or includes critical comments on the author's works--it would seem impossible, for example, to omit George Sherburn's The Early Career of Alexander Pope (1934), a work that has yet to be superseded. Equally rigorous has been the decision to omit textual and bibliographical material, however essential that material might be for the student of the period: the exceptions again have to do with those works that seem to shed light on the meaning or interpretation of the literature, or that have achieved recognition as significant contributions to scholarship. The exceptions have been few. Not the least difficult aspect of the project has been the necessity of restricting the scope of the bibliography, of limiting the number of entries chiefly to the more extensive and substantial comments. In other words, very brief explications, letters to the editor, and abbreviated notes, in such journals as The Explicator, the Times Literary Supplement, and Notes and Queries, have been omitted. Their omission does not imply that they are considered insignificant or redundant, since obviously length cannot be an acceptable criterion of value; rather, it indicates that, generally speaking, the longer contribution has been deemed more useful to the student and scholar who are mainly interested in detailed criticism. For the same reason, unpublished dissertations have not been listed; their usefulness has not yet been tested by widespread circulation through publication. Within the limitations imposed by these exclusions, the items included are intended to represent the full range of scholarship and criticism that have appeared during the past fifty years, primarily among English-speaking peoples. Undoubtedly, any user of this bibliography will find omissions and lacunae that he will think indefensible, yet practical necessity as well as the reader's convenience dictates that kind of limitation.

A further limitation has been accomplished by including, again for the sake of the user's need, a list of General Works introductory to the period but without annotation; they are for the most part recognized authorities or works that may be useful as background material. Collected Studies, both for the period as a whole and for each individual author, are likewise not annotated under that heading, but relevant essays within those volumes have been annotated and listed under individual authors. Neither the list of General Works nor that of Collected Studies is intended to be complete--they merely suggest possible further sources of investigation. When an entry refers to more than one author, or to more than one work by the same author, it will be annotated under one heading only and reference will be made to that annotation by cross-referencing. Since the purpose of the bibliography is to provide information about the contents of various books and articles, and to suggest the range of possible material on a given topic, the annotations are seldom evaluative except by implication; they are intended to indicate, beyond the information contained in the title, the main subject of the work, the author's purpose, and usually the conclusions at which he arrives. Under each literary figure, the names of critics are listed alphabetically, but if there is more than one work by the same scholar for a particular topic, then the entries are arranged in reverse chronological order, from 1980 to 1925, so that the inquirer may locate instantly the most recent work by a critic on a piece of literature.

Like anthologies of poetry, whose compilers are always liable to the charge of omitting someone's favorite poem or author, this bibliography represents to a large extent one person's judgement as to which works are significant in the sense of making a worthwhile contribution to our knowledge or understanding of an author. The resulting compilation represents, therefore, a combination of received opinion and personal taste. To those who might criticize the omission of a particular work or author, or who might question the inclusion of an item as irrelevant or uncritical, one can only respond by remarking that, in spite of the limitations enumerated previously, the hope is that enough remains of value to serve the interest or use of a great variety of readers. Much material necessarily has been omitted; yet the conviction remains that few references have been neglected unintentionally.

AB	American Bookman
Antig. Rev.	Antigonish Review
ArielE	Ariel: A Review of International English Literature
AUMLA	Journal of the Australasian Universities Language and Literature Association
BA	Books Abroad
BJA	British Journal of Aesthetics
BJECS	British Journal for Eighteenth-Century Studies
BNYPL	Bulletin of the New York Public Library
BRH	Bulletin of Research in the Humanities
BSM	British Studies Monitor
BSUF	Ball State University Forum
BUSE	Boston University Studies in English
C & L	Christianity and Literature
CE	College English
CEA	CEA Critic: An Official Journal of the College English Association
Cent. Rev.	Centennial Review
CF	Classical Folia
CJIS	Canadian Journal of Irish Studies
CLAJ	College Language Association Journal
Clio	CLIO: An Interdisciplinary Journal of Literature, History, and the Philosophy of History
CLS	Comparative Literature Studies
Coll. L.	College Literature
Comp. Lit.	Comparative Literature
Conn. Rev.	Connecticut Review
Cont. Rev.	Contemporary Review
CP	Concerning Poetry
CQ	Cambridge Quarterly
CR	Critical Review
CRCL	Canadian Review of Comparative Literature
CREL	Cahiers Roumains d'Etudes Littéraires
Crit. Quart.	Critical Quarterly
DidS.	Diderot Studies
DR	Dalhousie Review
DUJ	Durham University Journal
DVLG	Deutsche Vierteljahrsschrift für Literatur-wissenschaft und Geistesgeschichte

E & S	Essays and Studies
EA	Etudes Anglaises: Grande-Bretagne, Etats-Unis
ECent.	The Eighteenth Century: Theory and Interpretation
ECLife	Eighteenth-Century Life
ECS	Eighteenth-Century Studies
EHR	English Historical Review
EIC	Essays in Criticism
ELH	English Literary History; formerly A Journal of ...
ELN	English Language Notes
ELS	English Literary Studies
ELWIU	Essays in Literature (Western Illinois University)
Eng. Misc.	English Miscellany: A Symposium of History, Literature and the Arts
Enl. E.	Enlightenment Essays
ES	English Studies: A Journal of English Language and Literature
ESA	English Studies in Africa: A Journal of the Humanities
ESC	English Studies in Canada
ESRS	Emporia State Research Studies
ETJ	Educational Theatre Journal
Explor.	Exploration (Normal, Illinois)
FMLS	Forum for Modern Language Studies
Fort. Rev.	Fortnightly Review
FR	French Review
GRM	Germanisch-romanische Monatsschrift, Neue Folge
GyS	Gypsy Scholar
HAB	The Humanities Association Review; formerly Humanities Association Bulletin (Canada)
HLB	Harvard Library Bulletin
HLQ	Huntington Library Quarterly
HR	Hudson Review
HSL	Hartford Studies in Literature
HumLov	Humanistica Lovaniensia
HUSL	Hebrew University Studies in Literature
I & L	Ideologies and Literature
JEGP	Journal of English and Germanic Philology
JEn	Journal of English (Sana'a University)
JFI	Journal of the Folklore Institute
JHI	Journal of the History of Ideas
JNT	Journal of Narrative Technique
JRUL	Journal of the Rutgers University Libraries
JWCI	Journal of the Warburg and Courtauld Institute
JWSL	Journal of Women's Studies in Literature
KPAB	Kentucky Philological Association Bulletin
KR	Kenyon Review

L & H	Literature and History
L & P	Literature and Psychology
LJHum.	Lamar Journal of the Humanities
McNR	McNeese Review
MCR	Melbourne Critical Review
Mich. A.	Michigan Academician: Papers of the Michigan Academy of Science, Arts, and Letters
ML	Modern Languages: Journal of the Modern Language Association (London)
MLN	Modern Language Notes
MLQ	Modern Language Quarterly
MLR	Modern Language Review
MLS	Modern Language Studies
MP	Modern Philology
N & Q	Notes and Queries
NDEJ	Notre Dame English Journal
NR	The Nassau Review
NRP	Nueva Revista del Pacífico
OL	Orbis Litterarum
PAPA	Publications of the Arkansas Philological Association
PBSA	Papers of the Bibliographical Society of America
PLL	Papers on Language and Literature
PMASAL	Papers of the Michigan Academy of Science, Arts and Letters
PMLA	Publications of the Modern Language Association of America
PMPA	Publications of the Missouri Philological Association
PQ	Philological Quarterly
PR	Partisan Review
Psycul R	Psychocultural Review
PTL	PTL: A Journal for Descriptive Poetics and Theory
PUASAL	Proceedings of the Utah Academy of Sciences, Arts, & Letters
PVR	Platte Valley Review
RBPH	Revue Belge de Philologie et d'Histoire
REL	Review of English Literature
RES	Review of English Studies
RMMLA Bull.	Rocky Mountain Modern Language Association Bulletin
RMS	Renaissance & Modern Studies
SAB	South Atlantic Bulletin
SAQ	South Atlantic Quarterly
SB	Studies in Bibliography
SBHT	Studies in Burke and His Time
SCB	South Central Bulletin
ScLJ	Scottish Literary Journal
S. C. Rev.	South Carolina Review
SECOLB	The SECOL Bulletin

SEL	Studies in English Literature
SHR	Southern Humanities Review
SIR	Studies in Romanticism
SNL	Satire Newsletter
SoQ	The Southern Quarterly
SP	Studies in Philology
SR	Sewanee Review
SSEng.	Sidney Studies in English
SSL	Studies in Scottish Literature
StHum	Studies in the Humanities
Std. in Lit. Imag.	Studies in the Literary Imagination
SVEC	Studies on Voltaire and the Eighteenth Century
TLS	Times Literary Supplement (London)
TSE	TSE: Tulane Studies in English
TSL	Tennessee Studies in Literature
TSLL	Texas Studies in Literature and Language
UDR	University of Dayton Review
UES	Unisa English Studies
UFMH	University of Florida Monographs, Humanities Series
UKCR	University of Kansas City Review
Univ. Rev.	University Review
UTQ	University of Toronto Quarterly
VQR	Virginia Quarterly Review
W & L	Women and Literature
WHR	Western Humanities Review
WTW	Writers and Their Works (published by the British Council)
W. Va. Univ. Phil. Papers	West Virginia University Philological Papers
XUS	Xavier University Studies
YES	Yearbook of English Studies
YR	Yale Review
ZAA	Zeitschrift für Anglistik und Amerikanistik (Leipzig, E. Germany)

COLLECTED STUDIES

1   ANDERSON, HOWARD, PHILIP B. DAGHLIAN, and IRVIN
EHRENPREIS, eds.
The Familiar Letter in the Eighteenth Century.   Lawrence:
Univ. Kansas Press, 1966.

2   ANDERSON, HOWARD and JOHN S. SHEA, eds.
Studies in Criticism and Aesthetics, 1660-1800: Essays in
Honor of Samuel Holt Monk. Minneapolis: Univ. Minn. Press,
1967.

3   BACKSHEIDER, PAULA, ed.
Probability, Time, and Space in Eighteenth-Century Literature.
New York: AMS, 1979.

4   BENTLEY, G(erald) E., JR., ed.
Editing Eighteenth Century Novels (Papers on Fielding, Lesage,
Richardson, Sterne and Smollett Given at the Conference on
Editorial Problems, Univ. Toronto, Nov. 1973). Toronto:
Hakkert, 1975.

5   BOND, DONOVAN H. and W. REYNOLDS McLEOD, eds.
Newsletters to Newspapers: Eighteenth-Century Journalism.
(Papers Presented at a Bicentennial Symposium at West Vir-
ginia Univ., Mar. 31-Apr. 2, 1976). Morgantown, W. Va.:
West Va. Univ. School of Journalism, 1977.

6   BOND, W. H., ed.
Eighteenth-Century Studies in Honor of Donald F. Hyde.
New York: Grolier Club, 1970.

7   BOYS, RICHARD C., ed.
Studies in the Literature of the Augustan Age: Essays Collected in Honor of Arthur Ellicott Case. Ann Arbor: George
Wahr Publishing Co. for the Augustan Reprint Society, 1952;
rpt. New York: Gordian Press, 1966.

8   BRISSENDEN, R. F. and J. C. EADE.
Studies in the Eighteenth Century III: Papers Presented at the
Third David Nichol Smith Memorial Seminar, Canberra, 1973.
Toronto: Univ. Toronto Press, 1976.

9   BRISSENDEN, R. F., ed.

Studies in the Eighteenth Century II: Papers presented at the Second David Nichol Smith Memorial Seminar, Canberra, 1970. Toronto: Univ. Toronto Press, 1973.

10   Studies in the Eighteenth Century I: Papers presented at the David Nichol Smith Memorial Seminar, Canberra, 1966. Canberra: Australian National Univ. Press, 1968.

11   BROWER, REUBEN A. and RICHARD POIRIER, eds. In Defense of Reading: A Reader's Approach to Literary Criticism. New York: Dutton, 1962.

12   BUTT, JOHN, ed. Of Books and Humankind: Essays and Poems Presented to Bonamy Dobrée. London: Routledge & Kegan Paul, 1964.

13   CAMDEN, CARROLL, ed. Restoration and Eighteenth-Century Literature: Essays in Honor of Alan Dugald McKillop. Chicago: Univ. Chicago Press, 1963.

14   CARLSON, LELAND H. and RONALD PAULSON, eds. English Satire: Papers Read at a Clark Library Seminar, January 15, 1972. Los Angeles: William Andrews Clark Memorial Library, U. C. L. A., 1972.

15   CHAMPION, LARRY S., ed. Quick Springs of Sense: Studies in the Eighteenth Century. Athens: Univ. Georgia Press, 1974.

16   CHESNUTT, MICHAEL, CLAUS FAERCH, TORBEN THRANE, and GRAHAM D. CAIE, eds. Essays Presented to Knud Schibsbye on His 75th Birthday, 29 Nov. 1979. (Pubs. of Dept. of English, Univ. of Copenhagen 8). Copenhagen: Akademisk, 1979.

17   CLIFFORD, JAMES L. and LOUIS A. LANDA, eds. Pope and His Contemporaries: Essays Presented to George Sherburn. Oxford: Clarendon Press, 1949.

18   CLIFFORD, JAMES L., ed. Eighteenth-Century English Literature: Modern Essays in Criticism. New York: Oxford Univ. Press, 1959.

19   DAGHLIAN, PHILIP B., ed. Essays in Eighteenth-Century Biography. Bloomington: Indiana Univ. Press, 1968.

20   DAVIES, HUGH SYKES and GEORGE WATSON, eds. The English Mind: Studies in the British Moralists Presented to Basil Willey. Cambridge: Cambridge Univ. Press, 1964.

21   DUCROCQ, JEAN, SUZY HALIMI, and MAURICE LEVY, eds.

Roman et société en Angleterre au XVIIIe siècle. Paris: Presses Univ. de France, 1978.

22   FRITZ, PAUL and DAVID WILLIAMS, eds.
      City and Society in the Eighteenth Century. Publication of the McMaster University Association for 18th-Century Studies, Vol. III. Toronto: A.M. Hakkert, Ltd., 1973.

23   The Triumph of Culture: Eighteenth Century Perspectives.
      Toronto: A.M. Hakkert, Ltd., 1972.

24   GAY, PETER, ed.
      Eighteenth-Century Studies Presented to Arthur M. Wilson.
      Hanover, N.H.: The Univ. Press of New England, 1972.

25   HIBBARD, GEORGE R., ed.
      Renaissance and Modern Essays Presented to Vivian de Sola Pinto. London: Routledge & Kegan Paul, 1966.

26   HILLES, FREDERICK W. and HAROLD BLOOM, eds.
      From Sensibility to Romanticism: Essays Presented to Frederick A. Pottle. New York: Oxford Univ. Press, 1965.

27   HILLES, FREDERICK W., ed.
      The Age of Johnson: Essays Presented to Chauncey Brewster Tinker. New Haven: Yale Univ. Press, 1949.

28   HILSON, J. C., M. M. B. JONES, and J. R. WATSON, eds.
      Augustan Worlds: New Essays in Eighteenth-Century Literature.
      New York: Barnes & Noble, 1978.

29   HUGHES, PETER and DAVID WILLIAMS, eds.
      The Varied Pattern: Studies in the 18th Century. Toronto: A.M. Hakkert, Ltd., 1971.

30   JENSEN, H. JAMES and MALVIN R. ZIRKER, JR., eds.
      The Satirist's Art. Bloomington: Indiana Univ. Press, 1972.

31   JONES, RICHARD FOSTER and Others Writing in His Honor.
      The Seventeenth Century: Studies in the History of English Thought and Literature from Bacon to Pope. Stanford, Calif.: Stanford Univ. Press, 1951.

32   KAY, DONALD, ed.
      A Provision of Human Nature: Essays on Fielding and Others in Honor of Miriam Austin Locke. University, Ala.: Univ. Alabama Press, 1977.

33   KORSHIN, PAUL J., ed.
      Studies in Change and Revolution: Aspects of English Intellectual History, 1640-1800. Menston, Yorkshire: Scolar Press, 1972.

34 Proceedings of the Modern Language Association Neoclassicism
    Conferences 1967-1968. New York: MLA, 1970.

35 MACDONALD, A. A. , P. A. FLAHERTY, and G. M. STORY,
    eds.
    A Festschrift for Edgar Ronald Seary: Essays in English
    Language and Literature Presented by Colleagues and Former
    Students. St. Johns: Memorial Univ. of Newfoundland, 1975.

36 MACK, MAYNARD and IAN GREGOR, eds.
    Imagined Worlds: Essays on Some English Novels and Novel-
    ists in Honour of John Butt. London: Methuen, 1968.

37 MacLURE, MILLAR and F. W. WATT, eds.
    Essays in English Literature from the Renaissance to the
    Victorian Age Presented to A. S. P. Woodhouse. Toronto:
    Univ. Toronto Press, 1964.

38 MARTZ, LOUIS L. and AUBREY WILLIAMS, eds.
    The Author in His Work: Essays on a Problem in Criticism.
    New Haven: Yale Univ. Press, 1978.

39 MAZZEO, J. A. , ed.
    Reason and the Imagination: Studies in the History of Ideas,
    1600-1800. New York: Columbia Univ. Press, 1962.

40 MIDDENDORF, JOHN H. , ed.
    English Writers of the Eighteenth Century: Essays in Honor
    of James Lowry Clifford Presented by His Students. New
    York: Columbia Univ. Press, 1971.

41 MILIC, LOUIS T. , ed.
    The Modernity of the Eighteenth Century. Studies in Eighteenth-
    Century Culture, Vol. I. Cleveland, Ohio: Case Western
    Reserve Univ. Press, 1971.

42 MILLER, HENRY K. , ERIC ROTHSTEIN, and G. S. ROUS-
    SEAU, eds.
    The Augustan Milieu: Essays Presented to Louis A. Landa.
    Oxford: Clarendon Press, 1970.

43 MINER, EARL, ed.
    Stuart and Georgian Moments: Clark Library Seminar Papers
    on Seventeenth- and Eighteenth-Century English Literature.
    Berkeley: Univ. Calif. Press, 1972.

44 NOVAK, MAXIMILLIAN E. , ed.
    English Literature in the Age of Disguise. Berkeley: Univ.
    Calif. Press, 1977.

45 PAGLIARO, HAROLD, ed.
    Racism in the Eighteenth Century (Studies in Eighteenth-Century
    Culture, Vol. III). Cleveland, Ohio: Case Western
    Univ. Press, 1973.

46   Irrationalism in the Eighteenth Century (Studies in Eighteenth-
        Century Culture, Vol. II). Cleveland, Ohio: Case Western
        Reserve Univ. Press, 1972.

47   PATTERSON, DANIEL W. and ALBRECHT B. STRAUSS, eds.
        Essays in English Literature of the Classical Period Pre-
        sented to Dougald Macmillan. Chapel Hill: Univ. N. C.
        Press, 1967.

48   PAULSON, RONALD, ed.
        Satire: Modern Essays in Criticism.   Englewood Cliffs, N. J. :
        Prentice-Hall, 1971.

49   ROGERS, PAT, ed.
        The Eighteenth Century (Context of English Literature).   New
        York: Holmes & Meier, 1978.

50   ROSBOTTOM, RONALD C. , ed.
        Studies in Eighteenth-Century Culture, Vol. VI.   Madison:
        Univ. Wisc. Press, 1977.

51   RUNTE, ROSEANN, ed.
        Studies in Eighteenth-Century Culture, Vol. VII.   Madison:
        Univ. Wisc. Press, 1978.

52   SCHILLING, BERNARD, N. , ed.
        Essential Articles: For the Study of English Augustan Back-
        grounds.   Hamden, Conn. : Archon Books, 1961.

53   SPECTOR, ROBERT D. , ed.
        Essays on the Eighteenth-Century Novel.   Bloomington: In-
        diana Univ. Press, 1965.

54   SUTHERLAND, JAMES R. and F. P. WILSON, eds.
        Essays on the Eighteenth Century Presented to David Nichol
        Smith in Honour of His Seventieth Birthday.   Oxford: Claren-
        don Press, 1945.

55   SWEDENBERG, H. T. , JR. , ed.
        England in the Restoration and Early Eighteenth Century:
        Essays on Culture and Society.   Berkeley: Univ. Calif.
        Press, 1972.

56   WASSERMAN, EARL R. , ed.
        Aspects of the Eighteenth Century.   Baltimore: Johns Hop-
        kins Press, 1965.

57   WATT, IAN, ed.
        The Augustan Age: Approaches to its Literature, Life, and
        Thought.   Greenwich, Conn. : Fawcett Premier Books, 1968.

58   WELLEK, RENE and ALVARO RIBEIRO, eds.
        Evidence in Literary Scholarship: Essays in Memory of James
        Marshall Osborn.   Oxford: Clarendon Press, 1979.

59   WILLIAMS, KATHLEEN, ed.
        Backgrounds to Eighteenth-Century Literature.   Scranton,
        Pa.: Chandler Publ. Co., 1971.

60   ABRAMS, M. H.
      The Mirror and the Lamp: Romantic Theory and the Critical
      Tradition.   London: Oxford Univ. Press, 1953; New York:
      Norton, 1958.

61   ADAMS, PERCY G.
      Graces of Harmony: Alliteration, Assonance, and Consonance
      in Eighteenth-Century Poetry.   Athens: Univ. Georgia Press,
      1977.

62   ALLEN, B. SPRAGUE.
      Tides in English Taste (1619-1800): A Background for the
      Study of Literature.   2 Vols. Cambridge: Harvard Univ.
      Press, 1937; New York: Pageant Books, 1958.

63   ARTHOS, JOHN.
      The Language of Natural Description in Eighteenth-Century
      Poetry.   (Univ. Michigan publications in Language & Litera-
      ture Series, Vol. 24).   Ann Arbor: Univ. Mich. Press,
      1949; rpt. 1966.

64   AUTY, SUSAN G.
      The Comic Spirit of Eighteenth-Century Novels.   Port Washing-
      ton, N. Y. : Kennikat Press, 1975.

65   BAKER, SHERIDAN.
      "The Idea of Romance in the Eighteenth-Century Novel. "
      PMASAL 49 (1964): 507-522.

66   BATE, WALTER J.
      From Classic to Romantic.   Cambridge: Harvard Univ. Press,
      1946.

67   BATTEN, CHARLES L. , JR.
      Pleasurable Instruction: Form and Convention in Eighteenth-
      Century Travel Literature.   Berkeley: Univ. Calif. Press,
      1978.

68   BATTESTIN, MARTIN C.
      The Providence of Wit: Aspects of Form in Augustan Litera-
      ture and the Arts.   Oxford: Clarendon Press, 1974.

69   BECKER, CARL L.
      The Heavenly City of the Eighteenth-Century Philosophers.
      New Haven: Yale Univ. Press, 1932.

70   BLOM, T. E.
      "Eighteenth-Century Reflexive Process Poetry." ECS 10
      (1976): 52-72.

71   BOND, DONALD F.
      "The Neo-Classical Psychology of the Imagination." ELH 4
      (1937): 245-264.

72   BRAUDY, LEO.
      "The Form of the Sentimental Novel." Novel 7 (1973): 5-13.

73   BREDVOLD, LOUIS I.
      The Natural History of Sensibility. Detroit: Wayne State
      Univ. Press, 1962.

74   "The Literature of the Restoration and the Eighteenth Cen-
      tury." In A History of English Literature, ed. H. Craig.
      New York: Oxford Univ. Press, 1950.

75   "A Note in Defense of Satire." ELH 7 (1940): 253-264.
      Rpt. in [7], pp. 2-12.

76   BRONSON, BERTRAND H.
      Facets of the Enlightenment: Studies in English Literature
      and Its Contexts. Berkeley & Los Angeles: Univ. Calif.
      Press, 1968.

77   "When was Neoclassicism?" In [2], pp. 13-35. Rpt. in
      above, pp. 1-25; [59], pp. 42-67.

78   "The Pre-Romantic or Post-Augustan Mode." ELH 20 (1953):
      15-28. Rpt. in [76], pp. 159-172.

79   "Personification Reconsidered." ELH 14 (1947): 163-177.
      Rpt. in [76], pp. 119-152; [1463], pp. 189-231.

80   BROWN, LAURA S.
      "Drama and Novel in Eighteenth-Century England." Genre
      13 (1980): 287-304.

81   BROWN, WALLACE C.
      The Triumph of Form. Chapel Hill, N. C.: Univ. N. C.
      Press, 1948.

82   BUTT, JOHN.
      "Science and Man in Eighteenth-Century Poetry." DUJ 39
      (1947): 79-88. Rpt. in [1907], pp. 91-110.

83   The Augustan Age. London: Hutchinson Univ. Library,
      1950.

84   BYRD, MAX.
      London Transformed: Images of the City in the Eighteenth
      Century. New Haven: Yale Univ. Press, 1978.

85 CARNOCHAN, W. B.
Confinement and Flight: An Essay on English Literature of the Eighteenth Century. Berkeley: Univ. Calif. Press, 1976.

86 CASSIRER, ERNST.
The Philosophy of the Enlightenment. Trans. F. C. A. Koelln and J. P. Pettegrove. Princeton, N. J.: Princeton Univ. Press, 1951.

87 CHALKER, JOHN.
The English Georgic: A Study in the Development of a Form. London: Routledge & Kegan Paul; Baltimore: Johns Hopkins Press, 1969.

88 CHAPIN, CHESTER F.
Personification in Eighteenth-Century English Poetry. New York: Columbia Univ. Press; London: Oxford Univ. Press, 1955. Rpt. New York: Octagon Books, 1968.

89 CLARK, KENNETH.
The Gothic Revival, an Essay in the History of Taste. London: John Murray, 1928.

90 COHEN, MURRAY.
"Eighteenth-Century English Literature and Modern Critical Methodologies." ECent. 20 (1979): 5-23.

91 COHEN, RALPH.
"The Augustan Mode in English Poetry." ECS 1 (1967): 3-32. Rpt. in [10], pp. 171-192.

92 CONGLETON, J. E.
Theories of Pastoral Poetry in England, 1684-1798. Gainesville, Fla.: Univ. Fla. Press, 1952.

93 COX, STEPHEN D.
"The Stranger Within Thee": Concepts of the Self in Late-Eighteenth-Century Literature. Pittsburgh: Univ. Pittsburgh Press, 1980.

94 CRANE, RONALD S.
"Suggestions toward a Genealogy of 'The Man of Feeling.'" ELH 1 (1934): 205-230. Rpt. in The Idea of the Humanities (Chicago: Univ. of Chicago Press, 1967), I, pp. 188-213; in [7], pp. 62-87; in [59], pp. 322-349.

95 DEANE, CECIL V.
Aspects of Eighteenth Century Nature Poetry. Oxford: Blackwell, 1935; rpt. London: Frank Cass, 1967.

96 DOBREE, BONAMY.
English Literature in the Early Eighteenth Century, 1700-1740. The Oxford History of English Literature, Vol. 7. Oxford: Clarendon Press, 1959.

97   DUNCAN, JEFFREY L.
     "The Rural Ideal in Eighteenth Century Fiction." SEL 8
     (1968): 517-535.

98   DUSSINGER, JOHN A.
     The Discourse of the Mind in Eighteenth-Century Fiction
     (Studies in English Literature). The Hague: Mouton, 1974.

99   EHRENPREIS, IRVIN.
     Acts of Implication: Suggestion and Covert Meaning in the
     Works of Dryden, Swift, Pope, and Austen. Berkeley: Univ.
     Calif. Press, 1980.

100 ELTON, OLIVER.
     A Survey of English Literature, 1730-1780. 2 Vols. London:
     Edward Arnold & Co., 1928.

101 ERSKINE-HILL, HOWARD.
     "Augustans on Augustanism: England, 1655-1759." RMS 11
     (1967): 55-83.

102 FEINGOLD, RICHARD.
     Nature and Society: Later Eighteenth-Century Uses of the
     Pastoral and Georgic. New Brunswick, N.J.: Rutgers Univ.
     Press, 1978.

103 FRYE, NORTHROP.
     "Towards Defining an Age of Sensibility." ELH 23 (1956):
     144-152. Rpt. [59], pp. 312-321.

104 FUSSELL, PAUL.
     The Rhetorical World of Augustan Humanism: Ethics and
     Imagery from Swift to Burke. Oxford: Clarendon Press;
     New York: Oxford Univ. Press, 1965.

105 GAY, PETER.
     The Enlightenment: an Interpretation. Vol. I: The Rise of
     Modern Paganism (1966), Vol. II: The Science of Freedom.
     New York: Alfred A. Knopf, 1969.

106 GOLDGAR, BERTRAND A.
     Walpole and the Wits: The Relation of Politics to Literature,
     1722-1742. Lincoln: Univ. Nebr. Press, 1976.

107 GOLDSTEIN, LAURENCE.
     Ruins and Empire: The Evolution of a Theme in Augustan
     and Romantic Literature. Pittsburgh: Univ. Pittsburgh
     Press, 1977.

108 GREENE, DONALD J.
     "Latitudinarianism and Sensibility: the Genealogy of the 'Man
     of Feeling' Reconsidered." MP 75 (1977): 159-183.

109   The Age of Exuberance: Backgrounds to Eighteenth-Century
       English Literature. New York: Random House, 1970.

110   " 'Logical Structure' in Eighteenth-Century English Poetry. "
       PQ 31 (1952): 315-336.

111   HAGSTRUM, JEAN H.
       Sex and Sensibility: Ideal and Erotic Love from Milton to
       Mozart. Chicago: Univ. Chicago Press, 1980.

112   The Sister Arts: The Tradition of Literary Pictorialism and
       English Poetry from Dryden to Gray. Chicago: Univ. Chi-
       cago Press, 1958.

113   HALSBAND, ROBERT.
       "Women and Literature in 18th Century England. " In Woman
       in the 18th Century and Other Essays, Paul Fritz and Richard
       Morton, eds. (Toronto & Sarasota: Hakkert, 1976), pp. 55-
       71.

114   HAVENS, RAYMOND D.
       The Influence of Milton on English Poetry. Cambridge:
       Harvard Univ. Press, 1922; rpt. New York: Russell & Rus-
       sell, 1961.

115   HEIMANN, P. M.
       "Voluntarism and Immanence: Conceptions of Nature in
       Eighteenth-Century Thought. " JHI 39 (1978): 271-283.

116   HIPPLE, WALTER J. , JR.
       The Beautiful, the Sublime, and the Picturesque in Eighteenth
       Century British Aesthetic Theory. Carbondale: Univ. So.
       Ill. Press, 1957.

117   HOLUB, ROBERT C.
       "The Rise of Aesthetics in the Eighteenth Century. " CLS
       15 (1978): 271-283.

118   HORSLEY, L. S.
       "Rogues or Honest Gentlemen: The Public Characters of
       Queen Anne Journalists. " TSLL 18 (1976): 198-228.

119   HUGHES, PETER.
       "Allusion and Expression in Eighteenth-Century Literature. "
       In [38], pp. 297-317.

120   HUMPHREYS, A. R.
       The Augustan World: Life and Letters in Eighteenth–Century
       England. London: Methuen, 1954. Rpt. New York: Harper
       & Bros. , 1963.

121   HUNT, JOHN DIXON.
       The Figure in the Landscape: Poetry, Painting, and Garden-

ing during the Eighteenth Century.   Baltimore: Johns Hopkins
Univ. Press, 1976.

122   HUNTER, J. PAUL.
      "Biography and the Novel."   MLS 9, iii (1979):   68-84.

123   JACK, IAN.
      Augustan Satire: Intention and Idiom in English Poetry, 1660-
      1750.   Oxford: Clarendon Press, 1952.

124   JOHNSON, JAMES WILLIAM.
      The Formation of Neo-Classical Thought.   Princeton, N.J.:
      Princeton Univ. Press, 1967.

125   JONES, WILLIAM POWELL.
      The Rhetoric of Science: A Study of Scientific Ideas and
      Imagery in Eighteenth-Century Poetry.   London: Routledge
      & Kegan Paul; Los Angeles: Univ. Calif. Press, 1966.

126   KARL, FREDERICK R.
      The Adversary in Literature: The English Novel in the
      Eighteenth Century: A Study in Genre.   New York: Farrar,
      Straus & Giroux, 1974.

127   KORSHIN, PAUL J.
      "Probability and Character in the Eighteenth Century."   In
      [3], pp. 63-78.

128   KROPF, C. R.
      "Unity and the Study of Eighteenth-Century Literature."
      ECent.   21 (1980):   25-40.

129   LANDA, LOUIS A.
      Essays in Eighteenth-Century English Literature.   Princeton,
      N.J.:   Princeton Univ. Press, 1981.

130   LOVEJOY, ARTHUR O.
      The Great Chain of Being: A Study of the History of an Idea.
      Cambridge: Harvard Univ. Press, 1936.

131   LUCAS, F. L.
      The Search for Good Sense: Four Eighteenth-Century Char-
      acters.   New York: Macmillan; London: Cassell & Co.,
      Ltd., 1958.

132   LYONS, JOHN O.
      The Invention of the Self: The Hinge of Consciousness in the
      Eighteenth Century.   Carbondale: So. Ill. Univ. Press; Lon-
      don: Feffer & Simons, 1978.

133   McCULLOUGH, BRUCE.
      Representative English Novelists: Defoe to Conrad.   New
      York: Harper & Bros., 1946.

134   McKILLOP, ALAN DUGALD.
       The Early Masters of English Fiction.   Lawrence: Univ.
       Kansas Press, 1956.

135   MALINS, EDWARD.
       English Landscaping and Literature, 1660-1840.   London:
       Oxford Univ. Press, 1966.

136   MANLOVE, C. N.
       Literature and Reality 1600-1800.   New York: St. Martin's
       Press, 1978.

137   MARESCA, THOMAS E.
       Epic to Novel.   Columbus: Ohio State Univ. Press, 1974.

138   MILLER, NANCY K.
       "Novels of Innocence: Fictions of Loss."   ECS 11 (1978):
       325-339.

139   MONK, SAMUEL H.
       The Sublime: A Study of Critical Theories in XVIII-Century
       England.   New York: Modern Lang. Assoc. , 1935; 2nd. ed.
       Ann Arbor: Univ. Mich. Press, 1960.

140   MOORE, ROBERT E.
       Hogarth's Literary Relationships.   Minneapolis: Univ. Minn.
       Press, 1948.

141   NICHOL SMITH, DAVID.
       Some Observations on Eighteenth-Century Poetry.   London:
       Oxford Univ. Press, 1st. ed. , 1937; 2nd. ed. , 1964.

142   NICOLSON, MARJORIE.
       Mountain Gloom and Mountain Glory: The Development of
       the Aesthetics of the Infinite.   Ithaca: Cornell Univ. Press,
       1959.

143   Newton Demands the Muse: Newton's "Opticks" and the
       Eighteenth-Century Poets.   Princeton, N. J. : Princeton Univ.
       Press, 1946.

144   NOVAK, MAXIMILLIAN E.
       "The Extended Moment: Time, Dream, History, and Per-
       spective in Eighteenth-Century Fiction." In [3], pp. 141-166.

145   PAULSON, RONALD.
       Popular and Polite Art in the Age of Hogarth and Fielding.
       Notre Dame, Univ. Notre Dame Press, 1979.

146   Satire and the Novel in Eighteenth-Century England.   New
       Haven: Yale Univ. Press, 1967.

147   The Fictions of Satire.   Baltimore: Johns Hopkins Univ.
       Press, 1967.

148   PERRY, RUTH.
      Women, Letters, and the Novel (AMS Studies in the 18th
      Century 4). New York: AMS, 1980.

149   PIPER, WILLIAM BOWMAN.
      "Common Sense as a Basis of Literary Style." TSLL 18
      (1976): 624-641.

150   The Heroic Couplet. Cleveland, Ohio: Case Western Re-
      serve Univ. Press, 1969.

151   PRESTON, JOHN.
      The Created Self: The Reader's Role in Eighteenth-Century
      Fiction. London: Heinemann; New York: Barnes & Noble,
      1970.

152   PRESTON, THOMAS R.
      Not in Timon's Manner: Feeling, Misanthropy, and Satire
      in Eighteenth-Century England. University, Ala.: Univ. Ala.
      Press, 1975.

153   PRICE, MARTIN.
      To the Palace of Wisdom: Studies in Order and Energy from
      Dryden to Blake. Garden City, N.Y.: Doubleday, 1964.

154   REID, B. L.
      The Long Boy and Others. Athens: Univ. Georgia Press,
      1969.

155   RICHETTI, JOHN J.
      "The Portrayal of Women in Restoration and Eighteenth-
      Century English Literature." In What Manner of Woman:
      Essays on English and American Life and Literature, ed.
      Marlene Springer (New York: New York Univ. Press, 1977),
      pp. 65-97.

156   Popular Fiction before Richardson: Narrative Patterns 1700-
      1739. Oxford: Clarendon Press, 1969.

157   ROGERS, PAT.
      The Augustan Vision. London: Weidenfeld and Nicolson,
      1974.

158   SEIDEL, MICHAEL.
      Satiric Inheritance: Rabelais to Sterne. Princeton, N.J.:
      Princeton Univ. Press, 1979.

159   SELDEN, RAMAN.
      English Verse Satire 1590-1765. London: George Allen &
      Unwin, 1978.

160   SHERBO, ARTHUR.
      Studies in the Eighteenth-Century Novel. East Lansing:
      Mich. State Univ. Press, 1969.

161   SHERBURN, GEORGE.
      "The Restoration and Eighteenth Century (1660-1789)." In
      A Literary History of England, Vol. 3, ed. Albert C. Baugh
      (New York: Appleton-Century-Crofts, 1948; 2nd. ed. rev.
      Donald F. Bond, 1967).

162   SHERWOOD, IRMA Z.
      "The Novelists as Commentators." In [27], pp. 113-125.

163   SHROFF, HOMAI J.
      The Eighteenth Century Novel: The Idea of the Gentleman.
      Atlantic Highlands, N.J.: Humanities Press Inc., 1978.

164   SITTER, JOHN E.
      "Mother, Memory, Muse and Poetry after Pope." ELH 44
      (1977): 312-336.

165   SKILTON, DAVID.
      The English Novel: Defoe to the Victorians. Newton Abbott:
      David & Charles; New York: Barnes & Noble, 1977.

166   SPACKS, PATRICIA MEYER.
      Imagining A Self: Autobiography and Novel in Eighteenth-
      Century England. Cambridge: Harvard Univ. Press, 1976.

167   The Poetry of Vision: Five Eighteenth-Century Poets. Cam-
      bridge: Harvard Univ. Press, 1967.

168   STAUFFER, DONALD A.
      The Art of Biography in Eighteenth-Century England. 2 Vols.
      Princeton, N.J.: Princeton Univ. Press, 1941.

169   STEEVES, HARRISON R.
      Before Jane Austen: The Shaping of the English Novel in the
      Eighteenth Century. New York: Holt, Rinehart & Winston,
      1965.

170   STEPHEN, LESLIE.
      History of English Thought in the Eighteenth-Century. Lon-
      don: Smith, Elder, 1876; 3rd. ed. 1902 and subsequent re-
      prints.

171   SUTHERLAND, JAMES.
      English Literature of the Late Seventeenth Century. Vol.
      6 in Oxford History of English Literature, ed. Bonamy Dobrée
      & Norman Davis. Oxford: Clarendon Press, 1969.

172   A Preface to Eighteenth Century Poetry. Oxford: Clarendon
      Press, 1948; rpt. 1962.

173   SUTHERLAND, W. O. S., JR.
      The Art of the Satirist: Essays on the Satire of Augustan
      England. Austin: Humanities Research Center of Texas,
      1965.

174   TILLOTSON, GEOFFREY.
      Augustan Studies. London: Athlone Press, 1961.

175   Augustan Poetic Diction. London: Athlone Press, 1964;
      corrected reprint of Chaps. 1-4 of Augustan Studies, 1961.

176   TRICKETT, RACHEL.
      The Honest Muse: A Study in Augustan Verse. Oxford:
      Clarendon Press, 1967.

177   "The Augustan Pantheon." E & S 6 (1953): 71-86.

178   TROWBRIDGE, HOYT.
      From Dryden to Jane Austen: Essays on English Critics and
      Writers, 1660-1818. Albuquerque: Univ. N. M. Press, 1977.

179   TURBERVILLE, ARTHUR S.
      Johnson's England: An Account of the Life and Manners of
      His Age. 2 Vols. Oxford: Clarendon Press, 1933; rev. 1952.

180   UPHAUS, ROBERT W.
      The Impossible Observer: Reason and the Reader in 18th-
      Century Prose. Lexington: Univ. Ky. Press, 1979.

181   WASSERMAN, EARL R.
      "The Inherent Values of Eighteenth-Century Personification."
      PMLA 65 (1950): 435-463.

182   WATKINS, W. B. C.
      Perilous Balance: The Tragic Genius of Swift, Johnson, and
      Sterne. Princeton, N. J. : Princeton Univ. Press, 1939; rpt.
      Cambridge: Walker-de Berry, 1960.

183   WATT, IAN.
      The Rise of the Novel: Studies in Defoe, Richardson and
      Fielding. London: Chatto & Windus, 1957.

184   WEINBROT, HOWARD.
      Augustus Caesar in "Augustan" England: The Decline of the
      Classical Norm. Princeton, N. J. : Princeton Univ. Press,
      1978.

185   The Formal Strain: Studies in Augustan Imitation and Satire.
      Chicago & London: Univ. Chicago Press, 1969.

186   WELLEK, RENE.
      A History of Modern Criticism, 1750-1950. Vol. I: The
      Later Eighteenth Century. New Haven: Yale Univ. Press,
      1955.

187   WILLEY, BASIL.
      The Eighteenth-Century Background: Studies on the Idea of
      Nature in the Thought of the Period. London: Chatto &

Windus, 1940; New York: Columbia Univ. Press, 1941; rpt.
Harmondsworth: Penguin Books, 1962.

188   WIMSATT, W. K. , JR.
        Rhetoric and Poems: The Example of Pope. (English In-
        stitute Essays, 1948, ed. D. A. Robertson. New York:
        Columbia Univ. Press, 1949), pp. 179-207; rpt. in The Ver-
        bal Icon (Lexington, Ky. : Univ. Press of Ky. , 1954), pp.
        169-185.

Collected Studies

189   BLOOM, EDWARD A. and LILLIAN D. BLOOM.
Addison and Steele: The Critical Heritage. London: Routledge & Kegan Paul, 1980.

General Studies

190   ARAKELIAN, PAUL G.
"The Myth of a Restoration Style Shift." ECent. 20 (1979):
227-245.

Analyzes the grammatical style of Addison's de Coverley
Papers and Pope's "Preface to the Iliad" and compares them
with works by Thomas Browne, Isaac Newton, and Joseph
Glanvill to show the change in language "from the complacent
years before the Restoration, through turbulent years of challenge and change, to the self-conscious years after the Restoration."

191   BAKER, DONALD C.
"Witchcraft, Addison, and The Drummer." Studia Neophilologica 31 (1959): 174-181.

Examines The Drummer's intellectual milieu, analyzes its
purpose, and suggests that it is an excellent illustration of
literary theory being put into practice; describes the famous
Mompesson affair, which it is the purpose of the play to make
light of, and suggests that Addison used the opportunity to
present a common-sense and rational view of witchcraft without denying the supernatural.

192   BATTERSBY, JAMES L.
"Johnson and Shiels: Biographers of Addison." SEL 9 (1969):
521-537.

Examines Samuel Johnson's Prefaces and Robert Shiels's
biography of Addison in his Lives of the Poets (1753) to show

that Johnson was merely reclaiming his own material when
he borrowed from Shiels's biography.

193   BLOOM, EDWARD A. and LILLIAN D. BLOOM.
       Joseph Addison's Sociable Animal: In the Market-Place, On
       the Hustings, In the Pulpit.   Providence, R. I. : Brown Univ.
       Press, 1971.

       A study of Addison's thought as it relates to man as a
       "sociable animal"; attempts to argue that Addison was not
       merely an apologist and propagandist for the thought of his
       day, but also set out to judge it morally.   Suggests the range
       and extent of Addison's intellectual interests, particularly
       "In the Market Place," "On the Hustings," and "In the Pul-
       pit. "

194   "Addison on 'Moral Habits of the Mind. ' "   JHI 21 (1960):
       409-427.

       Argues that Addison sought to fuse man's rational and re-
       ligious faculties, to create a rational bond between intellect
       and belief; that, specifically, he wanted the individual to ac-
       quire "moral habits of the mind" out of which could arise a
       "code of rational-ethical behavior for all men. "   He postulates
       an intimate relationship between virtue and knowledge, arguing
       that virtue is essentially an intellectual quality capable of de-
       velopment through discipline and learning; therefore, Addison
       emphasized the importance of education.   The passions, further-
       more, are an acceptable part of the total man, if maintained
       under rational control: "The passions under reasonable con-
       trol were for Addison inseperable from virtue and knowledge,
       and with these faculties a means to 'project' the mind 'on
       its lone way. ' "

195   "Joseph Addison and Eighteenth-Century 'Liberalism. ' "   JHI
       12 (1951):   560-583.

       Addison, "a foremost governmental theorist in his day,"
       was influenced in his political thought by two groups of think-
       ers: those noted for their rational liberalism, the Stoics and
       their seventeenth-century followers, and those who shared
       popular Augustan beliefs molded by the Revolution of 1688 and
       the consequent threat of a Jacobite rebellion.   Addison's be-
       lief in human rights was based most substantially on the law
       of nature as the basic ingredient of civil government; these
       natural rights included those of equality and property, and
       the broader natural right to resist any form of tyranny.   The
       last right that Addison supported was the right to religious
       toleration, a right, though, that he was unprepared to extend

to Catholics. Concludes that the value of Addison's political
thought is largely one of synthesis, "the original arrangement
of acquired ideas which he made readily accessible to his
contemporaries and those who followed him."

196   "Addison's 'Enquiry After Truth': The Moral Assumptions
        of His Proof for Divine Existence." PMLA 65 (1950): 198-
        220.

        Sees Addison as representative of a new spirit of rational
        inquiry concerning proofs for the existence of God; he repre-
        sented the eclectic religious temper of the age.   Like the
        Cambridge divines, he advocated a moral philosophy based
        upon a close personal union between God and man; he arbi-
        trarily divided religion into two categories: faith or "re-
        vealed religion" was the counterpart of established orthodoxy,
        and morality or "natural religion" was the fundamental good-
        ness that went beyond creed or church.   Addison always laid
        greater stress upon morality.   Since all order, furthermore,
        flowed from God, and derived from the soul's search for di-
        vine truth, it became necessary for Addison to provide proof
        for the existence of God, proof that depended on evidence of
        the physical universe as to, among other things, the great
        chain of being, on the psychological fact of man's volitive
        inadequacy and emotional awareness of the divine presence
        within himself, and on a metaphysical proof based on the
        philosophical concept of eternity.

197   BLOOM, LILLIAN D.
        "Addison's Popular Aesthetic: The Rhetoric of the Paradise
        Lost Papers."   In [38], pp. 263-281.

        Mainly concerned with the rhetorical strategies and ap-
        proaches that Addison adopted in his Spectator papers on
        Paradise Lost to engage the interest and understanding of a
        less than learned audience: he "planned an approach to the
        poem that, while often using familiar critical language and
        authority, skirted intellectual rigor and instead elicited the
        delights of the imagination...."

198   "Addison as Translator: A Problem in Neo-Classical Scholar-
        ship."   SP 46 (1949): 31-53.

        Looks at the classical texts which Addison used for his
        translation of Virgil and Ovid and refutes the argument that
        Addison lacked scholarly accuracy in his translations.   "By
        the interpolation of the pertinent and by the omission of the
        extraneous, Addison helped to make the work of the two Ro-
        man poets not foreign and dead classics, but part of the main
        tide of English literature. [His] ... changes ... still remain

relatively few in number when viewed against the main body
of Addison's translations. "

199   BOND, DONALD F.
      "Addison in Perspective." MP 54 (1956): 124-128.

      Review of Peter Smithers' The Life of Joseph Addison.

200   "The First Printing of the Spectator." MP 47 (1950): 164-
      177.

      A detailed examination of the original 555 numbers of the
      Spectator as a clue to understanding the collaboration of Ad-
      dison and Steele.

201   BOND, RICHMOND P.
      "The Spectator: Two Notes." SP 42 (1945): 578-580.

      Provides information on early editions of the Spectator
      which stated that "this paper will be sent Gratis for a week,
      for a Taste to those who have not yet seen it.   It will con-
      tinue to be Published Daily. " Regular editions did not have
      this promise.

202   BRADNER, LEICESTER.
      "The Composition and Publication of Addison's Latin Poems."
      MP 35 (1938): 359-367.

      Concerned with the factual problems connected with the
      writing and publication of Addison's Latin poems; concludes
      that the bulk of the Latin poems was composed during the
      years 1689-94, with the exception of "Pax Gulielmi auspiciis,"
      and that they were thoroughly revised, almost to the extent
      of becoming new versions, some time previous to the publica-
      tion of the second volume of the Musarum anglicanarum an-
      alecta in 1699.   After that date Addison apparently wrote no
      more Latin poems.

203   BROWN, F. ANDREW.
      "Addison's 'Imagination' and the 'Gesellschaft der Mahlern. ' "
      MLQ 15 (1954): 57-66.

      Shows that the Swiss writers Johann Jakob Bodmer and
      Johann Jakob Breitinger were influenced greatly by Addison's
      "Pleasures of the Imagination" until he departed from Locke's
      Essay Concerning Human Understanding; then they departed
      from Addison and followed Locke's argument.

204   CARDWELL, GUY A. , JR.
        "The Influence of Addison on Charleston Periodicals, 1795-
        1860. " SP 35 (1938): 456-470.

        Illustrates "in concrete ways the modes and, to an extent,
        the scope of Addison's influence as it applied in a rather re-
        stricted way--that is, to the periodicals published in Charles-
        ton, South Carolina, before 1860. " Deals only with the Tatler
        and Spectator papers, and shows that Addison's neo-classicism
        had a great influence on the periodical literature of antebellum
        Charleston.

205   CARRITT, E. F.
        "Addison, Kant, and Wordsworth. " In E & S 22 (1937): 26-36.

        Argues the thesis that, on the whole, "it was the critical
        theories which anticipated and stimulated the change in cre-
        ative writing rather than the reverse"; in particular, Addison
        "foreshadowed Wordsworth's and Coleridge's theories of the
        Imagination and of Sublimity much more closely than any of
        his contemporary poets foreshadowed their practice. " The
        author mainly surveys Addison's influence, and that of Eng-
        lish theorists who derived from him, on Kant, who influenced,
        by way of Coleridge, the poetic theory and practice of Words-
        worth; concludes that Addison may justly be regarded as the
        father of modern critical theory, and that Wordsworth's and
        Coleridge's critical theories, and to some extent their poetry,
        were influenced by the critical speculations of the previous
        century which had created a taste to appreciate them.

206   CHAMBERS, ROBERT D.
        "Addison at Work on the Spectator. " MP 56 (1959): 145-
        153.

        Making use of the Dykes Campbell MS and the Bodleian
        MS, the author examines Addison's method of writing forty-
        one Spectator papers by using earlier essays and materials
        that he had "stockpiled" for just such an occasion.

207   COOKE, ARTHUR L.
        "Addison's Aristocratic Wife. " PMLA 72 (1957): 373-389.

        Presents facts about Addison's wife, the Countess of War-
        wick, to refute the traditional view that she was haughty and
        treated Addison badly. Presents evidence to show that their
        marriage was apparently a happy one.

208   "Addison vs. Steele, 1708." PMLA 68 (1953): 313-320.

Deals with the question as to whether Addison foreclosed
a mortgage on his friend Steele for a £1000 debt. New evidence from the Public Record Office shows that the mortgage
was on the Barbados plantations, not on Hampton House, and
that it is doubtful that Steele ever repaid the debt.

209   DAMROSCH, LEOPOLD, JR.
"The Significance of Addison's Criticism." SEL 19 (1979):
421-430.

Addison took the humanist view toward criticism, helping
the reader to understand and appreciate works of literature
rather than analyzing their structure. He knew that his remarks were informal and superficial, but he believed that a
critic's role was "to help the reader clarify what he thinks
about a poem he already knows well or should seek to know
well, not to create meaning for him."

210   ELIOSEFF, LEE ANDREW.
The Cultural Milieu of Addison's Literary Criticism.   Austin:
Univ. Texas Press, 1963.

A study of Addison's criticism and its historical setting.
Focuses on Addison's theories as they are related to ballad,
epic, and tragedy, to cosmological and political problems,
and to psychology and The Pleasures of the Imagination.

211   FRIEDMAN, ALBERT.
"Addison's Ballad Papers and the Reaction to Metaphysical
Wit." Comp. Lit. 12 (1960): 1-13. Rpt. as "Addison's
'Chevy Chase' Papers" in The Ballad Revival: Studies in the
Influence of Popular on Sophisticated Poetry (Chicago: Univ.
Chicago Press, 1961), pp. 84-113.

Argues that, contrary to the belief of Romantic critics,
the ballad revival in the first half of the eighteenth century
was sponsored by neoclassicism, and that it was not Addison's
latent romanticism that dictated his selection of "Chevy Chase"
and "The Two Children in the Wood" to praise, but rather
his doctrine of simplicity which they perfectly exemplified:
" ... it was by a doctrinaire extension of neoclassic tenets
that Addison became the momentary champion of popular poetry." Argues further that the three ballad papers (Nos. 70,
74, and 85) are not complete in themselves, but are pendants
to the extended essay on true and false wit in Spectator Nos.
58-63; Addison, in other words, contrasts the ballads with
meretricious metaphysical verse, so that by criticizing the

"inanities of the Metaphysicals, [he] is advocating by indirection the program of neoclassical, regular poetry."

212   FURTWANGLER, ALBERT.
       "Addison Among the Quidnuncs." ESC 6 (1980): 13-21.

       Even though the Spectator lacks a clear sense of purpose
       and of authorial control, it is still the work in which Addison
       is "best seen and understood ... his editing ... is innovative,
       imaginative, and consistent in addressing a new and trouble-
       some problem in literate culture." That is, he exploited the
       new technologies of news publishing by making traditional
       literature appealing to a wider public of common readers,
       thereby effecting an integration between popular and enduring
       literature; his problem was that of bridging the gap between
       literature and journalism. Addison attempted to meet the
       quidnuncs on their own ground: " ... the Spectator literally
       followed news into the hands of the most avid quidnuncs and
       challenged them on their own grounds to see the world a bet-
       ter way."

213   "The Making of Mr. Spectator." MLQ 38 (1977): 21-39.

       The creation of Addison's and Steele's eidolon reveals that
       "their conscious, deliberate touches in this character [Mr.
       Spectator] were determined, limited, and enhanced by larger
       choices and circumstances affecting the entire periodical."
       Through him they are able to speak to their audience, es-
       pecially about public education.

214   "Addison's Editing of the Papers on Imagination." Wascana
       Rev. 11, ii (1976): 3-18.

       A recent discovery of another Addisonian notebook (Har-
       vard) shows that his papers on pleasures of the imagination,
       Spectator Nos. 411-421, should be viewed "as part of the
       fabric of Addison's journalism and not as a critical treatise
       standing by itself." Compares the papers with this Harvard
       notebook showing that the various stages of revision make it
       difficult to trace a single development of thought and that they
       were "peculiarly adapted to the time and occasion of printing
       them." From these papers we can now see a "deliberate re-
       view of [Addison's] principles as an editor of the Spectator."

215   "Mr. Spectator, Sir Roger and Good Humour." UTQ 46
       (1976): 31-50.

       Addison develops Sir Roger as a "major example of good

humour" whereas Mr. Spectator "absorbed" from Sir Roger
"an uncanny range of agreeable authority." He was a "figure
born of journalistic convention and bred to journalistic convenience ... and his origins and development provide a handy
and revealing pattern against which Mr. Spectator can be
measured." Discusses how Addison used Sir Roger in comparison with Steele's use.

216   "Addison's Comedy and Control in two Spectator Essays [Nos.
29 [sic] and 329]." In Der Englische Essay Analysen, Horst
Weber, ed. (Darmstadt: Wissenschaftliche Buchgesellschaft,
1975), pp. 109-117.

A comparison of two linked essays, Nos. 26 and 329, both
on Westminster Abbey, that together reveal some of Addison's
characteristic habits as an essayist: "they show him sustaining a single theme, adding touches to two different characters, and drawing upon different resources for essays early
and late in the run of this periodical."

217   GAY, PETER.
"The Spectator as Actor: Addison in Perspective." Encounter 29, No. 6 (1967): 27-32. Rpt. in [57], pp. 283-294.

A review of Donald F. Bond's edition of The Spectator,
this article considers the contrast in views about Addison as
the first Victorian (Bonamy Dobrée) and as a classical moralist (Samuel Johnson); and argues that Addison is not the "bland
ideologist of the Establishment" that many modern readers
accept, but a "leading actor in a great moral drama." We
must recognize in the genteel journalist who sought, in the
traditional view, to do nothing more than to divert the ladies
and amuse the gentlemen, the serious moralist.

218   GRAHAM, WALTER.
"Addison's Travel Letters in the Tatler and Guardian." PQ
15 (1936): 97-102.

Gives evidence to show that the excerpts from eight of
Addison's travel letters which were printed in the Tatler and
Guardian were taken from the Tickell Letter Book. All the
letters were written between August, 1699 and September,
1703 and copies are in Letter Book No. 1 of the Tickell Papers, a book filled with transcripts made by Addison himself.

219   HAMM, VICTOR M.
"Addison and The Pleasures of the Imagination." MLN 52
(1937): 498-500.

A close analysis of Spectator 411 shows that Addison's
belief that the "distinction between primary and secondary
pleasures of the imagination is identical, on the esthetic level,
with that of Locke" is an ill-founded assumption.

220   HANSEN, DAVID A.
      "Addison on Ornament and Poetic Style." In [2], pp. 94-127.

      Suggests that Addison assigns a variety of functions to
ornament: in his earliest criticism he says that it has the
function of painting vivid images and of "giving the imagination and the understanding the pleasure of discovering in the
image some truth or complex idea about the nature of things."
Later he accepts the function of diverting the mind by recognizing surprising similarities between ideas, while at the
same time he suggests that ornament assists the writer in
departing from the idiomatic way of writing and in forming
the sublime style--to that latter style he assigns the function
of filling the mind with strong emotions and of revealing the
power and wisdom of God in the creation and design of the
universe.

221   HODGART, M. J. C.
      "The Eighth Volume of the Spectator." RES 5 (1954): 367-
      387.

      Analyzes the contents of the Eighth volume and attempts
to assign authorship to the various papers. Concludes that
Thomas Tickell was the sole editor during the Spectator's
last months, and that Addison himself had a hand in more
than the twenty-four essays previously attributed to him.

222   HORN, ROBERT D.
      "Addison's Campaign and Macaulay." PMLA 63 (1948): 886-
      902.

      Discusses Macaulay's uncritical fusion of two accounts of
Addison's writing and publishing of the Campaign, one by
Tickell and one by Budgell, and his elaboration of those two
accounts by details of his own. New evidence suggests that
Tickell's is the more accurate version; Macaulay's invention
tends to bolster Budgell's fanciful elaboration: "Macaulay
alone stands with Budgell for sheer dramatic invention....
Macaulay warms the imagination and disarms suspicion with
the best of his severe and bold artistry of persuasive rhetoric."

223   HUMPHREYS, A. R.
      Steele, Addison and Their Periodical Essays. (WTW) Lon-
      don: Longmans, 1959.

A brief study of the historical and literary importance of
The Tatler and The Spectator, with a short survey of the
essay-form and of Addison's and Steele's subsequent periodicals.

224   JACKSON, WALLACE.
       "Addison: Empiricist of the Moral Consciousness." PQ 45
       (1966): 455-459.

       A close scrutiny of Addison's argument in "On the Pleas-
       ures of the Imagination" as it " ... bears upon the relation
       between the great and the uniform and the relation between
       nature and art." Proposes that Addison avoided using the
       word "sublime" because " ... the connotations of the word
       could only confound his intentions and confuse the synthesis
       he achieves. Though he distinguishes between the 'natural'
       and 'rhetorical' sublime, his interest lies essentially in recon-
       ciling and integrating them."

225   KALLICH, MARTIN.
       "The Association of Ideas and Critical Theory: Hobbes,
       Locke, and Addison.", ELH 12 (1945): 290-315.

       Purpose of the study " ... is to show how this psychology
       [association of ideas] was used in the early period of what
       may be called associationist critical theory and incidentally
       to provide evidence for belief in the continuity of the as-
       sociationist method in critical thought." Shows how Addison
       used this critical theory in his writings which made him
       " ... prophetic of the future importance of associationism
       in romantic aesthetics." Addison, by relating the scientific
       psychology of his day to taste and pleasures of the imagina-
       tion, contributed to the " ... tendency of supporting critical
       theory by reference to mental processes."

226   KELSALL, M. M.
       "The Meaning of Addison's Cato." RES 17 (1966): 149-162.

       Analyzes the importance of the Cato-figure to Addison and
       other writers of the first half of the eighteenth century: Cato's
       character was very much the subject of controversy at the
       time. Addison chose Cato over Socrates because he was not
       only an example of pagan philosophical virtue, but a political
       hero as well. Cato is mainly concerned with ideas--"virtue,
       liberty, and Rome" (I. i. 32) are the key words of the play.

227   KENNEY, WILLIAM.
       "Addison, Johnson, and the 'Energetick' Style." Studia Neo-

philologica 33 (1961): 103-114.

Comments on the late eighteenth-century opinions about
Addison's style as compared to Johnson's.

228   KINSLEY, WILLIAM.
       "Meaning and Format: Mr. Spectator and his Folio Half-
       Sheets. " ELH 34 (1967): 482-494.

       Investigates two reasons for the success of the Spectator:
       the nature of its medium, the printed folio half-sheet, and
       the character of Mr. Spectator, especially as it is influenced
       by that medium. Mr. Spectator achieved a remarkable rap-
       port with his readers, so much so, in fact, that one of his
       greatest achievements consisted of the "way he persuaded
       his readers to co-operate in his program of social reform";
       yet he prides himself on his ability not to get involved. The
       resolution of the contradiction lies in the success with which
       Addison and Steele exploited the literary possibilities of the
       folio half-sheet: "although Mr. Spectator himself remains
       silent and uninvolved, his periodical (the object, the material
       sheet of paper), by its agility, ubiquity, and convenience be-
       comes closely involved with its audience. ... Addison and
       Steele succeeded in equating their narrator's personality with
       its printed manifestation: Mr. Spectator and the Spectator
       are one. "

229   LANNERING, JAN.
       Studies in the Prose Style of Addison (Uppsala Essays &
       Studies on English Lang. & Lit. , vol. 9). Uppsala: Lun-
       dequistska, 1951.

       Attempts "to discover the fundamental characteristics of
       Addison's style" and his contribution to the development of
       English prose by analyzing his sentence structure and its
       component parts as well as his theory and practice in the
       use of simile and metaphor. Concludes that "pleonastic paral-
       lelism" is the "most characteristic formal feature" of Addi-
       son's style.

230   LEHENY, JAMES.
       "The Essayist as Hangman: Joseph Addison and Political In-
       vective. " In Der Englische Essay Analysen, Horst Weber,
       ed. (Darmstadt: Wissenschaftliche Buchgesellschaft, 1975),
       pp. 118-134.

       Discusses the influence of both the essay and the "char-
       acter" on the writers of political invective, and concentrates
       on Swift's most effective ad hominem attacks before present-

ing Addison's comments in The Spectator on political writing.
Addison condemns invectives in a variety of arguments, and
his campaign played an important role in the decline in their
popularity during the second decade of the century. Addison's arguments can be classified as moral, social, and literary. His most fundamental arguments against political invectives are humanitarian, and most of his papers deal with
subjects that interested him--religion, social customs, and
literature.

231   LEWIS, C. S.
       "Addison." In [54], pp. 1-14; rpt. in [18], pp. 144-157.

       Attempts to sketch in and define the essential character-
istics of Addison the writer, especially in contrast to Pope
and Swift; suggests, among other qualities, that Addison is
significant for "his open-mindedness, his readiness to recognize excellence wherever he finds it.... Addison wants to
hear about everything ... but he does not live in the Humanist prison." Discusses, further, Addison as standing at a
turning-point in the history of feeling, especially with regard
to his essays on the ballad and Spectator, No. 160; sees him,
finally, as representing everything that once was ignorantly
called Victorian--the vague religious sensibility, the emphasis
on Good Form, the untroubled faith in the beneficence of
trade, the comfortable sense of security that makes possible
the romantic enjoyment of wildness and solitude.

232   McDONALD, DANIEL.
       "The 'Logic' of Addison's Freeholder." PLL 4 (1968): 20-
       34.

       Shows that the Freeholder " ... was clearly a work of
wartime propaganda, intended rather to beat down rebel arguments than to reason against them." Addison's purpose in
the Freeholder was to justify the reign of Hanover to Englishmen and in so doing he was " ... content to accuse the Jacobites of villainy, to dismiss their principles as idle theories,
to distort the controversy with fallacious arguments, and to
criticize rebel authors for employing the same fallacies as
he used himself."

233   MORRIS, ROBERT L.
       "Addison's mixt wit." MLN 57 (1942): 666-668.

       "An examination of Addison's doctrine of comparison, or
agreement, as expressed in his papers on 'The Pleasures of
the Imagination' to show why Addison applied the term 'mixt
wit' to Cowley's verse in Spectator 62."

234   RAMSEY, ROGER.
       "The Ambivalent Spectator." <u>PLL</u> 9 (1973): 81-84.

       Analyzes "a curious dichotomy of intentions conveyed by
       an image in the first <u>Spectator</u> paper" in which "the Spectator
       appears to identify not only with the 'standers-by,' but with
       the 'Blots' as well." This ambivalence "is well supported
       with an appropriate double pattern of statements having to do
       with sight."

235   RAU, FRITZ.
       "Zum Gehalt des <u>Tatler</u> und <u>Spectator</u>: Forschungsbericht."
       <u>Anglia</u> 88 (1970): 42-93.

236   ROGAL, SAMUEL J.
       "Hurd's Editorial Criticism of Addison's Grammar and Usage."
       <u>Costerus</u> ns 3 (1975): 13-47.

       Bishop Richard Hurd's edition of <u>The Works of the Right
       Honourable Joseph Addison</u>, 1811, contained almost no his-
       torical and biographical commentary but did include Hurd's
       criticism of Addison's style and grammar.   Hurd's apprecia-
       tion was based on his supposing that Addison preferred and
       followed traditional principles of composition, rather than the
       easy conversational style praised by Johnson.   Hurd's method
       of criticism consisted of measuring a passage of prose against
       the criteria established by Cicero, Quintilian, Aristotle, and
       Longinus; his notes chiefly reveal his pedantry and his pur-
       ism: he eagerly pounces on all of Addison's departures from
       strict principles of grammar.   Hurd's annotations are sig-
       nificant because they are representative of the dominant criti-
       cal opinion of the eighteenth century.

237   SALTER, C. H.
       "Dryden and Addison." <u>MLR</u> 69 (1974): 29-39.

       Compares Addison's and Dryden's views on drama, wit,
       and ballads, and on <u>Paradise Lost</u>.   Concludes that Addison
       " ... is a much less intelligent and original critic than Dry-
       den ... [that] his sense of his own unoriginality appears in
       his concealment of his sources and his attempts to disagree
       with them, if necessary by misrepresenting them." Also
       suggests that Addison follows Aristotle literally whereas Dry-
       den does not.

238   SHAHEEN, ABDEL-RAHMAN.
       "Joseph Addison's Views on Tragedy: Theory and Practice."
       <u>JEn</u> 4 (1977): 14-23.

239   SHAW, CATHERINE M.
       "Addison and the Drammatick Rules. "   Enl. E. 1 (1971):
       190-196.

              Analyzes the relationship between The Spectator essays
       and Addison's play, Cato, in order to establish links between
       his "dramatic criticism and his 'new' imaginative approach
       to literature. "

240   SMITHERS, PETER.
       The Life of Joseph Addison.   Oxford: Clarendon Press,
       1954.

              An account of Addison's public and private life, well
       documented.   Presents him, not primarily as a man of let-
       ters, but as a statesman and administrator who lived his
       life on "the concept of the Roman citizen and statesman, a
       man of public business with elegant accomplishments of learn-
       ing and letters. "

241   STEPHENS, JOHN C. , JR.
       "Addison as Social Critic. "   Emory Univ. Quart. 21 (1965):
       157-172.

              Addison's ideas about society--a cosmic chain of being, a
       gentleman, the social position of women, marriage--as ex-
       pressed in the Spectator papers had a great deal of influence
       on the social development of England and "on more than a
       century of English manners. "

242   STEVICK, PHILIP.
       "Familiarity in the Addisonian Familiar Essay. "   Coll. Comp.
       & Comm. 16 (1965):   169-173.

              Discusses the tenth Spectator from the point of view of its
       familiarity, in the special sense of belonging, of obtaining
       membership in a group; the reader is "constantly encouraged
       to recognize kinship, to distinguish himself from one group
       and ally himself with another, to separate himself from 'cer-
       tain young gentlemen' and to join the author. "   Addisonian
       familiarity draws the reader into the rhetoric of the essay
       and compels him to participate in an alliance with the author;
       it suggests endless distinctions between "they" and "we," "he"
       and "I, " contributing to the rhetoric of ingratiation.

243   THORPE, CLARENCE D.
       "Addison's Contribution to Criticism. "   In [31], pp. 316-329.

Argues that Addison's criticism belongs to his age, but not in the way that Pope's Essay on Criticism belonged to it, and to the future: "Unlike Pope, Addison's peculiar service to aesthetics and criticism was not to utilize the old-- though he did some of that, too--but to accept and adopt and transmit the new, and in such a way and to such a degree that he became thereby one of the chief constructive forces in the literary theory of the century that followed." Sees Addison, in other words, as one of the most important "grandfathers" of Romantic criticism.

244   "Addison and Some of His Predecessors on 'Novelty.'"
        PMLA 52 (1937): 1114-1129.

        Discusses the view of novelty as a source of aesthetic delight by such writers as Hobbes, Dennis, Du Bos, Dryden, and Longinus, and compares these views with those expressed by Addison.

245   "Addison and Hutcheson on the Imagination." ELH 2 (1935):
        215-234.

        Hutcheson, whose name is usually associated with Shaftesbury, is here compared with Addison, especially as he gave Addison's ideas on the Imagination wider circulation and added dignity and influence; concludes that Hutcheson, the leading aesthetician of the day, approved of Addison's theories and therefore "must have had much to do with directing attention to them and spreading their influence among later writers and thinkers."

246   "Addison's Theory of the Imagination as 'Perceptive Response.'"
        PMASAL 21 (1935): 509-530.

        A discussion of Addison's theory of the imagination as the organ of taste and "perceptive response," with particular attention to the psychological bases upon which the theory is built and the sources from which it derives. In addition to Addison's indebtedness to Hobbes, Descartes, and Locke, he owes his basic idea of imagination as the organ of taste to Gracian and St. Evremond, and possibly to Shaftesbury; concludes that his contribution is not so much in the discovery of new ideas as in the combination of old ones, and especially in the adoption of the introspective methods of the new philosophy: "What was new here, and even this was not entirely new ... was the conscious purpose to apply this scientific-philosophic method to the problems of literary merit and appeal."

247   "Two Augustans Cross the Alps: Dennis and Addison on
        Mountain Scenery." SP 32 (1935): 463-482.

        Discusses passages in "The Epistle to Lord Halifax," "The
        Remarks on Italy," and in The Tatler No. 161 which show
        Addison's affection for mountain scenery: "he found mountain
        scenery not only interesting and pleasant, but productive of
        the aesthetic delight he was later to hold sublime."

248   TIMMERMAN, JOHN.
        "Divinity and Creativity: The Aesthetic Framework of Joseph
        Addison." UDR 8 (1971): 17-28.

        Discusses the aesthetic framework, the qualities of the
        creative man, and three areas of Addison's aesthetic theory
        regarding the nature of the artist and his art: 1) "the divine
        framework of creativity and the physical framework of the
        creative man," 2) "the qualities of the artist who creates,"
        and 3) "the qualities of the art created." Addison's theory
        is formulated mainly in The Spectator, Nos. 409-421, and
        gives art meaning and permanence because it accounts for
        its value rather than for its mere mechanical structure.

249   TURNER, MARGARET.
        "The Influence of La Bruyère on the 'Tatler' and the 'Specta-
        tor.'" MLR 48 (1953): 10-16.

        Gives evidence to show "that the character-sketches of
        Steele and Addison were, in the first instance, modelled upon
        those of La Bruyère, and although they were not content to
        remain mere imitators, but expanded and developed the form
        in their own way, they owed their initial inspiration to him."
        Suggests further that "sketches in the manner of La Bruyère
        are to be found throughout the Tatler and the Spectator--for
        example, Steele's Tom Tercett in Tatler No. 219, Addison's
        Eubulus and Nemesis in Spectator, Nos. 49 and 483...."

250   WHEATLEY, KATHERINE E.
        "Addison's Portrait of the Neo-Classical Critic (The Tatler,
        No. 165)." RES 1 (1950): 245-247.

        Although this portrait " ... is a transposition to a more
        farcical key of parts of two scenes from Molière's Critique
        de l'Ecole des femmes," Addison's "idea of having his critic
        complain of being worn out because the action of the play he
        was watching shifted from place to place" did not come from
        Molière.

See also: 88, 257, 259, 261, 990, 1844, 1914, 2004, 2247, 2345, 2805

General Studies

251   ALDRIDGE, ALFRED O.
"Akenside and Imagination." SP 42 (1945): 769-792.

       Takes exception to the view that Akenside, like Collins,
is a forerunner of the coming age of romanticism. Traces
his attitudes toward nature, the past, and his own time and
analyzes his philosophical concepts. Notes his emphasis on
the creative act as compounding various elements into a unique
whole.

252   "The Eclecticism of Mark Akenside's 'The Pleasures of Imagination.'" JHI 5 (1944): 292-314.

       Aldridge feels that Akenside presents in his poem a hodge-
podge of philosophical concepts drawn from many sources,
not necessarily compatible; that his combining of imaginary
arts, science, and philosophy led to a further forcing of rationalism and empiricism to lie down together. The poem
also fuses concepts from the stoic and epicurean philosophies.
With all this, Aldridge considers it a real contribution to
eighteenth-century thought.

253   BUCK, HOWARD.
"Smollett and Akenside." JEGP 31 (1932): 10-26.

       Discusses the relationship of these two physician-writers
from the point of view of critical and biographical evaluation
of Smollett, whose novel Peregrine Pickle caricatures Mark
Akenside. Buck argues that the lampoon of Akenside is done
without personal malice.

254   HART, JEFFREY.
"Akenside's Revision of The Pleasures of Imagination." PMLA
74 (1959): 67-74.

       Discusses the changes made by Akenside in his revision
of The Pleasures of Imagination showing changes in Akenside's
politics, general attitudes, and altered sensitivity to diction,
and also the altered taste of his times.

255   HOUPT, CHARLES THEODORE.
       Mark Akenside: A Biographical and Critical Study.   Philadel-
       phia: Univ. Penn. Press, 1944; New York: Russell & Rus-
       sell, 1970.

            Draws together, summarizes, and evaluates what critics
       have said about Akenside since 1744.   Attempts a reappraisal
       of his contribution to English literature.

256   KALLICH, M.
       "The Association of Ideas and Akenside's The Pleasures of
       Imagination."   MLN 62 (1947): 166-172.

            Akenside's The Pleasures of Imagination is the first dis-
       tinguished poem to give expression to the psychological theory
       of association of ideas.   This theory is essential to an under-
       standing of Akenside's handling of the functions of imagination
       in the poem.

257   MAHONEY, JOHN L.
       "Addison and Akenside: The Impact of Psychological Criti-
       cism on Early English Romantic Poetry."   BJA 6 (1966):
       365-374.

            Suggests that Akenside probably did not read Locke him-
       self, but was greatly influenced by what he read of Locke in
       the writings of Addison.   Mahoney traces a movement in Eng-
       lish aesthetic theory sparked by Lockean psychology, popu-
       larized by Addison and illustrated by Akenside.

258   "Akenside and Shaftesbury: The Influence of Philosophy on
       English Romantic Theory."   Discourse 4 (1961): 241-247.

            Suggests that Akenside took from Shaftesbury the theory of
       benevolence, the identification of truth, goodness, and beauty
       --and the concept of the moral sense--and shaped them into
       the beginnings of Romantic theory.

259   MARSH, ROBERT.
       "Akenside and Addison: The Problem of Ideational Debt."
       MP 59 (1961): 36-48.

            Compares Addison and Akenside as to intentions, principles,
       and methods in order to "solve at least part of the general
       problem of Akenside's ideational debt to Addison."

260   NORTON, JOHN.
       "Akenside's The Pleasures of Imagination: An Exercise in
       Poetics."   ECS 3 (1970): 366-383.

Norton demonstrates that nearly all previous critical readings seriously misconstrue The Pleasures of Imagination,
which was not intended as a descriptive poem or as a versification of several of Addison's Spectator papers. "The
poem is not about the natural world; it concerns the processes
involved when the mind confronts the natural world...." Akenside intended to deal with the problems of value and knowledge that interested his contemporaries.

261   POLLARD, ARTHUR.
       "Keats and Akenside: A Borrowing in the 'Ode to a Nightin-
       gale.'"   MLR 51 (1956): 75-77.

       Shows the similarity between the fourth and fifth stanzas
       of Keats's poem and the seventh stanza of Akenside's ode--
       "a relationship which is much too close to be merely coin-
       cidental."

262   POTTER, GEORGE R.
       "Mark Akenside, Prophet of Evolution."   MP 24 (1926): 55-
       64.

       Akenside in The Pleasures of Imagination, while assuming
       the eighteenth-century idea of the "scale of being," also ad-
       vances the evolutionary theory of generation, which he called
       "epigenesis." "A comparison between the earlier and the
       later versions of the Pleasures of the Imagination gives an
       interesting probability as to the direct effect on Akenside's
       poetry of his scientific reasoning."

263   RENWICK, W. L.
       "Akenside and Others."   DUJ 3 (1942): 94-102.

       The eighteenth-century poets showed their appreciation of
       nature as formalized by the "creative pictorial" technique
       of the landscape poems.   But nature was often tied to
       a "reflective moralizing" theme.   Akenside, a Newcastle
       poet, followed this pattern, but his fresh sense of beauty
       makes him a link between the eighteenth century and Words-
       worth.

264   SILBER, C. ANDERSON.
       "The Evolution of Akenside's The Pleasures of The Imagina-
       tion: The Missing Link Established."   PBSA 65 (1971): 357-
       363.

       An attempt to define the hereditary connection between
       The Pleasures of Imagination (1744) and an incomplete ver-

sion, The Pleasures of the Imagination (1757)--a textual link
that was a turning point in Akenside's career.

See also: 143, 3698

Collected Studies

265   CLIFFORD, JAMES L. , ed.
Twentieth Century Interpretations of Boswell's "Life of Johnson." Englewood Cliffs, N. J.: Prentice-Hall, 1970.

General Studies

266   ABBOTT, CLAUDE COLLEER
"Boswell.   The Robert Spence Watson Memorial Lecture for
1945-46." Newcastle-Upon-Tyne: Literary and Philosophical
Society, 1946; rpt. Folcroft, Pa.: Folcroft Press, Inc.,
1969.

   A discussion of Boswell and the Boswell papers by the
discoverer of Boswelliana at Fettercairn House.

267   ALKON, PAUL K.
"Boswellian Time." SBHT 14 (1973): 239-256.

   Boswell's biography of Johnson is huge and heavy partly
because of Boswell's concept of time and proportion; he yearns
for an ideal "one-to-one correspondence between life and its
representation," and seems to believe that authenticity cannot
be achieved when there is a disproportion between the length
of a man's life and the time it takes a person to read an
account of it.   Boswell's solution to the problem of attaining
an ideal balance between "recorded and lived experience" is
to suggest that the attempt is possible if it is confined to
significant actions: "But I mean only to record what is excellent."   Boswell's conception of biography gradually shifted
from a static or pictorial motive to a dramatic or kinetic
one, and though he retained a moral justification for his biography, he emphasized authenticity as the defining technique of
the new biography.

268   "Boswell's Control of Aesthetic Distance." UTQ 38 (1969):
174-191.

Discusses how Boswell's control of aesthetic distance makes his Life of Johnson one of the best biographies ever written and points out how the Life fails when he loses control of this ideal.

269   ALTICK, RICHARD D.
"Johnson and Boswell." From Lives and Letters (New York: Alfred A Knopf, Inc. , 1965), pp. 60-70. Rpt. in [265], pp. 104-111.

Evaluates Boswell as a biographer and concludes that in spite of Boswell's "scrupulous authenticity," the Life is full of disorderliness and that Boswell "was so engrossed in his wealth of source material that he could not see it in perspective. "

270   AMORY, HUGH.
"Boswell in Search of the Intentional Fallacy." BNYPL 73 (1969): 24-39.

Johnson portrayed by Boswell, in his conversations, compared to Socrates portrayed by Plato. The purpose as stated by Amory is to explore Boswell's intentions in the Life.

271   BAILEY, M.
"Boswell as Essayist. " JEGP 22 (1923): 412-423.

Bailey's review of "James Boswell as Essayist," by Dr. J. T. T. Brown, which appeared in the Scottish Historical Review. Brown's thesis was that the Hypochondriac series of essays is intimately related to the Life of Samuel Johnson. He goes on to intimate that these essays were merely exercises in style, a warming-up for the writing of the Life, which Boswell even then had firmly in mind. Bailey accepts the original premise but argues against Brown's interpretations of it.

272   BALDWIN, LOUIS.
"The Conversation in Boswell's 'Life of Johnson. ' " JEGP 51 (1952): 492-506.

Examines evidence for and against Boswell's accuracy in reporting Johnson's conversation.

273   BELL, ROBERT H.
"Boswell's Notes toward a Supreme Fiction: From London Journal to Life of Johnson." MLQ 38 (1977): 132-148.

Discusses the degree to which Boswell achieved aesthetic distance and control over adventitious experience in the London Journal, and how his success as an autobiographer affected his success as a biographer. Shows how Boswell progresses from an "engaging, unreliable narrator" to a credible biographer who was able to subordinate himself to his subject. Boswell, in developing a "double consciousness of himself" becomes more constant and consistent in the Life than he was in the London Journal.

274   BRADHAM, JO ALLEN.
       "Comic Fragments in the Life of Johnson." Biography 3
       (1980): 95-104.

Gives several illustrations of how Boswell through "the delicate equipoise of timing, contrast, insinuation, diction, and spirited participation ..." takes small insignificant happenings and turns them into "finely scaled comic interludes." It is Boswell's sense of humor, his sense of timing, and his ability to develop tension which give him the light touch of a comic genius.

275   "Boswell's Narrative of Oliver Edwards." JNT 8 (1978):
       176-184.

Boswell's narrative reveals "how a biographer takes highly unpromising materials and by a series of artistic plays produces sustained and fascinating narrative." Edwards becomes a foil to Johnson, both of whose roles are supported and controlled by Boswell; the latter uses theatrical conventions, imagery, contrast, and allusion to create a fast-paced scene with beginning, middle, and end.

276   BRADY, FRANK.
       "Boswell's Self-Presentation and His Critics." SEL 12 (1972):
       545-555.

In presenting his portrayal of Johnson, Boswell the literary craftsman puts himself into the book as a persona whom we might today identify as "Watson." Boswell is to Johnson as Watson is to Holmes. This naive and subordinate character was taken by many to be a true picture of Boswell, and has resulted in a patronizing attitude toward Boswell which he did not deserve.

277   Boswell's Political Career (Yale Studies in English, 155).
       New Haven: Yale Univ. Press, 1965.

Though Boswell avidly sought political fame, his political

career was essentially a series of disappointments and frustrations.   Some account of political affairs in eighteenth-
century Scotland.

278   BRONSON, BERTRAND H.
       "Boswell's Boswell."   In [1485], pp. 53-99.

       Examines Boswell's personality and dismisses most of the
       former attempts at analysis, stating that "they go down like
       ninepins before Boswell's own records."   Suggests need of
       approval from a father figure.

279   BROOKS, A. RUSSELL.
       James Boswell.   New York: Twayne, 1971.

       Attempts to "provide a fuller view of Boswell's career as
       a writer than hitherto has been encompassed in a single study
       and to emphasize the unique coalescence of his personal ex-
       periences with his artistic outlook."   Sees Boswell as suffer-
       ing from an inner conflict that affected both his personality
       and the style and substance of his writings.

280   "Pleasure and Spiritual Turmoil in Boswell."   CLAJ 3 (1959):
       12-19.

       Boswell's intellectual, moral, and spiritual character and
       its influence on his biography of Johnson.

281   BROWN, ANTHONY E.
       Boswellian Studies.   Hamden, Conn.:   Archon, 1972.

       A valuable commentary on Boswell and his work, mainly
       bibliographic, but also containing eighteenth- and nineteenth-
       century reviews, extracts (and parodies) of Boswell's writ-
       ings.   Annotated, cross-referenced, and contains a subject
       index.

282   BROWN, J. T. T.
       "James Boswell as Essayist."   Scottish Historical Rev. (Jan.
       1921):   102-116.

       Deals with the collection of essays in "The Hypochondriack"
       and their value for the study of Boswell and the Life of John-
       son.

283   BRUSS, ELIZABETH W.
       "James Boswell: Genius and Stenography."   In Autobiographi-

cal Acts: The Changing Situation of a Literary Genre (Baltimore: Johns Hopkins Univ. Press, 1976), pp. 61-92.

A detailed study of Boswell's autobiographical writings, especially the London Journal and the Life of Johnson, placed in the historical context of "autobiographical acts" which in Boswell have become secularized. Boswell's journal becomes a companion and a confessor, ministering to his need for indulgence, approval, and forgiveness. The characteristic note of the London Journal is intimacy, since we overhear Boswell speaking to himself; and since the journal reflects the fluidity of the self, Boswell does not shatter the "utter privacy of his act."

284   BUCHANAN, DAVID.
The Treasure of Auchinleck: The Story of the Boswell Papers.
New York: McGraw-Hill, 1974.

A detailed history of the Boswell papers, done by a member of the law firm which had represented Isham in his fight to assemble the scattered papers of James Boswell.

285   BUTT, JOHN.
Biography in the Hands of Walton, Johnson, and Boswell (Ewing Lectures). Los Angeles: Univ. Calif. Press, 1966.

A consideration of the problems and their solutions that the three authors shared, and of the theories and purposes that governed their biographies. In the essay on Johnson the author first surveys Johnson's views on how biographies should be written, and then considers how far he succeeded in writing lives that illustrate his theories; in the essay on Boswell he emphasizes Johnson's influence on Boswell and the salient characteristics of his biographical writing.

286   CHAPMAN, R. W.
"Johnson's Letters to Boswell." RES 18 (1942): 323-328.

Examines the mysterious disappearance of those letters from Johnson to Boswell which were quoted in the Life; only one original has been found.

287   COLEMAN, WILLIAM H.
"The Johnsonian Conversational Formula." Quarterly Rev. 282 (1944): 432-445.

Discusses Johnson's formula for accomplished conversation: knowledge, command of words, imagination, presence of mind, and a resolution that is not to be overcome by failures.

288   COLLINS, PHILIP A. W.
       James Boswell. (WTW) London: Longmans, 1956.

           Contains chapters on the Life, the journals and corres-
       pondence, and the published works; also a select bibliography.

289   "Boswell's Contact with Johnson. " N & Q 201 (1956): 163-166.

           Estimates that "Boswell and Johnson met on about 425
       days in all. "

290   COPELAND, THOMAS W.
       "Boswell's Portrait of Burke. " In [27], pp. 27-39.

           Considers the nature of Boswell's relationship with Burke,
       the quality of Burke's conversation, and the reasons for the
       blurred portrait that Boswell painted of him.

291   CORE, GEORGE.
       "The Boswellian Aether. " SR 76 (1968): 686-690.

           A long and favorable review of Frederick Pottle's James
       Boswell: The Earlier Years.

292   DAICHES, DAVID.
       James Boswell and His World.   London: Thames & Hudson;
       New York: Scribner's, 1976.

           A popular account, lavishly illustrated.

293   DAMROSCH, LEOPOLD, JR.
       "The Life of Johnson: An Anti-Theory. " ECS 6 (1973):
       486-505.

           Takes opposite view of Macaulay; examines some of the
       defects and limitations of the Life suggesting that it is not
       a fully realized work of art and that the excellence of the
       dramatic episodes stands out from the mass of boring edi-
       torial material.

294   DOWLING, WILLIAM C.
       Language and Logos in Boswell's LIFE OF JOHNSON.   Prince-
       ton, N. J. : Princeton Univ. Press, 1981.

           An analysis of narrative and thematic structure in the Life;
       the aim is "avowedly syncretist," to reconcile the rival theor-
       ies of the objective or formal tradition and the deconstructiv-
       ist school of Jacques Derrida and the Yale critics.   The author

is primarily concerned with the implications of an implicit critique in deconstructivist theory of "certain assumptions about
literary structure associated with the objective mode of interpretation." The purpose of the study is to examine the challenge
posed by the <u>Life</u> to the traditional notion of continuity in narrative structure.

295   "Biographer, Hero, and Audience in Boswell's <u>Life of John-
       son.</u>" <u>SEL</u> 20 (1980): 475-491. Expanded and reprinted in
       [296], Chap. 3.

       A consideration of the internal audience in Boswell's <u>Life</u>
       which argues that the biography "posits the existence of an
       inner world of moral stability--as opposed to an outer world
       of skepticism and infidelity and doubt--that takes Johnson as
       its central figure, and that this world is sustained by a shared
       perception of Johnson as moral hero." Boswell's aim is to
       draw the reader into the "inner circle" where he is able to un-
       derstand both the moral and social sphere of Johnson's world.

296   <u>The Boswellian Hero.</u>   Athens: Univ. Georgia Press, 1979.

       Attempts to define, behind Boswell's portrayal of Paoli
       and the two portraits of Johnson, Boswell's conception of the
       heroic character, and therefore seeks to reach "beyond the
       particular narrative situation to a final vision of man's di-
       lemma in the modern world." Suggests that Boswell's great
       subject is the hero in an unheroic world, and that each of
       his three narratives also dramatizes the character of the age
       that has placed men like Johnson and Paoli in a condition of
       spiritual isolation.

297   "Boswell and the Problem of Biography." In <u>Studies in Biog-
       raphy,</u> Aaron Daniel, ed. (Cambridge: Harvard Univ. Press,
       1978), pp. 73-93.

       Raises certain questions about biography as a genre, es-
       pecially the question whether the usual distinction between
       fiction and nonfiction is valid: "The question of whether the
       <u>Life of Johnson</u> may be approached as a literary work is ...
       a question of whether Johnson as he exists in the pages of
       the <u>Life</u> is a hero in the sense that Hamlet or Lear are he-
       roes, one whom we must dissociate from the historical John-
       son...." As a way out of that dilemma, Dowling suggests
       that the <u>Life</u> should be read as literature, with a "controlling
       awareness of its self-contained nature as a work of art--
       something that is in no way inconsistent with its being simul-
       taneously a repository of facts about the 'real' Samuel John-
       son." It becomes a self-contained world of image, speech, and
       action that emphasizes the literary or symbolic meaning, a spe-
       cial kind of meaning that belongs to literature alone.

298   "The Boswellian Hero." SSL 10 (1972): 79-93.

Considers the Life of Johnson, The Tour to Corsica, and
the Tour to the Hebrides as presenting a "single conception
of heroic character, one which reaches beyond the particular
narrative situation to a final vision of man's dilemma in the
modern world."

299   DUNN, WALDO H.
"Jamie Boswell's Thorn in the Flesh." SAQ 28 (1929): 71-82.

Comments on the relationship between Boswell and John
Wolcot (Peter Pindar), with examples of Wolcot's satire on
Boswell.

300   FIFER, C. N.
"Boswell and the Decorous Bishop." JEGP 61 (1962): 48-56.

Explores Boswell's relations with the Bishop Percy who
"appears in the Life in three different functions: as a character, as a source of early Johnsoniana, and as a commentator on certain of Johnson's opinions." There is plenty of
possibility here for the estrangement of Boswell and Bishop
Percy, for which no authoritative explanation has survived.

301   FUSSELL, PAUL, JR.
"The Force of Literary Memory in Boswell's London Journal."
SEL 2 (1962): 351-357.

A chronicle of Boswell's mental processes in building his
image of himself. Based on letters and the London Journal
of 1762-1763, it shows Boswell identifying with various heroes,
real or literary, and modeling himself upon them.

302   GOLDEN, JAMES L.
"James Boswell on Rhetoric and Belles-Lettres." Quart.
Jour. of Speech 50 (1964): 266-276.

Explores Boswell's sayings about rhetoric and belles-
lettres, his opinions on style, on speech content and delivery,
on poetry and drama, and on historical writing. Supports
Boswell's reputation as a significant literary man.

303   GOW, A. S. F.
"The Unknown Johnson." From Life and Letters, VII (September 1931): 200-215. Rpt. in [265], pp. 79-89.

Looks at aspects of Johnson's life which are not covered
by Boswell and suggests that Boswell's portrait of Johnson is

incomplete, not because of his inability to write the biography but because Johnson was such a complex character.

304   GRAY, JAMES.
       "Boswell's Brother Confessor: William Johnson Temple. "
       TSL 4 (1959):   61-71.

       Discusses correspondence between Boswell and Temple; suggests that the correspondence reveals "Gradually but noticeably a much more serious Boswell than that of the London Journal ... still a flirtatious and roistering fanfaron, but now clearly possessed of a greater awareness of the need to fashion his life to important ends. "

305   GRAY, W. FORBES.
       "James Boswell in the Newer Light. "   Quarterly Rev. 283 (1945):   456-467.

       Maintains that Boswell's literary career has been misinterpreted--that he was more than the "biographer" of Johnson.

306   "New Light on James Boswell. "   Juridical Rev. 50 (1938): 142-164.

       Discusses mainly biographical material on Boswell revealed by the Fettercairn papers.

307   GREENE, DONALD J.
       "Do We Need a Biography of Johnson's 'Boswell' Years?"
       MLS 9, iii (1979):   128-136.

       Boswell's Life of Johnson, especially the "Boswell" years from 1763 to 1784, is not a biography at all, i. e. , it is not "a systematic attempt to trace the life of an individual fully and continuously between a certain set of dates. " It is rather Table-Talk, as Boswell himself seems to suggest.   Greene estimates that Boswell and Johnson met for a total of 227 days as recorded in the Life, or perhaps the portions of 250 days.   Since the total number of days intervening between their first meeting and Johnson's death is 7,783, the task of a biographer is to indicate what happened to Johnson on the remaining 7,500 or so days.   Greene plans to write a biography of Johnson during the "Boswell years" in which Boswell is seen through Johnson's eyes and appears as infrequently as he did in life.

308   " 'Tis a Pretty Book, Mr. Boswell, But--. " Georgia Rev. 32 (1978):   17-43.

The thesis of this article is that "It will not hurt Boswell's reputation--indeed, it may help it--if we stop trying to bolster it by the absurd contention that, as biography, the Life has unique merits that have never been equalled, and closing our eyes to the very plain fact that, by modern standards of biography, it has grave faults indeed; that in 1978 it is a most inadequate biography of Samuel Johnson." The Life ought not, therefore, to be praised as a biography, for its true merit lies in Boswell's accounts of his meetings with Johnson; and these do not, by modern standards, constitute a biography, but a memoir similar to Eckermann's Conversations with Goethe. Boswell's reports of Johnson's conversations are not biography: they are material for biography.

309   "The Making of Boswell's Life of Johnson." SBHT 12 (1970-71): 1812-1820.

A review article on Marshall Waingrow's book [363]. Greene considers this the most valuable volume of the series to come out as of 1970, "an important new primary source for future work on Johnson," containing much material which Boswell had compiled but decided not to use.

310   "Reflections on a Literary Anniversary." Queen's Quarterly 70 (1963): 198-208. Rpt. in [265], pp. 97-103.

Maintains that as a diary, the Life is "a minor masterpiece," but as a biography it cannot compare to Hawkins's Life of Johnson. Points out some of Boswell's inaccuracies and his attempts to picture Johnson as something he wasn't-- " ... to make Johnson a much simpler person than, in his complexity, he really was--simple-minded in his uncritical devotion to his wife, the Church, the monarchy; simple-minded, lovable, and ... slightly ridiculous."

311   HART, EDWARD.
"The Contributions of John Nichols to Boswell's Life of Johnson." PMLA 67 (1952): 391-410.

Demonstrates that Boswell was indebted to Nichols for material included in the Life, for items that appeared in the Gentleman's Magazine, and claims that his investigation "will add a new degree of authenticity to the parts of the Life concerned, and will ... illustrate the pains taken by Boswell to make his work the most complete and accurate of its kind in the English language."

312   HART, FRANCIS R.
"Boswell and the Romantics: A Chapter in the History of Biographical Theory." ELH 27 (1960): 44-65.

31   Concerned with Boswell's immediate influence on biography;
            explains why Boswell was popular with the Romantics; and
            considers effects of and reactions to "Boswellism."

313   HYDE, MARY.
       The Impossible Friendship: Boswell and Mrs. Thrale.   Cam-
       bridge: Harvard Univ. Press, 1972.   Also in HLB 20 (1972):
       5-37, 188-221, 270-317, 372-429.

            Traces the uneven history of the friendship (if such it can
       be called) between James Boswell and Mrs. Thrale, in which
       the figure of Samuel Johnson is either the force holding them
       together or the divisive element making their friendship "im-
       possible."

314   JAARSMA, RICHARD J.
       "Boswell the Novelist: Structural Rhythm in the London Jour-
       nal." North Dakota Quarterly 34 (1966): 51-60.

            "If Aristotle's definition of tragedy may be applied also to
       nondramatic literature," Boswell's London Journal appears
       Aristotelian in its structure. A series of scenes, each com-
       plete in itself, reveals the theme of Boswell's search for
       happiness in a rhythmic alternation of scenes that illustrates,
       for example, moderation versus immoderation, innocence
       versus experience, the intellect versus the passions.   The
       Journal account of the affair with Louisa is an example of
       this technique, revealing Boswell's innocence and immodera-
       tion. The other "focal episode" of the work, the relation-
       ship with Johnson, shows Boswell "tempered by experience
       and more moderate in his expression of his natural vitality."

315   KAY, DONALD.
       "Boswell in the Green-Room: Dramatic Method in the London
       Journal, 1762-1763." PQ 57 (1978): 195-212.

            Boswell's association with the theater and with individuals
       in the theater strongly influenced his imagination in the Lon-
       don Journal.   "It is the metaphor of the theater that allows
       [him] the freedom and easiness necessary to observe himself,
       and ... provides a method of letting us observe him viewing
       his activities and reviewing his motives.   Role-playing func-
       tions to give shape and direction to the work even as it is
       giving form" to his life. Boswell's use of the dramatic method
       causes the Journal to succeed as a narrative autobiographical
       journal.

316   "Purposeful Contrarieties in Boswell's Tour to the Hebrides
       and in Johnson's Journey to the Western Islands." Aevum
       (Milan) 50 (1976): 588-596.

By contrasting the features of the two closely related works inspired by the same event, one can better understand and appreciate Johnson and Boswell as individual artists and realize that the two works "blend together like the component parts of a Flemish portrait." Dr. Johnson gives us a "travelogue study of Scotland, and Boswell gives us an invaluable and unusually dramatic look at Johnson on strange and alien territory: together the Tour by Boswell and Journey by Johnson make a splendid tour de force of engaging contrarieties."

317   KILEY, FREDERICK S.
       "Boswell's Literary Art in the London Journal." CE 23
       (1962): 629-632.

       Comments from the Journal to show that it is a "rare
       combination of fact, fiction, and poetry: fact, in that Boswell's actual observations and experiences form the basis of
       the book; fiction, in that he expresses these observations and
       experiences in a meaningful narrative form; poetry, in that
       internal structures function as parts of a larger design."

318   KIRKLEY, HARRIET.
       "Boswell's Life of the Poet." JNT 9 (1979): 21-32.

       A discussion of Boswell's techniques, themes, and devices
       especially with reference to his development of his account
       of Johnson's early years to 1750; suggests that Boswell conceived of the first section of the Life as his own life of the
       poet, in order to emphasize the influence of the Lives on
       Boswell's technique of composition. Johnson had, in the Lives
       of the Poets, described the slow growth of the poet as a professional man: Boswell's Johnson becomes the figure who
       completes the process he himself had described. Suggests,
       furthermore, that Boswell borrows Johnson's own "rhetorical
       techniques to enhance his fusion of man and hero" and that,
       in general, he skillfully adapts Johnsonian material to help
       him illumine dark periods in Johnson's own life: e.g., the
       Life of Thomson provides Boswell with Johnson's reflections
       on the London of his youth.

319   LAITHWAITE, PERCY.
       "A Boswellian Interlude." Johnson Society Transactions,
       1951-52, Lichfield, England.

       Discusses the character and motives of Anna Seward and
       her hitherto inexplicable refusal to give Boswell reliable information about Johnson's early years. Laithwaite, with the
       help of the Fettercairn Papers, establishes facts about the
       "Swan of Lichfield" which account for her "campaign of defamation" and disclose Boswell's reasons for discarding her

anecdotes about Johnson and the malicious statements she
made about him.

320   LEIGH, R. A.   "Boswell and Rousseau."   MLR 47 (1952):
       289-318.

       Rousseau's relations with and influence upon Boswell.
       Shows Boswell's self-estimate to be, "I was as a board on
       which fine figures had been painted, but which some corrosive
       application had reduced to the original nakedness."

321   LONGAKER, JOHN MARK.
       "Boswell's Life of Johnson."   In English Biography in the
       Eighteenth Century (Philadelphia: Univ. Pa. Press, 1931;
       New York: Octagon Books, 1971), pp. 407-476.

       An historical and critical account of the Life, and a full
       consideration of Boswell the man.

322   LUSTIG, IRMA S.
       "The Friendship of Johnson and Boswell: Some Biographical
       Considerations."   In [50], pp. 199-214.

       Lord Auchinleck, an austere and remote father, had ac-
       customed Boswell to authority, but also provoked him to re-
       sistance, even though he was deeply troubled by respect for
       his father's virtues and attainments.   Boswell turned for sup-
       port and guidance to men of strong character, of whom "John-
       son was the father-surrogate supreme."   Boswell's "reverence
       for Johnson as moral and intellectual hero never failed....
       [T]hough the friendship of Johnson and Boswell is not equal,
       it is more balanced than many have assumed."

323   "Boswell at Work: the 'Animadversions' on Mrs. Piozzi."
       MLR 67 (1972):   11-30.

       Working with the Malahide Castle manuscript of the Life
       of Samuel Johnson and "related documents," Lustig refutes
       the theory that the revised editions of the Life, in which the
       attack on Mrs. Piozzi has been materially softened, were re-
       vised mainly through the influence of Courtenay.   Her analysis
       tends to establish Boswell's prime responsibility for the final
       text, and her study of the revisions is also used to demon-
       strate the working of Boswell's literary skills.

324   "Boswell's Literary Criticism in The Life of Johnson."   SEL
       6 (1966):   529-541.

An analysis of Boswell's literary opinions, showing his
modernity of ideas and critical finesse; his criticism is characterized by the union of didacticism, sentimentality, and
common sense.

325   "Boswell on Politics in The Life of Johnson." PMLA 80
       (1965): 387-393.

Shows Boswell, the Tory Laird of Auchinleck, firmly committed to order, subordination, and the feudal laws of entail
and primogeniture; yet nonetheless a man swept up into the
excitement of Britain's commercial expansion. This gives
him a "Janus" stance. Analyzes the conflicting influences
on Boswell which make him "an amalgam of traditionalist
and rebel."

326   McCOLLUM, JOHN I. , JR.
       "The Indebtedness of James Boswell to Edmond Malone."
       New Rambler 1, Ser. C (June 1966): 29-45.

Discusses their collaboration in preparing the Tour to the
Hebrides for publication, and Boswell's dependence on Malone
for guidance in personal matters as well as in his writings
about Johnson.

327   McLAREN, MORAY.
       Corsica Boswell. London: Secker and Warburg, 1966.

Mr. McLaren follows in Boswell's footsteps, writing a
book that involves both history and travel. Describes Corsica and General Paoli.

328   MOLIN, SVEN ERIC.
       "Boswell's Account of the Johnson-Wilkes Meeting." SEL
       3 (1963): 307-322.

Argues that the account was consciously shaped in terms
of a comedy of manners.

329   MORGAN, H. A.
       "Boswell on the Grand Tour." New Rambler (June 1961):
       14-19.

Passages from Boswell's notes on his European travels
which best illustrate his character and the social environment
in which he was living at any given time.

330   MORLEY, EDITH J.
       "Boswell in the Light of Recent Discoveries." Quarterly Rev.
       272 (1939): 77-93.

          Records the history of the discovery of Boswell's papers,
       and briefly states contents of Volumes VII to XVIII edited by
       Professor Pottle.

331   MURDICK, MARVIN.
       "The Entertainer." HR 30 (1977): 270-278.

          Discusses Boswell's Journals and how they portray his de-
       votion to Johnson.

332   NICOLSON, SIR HAROLD.
       "The Boswell Formula, 1791." From his The Development
       of English Biography (London: The Hogarth Press, 1927),
       pp. 87-108. Rpt. in [265], pp. 74-78.

          Compares Boswell's formula for writing the Life with the
       cinematograph because of his ability to "project his detached
       photographs with such continuity and speed that the effect
       produced is that of motion and of life." His great achieve-
       ment was that he perfected the "annotative and analytical
       methods of biography," and combined them with the synthetic.

333   NUSSBAUM, FELICITY A.
       "Father and Son in Boswell's London Journal." PQ 57 (1978):
       383-397.

          The London Journal, perhaps the first memorable diary to
       record adolescent conflicts between one's own identity and
       the roles he wishes to assume, is the creation of a self in
       rebellion against his father. Boswell displays excessive iden-
       tification with others: he uses the "factual materials of his
       life to create an image of himself as a child becoming a man,
       a son becoming a father...."

334   "Boswell's Treatment of Johnson's Temper: 'A Warm West-
       Indian Climate." SEL 14 (1974): 421-433.

          In writing Johnson's Life, Boswell found it necessary to
       "counterpoise Johnson's reputation for irritability with his
       warmth and kindness." By comparing his journal entries
       with the Life manuscript, we can see Boswell the artist at
       work, taking actual facts and molding them into a larger
       thematic structure which is his interpretation "of a life well-
       lived."

335   OSBORN, JAMES M.
       "Edmond Malone and Dr. Johnson." In [1464], pp. 1-20.

       Inquires into the credentials of Edmond Malone for Bos-
       well's prestigious identification of him as "an acute and know-
       ing critic, Johnsonianissimus."

336   PASSLER, DAVID L.
       Time, Form, and Style in Boswell's Life of Johnson.   New
       Haven: Yale Univ. Press, 1971.

       Passler views Boswell's Life as imaginative literature.
       After years of critical discounting of Boswell, accompanied
       by attempts to solve the "Boswell paradox"--why such a good
       book could have been produced by a nonentity--the discovery
       of the Boswell private papers at Malahide Castle forced a
       reevaluation of Boswell as an able writer, and of the Life
       as "a product of the creative imagination." Suggests that
       Boswell treated the temporal sequence of events more as a
       spatial composition than as an arrangement in time.

337   PEARSON, HESKETH.
       "Boswell as Artist." Cornhill 73 (1932): 704-711.

       Maintains that Boswell was an artist, not a chronicler,
       and, as such, he portrayed Johnson as he wished--that he
       suppressed, selected, and enlarged his material with absolute
       freedom and that he was a master of evasion as well as a
       dramatic genius. Compares two accounts, Anna Seward's
       and Boswell's, of an altercation between Mrs. Knowles and
       Johnson on April 15, 1778.

338   POTTLE, FREDERICK A.
       "The Life of Johnson: Art and Authenticity." In [265], pp.
       66-73.

       Discusses Boswell's ability to record Johnson's conversa-
       tions and concludes that he "reconstructed the conversations
       in the first place to complete portions of his own life..."
       and that although the conversations appear to be pure John-
       son, they are in fact "the quintessence of Boswell's view of
       Johnson."

339   James Boswell: The Earlier Years, 1740-1769. New York:
       McGraw-Hill; London: Heinemann, 1966.

       The first half of a definitive life of Boswell. Emphasis
       on his origin in a distinguished Scotch family, his active law
       career, and his career as man of letters.

340   "Boswell Revalued." In Literary Views: Historical and Criti-
        cal Essays, ed. Carroll Camden (Chicago: Univ. Chicago
        Press for Rice Univ. , 1964), pp. 79-91.

        Emphasizes important points emerging in present-day criti-
        cal thinking about Boswell; describes recent additions to his
        writings.

341   "James Boswell, Journalist." In [27], pp. 15-25.

        Boswell's journals are the source of much of the most in-
        teresting and characteristic parts of the Life, which owes its
        literary distinction to the conversations.   Boswell's primary
        literary achievement, according to Pottle, is to be found else-
        where than in the Life, much of it in the journals.

342   "The Power of Memory in Boswell and Scott." In [54], pp.
        168-189.

        A comparison between Boswell and Scott: suggests that
        Scott perceived the same normal, average world as did Bos-
        well, though he did perceive a romantic world behind it.   In
        the uses that Scott made of his perceptions he reveals a
        striking difference between his mind and Boswell's: Boswell
        in the power of his memory possessed, given a written clue
        to jog his recollection, almost total recall; " ... he has com-
        bined the full recall of the savage or the moron with the
        selectivity of the artist." Scott, on the other hand, pos-
        sessed an inaccurate memory, for imagination was always at
        work in it: his memory "has blended a collection of impres-
        sive objects and given something more striking and romantic
        than actual fact." Scott, therefore, had a double vision:
        his perceptions are of the eighteenth century, his imagination
        is Romantic.

343   The Literary Career of James Boswell, Esq. :   Being the
        Bibliographical Materials for a Life of Boswell.   Oxford:
        Clarendon Press, 1929; reissued with a new introduction,
        1966.

        This book performs a crucial function for a writer attempt-
        ing preparation of a biography of Boswell; it ensures that
        he will have complete information from which to form his
        mental image of the man.

344   POWELL, L. F.
        "Boswell's Original Journal of his Tour to the Hebrides and
        the Printed Version." E & S 23 (1938):   58-69.

Brief discussion of differences between Boswell's original journal of the Tour and the printed book of 1785.

345   PRIMEAU, RONALD.
"Boswell's 'Romantic Imagination' in the London Journal."
PLL 9 (1973): 15-27.

A reading of the London Journal and The Prelude to see how "similarities in the sensibilities of Boswell and Wordsworth cut across what have generally been accepted ... as major movements in the English cultural tradition," and how "Boswell's complexity as a writer arises in part from a 'romantic imagination.' "

346   RADER, RALPH W.
"Literary Form in Factual Narrative: The Example of Boswell's Johnson." In [19], pp. 3-42.

Using Boswell's Life as his example, the author seeks an answer to the question, how do "works whose primary commitment is distinctly non-literary nevertheless become literature?" Suggests that factual narratives become literature by transcending while fulfilling their usual purpose of providing useful knowledge of the human past; they must raise their subjects creatively out of the past and "represent them to the imagination as concrete, self-intelligible causes of emotion." Argues that the Life of Johnson has a structure that is the cause of its greatness and that its purpose is to "reconstruct and present as concrete and universal an aspect of human fact so as to render it inherently the cause of a distinct effect"--the aspect of fact that Boswell reconstructs, and the subject of his book, is the character of Johnson.

347   REIBERG, RUFUS.
"James Boswell's Personal Correspondence: The Dramatized Quest for Identity." In [1], pp. 244-268.

Briefly discusses three types of Boswellian letters: the social letter, the highly contrived, or artificial letter, and the personal letter written to intimate friends; deals with some aspects of the letters-journal relationship and elements of style and theme.

348   REICHARD, HUGO M.
"Boswell's Johnson, the Hero Made by a Committee." PMLA 95 (1980): 225-233.

Johnson's life--his conversation, his writing, his activities --are largely controlled by his associates. His greatness he did not achieve or have thrust upon him but rather it was a coproduction by his circle of friends.   The art of Boswell consists of his ability to disguise Johnson's dependency on others while at the same time suggesting the role that Johnson's "stimulating and sustaining" friends played by influencing him "to live the life that one will record."

349   REID, B. L.
        "Johnson's Life of Boswell."   KR 18 (1956):   546-575.   In
        [154], pp. 1-30.

        Sees Johnson as "Compleat Father" to one who could not grow up.

350   REWA, MICHAEL.
        "Some Observations on Boswell's Earlier Satiric Ambitions."
        SSL 13 (1978):   211-220.

        Boswell failed as a satirist because he was incapable of seeing himself as his own object of satire for seeking to make a reputation as a satiric "Genius."   Boswell lacked the courageously aggressive wit needed for satire, and the lucidity of his style gave no hint of satiric irony.   After his meeting with Johnson, he came to realize that the mode of writing that best accorded with his character and offered the possibility of fame was that of the irrepressibly genial; he perceived that literary success was more likely to be won by celebrating virtue in a manly fashion rather than by criticizing occasional lapses from literary good taste.

351   ROSS, IAN.
        "Boswell in Search of a Father? or a Subject?"   REL 5, i
        (1964):   19-34.

        Explores Boswell's apparent Oedipus complex and his fortunate release from it through writing.   "Boswell dramatized his need of a satisfactory father and so made articulate the values of the Age of Enlightenment...."

352   SCHWALM, DAVID E.
        "The Life of Johnson: Boswell's Rhetoric and Reputation."
        TSLL 18 (1976):   240-289.

        A rhetorical analysis of the Life shows that the "Boswellian Paradox" is "not really paradoxical but merely ironic." Because Boswell chooses to sacrifice his reputation in order to enhance the credibility and authenticity of his record and to become a participant, he is not considered to be a great author even though the Life is considered to be a great work.

Shows that "Boswell deliberately adopted a rhetorical strategy
... which was necessary to his biographical aims" even
though at times it draws the reader away from his literary
artistry.

353   SCHWARTZ, RICHARD B.
       Boswell's Johnson: A Preface to the LIFE.   Madison: Univ.
       Wisc. Press, 1978.

       The chief purpose is to describe those contexts that best
    elucidate the nature of Boswell's achievement in the Life of
    Johnson, and to argue that " ... modern discussions of biog-
    raphy and autobiography are more useful than the theoretical
    commentary of Boswell's predecessors and contemporaries."
    Among topics covered are Boswell's theory of biography in
    the context of eighteenth-century scientific methodology; the
    "epistemological analogy" as displayed in individual "scenes"
    or sections of the Life; the seldom discussed issue of setting,
    or the type of specific context in which Boswell presents his
    subject; "Johnson's Johnson," the image that emerges in the
    self-portraits scattered throughout Johnson's works; and the
    uses to which the Life should be put.

354   SCOTT, GEOFFREY.
       The Making of the Life of Johnson, Vol. VI of The Private
       Papers of James Boswell from Malahide Castle in the Collec-
       tion of Lt. Colonel Ralph Heyward Isham, Geoffrey Scott &
       Frederick A. Pottle, eds. (Mt. Vernon, N.Y.:   privately
       printed, 1929).   Partly rpt. in [265], pp. 27-39.

       Examines Boswell's method of gathering material for the
    Life of Johnson: his technique of recalling and recording
    Johnson's conversation, giving reasons for insisting that Bos-
    well did not take notes during a conversation; his accumula-
    tion of Notes, usually taken down shortly after the events re-
    corded; and, finally, his "journalising," the next stage in
    which a continuous narrative is built up from the notes, at
    an interval usually of from one to four weeks.   Scott's main
    purpose is to define Boswell's role as editor of his own papers.

355   SHERBO, ARTHUR.
       "Gleanings from Boswell's Notebook."   N & Q 201 (1956):
       108-112.

       Discusses some of Boswell's "discarded gems," the ma-
    terials he collected but decided not to use.   Sherbo finds
    many of them well worth reading, and regrets that they were
    not in the Life and that some of the anecdotes which did get
    in were so thoroughly edited.

356   SIEBENSCHUH, WILLIAM R.
       "The Relationship between Factual Accuracy and Literary
       Art in the Life of Johnson." MP 74 (1977): 273-288.

       Although Boswell creates the impression of "almost slavish
       attention to factual accuracy and total candor," his "control-
       ling purpose as interpretive artist as well as biographer re-
       veals a systematic and highly sophisticated use of the ap-
       parent nature and limitations of the factual genres and the
       stuff of which they are made in order uniquely to amplify
       the effects of his art." The power of the biography comes
       from Boswell's ability to combine "facts" with imagination
       and to make Johnson "a character in [his] book."

357   Form and Purpose in Boswell's' Biographical Works. Berke-
       ley: Univ. Calif. Press, 1972.

       "What emerges from a close comparative study of Bos-
       well's major biographical works is the fact that each is a
       separate and formally distinct literary achievement." Identi-
       fication of some of the formal and stylistic characteristics
       of each work, emphasizing his "selective and interpretive
       dramatization" of his primary factual materials.

358   SPACKS, PATRICIA MEYER.
       "Young Men's Fancies: James Boswell, Henry Fielding."
       In [166], pp. 227-263.

       Both Boswell and Fielding insist that writing partakes of
       the drama of individual experience and they also investigate
       the importance of the imagination in psychic life by recogniz-
       ing its dual role as literary and personal resource. They
       discuss the same crucial issues: "the relation of the internal
       to the external world and of life to art; how the imagination
       guides one to reality; how and when the imagination deceives."
       The London Journal and Tom Jones are both concerned with
       the effort to achieve selfhood in youth.

359   STEESE, PETER.
       "Boswell 'Walking upon Ashes.' " English Symposium Papers
       (State Univ. of New York College at Fredonia). 1 (1970):
       46-69.

       Comparison of Boswell's first meeting with Dr. Johnson
       as reported in his London Journal and in the Life of Johnson.

360   STEWART, MARY MARGARET.
       "Boswell and the Infidels." SEL 4 (1964): 475-483.

Examines Boswell's religion in the light of his attitudes
toward nonbelievers. The violence of his reaction to them
is an indication of the depth of his distress at having on
several occasions been unable to refute their arguments.

361   TILLINGHAST, A. J.
        "Boswell Playing a Part." RMS 9 (1965): 86-97.

        Shows effect on Boswell's writing of his ability to play a
        part and at the same time to observe himself playing it.

362   TRACY, CLARENCE.
        "Boswell: The Cautious Empiricist." In [23], pp. 225-243.

        Evaluates the Life in the light of Johnson's criteria for
        biography and Boswell's effort to meet those standards.
        Tracy is cautious, too, and sparing of praise for the Life.

363   WAINGROW, MARSHALL.
        "Boswell's Johnson." From The Correspondence and Other
        Papers of James Boswell Relating to the Making of the Life
        of Johnson (New York: McGraw-Hill, 1969). Partly rpt. in
        [265], pp. 45-50.

        Discusses Boswell's portrayal of Johnson's intellectual
        powers and weaknesses, and tests Boswell's editorial prac-
        tices against the finished work.

364   WARNOCK, ROBERT.
        "Boswell on the Grand Tour." SP 39 (1942): 650-661.

        Chiefly biographical, recreating Boswell's adventures in
        Italy in 1765 and casting light on his personality development.

365   WECTER, DIXON.
        "The Soul of James Boswell." VQR 12 (1936): 195-206.

        An account of Boswell's religious opinions.

366   WIMSATT, WILLIAM K., JR.
        "James Boswell: The Man and the Journal." YR 49 (1959):
        80-92. Revised as "The Fact Imagined: James Boswell" in
        Hateful Contraries (Lexington: Univ. Ky. Press, 1965), pp.
        165-183.

        Boswell's attitude towards his journals and characteristics

of the journals as literary art. On the one hand, he emphasizes Boswell's concern for "the very fact," and on the
other, he makes some penetrating observations in the course
of his search for "the real imaginative principle in Boswell."

367   WOODWARD, A. G.
       "The Emergence of the Self: James Boswell in His Jour-
       nals." ESA 19 (1976): 57-63.

       Boswell's entries in his journals reveal his "emergence
       of the self" attitude which was beginning to surface in the
       eighteenth century. Especially impressive is "his brio, the
       vitality of his prose even when he is in the dumps, his sheer
       zest for existence."

368   WOOLLEY, JAMES D.
       "Johnson as Despot: Anna Seward's Rejected Contributions
       to Boswell's Life." MP 70 (1972): 140-145.

       Prints Anna Seward's account of Johnson's angry and ran-
       corous conversation of April 15, 1778, which was rejected
       by Boswell, and suggests that Boswell did not use the letter
       because its hostility to Johnson would be contrary to the char-
       acter of the man worthy of such admiration as portrayed in
       the Life.

See also: 1204, 1464, 1507, 1561, 1798

General Studies

369   ADELSTEIN, MICHAEL E.
Fanny Burney. New York: Twayne, 1968.

Describes, examines, and evaluates Fanny Burney's writings, integrating the writings with biographical material because much of what she wrote had to do with her family and her friends and is a reflection of her own social and economic problems. Author's purpose is to guide readers in an understanding of Fanny's "strengths and weaknesses as a writer, and to help them in appreciating her literary achievement and in realizing her historical significance."

370   ANDERSON, EARL R.
"Footnotes More Pedestrian than Sublime: A Historical Background for the Foot-Races in Evelina and Humphry Clinker."
ECS 14 (1980): 56-68.

A look at the foot race between Lord Merton and Mr. Coverley from the standpoint of literary background, background in the history of gambling and gambling law, and background in the history of pedestrianism shows that hundred-pound wagers were beyond the limit of the gambling statutes, that "the two gentlemen ... made fools of themselves, and abused two poor old women," and that "the ludicrous details of both foot-races [in Evelina and in Humphry Clinker] showed a class-consciousness."

371   BARKER, GERARD A.
"The Two Mrs. Selwyns: Evelina and The Man of the World."
PLL 13 (1977): 80-84.

Mrs. Selwyn, Evelina's chaperone, possesses the same name as one of Mackenzie's minor characters in The Man of the World but the contrast in treatment differs because of the two novelists' attitudes toward feminism. Burney uses Mrs. Selwyn as a primary agent for manipulating and resolving the action of her novel and a dominant force in precipitating the action. Because Burney has a more enlightened conception of women's role in society, her Mrs. Selwyn as-

sumes an importance and complexity that Mackenzie's character does not possess.

372   BEASLEY, JERRY C.
       "Fanny Burney and Jane Austen's Pride and Prejudice."
       Eng. Misc. 24 (1973-74): 153-166.

       Investigates the differences and the similarities of the two
       authors with regard to plots and characters, especially the
       influence of Evelina and Cecilia on Jane Austen.

373   BENKOVITZ, MIRIAM.
       "Dr. Burney's Memoirs." RES 10 (1959): 257-268.

       Examines the manuscript remnants of Dr. Burney's auto-
       biography to prove that Fanny Burney's (Mme. d' Arblay)
       memoirs of her father were unjust and that they present an
       untrue picture of him; also that the book fails to focus on
       Dr. Burney and that it is full of pompous language.

374   BLOOM, LILLIAN D.
       "Fanny Burney's Camilla: the Author as Editor." BRH 82
       (1979): 367-393.

       Discusses the relationship between scraps of paper on
       which Fanny Burney jotted down bits of dialogue, lists of
       characters and suggestions for plot and themes and the two
       printed versions of Camilla; presents much information con-
       cerning the printing and editorial history of the novel, em-
       phasizing in particular Mme d'Arblay's "cutting and correct-
       ing" for the second edition of 1802, reducing the original by
       over five hundred octavo pages. Most of the revisions were
       intended to increase the narrative speed of the story. The
       comparison between the two versions involves a number of
       critical comments on the qualities and characteristics of Ca-
       milla.

375   BLOOM, LILLIAN D. and EDWARD A. BLOOM.
       "Fanny Burney's Novels: the Retreat from Wonder." Novel
       12 (1979): 215-235.

       An examination of Fanny Burney's four novels shows that,
       although the "surface narrative does not alter significantly,"
       Cecilia and Evelina were highly successful whereas Camilla
       and The Wanderer were failures. Perhaps the reason for
       the failure of the last two novels was because she no longer
       lived in a fairy-tale world, no longer needed to become "some-
       body" or to please her father, and her life no longer allowed
       her to fantasize or write with that "creative zest" that was
       evident in her earlier work.

376   CECIL, LORD DAVID.
        "Fanny Burney." In Poets and Story-Tellers (London: Con-
        stable, 1949), pp. 77-96.

        An essay dealing with reasons why Fanny Burney was not
        as successful a novelist as Fielding, Richardson, and others
        in the eighteenth century and showing how she translated the
        "Fielding-type novel into the feminine key." She was able
        to examine in greater detail what she saw than were other
        novelists and therefore made social distinctions the dominant
        subject of her stories. Also for the first time in an English
        novel, courtship becomes the central theme.

377   "Fanny Burney's Novels." In [54], pp. 212-224.

        Illustrates how Fanny Burney combined the methods of
        Fielding and Richardson, and her influence on the course of
        the English novel. "She is the first novelist ... to make a
        thorough study of snobbery."

378   COPELAND, EDWARD W.
        "Money in the Novels of Fanny Burney." Studies in the Novel
        8 (1976): 24-37.

        Argues that the "insistent exploration of women's peculiar
        relationship to money defines the new female fiction" of the
        eighteenth century, and that the dramatic tension in women's
        novels is caused by the presence of two kinds of money--
        fantasy money and real money: "it is the changing relation-
        ship between the fantasy money and the real money that pro-
        vides a focus for plotting the growth of a new consciousness
        and self-awareness in women's literature of the last years
        of the century." In particular, the author argues that the
        alteration of Fanny Burney's style in her later novels follows
        her changing response to the relationship in her novels be-
        tween real and fantasy money.

379   CUTTING, ROSE MARIE.
        "Defiant Women: The Growth of Feminism in Fanny Burney's
        Novels." SEL 17 (1977): 519-530.

        Fanny Burney is allied with those women who applied revo-
        lutionary ideas to their own sex: Mary Wollstonecraft, Char-
        lotte Smith, Mary Hays, and the unknown author of The Fe-
        male Aegis. Her novels reflect her growing resentment a-
        gainst the restrictions imposed upon women; her heroines in-
        creasingly develop attitudes of self-reliance, and other fe-
        male characters develop strong traits of independence--Mrs.
        Selwyn in Evelina, for instance. Fanny Burney demands self-
        sufficiency for both sexes--that is the essential characteristic
        in her plea for improved conditions for women.

380   "A Wreath for Fanny Burney's Last Novel: The Wanderer's
       Contribution to Women's Studies." CLAJ 20 (1976): 57-67;
       Agora 3, i-ii (1976): 80-90.

       Fanny Burney seriously examined the problems of sex in
       her last novel, The Wanderer, which analyzes the "mental,
       economic, and social bondage of women and predicts their
       struggle towards independence."

381   DEITZ, JONATHAN and SIDONIE SMITH.
       "From Precept to Proper Social Action: Empirical Matura-
       tion in Fanny Burney's Evelina." ECLife 3 (1977): 85-88.

       Discounts the theory that the Reverend Mr. Villars is
       Evelina's guiding moral light but suggests that his guidance
       becomes less important as she learns to adjust to society.
       Evelina learns to cope in the empirical world of Lord Orville
       and in so doing leaves the sheltered and isolated world im-
       posed upon her by Villars. When we understand the terms
       of Evelina's growth, we accept her marriage to Orville as
       the only logical conclusion.

382   DOODY, MARGARET ANNE.
       "Deserts, Ruins and Troubled Waters: Female Dreams in
       Fiction and the Development of the Gothic Novel." Genre 10
       (1976): 529-572.

       Fanny Burney's Cecilia, or Memoirs of an Heiress (1782),
       discussed among other popular novels.

383   ERICKSON, JAMES P.
       "Evelina and Betsy Thoughtless." TSLL 6 (1964): 96-103.

       Examines the similarities between the two novels and con-
       siders to what extent Fanny Burney may have been influenced
       by Mrs. Haywood and the nature of her achievement; con-
       cludes that Evelina is more original than Betsy Thoughtless.

384   GLOCK, WALDO S.
       "Evelina: The Paradox of the 'Open Path.'" SCB 39 (1979),
       129-134.

       The paradox of the "open path," which Evelina usually
       identifies with conventional behavior, suggests that "'guile-
       less sincerity' is more frequently found in the vagaries and
       contradictions of private judgment, as in Evelina's openly
       expressed liking for Orville, than in the traditional codes of
       accepted behavior." She has to learn that the "open path"
       of candor which she aspires to follow is not often found apart
       from the natural virtue of instructive action.

385   "Appearance and Reality: The Education of Evelina." <u>ELWIU</u>
       2 (1975): 32-41.

       Suggests that Evelina's education consists of her learning
       the paradoxical nature of experience: that knowledge of the
       world involves a recognition that hypocrisy may often be a
       virtue. But Evelina, after happily marrying Lord Orville,
       appears to forget all that she had learned from her numerous
       episodes of social embarrassment: she cheerfully reverts to
       her former tendency to assume that appearance and reality
       coincide.

386   HAHN, EMILY.
       <u>A Degree of Prudery</u>. New York: Doubleday & Co. , 1950;
       London: Arthur Barker, 1951.

       A rather unsympathetic treatment of Fanny Burney's biog-
       raphy.

387   HEMLOW, JOYCE.
       <u>The History of Fanny Burney</u>. Oxford: Clarendon Press,
       1958.

       A comprehensive study of Fanny Burney's life and writings
       based largely on her "journal-letters, notebooks, unpublished
       works, and voluminous correspondence." The standard biog-
       raphy, with extensive chapters on the novels.

388   "Fanny Burney and the Courtesy Books." <u>PMLA</u> 65 (1950):
       732-761.

       Describes the courtesy books which Fanny Burney was
       familiar with, their influence in the age, and their influence
       on her, expecially in <u>Camilla</u>--an influence which contributed
       to its failure as a novel in comparison to <u>Evelina</u>.

389   "Fanny Burney: Playwright." <u>UTQ</u> 19 (1950): 170-189.

       A survey of Fanny Burney's dramatic activity, especially
       of her "methods of work, and ... her mind, purposes, and
       abilities."

390   HORNER, JOYCE M.
       <u>The English Women Novelists and Their Connection with the</u>
       <u>Feminist Movement (1688-1797)</u>. Northhampton, Mass. :
       Smith College Studies in Modern Languages, Vol. 11, Nos.
       1-3 (1929-1930), 1930, pp. 59-65; 133-142.

       Analyzes Fanny Burney as the first important woman novel-

ist, and attempts to define those qualities in her heroines--
Evelina, Camilla, and Cecilia--that reflect a specifically
feminine sensibility.

391   JEFFREY, DAVID K.
       "Manners, Morals, Magic, and Evelina." Enl. E. 9 (1978):
       35-47.

       Compares the epistolary method used by Burney with that
       of Richardson and Smollett, and then compares the three
       heroines, Evelina, Pamela, and Lydia Melford to "suggest
       the originality of Burney's heroine and the uniqueness of
       [her] examination of sexual roles."

392   LLOYD, CHRISTOPHER.
       Fanny Burney. London: Longmans, 1936.

       A readable biography, with almost no criticism of the
       novels.

393   LUSTIG, IRMA S.
       "The Prudent Heart: Fanny Burney's Journals Restored."
       SBHT 15 (1973-74): 287-296.

       A discussion of Joyce Hemlow's editions of The Journals
       and Letters of Fanny Burney.

394   MacCARTHY, BRIDGET G.
       "The Domestic Novel and the Novel of Manners." In The
       Later Women Novelists, 1744-1818. (Cork, Ireland: Cork
       Univ. Press, 1947; New York: William Salloch, 1948), pp.
       89-128.

       Emphasizes the personal and family influences that helped
       to shape Fanny Burney's literary career; contains extensive
       analysis of the novels, and attempts to define the new char-
       acteristics of Evelina that separate Fanny Burney from the
       four great male novelists of the period.

395   MALONE, KEMP.
       "Evelina Revisited." PLL 1 (1965): 3-19.

       Considers such matters as Fanny Burney's conception of
       nature, the time-scheme and the place-scheme of the novel,
       and the characters; concludes that the basic plot is highly
       conventional, and that the author made it "individual by the
       setting she gave it, and by a masterly elaboration of char-
       acters and events.... Through this elaboration she turned
       a simple tale into a richly freighted novel."

396   MONTAGUE, EDWINE and L. L. MARTZ.
       "Fanny Burney's Evelina." In [27]: pp. 171-181.

          A pro and con discussion of the literary merits of Evelina.
       Suggests, among other perceptions, that "the whole novel
       seems to insist that the standards and demands of manners
       must be and should be met. The book seems to be built on
       the assumption that a society ... stands or falls by its ability
       to express and maintain a code of manners."

397   MORLEY, EDITH J.
       Fanny Burney. The English Assoc. Pamphlet No. 60, April
       1925.

          A general study of Fanny Burney, especially of the Diary
       and Letters which are taken as the best commentary on the
       novels as well as the best illustration of the society that they
       depict; suggests that she added realistic conversation to the
       English novel; she "theatricalizes the dialogue." Emphasizes
       that she presented the feminine point of view and that, as a
       writer of the novel of manners, she introduces the common-
       places of middle-class life into her works.

398   NEWTON, JUDITH.
       "Evelina: Or, The History of a Young Lady's Entrance into
       the Marriage Market." MLS 6, i (1976): 48-56.

          A feminist reading which attempts to avoid stereotypes and
       to define "what is peculiar to Burney's perception of women's
       experience." The world of Evelina is the world of Fanny
       Burney--a world in which the female is on display in the mar-
       riage market, and "men appear licensed to abuse women."

399   PATTERSON, EMILY H.
       "Family and Pilgrimage Themes in Burney's Evelina." New
       Rambler 18 (1977): 41-48.

          Traces Evelina's pilgrimage--from birth until her marriage
       to Lord Orville--in which she is finally successful in obtain-
       ing her father's recognition which brings her fame and for-
       tune. Discusses how Villars manipulates the development of
       the story--the three pilgrimages which Evelina makes, al-
       though they are with surrogate parents or chaperones, are
       always controlled by Villars. In the end, Evelina's pilgrim-
       age wins her a lost Eden--one which she had been unfairly
       deprived of.

400   "Unearned Irony in Fanny Burney's Evelina." DUJ 36 (1975):
       200-204.

Evelina's "failure to discriminate among her facts and observations and to project consequences allows an irony of
situation to infiltrate Evelina, wholly unstrived for, hence
unearned, and even more, undesired, because Miss Burney
owes it, not to a deliberate stroke, but to her loss of control
over the materials of her art." Mr. Villars, for instance,
is portrayed as a wise and benevolent protector, shielding
Evelina from an unscrupulous world, yet he ignores these
excellent intentions to plan a project that will expose her to
the cruelty and malice of the world in order to secure for
her two fortunes to which she is legally entitled: "Miss
Burney never grasps the incongruity of Villars's professed
aims with his overt actions." The resulting "unearned irony"
compromises Fanny Burney's art.

401   RUBENSTEIN, JILL.
        "The Crisis of Identity in Fanny Burney's Evelina." New
        Rambler 112 (1972): 45-50.

        Sees the theme of Evelina as residing in the dialectical
        conflict between the claims of environment (Mr. Villars and
        Lord Orville) and of heredity (Sir John Belmont and Mme.
        Duval): Evelina seeks her identity and her place in the world
        by having to choose between the two. Her love for Lord
        Orville helps her to resolve her conflict; however, "she learns
        that she cannot completely discount her heredity and, with
        Lord Orville's help, manages to come to terms with it."

402   SHROFF, HOMAI J.
        " 'A Young Lady's Entrance into the World' of the Gentleman
        --Fanny Burney." In [163], pp. 236-253.

        Fanny Burney's concept of a gentleman as portrayed in
        her novels. Her "most outstanding achievement in Evelina
        is the study of the manners of the two divisions of the Lon-
        don society of the time, the town and the City." She was a
        great advocate of the ideal way of life " ... in which urbanity
        elegance and intelligence lend grace to upright and humane
        conduct...."

403   SPACKS, PATRICIA MEYER.
        "Dynamics of Fear: Fanny Burney." In [166], pp. 158-192.

        Fanny Burney's fiction and diaries emphasize the importance
        of order and pattern; the entire mass of her work exhibits per-
        vasive female fear--"not of the absence of power but of failure
        of goodness and consequent loss of love." Where Tristram's
        fear of impotence reduces his life to disorder, Miss Burney's
        fears have the power to create order, defending against chaos;
        her novels and journals reveal the "dynamics of fear" in a

woman's experience. In life and literature she sought moral
structures that would assure her that virtue would be rewarded, and in her fiction especially she uses her fantasies
to communicate her feelings and conflicts, the psychological
drama that her virtuous life largely concealed.

404   " 'Ev'ry Woman is at Heart a Rake.' " ECS 8 (1974): 27-
46.

A discussion of what women writers of the eighteenth century thought about women's sexuality and how they handled
the subject in their novels and autobiographies. Both novelists
and autobiographers investigated "the question of how much
lechery is inherent in the female nature and what should be
done about it," particularly Fanny Burney, whose central subject concerns the "ambiguities of innocence"; refers to her
girlish devotion to her father and Mr. Crisp, a surrogate
father, a father-daughter relationship that provided, for Fanny
as for many women, a model of emotional satisfaction and
safety.

405   STAVES, SUSAN.
"Evelina: or Female Difficulties." MP 73 (1976): 368-381.

An analysis of what Evelina's difficulties were and what
they were created out of to suggest a vital relationship between the plot and the incidental comedy. Concludes that
Fanny Burney " ... could not finally deny the self-abnegation
society required of ladies, and so, in rejecting the laughter,
the irony, the satire, and the spirit of criticism, which seem
to have been her natural gifts, she ultimately weakened her
art."

406   STEEVES, HARRISON R.
"A Young Lady's Entrance into the World." In [169], pp.
204-225.

Chiefly about Evelina, which the author sees as of "lasting
importance ... as the first novel to examine seriously, through
a woman's eyes, the effects of the usages of the time upon the
position and the life of a woman." A rather uncritical survey.

407   VOPAT, JAMES B.
"Evelina: Life as Art--Notes Toward Becoming a Performer
on the Stage of Life." ELWIU 2 (1975): 42-52.

Argues that Evelina is a "durable" novel " ... because of
the strength of Burney's theme that life, after all, can be
controlled and, in fact, be lived as art."

408   WHITE, EUGENE.
"Fanny Burney." In Minor British Novelists, ed. Charles
Alva Hoyt (Carbondale & Edwardsville: Southern Ill. Univ.
Press, 1967), pp. 3-12.

The author's reasons for considering Fanny Burney a good
novelist, and the relationship of Evelina to the development of
the novel as a genre.

409   Fanny Burney, Novelist: A Study in Technique: "Evelina,"
"Cecilia," "Camilla," "The Wanderer." Hamden, Conn.:
Shoe String Press; London: Mark Patterson, 1960.

Discusses Fanny Burney's technical achievement, in order
to see how she worked and to evaluate her contributions to
the development of the English novel. Concludes that an analysis of such aspects of her work as "plot and characterization; manner of presentation, including her use of the pictorial and dramatic methods, her handling of the center of
interest and point of view, and her use of setting; and style,
dealing with such elements as diction, sentence structure,
dialogue and its uses, humor and satire, sentiment, and moral
tone, will reveal that hers was a considerably sophisticated
craft."

See also: 885

Collected Studies

410   LOW, DONALD A. , ed.
       Critical Essays on Robert Burns.   London: Routledge &
       Kegan Paul, 1975.

411   Burns: The Critical Heritage.   London: Routledge & Kegan
       Paul, 1974.

General Studies

412   BAIRD, JOHN D.
       "Two Poets of the 1780s: Burns and Cowper."   In [410], pp.
       106-123.

       Attempts to suggest reasons why Burns and Cowper estab-
       lished themselves almost simultaneously as important and
       popular poets, concentrating on three points: 1) the relation
       between the biographies of Burns and Cowper and their poetry;
       2) the disappearance of the notion of poetic kinds; and 3) the
       attitudes of late-eighteenth-century readers toward poetry.

413   BEATY, FREDERICK L.
       "Burns' Comedy of Romantic Love."   PMLA 83 (1968): 429-
       438.

       Burns's poetry anticipates and illustrates the tenets developed
       in later years by critics analyzing humor and comic love.
       Carlyle especially takes delight in this talent of Burns, valuing
       his humor above the more prestigious wit and satire of the
       eighteenth-century poets.

414   "Ae Spark o' Nature's Fire."   ELN 1 (1964): 203-207.

       Presents Burns as an intuitive, inspirational poet, in con-
       trast to scholarly poets working within structured concepts of
       form.   In this he draws distinguished support from Addison's
       Spectator No. 160.   Burns "rejected Pope's mirror in favor
       of Addison's lamp."

415   BENTMAN, RAYMOND.
       "Robert Burns's Declining Fame." SIR 11 (1972): 207-224.

           Argues that Burns is being denied his rightful place in the
       tradition of British poetry; that he is significant in the transi-
       tion from eighteenth- to nineteenth-century styles of poetry.

416   "Robert Burns's Use of Scottish Diction." In [26], pp. 239-
       258.

           Points out that "The 'Scottish' poems are written in a
       literary language, which was mostly, although not entirely
       English, in grammar and syntax, and, in varying proportions,
       both Scottish and English in vocabulary"; Burns did not write
       as he spoke.

417   BROGAN, HOWARD O.
       "Satirist Burns and Lord Byron." Costerus 4 (1972): 29-47.

           Discusses Burns's religious and political satires emphasizing
       "how his satire of the Auld Licht in religion is related to his
       later satire of Tory domestic and foreign policy, [and] how
       decisive a turning point in his view of himself and his world
       was his triumph in Edinburgh."

418   BROWN, EVERETT S.
       "The Political Ideas of Robert Burns." PMASAL 19 (1934):
       477-491.

           The keynote of all of Burns's political thinking is a pas-
       sionate devotion to the principle of liberty.   Discusses his
       contempt for class distinctions, his attitude toward the Ameri-
       can and the French Revolutions, his interest in politics and
       religion, and the extent of his reading in works on economics
       and government.

419   BUCHAN, A. M.
       "Word and Word-Tune in Burns." SP 48 (1951): 40-48.

           Analyzes sound and meaning in Burns's dialect poems:
       " ... the surface meaning, as always in poetry, is only a
       part of the effect of the lines.   The tune of the poem depends
       much more upon the Scottish pronunciation of familiar English
       words than upon an unfamiliar vocabulary." Suggests, further,
       that the poetic essence of Burns's poetry derives from the
       qualities of the Scottish words--"the drawl with which they
       are spoken, their earthiness and roughness on the tongue,
       and the idiomatic practice by which any one of them may be
       changed into a term of affection...."

420   CAMPBELL, IAN.
       "Burns's Poems and Their Audience." In [410], pp. 39-53.

          Burns was the center of his social community in Ayrshire,
       a sociable man who loved fun and conviviality. He looked at
       life from inside such a community, without limiting his world-
       view to the values of that community: an example is Tam
       O' Shanter who sees life from the "cosy intimacy" of such a
       community. A reader must place himself in the position of
       such a person, and try to follow Tam's drunken thought proc-
       esses at their own speed. That approach is applied to "Death
       and Doctor Hornbook," which illustrates a similar application
       of biography and social history to the criticism of literature.

421   CRAWFORD, THOMAS.
       Burns: A Study of the Poems and Songs.   Stanford, Calif. :
       Stanford Univ. Press, 1960; Edinburgh: Oliver & Boyd,
       1965.

          Refutes "current critical judgements" on the poems of
       Burns: for example, that he was an excellent user of the
       Scots language but mediocre in English.   Shows an aspect of
       Burns separate from Scottish tradition.

422   DAICHES, DAVID.
       "Robert Burns and Jacobite Song." In [410], pp. 137-156.

          Surveys Burns's attitude toward the exiled House of Stuart,
       emphasizing his life-long interest in Jacobite song; his in-
       terest in collecting and restoring popular Scottish songs ex-
       tended to the attempt to preserve Jacobite airs by writing
       inoffensive words to them.   Even more important are the
       some 30 songs Burns wrote or adapted which are directly
       Jacobite in subject; these are critically examined, and Daiches
       concludes that Burns gave Jacobite song a new lease on life
       by his ability to respond to and capture the different moods
       evoked in Scottish breasts by the Jacobite movement.

423   Robert Burns and His World.   London: Thames & Hudson,
       1971; New York: Viking Press, 1972.

          A popular, lavishly illustrated account of his life.

424   Robert Burns.   New York: Rinehart & Co. , 1950; London:
       Andre Deutsch, 1952; rev. ed. , 1966.

          Emphasis on critical examination of the poet's work, rather
       than the biography, which Daiches included to clarify his criti-
       cal effort.   Pays particular attention to " ... Burns's relation

to the older Scottish 'makers' ... and with the place of Burns
in the Scottish literary tradition...."

425   "The Identity of Burns." In [13], pp. 323-340; rpt. in More
        Literary Essays (London: Oliver & Boyd; Chicago: Univ. Chi-
        cago Press, 1968), pp. 164-183.

        A biographical as well as critical analysis of Burns. He
        is shown as an idealistic liberal, hampered by a class-ridden
        society; his best work is great, his worst is sentimental-
        rhetorical.

426   Robert Burns. (WTW) London: Longmans, 1957.

        A short biographical account and bibliography.

427   DAMICO, HELEN.
        "Sources of Stanza Forms Used by Burns." SSL 12 (1975):
        207-219.

        Traces stanzas used by Burns back to medieval sources
        for a better understanding of the tradition out of which he
        worked. In addition to using these models, "he assimilated
        them, and through their structures expressed his personality"
        which perhaps indicates "a temperament closer to the Middle
        Ages than to the eighteenth century."

428   DAVIE, CEDRIC THORPE.
        "Robert Burns, Writer of Songs." In [410], pp. 157-185.

        Insists that Burns's songs cannot be critically appreciated
        solely as poetry, apart from the music to which they are
        set; they are integrated works of art. Argues for five propo-
        sitions: 1) an effective tune did not always draw highly in-
        spired words from the poet, and conversely, some of the fin-
        est words were linked with indifferent tunes; 2) songs in-
        cluded in The Scots Musical Museum are generally superior
        to those in George Thomson's A Select Collection of Original
        Scotish Airs; 3) songs written in the vernacular are in general
        superior to those written entirely in English; 4) everyone,
        including Burns, accepted the practice of publishing a song
        to a tune other than that which the poet intended; and 5) Burns
        was indifferent to the form in which his songs were published,
        so that he failed to realize that, for instance, the harmoniza-
        tions in The Scots Musical Museum were undistinguished and
        the accompaniments in Thomson were often ludicrously inept.

429   DENT, ALAN.
        Burns in His Time. London: Nelson, 1966.

A popular, illustrated "attempt to set Robert Burns in his period and to communicate the flavour and tang of that period" by an Ayrshire-born critic. Includes a collection of the "wisest and shrewdest and most eloquent appraisals" of Burns during his lifetime and afterwards.

430   DEWAR, R.
      "Robert Burns." In [54], pp. 190-211.

A general survey of Burns's life and career, especially concerned with the conflict in Burns and among his contemporary readers between the simple Bard and the "book-taught, derivative Poet." Concludes that "Burns is nothing if not the poet of the folk among whom he was born, the folk of the harvest-field of 1773, the simple folk of his native Kyle and their likes elsewhere in the workaday Scotland of his time. And for all who would know him rightly and appreciate his peculiar virtue, the true path of approach must be--Johnson, Thomson, the Poems."

431   EDGAR, IRVING.
      "Robert Burns: A Literary Evaluation." In Essays in English Literature and History (New York: Philosophical Library, 1972), pp. 15-34.

Considers Burns as a "poet in the light of the times in which he lived"; seeks to discover the source of his power over the human heart.

432   EGERER, J. W.
      "Robert Burns and 'Guid Black Prent.'" In [27], pp. 269-279.

A partly bibliographical account of the publishing history of Burns's poems, emphasizing in particular his search for an appreciative audience and a publisher who realized his worth; had he been more successful, the world would have been richer by many poems. Burns was partly successful in achieving his ideal of being a Scottish bard when he became associated with James Johnson and George Thomson in the compilation and production of song anthologies; but the general picture remains clear: "the Poet wanting passionately to be read and, when he discovered that his public had reached the saturation point, seeking other means of expressing himself. Indeed, we are richer by having the songs ... but we might have had other lyrics and satires and narratives if Burns had only realized that his dream of a large and appreciative audience was a reality."

433   ERICSON-ROOS, CATARINA.

The Songs of Robert Burns: A Study of the Unity of Poetry and Music. (AUUSAU 30) Stockholm: Almqvist & Wiksell, 1977.

Insists that a true appreciation of Burns's art requires that "the lyric texts should ... always be analysed in conjunction with their respective tunes and the songs be dealt with as unities of poetry and music"; the aim is "to show how an essential part of the expression of the songs lies in their music as well as in the interaction between words and music, how a kind of synergism is created cooperatively by the lyric and music, and how most songs suffer from being only read." The study is limited to the songs printed in James Johnson's six volumes of The Scots Musical Museum (Edinburgh, 1787-1803), and concentrates especially on their literary themes.

434   FERGUSON, J. DeLANCEY.
Pride and Passion: Robert Burns 1759-1796. New York & London: Oxford Univ. Press, 1939; rpt. New York: Russell & Russell, 1964.

Attempts to answer the question, What sort of man was Robert Burns? by avoiding chronological narrative and emphasizing the relationships of everyday life: education, men, women, livelihood, and song.

435   "Some Aspects of the Burns Legend." PQ 11 (1932): 263-273.

Through a study of Burns's letters, the author attempts to show how editors and owners of Burns's manuscripts have distorted the picture of the poet--that he "was neither a Galahad nor the raffish scamp of the oral tradition, but, in his own phrase, 'a frail, backsliding mortal merely.'"

436   "Burns and Hugh Blair." MLN 45 (1930): 440-446.

Discusses changes in Burns's Kilmarnock Poems which were suggested by Blair, and refused by Burns.

437   FITZHUGH, ROBERT T.
Robert Burns: the Man and the Poet: A Round Unvarnished Account. Boston: Houghton Mifflin, 1970; London: Allen, 1971.

Burns is here presented with heavy reliance upon quotations from his own works and letters and from those of his close friends, with the intent of staying close to the most accurate sources. "Attempts to deal straightforwardly with controversies, presenting the evidence, indicating probabilities, but not forcing conclusions." Quotes the poems and songs extensively, both as a source of biographical material and as a delight in themselves.

438   "Burns' Highland Mary." PMLA 52 (1937): 829-834.

Substantiates stories of Burns's relationship with Highland Mary as told by John Richmond and Joseph Twain based on new evidence to prove that such a relationship did exist.

439   "The Composition of 'Scots Wha Hae.'" MLN 51 (1936): 423-426.

A study of the original manuscript shows that Dr. Currie's account of the composition of "Scots Wha Hae" was inaccurate --that he was inclined to "change documents when they conflicted with his theories."

440   "The Paradox of Burns' Character." SP 32 (1935): 110-119.

An attempt to "put several unpleasant traits of Burns in their proper light"--his bawdy, caustic, and resentful side-- and "to emphasize the paradox of his character"--the other side well-received, friendly, brilliant, and generous--during the period 1791-96 when he resided in Dumfries. Although most writers only look at Burns " ... as the ideal figure of romantic tradition ... ," it is evident that he was " ... at the same time, a man of bitter moods and violent, uncontrolled impulses."

441   FRASER-HARRIS, D. F.
       "Burns as a Writer of Prose." Dalhousie Rev. 14 (1934): 203-213.

Examines Burns's vigorous prose style, written in the purest English, and asks, where did Burns acquire a style of such assurance, elegance, and dignity? Suggests that he did not become a writer of good English prose by any amount of reading: he had a "latent capacity for literary expression in the form both of verse and of prose."

442   GRANGER, BYRD H.
       "Folklore in Robert Burns' 'Tam O' Shanter.'" In Folklore International: Essays in Traditional Literature, Belief, and Custom in Honor of Wayland Debs Hand, Professor of German and Folklore, University of California, Los Angeles, ed. D. K.

Wilgus (Hatboro, Pa.: Folklore Associates, Inc., 1967),
pp. 83-88.

Explains some of the folklore elements known to Burns's
contemporaries but unknown to modern readers; elements essential to the understanding of the poem, especially its ending.

443   HECHT, HANS.
       Robert Burns, the Man and His Work.   Jane Lymburn, trans.
       Edinburgh: Hodge, 1936; 2nd ed. 1950.

Originally appearing in 1919, this work in translation is
revised and enlarged; its aim is "to show the universal aspect of Burns by presenting him against the broad backgrounds
of British civilization, of the eighteenth century, and of European culture in general," while "leaving out of account ...
much that is merely ephemeral...." Among many insights,
Hecht suggests that Burns sought to eliminate the boundary
between the one who made the song and those who sang it:
"The magnitude of this idea ... is tremendous and unique,
and the manner of its execution of inexhaustible interest."
Burns's career reflects the characteristics of his age: "...
at its best his poetry rises to the typical expression of the
highest ideas that the eighteenth century was called upon to
communicate to mankind." Argues, finally, that his poetry
possessed the same passion, pride, and manliness as his
character.

444   HELLER, OTTO.
       "Robert Burns: A Revaluation."   Wash. Univ. Stds.   12
       (April, 1925): 171-199.

General reflections on Burns's poetry and poetic achievement, emphasizing that Burns was not so much a "natural
poet" as a conscious and studious artist and that the traditional allegation that he is a "poet of nature" needs qualifica-
tion: he did not expand the scope of the poetic treatment of
nature, but deepened and enriched it.   His claim to greatness resides in the universality of his appeal to humanity.

445   KEITH, CHRISTINA.
       The Russet Coat: A Critical Study of Burns' Poetry and of
       Its Background.   London: Hale, 1956.

Emphasizes such topics as Burns as a satirist, the background of Burns's thought, his qualities as a poet, the basis
of his lyrical art in Scots folksong, and extended analyses of
the poems.

446   KINSLEY, JAMES.

"A Note on 'Tam O' Shanter.'" English 16 (1967): 213-217.

Discusses ambivalences in the poem: ironic attitude at beginning and end, but "at the core of the poem ... Burns and his audience willingly suspend their disbelief."

447   "Burns and the Merry Muses." RMS 9 (1965): 5-21.

The Merry Muses of Caledonia identified as a "collection of bawdry" whose authorship is still a matter of controversy. Burns's authorship of some of them is accepted, and Kinsley discusses textual evidence linking most but not all of the rest to a collection compiled by Burns.

448   LEGMAN, G.
       The Hornbook: Studies in Erotic Folklore and Bibliography.
       New Hyde Park, N.Y.: University Books, 1964.

Includes a chapter on The Merry Muses of Caledonia, using it as a printed source of Scottish and English folksong.

449   LEWIS, MARY B.
       "Burns' 'Tale O' Truth': A Legend in Literature." JFI 13
       (1976): 241-262.

A study of Burns's artistic use of folklore in "Tam O' Shanter." Suggests that "Knowing what a legend is, how it operates as a communicative event among peoples, is ... a key to understanding" the poem. It is Burns's "ability to infuse 'Tam o' Shanter' internally with dialectic elements and to evoke externally appropriate responses from the poem's audiences that indicates not only his own power as poet but his links with his own traditional environment."

450   LINDSAY, MAURICE.
       The Burns Encyclopaedia. London: Hutchinson, 1959; rev.
       ed., 1970.

451   Robert Burns: The Man, His Work, The Legend. London:
       MacGibbon & Kee, 1954; rev. ed., 1968.

A popular study of Burns and his work.

452   McGUIRK, CAROL.
       "Sentimental Encounter in Sterne, Mackenzie, and Burns."
       SEL 20 (1980): 505-515.

Burns uses the techniques of "ironist Sterne" and "benevolist Mackenzie in 'To a Louse' and 'To a Mouse' in which
he is able to milk 'significance' from a stage-prop world ...
to circumscribe [his] bare peasant world with an aura of
warmth and idealism."

453   MacKENSIE, M. L.
        "A New Dimension for 'Tam O' Shanter.'"   SSL 1 (1964):
        87-92.

        Supports the position that "Tam O' Shanter" is not only a
        narrative poem but belongs in the genre of the mock-heroic.
        Demonstrates its relationship to The Rape of the Lock in
        techniques and incidents.

454   McKILLOP, ALAN D.
        "The Living Burns."   Rice Inst. Pamphlet 47, No. 3 (1960):
        1-16.

        A general attempt to define the "living Burns" within the
        context of his age and country, emphasizing in particular that
        he "imposes a unity upon his best work which overrides the
        matter of language."

455   MacLAINE, Allan H.
        "Radicalism and Conservatism in Burns's The Jolly Beggars."
        SSL 13 (1978): 125-143.

        An analysis of the poem--its literary background, tight
        dramatic organization, language, and stylistic effects--to
        show that it is "a radical-conservative paradox" which pre-
        sents both the radical philosophy of the beggars and the con-
        servative, realistic, and socially orthodox view of the nar-
        rator.   It is this conflict of ideas that gives the poem its
        tension and its unique appeal.

456   "Burns's Use of Parody in 'Tam O' Shanter.'"   Criticism 1
        (1959): 308-316.

        A supportive response to David Daiches' treatment of "Tam
        O' Shanter" in his 1950 work on Burns [424].   MacLaine's
        emphasis is on the style of the poem and how the element of
        parody operates in it.

457   MORTON, RICHARD.
        "Narrative Irony in Robert Burns' Tam O' Shanter."   MLQ
        22 (1961): 12-20.

Discusses Burns's control of ironic distance, and shows
that the ironic effect is maintained in the poem by the tension between the action as it tries to unfold and the hinder-
ing of this unfolding by the garrulous narrative style of the
character telling the story.   Morton analyzes this tension
from two points of view: first, the narrator's understanding
of the moral significance of the tale; and, second, the narrator's skill in rhetoric.

458   MURISON, DAVID.
       "The Language of Burns."   Burns Chron. 25 (1950):   39-47;
       rpt. in [410], pp. 54-69.

       Emphasizes the "strict training Burns gave himself in
language, the careful weighing up of each word, the ordering
of the thought, the choice of imagery...." Discusses, among
other topics, the models for some of the Kilmarnock poems,
Burns's skill in turning conversational prose into poetry, the
influence of homiletic Scots on such poems as "Tam O' Shanter" and "The Cotter's Saturday Night," and the nature and
extent of Burns's use of the Scots language.

459   RENWICK, W. L.
       "Notes on a Poem of Burns." In [12], pp. 109-116.

       "Epistle to Major Logan": concerned with textual varia-
tions in an autograph manuscript in the Edinburgh University
Library.

460   ROBOTHEN, JOHN S.
       "The Reading of Robert Burns."   BNYPL 74 (1970):   561-
       576.

       List of books, individual plays, poems, letters, and es-
says which Burns mentioned in his writings.   Refers to quotations which Burns used.

461   SCOTT, ALEXANDER.
       "The Satires: Underground Poetry." In [410], pp. 90-105.

       An account of several satires--"The Holy Tulzie," "Holy
Willie's Prayer," and "The Ordination"--that contained personal satire too libelous to be included in the Kilmarnock
edition, in addition to which Burns's sexual irregularities,
even including bigamous marriages to Jean Armour and Mary
Campbell, might have further increased the chances that the
kirk would censure Burns if those satires also aroused anta-
gonism.   "The Holy Fair" and "Address to the Deil," both

of which contained public and general satire, and "The Twa
Dogs," whose satire is not religious, found a place in the
Kilmarnock volume.

462   SMITH, SYDNEY G.
       "Burns and The Merry Muses." HR 7 (1954): 327-349.

       Burns saw as one of his most important achievements the
       work he did as compiler of the songs of Scotland. With the
       assistance of James Johnson, he put together The Merry
       Muses of Caledonia which was published at Dumfries in 1800,
       four years after his death. Smith discusses this epoch-making
       book and the many imitations and plagiarisms of it.

463   SNYDER, FRANKLYN B.
       Robert Burns: His Personality, His Reputation, and His Art.
       Toronto: Univ. Toronto Press, 1936; rpt. Port Washington,
       N. Y.: Kennikat Press, 1970.

       Attempts to reinterpret Burns and his poetry; sees him as
       exemplifying the "glory of the commonplace, the significance
       of the ordinary."

464   The Life of Robert Burns. New York: Macmillan, 1932;
       rpt. Hamden, Conn: Shoe String Press, 1968.

       A workmanlike biography, scholarly, accurate, and com-
       prehensive. Has as one of its aims the sifting of evidence
       to identify historical fact and separate it from Burnsian myth.

465   "A Note on Burns's Language." MLN 43 (1928): 511-518.

       Discusses Burns's dialect and suggests " ... that the dia-
       lect of [his] first volume was not precisely the dialect in
       which he conversed with his Ayrshire friends and neighbors,
       and also that his use of a Scottish dialect for his poetry was
       a distinctly revolutionary proceeding." Concludes by agreeing
       with Burns's brother, Gilbert, that the use of "Scotticisms"
       in poetry would have seemed an affectation, and that Burns
       wrote so well that there was no affectation in his poetry;
       also that the dialect of the poems was not Burns's natural
       dialect and that it was only his skill in handling it that make
       it appear so.

466   SPEIRS, JOHN.
       "Revaluations. III. Burns." Scrutiny 2 (1934): 334-347.

       Discusses Burns's use of Scottish vernacular verse (which

has no connection with English verse) to show its relationship
to conversation and to Scottish folk dance, and concludes that
"The world of Burns' vernacular poetry is a single complete
world and, essentially, a world of comedy. "

467   THORNTON, ROBERT D.
       "Robert Burns and the Scottish Enlightenment. "   SVEC 58
       (1967): 1533-1549.

       Discusses the effects of Burns's visit to Edinburgh, 1786-
       88, and of the Scottish Enlightenment upon his production of
       poetry.   Considers the degree of Burns's allegiance to the
       Enlightenment, and the importance of pride and passion in
       his poetry; concludes that "as a result of some months in
       Edinburgh face to face with the Scottish Enlightenment, literary
       fame through neo-classical poetry became Burns's dream to
       his dying days.... "

468   James Currie, the Entire Stranger, and Robert Burns.   Edin-
       burgh & London: Oliver & Boyd, 1963.

       Dr. James Currie, the biographer and editor of Burns,
       was not "an entire stranger," though almost unknown to
       twentieth-century Burns scholars; not an evaluation of Currie's
       edition, but a straightforward life of a man interesting in his
       own right.

469   "Twentieth-Century Scholarship on the Songs of Robert Burns. "
       Univ. Colo. Stds. , Series in Lang. & Lit. , No. 4 (July
       1953): 75-92.

       After scanning nineteenth-century reactions to Burns, Thorn-
       ton discovers a work he can respect, Songs of Robert Burns
       by James E. Dick (1903).   From here on scholars make gains
       in uncovering factual material in spite of Scotch literary cri-
       tics, who want to keep Burns conventionally respectable and
       preserve his aura of myth.

470   TUTTLETON, JAMES W.
       "The Devil and John Barleycorn: Comic Diablerie in Scott
       and Burns. " SSL 1 (1964): 259-264.

       Examines the evidence for David Daiches' theory that Sir
       Walter Scott was inspired by Burns's narrative poem, "Tam
       O'Shanter," when he wrote his "Wandering Willie's Tale. " Con-
       cludes cautiously that Daiches' proposition is "not unreason-
       able. "

471   WAUGH, BUTLER.

"Robert Burns' Satires and the Folk Tradition: 'Halloween.' "
SAB 32, No. 4 (1967): 10-13.

Reevaluates "Halloween" and reinstates it as a significant
poem in showing the development of Burns as a satirist and
his use of folklore as a strategy of satire.

472   WESTON, JOHN C.
"Robert Burns' Satire." ScLJ 1, No. 2 (1974): 15-28.

Discusses the savagery that lurks behind Burns's comic
and ironic verse.

473   "Robert Burns' Use of the Scots Verse-Epistle Form." PQ
(1970): 188-210.

Examines the development of the Scots verse epistle genre
before Burns, its limitations caused by Scotland's divided
culture, how Burns used it, and the extent to which he modi-
fied it; Burns exploited the form in order to express a personal viewpoint and his innovation was significant: "the introduction of serious subject matter in the expression of full
personal vision."

474   "The Narrator of 'Tam O' Shanter.' " SEL 8 (1968): 537-
550.

Weston analyzes "Tam O' Shanter" as symbolizing the schizoic
problems of the age, torn between pleasure and Puritan duty;
of the narrator's mind as he wrestles with native Scots and
Scots-English culture; and of Burns's own divided self. "This
essay offers [the] idea ... that the narrator of the tale is
divided in a very Scottish way ... it is the first, I believe,
to relate Tam O' Shanter to this split [in the Scottish char-
acter] and thus to show how it is of all or almost all of
Burns's poems the most distinctively national."

475   "An Example of Robert Burns' Contribution to the Scottish
Vernacular Tradition." SP 57 (1960): 634-647.

Tries to answer the following questions about one of Burns's
poems, "Poor Mailie's Elegy": "What was the tradition Burns
inherited? What did Burns keep, add to, or change in the
tradition? ... what are some of the distinctive qualities of
Burns' poetry? And from what source, if any, did Burns
derive his innovation?"

476   "The Text of Burns' 'The Jolly Beggars.' " SB 13 (1960):
239-247.

Argues that the Merry-Andrew section should not be printed
with the poem because it was part of an earlier version rejected by Burns.

See also: <u>3664</u>

General Studies

477   BEATTY, JOSEPH M., JR.
"Churchill's Influence on Minor Eighteenth-Century Satirists."
PMLA 42 (1927): 162-176.   See also: Robert C. Whitford,
MLN 43 (1928): 30-34.

Traces Churchill's "posthumous influence upon the minor
controversial writers between 1764 and 1783," and includes a
bibliography of works occasioned by Churchill's works or influenced by them, some written during his lifetime.

478   "An Essay in Critical Biography--Charles Churchill."   PMLA
35 (1920): 226-246.

A biographical sketch based on materials available in America at the time in which the author's purpose was to state
" ... as concisely as possible what [was] known of Churchill's
life, and ... indicating in every case the source of the information."

479   "Charles Churchill's Treatment of the Couplet."   PMLA 34
(1919): 60-69.

Shows how Churchill, although greatly influenced by Dryden
and Pope, deviated from their style of rhymed couplets and
at times " ... poured out all his emotion in powerful couplets
which were almost blank verse."

480   "The Battle of the Players and Poets, 1761-1776."   MLN 35
(1919): 449-462.

Discusses the literary-historical context of The Rosciad.

481   "The Political Satires of Charles Churchill."   SP 16 (1919):
303-333.

Discusses The Prophecy of Famine, An Epistle to William
Hogarth, and The Duellist as commentary upon the political

situation in London in 1763; also discusses Churchill's part
in the political battles waged in The North Briton.

482   BROWN, WALLACE CABLE.
       Charles Churchill: Poet, Rake, and Rebel.   Lawrence: Univ.
       Kansas Press, 1953.

       A critical biography which combines " ... factual narrative
       with evaluative interpretation: the man's life and the approach
       to his works." Includes a discussion of most of Churchill's
       major works.

483   "Churchill: The Triumph of Irony." In [81], pp. 87-119.

       An examination of the influence of Dryden and Pope on
       Churchill's style, and a critical analysis of some of his major
       poems.

484   "Churchill's Mastery of the Heroic Couplet." JEGP 44 (1945):
       12-23.

       Maintains that in "Dedication," "The Prophecy of Famine,"
       "The Author," and "The Candidate," Churchill is one of the
       masters of the couplet and the last great neoclassical satir-
       ist.

485   "Charles Churchill and Criticism in Transition." JEGP 43
       (1944): 163-169.

       Churchill's critical remarks are scattered throughout his
       works and are inconsistent; as a neoclassic he supports
       Johnson, Pope, and Dryden, but when he is anti-neoclassic
       his views are similar to those of Joseph Warton and Young.

486   CARNOCHAN, WALTER BLISS.
       "Satire, Sublimity, and Sentiment: Theory and Practice in
       Post-Augustan Satire." PMLA 75 (1970): 260-267.

       Looks at some of the corollaries of the decline of ridicule
       in the eighteenth century, especially "at the post-Augustan
       image of Juvenal; and ... at satiric practice in the latter
       half of the century." Sees Churchill's "Dedication to War-
       burton" as an exception to the typical "pseudo-Juvenalian"
       satire.

487   CUNNINGHAM, WILLIAM F. , JR.
       "Charles Churchill and the Satiric Portrait." In Essays &

Studies in English Literature, Herbert H. Petit, ed. (Du-
quesne Studies, Philological Series 5, Pittsburgh, 1964), pp.
110-132.

The Johnson-Boswell discussion of Churchill's poetry, the
satiric portrait and Churchill's contribution to this aspect of
formal verse satire.

488   FISHER, ALAN S.
      "The Stretching of Augustan Satire: Charles Churchill's
      'Dedication' to Warburton. "   JEGP 72 (1973): 360-377.

      Whereas Augustan satirists, especially Pope, packed their
      poems with specific details that they regarded as symbolic,
      Churchill used details primarily for their literal meaning:
      "he often is so interested in sheer detail that the coherence
      of his general meaning breaks down. " Churchill, in fact,
      was attempting to create a new, literal approach to satire,
      a kind of satire in which objective things acquire subjective
      associations from the mind of the poet, and he succeeds in
      creating it in one poem, the "Dedication" to Bishop Warbur-
      ton.

489   GOLDEN, MORRIS.
      "Sterility and Eminence in the Poetry of Charles Churchill. "
      JEGP 66 (1967): 333-346.

      Asks why he was so distinctly a minor poet? Surveys
      Churchill's work for attitudes which underlie his poetic tech-
      nique.   His thematic preoccupation with superiority and ster-
      ility occurs in all of Churchill's poems, and contributes to
      his "minorness. " Churchill's lack of lasting impact can be
      attributed to his failure to hold strongly to some positive
      values; " ... he is unable to project his imagination and sym-
      pathies beyond himself to encompass all men, and sometimes
      he does not believe in himself. "

490   HOPKINS, KENNETH.
      Portraits in Satire (London: Barrie Books Ltd. , 1958): 1-
      75.

      Biographical sketch of Churchill to indicate the background
      in which he wrote; includes discussion of most of his major
      poems.

491   JEFFERSON, D. W.
      " 'Satirical Landscape': Churchill and Crabbe. "   YES 6
      (1976): 92-100.

Attempts to show that Churchill provides a link between
Crabbe and earlier poets, that he "has elements in common
with Pope which do not recur in Crabbe, and elements in
common with Crabbe which he did not derive from Pope."
Churchill's satirical landscape in The Prophecy of Famine
"is partly achieved by a reversal of conventional landscape
effects." Crabbe's nature poetry "is best understood if his
central characteristic is recognized not as harsh realism ...
but as wit."

492   LOCKWOOD, THOMAS.
      Post-Augustan Satire.   Seattle: Univ. Wash. Press, 1979.

Churchill is the focus of this study of some of the "distinctions between the earlier and later character of verse
satire during the eighteenth century" in an attempt "to see
satire after Pope as the realization of a certain potential in
the satire before Pope...." Churchill and the satire of the
latter half of the century is set alongside the established
Augustan habits of form and content to show a certain mutuality between the two.

493   SCHAEFFER, NEIL.
      "Charles Churchill's Political Journalism."   ECS 9 (1976):
      406-428.

A study of Churchill's contributions to the North Briton,
which are interesting for several reasons: "for their literary merit as examples of sophisticated irony, for their relevance to the development of the reform movement in politics,
and for their biographical interest as constituting a salient
episode in Churchill's meteoric and tragic career."

494   SIMON, IRENE.
      "An Eighteenth-Century Satirist: Charles Churchill."   RBPH
      37 (1959): 645-682.

Takes issue with Yvor Winters's high estimate of Churchill
and says that, although Churchill was a competent versifier,
he was superficial, that his poetry was loose and rambling
with structural problems. Thinks that Churchill tried to bring
force and power back into eighteenth-century satire with his
use of personal attack.

495   SMITH, RAYMOND J.
      Charles Churchill.   New York: Twayne, 1977.

"An attempt to describe, analyze and evaluate the writings

of Churchill ... this study treats each of the major poems, together with his prose contributions to The North Briton, in terms of structure, technique, and characteristic themes." Each poem is considered in the context of Churchill's times and his work as a whole.

496   WALDHORN, ARTHUR.
       Charles Churchill: Conservative Rebel.   New York: New York Univ. Press, 1955.

       Deals mainly with his political views.

497   WEATHERLY, EDWARD H.
       "Charles Churchill: Neo-Classic Master."   UKCR 20 (1954): 266-271.

       Churchill enjoyed an immense reputation in his lifetime, then dropped out of literary-critical sight.   Weatherly reviews a biography of Churchill by Wallace C. Brown [482] which is part of an attempt to rehabilitate and reassess Churchill.

498   "Churchill's Literary Indebtedness to Pope."   SP 43 (1946): 59-68.

       Presents evidence, in addition to that presented by Brown [482], to "justify the conclusion that the most important single literary influence on Churchill's poetic career was the work of Alexander Pope."   Shows close similarities between their ideas (especially the use of personal interests as theme), their use of satire, and their use of versification.

499   WINTERS, YVOR.
       "The Poetry of Charles Churchill."   Poetry 98 (1961): 44-53, 104-117.   Rpt. in Forms of Discovery: Critical and Historical Essays on the Forms of the Short Poem in English. (Denver: Alan Swallow, 1967), pp. 121-145.

       A critical study of Churchill's poetry with a thorough analysis of the "Dedication."

See also: 561, 1578

General Studies

500 AINSWORTH, EDWARD G. , JR.
Poor Collins: His Life, His Art, and His Influence. Ithaca,
N. Y. : Cornell Univ. Press, 1937.

A study of Collins as man and poet, including biographical
material not previously published. An exhaustive study of
his poetry and the influence of Collins upon nineteenth-century
poets.

501 BAINE, RODNEY M.
"Warton, Collins, and Skelton's Neocramancer." PQ 49
(1970): 245-248.

Supports previously dubious evidence as strongly indicative,
though not conclusive, that Collins had been the owner of a
very rare book, John Skelton's Neocramancer.

502 BROOKS, E. C.
"William Collins's 'Ode on the Poetical Character.' " CE 17
(1956): 403-404.

An analysis of the myth Collins creates about the Cestus
of Poethood, ll. 23-50; argues that God created the poetical
character on a loom rather than begot it on a female, and
that when the Cestus of Poethood was completed, He gave it
to Fancy to dispose of as she wished; she gave it to Milton.
The "rich-hair'd Youth of Man," moreover, was not born of
the union of God and Fancy, and is neither a mortal poet nor
an Ideal or Abstract poet; rather he is the sun. Defends
Collins's handling of the poem's conclusion.

503 BROWN, MARSHALL.
"The Urbane Sublime." ELH 45 (1978): 236-254.

Satiric and sublime poets displayed common stylistic pre-
suppositions: they used "similar kinds of verbal artifice,
entertained similar conceptions of formal organization, and
envisioned similar purposes with respect to much the same

audience." Since a continuity exists between the satiric and
the sublime modes, the early eighteenth century possessed
a unity within diversity that still allowed for a remarkable
range of tone and subject matter. The article deals with the
style of sublime poetry, emphasizing its artificial and inflated
diction, as in Gray's Eton College ode; it considers The Seasons and Collins's Odes in order to examine the age's formal
sense; and it concludes with an examination of Young's Night
Thoughts, in order to describe the purpose of the style and
to explain its fascination with the supernatural.

504   BROWN, MERLE E.
        "On William Collins' 'Ode to Evening.'" EIC 11 (1961): 136-
        153.

        Ode to Evening is analyzed and declared to be "one of the
        richest poems in the English language." The power of the
        poet to capture Beauty and make his vision of it eternal is
        the messages delivered more strongly and with more vitality
        than is usual in poems about evening.

505   CARVER, P. L.
        The Life of a Poet: A Biographical Sketch of William Col-
        lins. London: Sidgwick and Jackson, 1967; The Life of a
        Poet: A Biography of William Collins. New York: Horizon
        Press, 1967.

        Based on new material, the book seeks to find the real
        Collins.

506   "Collins and Alexander Carlyle." RES 15 (1939): 35-44.

        Speculates on relationship between "Ode to Evening" and
        "How Sleep the Brave."

507   COLLINS, MARTHA.
        "The Self-Conscious Poet: The Case of William Collins."
        ELH 42 (1975): 362-377.

        Discusses Collins's self-consciousness as manifested in
        the thematic structure and stylistic qualities of his poems,
        his obsession with the subject of poetry, and his preoccupation
        with and lack of confidence in his own poetic role.

508   CRIDER, JOHN R.
        "Structure and Effect in Collins' Progress Poems." SP 60
        (1963): 57-72.

Shows how Collins's "Verses Humbly Address'd to Sir
Thomas Hanmer on His Edition of Shakespeare's Works"
served as a background for his odes on Pity, Fear, and
Simplicity. "The central idea of odes such as Pity, Fear
and Simplicity exists in embryo in this piece. And, more
important here, the progress structure and the revival of the
arts theme carry over, transformed, into the later poems."
Especially discusses the critical ideas in the Ode to Simplicity.

509   DELAMARE, MARCEL.
       "L'originalité de Collins." Revue Anglo-Américaine 9 (1931):
       16-28.

       Though Collins has not "the hallucinating vision of a Cole-
       ridge or a Poe" he has the ability to bring life to his char-
       acters, even mythological ones, and to create intensely vivid
       word-pictures. He does this with the use of action more than
       description. Ode to Evening is considered his masterpiece;
       Swinburne rated him above Gray in lyricism but not in elegy;
       he was a forerunner of the Age of Romanticism.

510   DOUGHTY, OSWALD.
       William Collins. (WTW) London: Longmans, 1964.

       Biographical sketch and literary criticism of a "poet of
       transition" who links the eighteenth and nineteenth centuries
       not because his lifetime (1721-1759) crossed the century line,
       but because his poetry appealed to the Romantics of the nine-
       teenth century. His fame and reputation grew greater after
       his death.

511   FRY, CHRISTOPHER.
       "William Collins (1721-1759)." Cont. Rev. 227 (1975): 142-
       145.

       Brief sketches of some of Collins's poetry as an insight
       into his love of music. Suggests that "we can gain most
       pleasure from him now if we ... listen to him as we would
       listen to the sound of a musical instrument."

512   FRY, PAUL H.
       "The Tented Sky in the Odes of Collins." In: The Poet's
       Calling in the English Ode (New Haven: Yale Univ. Press,
       1980), pp. 97-132.

       Collins set out to explore (and restore) the origin of con-
       tentment. "His odes invoke the ground of freedom rather
       than the impersonality of form. They are meant ... to re-

assert the freedom of the creative will in times that are
hagridden by spleen. " Chastity, for example, the state of
freedom from sensual tyranny, is an emblem of "originary
freedom and of absence from natural origins. " An important
motif is that of incest, especially in the "Ode on the Poetical
Character"; in Collins's odes there is a dramatic conflict between the independence of chastity and the intricate pattern
of incest. The odes of Collins (and Gray) exemplify a willing
submission to the conventions of "vocal" writing; they employ
a circumscriptural imagery based on a central paradox: the
more a circle closes, the more it closes off its content from
the viewer.

513   GARROD, H. W.
       Collins. Oxford: Oxford Univ. Press, 1928; rpt. New York:
       Octagon Books, 1973.

       Collins the man and his poetry realistically treated in
what the author calls a "minute study" in literary criticism.
Discusses the earlier odes, Ode to Evening, patriotic Odes,
and The Passions.

514   GEARIN-TOSH, MICHAEL.
       "Obscurity in William Collins. " Studia Neophilologica 42
       (1970): 25-32.

       Takes exception to Roger Lonsdale's discussion of obscurity
in Collins's poetry (Poems of Gray, Collins and Goldsmith,
1969), that his use of words required the reader's knowledge
of earlier literature, and that some of his obscurity "is little
more than editorial euphemism" for Collins's ignorance.
Suggests that a knowledge of classical studies would make
Collins's poetry less obscure.

515   HAGSTRUM, JEAN H.
       "William Collins. " In [112], pp. 268-286.

       Deals with the pictorial elements of Collins's poetry and
"Where in this form, is the pictorial most prominently and
effectively present?" Discusses Collins's Odes, his allegorical personifications, and his relationship with the plastic arts.

516   HAMMER, MICHELE.
       "A Propos d'une Vie: William Collins. " EA 23 (1970): 302-
       310.

       Review of a biographical sketch of William Collins written
by P. L. Carver [505]. Notes that Carver had to fill in the
gaps caused by lack of documentation on Collins with unsup-
ported theorizing, but concurs with the tribute to Collins.

517   JACKSON, WALLACE.
      The Probable and the Marvelous: Blake, Wordsworth, and
      the Eighteenth-Century Critical Tradition.   Athens: Univ.
      Georgia Press, 1978.

      Proposes a new approach to the study of the poetry and
      criticism between the years 1750 and 1800, discovering in
      the poetry of Collins, Gray, and the Wartons a "revolution"
      whose touchstone was a "decidedly more radical interest in
      the poetic marvelous than had been tolerated by the literary
      Augustans.   The poets of mid-century ... sought an enlarge-
      ment of poetic license to delineate the unbodied realities of
      the human spirit that the eighteenth century called the pas-
      sions. " By embodying the "furies and beneficent deities of
      the human mind" in their pageants and processions, they
      created images of human nature different from those em-
      bodied in the poetry of Spenser, Shakespeare, and Milton.
      The major poets of mid-century are informed by one dom-
      inant theme, the exploration of the permissible limits of the
      marvelous consistent with the presentation of probable human
      action and response.

518   JOHNSTON, ARTHUR.
      "The Poetry of William Collins. "   Proc. of British Academy
      59 (1973): 321-340.

      A general discussion of Collins as a poet needing the stim-
      ulus of another person's poem, novel, or article to excite
      him to write; discusses themes, diction, and structure of the
      Odes.

519   KALLICH, MARTIN.
      " 'Plain in Thy Neatness': Horace's Pyrrha and Collins'
      Evening. " ELN 3 (1966): 265-271.

      A study of the large number of rhetorical similarities be-
      tween Odes 1 and 5, in Milton's translation, and Collins's
      poem.

520   LAMONT, CLAIRE.
      "William Collins's 'Ode on the Popular Superstitions of the
      Highlands of Scotland'--A Newly Recovered Manuscript. " RES
      19 (1968): 137-147.

      Prints the text of Collins's Ode from the manuscript given
      by Collins to John Home in 1750, and not recovered until
      1784 when it was read by Dr. Alexander Carlyle to the Royal
      Society of Edinburgh; this is the manuscript newly discovered
      in 1967, and printed here: "The manuscript shows the text
      as printed in the Transactions of the Royal Society of Edin-
      burgh to be remarkably accurate.... The Aldourie manuscript

makes few changes in our reading of Collins's Ode, although some of these changes are of interest. Its significance is that it gives a new authority to the text of the poem as it had previously come down to us."

521   McKEEN, JOAN LEE.
       "William Collins." Nota Bene 2 (1959): 14-17.

       Collins's use of poetic devices in "Ode to Evening" makes the verses live and speak for themselves, not only through the words but also through the sound.

522   McKILLOP, ALAN D.
       "Collins's Ode to Evening--Background and Structure." TSL 5 (1960): 73-83.

       Sets forth a simple analysis quoted from the early critics, who evaluated the poem for (1) enlivened natural detail, (2) animated "proper allegorical personages," and (3) the sympathetic response of a meditative observer. McKillop then explores the relative priority of these elements and their interaction.

523   "The Romanticism of William Collins." SP 20 (1923): 1-16.

       The place of Collins in the Romantic revival is discussed. Shows how Collins is held as a victim of extreme sensibility on the one hand and the victim of his imagination on the other.

524   MIYASHITA, CHUJI.
       "A Note on William Collins' Theory of Art." Hitotsubashi Jour. of Arts & Sciences (Tokyo) 8, i (1967): 1-6.

       Suggests that Collins wanted to assert the universality of beauty all the more effectively by arranging the beauty odes alongside the political ones.

525   PETTIT, HENRY.
       "Collins's 'Ode to Evening' and the Critics." SEL 4 (1964): 361-369.

       In literary criticism Collins's Ode to Evening has led a roller-coaster existence. It was very popular from his lifetime until 1928, when H. W. Garrod "did a remarkable hatchet-job" on it. But Pettit sees in Garrod an opposite bias, and brings the poem back to at least qualified approval. "The success of Collins is his originality within perfectly traditional patterns."

526   QUINTANA, RICARDO.
       "The Scheme of Collins's Odes on Several ... Subjects." In
       [13], pp. 371-380.

       Quintana undertakes to show that Collins had a scheme in
       mind in composing much of Odes on Several Descriptive and
       Allegoric Subjects, and that this reveals the shape of the
       book, "establishing the relationship of the twelve odes to one
       another, and [illuminating] how Collins's creative powers
       were channeled."

527   SHERWIN, PAUL S.
       Precious Bane: Collins and the Miltonic Legacy.   Austin:
       Univ. Texas Press, 1977.

       An interpretation of Collins and his poetry demonstrating
       "that an interpretation of Collins which aims at completeness
       cannot ignore Milton's importance for him, and that reading
       Collins in continual awareness of Milton enriches one's under-
       standing of descendant and precursor alike." Also demon-
       strates how Collins "malforms and individuates himself in
       relation to the 'precious bane' of the Miltonic legacy."

528   SIGWORTH, OLIVER F.
       William Collins. New York: Twayne, 1965.

       "A guide to the appreciation of the poetry of William Col-
       lins and ... to the appreciation of a certain kind of eighteenth-
       century poetry the possible pleasures of which are today or-
       dinarily overlooked." This extended study of Collins, his
       life and his poetry, makes use of new material, "Drafts and
       Fragments" by Collins, discovered among the Warton papers
       at Oxford.

529   SPACKS, PATRICIA M.
       "Collins' Imagery." SP 62 (1965): 719-736.   Rpt. with al-
       terations and additions as "William Collins: The Controlling
       Image" in [167], pp. 66-89.

       Discusses Collins's poetic theory and practice, his use of
       imagery and emotion in the odes; suggests that Collins's
       theory, that "poetry is the product of the image-making power
       and of divine inspiration," has great significance: "Collins's
       concept of the poet as literally a seer--one who sees deep
       into the heart of things, and who also sees surfaces meaning-
       fully--gains new importance from the way he uses imagery:
       as a mode of achieving insight as well as of recording it."
       When Collins's odes are successful, their visual images de-
       rive from and define emotion; when they are unsuccessful,
       the relation between vision and feeling is tenuous.

530   STEWART, MARY M.
        "Further Notes on William Collins." SEL 10 (1970): 569-
        578.

        A new examination of records leads to the discrediting of
        a long-held belief of Collins scholars. The genealogy of his
        grandmother Collins, née Duffield, is established. May
        Thomas's story of John Caryll's buying hats at the shop of
        Collins's parents is upheld, however, and corroboration is
        found for John Ragsdale's stories of the Collins parents and
        their financial problems.

531   "William Collins and Thomas Barrow." PQ 48 (1969): 212-
        219.

        Interprets the final lines of "Ode on Popular Superstitions
        of the Highlands," supporting "the assumption that Collins
        was acquainted with John Blair and others of the Scottish
        circle in London and through them met John Home."

532   STITT, PETER A.
        "William Collins's 'Ode to Evening.'" CP 5 (1972): 27-33.

        Collins's skillful use of poetic devices--assonance, con-
        sonance, metrical variation, alliteration, syntax, poetic dic-
        tion, and progression in the imagery--makes the ode a "su-
        perb lyrical achievement in an age not noted for lyric poetry."
        Suggests that poem is divided into three parts, each part of
        which flows so fluently together as to create a sense of the
        progress of evening. It also shows a movement from the
        specific to the general--e. g. , from one summer evening to
        evenings in general--and from concrete to vague imagery.

533   SYPHER, WYLIE.
        "The 'Morceau de Fantaisie' in Verse: A New Approach to
        Collins." UTQ 15 (1945): 65-69.

        Associates Collins's plastic fantasy of approximate and
        dynamic order with a special development within the decora-
        tive arts that occurred between 1730 and 1750; an insight into
        Collins as a rococo artist.

534   TILLOTSON, GEOFFREY.
        "Notes on William Collins." In Essays in Criticism and Re-
        search (London: Cambridge Univ. Press, 1942; rpt. New
        York: Archon Books, 1967), pp. 127-129.

        Deals primarily with Collins's diction.

535   TILLYARD, E. M. W.
       "William Collins's 'Ode on the Death of Thomson.'" REL 1,
       iii (1960): 30-38. Rpt. in Essays Literary and Educational
       (London: Chatto & Windus, 1962), pp. 89-98.

       Collins's Ode on the Death of Thomson is examined and
       described as being "at ease with its audience." Collins is
       identified as truly a man of the Augustan Age, rather than
       as a Romantic born too soon.

536   TOMPKINS, J. M. S.
       "In Yonder Grave a Druid Lies." RES 22 (1946): 1-16.

       Examines the significance of the word "Druid" in Collins's
       Ode Occasion'd by the Death of Mr. Thomson. Concludes
       that it was not unusual "for Collins to see in Thomson, the
       modern Druid ... because he embodied in a modern form al-
       most all the characteristics of the idealized Druids of con-
       temporary conceptions."

537   WASSERMAN, EARL R.
       "Collins' 'Ode on the Poetical Character.'" ELH 34 (1967):
       92-115.

       Discusses relationship of first stanza of the Ode to the
       rest of the poem--the significance of the tripartite structure
       --and "the clash between the careful thematic organization
       and the abrupt, irregular Pindaric surface of the poem."

538   WENDORF, RICHARD.
       William Collins and Eighteenth-Century English Poetry. Min-
       neapolis: Univ. Minn. Press, 1981.

       Chiefly a book of criticism of Collins's poetry, not a criti-
       cal biography; but the book includes a chapter on Collins's
       madness and the biographical and critical myths that have
       grown around it. Argues that the "notorious difficulties of
       [the "Ode on the Poetical Character"]--in its syntax, imagery,
       and formal structure--are neither accidental nor perverse";
       they are intended to allow Collins's readers to experience the
       obstacles and frustrations that thwart any ambitious writer.
       Emphasizes Collins's investigation of the passions and his
       explanation of external nature, with particular stress on his
       achievements rather than his limitations.

539   "Collins's Elusive Nature." MP 76 (1979): 231-239.

       An examination of Collins's ode, "The Manners," which

is used to find an answer to the question of why Collins had
to go beyond the bounds of nature for poetic material. The
importance of the poem lies in the fresh perspective it provides of Collins's conception of nature, for it suggests that
"manifestations of nature such as Evening, despite their traditional associations, remain essentially elusive forces capable of withstanding our critical attempts to pin them down."
After "The Manners" the poet must either celebrate nature
or accept the invitation to explore beyond its "seductive sur-
faces." But in the ode itself, Collins celebrates external
nature as well as questioning our ability to perceive that
world in its myriad shapes and colors.

540   " 'Poor Collins' Reconsidered." HLQ 42 (1979): 91-116.

A reconsideration of Collins's madness, based on all the
relevant material for the first time; discusses three related
problems: "in the first section the conclusions that have
been (and can be) drawn about Collins's illness are balanced
against a close narrative of the last ten years of his life;
the second section illustrates how these facts have been re-
worked into influential fictions; and the final section analyzes
the ways in which the fictions and half-truths surrounding
Collins have had an influence on the way his poetry has been
read." Concludes that Collins was not mad or ill during the
years in which he wrote poetry, and therefore his poetry
should not be read as either that of a madman or as an anticipation of his future insanity.

541   WOODHOUSE, A. S. P.
        "The Poetry of Collins Reconsidered." In [26], pp. 93-137.

Collins is examined as a pre-Romantic for a second time.
Woodhouse takes up essential elements in the background of
Collins's poetry, goes more deeply into his artistry, and
takes care to differentiate him from his near stylistic rela-
tives, the Wartons. He corrects what he sees as defects in
his earlier work [542]. Concludes that for Collins the imagination bears some relation to truth, and can seize on and present the "idea" of things--of pity, of liberty, of evening; the
means by which that end is achieved is through symbol--and
that is "Collins' great discovery, and ... the basis of his
best achievement in poetry."

542   "Collins and the Creative Imagination: A Study in the Critical
        Background of His Odes (1746)." In Studies in English by
        Members of University College, Toronto, ed. Malcolm W.
        Wallace (Toronto: Univ. Toronto Press, 1931), pp. 59-130.

Analyzes the Ode on the Poetical Character as an allegory

depicting the creative imagination and the poet's passionate
desire for its power; sketches the history of the imagination
in English criticism; indicates some of the ways in which
the theories of the imagination throw light on Collins's Odes
(1746), and especially on the effects at which he aims; and
suggests the place of those theories in the history of eighteenth-
century poetry and of developing Romanticism.

See also: 1365, 1400, 1412

General Studies

543   BAIRD, JOHN D.
"Cowper's Concept of Truth." In [51], pp. 367-373.

Describes Cowper's attitude toward salvation especially as displayed in the poems "Truth" and "The Progress of Error." Links Cowper's suicidal tendencies to his belief that God had condemned his soul to annihilation, and discusses how this belief influenced his writing.

544   BLOM, THOMAS E.
"The Structure and Meaning of The Task." Pacific Coast Philology 5 (1969): 12-18.

Blom reassesses The Task without the bias of earlier generations that resulted from their belief that the poem was written by a madman. He finds that The Task has organization and a unifying structure as a pilgrimage poem--certainly a long and frequently honored tradition. "The Task is the journey of the Christian pilgrim in the fallen world...."

545   BOYD, DAVID.
"Satire and Pastoral in The Task." PLL 10 (1974): 363-377.

Argues that when Cowper fears his moral security to be threatened, he interrupts the apologia for pastoral withdrawal that is the ostensible subject of the poem, abandons the persona of a rural recluse, and adopts the antithetical role of public satirist--that alternation between satire and pastoral poetry provides the basic structural principle of The Task.

546   BROWN, MARSHALL.
"The Pre-Romantic Discovery of Consciousness." SIR 17 (1979): 387-412.

Includes an analysis of "stylistic impasse" in the urbane sublime and its consequences in The Task.

547   CAGLE, WILLIAM R.
        "Cowper's Letters: Mirror to the Man." In [1], pp. 210-
        223.

            Cowper's letters dwell on his personal life and feelings,
        on the state of his soul, his attitude toward God, and what
        he thought to be God's attitude toward him; they are excellent
        examples of good narrative technique and spontaneity.

548   CECIL, LORD DAVID.
        The Stricken Deer; or, the Life of Cowper.   London: Con-
        stable, 1929; New York: Oxford Univ. Press, 1935; London:
        Collins, 1965.

            A finely written biography, emphasizing the duality in
        Cowper's life and work.

549   COX, STEPHEN D.
        "Self and Perception: William Cowper." In [93], pp. 113-
        126.

            Cowper exemplifies in his poetry the concept that "the
        self can discover its nature and significance by sympathetic
        identification with something in the outside world"; not only
        does he praise sympathy as a moral force, but he also em-
        ploys images based on sympathetic identification--with, for
        instance, the striken deer, the Yardley Oak, the Castaway,
        and even God.   He found in Nature and the Bible those images
        that would provide him with an accurate reflection of his own
        elusive self, yet he was never able to free himself from his
        own subjectivity: sympathy was not a liberating force.   His
        poetry suggests that sympathy and sensibility can actually
        reinforce the isolation of the self.

550   DANCHIN, PIERRE.
        "William Cowper's Poetic Purpose as Seen in His Letters."
        ES 46 (1965): 235-244.

            Argues that poetry was useful to Cowper as a safety valve,
        a means of expression needed for the maintenance of his
        mental balance; but that is not a complete explanation of his
        urge to write poetry.   Danchin explores overt and unconscious
        motives.

551   DAVIE, DONALD A.
        "Homage to Cowper."   PNReview 6, vi (1980): 21-24.

            An examination of the Olney Hymns convinces Davie that
        Cowper is "one of the four greatest poets of Christianity in
        the language...."

552   "The Critical Principles of William Cowper." Cambridge
        Jour. 7 (1953): 182-188.

        Cowper appealed to "the Strength of Denham"; he stood
        for taste and judgment; he was very consciously and deliber-
        ately a neoclassical poet.

553   DESAI, RUPIN W.
        "William Cowper and the Visual Arts." BNYPL 72 (1968):
        359-372.

        Examines Cowper's relationship with art and poetry and
        his knowledge of drawing which had an influence on his poetry.

554   ENRIGHT, D. J.
        "William Cowper." In Pelican Guide to English Literature,
        ed. Boris Ford, Vol. 4 (Baltimore: Penguin Books, 1966),
        pp. 387-398.

        Takes the position that although Cowper's quality of poetry
        is uneven he "speaks with an individual, if quiet, voice ... he
        has something to offer which will never fall entirely out of
        fashion or out of date."

555   FAUSSET, HUGH I'ANSON.
        William Cowper. London: Jonathan Cape, 1928.

        Emphasizes biography over literary criticism, regarding
        the poetry as more of a literary than a vital activity. At-
        tempts to explore Cowper's mental darkness.

556   FEINGOLD, RICHARD.
        "Art Divorced from Nature: The Task and Bucolic Tradition."
        In [102], pp. 155-192.

        Deals with Cowper's use of bucolic tradition in his com-
        plex interpretation of the public world in The Task; suggests
        that the poem, though remarkable for its treatment of con-
        temporary public issues, fails to "achieve a resolution, within
        the domains of nature and art, of the problems it raises ... ",
        a failure that emphasizes the "unsentimental clarity" of Cow-
        per's perception of those problems.

557   "William Cowper: State, Society, and Countryside." In
        [102], pp. 121-153.

        Considers the expression and intention of those elements

in The Task which deal with public issues, and especially
emphasizes the "stance and purpose" that influence the public
form of the poem.   In addition, the author examines some
of the major themes of Cowper's social outlook, and seeks
to determine the ways in which his ideas about the nature of
the social bond affected his treatment of the bucolic topics of
retirement, nature, and art in his criticism of contemporary
English life.   Concludes that "The Task needs to be understood, not as a simple and sentimental statement of the pleasures of retirement, but as a tortured, and often self-con-
tradictory attempt to speak in a public voice."

558   FREE, WILLIAM N.
       William Cowper.   New York: Twayne, 1970.

       Concentrates on Cowper's literary achievements, using
       biographical material primarily to explain and interpret the
       writings.   Tries to show how "the residue of [Cowper's] ex-
       perience appears in such formal aspects of his poetry as
       theme, structure, tone, and metaphor ... and that his tem-
       perament accounts for much that was new in his use of con-
       ventional themes and forms."

559   GILBERT, DOROTHY L. and RUSSELL POPE.
       "The Cowper Translation of Mme. Guyon's Poems."   PMLA
       54 (1939): 1077-1098.

       Analyzes the translation and discusses its ingenuity and
       technical excellence, and shows how Cowper modified the
       erotic imagery of the originals.

560   GOLDEN, MORRIS.
       In Search of Stability: The Poetry of William Cowper.   New
       York: Bookman Assoc. , 1960.

       Considers Cowper's various mental preoccupations as shap-
       ing influences on his poetry; is chiefly concerned with his
       attitude toward himself and society, toward stability and con-
       fusion, and toward authority and freedom.

561   "Churchill's Literary Influence on Cowper."   JEGP 58 (1959):
       655-665.

       Parallel passages are compared to show similarities in
       thought, opinions, factual material and, very rarely, a "ver-
       bal echo."   Cowper's care about plagiarism ruled out sim-
       ilarities in wording.   It is clear that for satire and other
       secular poetry, Cowper's mind was prepared by Churchill.

562   GREGORY, HOOSAG.
      "The Prisoner and His Crimes: Summary Comments on a
      Longer Study of the Mind of William Cowper." L & P 6
      (1956): 53-59.

      A detailed study of Cowper's mental defects and hazards,
      and his psychotic derangements, delusions, and the barriers
      in his daily environment.

563   GREW, SYDNEY and EVA MARY GREW.
      "William Cowper: His Acceptance and Rejection of Music."
      ML 13 (1932): 31-41.

      Analyzes some of Cowper's poetry in light of his comments
      on music and suggests how his philosophical ideas influenced his
      attitude toward music.

564   HARTLEY, LODWICK.
      "Harlequin Intrudes: William Cowper's Venture into the Sa-
      tiric Mode." In The Dress of Words: Essays on Restora-
      tion and Eighteenth Century Literature in Honor of Richmond
      P. Bond, Robert B. White, Jr., ed. (Univ. Kansas Pubs.,
      Lib. Ser. 42) Lawrence: Univ. Kansas Libr., 1978, pp.
      127-137.

      Cowper's satire against his cousin's three-volume work
      Thelyphthora: Or a Treatise on Female Ruin in a mock-
      heroic piece which he called "Anti-Thelyphthora: A Tale in
      Verse" launched him into a major literary effort which was
      to make him a major poet.

565   William Cowper: The Continuing Revaluation: An Essay and
      a Bibliography of Cowperian Studies from 1895 to 1960.
      Chapel Hill: Univ. N.C. Press, 1960.

      A thorough-going expansion of an earlier edition published
      in 1950. Extensively annotated and cross-referenced. Re-
      views critical background and discusses reasons for Cowper's
      permanence.

566   "Cowper and the Evangelicals: Notes on Early Biographical
      Interpretations." PMLA 65 (1950): 719-731.

      Before Hayley was commissioned by Lady Hesketh to write
      a biography of her cousin William Cowper, a number of
      writers of the Evangelical persuasion moved quickly to ex-
      ploit Cowper as a famous Evangelical writer and to clear
      their skirts of responsibility for his mental aberrations.

567   "The Worm and the Thorn: A study of Cowper's Olney Hymns."
       Jour. of Religion 29 (1949): 220-229.

       Traces indications of Cowper's spiritual struggle, his per-
       iods of depression or preoccupation with certain aspects of
       Christian living, through the hymns.   Their literary value
       as poetry is only faintly praised.

568   " 'The Stricken Deer' and his Contemporary Reputation."   SP
       36 (1939):   637-650.

       Surveys the popular reaction to Cowper in his lifetime,
       and the literary criticism for the same period, which was
       more often good than bad.

569   William Cowper, Humanitarian.   Chapel Hill: Univ. N. C.
       Press, 1938.

       "This study attempts to demonstrate the vitality of Cow-
       per's thought by presenting his poetry against the rich and
       dramatic background of eighteenth-century humanitarian ac-
       tivity."   The problem of the relation of the poet's religion
       to his insanity is regarded as sufficiently treated by others
       and as basically incapable of solution.

570   HUANG, RODERICK.
       William Cowper, Nature Poet.   London: Oxford Univ. Press,
       1957.

       " ... Aims at being a critical work on one particular
       phase of Cowper's poetry--his nature poetry ... [which] has
       been eclipsed by the brighter stars of English Romanticism...."
       Suggests that "Cowper's poetry of nature, in combining moral
       didacticism with depiction of country life and rural scenery,
       follows the Georgic tradition ... of Philips, Thomson, Young,
       and Goldsmith."

571   JONES, MYRDDIN.
       "Wordsworth and Cowper: The Eye Made Quiet."   EIC 21
       (1971):   236-247.

       Compares a passage from The Task with a passage from
       Tintern Abbey in an attempt to show the difference in the
       two poets' attitudes toward nature.   Cowper uses the land-
       scape technique as a means of "showing the divine actually
       present in the natural," whereas Wordsworth "finds his heaven
       on earth."

572   KROITOR, HARRY P.
       "The Influence of Popular Science on William Cowper." MP
       61 (1964): 281-287.

           Maintains that Cowper's desire to be as scientifically ac-
       curate as possible without sacrificing his poetic aims "helped,
       in part, to free his verse of much of the 'poetic diction' as-
       sociated with the generation of poets preceding him, to create
       precise, realistic description of a kind too seldom seen prior
       to The Task."

573   "Cowper, Deism, and the Divinization of Nature." JHI 21
       (1960): 511-526.

           Cowper's theological position is examined in the light of
       the burning issues of his times: science in apparent opposi-
       tion to religion.

574   LONG, ADA.
       "Quantitative Stylistics: A New Look at the Poetry of William
       Cowper." Style 12 (1978): 319-325.

           Seeks to find a comparative method which can distinguish
       between differences in styles, and selects for that purpose
       the traditional catalogues of rhetorical figures.   The author
       identifies 89 figures in 774 lines of Book I of The Task and
       subgroups them into 23 groups; she then identifies six basic
       categories: 1) mock epic, 2) personal narrative, 3) natural
       description, 4) philosophical doctrine, 5) social commentary,
       and 6) character description.   Comparing the stylistic dif-
       ferences between the first two categories, the author empha-
       sizes the various rhetorical figures that Cowper employs,
       and concludes that a "computer-assisted analysis of rhetorical
       figures can provide more precise terminology for the dis-
       cussion of style...."

575   MacLEAN, KENNETH.
       "William Cowper." In [27], pp. 257-267.

           Sees Cowper's writings as "a record of terror"; argues
       that "Neurosis and not the romantic movement was responsible
       for everything that he was as a writer."

576   MANDEL, BARRETT J.
       "Artistry and Psychology in William Cowper's Memoir."
       TSLL 12 (1969): 431-442.

           The Memoir presents two William Cowpers--"one who
       emerges from the shadows and has become the 'truth' of the

autobiography behind the author's back, and one consciously
created by the author to stand as his testimony to the first
three decades of his life. "

577   MANNING, B. L.
        "History, Politics, and Religion in Certain Poems of William
        Cowper. " Congregational Quart. 7 (1929): 326-343.

        Manning's article first sets forth what it does not intend
to do: it will not whitewash the Rev. John Newton, whose
religious slant is admittedly that of diseased Puritanism, and
it will not campaign to revive or popularize Cowper, whose
writing is heavy with "endless moralization and edification. "
The chronological account of Cowper's life exonerates religion
in general and Newton in particular from anything more than
a peripheral effect on his mental balance. His Whig politics
are reviewed by Manning in the context of history, and he is
shown to be a gentle man with clear insight in his lucid moments.

578   MARTIN, L. C.
        "Vaughn and Cowper. " MLR 22 (1927): 79-84.

        Suggests that a reading of Vaughn may have influenced
Cowper's change of attitude toward external nature which first
appears in his Retirement (1782).

579   MORRIS, JOHN N.
        "The Uses of Madness: William Cowper's Memoir. " Ameri-
        can Scholar 34 (1965): 112-126.

        Regards the Memoir "as a work in its own right, as a
literary production with its own peculiar virtue, its own claim
on our attention. " Cowper deals with "extreme experience--
the experience of religious conversion ... preceded and ...
determined by madness. "

580   MUSSER, JOSEPH F. , JR.
        "William Cowper's Rhetoric: The Picturesque and the Per-
        sonal. " SEL 19 (1979): 515-531.

        The lack of unity in Cowper's poetry parallels the aesthetic
assumptions of the picturesque. In picturesque art the audience assumes great importance, for it "must work to perceive the whole, it must integrate the perspectives if only
as a vague feeling of the appropriateness of each part to
some imprecisely defined whole. " The chief assumption of
the picturesque movement is that man is pleased by variety
and by motion rather than by stasis; good art therefore must

arouse energetic responses in the audience. Cowper combines homiletic and confessional rhetoric to create a rhetoric of engagement; in other words, the "intent to preach [and] the desire to confess encourage an active response...."

581   "William Cowper's Syntax as an Indication of His Relationship to the Augustans and Romantics." Style 11 (1977): 284-302.

Analyzes Cowper's poetry on the basis of its "prismatic" mode, defined as "a conflict between syntax and verse form, as a characteristic type of modification within his sentences, and as development based on contrast, negation, or denial." Cowper's syntax demonstrates that he was typical of an age that was moving toward the Romantic mode, and that his heroic couplets reveal his reluctance to accept the implications of the couplet--that is, he does not assume a communal moral vision based on accumulation of detail, but insists on the necessity of grace, a belief reflected in his refusal to depend on "the reader's prehensile activity with syntax...."

582   NEWEY, VINCENT.
"Cowper and the Description of Nature." EIC 23 (1973): 102-108.

Takes exception to Myrdden Jones's interpretation of Cowper [571] as a landscape poet: " ... many of his statements ... [are] underdeveloped to the extent of producing a false view of Cowper's involvement with the natural world, particularly a disregard for its complexity and depth." Argues that it is more important to emphasize, not Cowper's "picturesque" qualities, but his "decisive freshness, an exceptional subjectivity of response accommodated in an intimacy and naturalness of tone."

583   NICHOLSON, NORMAN.
William Cowper.   (WTW) London: Longmans, 1960.

A brief biographical and critical survey.

584   William Cowper.   London: John Lehmann, 1951.

A brief biographical account which quotes many of Cowper's poems. It includes some hymns which have built themselves into English-speaking Protestant culture, well known to millions who would not recognize the name of Cowper.

585   PALEY, MORTON D.
"Cowper as Blake's Spectre." ECS 1 (1968): 236-252.

Argues that the Spectre's speech was suggested by Blake's knowledge of and compassion for Cowper's sufferings.

586   POVEY, KENNETH.
       "The Banishment of Lady Austen." RES 15 (1939): 392-400.

Intended as sequel to "Cowper and Lady Austen" [587], and attempts to reconcile the various accounts of Cowper's final breach with Lady Austen in June, 1784.

587   "Cowper and Lady Austen." RES 10 (1934): 417-427.

The material comes from the letters of a Reverend Samuel Greatheed who was a friend of and frequent visitor to Cowper from 1785 to 1795. The letters were written to inform William Haley, Cowper's biographer, and contain an account of Lady Austen's character which is valuable in its application to the puzzle of Cowper's breach with Lady Austen.

588   "Some Notes on Cowper's Letters and Poems." RES 5 (1929): 167-172.

Discusses the letters and poems after 1778, discussing several individually with some textual criticism. Considers the possibility of Cowper as author of some anonymous short works of the time.

589   "The Text of Cowper's Letters." MLR 22 (1927): 22-27.

Gives evidence of the incompleteness and inaccuracy of the existing collection of letters.

590   QUINLAN, MAURICE J., ed.
       "Memoir of William Cowper: An Autobiography." Proc. of
       Amer. Phil. Soc. 97 (1953): 359-382.

Quinlan's preface emphasizes Cowper's mental illness and surveys its contributing factors. The Memoir itself is an interesting self-portrait, with emphasis on religion.

591   William Cowper: A Critical Life. Minneapolis: Univ. Minn.
       Press, 1953.

Endeavors to show "the man in relation to his works and his works in relation to his life." Uses material not available to earlier writers, making possible a reappraisal of Cowper.

592   "William Cowper and the French Revolution." JEGP 50
      (1951): 483-490.

      Examines apparent contradictions in Cowper's attitude
      toward the French revolutionary cause, showing how the ex-
      cesses of the revolutionaries alienated him from his original
      liberalism.

593   "Cowper's Imagery." JEGP 47 (1948): 276-285.

      Demonstrates (1) that certain of Cowper's biblical images
      appear throughout his verse, (2) that the same imagery some-
      times occurs both in his verse and in his prose, and (3) that
      the recurrence of certain images indicates that they bore a
      special relationship to his religious fears and melancholy ob-
      sessions.

594   "William Cowper and the Unpardonable Sin." Jour. of Re-
      ligion 23 (1943): 110-116.

      While admitting that Calvinistic Evangelicalism had an un-
      healthy influence upon the poet, Quinlan says that his obses-
      sion predated his religious conversion by about seven months.
      Upon embracing Evangelicalism he was relieved of this anxiety
      for several years, until the obsession returned.

595   RUSSELL, NORMA.
      "A Bibliography of William Cowper to 1837" (Oxford Biblio-
      graphical Society Publications). Oxford: Clarendon Press,
      1963.

      Includes much background information, such as reviews in
      contemporary journals, and provides specific evidence con-
      cerning Cowper's reception and subsequent reputation.

596   RYSKAMP, CHARLES.
      William Cowper of the Inner Temple, Esq.: A Study of His
      Life and Works to the Year 1768. Cambridge: Cambridge
      Univ. Press, 1959.

      Containing much new material, this biography is intended to
      supplement and correct earlier biographies and critical studies
      Emphasizes, not the Evangelical connection, but Cowper's
      activities as a templar.

597   SHERBO, ARTHUR.
      "Cowper's Connoisseur Essays." MLN 70 (1955): 340-342.

These few essays from Cowper's lighthearted youth are not significant in themselves, but are of some interest because Cowper in later years incorporated some of their ideas in his poetry, particularly the poem Conversation.

598   SPACKS, PATRICIA M.
        "William Cowper: The Heightened Perception." In [167], pp. 165-206.

A discussion and analysis of the imagery of the hymns; observes that the significant aspect of Cowper's hymns is their slight dependence on imagery and that their strength derives from their psychological insight.   Contains a lengthy analysis of The Task, and concludes that for Cowper the act of visual perception assumes metaphysical importance; seeing itself implied a transcendental truth, and the "physical power of vision became a spiritual reality."

599   THOMAS, GILBERT.
        William Cowper and the Eighteenth Century.   London: Nicholson & Watson, 1935; London: Allen & Unwin Ltd. , 1948; New York: Macmillan, 1949.

Emphasizes the charm of Cowper's personality and attempts to see him in relation to his time, especially in relation to the Evangelical Revival.

600   "William Cowper." Cont. Rev. Nov. (1931):   621-628.

A look at Cowper's life and his weaknesses and how these were reflected in his poetry.

601   WAUGH, ARTHUR.
        "William Cowper." Fort. Rev. 86 (1931):   590-603.

Discusses Cowper's life and the way in which his poetry reveals his innermost thoughts.

See also: 412, 769, 1954, 2232

Collected Studies

602   POLLARD, ARTHUR, ed.
     Crabbe: the Critical Heritage.   London: Routledge & Kegan
     Paul, 1972.

General Studies

603   BAREHAM, TERENCE.
     George Crabbe.   New York: Barnes & Noble, 1977.

     If Crabbe is viewed as a "Regency" poet, as a writer very
much aware of the atmosphere, the problems, and the literary
trends from 1780 to 1830, the modern reader should come to
respect him.   The author, therefore, tries to "place him
within the context of the church he served as an ordained
minister for fifty years, of the political upheavals he wit-
nessed--and, as serving magistrate, helped to alleviate--as
a writer making a substantial contribution to the investigation of the human mind which so preoccupied his fellow authors
in those years, and as 'pure' artist as well."   The approach
is not strictly biographical.

604   "Crabbe's Studies of Derangement and Hallucination."   OL
     24 (1969):   161-181.

     Crabbe's poetry often is concerned with the causes and
effects of derangement and hallucination, which are closely
related to sleep and ghosts; his poetry contrasts with that of
his contemporaries by its quality of insight and by its near-
clinical yet imaginative treatment.   Considers image patterns
and symbols of delusion and madness.

605   BRADY, MARION B.
     "Crabbe, 'Clutterbuck and Co.' "   Brigham Young Univ. Std.
     5 (1962):   19-30.

     Seeks to show how Crabbe uses tone in the "Elder Brother's
Tale" in Tales of the Hall to contribute meaning; argues that

he consciously moves from a deliberately heightened, romantic tone to a deliberately lowered, prosaic tone, so that the
poem may be regarded as unified by a brilliant handling of
varying tones.

606   BRETT, R. L.
       George Crabbe. (WTW) London: Longmans, 1956.

       A brief, general survey of the man and his work, attempt-
ing particularly "to lay bare his 'system,' the rationale of
his work, and to illustrate from its vast bulk those qualities
which give his poetry literary distinction."

607   BREWSTER, ELIZABETH.
       "George Crabbe and William Wordsworth." UTQ 42 (1973):
       142-156.

       Suggests that Crabbe and Wordsworth had much in common
and that they might have had more sympathy for each other's
work if they hadn't been so frequently placed in opposition by
their reviewer, Francis Jeffrey. Although the two poets had
many differences, they also had several points of likeness,
and their work became more similar with the years. "Wordsworth's Excursion has more of Crabbe's realism than have
the Lyrical Ballads. The Tales of the Hall has more of
Wordsworth's lyricism and pathos than have Crabbe's earlier
poems."

608   BROMAN, WALTER E.
       "Factors in Crabbe's Eminence in the Early Nineteenth Cen-
       tury." MP 51 (1953): 42-49.

       A reexamination of Crabbe's work and reactions to it by
his contemporaries that emphasizes his relationship to early
nineteenth-century poetic trends. Gives Crabbe more credits
as a poet than do most literary histories.

609   BROWN, WALLACE C.
       "Crabbe: Neo-Classic Narrative." In [81], pp. 161-187.

       An analysis of how Crabbe adapted the heroic couplet to
the art of narrative and his management of content and structure.

610   CHAMBERLAIN, ROBERT L.
       George Crabbe. New York: Twayne, 1965.

       A chronological approach dealing with "Crabbe's particular

claims to greatness as a poet and ... identifying ... his
peculiar place in English literary history. " Study emphasizes
"his poems and the life of the spirit they reflect" and deals
at some length with the Tales of the Hall.

611   "George Crabbe and Darwin's Amorous Plants. " JEGP 61
       (1962): 833-852.

       An examination of the poetry of Crabbe and Darwin to show
       that Crabbe had no intention of resembling Darwin and took
       great pains to avoid any resemblance. Most of the discus-
       sion refers to "The Library. "

612   CRUTTWELL, PATRICK.
       "The Last Augustan. " HR 7 (1955): 533-554.

       A discussion of Crabbe's poetry as that "of a true Augus-
       tan: an Anglican Christian of the eighteenth century," who
       was successful in combining "the stoicism of the classics
       with the 'rational piety,' the 'good humour which is never at
       cuffs with true religion,' that descends from Shaftesbury and
       Addison down through the central backbone of the eighteenth
       century. "

613   DIFFEY, CAROLE T.
       "Journey to Experience: Crabbe's 'Silford Hall. ' " DUJ 30,
       No. 3 (1969): 129-134.

       Deals with the emotional structure of the poem--the pattern
       of the symbolic progress from Innocence to Experience--with
       a close analysis of the introductory section and its relation
       to Peter's adventures at the Hall.

614   EDWARDS, GAVIN.
       "The Grimeses. " EIC 27 (1977): 122-140.

       Discusses Crabbe's use of language in the poem "Peter
       Grimes" in which he talks "as if Grimes had a real life out-
       side the poem ... and as if the poet were not in control of
       the meaning of the poem. "

615   EVANS, J. H.
       The Poems of George Crabbe: A Literary and Historical
       Study. London: The Sheldon Press, 1933.

       Attempts to describe the "main features, associations,
       traditions, and legends" concerning the writer and his poems,
       based upon such sources as his son's biography, county and
       local histories, parochial records and family manuscripts.

616   FORSTER, E. M.
       "George Crabbe and Peter Grimes." In Two Cheers for
       Democracy (London: Edward Arnold, 1951), pp. 171-187.

          Relates how Crabbe's antipathy to Aldeburgh played an es-
       sential role in his creation of Peter Grimes and shows how
       "the poet and his creation share the same inner tension, the
       same desire for what repels them."

617   GALLON, D. N.
       " 'Silford Hall or the Happy Day.' "   MLR 61 (1966):   384-
       394.

          Interprets "Silford Hall" as a "knightly quest" or a great
       adventure.

618   GREGOR, IAN.
       "The Last Augustan: Some Observations on the Poetry of
       George Crabbe (1775-1832)." Dublin Rev. 179 (1955): 37-
       50.

          Considers Crabbe's realism in the light of three phases
       of his poetic career: the use of the pastoral convention in
       The Village; the moral and regional interests in one of the
       tales in The Borough; and finally the relationship of Crabbe,
       the "late Augustan," with Romantic expectations of the age.

619   HADDAKIN, LILIAN.
       The Poetry of Crabbe.   London: Chatto & Windus, 1955.

          Points out the distinctive qualities of Crabbe's work with
       ample quotations to illustrate the points made; more concerned
       with his "experiencing mind" than his life and career, and
       seeks to show by examining his aims and assumptions his
       characteristic mode of writing and the poetic tradition to
       which he belonged.

620   HATCH, RONALD B.
       Crabbe's Arabesque: Social Drama in the Poetry of George
       Crabbe.   Montreal; London: McGill-Queen's Univ. Press,
       1976.

          A major characteristic of Crabbe's poetry is his manner
       of handling conflicting social, moral, and religious questions
       as a drama in which ideas exist independently of any coherent
       theory.   Crabbe includes within a single poem several dif-
       ferent and often contradictory social attitudes or human prob-
       lems without committing himself to one point of view.   In
       numerous poems he employs different "voices" to represent
       different opinions.   The purpose of this book is to emphasize

the recurring patterns created by Crabbe's contrasting attitudes, and "to suggest how these give his poems a richness
and variety which is ultimately far more satisfying than sim-
plistic answers." In order to trace the development of Crabbe's
artistic handling of dramatic structure, the author concentrates on one topic, that of social problems.

621   "George Crabbe and the Tenth Muse." ECS 7 (1974): 274-294.

Discusses Crabbe's attempt to destroy the false picture
created by the pastoral myth and to come to grips with "the
real world" in The Village, which "combines [his] perceptions
of an empirically based world with his belief in man's ability
to find values and goals."

622   HIBBARD, G. R.
       "Crabbe and Shakespeare." In [25], pp. 83-93.

Demonstrates how Crabbe took material from Shakespeare
and adapted it to his own age and to the life and society that
he knew. The influence of Shakespeare's attitude makes his
poetry more dramatic: " ... a sense of the tragic ... gives
depth and resonance to the moralizing; reproof is sweetened
with compassion."

623   HSIA, C. T.
       "Crabbe's Poetry: Its Limitations." Tamkang Rev. 1 (1970):
       61-77.

While admitting Crabbe's metaphorical and structural weaknesses, the author claims distinction for Crabbe on the lower
level of "good diction, ease and variety of movement, coherence and power of statement." The chief accomplishment
of Crabbe is to achieve a personal idiom within the stylized
form of the couplet convention.

624   HUCHON, RENE.
       George Crabbe and His Times, 1754-1832: A Critical and
       Biographical Study. London: Cass, 1968.

A revision of the biography of Crabbe, published in 1834
by his son, and a detailed critical analysis of his poetry.

625   KER, W. P.
       "George Crabbe." In On Modern Literature: Lectures and
       Addresses. Terence Spencer and James Sutherland, eds.
       (Oxford: Clarendon Press, 1955), pp. 62-77.

A general discussion of Crabbe, his style, and his success

as a narrative poet. Considers Crabbe "a chronicler of human
life without any prejudice in favor of misery."

626   LANG, VARLEY.
      "Crabbe and the Eighteenth Century." ELH 5 (1938): 305-
      333.

      Briefly traces history of the Pastoral and discusses The
      Village as a link in a series of changes and additions in the
      Pastoral form. Discusses Crabbe's theory of poetry and its
      connection with neoclassicism and his masterly treatment of
      character and psychological realism.

627   LOOKER, SAMUEL.
      "In Praise of Crabbe." Nineteenth Century 110 (1931): 489-
      502.

      Suggests that Crabbe's real strength comes from his psy-
      chological insight and from his "profound knowledge of human
      character and his mastery and understanding of the tragi-
      comedy of life in a wide sense."

628   NELSON, BETH.
      George Crabbe and the Progress of Eighteenth-Century Nar-
      rative Verse. Lewisburg, Pa.: Bucknell Univ. Press, 1976.

      The last Augustan satiric poet, Crabbe undertook "ingenu-
      ous experiments" in the service of literary values he had ac-
      cepted from Pope; no experiment was more radical than his
      fusing the novel of the 1790s with the short verse tales of
      the eighteenth century. He instinctively realized that only in
      the novel could anything be salvaged from Augustan verse
      satire. He was therefore an eccentric--the "conservative
      poet, who, in his determination to survive as an artist, ven-
      tures on extreme, seemingly improbable measures that re-
      flect his dilemma and his times." Crabbe was involved with
      the same moral and technical problems that confronted George
      Eliot: the "movement from Godwin and Inchbald and Edge-
      worth to Crabbe and then to Eliot and on to James is some-
      thing of a full circle in the history of English fiction."

629   NEW, PETER.
      George Crabbe's Poetry. New York: St. Martin's, 1976.

      A thorough and detailed discussion of the "Literary and
      Ethical Context of Crabbe's Poetry," "Poems up to 1807,"
      "The Borough," "Tales, 1812," and "Tales of the Hall."

630   SALE, ARTHUR.

"The Development of Crabbe's Narrative Art." Cambridge
Jour. 5 (1952): 480-498.

   An examination of Crabbe's work proves that The Village,
"which has no narration and not even a character study, gives
no indication whatever that Crabbe is almost the only, and
almost the greatest, practitioner of the realistic short story
in English verse."

631   SIGWORTH, OLIVER F.
      Nature's Sternest Painter: Five Essays on the Poetry of
      George Crabbe. Tucson: Univ. Ariz. Press, 1965.

   Examines Crabbe as a nature poet and a narrative poet
and tries to place him in relation to the poetry and thought
of the eighteenth century and to his romantic contemporaries.
Looks at criticism of Crabbe from Jeffrey to present. Concludes that Crabbe's characters become, under the influence
of his Christian ethic, generalizations; "without losing their
fictional reality, [they] become general comments on humanity."

632   SPEIRS, JOHN.
      "Crabbe as Master of the Verse Tale." Oxford Rev. 2
      (1966): 3-40.

   An analysis of Crabbe's Tales (1812) and The Village showing his mastery of the short story in verse. Suggests that
Crabbe has as much in common perhaps with Jane Austen
and Wordsworth as with Johnson and Pope.

633   SPINGARN, LAWRENCE P.
      "George Crabbe as Realist." UKCR 17 (1950): 60-65.

   Crabbe broke with the idea that nature was subordinate
to man. His nature was based on his botanical studies, and
he divided the eighteenth century into two parts: he retained
the style but dispensed with the artificiality. He retained
the descriptive power of the couplet to observe a changing
England during the Agricultural Revolution. He also introduced a new attitude of common sense toward common things.

634   SWINGLE, L. J.
      "Late Crabbe in Relation to the Augustans and Romantics:
      The Temporal Labyrinth of His Tales in Verse, 1812." ELH
      42 (1975): 580-594.

   An analysis of the Tales in an attempt to measure "the
extent to which Crabbe's artistic vision developed beyond his
early Augustanism," and a discussion of Crabbe's handling of
the challenge of time.

635   THALE, ROSE MARIE.
        "Crabbe's Village and Topographical Poetry." JEGP 55
        (1956): 618-623.

        Relates the "anomalies" of the poem to its topographical
        structure. The poem contains descriptive elements, moraliz-
        ing characteristics, and stylistic adornments common to topo-
        graphical poems and by these means "Crabbe calls into ex-
        istence a village that is probably the most individual and
        concrete spot in all of eighteenth-century poetry."

636   THOMAS, W. K.
        "Crabbe's Workhouse." HLQ 32 (1969): 149-161.

        A discussion of Crabbe's "Selectivity" in words and detail
        which he employed in The Village to create a poetic descrip-
        tion which would move his readers to be sympathetic toward
        the poor.

637   "George Crabbe: Not Quite the Sternest." SIR 7 (1968):
        166-175.

        Argues that Crabbe was neither "stern" in his depiction
        of life nor as original as most of his contemporaries. Pre-
        sents interesting facts about the economic condition of the
        rural poor, and suggests that Crabbe was much indebted for
        his subject matter to John Langhorne.

638   "Crabbe's Borough: The Process of Montage." UTQ 36
        (1967): 181-192.

        A close analysis of the poem showing that it was a com-
        posite of several locales--the church bells, the inns, the
        schools, the streets, and docks--details all added to the site
        and natural scenery of Aldborough.

639   "The Flavour of Crabbe." Dalhousie Rev. 11 (1961): 489-
        504.

        An analysis of Crabbe's poetry showing the effect of his
        moralism, his humor as well as his pathos, his satire, and
        his use of natural description. Argues that one of Crabbe's
        most distinctive merits is his ability to write equally well in
        both the humorous and the pathetic veins, occasionally in the
        same poem.

640   UNWIN, RAYNER.
        "George Crabbe: The Real Picture of the Poor." In The

Rural Muse: Studies in the Peasant Poetry of England. (London: Allen & Unwin, 1954).

A study of the English peasant-poet. Maintains that Crabbe's "power lies in his faithfulness to the spirit of the times--to a narrow and precise portrait of the life around him--rather than to a generalized or imaginative commentary upon it."

641   WILSON, P. B.
       "Crabbe's Narrative World." DUJ 37 (1976): 135-143.

The main elements of Crabbe's narrative poems are "the narrator and his function, dynamic shape or structure, and the presentation of character." He solved his structural dilemma by concentrating the significance of each poem upon a single point--of character, or moral process, or dilemma, or human experience. He persuades the reader to accept the narrator's version, and uses a narrative method to imitate the dynamism that exists in the world of social man.

See also: 491, 1954, 3183

Collected Studies

642 BYRD, MAX, ed.
Daniel Defoe: A Collection of Critical Essays. Twentieth
Century Views. Englewood Cliffs, N.J.: Prentice-Hall,
1976.

643 ROGERS, PAT, ed.
Defoe: The Critical Heritage. London & Boston: Routledge
& Kegan Paul, 1972.

General Studies

644 ALKON, PAUL K.
Defoe and Fictional Time. Athens: Univ. Georgia Press,
1979.

Partly intended to show how extensively Defoe's narratives
deal with time before modern developments in the novel created new temporal concepts, and partly argues that Defoe's
treatment of time points to the future as well as marking
the end of an older tradition. His narratives "invite exploration of three issues that are now central to the problem of
fictional time: the question of how temporal settings within
narratives may be related to the outside world of clock- and
calendar-time, the question of how time-concepts shared within a culture may influence expectations about the writing and
reading of fiction, and above all the question of how narratives shape the phenomenal time experienced by their readers."

645 ANDERSON, HANS H.
"The Paradox of Trade and Morality in Defoe." MP 39
(1941): 23-46.

A consideration of the conflict between commercialism
and morality in Defoe's attitude toward slavery and luxury;
in the eighteenth century the objections to both slavery and
luxury had mainly a religious origin, yet Defoe (and others)
recognized that they encouraged trade. Defoe's inconsistent
approach to the problem is explained by his recognition of
the distinction between economic and ethical ends.

646   BACKSCHEIDER, PAULA.
        "Defoe's Women: Snares and Prey." Studies in 18th-Cent.
        Culture 5 (1976): 103-120.

            A presentation of Defoe's women as they are "entrapped
        by circumstances and by social codes" and as they "fight
        back against the social evils which victimize them." Dis-
        cusses their role as "predators" and the "snare images"
        which Defoe sets for them.

647   BAINE, RODNEY M.
        Daniel Defoe and the Supernatural. Athens: Univ. Georgia
        Press, 1968.

            An examination of Defoe's occult writings that attempts
        to prove his belief in the reality of the unseen world and of
        the existence of a Particular Providence.

648   "Defoe and the Angels." TSLL 9 (1967): 345-369.

            A study of Defoe, his angelology, and his angelic com-
        munion. To understand his angelology is to understand his
        angelic ministry to his heroes and heroines as well as the
        serious themes and purposes of his fiction: "Such an under-
        standing will reveal a sincere Puritan trying both in his oc-
        cult works and in his fiction to retain and strengthen all
        meaningful and credible evidence of Providence, of an in-
        visible world of spirits, and of a communion thereby with
        God."

649   "Daniel Defoe and The History and Reality of Apparitions."
        Proc. of Amer. Phil. Soc. 106 (1962): 335-347.

            Defoe's collection of ghost stories and other supernatural
        phenomena studied to determine his attitudes and beliefs and
        their contribution to the understanding of the novels.

650   BAIRD, THEODORE.
        "The World Turned Upside Down." American Scholar 27
        (1958): 215-223.

            Discusses Defoe's remarkable believability and the part
        played in it by his deceptively simple style. Notes Defoe's
        "achievement in ... relocating the place of the imagination
        by seeming to deny its very existence."

651   BISHOP, JONATHAN.
        "Knowledge, Action, and Interpretation in Defoe's Novels."
        JHI 13 (1952): 3-16.

Sees a Lockean tabula rasa in the anonymous births and many new starts from a destitute condition which occur in the lives of some of Defoe's characters. In Defoe's realism the action of the novel is directed to problem-solving.

652   BLEWETT, DAVID.
Defoe's Art of Fiction: ROBINSON CRUSOE, MOLL FLANDERS, COLONEL JACK, and ROXANA.   Toronto: Univ. Toronto Press, 1979.

By examining Defoe's social and moral views, the author outlines Defoe's vision of human experience within the historical context, especially emphasizing his preoccupation with social issues that grew as the novels advanced.   In the discussion of the four novels he suggests how that vision informs all of Defoe's fiction: he traces the "evolution of Defoe's attitude to fiction from Puritan dislike to a more open acceptance of what he is really doing." He also wants to emphasize Defoe's fictional techniques and to demonstrate his artistic achievement by revealing in the four novels a "unity of theme and structure, an effective use of imagery and of language, a depth of concern with craft...."

653   BOULTON, JAMES T. , ed.
"Daniel Defoe: His Language and Rhetoric."   Introduction to Daniel Defoe.   New York: Schocken, 1965.

Defoe's theory and practice of language, and the nature of his stylistic achievement.

654   BOYCE, BENJAMIN.
"The Question of Emotion in Defoe."   SP 50 (1953): 45-58. Rpt. in [642], pp. 40-50.

Suggests "first, that attention to Defoe's realistic method has caused critics to ignore one other source of his power-- his representation of anxiety--and, second, that Defoe's success in this latter phase of his art was a result of his own problems of morality."

655   BRAUDY, LEO.
"Daniel Defoe and the Anxieties of Autobiography."   Genre 6 (1973): 76-97.

Considers Defoe's "first-person novels" as the record of his exploration of what constitutes human individuality and how to write about it, and concludes that Defoe's novels "change the basic nature of autobiography and announce one of the most important preoccupations of eighteenth-century literature"--the preoccupation with the possibility of retreat.

Defoe's final ideal may well be "an introspection without society, a replenishing of human insides that ... is basically pastoral and pagan in impulse."

656   BROWN, HOMER O.
"The Displaced Self in the Novels of Daniel Defoe." ELH 38 (1971): 562-590. Rpt. in Studies in 18th Cent. Culture 4 (1975).

Considers the fact that "Names, false names, absence of names" have a special importance in Defoe's novels, that the narrators "seem under a double compulsion to expose and to conceal themselves": secrecy is a precondition of self-revelation.   Concentrating on Robinson Crusoe, the author concludes that while Defoe is impersonating Robinson Crusoe, he is also impersonating Providence itself: "Just as the double vision made possible by the Christian conversion is replaced by the double vision of narration, the structure of narration has stood in place of providence." Defoe's discoveries about the nature of narrative made the novel the proper vehicle for the study of a society of isolated and mutually suspicious individuals.

657   BROWN, LLOYD W.
"Defoe and the Feminine Mystique." Trans. of the Samuel Johnson Society of the Northwest 4 (1972): 4-18.

An examination of Defoe's image of women as liberated-but-unequal individualists in Moll Flanders and Roxana as related to his pronouncements in An Essay Upon Projects.

658   BURCH, CHARLES EATON.
"The Moral Elements in Defoe's Fiction." London Quart. & Holborn Rev. 6 (April, 1937): 207-213.

Argues that Defoe was not using moral tags in his novels to placate pious middle-class readers: throughout his entire career he had promoted a practical, if not lofty, standard of morality.

659   COOK, RICHARD I.
" 'Mr. Examiner' and 'Mr. Review': The Tory Apologetics of Swift and Defoe." HLQ 29 (1966): 127-146.

Deals with Swift and Defoe "as Tory apologists, paying particular attention to their respective audiences, in an attempt to show how the conspicuous differences between each man's tracts can best be understood by reference to the varying requirements of their readers," and concludes that "De-

foe's arguments reflect ... a compromise between extremes
which was far more real than Swift's professed moderation."

660   DAMROSCH, LEOPOLD, JR.
       "Defoe as Ambiguous Impersonator." MP 71 (1973): 153-
       159.

       An examination of three of Defoe's brief prose works shows
that even though they were not presented as fiction, Defoe
leaves the reader confused; the works exhibit the same kinds
of ambiguity as his novels.

661   DOBREE, BONAMY.
       "Defoe and the Novel." In [96], pp. 395-432.

       An overall view of Defoe's work showing that his main
interest was in trade and morals, and that his "fictional works
are the outcrop of his puritan conduct-books." Defoe's
characters "share a characteristic which seems to be peculiar to [his] idea of life. It was manifest to him that there
is in man an intractable impulse, an irresistible itch to go
on that no preaching can tame, a tireless daemon driving
him to hazards and disaster. Defoe seems to be in some
doubt whether this is a virtue or a moral defect, though, to
be sure, his characters assign their misfortunes to it." Discusses Defoe's works, not only from a moral standpoint, but
also as artistic endeavors.

662   "The Writing of Daniel Defoe." Jour. Royal Soc. Arts. 108
       (1960): 729-742.

       A lecture on the 300th anniversary of Defoe's birth; analy-
zes Defoe's prose style, pointing out that it is not one but
many styles, as he writes differently for different characters,
genres, or purposes. Dobrée feels that it is unfair to Defoe
to categorize him as "master of the plain simple style," and
gives many quotations to support his argument.

663   "Some Aspects of Defoe's Prose." In [17], pp. 171-184.

       Analyzes Defoe's prose styles, giving him highest marks
for those six late years in which he wrote novels. Here he
achieves a more natural style than that shown in persuasive
nonfiction.

664   DOTTIN, PAUL.
       The Life and Strange and Surprising Adventures of Daniel De
       Foe, trans. Louise Ragan. New York: Macaulay, 1929.

A biography which takes its tone from Robinson Crusoe.
Endeavors "to re-create life, conjuring up the whole pageantry
of the late Seventeenth and the early Eighteenth centuries in
order to make De Foe live again in the midst of his contemporaries and against his own background." Takes its material from journals and pamphlets that Defoe himself might
have read, and from a few older and "more intimate" historians; anecdotal, with no attempt at literary criticism.

665   Daniel Defoe et ses romans.   3 Vols. Paris: Les Presses
       Universitaires de France, 1924.

       Largely biographical, though Vol. II contains a study of
       Robinson Crusoe, and III includes commentary on the other
       novels; Vol. I has been translated into English by Louise
       Ragan: see above entry.

666   EARLE, PETER.
       "The Economics of Stability: The Views of Daniel Defoe."
       In Trade, Government and Economy in Pre-Industrial Eng-
       land: Essays Presented to F. J. Fisher. D. C. Coleman
       and A. H. John, eds. (London: Weidenfeld & Nicolson,
       1976), pp. 274-292.

       Defoe was an economic conservative, arguing that no changes
       should be allowed that would undermine the prosperity Eng-
       land enjoyed more than other nations. He believed that the
       economic structure was supported by three pillars: 1) God
       provided England with the best wool in the world; 2) the Eng-
       lish were paid higher wages than other people; and 3) the
       circulation and distribution of goods created an enormous
       amount of employment. Defoe did, however, contemplate with-
       out hesitation the possibility of expansion so long as the over-
       all structure was not disturbed; but as a moralist he was
       disturbed by the paradox that high consumption was linked
       with an increase in vice.

667   FITZGERALD, BRIAN.
       Daniel Defoe: A Study in Conflict.   Chicago: Regnery, 1955.

       A biography emphasizing character and motive rather than
       a wealth of factual or anecdotal detail. The slant is inter-
       pretative, seeking "to relate the works to the man, and both
       to the times in which he lived."

668   FLETCHER, E. G.
       "Defoe and the Theatre."   PQ 13 (1934): 382-389.

       An account of Defoe's attack, in his Review, upon the

lamentable morals of the theatre.   He wants a group of the
Righteous to buy the theatres and close them, pensioning off
the players, to "put a stop to their future acting such scenes
of Lewdness, Immorality and Prophaneness, which has been
the great scandal of the Protestant Religion, and the happy
Government under which we live. "

669   FREEMAN, WILLIAM.
      The Incredible Defoe.   London: Jenkins, 1950.

         Biographical.

670   GOLDKNOPF, DAVID.
      "The I-Narrator in the Pseudomemoir: Daniel Defoe. "   In
      The Life of the Novel (Chicago: Univ. Chicago Press, 1972),
      pp. 421-458.

         Concerned with the manner in which Defoe used the pseudo-
      memoir to convey central meaning of his novels; argues against
      the point of view that Defoe was an ironist, suggesting in-
      stead that his attitude is basically journalistic, an attitude
      that irony would have compromised; and concludes, finally,
      that although the basic orientation in Defoe's novels is em-
      pirical or realistic, he provided a "subjective counterpoint to
      this outlook by means of the pseudomemoir format.   That
      contrapuntal relationship may, therefore, properly be called
      the 'message' of I-narration in those works. "

671   GRAY, CHRISTOPHER W.
      "Defoe's Literalizing Imagination. "   PQ 57 (1958):   66-81.

         Defoe's narrators respond to the fear they feel toward
      people and society by "enacting" elaborate strategies of iso-
      lation and withdrawal, a failure to maintain permanent social
      relationships that has a verbal analogue: "For Defoe treats
      objects rhetorically as, by implication, he would like society
      to deal with his characters. . . .   He wants the definitions of
      words fixed in meaning so that no object will be turned into
      another, so that there will be no promiscuous conflation of
      objects through metaphoric activity.   Defoe does not, that is
      to say, want objects cannibalized metaphorically by investing
      them with figurative significance. . . . "

672   HAHN, H. G.
      "An Approach to Character Development in Defoe's Narrative
      Prose. "   PQ 51 (1972):   845-858.

         An examination of Defoe's technique, his use of organic
      character, and his emphasis on verisimilitude reveals a three-

phase pattern of character development: character dominating event, event dominating character, and variations of an interplay between the two.

673   HARLAN, VIRGINIA.
"Defoe's Narrative Style." JEGP 30 (1931): 55-73.

An "attempt to discover something about the art or craft by which Defoe has written history that sounds like fiction and fiction with the verisimilitude of history." Defoe's style, his use of rhetorical devices, and his universal themes are examined.

674   HOWARD, WILLIAM J. , C. S. B.
"Truth Preserves Her Shape: An Unexplored Influence on Defoe's Prose Style." PQ 47 (1968): 193-205.

Defoe, in the effort to protect and defend political figures who were seen as enemies to the party in power, learned to write fictional histories, memoirs and similar items which were presented to the British public as authentic, and which could thus be used to exonerate the suspected political figure. This new skill, developed to avoid entanglement with libel laws which were acting to constrain the traditional use of "satyr," was then applied to great advantage in the writing of Robinson Crusoe.

675   JAMES, E. ANTHONY.
Daniel Defoe's Many Voices: A Rhetorical Study of Prose Style and Literary Method. Amsterdam: Rodopi NV, 1972.

Reviews Defoe's literary values and their sources, followed by a critical analysis based on a close textual explication of several representative works; discusses such topics as Defoe writing in his own voice, Defoe as mimic and ironist, his narrative style and method, and concludes with chapters on Robinson Crusoe, Moll Flanders, and Roxana.

676   JOYCE, JAMES.
Daniel Defoe. Edited and translated from the Italian MSS by Joseph Prescott. Buffalo Studies I, i. Buffalo: (State Univ. of New York, 1964.

A perceptive analysis of Defoe's realism.

677   McVEAGH, JOHN.
"Defoe and the Romance of Trade." DUJ 70 (1978): 141-147.

A look at Defoe's "idealizing"--his "firm and vivid grasp of the vital abundance of the world and [his] insistence on man's role in relation to it"--in his commercial writings. Defoe's sanction of "the discovery, colonisation and exploitation of new lands" is based on his belief that "God made the whole created system for man's 'use, delight, and blessing.' "

678   MASON, SHIRLENE.
       Daniel Defoe and the Status of Women (Monographs in Women's Studies). St. Albans, Vt.: Eden Press, 1978.

The purpose of this study is "to examine Defoe's attitude toward women in light of their legal and social status, with a comparison of eighteenth-century law and social conditions to the ideas Defoe sets forth in his didactic works, in his journalism, and in his fiction." Concludes that Defoe's attitude remains paradoxical: although he desires to see women's condition improved and regards women as equal in ability to men, he is unwilling to grant them equality of status.

679   MOORE, JOHN ROBERT.
       A Checklist of the Writings of Daniel Defoe.   2nd. ed. Hamden, Conn.: Archon Press, 1971.

Attempts to tell "what Defoe wrote, when and often why he wrote and published it, who printed and sold it, and where copies of first editions are to be found in accessible libraries."

680   "Defoe and Shakespeare." Shakespeare Quart. 19 (1968): 71-80.

Researches Defoe's knowledge of Shakespeare and the allusions in his writings to the works of Shakespeare. Finds some derivative plot situations as well as allusions in Robinson Crusoe, the work which shows the most Shakespearean influence.

681   "Daniel Defoe: Precursor of Samuel Richardson." In [13], pp. 351-369.

Considers the various ways in which Defoe was a precursor of Richardson: he was uniquely connected with printers and publishers, and he anticipated Richardson not only in being a novelist of real life but in his narrative method. Particularly concerned with "Defoe's training in the composition of letters, and his use (in many of his writings) of something of the epistolary method so intimately associated with the novels of his successor."

682   Daniel Defoe: Citizen of the Modern World.   Chicago: Univ.
      Chicago Press, 1958.

          A biographical study, with extensive critical comments on
      the writings, that attempts to correct misconceptions and to
      distinguish Defoe's authentic works; makes "no consistent at-
      tempt ... to trace the minute details of Defoe's personal
      life, except where these seem significant for understanding
      him as a citizen of the modern world." Not based on a strict
      chronological sequence.

683   "Defoe, Stevenson, and the Pirates." ELH 10 (1943): 35-
      60.

          Examines the influence of Defoe upon Stevenson and rea-
      sons for their similarities and differences.

684   "Defoe and Scott." PMLA 56 (1941): 710-735.

          Sir Walter Scott was responsible for the revival of Defoe's
      reputation, which had declined sharply after his death. "As
      editor, critic, collector, and admirer, he did pioneer service
      for Defoe ... [and] ... the ultimate influence of Defoe on
      Scott's writings is more significant than that of Dryden or of
      Swift."

685   Defoe in the Pillory and Other Studies (Indiana University
      Publications, Humanities Series No. 1). Bloomington: Univ.
      Indiana Press, 1939.

          Deals primarily with historical and bibliographical matters:
      e. g. , the reason why Defoe was so severely punished in the
      pillory, two sources for Roxana, the authenticity of the "spur-
      ious" collected edition of Defoe's works in 1703, and the au-
      thorship of Robert Drury's Journal and A General History of
      the Pirates.

686   NEW, MELVYN.
      " 'The Grace of God': The Form of Eighteenth-Century Eng-
      lish Fiction." PMLA 91 (1976): 235-243.

          Examines the idea that Providence always intervenes in
      eighteenth-century fiction to support a good cause or protect
      innocence; and asks whether or not this providential world
      is paramount in the novels of Defoe, Fielding, Smollett, and
      Richardson. Argues that "a proper 'conceptual context' for
      [these novelists] must embody not only the providential de-
      sign, but also what was happening to that design ... ; [they]
      imaged forth in their writings neither the Christian world view

... nor the secular world view"--but rather reflected "that
historical moment when the intellectual and imaginative resources of their culture were transferred from one system
of ordering experience to another."

687   NOVAK, MAXIMILLIAN E.
        "Defoe's Use of Irony." In The Uses of Irony: Papers on
        Defoe and Swift Read at a Clark Library Seminar, April 2,
        1966 (Berkeley & Los Angeles: Univ. Calif. Press, 1966),
        pp. 5-38. Rpt. in [43], pp. 189-220.

        Argues that the image of Defoe as a simple, honest man
        who wrote in a plain style should be replaced by that of De-
        foe as an ironist. Considers the question of Defoe's character
        in relation to that of the ironist; examines some examples of
        his irony; and discriminates between techniques which are en-
        tirely ironic and devices of fiction which may be part of an
        ironic work but which may exist independently.

688   " 'Simon Forecastle's Weekly Journal': Some Notes on Defoe's
        Conscious Artistry." TSLL 6 (1965): 433-440.

        Argues against Watt's view that apparently ironic effects
        in Defoe are actually the result of his ineptness as a writer;
        in fact, according to Novak, Defoe consciously intended to
        create irony by a careful selection and juxtaposition of real-
        istic details.

689   "Defoe's Theory of Fiction." SP 61 (1964): 650-668.

        Discusses three aspects of Defoe's fiction: 1) his "attitude
        toward fiction as a genre practiced by his contemporaries
        and to the taste of his audience"; 2) "his theory of reality
        and its effect on his realistic technique"; and 3) "his concept
        of the uses of fiction and efforts to defend it on moral gounds."
        Notes Defoe's labor to justify fiction as more than mere sin-
        ful entertainment; calls him an early master of realism.

690   Defoe and the Nature of Man (Oxford English Monographs).
        London: Oxford Univ. Press, 1963.

        Considers the ideological basis for some of Defoe's themes
        and stories; deals with such topics as the laws of Nature,
        the problem of Necessity, love and marriage, the meaning
        of gratitude, and the search for a hero.

691   Economics and the Fiction of Daniel Defoe (Univ. Calif.
        Publications, English Std. 24.). Berkeley: Univ. Calif.
        Press, 1962.

Attempts to provide an explanation and interpretation of Defoe's economic thought and to comment on the novels in the light of that thought. Defoe's ideas are related to contemporary mercantile economists.

692   "The Problem of Necessity in Defoe's Fiction."   PQ 40 (1961) 513-524.

Traces "a pattern of thought underlying Defoe's fiction," in which he justifies criminal action taken in self-defense or extreme necessity; asserts that Defoe's characters must be judged before the "Bar of Nature" before they can be called innocent or guilty, and concludes that "None of the main characters fall into necessity through vice, and therefore they cannot be charged with guilt for their original crimes."

693   PAYNE, WILLIAM LYTTON.
        Mr. Review: Daniel Defoe as Author of "The Review."   New York: King's Crown Press, 1947.

A selection of Defoe's comments, gleaned from The Review, on the subjects of authorship, journalism, economics, and social relationships, as well as his autobiographical references. A cross-index of over 30,000 items.

694   PRAZ, MARIO.
        "De Foe and Cellini."   ES 13 (1931): 75-87.

Draws parallels between the two men showing similarity in their styles and suggests that Defoe would have been the man to write Cellini's biography if Cellini had not written his own.

695   PRICE, MARTIN.
        "Defoe's Novels."   From [153], pp. 263-276; in [642], pp. 23-39.

Considers Robinson Crusoe, Moll Flanders, and Colonel Jack as novels in which "Defoe gives us the great myth of the isolated man bringing order out of unfamiliar materials... All these characters aspire to some kind of morality; all have a glimpse of some kind of redemption."

696   RAY, J. KAREN.
        "The Feminine Role in Robinson Crusoe, Roxana, and Clarissa."   ESRS 24, iii (1976): 28-33.

In spite of many differences, the position of woman as

portrayed in these three novels exhibits many similarities
especially when considered from these standpoints: " ...
economic position; ... woman's role, both sexual and social
as circumscribed by the prevailing social code; and ... the
psychological position of woman in relation to herself and
her world. " The tensions created by the rigid restrictions
against women in the eighteenth century and "the rejection
of and struggle against them function as major formative devices in each of the novels. "

697   RICHETTI, JOHN J.
       Defoe's Narratives: Situations and Structures.   Oxford:
       Clarendon Press, 1975.

       A close reading of Defoe's major narratives as they un-
       fold tracing the exact line of each narrative "to recreate and
       summarize in their own sequence the local effects that occur. "
       Discusses "the self as Master" in Robinson Crusoe, "the
       dialectic of power" in Moll Flanders, "the self enters history"
       in Colonel Jack, and "nature, knowledge, and power" in Rox-
       ana, with chapters on Captain Avery and Captain Singleton
       and A Journal of the Plague Year.

698   "Defoe. "   In Popular Fiction before Richardson: Narrative
       Patterns 1700-1739 (Oxford: Clarendon Press, 1969), pp.
       60-118.

       Opposes the teleological interpretation of the development
       of the novel as progressing toward realism, and argues that
       that development must be viewed as a significant step in the
       emergence of "mass art. "   Studies the pre-Richardson fic-
       tional milieu and attempts to understand the values the orig-
       inal audience attached to fiction; interprets the novels (in-
       cluding Robinson Crusoe) as ideological structures reflecting
       an "eighteenth-century version of the traditional confrontation
       of the secular and the religious. "

699   ROGERS, KATHARINE.
       "The Feminism of Daniel Defoe. "   In Woman in the 18th
       Century and Other Essays, Paul Fritz and Richard Morton,
       eds. (Toronto: Hakkert, 1976), pp. 3-24.

       Surveys Defoe's writings that depict his attitude toward
       the relationship between men and women in marriage; refers
       to his journalism and his three manuals on family life, and
       uses extensively the evidence from Moll Flanders and Roxana,
       concluding that "although Defoe's presentation of women and
       women's relationships with men was unsentimental to the point
       of crudity, it was admirably fair-minded and actually opened
       up possibilities of freedom which anticipate those of modern
       times. "

700   ROORDA, GERRIDINA.
      Realism in Daniel Defoe's Narratives of Adventure.   Wagen-
      ingen: H. Veenman & Zonen, 1929.   Rpt. Folcroft, Pa. :
      Folcroft Library Edition, 1970.

           After a survey of Defoe and his age--the religious, politi-
      cal, philosophical, and literary conditions--the author dis-
      cusses Robinson Crusoe, Captain Singleton, and A New Voyage
      Round the World.

701   SCHONHORN, MANUEL.
      "Defoe: The Literature of Politics and the Politics of Some
      Fictions. " In [44], pp. 15-56.

           An account of Defoe's political thought as essentially con-
      servative, rejecting the concept of the supremacy of Parlia-
      ment; he rejects also the concept of "mixed monarchy" be-
      cause it tended to reduce the authority and independence of
      the crown.   Defoe's defense of patriarchally divine kingship
      is staunchly traditional, partly derived from his reading of
      the Old Testament.   His concept of royal government, there-
      fore, is inseparable from theological considerations; Crusoe
      becomes an Adamic figure, a king divinely ordained to rule
      over his island, both secular ruler and military leader.

702   SECORD, ARTHUR W.
      Studies in the Narrative Method of Defoe (Univ. Ill. Studies
      in Language & Literature, 9, No. 1).   Urbana: Univ. Ill.
      Press, 1924.

           A study of the sources of Robinson Crusoe, Captain Single-
      ton, and the Memoirs of Captain Carleton (also the author-
      ship of the Memoirs); also looks at Defoe's method of com-
      position by analyzing A Journal of the Plague Year.

703   SEN, SRI C.
      Daniel Defoe: His Mind and Art.   Calcutta: Univ. Calcutta
      Press, 1948.   Rpt. Folcroft, Pa. : The Folcroft Press,
      1969.

           Emphasis on the art and technique of Defoe's novels.   Ex-
      amines A Journal of the Plague Year for the light it throws
      on his memory and imagination; Defoe's ideas on education;
      his ideas on trade as reflected in Complete English Trades-
      man; his social criticism as presented in Essay upon Proj-
      ects; his political conduct; his narrative and dramatic quali-
      ties, and the importance of didacticism in Robinson Crusoe;
      and, finally, Defoe's conception of character and the plot of
      Robinson Crusoe.

704   SHINAGEL, MICHAEL.
       Daniel Defoe and Middle-Class Gentility.   Cambridge: Har-
       vard Univ. Press, 1968.

       An examination into Defoe's values and philosophy, based
       particularly on The Compleat English Gentleman, constitutes
       the third part of a longish biography and critical evaluation
       of Daniel Defoe. Defoe's Compleat English Gentleman shows
       his democratic bias; he looked on ignorant men of gentle
       birth as outmoded and advocated a society in which a man
       might achieve high social rank through hard work and a gentle-
       man of birth might discover true gentility by educating him-
       self properly.

705   SILL, GEOFFREY M.
       "Rogues, Strumpets, and Vagabonds: Defoe on Crime in the
       City." ECLife 2 (1976): 74-78.

       Because Defoe considered the city both a blessing and a
       curse he "could celebrate in his fictional narratives the liber-
       ating effect of the free market on the human personality,
       while at the same time calling in his treatises for the sup-
       pression of the consequences of that liberation." To Defoe
       the novelist, the city and the free market operating within it
       represent freedom from serving a master; to Defoe the crim-
       inologist, the city and the free market appear as "the domain
       of vagrants, strumpets, dishonest merchants, stock-jobbers,
       and insubordinate rogues." Defoe's characters often act in
       contradiction to his beliefs about crime, and they continue to
       steal and cheat after there is no need for it.

706   SKILTON, DAVID.
       "Defoe and the Augustan Age." In [165], pp. 7-18.

       Defoe is seen as a "progressive" writer, as opposed to
       the Augustan mode of thought in such a writer as Richardson;
       he "represented at once a social, literary and intellectual
       challenge to the Augustan world, and the Augustans reacted
       to him accordingly."

707   SKYDSGAARD, NIELS JØRGEN.
       "Defoe on the Art of Fiction." In [16], pp. 164-171.

       Examines Defoe's prefaces and suggests "that Defoe was
       more consistent when writing about his craft as a novelist
       than when insisting on authenticity or, even, on morality."
       Shows that he found it "more important to assert the moral
       purpose of his stories than their authenticity ... that he was
       highly conscious of the aesthetic qualities of his art, and

made his concern for authenticity, so frequently expressed,
serve his aesthetic purposes."

708   SNOW, MALINDA.
      "The Origins of Defoe's First-Person Narrative Technique:
      An Overlooked Aspect of the Rise of the Novel." JNT 6
      (1976): 175-187.

      Argues that Defoe's first-person narrative method is very
      similar to seventeenth-century scientific writing, especially
      that of Robert Hooke and Robert Boyle. Shows that the two
      narrative techniques used by Defoe--the selection and descrip-
      tion of specific objects so that the reader can instantly see
      them and the portrayal of his hero or heroine handling, ap-
      praising, or reacting to these objects in such a way that the
      reader vicariously participates in the narrator's experience--
      are identical to the major techniques used by Hooke and Boyle.

709   STAMM, RUDOLF G.
      "Daniel Defoe: An Artist in the Puritan Tradition." PQ 15
      (1936): 225-246.

      Defoe as a Presbyterian had problems with the aesthetics
      of the novel. There was "a desperate battle between Defoe's
      creative impulses and his Puritan views concerning art," but his
      experience of life did not reinforce the teachings of his re-
      ligion. Indicates that Defoe's conflicts may have been solved
      by self-deception.

710   STARR, G. A.
      "Defoe's Prose Style, I: The Language of Interpretation."
      MP 71 (1974): 277-294.

      Analyzes Defoe's language and style; supports thesis that
      "Defoe's prose is indeed 'realistic,' but in a special and
      limited sense: his characters tell us directly rather little
      about themselves or their external world, but they create an
      illusion of both by projecting themselves upon their world in
      the act of perceiving it."

711   Defoe and Casuistry. Princeton, N. J.: Princeton Univ.
      Press, 1971.

      Examines the influence of traditional casuistry on Defoe's
      subject matter, narrative technique, and ethical outlook. Also
      emphasizes the role of "Seventeenth century casuistical divin-
      ity" in the genesis of his writings, and argues that the in-
      fluence of the casuistical tradition tends to break the novels
      into episodes, each with its own crisis, and to make the char-

acters as concerned with the motives of their actions as with
the eventual actions themselves.

712   Defoe and Spiritual Autobiography.   Princeton, N. J. :   Prince-
       ton Univ. Press, 1965.

       Robinson Crusoe and, to a lesser extent, Moll Flanders
       are interpreted as examples of a humble form of literature
       taken over and transformed by writers of genius.   The author
       seeks to show that Defoe's moral and religious principles,
       as embodied in the spiritual autobiographies of the Restora-
       tion, are reflected also in the structure of his own novels.
       The book describes the main characteristics of spiritual auto-
       biography as a genre; analyzes Robinson Crusoe's structure
       to prove that it was strongly influenced by the autobiographies
       already described; and similar claims are made for Moll
       Flanders and Roxana.

713   SUTHERLAND, JAMES.
       Daniel Defoe: A Critical Study.   Cambridge: Harvard Univ.
       Press, 1971.

       A "critical account of Defoe's varied achievements as a
       writer."   Although most space is devoted to fiction, this
       book is notable for its consideration of Defoe as journalist;
       includes biographical material and a list of modern critical
       studies.

714   "The Relation of Defoe's Fiction to his Non-Fictional Writ-
       ings. "   In [36], pp. 37-50.

       A study of several devices used in his fiction--the persona,
       dialogue--that Defoe previously used in his nonfictional writ-
       ings; analyzes the nonfictional elements in A True-Relation
       of the Apparition of one Mrs. Veal to one Mrs. Bargrave,
       and the way in which Defoe makes his account more circum-
       stantial and vivid.

715   Defoe.   (WTW) London: Longmans, 1954.

       A perceptive evaluation of Defoe and his work by a recog-
       nized Defoe scholar.

716   Defoe.   London: Methuen, 1937.

       A biography primarily, rather than a volume of literary
       criticism.   In the pro-Defoe, anti-Defoe controversy, the
       author adopts a middle position.

717   "Some Early Troubles of Daniel Defoe." RES 9 (1933): 275-
        290.

        The lawsuits recorded in the Chancery records show the
        author of the Complete English Tradesman involved in some
        of the difficulties against which he was ready to warn others.
        They suggest sources of information for some of the novels.

718   SWALLOW, ALAN.
        "Defoe and the Art of Fiction." WHR 4 (1950): 129-136.

        Sees Defoe's contribution to the art of fiction as that of
        adding theme to narrative, and of using the one great theme
        of modern literature--"Man's isolation, the quality and degree
        of his commitment to society, the moral choice involved in
        balancing between anarchism and too much involvement."

719   TITLEBAUM, RICHARD.
        "Some Notes Toward a Definition of Defoe's Demonology."
        UES 14, ii-iii (1976): 1-7.

        Defoe's The Political History of the Devil and A System
        of Magic are based on the Bible and are the consummation
        of his religious beliefs.   He attributes much of what has
        happened in history to the influence of the Devil, and many
        of his assumptions are based on the famous Daemonologie of
        King James I.   Many of Defoe's novels contain aspects of
        his demonology and especially The Apparition of Mrs. Veal
        and The Secret Memoirs of the Late Duncan Campbell con-
        tain his ideas on the spiritual world; according to the theor-
        ies contained in his demonology books, Mrs. Veal would have
        seen an angel rather than a ghost.

720   UPHAUS, ROBERT W.
        "Defoe, Deliverance, and Dissimulation." In [180], pp. 46-
        70.

        Defoe's novelistic strategy is to draw the reader into his
        characters' processes of thought, in order to decrease the
        distance between the reader and the characters he is observ-
        ing.   That authorial procedure is called "dissimulation,"
        which destroys the sense of narrative distance by projecting
        the author completely into a character and by luring a reader
        to participate in the way a character's mind works.   The re-
        sult of this strategy is that "both author and reader are led
        into a mutual process of dissimulation whereby, voluntarily
        or involuntarily, we become ... active participants in thoughts
        and actions which in our conscious life and in our conventional
        moral habits we might otherwise reject."

721   WALTON, JAMES.
       "The Romance of Gentility: Defoe's Heroes and Heroines."
       Literary Monographs 4 (1971): 89-135.

       Defoe's novels seen as combination of romance and real-
       ism, often treated ironically, and based on the theme of the
       child exile.   They represent a conflict between the demand
       of one's ideal self to triumph over circumstances and the
       equally insistent need to make moral judgments.   That con-
       flict, the author argues, is intrinsic to all novels.

722   WATT, IAN.
       "Defoe as Novelist."   In The Pelican Guide to English Litera-
       ture, Vol. 4, From Dryden to Johnson, ed. Boris Ford
       (Baltimore: Penguin, 1965), pp. 203-216.

       Emphasizes Defoe's narrative realism, his plain style, his
       religious beliefs; sees Robinson Crusoe as one of the myths
       of modern civilization prefiguring man's spiritual loneliness.
       Defoe's chief failure is the lack of serious order or design;
       his forte is the brilliant episode.

723   "Defoe and Richardson on Homer: A Study of the Relation
       of Novel and Epic in the Early Eighteenth Century."   RES
       3 (1952):   325-340.

       Defoe and Richardson seen as establishing, though not pur-
       posely, the independence of the novel genre from the tradi-
       tions of the epic.   Watt explores the background of the un-
       favorable bias toward Homer shown by these authors.

724   "The Naming of Characters in Defoe, Richardson, and Field-
       ing."   RES 25 (1949):   322-338.

       The names of Defoe's characters all sound real, as befits
       his "true-confession" novels: this is a departure from earl-
       ier practice in which characters often had generalized names
       denoting traits of character.   This and other considerations
       in the matter of naming are followed through Defoe's, Richard-
       don's and Fielding's novels, noting the aura of associations
       gathering around certain names, and the conscious and ap-
       parently unconscious choices made by the authors.

725   WRIGHT, TERENCE.
       " 'Metaphors for Reality':   Mind and Object and the Problem
       of Form in the Early Novel."   DUJ 38 (1976):   239-248.

       The history of the novel may be defined as a history of

the images that project the discovery of the relations between mind and object, Man and his world; this empirical approach to reality can be exemplified in three early novels. In Robinson Crusoe, the world is presented as a succession of phenomena interesting for their own sake; in Clarissa, man is not naked and alone, but exists within a subtle social structure in which a system of signs and props help men to live together; and in Tristram Shandy, a new dimension, time, is added to the mind's relationship to the world of objects, so that man's knowledge of his world is essentially remembering in time.

726   ZIMMERMAN, EVERETT.
      Defoe and the Novel. Berkeley: Univ. Calif. Press, 1975.

      An analysis of Defoe's fictional technique that attempts to define some of the literary, intellectual, and religious traditions to which the novels are related. Argues that his "authorial position changes: he gradually introduces himself as an implied ironic presence.... Defoe's developing irony reveals his clearer understanding of the failures not only of his characters but also of the values by which they are judged. "

See also: 916, 991, 3168

                              Robinson Crusoe

727   ALKON, PAUL K.
      "The Odds Against Friday: Defoe, Bayes, and Inverse Probability. " In [3], pp. 29-61.

      Part of Robinson Crusoe's meaning concerns the problem of probability, either explicit or implied: if objective probabilities do exist, and can't be "accounted for in terms of our subjective lack of perfect information," then we must abandon the "idea that, because time is conceptually reversible, retrodiction may be as valid as prediction. " Defoe uses non-mathematical statements about probability to demonstrate how infrequently probability is the most prudent guide to future action; at the same time Crusoe progresses from an almost completely thoughtless state to an awareness that rational foresight based on probabilities can often be useful, and finally develops a prudence that is firmly based on faith.

728   AYERS, ROBERT W.
      "Robinson Crusoe: 'Allusive Allegorick History. ' "   PMLA 82 (1967): 399-407.

A reading of Robinson Crusoe which differs from popular
"economic quest and conquest" interpretations; interprets it
as "Allusive Allegorick History." It orients the symbolic elements of the work within the context of Defoe's other works
and of traditional Bible exegesis, particularly as expressed
in the Puritan literature of the time.   Finds Robinson Crusoe
to be a "symbolic account of a spiritual experience, compar-
able to a Biblical parable or The Pilgrim's Progress....
We may further find that the principal individuals, objects,
and incidents in the story are literal corollaries to a metaphorical story of the Christian wayfarer and warfarer...."

729   BENJAMIN, EDWIN B.
       "Symbolic Elements in Robinson Crusoe." PQ 30 (1951):
       206-211. Rpt. in [733], pp. 34-38.

       Discussion of allegorical symbolism in the novel and a
       look at the book as a symbolic account of a spiritual exper-
       ience.

730   BERNE, ERIC.
       "The Psychological Structure of Space with Some Remarks on
       Robinson Crusoe." Psychoanalytic Quarterly 25 (1956): 549-
       567. Rpt. and abridged in [768], pp. 332-335 and [733], pp.
       94-97.

       Robinson Crusoe represents a detailed account of the psy-
       chological process of organizing space into a structure; De-
       foe describes Crusoe's adventures with insular fear and anx-
       iety and Crusoe himself shows an intense oral fixation that
       causes his explorations to be incomplete and inefficient.

731   BOREHAM, FRANK WILLIAM.
       The Gospel of Robinson Crusoe.   London: Epworth Press,
       1955.

       Discusses Crusoe as convert, philosopher, evangelist, and
       mystic.

732   EGAN, JAMES.
       "Crusoe's Monarchy and the Puritan Concept of Self." SEL
       13 (1973):   451-460.

       An examination of Crusoe's treatment of his fellow men
       after his spiritual rebirth establishes a relationship between
       Robinson Crusoe and the Puritan homiletic tradition.   The
       monarch image in the novel represents metaphorically Cru-
       soe's regenerate self-image.

733   ELLIS, FRANK H.
       Twentieth Century Interpretations of "Robinson Crusoe": A
       Collection of Critical Essays.   Englewood Cliffs, N. J. :
       Prentice-Hall, 1969.

734   GANZEL, DEWEY.
       "Chronology in Robinson Crusoe. "   PQ 40 (1961):   495-512.

       Offers a new interpretation of the inconsistencies in Robin-
       son Crusoe which militated against Defoe's desire to have it
       accepted as fact.   He "postulates two chronologies, each con-
       sistent in itself, the second interpolated into the first. "

735   GREIF, MARTIN J.
       "The Conversion of Robinson Crusoe. "   SEL 6 (1966):   551-
       574.

       The Protestant scheme of salvation and the opinions of
       Defoe's contemporary divines applied to Crusoe's conversion
       to Christianity and a discussion of the novel as a Christian
       allegory which draws heavily on biblical metaphors.

736   HALEWOOD, WILLIAM H.
       "Religion and Invention in Robinson Crusoe. "   EIC 14 (1964):
       339-351.   Rpt. in [733], pp. 79-89.

       Challenges the view that Defoe is lacking in imagination,
       creativity, and technique and that his characters are all facets
       of his own personality.   "Behind Crusoe's warmth ... is a
       cool-headed Defoe intent upon his novelist's work. "   Suggests
       that for action and plot in the novel, Crusoe's religious con-
       flicts are made to substitute for the other human beings ab-
       sent from the island.   "The 'discontinuity between religion
       and action' ... is made to serve the ends of the novelist's
       art. ...   It gives the book its structure, justifies its length
       and method, contributes to its air of authenticity, provides
       emotional complexity and depth, and enlivens its language. "

737   HARTOG, CURT.
       "Authority and Autonomy in Robinson Crusoe. "   Enl. E. 5
       (1974):   33-43.

       Discusses Crusoe's conflict in forging "an identity that
       can balance the demands of religious authority ... against
       the demands of the self for independence and autonomy ...
       gives the novel a coherent, dramatic pattern of action, and
       illuminates the paradox of a character who is, often at the
       same time, a religious prodigal and a shrewd entrepreneur. "

738   HAUSERMANN, HANS W.
       "Aspects of Life and Thought in Robinson Crusoe." RES 11
       (1935): 299-312, 439-456.

       A systematic survey of the points of view of Dottin, Hü-
       bener and other Defoe critics who have dealt with the influ-
       ence on Defoe's writing of his life and thought.   Discusses
       the religious, commercial and social elements of the novel,
       and concludes that "the religious aspect of Robinson Crusoe
       is strongly marked and the spirit of the Puritan permeates
       the whole novel.   Calvinistic theology often furnishes explana-
       tions for phenomena which it would be hard to explain in any
       other way.   The commercial and social elements ... are
       ... the substance of the book and constitute also the larger
       part of its literary value."

739   HEARNE, JOHN.
       "The Naked Footprint: An Inquiry into Crusoe's Island."
       REL 8, No. 4 (1967): 97-107.

       Criticizes Robinson Crusoe from standpoint of " ... tex-
       ture, technical development and [its] implicit necessity...."
       Discusses the fact that "Loss of identity and assertion of the
       identity that can exist only within a sort of seamless, un-
       yielding insulation" are the twin themes of the novel.

740   HONIG, EDWIN.
       "Crusoe, Rasselas, and the Suit of Clothes." UKCR 18 (1951):
       136-142.

       A comparison of Robinson Crusoe and Rasselas as examples
       of irony that attempts to get at the nature of man, to get be-
       hind his representation as a suit of clothes.

741   HOWES, RAYMOND F.
       "Robinson Crusoe: A Literary Accident." Eng. Jour. 16
       (1927): 31-35.

       Argues that Defoe's literary greatness lies exclusively with
       Robinson Crusoe and that the two best things about the novel
       are the central theme and the method of treatment, both of
       which are a "product of circumstances."

742   HUNTER, J. PAUL.
       "The Conclusion of Robinson Crusoe." In [642], pp. 92-103.
       Excerpted from [743], pp. 188-201.

       By viewing the last major episode, the attack by wolves

in the Pyrenees, in "relation to Crusoe's maturation and the novel's emblematic method, ... the episode takes on significant meaning and provides a dramatic climax to the previous physical and spiritual adventures."

743   The Reluctant Pilgrim: Defoe's Emblematic Method and Quest for Form. Baltimore: Johns Hopkins Press, 1966.

Focuses on Robinson Crusoe to "offer a detailed critical reading ... to define and describe several kinds of Puritan subliterary materials; and to suggest the relationship between characteristic Puritan ways of thinking in the seventeenth century and the new prose fiction of the eighteenth."

744   "Friday as a Convert: Defoe and the Accounts of Indian Missionaries." RES 14 (1963): 243-248.

Discusses how Defoe uses Friday's conversion to Christianity to give the reader dramatic insight into Crusoe's spiritual accomplishment.

745   JAMES, E. ANTHONY.
"Defoe's Narrative Artistry: Naming and Describing in Robinson Crusoe." Costerus 5 (1972): 51-73.

Concerned with Defoe's literary imagination and craftsmanship, concentrating on several aspects of style and method. Patterns of epithets are used to suggest Crusoe's attitude toward the island, himself, and his situation: "Crusoe's habits of style reflect his growth and development along logical lines and through recognizable stages...."

746   JOHNSON, ABBY A.
"Old Bones Uncovered: A Reconsideration of Robinson Crusoe." CLAJ 17 (1973): 271-278.

Argues against critics who have maintained that Defoe was unbiased toward race and that Crusoe was "Everyman."

747   KAVANAGH, THOMAS M.
"Unraveling Robinson: The Divided Self in Defoe's Robinson Crusoe." TSLL 20 (1978): 416-432.

"I propose to examine ... the way in which this form, this overall patterning of explicit statement, centers on an always troubled representation of coherence within consciousness, of the self as unified. As concerns this problematic, the process of an individual consciousness defining itself within

space and time, Robinson Crusoe exists as a veritable test
case. What better way to identify the nature of the self than
to examine it as radically cut off from the fluctuations of
intersubjectivity, the multiple influences of the Other upon
the self? Robinson Crusoe is the story of a man alone; a
story of how, within that solitude, he achieves an awareness
of self denied him during his time among men. "

748   KRAFT, QUENTIN G.
       "Robinson Crusoe and the Story of the Novel. " CE 41 (1980):
       535-548.

       Since the way a story ends "is crucial in defining a novel,"
       it is the "second, problematic ending," in which Crusoe re-
       turns home to find he no longer has a home and to trade his
       religion for money, that makes Robinson Crusoe the first
       novel. Focuses primarily on the narrative elements--the two
       stories of Robinson Crusoe, the irony, and the radical end-
       ing--which make up the story of the novel.

749   MacDONALD, ROBERT H.
       "The Creation of an Ordered World in Robinson Crusoe. "
       Dalhousie Rev. 56 (1976): 23-34.

       Explores from an archetypal viewpoint Crusoe's dual con-
       quest of the outer space of the island and the inner space of
       the self, emphasizing that the novel is about both physical
       and psychic order: the establishment of that order is the
       dominant myth. Crusoe's quest is to find himself; his quest
       is "both extraordinary and commonplace, heroic and human.
       He is the exceptional man, yet one of us; no neurotic, but
       a man undergoing the archetypal crises of life. " Crusoe be-
       comes more than homo economicus, more than the Wanderer:
       he becomes every man who has struggled to surmount the
       hostility of a chaotic world.

750   MacLAINE, ALLAN H.
       "Robinson Crusoe and the Cyclops. " SP 52 (1955): 599-604.

       Suggests the Odyssey as a source for Robinson Crusoe and
       that "Homer's account of the Cyclops' cave had much to do
       with Defoe's conception of Crusoe's 'castle' on the island. "

751   McVEAGH, JOHN.
       "Rochester and Defoe: A Study in Influence. " SEL 14 (1974):
       327-341.

       The nature of the relationship between Defoe and Rochester.
       "As man and poet ... Rochester captured Defoe's imagination.

As philosopher, his influence slid into Defoe's mind where it did not belong and where it was never properly assimilated; and certain inconsistencies in Defoe's theory of man and society are due to this influence."

752   MOORE, CATHERINE S.
"Robinson Crusoe's Two Servants: The Measure of His Conversion." In A Fair Day in the Affections: Literary Essays in Honor of Robert B. White, Jr., Jack D. Durant and M. Thomas Hester, eds. (Raleigh, N.C.: Winston Press, 1980), pp. 111-118.

Discusses the parallel relationships of Crusoe with his two servants Xury, the African Moor, and Friday, the American Indian, to "illustrate not only Crusoe's spiritual progress but also the theme of civilized man's relationship to primitive man." Both characters exist for Crusoe's benefit. They are "the primitives required for a major thematic function--the measurement of the spiritual distance between the sinful and the saved Crusoe."

753   MOORE, JOHN ROBERT.
"The Tempest and Robinson Crusoe." RES 21 (1945): 52-56.

Argues that many details of the plots are alike, especially the manner in which Crusoe and Prospero leave their respective islands.

754   NOVAK, MAXIMILLIAN E.
"Imaginary Islands and Real Beasts: The Imaginative Genesis of Robinson Crusoe." TSL 19 (1974): 57-78.

Seeks to discover, not sources, but what may have moved Defoe's imagination; "what I want to show is that Crusoe is in many ways the product of certain contemporary events, and that Defoe's imagination was particularly stirred toward a depiction of the terrible and the sublime."

755   "Robinson Crusoe and Economic Utopia." KR 25 (1963): 474-490.

Analyzes Robinson Crusoe for evidence of Defoe's economic theories and their sources; divides Defoe's economic principles into three parts: a theory of invention, a theory of value, and an economic theory of society, and concludes, rather generally, that Defoe created his novels from ideas rather than incidents.

756   "Crusoe the King and the Political Evolution of His Island."
        SEL 2 (1962): 337-350.

        Discusses why Defoe, an ardent opponent of tyranny, makes
        Crusoe into a despot and also shows how he uses him to pre-
        sent the solitary man in the state of nature but finds Crusoe
        an obstacle in his attempt to present his theories on the poli-
        tical evolution of society.

757   "Robinson Crusoe's Fear and the Search for Natural Man."
        MP 58 (1961): 238-245.

        Examines emotional states of Robinson Crusoe, and of his-
        torical figures who have lived in a wild, isolated state, in
        the light of the power of complete isolation to invoke fear.

758   "Robinson Crusoe's 'Original Sin.' "   SEL 1 (1961):   19-29.
        Rpt. in [691], pp. 32-48; [642], pp. 60-77.

        Challenges the popular view that "the real key to Defoe
        lies in an understanding of capitalism and economic individual-
        ism." There is indeed an economic problem, one which gives
        Robinson Crusoe a constant sense of sin.   Novak suggests
        that "Crusoe's sin is his refusal to follow the 'calling' chosen
        for him by his father, and that the rationale for this action
        can be found in Crusoe's personal characteristics."

759   PEARLMAN, E.
        "Robinson Crusoe and the Cannibals."   Mosaic 10, i (1976):
        39-55.

        A psychological study of Crusoe's character reveals him
        to be both authoritarian and childishly violent.   His battles
        with the cannibals are unnecessary but are fought because of
        his need to dominate and destroy; he kills to satisfy his own
        psychological needs in the same way that he subjugates Friday
        and strips him of his identity.

760   PECK, H. DANIEL.
        "Robinson Crusoe: The Moral Geography of Limitation."
        JNT 3 (1973): 20-31.

        Bases discussion on assumption "that in the character of
        Crusoe, Defoe is expressing a level of motivation and mean-
        ing that is more fundamental to his experience than either
        economic or religious theory, one which he may not have
        been entirely aware of, namely, the need for 'place' ...

[P]lace becomes in the novel not a mythic setting but an active force in 'grounding' the hero and creating in him a sense of personal identity."

761   ROBERT, MARTHE.
        Origins of the Novel. Bloomington: Indiana Univ. Press, 1980. Publ. in France as Roman des Origines et Origines du Roman, Sacha Rabinovitch, trans. (Paris: Editions Bernard Grasset, 1972), Chap. 3.

        Contains a chapter on "Crusoism and Quixotery" in which the novel, as exemplified by Robinson Crusoe and Don Quixote, leaves its fairyland and learns " ... to see the world as it is and to take an interest in what is going on."

762   ROBINS, HARRY F.
        "How Smart was Robinson Crusoe?" PMLA 67 (1952): 782-789.

        Speculates why Defoe allows the reader to believe that Crusoe has little in the way of tools and equipment, when actually he had all the ship's supplies, and why Defoe caused his hero to err. Was it an artistic impulse?

763   ROGERS, PAT.
        Robinson Crusoe. London: Allen & Unwin, 1980.

        Robinson Crusoe is the culmination of a long literary career, and did not just happen; its cultural roots are many and complex: "Subsequent chapters of this book will explore particular aspects of the novel, as they were informed by Defoe's concerns and those of the age at large. These topics range from attitudes towards travel, discovery and colonialism to social, philosophical and religious themes such as solitude and self-help." The purpose is not to explain away the novel's originality, but to show the density of its imaginative world.

764   SCHOLTE, J. H.
        "Robinsonades." Neophilologus 35 (1951): 129-138.

        The central idea of Robinson Crusoe, the building up of a new life in solitude, is traced back in literature.

765   SCHROCK, THOMAS S.
        "Considering Crusoe: Part II. Interpretations 1 (1970): 169-232.

        Comments on such subjects as the law of nature, nature's

indifference to man, Crusoe as Saviour, Crusoe's rescue of
Friday and subjection of him, what Crusoe needs from society,
his apparent irrationality in preferring not to live on the more
bountiful side of the island, the necessity of civil society, the
importance of solitude, and Crusoe's boredom.

766   SEEBER, EDWARD D.
       "Oroonoko and Crusoe's Man Friday." MLQ 12 (1951): 286-
       291.

       Provides evidence for believing that Defoe patterned his
       "noble savage" after Mrs. Behn's famous hero and that he
       situated Crusoe's island near Guiana, the scene of Oroonoko.

767   SIEGEL, SALLY D.
       "Everyman's Defoe: Paradox as Unity in Robinson Crusoe."
       Thoth 14 (1974): 51-56.

       Considers the "ambiguous nature of Crusoe's 'original sin'
       and its relation to thematic unity," and suggests "an inclusive
       interpretation that accounts for economics, religion, and ad-
       venture."

768   SHINAGEL, MICHAEL.
       Daniel Defoe: ROBINSON CRUSOE (Norton Critical Edition).
       New York: W. W. Norton & Co., 1975.

       An authoritative text, background and sources, and criti-
       cism.

769   SPACKS, PATRICIA MEYER.
       "The Soul's Imaginings: Daniel Defoe, William Cowper."
       In [166], pp. 28-56.

       Examines a late eighteenth-century spiritual autobiography
       (Cowper's Memoir) and a fictional analogue (Robinson Crusoe),
       chronologically earlier but psychologically contemporaneous,
       that together suggest the complexities inherent in a highly
       conventionalized form. Both Defoe and Cowper use spiritual
       autobiography to contain and justify "imaginative self-investiga-
       tion"; the concern in both authors for imaginative growth sug-
       gests that the "given" identity of the Christian soul cannot
       provide adequate substance for literary treatment. For the
       eighteenth century, imagination contributed to the growth of
       the soul; it was a means of drawing man toward God, and of
       defining his ultimate identity.

770   STARR, GEORGE A.

"Robinson Crusoe's Conversion." In [642], pp. 78-91. Selections from "Robinson Crusoe" in [712], pp. 74-123.

Discusses Crusoe's "original sin," his running away to sea, his further progression in sin before conversion, and his relationship with Friday.

771   STEEVES, HARRISON R.
"Man on an Island." In [169], pp. 22-42.

An overall view of Defoe's writing with special emphasis on "Robinson Crusoe, because it is still one of the best examples--if not the best--of circumstantial realism; and Moll Flanders, because it conforms so closely to the general view of what goes to the making of a novel that many scholars and critics have called it, without reservation, the first English novel." Discusses Defoe's simplicity of style and his tendency to "emphasize the event, the adventure, the material gain or loss, rather than the personality concerned."

772   STEIN, WILLIAM BYSSHE.
"Robinson Crusoe: The Trickster Tricked." Cent. Rev. 9 (1965): 271-288.

Argues that Robinson Crusoe was written to sell: "It was and still is the consumer product par excellence.... Defoe's refusal to acknowledge the writing of his 'honest cheat' cheated posterity of a valid appreciation of his genius. So the trickster tricked himself."

773   STEPANIK, KAREL.
"Fact and Fiction in the Novels of Daniel Defoe." Philologica Pragensia 3 (1960): 227-240.

A discussion of Defoe's presentation of reality, and of his theory of literature and of how he came to produce his novels; a Brief survey of his life. Primarily a detailed analysis of Robinson Crusoe, and of its three levels of significance.

774   SWADOS, HARVEY.
"Robinson Crusoe: The Man Alone." Antioch Rev. 18 (1958): 25-40. Rpt. in Twelve Original Essays on Great English Novels, ed. Charles Shapiro (Detroit: Wayne State Univ. Press, 1960), pp. 1-21.

Discusses Defoe's adaptation of Alexander Selkirk's life and how Robinson Crusoe parallels both his life and that of Defoe. Discusses the problem of loneliness.

775   THORNBERG, THOMAS R.
       "Robinson Crusoe." BSUF 15 (1974): 11-18.

       Personal reflection on Robinson Crusoe and much else,
       concluding that Defoe's book is about how to survive, how to
       keep one's eye on the main chance.

776   TILLYARD, E. M. W.
       "Defoe." From The Epic Strain in the English Novel (Lon-
       don: Chatto & Windus, 1958), pp. 25-50; rpt. in [733], pp.
       62-78.

       Suggests that Robinson Crusoe is a greater work of art
       than Moll Flanders, Colonel Jacque, and Roxana, for it is
       "constructed with a closeness that the other novels ... do
       not attempt, and it touches greater depths of the mind." Dis-
       cusses several possible themes--a version of the story of
       the Prodigal Son, a progression from the practical to the
       contemplative life wherein a combination of both types pre-
       pares man for existence, or a theological version of Crusoe
       as Everyman abounding in Original Sin; and finally, after
       sketching in the symbolic overtones in Defoe's plot, concludes
       that Robinson Crusoe is an "epic, but an epic having some
       of the limitations of the middle-class ethos whose choice ex-
       pression it was."

777   WATT, IAN.
       "Robinson Crusoe." In [183], pp. 85-92.   Rpt. in [642], pp.
       51-59.

       A consideration of the novel's greatness and the way it
       "reflects the deepest aspirations and dilemmas of individual-
       ism."

778   "Robinson Crusoe as a Myth." EIC 1 (1951): 95-119.   Rpt.
       in [18], pp. 158-179.   Rev. and rpt. in [768], pp. 311-332.

       Examines relationship of Crusoe's story to three essential
       themes of modern civilization: " 'Back to Nature,' 'The Dig-
       nity of Labour,' and 'Economic Man.'   Robinson Crusoe
       seems to have become a kind of culture-hero representing all
       three of these related but not wholly congruent ideas."

779   WOOLF, VIRGINIA.
       "Robinson Crusoe." In The Second Common Reader (New
       York: Harcourt, Brace, 1932), pp. 50-58.   Rpt. in [768],
       pp. 306-311.

       Defoe, with his genius for fact, forces us to accept his

perspective on the world; he persuades us to abandon our
preconceptions and to see far islands and the solitudes of
the human soul.

780   ZIMMERMAN, EVERETT.
       "Defoe and Crusoe." ELH 38 (1971): 377-396. Rpt. with
       additions in [726] as Chapter II.

       An analysis of the Robinson Crusoe persona; considers
       how much of it is Defoe, if any, the emotional problems
       which affect the language of the novel, and Crusoe's and De-
       foe's struggles with the workings of an inexplicable Providence.

See also: 652, 656, 664, 665, 675, 695, 696, 697, 700, 701, 702,
    703, 712, 722, 725, 841, 853, 949, 2493, 3647

Moll Flanders

781   ALTER, ROBERT.
       "A Bourgeois Picaroon." In Rogue's Progress: Studies in
       the Picaresque Novel (Cambridge: Harvard Univ. Press,
       1964), pp. 35-57.

       Examines several picaresque novels, including Moll Flan-
       ders, "to see what are the possibilities of the picaresque ex-
       perience, what is ... and what is not picaresque." In "A
       Bourgeois Picaroon," Alter argues that Moll's childhood en-
       vironment of gentility is in conflict with her career. Her
       literal-mindedness and tough realism prevent her from ra-
       tionalizing away this conflict. So she appears as a qualified
       picaroon-"bourgeois": "It would seem, then, more mislead-
       ing than instructive to call Moll Flanders a picaresque novel."

782   BELL, ROBERT H.
       "Moll's Grace Abounding." Genre 8 (1975): 267-281.

       Explores the difficulties Moll, as narrator, experiences
       in trying to fulfill the demands of two literary genres--rogue's
       life and spiritual autobiography--and proposes a way of fitting
       together the very disparate elements of the whole.

783   BISHOP, JOHN PEALE.
       "Moll Flanders." In Collected Essays, ed. Edmund Wilson
       (New York: Scribner's, 1948), pp. 47-55. Originally pub-
       lished in Story, 1937.

       Argues that, as in novels of Hardy, Dostoevsky, and many

others, it is the criminal and not the "rightful protectors of society," who has our sympathetic interest. This, Bishop says, is precisely the greatness of these novels; they have been able to find "tragic possibilities, not in what was done, but in the failure of accomplishment," in "the disparity between what is willed and what is done." Discusses Moll's morality and her ability to rise above her station in life and Defoe's ability to convince the reader of Moll's innate goodness in spite of the life she led. Sees the novel as the literary expression of the middle classes.

784   BJORNSON, RICHARD.
"The Ambiguous Success of the Picaresque Hero in Defoe's Moll Flanders." In The Picaresque Hero in European Fiction (Madison: Univ. Wisc. Press, 1977), pp. 188-206.

The difficulty of deciding whether Defoe or the narrator is the source of any irony compounds the novel's ambiguity, but an analysis of Defoe's skill as a consummate creator of masks can contribute to a better understanding of the way in which the narrative perspective is manipulated. Since Moll is a biased and limited observer of her own past, her judgments cannot represent an ultimate standard of truth and moral value. The criteria for evaluating her comments are not clearly established, with the result that the moral significance of her example remains unclear: "readers are left in the ambiguous position of sympathizing with a character whose unreliability they have been warned against but whose arguments often seem to coincide with those of the author and the implied reader." Defoe never questions Moll's material success, a fact that partly explains the novel's popularity among middle- and lower-class Englishmen; yet Moll Flanders also reflects the bourgeois ideology and the ambiguity of bourgeois attitudes toward success.

785   BROOKS, DOUGLAS.
"Moll Flanders: An Interpretation." EIC 19 (1969): 46-59.

A structural analysis of Moll Flanders, begun as a refutation of the common interpretation of the novel in socio-economic terms (Moll, the countinghouse mind), discovers hitherto unexamined patterns in the unfolding of the plot.

786   COLUMBUS, ROBERT R.
"Conscious Artistry in Moll Flanders." SEL 3 (1963): 415-432.

Contrary to some critical opinion, Moll Flanders does have a plot, which "can be apprehended three ways: through the technique of the point of view, through Defoe's dramatization of the influence upon Moll of the values of security, love, and money, and through Defoe's own moral perception of his heroine."

787   DAY, ROBERT ADAMS.
       "Speech, Acts, Orality, and the Epistolary Novel." ECent.
       21 (1980): 187-197.

           Considers three novels--Moll Flanders, Clarissa, and
       Tom Jones--and applied to them "some considerations from
       speech-act philosophy and from our new awareness of the resi-
       dual presence of orality in post-Gutenberg literature."

788   DOLLERUP, CAY.
       "Does the Chronology of Moll Flanders Tell Us Something
       About Defoe's Method of Writing?" ES 53 (1972): 234-235.

           Dollerup concludes that Defoe seems to have made a "chron-
       ological table on which he checked Moll's age every time she
       was married or started a prolonged affair," but he failed to
       count time spent on husband-chasing and other incidents.
       Many discrepancies show under Dollerup's microscope, but
       he admits they are minor flaws in a good novel.

789   DONOGHUE, DENIS.
       "The Values of Moll Flanders." SR 71 (1963): 287-303.

           Defoe's ethic of trade was acknowledged by many Puritans--
       up to a point. His philosophy, dominated by thoughts of trade,
       shows in Moll Flanders' attitude that society, in presenting
       her with grim necessity, is more guilty than she is.

790   DONOVAN, ROBERT A.
       "The Two Heroines of Moll Flanders." In The Shaping Vision
       (Ithaca, N. Y.: Cornell Univ. Press, 1966), pp. 21-46.

           Defoe seen as accomplished artist: "The apparent artless-
       ness actually conceals Defoe's special kind of art." Moll's
       shady career contrasts with her early ambition, never for-
       gotten by her, to be a "gentlewoman." Therefore, "the or-
       ganizing principle of the novel, the principle that ultimately
       controls order, proportion, and emphasis, is implicit in this
       double function of Moll to serve ... as both subject and ob-
       ject.... The fundamental irony, produced by the reader's
       continuous and simultaneous awareness of the two sides of
       Moll's nature, transforms what would otherwise be a dreary
       and tedious chronicle of petty deceptions and crimes ... into
       a clearly focused and coherent story."

791   EDWARDS, LEE.
       "Between the Real and the Moral: Problems in the Structure
       of Moll Flanders." In [792], pp. 95-107.

A study of the novel's structure emphasizes that "the moral structure and the structure of reality remain divorced because Defoe had failed to coordinate the two aspects of his narrative purpose." Because the relationship between the real world and a surrounding moral universe is not completely controlled, Moll Flanders is a "perpetually anomalous and problematic prose fiction."

792   ELLIOTT, ROBERT C. , ed.
       Twentieth Century Interpretations of Moll Flanders: A Collec-
       tion of Critical Essays.   Englewood Cliffs: Prentice-Hall,
       1970.

793   ERICKSON, ROBERT A.
       "Moll's Fate: 'Mother Midnight' and Moll Flanders."   SP
       76 (1979): 75-100.

       An examination of the influence of Moll's "Governess" (or
       "Mother Midnight") shows a close analogy between Moll's
       practice of thievery and the lore of midwifery.   To under-
       stand the influence of Mother Midnight on Moll's "fate" helps
       us to understand "who the real Moll Flanders is for herself,"
       and also "entails a final analysis of Moll's 'grand Secret,'
       her 'true Name' ... and actual origin.   Moll Flanders is in
       many ways a searching examination of the meaning of 'name'
       and 'fate' in the role of a 'woman of the world. ' "

794   GASKIN, BOB.
       "Moll Flanders: Consistency in a Psychopath."   LJHum. 6,
       i (1980):   5-18.

       Advocates that Moll's consistent inconsistencies give her
       those personality characteristics found in psychopaths, and
       when so considered, she "has more coherence as a character
       than some have allowed, and her fragmented pseudo-ethics
       become meaningful parts of a larger, more integrated pic-
       ture." Discusses various interpretations of Moll's character
       by E. M. Forster, Sutherland [713], Van Ghent [836], Gold-
       berg [795], Edwards [791], Watt [183], and Koonce [802].

795   GOLDBERG, M. A.
       "Moll Flanders: Christian Allegory in a Hobbesian Mode."
       Univ. Rev. 33 (1967):   267-278.

       Sees the story as Christian allegory in a late-seventeenth-
       century mode: Moll, born at Newgate in sin, "continues to
       live in sin until, once more at Newgate, she can be reborn
       in Christ." She makes a journey like many another Christian

wayfarer: "her relentless emphasis upon the external gives
to Moll the appearance of one of those lost souls in Dante's
Inferno, aimlessly wandering...."

796   HAMMOND, BREAN S.
       "Repentance: Solution to the Clash of Moralities in Moll Flan-
       ders." ES 61 (1980): 329-337.

       A closer look at Defoe's concept of repentance in the novel
       shows that he "was neither ironic about the expediency of his
       characters nor insensitively blind to it, but rather felt it to
       be an ineluctable consequence of their social circumstances,
       which only the key concept of repentance could render toler-
       able." Moll's conflict between her repentance for her former
       actions and her need to vindicate herself makes her "unusually
       sensitive to her moral position."

797   HARTOG, CURT.
       "Aggression, Femininity, and Irony in Moll Flanders." L & P
       22 (1972): 121-138.

       Argues that the feminine viewpoint in Moll Flanders repre-
       sents an advance for Defoe, and suggests a "regression from
       the assertion of Crusoe." The feminine point of view is the
       "principal mode for expressing aggression without seeming
       to, or while pretending to disapprove of it."

798   HOCKS, RICHARD.
       "Defoe and the Problem of Structure: Formal 'Ropes' and
       Equivalent Technique." Literatur in Wissenschaft und Unter-
       richt 3 (1970): 221-235.

       Moll Flanders is a "structureless" novel, though not with-
       out some formal qualities: it possesses what the author calls
       "little histories," an equivalent technique that reflects back
       on Moll and flatters her.

799   KARL, FREDERICK R.
       "Moll's Many-Colored Coat: Veil and Disguise in the Fiction
       of Defoe." Studies in the Novel 5 (1973): 86-97.

       A study of the imagistic patterns and recurring themes in
       Defoe's work as related to the image of Proteus. A discus-
       sion of the "contours of Moll's career, within the novel's
       overall structure and imagistic frame of reference."

800   KELLY, EDWARD, ed.
       Daniel Defoe: MOLL FLANDERS (Norton Critical Edition),
       New York: W. W. Norton & Co., 1973.

An authoritative text, background and sources, and criticism.

801   KETTLE, ARNOLD.
       "In Defence of Moll Flanders." In [12], pp. 55-67. Rpt. in
       [800], pp. 385-396.

       Disagrees with Ian Watt's estimate of Defoe as a novelist
       and argues that Moll Flanders is a great novel. A Marxist
       interpretation of Moll's behavior as caused by social evil.

802   KOONCE, HOWARD L.
       "Moll's Muddle: Defoe's Use of Irony in Moll Flanders."
       ELH 30 (1963): 377-394. Rpt. in [792], pp. 49-59.

       Refutes the view of Ian Watt that much of what is seen
       as "ironic masterstrokes" is a perception brought to the novel
       by the critic, unintended by Defoe. " ... This is a work of
       comic excellence because it is basically ironic in structure."

803   KRIER, WILLIAM J.
       "A Courtesy Which Grants Integrity: A Literal Reading of
       Moll Flanders." ELH 38 (1971): 397-410.

       An explanation of Moll Flanders in terms of the book's
       reality created by its language--an explication of Moll's world.

804   LEGOUIS, PIERRE.
       "Marion Flanders est-elle une victime de la Societé?" Revue
       de l'Ensignement des Langues Vivantes 47 (1931): 288-299.

       Argues that Moll is not the victim of society, but rather
       that society is Moll's victim.

805   LERANBAUM, MIRIAM.
       "Moll Flanders: 'A Woman on Her Own Account.'" In The
       Authority of Experience: Essays in Feminist Criticism, Arlyn
       Diamond and Lee R. Edwards, eds. (Amherst: Univ. Mass.
       Press, 1977), pp. 101-117.

       Using evidence from the novel itself, from social histories
       of the period, and from recent biological and psychological
       writings, the author argues that Moll Flanders represents an
       extremely accurate rendering of an "involuntary involvement"
       in the feminine role. Defoe, in other words, has "contrived
       a narrative in which the major turning points of the heroine's
       life and her responses to them are in great part peculiarly
       feminine"; the essence of her character is not, as Watt avers,
       essentially masculine.

806   McCOY, KATHLEEN.
       "The Femininity of Moll Flanders." In [51], pp. 413-422.

       Discusses various critics and their views on whether or
       not Moll Flanders is a feminine character. Although there
       are many differences in opinion, the conclusion is that "Moll
       belongs more to the tribe of her class than to the tribe of
       her sex." Her use of feminine wiles is "more readily ap-
       plied to her self-deceptions than to her self-knowledge and
       self-aggrandizement.... Moll's character is a product of a
       set of vital ideas, lower-middle-class dissenting Protestant
       ideas, which are extra-literary but through which Defoe found
       an original concept of characterization."

807   McCULLOUGH, BRUCE.
       "The Conquest of Realistic Incident--Daniel Defoe." In [133],
       pp. 3-22.

       Discusses Defoe's "technique of circumstantial narration
       which enabled him to secure an unparalleled appearance of
       credibility and validity in the depiction of wholly imaginary
       events." Analyzes Defoe's contributions to fiction, especially
       through Moll Flanders, and suggests what, in spite of his
       shortcomings, he did manage to achieve.

808   McMASTER, JULIET.
       "The Equation of Love and Money in Moll Flanders." Studies
       in the Novel 2 (1970): 131-144.

       Considers how Defoe persistently develops the theme of
       the confusion between love and money in the incidents and
       in the language and imagery of the novel. Moll Flanders
       presents an economic version of the Christian order of values.

809   MARTIN, TERENCE.
       "The Unity of Moll Flanders." MLQ 22 (1961): 115-124.
       Rpt. & abridged [800], pp. 362-371.

       A study of cyclical repetition in the plot. Is Moll Flan-
       ders' journalistic, episodic account of her life a kind of form,
       or is the novel formless? Martin suggest "that the episodes
       themselves ... afford a unity which complements structurally
       the unity supplied by the novel's heroine.... In conjunction
       with the natural psychological progression in the book, there
       exists ... a formal pattern of circumstance shaped coherently
       by the episodes which make up Moll's experience."

810   MICHIE, J. A.
       "The Unity of Moll Flanders." In Knaves and Swindlers:

Essays on the Picaresque Novel in Europe, ed. Christine J.
Whitbourn (London & New York: Oxford Univ. Press, for
Univ. of Hull, 1974), pp. 74-92.

Attempts to show that this "novel has a stronger claim to
structural unity, involving theme, character and action, than has
hitherto been acknowledged." The unity of the novel is rooted
in the tensions between the social and economic aspirations
of Moll and her moral or religious scruples, in the difficulties of being good in the process of "making good."

811   MILLER, NANCY K.
       "A Harlot's Progress: I. Moll Flanders." In The Heroine's
       Text (New York: Columbia Univ. Press, 1980), pp. 3-20.

       A feminist interpretation of Moll Flanders, insisting upon
the importance of conventional ideas about women and female
psychology, or the eighteenth-century female codes, in affecting the plot and thematic structure of the novel.   Moll always defines her situation in terms of a generalized feminine
condition, which in turn is defined by opposition to masculine
self-sufficiency.   Moll's story is a quest for female autonomy,
an interpretation that implies the need for telic structure and
a clear sense of an ending or closure; the ending is then complete and consequential: Moll has achieved her goal of becoming a gentlewoman.

812   NEEDHAM, J. D.
       "Moll's 'Honest Gentleman.' "   Southern Rev. (Adelaide) 3
       (1969): 366-374.

       Analyzes some of the ambiguities of Moll's idiom and sug-
gests that "the implications of the stock praise, 'Defoe handles
colloquial speech well,' have not been sufficiently brought out;
and that the typical structure of meaning of some key words
are [sic] not for Defoe what they are for Moll."

813   NOVAK, MAXIMILLIAN E.
       "Defoe's 'Indifferent Monitor': The Complexity of Moll Flan-
       ders." ECS 3 (1970): 351-365.

       Examines in detail some of the complexities of language
and narrative in Moll Flanders which indicate irony of a type
influenced by picaresque fiction, or by criminal biography
which showed the influence of the picaresque.

814   "Conscious Irony in Moll Flanders." CE 26 (1964): 198-204.

       Refutes the opinions of many critics that Defoe either failed to write successful irony or that his irony was unintentional, a product of naiveté. Gives a summary of the themes in Moll Flanders, demonstrating "that the underlying irony of the work is to be found in Moll's blindness...." Defends the author from imputations of puritanism and moral insensitivity.

815   "Moll Flanders' First Love." PMASAL 46 (1961): 635-643.

Examines Moll Flanders' "first love" in order to show how Defoe uses first person narrative to present social satire; and suggests that the episode involves a conflict between "two self-interested characters--the rake and the clever maid."

816   ODA, MINORU.
"Moll's Complacency: Defoe's Use of Comic Structure in Moll Flanders." SEL (Tokyo) 58 (Oct. 1971): 31-42.

817   OLSHIN, TOBY A.
" 'Thoughtful of the Main Chance': Defoe and the Circle of Anxiety." HSL 6 (1974): 117-128.

A psychoanalytic approach to several problems in Defoe criticism: 1) how does he achieve his effects? 2) the question of ironic tone in Moll Flanders; and 3) the question of whether or not the protagonist of Roxana is a sympathetic projection of Defoe and the question of the enigmatic ending. The author seeks to find an underlying unity of pattern in Defoe's life and a similar uniformity of emotional tone in the works.

818   PIPER, WILLIAM BOWMAN.
"Moll Flanders as a Structure of Topics." SEL 9 (1969): 489-502.

Calls into question the argument of Terence Martin for a circular unity in Moll Flanders, marked by her return to scenes of earlier action, to Colchester, to Virginia, to Newgate. Moll's account of these is "imprecise and unemphatic" and does not support the idea of circular unity. Piper contends that the novel is organized under three topics--Moll's sexual adventures, her adventures in theft, and her Virginia adventures. Defoe does not remain true to this topical organization, but this failure has "an extremely lucky expressive effect." In other words, Moll's "imperfect achievement of order in her narrations" corresponds "with her imperfect achievement of order in her life."

819   PRESTON, JOHN

"Moll Flanders: 'The Satire of the Age.'" In [151], pp. 8-
37.

An analysis of Defoe's irony, which the author sees as a
"social act, a way of improving the public conscience," with
the result that Moll Flanders deals with the need for honesty
and the need for deceit: Defoe, therefore, is really testing
the different ways of using language; concludes not only that
Moll's whole way of life is an irony but also that Defoe is
largely concerned with the way in which "truth is mixed up
with deceit": i.e., "Moll Flanders provides ... an ironic
experience, the approach to truth through deceit."

820   PRICE, MARTIN.
       "Defoe's Novels." In [153], pp. 262-275; rpt. in [642], pp.
       23-39.

       General comments mainly on Moll Flanders; sees as the
       one constant in Moll's character the energy of life itself, the
       "exuberant innocence that never learns from experience and
       meets each new event with surprise and force."

821   RADER, RALPH W.
       "Defoe, Richardson, Joyce, and the Concept of Form in the
       Novel." In Autobiography, Biography, and the Novel: Papers
       Read at a Clark Library Seminar, May 13, 1972, ed. William
       Matthews & Ralph W. Rader (Los Angeles: William Andrews
       Clark Memorial Library, 1973), pp. 31-72.

       Attempts to resolve certain confusing problems concerning
       the form of Moll Flanders as contrasted to the form of Pam-
       ela by defining a standard "realism-plot-judgment" form of
       the novel that includes Pamela but excludes Moll as one in
       which the "author pits our induced sense of what will happen
       to a character against our induced sense of what we want to
       happen to him...." Moll is defined as a "naive incoherent
       autobiography."

822   RODWAY, A. E.
       "'Moll Flanders' and 'Manon Lescaut.'" EIC 3 (1953): 303-
       320.

       Compares the two novels as to the different way in which
       essentially the same material is handled. " ... Prévost had
       recourse to the master realist, Defoe. Consequently, Moll
       Flanders throws much light on Manon Lescaut."

823   ROGAL, SAMUEL J.
       "The Profit and Loss of Moll Flanders." Studies in the Novel
       5 (1973): 98-103.

Defoe's attention to the financial details of Moll's life makes
the novel "read as pages from a London merchant's ledger"
and in the end she achieves a financial security and independence which Defoe once had but never again attained.

824   ROGERS, HENRY N., III.
       "The Two Faces of Moll." JNT 9 (1979): 117-125.

Considers the possibility that Moll, as a first-person narrator, has a meaningful view of her own story; that she is
a reflective narrator who observes her former life from a
position separated from it by time and attitude. Is Moll capable of looking back on her infamous life and reflecting upon
its significance from an enlightened point of view? The answer appears to be, yes, she does repent of her former conduct: "Moll's recognition and admittance of her earlier wrong-
doing makes her an effective commentator rather than a self-
righteous moralizer unaware of her own guilt.... It follows
that conscious irony in the novel must come through Moll."

825   ROGERS, PAT.
       "Moll's Memory." English 24 (1975): 67-72.

Argues that Moll's exceptional memory of the details of
her life destroys the imaginative coherence of the novel.

826   SCHORER, MARK.
       "A Study in Defoe: Moral Vision and Structural Form."
       Thought 25 (1950): 275-287. Rpt. in The World We Imagine:
       Selected Essays as "Moll Flanders" (New York: Farrar,
       Straus, 1968): pp. 49-60, and as Introduction to the Modern
       Library Edition of Moll Flanders (New York: Random House,
       1950), pp. x-xvii; rpt. [642], pp. 120-126.

Combines biographical information on Defoe with a critical
evaluation of the novel. Interestingly for us today, Schorer
criticizes the episodic structure and "monotonously summariz-
ing method"; he concludes by saying that Defoe "does not,
finally, judge his material, as a novelist must. He makes
us sort out his multiple materials for him and pass our judgment. Our judgment must therefore fall on him, not on his
creature, Moll."
Discusses such further matters as Defoe's method, his
matter-of-fact tone, and his ostensible moral purpose--asserts
that Defoe's profession, that he intends to warn us against
the cost of a life of crime, cannot be taken seriously: "The
actualities of the book ... enforce the moral assumption of
any commercial culture, the belief that virtue and worldly
goods form an equation." Moll's life is "savage," a life mo-
tivated solely by economic need.

827   SHERBO, ARTHUR.
       "Moll Flanders: Defoe as Transvestite?" In [160], pp. 136-
       167.

            Sherbo says, "What I want to try to show is that Defoe's
       characters are infinitely less individualized than some critics
       have asserted they are and that what individuality they may
       possess is not discoverable for the reasons advanced by these
       same critics." Also discusses repetitiousness in the novels,
       and Moll's use of imagery.

828   "Moll's Friends." In [160], pp. 168-176.

            Argues that at every critical juncture in her life someone
       has been on hand to take care of her; one of Moll's greatest
       fears in life is to be without a friend.

829   SHINAGEL, MICHAEL.
       "The Maternal Theme in Moll Flanders: Craft and Character."
       Cornell Library Jour. 7 (1969): 3-23.

            Discusses Moll's relationship with her children pointing
       out Defoe's poor craftsmanship. Concludes that "despite the
       moral muddlement of point of view and the errors and in-
       consistencies of narrative consciousness, Moll Flanders is
       a novel 'where the character is everything and can do what
       it likes.' "

830   SPADACCINI, NICHOLAS.
       "Daniel Defoe and the Spanish Picaresque Tradition: The
       Case of Moll Flanders." I & L 2, vi (1978): 10-26.

            Argues that Defoe's knowledge of Spanish picaresque fiction
       is far more thorough and direct than is commonly supposed:
       "In this article I shall first review those pieces of external
       evidence that point to that conclusion and I shall then examine
       the elaboration in Moll Flanders of two major concerns of
       traditional (i. e. , Spanish) picaresque authors: the relation-
       ship between delinquency and autobiography and the exploration
       of the interrelated themes of 'freedom,' 'survival,' and dis-
       illusionment." Concludes that Moll Flanders moves toward
       the secularization and Europeanization of picaresque, fictional
       autobiography.

831   STARR, GEORGE A.
       "Moll Flanders." In [711], pp. 111-164. Rpt. in [792], pp.
       78-94.

            A look at Moll's various marriages, her attitude toward

them, and the reader's conflict between sympathy and moral
judgment: "We are asked to distinguish between act and
agent--between what Moll does and what she essentially is:
without minimizing her culpability, the narrative seeks to de-
flect our severity from the doer to the deed, and to retain
sympathy for the erring heroine."

832   STRANGE, SALLIE MINTER.
       "Moll Flanders: A Good Calvinist." SCB 36 (1976): 152-
       154.

       Finds no irony, in tone or point of view, in Moll Flanders;
       if problems and confusions arise in interpretation, they re-
       sult from oversubtle readings by modern critics--George
       Chalmers, in The Life of Daniel Defoe (1785), finds the novel
       straightforward and clear.   The basic misunderstanding de-
       rives from indifference to the Calvinistic doctrine and eighteenth
       century concept of man that is at the center of the novel:
       "If we can understand and accept Defoe's notions of what man
       is, how man thinks, and how he relates to God and his world
       --in other words, his Calvinistic beliefs--we can read the
       work as Chalmers did and as Defoe wrote it." Concludes
       that Moll Flanders is a Calvinistic work, seriously conceived,
       philosophically consistent, and psychologically sound.

833   TAUBE, MYRON.
       "Moll Flanders and Fanny Hill: A Comparison." BSUF 9,
       No. 2 (1968): 76-80.

       "The epistolary form and the sleazy morality" of Fanny
       Hill may have derived from Pamela, but "the pattern of
       Fanny's life came from Defoe, and the treatment of the ma-
       terial was a revolt against what Defoe stood for."

834   TAYLOR, ANNE ROBINSON.
       "This Beautiful Lady Whose Words He Speaks: Defoe and
       His Female Masquerades." W & L 6, 2 (1978): 25-34.

       Concerned with the question, what is the female conscious-
       ness in Defoe like and what use does he make of it?   Sug-
       gests that when Defoe writes as a woman he explores for-
       bidden thoughts, desires, and problems in his own life; he
       uses female narrators to express his own fears concerning
       sex, poverty, and dependence on the great.

835   VAID, SUDESH.
       The Divided Mind: Studies in Defoe and Richardson.   New
       Delhi: Associated Pub. House, 1979.

A study, especially of Moll Flanders, Roxana, Pamela, and Clarissa, from a feminist perspective; attempts to analyze the novels from the "perspective of the political and social structures emanating from the ideological basis of patriarchy," and specifically argues two theses: that Defoe and Richardson are ambivalent in their "feminism" when viewed from the perspective of sexual politics and their own attitudes toward women, and that their ambivalence forms the shape and structure of their novels.

836   VAN GHENT, DOROTHY.
"On Moll Flanders." In The English Novel: Form and Function (New York: Rinehart, 1953; rpt. New York: Harper Torchbook, 1961), pp. 33-43. Rpt. in [642], pp. 127-139.

Is the irony and social comment in this novel deliberate, or is it "a collection of scandal-sheet anecdotes naively patched together with ... platitudes?" Van Ghent feels that Defoe was a better writer and man than the "impoverished soul" who might have written the tale naïvely. Discusses Moll Flanders as a structure consisting of a complex system of ironies or counterstresses that gives the novel significant unity.

837   WATSON, TOMMY G.
"Defoe's Attitude toward Marriage and the Position of Women Revealed in Moll Flanders." SoQ 3 (1964): 1-8.

Defoe presents Moll's irregular marriages and adulteries as deviations from the accepted standards of the middle class in order to bring into focus the injustices of the social system.

838   WATT, IAN.
"Moll Flanders." In [642], pp. 104-126. From "Defoe as Novelist: Moll Flanders" in [183], pp. 96-101, 104-106, 108-115.

Discusses lack of coherence and analyzes the novel's total structure and the relationship between plot, character, and moral theme.

839   "The Recent Critical Fortunes of Moll Flanders." ECS 1 (1967): 109-126.

After 1955 articles concerning Moll Flanders increased steadily and it became one of the world's great novels. A detailed study of the recent literature on the novel, and specifically on that which considers whether <u>Moll Flanders</u> is an intentionally ironic work.

840   WILSON, BRUCE L.
       " 'Sex and the Single Girl' in the Eighteenth Century: An Essay on Marriage and the Puritan Myth. " <u>JWSL</u> 1 (1979): 195-219.

       Argues that <u>Moll Flanders</u> and <u>Clarissa</u> reflect the common eighteenth-century assumptions that can be labeled the "Puritan Myth" concerning middle-class beliefs about women and marriage, but that their conclusions are essentially subversive of that myth.   Concludes that in <u>Moll Flanders</u> Defoe perceived women to be the equals of men in talent, intelligence, and industry, but that they must adopt socially divisive codes to compete with men at all effectively; in <u>Clarissa Harlowe</u> Richardson presents a "profoundly moral vision--a recognition that there can be no winners and only losers in the divisive wars of sexual power, no triumph for either women or men where money determines moral values or sex-role relationships. . . . "

841   WOOLF, VIRGINIA.
       "Defoe. " In <u>The Common Reader</u>, First Series (New York: Harcourt, Brace, 1925), pp. 125-135; rpt. Harvest Books, pp. 89-97. Rpt. in [642], pp. 15-22.

       Concerned mainly with <u>Moll Flanders</u> and especially with the question of the nature of Defoe's greatness; considers why <u>Moll Flanders</u> and <u>Roxana</u> are as great as <u>Robinson Crusoe</u>.

See also: 652, 657, 675, 695, 697, 699, 712, 771, 776, 853, 854, 2581

Roxana

842   BAINE, RODNEY M.
       "<u>Roxana's</u> Georgian Setting. " <u>SEL</u> 15 (1975): 459-471.

       Gives evidence to support the contention that <u>Roxana</u> was set in the time of George I and that the reader misses much of the contemporary satire and irony if the novel is read as being set during the reign of George II.

843   BLEWETT, DAVID.
       " 'Roxana' and the Masquerades. " <u>MLR</u> 65 (1970): 499-502.

"Defoe's habitual practice ... was to exploit his reader's interest in contemporary concerns, even while his work appears to be dealing with another time." Blewett demonstrates that the masquerade scenes in Roxana constitute a "slightly veiled attack upon the contemporary masquerades which were once again providing the occasion for a rise in luxury and immorality."

844   CASTLE, TERRY J.
       " 'Amy, Who Knew My Disease': A Psychosexual Pattern in Defoe's Roxana." ELH 46 (1979): 81-96.

       From the beginning of the novel to the very end "Amy's presence infiltrates Roxana's narrative in a curiously intense way, and modifies its complicated psychological structure." The relationship between the two women is such that Amy acts as a "double" for Roxana--a double "so close to Roxana herself that she cannot really see her. She merely assumes her eternal presence." A symbolic reading of the text reveals that "Roxana ... is doomed, with Amy, to act out over and over her acts of destruction and self-destruction.... She is suspended in a lethal matrix of fixation; she has failed to birth herself."

845   COHAN, STEVEN.
       "Other Bodies: Roxana's Confession of Guilt." Studies in the Novel 8 (1976): 406-418.

       The "helper" characters in the novel, Amy, Susan, the Dutch merchant, and the Quaker Friend are all used by Roxana in varying degrees as psychological surrogates in her fantasy world. Defoe has "established a model for the conservative moral structure that holds together subversive psychological content. The helper characters undermine Roxana's conventional moral intentions; and until the end of the novel Defoe keeps these two antithetical forces suspended in a tense psychological balance, allowing his narrative form to contain the story's guilt material even when his narrative voice cannot.... Defoe will not let Roxana escape her guilt, and she cannot face it by herself...."

846   GOLDSTEIN, LAURENCE.
       "Roxana and Empire." In [107], pp. 59-72.

       Arguing that political economy shares the ambiguities of personal salvation, Goldstein suggests that Roxana illustrates in her behavior the spiritual decay Defoe believed was facing England. Roxana possesses an episodic structure; each important stage of Roxana's narrative is prefaced by an argument of principles, either in her mind or between Roxana and her servant. These arguments are similar to those that agitated the nation itself: the uses of wealth, the limits of liberty, the avoidance of ruin. Her prescription for avoiding the ruin of her material wealth is the same as that of contemporary economists: an increase in trade.

847   HIGDON, DAVID LEON.
"The Critical Fortunes and Misfortunes of Defoe's Roxana."
Bucknell Rev. 20, No. 1 (1972): 67-82.

Argues that Roxana has "Defoe's most coherently designed, technically complex, and aesthetically pleasing structure.... Roxana, despite its talk of poverty, avarice, and pride, chronicles a crisis in self-identity ... a crisis having tragic dimensions."

848   HUME, ROBERT D.
"The Conclusion of Defoe's Roxana: Fiasco or Tour de Force?"
ECS 3 (1970): 475-490.

Argues that "Roxana is a different kind of novel than Moll Flanders, Colonel Jack, or Captain Singleton: ... that structurally it is more carefully wrought than the others; and ... that its much-criticized ending is artistically defensible." Concludes that the abrupt conclusion is intended "to jolt the reader and leave him, like Roxana, hanging in a state of suspense and suspendable expectation.... He is thrust into her perplexed condition and left to flounder--a device Defoe can well afford, for the novel's point is already complete."

849   JACKSON, WALLACE.
"Roxana and the Development of Defoe's Fiction." Studies in the Novel 7 (1975): 181-194.

Emphasizes Defoe's increasing artistic self-consciousness in Roxana, and suggests that, through the technique of assumed autobiographical narrative, he approaches the psychological novel. The abrupt ending of Roxana is regarded as unimportant.

850   JENKINS, RALPH E.
"The Structure of Roxana." Studies in the Novel 2 (1970):
145-158.

An analysis of the narrative and allegorical structure that attempts to show that the novel has "a conscious artistry, a command of structure, and a clarity of moral judgment" that are unequalled in Defoe's other novels.

851   KROPF, C. R.
       "Theme and Structure in Defoe's Roxana." SEL 12 (1972):
       467-480.

           Attempts to show that the novel has both a logical overall
       structure and a consistent thematic design. "The symmetry
       of structure and the clear definition of Roxana's progress
       through the various steps in sin from virtuous woman to dam-
       nation gives the work a unity and logical order of progression."

852   NOVAK, MAXIMILLIAN E.
       "Crime and Punishment in Defoe's Roxana." JEGP 65 (1966):
       445-465.

           Discusses Roxana as a "novel of moral decay, and sug-
       gest[s] that it represents Defoe's furthest advance in the form
       of the novel from four vantages: 1) the treatment of narra-
       tive point of view; 2) the moral complexity of crime and sin
       in relation to the interplay of natural, divine, and positive
       law; 3) the effort to investigate the individual conscience and
       passions; and 4) the focusing of all the moral and social im-
       plications of Roxana's career on a single action." Concludes
       that the "interplay between the individual conscience and the
       laws of God, nature, and men creates a psychological and
       moral complexity which is unique in early fiction."

853   ODA, MINORU.
       "Allegory and History: A Study of Daniel Defoe's Roxana."
       Memoirs of Osaka Gakugei University, A, No. 15 (1966):
       62-87.

           Compares Roxana to Robinson Crusoe, Moll Flanders, and
       Colonel Jack, and suggests that the life of Roxana is similar
       to Defoe's life.

854   PETERSON, SPIRO.
       "The Matrimonial Theme of Defoe's Roxana." PMLA 70
       (1955): 166-191.

           A discussion of Defoe's satiric comments on matrimonial
       law as evidenced by the marital or pseudo-marital relations
       on different levels of society in Roxana and in Moll Flanders.

855   PETTIGROVE, MALCOLM G.
       "The Incomplete English Gentlewoman: Character and Char-
       acterisation in Roxana." In Studies in the Eighteenth Century
       IV: Papers Presented at the Fourth David Nichol Smith Memor-
       ial Seminar, Canberra, 1979. R. F. Brissenden and J. C. Eade,
       eds. (Canberra: Australian National Univ. Press, 1979), pp.
       123-146.

It is in <u>Roxana</u> that "Defoe most consciously attempts,
and most nearly approaches, a real drama of character revelation.... [and] more emphatically than in any of [his] other
narratives, character determines fate and is meant to do so."
This study "has four main considerations: the theoretical
concept of perfect character that underlies the narrative; the
real, imperfect character of the narrative's protagonist; the
source and consequence of that character's imperfections;
the question of her integrity and our judgment." In Roxana's
incompleteness as an English gentlewoman "lie her character
and her fate."

856   RALEIGH, JOHN HENRY.
      "Style and Structure and Their Import in Defoe's <u>Roxana</u>."
      <u>UKCR</u> 20 (1953): 128-135.

      An analysis of the complex meanings of <u>Roxana</u> by looking
      at the "Protean mass of structural patterns, rhetorical de-
      vices, and stylistic levels" which Defoe uses to memorialize
      "an aspect of human experience in which all mankind is for-
      ever involved: the fight for life, the relations of man and
      woman, the merciless arbitrariness of circumstances, the
      courage ... to carry on."

857   SLOMAN, JUDITH.
      "The Time Scheme of Defoe's <u>Roxana</u>." <u>ESC</u> 5 (1979): 406-
      419.

      Defoe's treatment of time, including an apparent "error"
      in chronology, is perhaps a key to Roxana's character and
      to her failure to create a new identity for herself in the sec-
      ond half of the novel: Roxana, unlike Moll Flanders, stays
      in the old world and refuses to change. <u>Roxana</u> is essentially
      a subjective novel, with time being distorted and manipulated
      to reflect the narrator's personal needs. Defoe worked out
      the time scheme very carefully; it is Roxana, an unreliable
      narrator, who confuses the chronology. The distortion of
      time in the Restoration episode suggests that Roxana has
      "realized her desire to remain tied to the values of her past,
      at the cost of imprisoning herself in the identity of 'Roxana,'
      the dramatic heroine."

858   SNOW, MALINDA.
      "Diabolic Intervention in Defoe's <u>Roxana</u>." <u>ELWIU</u> 3 (1976):
      52-59.

      Discusses the interaction between Roxana and Amy as it
      fits the pattern of diabolic influence and the effect of that in-
      fluence on the characterization of the heroine.

859   STARR, G. A.
       "Sympathy v. Judgement in Roxana's First Liaison." In [42],
       pp. 59-76.

           Story of an unfortunate wife that merges into the tale of
       a fortunate mistress. A disastrous marriage leads into a
       story of seduction in order that we may first sympathize with
       Roxana before judging her.

860   SUTHERLAND, JAMES.
       "The Conclusion of Roxana." In [642], pp. 140-149.   From
       [713], pp. 205-216.

           Speculates that perhaps Defoe left Roxana's story unfinished
       because, when he brought her daughter upon the scene, "he
       had embarked ... on a course that could only lead to dis-
       aster for his heroine."

861   ZIMMERMAN, EVERETT.
       "Language and Character in Defoe's Roxana." EIC 21 (1971):
       227-235.   Rpt. with additions in [726], as Chap. 7.

           Supports the interpretations of Douglas Brooks rather than
       those of Arthur Sherbo in modern evaluations of Defoe. Brooks's
       finding of serious moral questions handled (in Moll Flanders) in
       "a set of passages that parallel each other in language and
       incident" applies to Roxana as well. Argues that Defoe's
       language, especially the imagery, creates a "psychologically
       complex and coherent narrator whose materialism is a de-
       fence against metaphysical terrors"; the linguistic patterns,
       though perhaps not entirely planned, yet reflect the author's
       conception of the central character.

See also: 652, 657, 675, 685, 696, 697, 699, 712, 776, 817, 834,
       835, 841, 2723

                          Journal of the Plague Year

862   BASTIAN, F.
       "Defoe's Journal of the Plague Year Reconsidered." RES 16
       (1965): 151-173.

           Discusses Defoe's sources for the Journal and the uses he
       made of them. Concurs with Sir Walter Scott in regarding
       the Journal "as one of that peculiar class of writing between
       history and romance."

863   BLAIR, JOEL.

"Defoe's Art in A Journal of the Plague Year." SAQ 72
(1973): 243-254.

Author states: "I wish to examine the character of Defoe's fictional persona, to describe his procedures of selecting and arranging, and to determine which truths about human nature the Journal suggests. In other words, what is
the nature of Defoe's craftsmanship and what are its effects?"

864   FLANDERS, W. AUSTIN.
        "Defoe's Journal of the Plague Year and the Modern Urban
        Experience." Cent. Rev. 16 (1972): 328-348. Rpt. in
        [642], pp. 150-169.

        Examines Journal from a literary point of view, arguing
        that it is concerned primarily with "certain aspects of
        eighteenth-century psychological and social experience common
        to all of Defoe's fiction." Views it as a "reflection of De-
        foe's experience of life as he perceived it in the 1720's pro-
        jected through an account of the plague of 1664."

865   JOHNSON, CLIFFORD.
        "Defoe's Reaction to Enlightened Secularism: A Journal of
        the Plague Year." Enl. E. 3 (1973): 169-177.

        Argues that Defoe's Christian piety was perfectly consis-
        tent with his interest in experimental science, that his inter-
        pretation of disaster is based as much on scientific fact as
        on divine wrath. "The Journal may be seen as part of the
        English Enlightenment's contribution to the tradition of Eng-
        lish piety."

866   KAY, DONALD.
        "Defoe's Sense of History in A Journal of the Plague Year."
        XUS 9, No. 3 (1970): 1-8.

        Defoe's historical sources, accuracy, and accomplishment;
        concludes that, though he makes mistakes and has an imper-
        fect sense of time, "his sense of history is a practical, an
        effective and subjective view of events which takes the reader
        right back to the heart of London during the Great Plague."

867   NOVAK, MAXIMILLIAN E.
        "Defoe and the Disordered Ctiy." PMLA 92 (1977): 241-
        252.

        Defoe's narrator H. F., in A Journal of the Plague Year,
        is an extremely humane character whose sympathy for human

suffering extends to everyone, and his survival in the end is the survival of London itself. The Journal is a novel with the poor being its collective hero, and Defoe argues that adversity, whether it be the South Sea Bubble or the plague of 1665, brings people together. Defoe's narrator does not blame or scold; instead, he tries to spread feelings of hope and charity.

868   SCHONHORN, MANUEL.
        "Defoe's Journal of the Plague Year: Topography and Intention." RES 19 (1968): 387-402.

        "All previous examinations of Defoe's Journal have been either historical or biographical, or both ... [this] examination ... is topographical. In addition ... some considerations about Defoe's handling of details which he found in his sources.... [h]is modifications of his sources, and the implications of his tonal variations ... " are discussed.

869   VICKERS, PETER.
        "Daniel Defoe's Journal of the Plague Year: Notes for a Critical Analysis." Filología Moderna 13 (1973): 161-170.

        Emphasizes the positive techniques used by Defoe to gain his effects; discusses both the atmosphere of realism in the book and the theme of dualism, especially in the person of the narrator: "Defoe presents us with a dramatic contrast between the dualism of the factual, realistic presentation of names, places and statistics through the faceless saddler-narrator and the emotive, impressionistic and subjective observations of the saddler-man."

870   ZIMMERMAN, EVERETT.
        "H. F.'s Meditations: A Journal of the Plague Year." PMLA 87 (1972): 417-423. Partly rpt. in [726], as Chapter V.

        Argues that it is the intense focus on the narrator that makes the Journal more like a novel that like the historical and religious writings on which it draws. In the "conflicts and mounting anxiety" of the narrator, we have "a psychologically complex and interesting central character." Although the Journal contains signs of hasty writing, the "aptness of the allusions and the clear development of H. F. imply a coherent design."

See also: 697, 702, 703

The Shortest Way with the Dissenters

871   ALKON, PAUL K.
      "Defoe's Argument in The Shortest Way with the Dissenters."
      MP 73, iv, part 2 (1976): S12-S23.

          An analysis, based on recent concepts of intentionality,
      of neglected relationships between fictive effects, metaphoric
      statements, and the method of Defoe's argument. Although
      the speaker's inhumanity and intolerance are quite obvious,
      it is not so clear how Defoe made the speaker's glaring in-
      tolerance appealing to readers who liked the argument but
      were later ashamed of their initial response. Defoe employs
      skillful rhetoric: "the reader's virtuous intentions ... dis-
      pose him to accept vicious means described in ways that sof-
      ten or conceal their true horror." The result was that Dis-
      senters immediately sensed their danger, while their oppon-
      ents were shocked to realize "how close the parodic argu-
      ments had brought them to discarding some moral restraints
      necessary to all civilized men."

872   BOARDMAN, MICHAEL M.
      "Defoe's Political Rhetoric and the Problem of Irony." TSE
      22 (1977): 87-102.

          Seeks to determine the internal structure of The Shortest
      Way with Dissenters, by distinguishing between the "internal
      system of inference Defoe established and external knowledge
      which tells us Defoe intended something like irony." In The
      Shortest Way Defoe used another rhetorical system that has
      been called irony, impersonation, and even satire, but that
      includes "no provision for its own unmasking." The Shortest
      Way lacks an internally coherent form that would reveal to
      readers that the persona does not mean exactly what he says;
      its internal structure is simply that of a non-ironic polemic.

873   BOYCE, BENJAMIN.
      "The Shortest Way: Characteristic Defoe Fiction." In [15],
      pp. 1-13.

          Argues that "The Shortest Way was not in all respects
      clever as an ironic satire and that the figure impersonated
      was not quite the sort of High Churchman readers of either
      party would be likely to expect." Defoe's speaker is imper-
      fect even as an invented human being: he is inconsistent and
      fails to conform to an expected pattern.

874   COOK, RICHARD I.
      "Defoe and Swift: Contrasts in Satire." DR 43 (1963): 29-
      39.

Suggests that, though The Shortest Way with the Dissenters and A Modest Proposal are similar in that each attempts to gain its end largely by using an outrageous proposal apparently put forward in sincerity, both pamphlets differ in technique, in effects sought, and in results achieved. Defoe employed a very subtle satire, whereas Swift used broad, bitterly indignant satire and heavy irony.

875   LERANBAUM, MIRIAM.
" 'An Irony Not Unusual': Defoe's Shortest Way with the Dissenters." HLQ 37 (1974): 227-250.

By examining the rhetoric of contemporary models, and Defoe's own statements, the author argues that The Shortest Way is not satire, but a "banter" or hoax.

876   NOVAK, MAXIMILLIAN E.
"Defoe's Shortest Way with the Dissenters: Hoax, Parody, Paradox, Fiction, Irony, and Satire." MLQ 27 (1966): 402-417.

Disagreeing with Ian Watt that The Shortest Way is merely a work of fiction, Novak argues that Defoe did indeed write an ironic satire.   Defoe "wrote to deceive and convince--to fool those who were secretly so committed to extremist arguments that they could not see the trick, and to inform his intelligent audience through irony."

Robert Drury's Journal

877   BAINE, RODNEY M.
"Daniel Defoe and Robert Drury's Journal." TSLL 16 (1974): 479-491.

Argues that the alleged similarities between Robert Drury's Journal and "Defoe's known work are conventional ones which could easily be matched in other contemporary writers. Moreover, striking differences in style and in ideas show that Defoe was neither author nor Transcriber."

878   MOORE, JOHN ROBERT.
Defoe's Sources for "Robert Drury's Journal" (Indiana Univ. Publications, Humanities Series, No. 9).   Bloomington: Indiana Univ. Press, 1943.

Considers, in addition to such matters as Defoe's artistry and dramatic sense, the chief sources of Robert Drury's Journal: Robert Knox's An historical relation of the island

of Ceylon and Knox's Autobiography, both of which constitute
Defoe's chief source; another important source was Robert
Everard's Relation (1732).

879   NOVAK, MAXIMILLIAN E.
       "Defoe, Thomas Burnet and the 'Deistical' Passages of Robert
       Drury's Journal." PQ 42 (1963): 207-216.

       Argues that "Defoe's love of paradox and his interest in
       the writings of Thomas Burnet led him to engage in an attack
       on the literal reading of the Bible, which, on the surface,
       appears little different from that of the very deists he so
       often criticized."

880   SECORD, ARTHUR WELLESLEY.
       "Robert Drury's Journal" and Other Studies.   Urbana: Univ.
       Ill. Press, 1961.

       Suggests hesitantly that Robert Drury's Journal was written
       by Defoe, and shows conclusively that Robert Drury did in-
       deed exist, and that the beginning and end of the Journal is
       an accurate account of the sinking of the Degrave and of Drury's
       shipwreck on Madagascar.   Also studies Defoe's sources for
       Memoirs of a Cavalier.

881   "Defoe and Robert Drury's Journal." JEGP 44 (1945): 66-
       73.

       The question of truth or fiction, or at least of the extent
       of Defoe's authorship vs. his reporting, is the subject of
       Secord's research.   The Journal, like Captain Carleton, is
       pronounced to have "a framework of fact within which Defoe
       invented freely."

See also: 685

Colonel Jacque

882   BLEWETT, DAVID.
       "Jacobite and Gentleman: Defoe's Use of Jacobitism in Co-
       lonel Jack." ESC 4 (1978): 15-24.

       Even though Colonel Jack becomes a Jacobite and joins
       the Jacobite rebels in 1715, most readers have usually re-
       garded the Jacobite material as "incidental." On the con-
       trary, Jack's Jacobite career is closely related to some of
       the main themes: "Defoe uses Jacobitism to emphasize those

aspects of his hero's character which ironically undercut his
progress to gentility." Jacobitism is presented as a doomed
cause, attracting men who are either misguided opportunists
or politically naïve or deluded.   The most important fictional
use of the theme is to further Jack's characterization as an
unthinking and naïve social climber; a secondary purpose is
to emphasize the related theme of gratitude, which defends
the Royal policy of pardoning former Jacobites.

883   McBURNEY, WILLIAM H.
       "Colonel Jacque: Defoe's Definition of the Complete Gentle-
       man." SEL 2 (1962): 321-336.

       Colonel Jack is not, as it is often considered, a comple-
       mentary picture to that of Moll Flanders; it is a contrasting
       one.   The "portrayal of an honest thief" presents a dilemma
       which Defoe solves by having the hero not understand the
       social implications of his deeds.

884   NOVAK, MAXIMILLIAN E.
       "Colonel Jack's 'Thieving Roguing' Trade to Mexico and De-
       foe's Attack on Economic Individualism." HLQ 24 (1961):
       349-353.

       A discussion of the final episode as one of the best illus-
       trations of Defoe's theory of commercial morality and as an
       example of Defoe's use of economic ideas in his novels.

885   STARR,   G. A.
       " 'Only a Boy': Notes on Sentimental Novels." Genre 10
       (1976): 501-527.

       Discussion of four novels: Defoe's Colonel Jack, Mac-
       kenzie's Man of Feeling, Sterne's Sentimental Journey, and
       Fanny Burney's Evelina.   The author is partly concerned with
       the form of the sentimental novel, partly with its relation to
       society, and partly with the responses the sentimental novel
       seeks to arouse.   His chief contention is that, "owing to dif-
       ferent social assumptions about masculinity and femininity
       the sentimental heroine can figure in conventional novelistic
       plots that end with wedding bells, since her role conforms
       to the popular sense of what a young lady should be; the sen-
       timental hero poses an implicit challenge to accepted notions of
       masculinity, and cannot be assimilated into the world repre-
       sented in the novels."

See also: 652, 695, 697, 776, 853

Captain Singleton

886   BLACKBURN, TIMOTHY C.
"The Coherence of Defoe's Captain Singleton." HLQ 41 (1978):
119-136.

Traces Singleton's progression through Locke's political
philosophy as expressed in Two Treatises of Government to
social maturity and spiritual salvation. Defoe achieves coherence in the novel by fictionalizing Locke's vision, by depicting Singleton's progress through states of development,
and by creating an environment reflecting these states. Defoe's art lies in his imaginative ability to turn Locke's philosophy into a "unified fictional world" by placing Singleton
in Africa, the original state of man, and in piracy, which
functions both as a state of war and a state of reason. Because of his environment, Singleton is able to "progress from
nature to reason to civil society, [and] ... from innocence
to rebellion to repentance."

887   SCHONHORN, MANUEL.
"Defoe's Captain Singleton: A Reassessment with Observations." PLL 7 (1971): 38-51.

Schonhorn's subject, he admits, is "partially negative; that
is, Captain Singleton bears little similarity to those piratical
records it was intended to resemble." But he intends a positive result from his conclusions and the material presented
with it; the reader may go back to Defoe's novel with "renewed interest and insight."

888   SCRIMGEOUR, GARY J.
"The Problem of Realism in Defoe's Captain Singleton." HLQ
27 (1963): 21-37.

Researches the sources of Captain Singleton and Defoe's
use of them, not to sift "fiction" from "fact" or to "acclaim
or deny [Defoe's] realism.... Rather, by studying what Defoe chose to emphasize either by inclusion or by omission,
we can learn the nature of his interests in writing fiction."

See also: 697, 700, 702

Mrs. Veal

889   BAINE, RODNEY M.
" 'The Apparition of Mrs. Veal'--A Neglected Account." PMLA
69 (1954): 523-541.

A study of the event based on an account given by the Reverend Thomas Payne which "makes feasible an analysis of Defoe's treatment of the affair; and ... gives ... much information concerning the dramatis personae ... " so that identification of almost all of them is possible.

890   "Defoe and Mrs. Bargrave's Story." PQ 33 (1954): 388-395.

Attributes authorship to Defoe but asserts that the story of the apparition was fabricated by Mrs. Bargrave.

891   SCOUTEN, ARTHUR H.
"At that Moment of Time: Defoe and the Early Accounts of the Apparition of Mistress Veal." Ball State Teachers College Forum 2, No. 2 (1961-62): 44-51.

Defoe's stylistic achievement at work in A True Relation-- how he altered the actual account of the ghostly visit to make a better story. Based on newspaper accounts of the time.

See also: 714, 719

A Tour Thro' the Whole Island of Great Britain

892   BARRINGER, GEORGE MARTYN.
"Defoe's A Tour Thro' the Whole Island of Great Britain." Thoth 9 (1968): 3-13.

The Tour regarded not as a guide book or an economic history but as a loving tribute paid by a patriot to his country; considers its history and the genre to which it belongs.

893   DAVIES, GODFREY.
"Daniel Defoe's A Tour Thro' the Whole Island of Great Britain." MP 48 (1950): 21-36.

Discusses changes in the various editions of the Tour and gives detailed examples of editorial alterations.

894   HACKOS, JO ANN T.
"The Metaphor of the Garden in Defoe's A Tour thro' the Whole Island of Great Britain." PLL 15 (1979): 247-262.

A Tour most directly displays Defoe's understanding that "art is nature methodized" and that art represents an artistic rearrangement or recreation of nature. For the early eight-

eenth century the garden represented nature controlled and
recreated; Defoe uses the metaphor of the garden to demonstrate the creative power of art.   When he equates garden
and landscape, he refers not only to the natural scene but
also to the verbal landscape that he creates imaginatively;
that creation becomes a verbal equivalent of the visual creation of the gardener.   Defoe, therefore, uses the metaphor
of the garden, through the structure of the Tour itself and
in descriptions of actual gardens, to focus upon a visual ordering of English landscape.

895   ROGERS, PAT.
       "Defoe at Work: The Making of A Tour thro' Great Britain,
       Volume I. "   BNYPL 78 (1975):   431-450.

       Suggests that Defoe's Tour thro' the Whole Island of Great
       Britain was not as extensively based on his early travels in
       the 1680s and 1690s as well as in the early 1700s as pre-
       viously supposed, and that he used a quantity of recent and
       firsthand information; suggests also that a working schedule
       can be drawn up to reveal the likely process of composition,
       thus showing a little of Defoe's working habits as a writer.

896   "Literary Art in Defoe's Tour: The Rhetoric of Growth and
       Decay. "   ECS 6 (1972-73):   153-185.

       A study of structure, voice, handling of language, and
       artistic detail; suggests that the "interest of the Tour is not
       confined to the social and economic data it provides.   The
       book deploys the resources available to a great imaginative
       writer, and it supplies less a picture of Britain than a vision
       of nationhood. "   Defoe gives us the "experiential equivalent"
       of a tour, and therefore achieves the true English epic.

897   "Defoe and Virgil: The Georgic Element in 'A Tour Thro'
       Great Britain. ' "   Eng. Misc. 22 (1971):   93-106.

       Parallels between the Tour and Virgil's Georgics show that
       the source for some of Defoe's ideas came from another age
       and another country.

Collected Studies

898   PAULSON, RONALD, ed.
Fielding: A Collection of Critical Essays. New York:
Prentice-Hall, 1962.

899   RAWSON, CLAUDE, J., ed.
Henry Fielding: A Critical Anthology. Harmondsworth:
Penguin, 1973.

General Studies

900   ALTER, ROBERT.
Fielding and the Nature of the Novel. Cambridge: Harvard
Univ. Press, 1968.

Defends Fielding as a self-conscious artist "for whom style
is not just the means of conveying or framing events but,
often, the event itself"; sees Fielding as an "architectonic"
novelist who arranges characters and episodes in symmetrical and antithetical patterns.

901   "Fielding and the Uses of Style." Novel 1 (1967): 53-63.
Rpt. in [900], pp. 27-59; [1092], pp. 97-109.

Explores Fielding's use of style, especially in his parodies
of epic devices in Tom Jones and Joseph Andrews, to show
how "he maneuvers us into seeing characters, actions, values,
society at large, from exactly the angle of vision he wants."

902   BAKER, SHERIDAN.
"Fielding's Comic Epic-in-Prose Romances Again." PQ 58
(1979): 63-81.

Argues that "neither Fielding nor his contemporaries thought
of his two books [Joseph Andrews and Tom Jones] as epics,
and that our calling them 'epics in prose' is actually a modern
misunderstanding, shutting from view their essential quality."
Fielding nowhere refers to his two novels as comic prose epics,

a term invented and overused by such modern critics as Ethel
Margaret Thornbury and Martin Battestin.   Baker surveys
recent criticism of Fielding to support his point.

903   "Fielding and the Irony of Form."   ECS 2 (1968):   138-154.

Argues "that the structure of Joseph Andrews derives principally from the repetitive structural impulse of simple narrative fiction whereas the structure of Tom Jones derives
from the formal outline of dramatic comedy, that in Joseph
Andrews structure emphasizes whereas in Tom Jones it
insulates, that in Joseph Andrews structure is more supportive
than ironic ... whereas in Tom Jones structure is much the
more ironic...."

904   "Henry Fielding's Comic Romances."   PMASAL 45 (1960):
        411-419.

Fielding's works are more appropriately regarded as comic
romances than as comic prose epics.   Traces influence of
Tom Brown's translation of Scarron's Comical Romance in
Tom Jones and Joseph Andrews.

905   "Henry Fielding and the Cliché."   Criticism 1 (1959):   354-
        361.

Discusses Fielding's use of proverbs and common figures
of speech; proverbs are often at the bottom of his mock-
heroic similes, which he frequently repeats.   Analyzes such
clichés as Nature and Fortune, Bill of Fare, "solid comfort"
(I, xi), and courtship as a hunting of hares or deers (V, x-
xii).   The cliché represents an epitome of experience, the
lasting truths of human nature; allows the author to chat fa-
miliarly.

906   BATTESTIN, MARTIN C.
        "Henry Fielding, Sarah Fielding, and 'the dreadful Sin of
        Incest.' "   Novel 13 (1979):   6-18.

Attempts to explain Henry and Sarah Fielding's fascination
with the sin of incest not only in literary terms, but also in
terms of Fielding's character and personal history.   Fielding's usual treatment of the incest theme is comic, but in
Amelia he resumed the theme obliquely and in a serious manner in Book II, Chapter iv, when Booth visits his dying sister, Nancy.   Perhaps the scene of Nancy's dying evokes a
well-known psychological phenomenon, the process by which
the individual "transcends the familiar pathology of the Oedipus complex--the process of displacing sexual desire from

mother, to sister, to a 'proper' object outside the family."
The process of "burying" the object of incestuous feelings
represents an aspect of attaining sexual maturity.

907   "Fielding and Ralph Allen: Benevolism and Its Limit as an
        Eighteenth-Century Ideal." MLQ 28 (1967): 368-377.

        Discusses benevolence as exemplified by Ralph Allen and
        advocated by Fielding, and discusses the analyses by Ben-
        jamin Boyce in his The Benevolent Man: A Life of Ralph
        Allen of Bath, by Malvin R. Zirker, Jr. , in Fielding's Social
        Pamphlets, and by Morris Golden in Fielding's Moral Psy-
        chology.

908   BEASLEY, JERRY C.
        "Romance and the 'New' Novels of Richardson, Fielding, and
        Smollett." SEL 16 (1976): 437-450.

        Although the three novelists wrote "anti-romantic" novels
        of familiar life, they yet made concessions to the romance
        tradition by borrowing some of its strategies and conventions,
        a concession that helped to increase their popularity.

909   "English Fiction in the 1740s: Some Glances at the Major
        and Minor Novels." Studies in the Novel 5 (1973): 155-175.

        Argues that Fielding, Richardson, and Smollett, in spite
        of differences in themes and methods, exploited several cur-
        rent modes of story-telling prevalent among their contem-
        poraries in the 1740s: they achieved great popularity by com-
        bining contemporary appeal with "excitingly original, utterly
        serious works of art."

910   BEATTY, RICHARD C.
        "Criticism in Fielding's Narratives and His Estimate of Cri-
        tics." PMLA 49 (1934): 1087-1100.

        Considers Fielding's views on the essentials of a good
        writer, his philosophy of character, his convictions about
        travel books and plagiarism, and his castigation of critics.
        Fielding believed that "novels should concern themselves with
        the affairs of this world. . . . "

911   BELL, MICHAEL.
        "A Note on Drama and the Novel: Fielding's Contribution."
        Novel 3 (1970): 119-128.

        Discusses Fielding's formal experimentation as influenced

by his dramatic practice in the proposal scene between Tom and Sophia in Tom Jones as an illustration of how Fielding's mixture of aesthetic modes influences later novelists, especially Jane Austen.

912   BISSELL, FREDERICK O.
Fielding's Theory of the Novel (Cornell Studies in English 22). Ithaca, N. Y. : Cornell Univ. Press, 1933; rpt. New York: Cooper Square Publishers, 1969.

Attempts to describe the chief sources of Fielding's theory of the novel, to interpret that theory, and to apply it to Joseph Andrews and Tom Jones. Concludes that, even though Fielding made "little effort to organize his rules into a complete code, they state all the essentials of the modern novel and constitute a sound and coherent body of doctrine."

913   BLANCHARD, FREDERIC T.
Fielding the Novelist: A Study in Historical Criticism. New Haven: Yale Univ. Press, 1926; rpt. New York: Russell & Russell, 1966.

A study of Fielding's fame as a novelist and of the "impress which his original genius has made upon the minds and hearts of English readers." Considers "kinships and antipathies" that illuminate not only Fielding's genius and achievement but also the development of the genre of realism.

914   BLAND, D. S.
"Endangering the Reader's Neck: Background Description in the Novel." Criticism 3 (1961): 121-139.

In an examination of the development of landscape description in the English novel, the author discusses two descriptions from Fielding, one from Joseph Andrews and one from Tom Jones: the one from Tom Jones (Bk. I, Ch. IV), the description of Allworthy's estate, is not a piece of natural description for its own sake, but the "panorama of a situation in which nature is so manipulated as to form a setting for man"; the passage from Joseph Andrews (Bk. III, Ch. V) describes a "natural amphitheatre" that underlines the romantic mood of Joseph and Fanny, and is therefore a "mood" landscape: it represents the next stage in the development of description in the novel. Fielding reminds the reader of visual experiences that derive from neoclassical landscape painting and the garden-design based on it.

915   BRAUDY, LEO.
Narrative Form in History and Fiction: Hume, Fielding, and Gibbon. Princeton, N. J. : Princeton Univ. Press, 1970.

Looks for a rationale of development and a unity of structure in which Hume, Fielding, and Gibbon have found a new
way of apprehending time and the way man lives within it;
and regards all four of Fielding's novels as "stages in the
development of a theory about the relation of the novel to the
public history of its own time as well as to the events of the
past."

916   BROOKS, DOUGLAS.
       Number and Pattern in the Eighteenth-Century Novel: Defoe,
       Fielding, Smollett and Sterne.   London: Routledge & Kegan
       Paul, 1973.

       Analyzes the formal structure in terms of symbolic mean-
       ing; argues that "our early novelists conceived of structure
       in what we would call numerological terms" that gave to those
       novels an ordered symmetry and harmony.

917   BURKE, JOHN J. , JR.
       "History without History: Henry Fielding's Theory of Fic-
       tion." In [32], pp. 45-63.

       Fielding's theory of fiction was greatly influenced by his
       disenchantment with the practice of historiography; he there-
       fore sought to create a new form of historiography, "history
       without historical content." He was disturbed by the popular
       assumption that history was truer than mere fiction, and by
       the convention that history was restricted to the affairs of
       the great; popular historiography encouraged readers to ad-
       mire qualities that ought to be repressed.   In Jonathan Wild,
       Fielding burlesques the compositional methods of historio-
       graphers and, even more emphatically, the subject matter
       of history, the affairs of the great.   Whereas in Jonathan
       Wild Fielding's role was largely negative, in Joseph Andrews
       he adopted a more positive and didactic attitude, directed
       toward people in the world of private affairs, and motivated
       by the desire to use the comic mode to make men happy.
       In Tom Jones, Fielding moves farther in the direction of auto-
       biography and expands the role of the narrator; goodness of
       heart is secularized, and the panoramic sweep of the nar-
       rative suggests that Tom Jones is indeed a History of Eng-
       land.

918   BUTT, JOHN.
       Fielding.   Revised ed. (WTW) London: Longmans, 1959.
       Rpt. in British Writers and Their Work: No. 6 (Lincoln:
       Univ. Nebraska Press, 1965), pp. 43-76.

       A brief and general survey of Fielding's career, emphasiz-
       ing the effect on the novels of his theatrical and journalistic
       experiences; suggests that the guiding principle of Joseph An-

drews is the "distinction between being and seeming," and
that the theme of Tom Jones concerns the need for maintaining the appearance of goodness; and concludes that Amelia
deals with the miseries and misfortunes typical of mid-eighteenth century London life: "No other novel provides such
a wide panorama of London society or better conveys what
it was like to live in London in the seventeen-fifties."

919   COLEY, W. B.
        "Notes Toward a 'Class Theory' of Augustan Literature: The
        Example of Fielding." In Literary Theory and Structure:
        Essays in Honor of William K. Wimsatt, ed. Frank Brady,
        John Palmer, & Martin Price (New Haven: Yale Univ. Press,
        1973), pp. 131-150.

        Presents a class theory (the two classes being the men
        of letters and their patrons) to account for some apparently
        unrelated aspects of Augustan literature, and argues that "any
        paradigm of the Augustan man of letters must emphasize his
        close dependency on the support of men in or around the seats
        of power and that this dependency presented him with two un-
        avoidable difficulties: ideological inconstancy and the threat
        of the loss of the dependency itself."

920   "Gide and Fielding." Comp. Lit. 11 (1959): 1-15.

        Discusses Gide's interest in the eighteenth-century novel,
        Fielding in particular, based on his "Travels in English Liter-
        ature" and "Notes en Manière d'un Préface à Tom Jones."
        Gide comments on Fielding's conception of Good Nature, the
        nature of his anti-religiousness, the significance of his epic
        "tone," and the value of the "poetics of the novel in the novel,"
        based on the essays in Tom Jones.

921   "The Background of Fielding's Laughter." ELH 26 (1959):
        229-252.

        Suggests that "for Fielding, as for Augustans generally,
        seriousness in literature was not a simple matter.... em-
        phasis on Fielding's seriousness may obscure not only the
        nature of the witty mode evolved for treating grave subjects,
        but also the nature of the important rhetorical pressures pres-
        ent in the background of such a mode." Reevaluates the in-
        fluences of South, Shaftesbury, and Swift on Fielding.

922   COOLIDGE, JOHN S.
        "Fielding and 'Conservation of Character.' " MP 57 (1960):
        245-259. Rpt. in [898], pp. 158-176.

Fielding's treatment of character follows Horatian principle of "conservation of character"--the essential reality of a person is a certain idea, which is his nature, and to which he conforms. Precludes change and development in character in some of Fielding's work, though in Amelia the characters develop more realistically, since they act in terms of social ideals of good and evil.

923   CROSS, WILBUR L.
       The History of Henry Fielding. New Haven: Yale Univ.
       Press, 1918.

Still a useful and authoritative life of Fielding, with chapters on the novels; e. g. , there are chapters on the publication and reception of Tom Jones, and one on its art.

924   DIGEON, AURELIEN.
       The Novels of Fielding. London: Routledge & Kegan Paul
       Ltd. , 1925; rpt. New York: Russell & Russell, 1962.

With only a brief look at Fielding's life, Digeon concentrates on a detailed analysis of the novels--their structure, characterization, plot, and moral philosophy.

925   DONALDSON, IAN.
       "High and Low Life: Fielding and the Uses of Inversion. "
       In The World Upside-Down: Comedy from Jonson to Fielding
       (Oxford: Clarendon Press, 1970), pp. 183-206.

Considers Fielding's treatment of a Scriblerian theme, the merger or levelling of the "high" and the "low": he "gradually connects the Tory satirist's despondent myth of a civilization falling to ruins to more optimistic comic ends; his mood becomes, on the whole, lighter and more amiable, and the levelling tends to be seen not with the savage energy of a satirist who proclaims the approach of the end of the world, but with the gentleness of a comic artist who reminds us of the artificiality of such distinctions in the first place. " Pursues this theme in Tom Thumb, Tumble-Down Dick, Pasquin, The Author's Farce, and Jonathan Wild, emphasizing the differences with Pope and his fellow-Scriblerians.

926   DUDDEN, F. HOMES.
       Henry Fielding, His Life, Works, and Times, 2 vols. Oxford: Clarendon Press, 1952.

An exhaustive life that does not supersede Cross's biography; especially good on the influence of Fielding's dramatic

writings on his later works and on Fielding's conception of
the comic epic in prose.

927   DUNCAN, JEFFREY L.
        "The Rural Ideal in Eighteenth-Century Fiction." SEL 8
        (1968): 517-535.

        "Fielding, especially in Joseph Andrews, focusses on [the
        rural ideal] as moral order; Smollett, in Humphry Clinker,
        as ecological and hence moral order; Goldsmith, in The Vicar
        of Wakefield, as aesthetic and religious order; Sterne, in both
        A Sentimental Journey and Tristram Shandy, as religious or-
        der." Concludes that the four writers tried to counter the
        capitalistic and individualistic values of the new social order,
        as embodied by Defoe and Richardson, by using the rural
        ideal to emphasize "group relationships rather than individual-
        ism, moderation rather than wealth, charity rather than cal-
        culation or hysterical virginity."

928   DYSON, A. E.
        "Fielding: Satiric and Comic Irony." In The Crazy Fabric:
        Essays in Irony (London: Macmillan, 1965), pp. 14-32.

        Sees Fielding as essentially a humorist, and emphasizes
        his large compassion and abundant engagement with life; he
        is too good-humored to be a satirist. The discussion of Tom
        Jones deals largely with its moral themes.

929   "Satiric and Comic Theory in Relation to Fielding." MLQ
        18 (1957): 225-237. Partly incorporated into [928].

        Examines "two literary modes in which ridicule plays a
        part--the satiric and comic modes--with a view to consider-
        ing their interrelation in the novels of Fielding, and to evalua-
        ting the particular nature of Fielding's success as a comic
        writer." Suggests that Tom Jones is superior because of the
        comic use of ridicule rather than the satiric.

930   EVANS, JAMES E.
        "The Social Design of Fielding's Novels." Coll. L. 7 (1980):
        91-103.

        Takes issue with Martin C. Battestin and Henry K. Miller
        who interpret Fielding's novels as emblem, allegory, or ro-
        mance in which plot and character illustrate various abstrac-
        tions. On the contrary, Fielding was more interested in so-
        cial mimesis than those readings would allow. The actions
        of his novels are set in communities which define their sig-
        nificance. In Joseph Andrews, most of the characters are

arranged in satiric gatherings or temporary social groups
that Joseph and Adams meet in coaches, inns, or houses;
in Tom Jones the community is formed by two patriarchal
families and their interlocking marital, judicial, and educational problems, while Tom and Sophia on the way to London
encounter small groups where self-love predominates; finally,
in Amelia Fielding combines his characters into an urban community joined by links of mutual dependence, with the Booths
forming a central conjugal family.

931   FARRELL, WILLIAM J.
       "Fielding's Familiar Style." ELH 34 (1967): 65-77.

       Shows how Fielding's biographical style echoes the language
of conventional history. Fielding must depend upon the be-
lievability of his narrator through whom the reader sees the
entire action because he focuses on the social relationships
rather than on the inner lives or physical environment of his
characters. "Important as its artificializing and distancing
function is, Fielding's familiar style plays a crucial role in
underlining his most important artistic end--fidelity to life
itself."

932   GOLDBERG, HOMER.
       "Comic Prose Epic or Comic Romance: The Argument of
       the Preface to Joseph Andrews." PQ 43 (1964): 193-215.

       An analysis of Fielding's literary theory as regards epics
and romances based on his thinking in the Preface to Joseph
Andrews.

933   GOLDEN, MORRIS.
       Fielding's Moral Psychology. Amherst: Univ. Mass. Press,
       1966.

       Describes Fielding's theory of psychology and its relation
to his morality, and attempts to analyze that relationship as
an effort to "resolve the paradox of an enclosed mind which
yet must establish outgoing sympathy...." Argues that for
Fielding the center of existence is the self; the mind is the
source of happiness or misery, and the world outside provides
the material for either condition; and that, while staying enclosed within the self is painful evil, virtuous joy consists
in escaping from the self by feeling and acting for others.

934   HASSALL, ANTHONY J.
       "Fielding and the Novel as Parody." Southern Rev. (Adelaide)
       13 (1980): 30-40.

One technique Fielding uses to expose hypocrites is a "new kind of fiction which will tell the truth as no others have done, and which can best explain its nature and purpose to the reader by describing how it differs from the various existing forms with which the reader is already familiar." Joseph Andrews and Tom Jones partly imitate comically forms like the epic and the romance, which Fielding admires, but at whose shortcomings he laughs; they provide him, however, with material for parody. Fielding's importance as a parodist is twofold: 1) he is unsurpassed, in the great age of English burlesque and parody, in his ability to mimic the dullness, bombast, or hypocrisy of authors who had aroused his sense of the ridiculous; and 2) he also successfully parodies exhausted traditions like that of heroic tragedy and the excesses of new genres like the novel of character.

935   "Fielding's Puppet Image." PQ 53 (1974): 71-83.

Attempts "to illustrate both the range and the depth of Fielding's interest in the puppet image by describing its frequent occurrence in his work, and by examining in some detail the three crucial contexts in which it appears."

936   HATFIELD, GLENN W.
Henry Fielding and the Language of Irony. Chicago: Univ. Chicago Press, 1968.

A study of Fielding's attitude toward corruption of language: "Debased language contributed to the undermining of society, but a debased society also contributed to the undermining of language...." The language of irony, then, becomes for Fielding a way of exposing the debasement of words and of rescuing them from the prostituted condition into which they have fallen.

937   "Quacks, Pettyfoggers, and Parsons: Fielding's Case Against the Learned Professions." TSLL 9 (1967): 69-83. Rpt. with alterations in [936], pp. 127-142.

Studies Fielding's war on the abuses of language, especially the specialized "learning" and specialized vocabularies of the doctors, lawyers, and clergymen. Fielding is not solely concerned with the proliferation of technical jargon; he is also concerned with the perversion of general words used for specialized and therefore corrupt purposes; for example, "if a 'good' man to a doctor could be a criminal and to a soldier a scoundrel, then there was reason to fear that its 'agreed meaning' was becoming lost and that the writer or speaker who tried to use it in this 'original' general sense might be interpreted differently by each order of society."

938   HEILMAN, ROBERT B.
       "Fielding and 'the First Gothic Revival.'" MLN 57 (1942):
       671-673.

           The development of the "first Gothic revival" in the 1740s
       is illustrated in several works of Fielding: e.g., Chapter 4
       of A Journey from This World to the Next and the description
       of Allworthy's home in Chapter 4 of Tom Jones.

939   HILL, ROWLAND M.
       "Setting in the Novels of Henry Fielding." Bull. of the Cita-
       del 7 (1943): 26-52.

           An account of Fielding's technique of putting out on a bare
       "stage" just enough properties to provide the illusion of a
       "somewhere" for dramatic action to occur; he experiments
       with description either by using the mock-heroic form or by
       making straightforward attempts to develop a technique to
       present interior and exterior settings.

940   HUGHES, LEO.
       "The Influence of Fielding's Milieu upon his Humor." In
       Studies in English, Dept. of English, No. 24, Univ. of Texas,
       1944 (Austin: Univ. Texas Press, 1945), pp. 269-297.

           Attempts "to select from [Fielding's] background some of
       the more obvious items which could have influenced his comic
       practice, and [tries] to assess the results of those influences";
       considers the influence of classical forms, of the literary
       factionalism of the period, of the Licensing Act, and of poli-
       tics on both Fielding's plays and novels.

941   HUMPHREYS, A. R.
       "Fielding's Irony: Its Methods and Effects." RES 18 (1942):
       183-196. Rpt. in [898], pp. 12-24.

           Defines Fielding's irony as "corrective and orthodox; it
       undermines deviations from a healthy, sensible, social moral-
       ity, it prunes society of perversions. Unlike the irony of
       Gibbon or Samuel Butler II, it does not unsettle traditional
       ethics and Christian orthodoxy--it is the irony of integration
       rather than disintegration." Compares Fielding's irony (in
       Jonathan Wild) with Swift's, and provides some comment on
       Tom Jones.

942   "Fielding and Smollett." In Pelican Guide to English Litera-
       ture, Vol. IV: From Dryden to Johnson (Harmondsworth:
       Penguin Books, 1957), pp. 313-332.

A general discussion of the two authors, emphasizing Fielding's qualities as those typically characteristic of eighteenth-
century England, and especially reflecting a "trust in the
good-natured impulses of life"; Fielding is seen as a faithful
portrayer of Augustan society.

943   HUNTER, J. PAUL.
Occasional Form: Henry Fielding and the Chains of Circumstance. Baltimore: Johns Hopkins Univ. Press, 1975.

Adopts a fairly narrow "historical" plan in attempting to
"place Fielding's career and his major works in relation to
historical forces operating on his mind and art, chronicling
his anxiety and adjustment to circumstance." Also considers
theoretical questions that transcend Fielding's career, for he
"stands between eras, a reactionary pioneer, and in his rest-
less commutings between rural and urban life he tracked a
path from very old values to very new ones, even while he
turned the nation's literary energies from the public modes
of drama toward the private ones of reflexive fiction." Specifically, the author seeks to place Fielding within a literary
and rhetorical context, but also refers to religious, political,
and psychological contexts as well.

944   IRWIN, MICHAEL.
Henry Fielding: The Tentative Realist. Oxford: Clarendon
Press, 1967.

Emphasizes that Fielding throughout his career was a
moralist, always interested in a number of specific social
and ethical issues. Makes no attempt to evaluate the plays,
the journalism, or the minor narrative works, all of which
are used illustratively; the main concern is with the three
major novels, and the author discusses how they came to be
the kind of works they are, and how they function for the
modern reader.

945   IRWIN, W. R.
"Satire and Comedy in the Works of Henry Fielding." ELH
13 (1946): 168-188.

A study of Fielding's use of literary satire and narrative
comedy to attack literary folly, not only among books and
authors, but also among actors, theatre-goers, theatrical
managers, book-sellers, readers, and scholars. Discusses
changes in Fielding's comic spirit as it progressed from
literary satire to the theory of the comic prose epic.

946   JENKINS, ELIZABETH.

Henry Fielding. London: Home and Van Thal, 1947; Denver: Alan Swallow, 1948.

A perceptive and imaginative little volume that has much useful comment on the novels.

947 JOHNSON, MAURICE.
Fielding's Art of Fiction: Eleven Essays on "Shamela,"
"Joseph Andrews," "Tom Jones," and "Amelia." Philadelphia: Univ. Pa. Press, 1961.

Examines technical features of Fielding's art by means of close textual analysis, and is especially concerned with his use of parody and structural analogy; theme is Fielding's concern with "life, literature, and the feigning through which life and literature seem to merge their identities."

948 KETTLE, ARNOLD.
["Fielding"] In An Introduction to the English Novel, Vol. I:
Defoe to George Eliot (London: Hutchinson Univ. Library,
1951); rpt. New York: Harper Torchbooks, 1960, pp. 71-81. Rpt. and abridged in [898] as "Tom Jones," pp. 84-88.

Contains perceptive insights into Fielding's method, characterization, and moral fables: the author comments on, inter alia, the importance of the journey in Joseph Andrews, a "journey not simply of adventure but of discovery," and on the novel as anti-romance; on Fielding's preoccupation with method in Tom Jones, on that novel's "carefully contrived but entirely non-symbolic plot," and on the central conflict between Tom and Sophia against conventional society; Kettle sees Tom Jones as a "panoramic commentary" on the England of 1745: "Tom and Sophia ... are rebels, revolting against the respectably accepted domestic standards of eighteenth-century society.... Tom and Sophia fight conventional society, embodied in the character of Blifil."

949 KNOWLES, A. S., JR.
"Defoe, Swift, and Fielding: Notes on the Retirement Theme."
In [15], pp. 121-136.

A comparison of the theme of retirement in Tom Jones, Joseph Andrews, and Jonathan Wild with Gulliver's Travels and Robinson Crusoe.

950 KROPF, C. R.
"Educational Theory and Human Nature in Fielding's Works."
PMLA 89 (1974): 113-120.

A study of Fielding's frequent use of educational theory to show to what extent his works present a consistent view of human nature.

951   LaFRANCE, MARSTON.
"Fielding's Use of the 'Humor' Tradition." Bucknell Rev. 17 (1969): 53-63.

Argues that the usefulness of Fielding's dramatic experience extends beyond his ability to write dialogue, that his use of humor characterization comes directly from his dramatic apprenticeship.

952   LEVINE, GEORGE R.
Henry Fielding and the Dry Mock: A Study of the Techniques of Irony in His Early Works (Studies in English Literature, 30). The Hague: Mouton, 1967.

A detailed examination of Fielding's comic irony in works written between 1728 ("The Masquerade") and August, 1742 (the second edition of Joseph Andrews), including Jonathan Wild but excluding Shamela; discusses eighteenth-century uses of irony, rhetorical irony (ironic masks and the techniques of verbal irony), and dramatic irony, and especially analyzes the verbal irony of Joseph Andrews: "In this novel, Fielding uses verbal irony primarily as a vehicle for satiric characterization, and ... as a structural support for the various thematic patterns ... and as a means of focusing on the parody that is potentially present in most of the highly stylized scenes."

953   MACALLISTER, HAMILTON.
Fielding (Literature in Perspective). London: Evans Bros., 1967; rpt. New York: Arco, 1971.

Deals with Fielding's reputation, background, and life; of the novels, Joseph Andrews and Tom Jones receive the greatest attention, especially on such matters as structure, characters, and themes.

954   McKILLOP, ALAN DUGALD.
"Henry Fielding." In [134], pp. 98-146.

A comprehensive survey, discussing such topics as the importance of humor in Fielding, the Preface to Joseph Andrews, the function of the narrator, the mock-heroic or burlesque element; the satiric method in Jonathan Wild; the role of the narrator in Tom Jones, the relation of plot structure to moral design, and the character of Tom; and, finally, the

importance of the narrator in Amelia and the character of
the heroine and of Booth. Concludes that Fielding (like Richardson) shows that technique is inseparable from theme and
intention; he is seriously concerned with "the moral issues
of character as raised within [his] own society, displayed ...
in the light of a broad and humane humor unmatched in its
toleration of man's limitations and possibilities save in Shakespeare and Cervantes."

955   MARESCA, THOMAS E.
       "Fielding." In [137], pp. 181-233.

       Whereas the "mock-epics" of Dryden, Pope, and Swift
have, among other purposes, mocked the epic itself, Fielding's novels, from Joseph Andrews through to Amelia, have
attempted to revive and restore the form: "epic meaning is
once again welded to epic action, and the internals and ex-
ternals of epic are made to coincide." Fielding's three novels
grow thematically, using more and more traditional epic material, until Amelia becomes simply epic: they deal with increasingly more generous conceptions of wisdom and with
"correspondingly greater sweeps of society."

956   MOORE, ROBERT E.
       "Hogarth's Role in Fielding's Novels." In [140], pp. 107-
       161.

       Concerned with the "broad currents of the age reflected
in both artists," as well as with the "particular paths into
which the painter led the writer." Perhaps Fielding's chief
debt to Hogarth is that the painter taught the novelist how to
avoid caricature.

957   MURRY, J. MIDDLETON.
       "In Defence of Fielding." In Unprofessional Essays (London:
       Cape; Fairlawn, N.J.: Essential Books, 1956), pp. 11-52.
       Rpt. partly in (898) as "Fielding's 'Sexual Ethic' in Tom Jones,"
       pp. 89-97.

       Defends Fielding against a depreciatory article in the Times
Literary Supplement and the adverse criticism of F. R. Leavis; praises the novels especially for their moral discrimination: Tom's behavior represents "not 'the genial tolerance
of the man-about-town' in his creator, but a positive moral
conviction, in the important sphere of the ethics of the sexual
relation."

958   PARK, WILLIAM.
       "What Was New about the 'New Species of Writing?'" Studies
       in the Novel 2 (1970): 112-130.

Seeks to prove that Fielding and Richardson were justified
in their claims of "newness," and that they shared a number
of assumptions and conventions about the novel.

959   "Fielding and Richardson." PMLA 81 (1966): 381-388.

Discusses the "common ground" the two authors share with
each other and with other novelists of the 1740s and '50s;
suggests that "these two masters, their contemporaries, and
followers have made use of the same materials and that as
a result the English novels of the mid-eighteenth century may
be regarded as a distinct historic version of a general type
of literature." Concludes that the "common ground" the novel
ists share includes the acceptance of hierarchical society, the
allegiance to custom and tradition, and the belief in a clearly
apprehensible moral world.

960   PAULSON, RONALD.
       Satire and the Novel in Eighteenth-Century England.   New
       Haven: Yale Univ. Press, 1967.

Considers the reciprocal effects of satire on the novel, a
conflict in which the novel triumphed because it represented
new values as opposed to the old ones of satire--values that
were "Lockean, Latitudinarian, Shaftesburyian, benevolist,
even deist ... ; it was middle-class, matter-of-fact, and
realistic in the sense of being interested in real people in
real-life situations." Contains three chapters on Fielding--
"Fielding the Satirist," "Fielding the Anti-Romanticist," and
"Fielding the Novelist"--in which the theory is applied: for
instance, "his progression toward Tom Jones can be said to
be from law and a study of actions (satire) to justice and an
interest in being (novel)...."

961   PIERCE, ROBERT B.
       "Moral Education in the Novel of the 1750's." PQ 44 (1965):
       73-87.

Shows how Fielding's handling of character development in
Tom Jones influenced the novels of the 1750s in the treatment of moral education, in that the "characters who are to
become truly moral must begin with innate good nature and
then learn by experience the prudential values of their society."

962   PRICE, MARTIN.
       "Fielding: The Comedy of Forms." In [153], pp. 285-311.

Suggests that the "central theme in Fielding's work is the
opposition between the flow of soul--of selfless generosity--

and the structures--screens, defenses, moats of indifference
--that people build around themselves. The flow is the active
energy of virtuous feeling; the structures are those forms
that are a frozen travesty of authentic order. "

963   RAMONDT, MARIE.
      "Between Laughter and Humour in the Eighteenth Century. "
      Neophilologus 40 (1956): 128-138.

      Discusses Molière, Goldoni, Marivaux, and Fielding, and
      attempts to analyze the latter's comedy of affectation: gives
      his definition of comedy.

964   RAWSON, C. J.
      "Language, Dialogue, and Point of View in Fielding: Some
      Considerations. " In [15], pp. 137-156.

      An analysis of Fielding's language that compares his pref-
      erence for a vocabulary drawn from the actual spoken idiom
      to Richardson's tendency to use "singular" and coined usages.
      Fielding prefers normal usages, and is often more particular
      than Defoe: "It is a particularity of the typical, celebrated
      not by the 'naked' truth but with the full honors of authorial
      'performances. ' "

965   Henry Fielding and the Augustan Ideal Under Stress.   London
      and Boston: Routledge & Kegan Paul, 1972.

      Using mainly Amelia and Jonathan Wild, Rawson explores
      Fielding's loss of certainty as the age exhibits increasing
      strain and anxiety; he is primarily concerned with the cultural
      and social changes reflected in the loss of confidence in Na-
      ture as norm and in the heroic ideal, and he suggests that
      Fielding occupies an "ambiguous position between an older
      world of aristocratic and neo-classic loyalties, and newer
      forces, one of whose literary manifestations is the novel-
      form itself. "

966   "Some Considerations on Authorial Intrusion and Dialogue in
      Fielding's Novels and Plays. " DUJ 32 (1971): 32-44.

      Examines the ways in which the narrator establishes a
      sense of his controlling presence and the implications of that
      effort in the field of dialogue.

967   "Nature's Dance of Death: Part I: Urbanity and Strain in
      Fielding, Swift, and Pope. " ECS 3 (1970): 307-338.

Concerns itself with a study of styles of writing which show "the strains of disorderly or 'unnatural' fact, of powerful or unbalancing emotions, and ... a painful scepticism of order," especially in Fielding's prose.

968   _Henry Fielding._ London: Routledge & Kegan Paul; New York: Humanities, 1968.

Consists of a short sketch presenting Fielding's life and works, followed by brief extracts from Fielding's fiction and nonfiction, under such headings as "Irony," "Dialogue," "Character: Two Sketches from Real Life," "Professions and Codes," "Snobbery and Class," and "Benevolence and Love."

969   "Gentlemen and Dancing-Masters: Thoughts on Fielding, Chesterfield, and the Genteel." ECS 1 (1967): 127-158. Rpt. in [965], pp. 3-34.

Attempts to define certain social attitudes of Fielding, especially his attitude on matters of rank and virtue, morals and manners, and good-nature and good-breeding; emphasizes that "the correlation between good-breeding and good-nature is one of the really unflinching and ineradicable elements in Fielding's entire moral outlook."

970   ROBINSON, ROGER. "Henry Fielding and the English Rococo." In [9], pp. 93-111.

Seeks to reconcile Fielding's "habitual diversity and virtuosity with the long-established claim of his mastery of composition"; concludes that Fielding sought to achieve diversity of form and unity of theme, so that digressions and interpolated narratives are fully relevant to the central themes of the novel: they "all contribute positively and coherently to the presentation of the theme of right judgment...."

971   ROGERS, PAT. _Henry Fielding: A Biography._ New York: Scribner's, 1979.

An up-to-date biography, making use of some fourteen completely new letters that illuminate Fielding's relations with the Duke of Bedford: they prove that Fielding was deeply involved in the "power structure" in the late 1740s, and that he was very dependent on the Duke for various unspecified favors. Not much in the way of literary criticism.

972   ROGERS, WINFIELD H. "Fielding's Early Aesthetic and Technique." SP 40 (1943): 529-551. Rpt. in [898], pp. 25-44.

Discusses Fielding's writing from 1729-1740 in which he developed the aesthetic and techniques upon which his later works were written. "Particularly important were: 1) his impatience with the restrictions of comedy and his consequent developing of farce as a satiric and moral medium for a criticism of life, 2) his adapting of the commonplace 'humour' as a basis for the study and analysis of the springs of human action, 3) his developing of words as symbols, which in context often carry allegorical meaning, and 4) his developing of a genuinely comprehensive and inclusive allegorical method of interpreting life, in which farce, 'humour,' and other word symbols, played an integral part."

973   SACKS, SHELDON.
      Fiction and the Shape of Belief: A Study of Henry Fielding
      with Glances at Swift, Johnson and Richardson.   Berkeley:
      Univ. Calif. Press, 1964.

      A "serious enquiry into a complex subject, the relation between belief and literary form"; argues that Fielding successfully includes his moral beliefs, opinions, and prejudices in coherently organized novels without damaging their artistic qualities.

974   SHERBURN, GEORGE.
      "Fielding's Social Outlook." PQ 35 (1956): 1-23. Rpt. in
      [18], pp. 251-273.

      Discusses Fielding's social philosophy, suggesting his various attitudes concerning the relation of the individual to the Whole, and analyzes and illustrates his doctrine of "good nature"; also considers Fielding's ethical and psychological theories, and concludes that "from first to last Fielding was the comic and moral satirist.... He is intellectual and analytical rather than sentimental in delineations of character; but both as man and as author he did not lack heart."

975   SHESGREEN, SEAN.
      Literary Portraits in the Novels of Henry Fielding.   DeKalb:
      Northern Illinois Univ. Press, 1972.

      Is primarily concerned with direct portraiture, which is defined as any "formal depiction of character that offers the reader a visual impression of a figure's physical appearance, a moral and psychological analysis, an evaluation of disposition, or a combination of these"; seeks in particular to isolate and comment upon the main influences, traditions, and conventions associated with Fielding's literary portraits.   Concludes that his characterization derives not from dialogue and action but, at least in his first three novels, from classical

and earlier native and continental literary genres; Fielding's
early depiction presented character as a finished product,
whereas his later novels are defined by the "disappearance
of classical methods of delineation and by the introduction of
techniques that describe character as a process or a developing psychological phenomenon."

976   SHROFF, HOMAI J.
       "Greatness, Goodness, Happiness--'A Great, Useful, and
       Uncommon Doctrine.'"   In [163], pp. 123-160.

       Fielding's ideas about the nature of man are presented
       through his heroes as he places them against a picture of
       brutality and depravity.   Squire Allworthy and Tom Jones,
       Dr. Harrison and Billy Booth, Parson Adams and Joseph
       Andrews--all are different kinds of men, not one of them
       perfect, but each picturing quite clearly a few of the qualities
       that Fielding demanded of an ideal person.   Fielding's ideas
       about life did not permit him to create perfect gentlemen and
       ladies but rather characters who were exceptionally good men
       and women--benevolent, prudent, charitable, and good-natured
       --and who must exist in a society full of lust, hypocrisy, and
       villainy.

977   SMITH, J. OATES.
       "Masquerade and Marriage: Fielding's Comedies of Identity."
       BSUF 6, No. 3 (1965): 10-21.

       Traces the themes of masquerade and marriage throughout
       Fielding's work--"The Masquerade," Love in Several Masques,
       The Modern Husband, The Wedding Day, Joseph Andrews,
       Tom Jones, and Amelia.   Concludes that his "treatment of
       the time-honored struggle of the morally virtuous in a hypo-
       critical world is sustained skillfully through his long career....
       What is significant and lasting ... is ... the painful struggle
       for identification (of others and of the self) in a socially and
       often psychologically complex world."

978   SMITH, LeROY W.
       "Fielding and 'Mr. Bayle's' Dictionary."   TSLL 4 (1962): 16-
       20.

       Indicates similarities between Fielding's thought and Bayle's
       and suggests that Fielding was familiar with the latter's Cri-
       tical and Historical Dictionary (1697).   That knowledge in-
       creases our sense of Fielding's "considerable sympathy with
       the point of view of the skeptical and anti-rationalist writers."

979   "Fielding and Mandeville: The 'War Against Virtue.'" Cri-
       ticism 3 (1961): 7-15.

Argues that the "skeptics, anti-rationalists, or self-love
psychologists" which included Hobbes, Bayle, and Mandeville
"strongly and directly influenced Fielding's thought"; suggests
that to establish that influence will clarify the nature of Fielding's indebtedness to the contemporary debate over the nature
of man and his fitness for society as well as show how he
resolved a personal problem, the conflict between an optimistic
view of human nature and a pessimistic view of the nature of
society.

980   SPEER, BLANCHE C. and ROBERT W. LOVETT.
       "Dialects and the Dialect in Fielding's Novels." SECOLB 3,
       ii (1979): 57-62.

Suggests that Fielding uses dialect to identify and develop
characters or to indicate social class.   Fielding writes re-
gional and social dialects carefully and accurately, but is
less accurate in handling the use of English by foreigners;
the latter, known as "Broken English," is analyzed at considerable length, both its pronunciation and its grammar.
Concludes that there is "a common core of phonological, grammatical, and lexical characteristics in the speech of all of
Fielding's non-English characters, justifying our designation
of their language as a special dialect."

981   STEEVES, HARRISON R.
       "A Manly Man: Henry Fielding." In [169], pp. 103-130.

A general and conventional survey of Fielding's novels;
suggests, among other insights, that Fielding's great art is
the ability to "see character ripening under his hand"; discusses comedy, satire, the "conservation of character," and
plot, especially in Tom Jones.

982   STERN, GUY.
       "A German Imitation of Fielding: Musäus' Grandison der
       Zweite." Comp. Lit. 10 (1958): 335-343.

Discusses Musäus's Grandison der Zweite, a satire of
Richardson's Sir Charles Grandison, that began the age of
Fielding in German fiction.   Contains a discussion of Field-
ing's irony.

983   STEVICK, PHILIP.
       "Fielding and the Meaning of History." PMLA 79 (1964):
       561-568.

"That Fielding's novels are so representative of their age
yet so different from anything else written in the eighteenth

century results, in part, from the fact that Fielding's view
of the possibilities of man in history was as free as it was
of the historical certainties of the philosophers of history."
Shows that Fielding's interest in history and its meaning led
him away from doctrine and toward skepticism. "The very
mode of Fielding's fiction ... is in itself a response to the
possibilities of man in history."

984   SWANN, GEORGE R.
       "Fielding and Empirical Realism." In Philosophical Parallel-
       ism in Six English Novelists: The Conception of Good, Evil,
       and Human Nature (Philadelphia: Univ. Pa. Press, 1929),
       pp. 46-64.

       Discusses influence of Shaftesbury and Hume on Fielding's
       thought and concludes that Shaftesbury was more influential
       than Hume.

985   THORNBURY, ETHEL MARGARET.
       Henry Fielding's Theory of the Comic Prose Epic. (Univ.
       Wisc. Studies in Lang. & Lit. , No. 30) Madison: Univ.
       Wisc. Press, 1931.

       Analyzes in great detail Fielding's theory of the comic
       prose epic and its origin; shows that his originality lay, not
       in inventing a new theory (for indeed it was a critical com-
       monplace in the eighteenth century), but in applying that theor
       to the "new province of writing" and thereby giving renewed
       life to the epic ideal. Argues that Fielding should be con-
       sidered not as the first English novelist but as the last of
       the Renaissance writers of epic.

986   TICHY, ALES.
       "Remarks on the Flow of Time in the Novels of Henry Field-
       ing." Brno Studies in English 2 (1960): 55-78.

       Analyzes Fielding's handling of time and assesses its im-
       portance for the "new province of writing" that he inaugurate
       suggests that the "uninterrupted flow of time ... a pattern
       imposed by the author on his material as a constructional
       principle, does not reflect any definite historical succession
       of days characterized by means of outstanding events and
       dates. ...   He paid no scrupulous attention to the dating in-
       volved in the historical allusions of his novels." Concludes
       that in Joseph Andrews and Amelia "the continuous chain of
       days, along which the story is developed ... is a principle
       inherent in Fielding's conception of the 'history' (i. e. the
       novel) as a literary kind." Also compares the similarities
       and differences between Fielding's handling of time in his
       novels and dramas, and suggests that the influence of the

dramatic time-scheme on the flow of time in the three novels was, with the exception of the last part of Tom Jones, negligible.

987   WALLACE, ROBERT M.
"Fielding's Knowledge of History and Biography." SP 44 (1947): 89-107.

Argues that Fielding's interest in history and biography was even stronger than his interest in the Greek and Latin epic poets, and may well have been the chief influence on the form and purpose of his novels.

988   WARNER, JOHN M.
"The Interpolated Narratives in the Fiction of Fielding and Smollett: An Epistemological View." Studies in the Novel 5 (1973): 271-283.

Suggests that Fielding's and Smollett's use of the interpolated story is not a simple throwback to earlier modes of fiction but is a foreshadowing of epistemological concerns expressed more clearly by the Romantics; that Fielding's early novels oscillate between an inductive and a deductive view of experience, emphasizing the principle of "epistemological uncertainty."

989   WARREN, LELAND E.
"History-as-Literature and the Narrative Stance of Henry Fielding." Clio 9 (1979): 89-109.

Argues that "Fielding shares with eighteenth-century history writers in the search to find a place from which the narrator can speak with some hope of influencing his readers. More important, Fielding's work shows him to have reached a solution paralleling that of men writing in a discipline that had rejected theology and not yet embraced science.   Far from rejecting the authoritative historian, Fielding emulates him. . . .   It is at least arguable that his example is pertinent to all attempts to write narratives that claim to describe real actions."   Concerned with the question of the narrator's personal authority in both history and fiction.

990   WATSON, GEORGE.
"The Augustans: Pope, Addison, Fielding." In The Literary Critics: A Study of English Descriptive Criticism, 2nd. ed. (Totowa, N.J.: Rowman & Littlefield, 1973), pp. 53-71.

Pope, Addison, and Fielding, as inheritors and continuers of Dryden's tradition of criticism; Fielding considered as a pioneer of novel criticism.

991   WATT, IAN.
      "Fielding and the Epic Theory of the Novel." In [183], pp.
      239-259.

      Considers the views of Defoe and Richardson on the sub-
      ject of the epic, and then evaluates Fielding's conception of
      the epic analogy and its influence on his novels.   Argues that
      "Fielding's attempts to bring [Joseph Andrews] into line with
      classical doctrine could not be supported either by existing
      literary parallel or theoretical precedent," and therefore not
      too much importance should be attached to its Preface; and
      that the epic analogy should not be exaggerated, even though
      Fielding introduced two epic features into a comic context:
      the use of surprise and of mock-heroic battles.

992   WEIDE, ERWIN.
      Henry Fieldings Komödien und die Restoration Komödien.
      Hamburg: Hansischer Gildenverlag, 1947.

      Argues that Fielding's comedies exemplify his belief that
      man is moved by emotion, that, in Hume's words, "senti-
      ments must touch the heart to make them control our pas-
      sions"; whereas Restoration comedy, influenced by the cyni-
      cal opinions of Mandeville and Shaftesbury's faith in reason,
      represents an entirely different conception of drama.

993   WILLIAMS, AUBREY.
      "Interpositions of Providence and the Design of Fielding's
      Novels." SAQ 70 (1971): 265-286.

      A "serious" look at Fielding's novels recognizing "the
      strong and intrinsic Christian elements in [his] work," and
      that amidst all the bawdiness and humor, there is also "a
      pattern of order, a providential design, a providential jus-
      tice." Fielding structures his novels so that "virtue is re-
      warded and vice is punished in this world and in worldly
      terms...." Coincidences and improbabilities are deliberate
      divine intervention.

994   WILLIAMS, MURIAL BRITTAIN.
      Marriage: Fielding's Mirror of Morality (Studies in Humani-
      ties, Literature).   University: Univ. Ala. Press, 1973.

      Arguing that no other author provided so rich and so com-
      prehensive a body of material for considering the contempor-
      ary marriage question as did Fielding, Murial Williams sur-
      veys courtship and marriage through the plays and the novels,
      and concludes that Fielding extolled the virtues of the ideal
      marriage and believed that "Rational love, that is, goodness
      as the object of love, is its foundation."

995   WILLIAMSON, EUGENE.
       "Guiding Principles in Fielding's Criticism of the Critics."
       In [32], pp. 1-24.

       Surveys the critical reception of Fielding's works between
       1728 and 1754, and suggests that much of his dissatisfaction
       with the critical practices of his contemporaries derives from
       the hostile treatment accorded his own dramas and novels.
       Fielding's criticism of the critics of his day consists of three
       points: 1) they are ignorant and generally unqualified; 2) they
       are guilty of pedantry and the mechanical application of criti-
       cal rules; and 3) they are unjust in their treatment of writers.
       He called, therefore, "for a criticism that was informed,
       genially responsive to creative practice, and fair"; and the
       critic himself must acquire critical responsibility, sensitivity,
       learning, and impartiality.

996   WORK, JAMES A.
       "Henry Fielding, Christian Censor." In [27], pp. 139-148.

       Argues that the "motivation of Fielding's activity as moral-
       ist and reformer lay at least in part, and perhaps in large
       part, in his Christian beliefs and feelings: in his conscious
       and conscientious, though unpublicized, intent to follow in his
       own life 'that total of all Christian morality ... "do unto all
       men as ye would they should do unto you," ' and to practice
       'the greatest virtue in the world (according to the tenets of
       [Christianity]) ... charity.' "

997   WRIGHT, ANDREW.
       Henry Fielding: Mask and Feast. London: Chatto & Windus;
       Berkeley: Univ. Calif. Press, 1965. Part of Chap. I rpt.
       as "Tom Jones: Life as Art" in [1092], pp. 56-67.

       By emphasizing the metaphor of art as feast, the author
       suggests that Fielding's comic mode is both a "celebration
       of life" and a civilizing force; that the narrator's role sup-
       ports the artificiality of the novel as a whole and that Field-
       ing's chief accomplishment is that he raised the novel to the
       level of serious playfulness: his "highest achievement lies
       in the realization of festive panorama rather than in the de-
       ployment of ideas within an epic structure."

See also: 376, 686, 724, 1559, 2146, 2450, 2470, 2482, 2490,
    2697, 2898

Plays and Miscellaneous Works

998   BAKER, SHERIDAN.
       "Political Allusion in Fielding's Author's Farce, Mock Doctor,
       and Tumble-Down Dick." PMLA 77 (1962): 221-231.

       A look at these plays reveals much of Fielding's political
       satire, especially against Walpole.

999   "Henry Fielding's The Female Husband: Fact and Fiction."
       PMLA 74 (1959): 213-224.

       Presents evidence to prove that The Female Husband was
       Fielding's work, even though he passes a great deal of fiction
       off as fact.   Points out parallels between this brief criminal
       biography and material in Tom Jones and Jonathan Wild.

1000   BRNO UNIVERSITY PHILOSOPHICAL FACULTY.   [On Field-
       ing]. Rada literárně vedná, 1955.

       Argues the Marxist view that Fielding's plays present a
       "ruthless satire" of the aristocratic-bourgeois society of
       eighteenth-century England.

1001   BROWN, JACK R.
       "Fielding's Grub-Street Opera." MLQ 16 (1955): 32-41.

       Traces the stage history of the play, examines critically
       the three printed versions on which any conclusions are based,
       and indicates the significance of The Grub-Street Opera on
       studies of Fielding and the theater.

1002   CRAIK, T. W.
       "Fielding's 'Tom Thumb' Plays." In [28], pp. 165-174.

       Suggests that The Tragedy of Tragedies is not essentially
       a work of ridicule, since it is not written with animosity;
       it is written with a Shakespearean gusto, and the satiric pas-
       sages serve as artistic inspiration.   The essential quality of
       the play, in all three versions, is enthusiasm, an expansive
       delight in the ridiculous that places Fielding in the great Eng-
       lish comic tradition.

1003   DURANT, JACK D.
       "The 'Art of Thriving' in Fielding's Comedies." In [32],
       pp. 25-35.

       The "Art of thriving," the capacity to look out for one's

own advantage, is a comprehensive organizing principle in
Fielding's theatrical comedies: the world of his stage is full
of thrivers of the most accomplished sort. The comedies
reflect the same moral phenomenon: "Ethical and social institutions developed for human safety and comfort fall prey
to the cruelties and sophistries of corrupt people, people void
of concern even for their own families. In effect the comedies dramatize a significant political conviction, the conviction
that anarchy within the family figures forth anarchy within
the state, that the public good is best served by the devoted
family man. . . . "

1004   GOGGIN, L. P.
        "Fielding's The Masquerade. " PQ 36 (1957): 475-487.

        A close examination of the poem as a satire on masked
balls, and of its materials and techniques. Shows Fielding's
purpose to be moral, and his theme to be one which pervades
his later works.

1005   "Development of Techniques in Fielding's Comedies. " PMLA
        67 (1952): 769-781.

        Traces improvements in the comedies' dramatic technique
that prepared the way for the great novels; especially concerned with questions of representation, those that pertain to
indirect representation, to characterization, and to the writing
of dialogue. Three general tendencies exist in Fielding's development: "greater verisimilitude, closer integration, more
vivid effect. "

1006   HUNTER, J. PAUL.
        "Fielding's Reflexive Plays and the Rhetoric of Discovery. "
        Std. in Lit. Imag. 5, No. 2 (1972): 65-100.

        Studies Fielding's development of a system of guiding com-
mentary in his rehearsal plays, foreshadowing methods and
techniques which were used later in his novels; Fielding, in
other words, "experimented with devices that pointed in the direction of self-consciousness about the making of fictional worlds
which men in more mundane worlds might need to relate to. "

1007   KERN, JEAN B.
        "Fielding's Dramatic Satire. " PQ 54 (1975): 239-257.

        A study of Fielding as a dramatic satirist shows that his
plays were "the best and most extensive attempts to adapt
the mode of satire to the stage in the first half of the eighteenth century. They kept alive a tradition of wit and irony
against the antithetical development of sentimental comedy and

thus pointed the direction of later developments in satire for
the theatre. "

1008   KISHLER, THOMAS C.
       "Fielding's Experiments with Fiction in the Champion."
       JNT 1 (1971): 95-107.

       Discusses various fictional aspects of the Champion: use
       of a persona, the non-ironic moral exemplum; fictionalized
       situations and incidents ironically reported as fact; and the
       imaginary journey.   Suggests that Fielding's essays in the
       Champion emphasize a "persistent problem for the Augustan
       satirist--the reconciliation of the didactic and the aesthetic. "

1009   LANE, WILLIAM G.
       "Relationships Between Some of Fielding's Major and Minor
       Works. " BUSE 5 (1961): 219-231.

       Deals with The True Patriot, The Covent-Garden Journal,
       A Journey from this World to the Next, and The Journal of
       a Voyage to Lisbon; argues that "certain elements of Field-
       ing's work are illuminated and enlarged by a reading of var-
       ious representative minor pieces. "

1010   LEWIS, PETER.
       "Fielding's The Covent-Garden Tragedy and Philip's The Dis-
       trest Mother. " DUJ 37 (1976): 33-46.

       The Covent-Garden Tragedy, one of the few masterpieces
       of Augustan dramatic burlesque, uses The Distrest Mother
       as a model for a satiric attack on contemporary tragedy; for
       that purpose Fielding uses the characters and some aspects
       of The Distrest Mother on which to build a mock-tragedy about
       prostitutes, ruffians, and drunkards.   Fielding's purpose is
       more serious than it was in The Tragedy of Tragedies, and
       the ridicule of contemporary tragedy seems more "relentless
       and uncompromising. "   Although the burlesque has never been
       popular with audiences, it is remarkable for its "sheer in-
       ventiveness and brilliance," and Fielding's skill in "controlling
       the deliberate bathos ... hardly falters. "

1011   LOFTIS, JOHN.
       Comedy and Society from Congreve to Fielding.   Stanford,
       Calif.: Stanford Univ. Press, 1959.

       Contains a discussion of Fielding's plays, primarily from
       the point of view of their treatment of social relationships;
       concludes that his plays reveal a certain conservatism, mainly
       in their rather strict insistence on the traditional relationships

between the classes: "Yet he has an eye to the irony of social distinctions, the huge disparity often existing between
rank and natural merit; and in at least two of his farces he
expresses ideas that can bear an egalitarian interpretation...."

1012   McCREA, BRIAN.
        "Fielding's Role in The Champion: A Reminder." SAB 42,
        i (1977): 19-24.

        In view of the problem presented by Fielding's apparent
change of politics in The Opposition: A Vision, the problem
of whether he switched to Walpole's side and accepted money
from the ministry, the author suggests that the debate has
been based on a false premise. The premise is that Fielding had firm political allegiances in 1739-40, just before its
publication, that support for Walpole would have compromised.
On the contrary, Fielding's role in The Champion was not
that of a dedicated Opposition propagandist and he did not
direct a strong anti-ministerial campaign. The conclusion is
that Fielding's political views tended to be uncertain and of
secondary interest to him; he had no firm political beliefs to
be compromised.

1013   MILLER, HENRY KNIGHT.
        Essays on Fielding's 'Miscellanies': A Commentary on Volume
        One. Princeton, N.J.: Princeton Univ. Press, 1961.

        Offers detailed analyses of the poems, essays, satires,
and translation in Volume One of the Miscellanies, and places
them in the broader context of Fielding's thought and that of
the literary and intellectual traditions upon which he drew.
Considers the material in relation to Fielding's total view of
man and society, and attempts to emphasize his comic view
of life.

1014   "Henry Fielding's Satire on the Royal Society." SP 57 (1960):
        72-86.

        Gives detailed explanation of Some Papers Proper to be
Read before the R---l Society. Notes that Fielding main-
tained an almost consistently satirical attitude towards the
Royal Society and the virtuosi.

1015   MORRISSEY, L. J.
        "Fielding's First Political Satire." Anglia 90 (1972): 325-
        348.

        Argues that Fielding's revision of The Tragedy of Tom
Thumb as The Tragedy of Tragedies alters and expands the

text in order to emphasize the political satire on the Court and on Walpole's government, particularly its economic and foreign policies.

1016   "Henry Fielding and the Ballad Opera." ECS 4 (1971): 386-402.

A discussion of the ballad opera before its suppression by Walpole, and particularly of Fielding's political ballad operas; suggests that three (really four) forces "influenced Fielding in his choice of music for The Grub-Street Opera. He had to take into account the taste of theatre managers and the printer John Watts, the taste of his audience, and he had some direct help from his friend James Ralph." Includes a lengthy discussion of how Watts printed ballads from woodblocks.

1017   MOSS, HAROLD G.
"Satire and Travesty in Fielding's The Grub Street Opera." Theatre Survey 15 (1974): 38-50.

Argues that Fielding "arranged a melange of bits and pieces from the popular entertainment of his time--the 'Grub-Street' hack-writing--to 'disguise' his satire on Walpole and the Royal Family in hopes of avoiding the legal conviction such satire might cause. This disguise used during the period by other political writers, was designed to confuse legal proceedings, not to mislead members of his audience."

1018   ROGERS, WINFIELD H.
"The Significance of Fielding's Temple Beau." PMLA 55 (1940): 440-443.

Discusses Fielding's use of the pedant symbol in The Temple Beau to express his attitude toward life.

1019   RUDOLPH, VALERIE C.
"People and Puppets: Fielding's Burlesque of the 'Recognition Scene' in The Author's Farce." PLL 11 (1975): 31-38.

A discussion of how Fielding burlesques contemporary abuse of the "recognition scene" by manipulating "two distinct planes of theatrical illusion--one realistic and one fantastic." In his recognition scene in The Author's Farce he "creates deliberate chaos by no longer providing his audience with clear indications of what it is to accept as real." Fielding's genius lies in his ability to depict eighteenth-century cultural and moral anarchy through the controlled chaos of his recognition scene, and in the end Fielding, like his character Harry

Luckless, " ... becomes the victim of his own satire, and his downfall ironically proves the empirical confirmation of his satiric vision. "

1020   WILNER, ARLENE.
       "History as Private Perspective: Fielding's Journal of a Voyage to Lisbon. " MLS 10, ii (1980): 26-36.

       Examines the narrative voice of the Journal, a voice whose complexity derives from a unique fusion of the techniques of autobiography, travelogue, sociopolitical commentary, and imaginative fiction; the narrative tension informing the work comes from "the interplay between public and private history. " Fundamentally Fielding attempts to mediate between the "conscientious historian and the artful story-teller. "

1021   WOLFE, GEORGE H.
       "Lessons in Evil: Fielding's Ethics in The Champion Essays. " In [32], pp. 65-81.

       The Champion essays present an early form of Fielding's moral ideas that are based on the orthodox view that men are born with an inherent capacity for sinning, but capable at the same time of doing good. Fielding's ethic was always informed by a strong sense of social responsibility; virtue consists in positive action combined with restraint, and in directing destructive tendencies toward useful, benevolent ends: virtue is "a delight in doing good. " Fielding opposes in The Champion the familiar proscriptive aspects of Christian morality, yet endorses the permanent felicity of a virtuous life. His concept of good nature includes an aspect often overlooked: good-natured men possess a toughness of fiber and a resolution that inspires them to pugnaciously resent any injury: e. g. , Tom's defense of Molly in the graveyard battle.

See also: 925, 966, 977, 1153, 2372

Shamela

1022   AMORY, HUGH.
       "Shamela as Aesopic Satire. " ELH 38 (1971): 239-253.

       Attempts to prove that Fielding aesopically implies that the "real" author of Pamela was "no other than Sir Robert Walpole," and that "the parallels between Mr. Booby and King George, Shamela and Walpole, and Parson Williams and [Bishop Edmund] Gibson are highly persuasive. " Also suggests that Shamela is a "political romance" as well as a literary parody.

1023   ROTHSTEIN, ERIC.
        "The Framework of Shamela." ELH 35 (1968): 381-402.

        A study of the relationship of Shamela to the three fictional
        letters that preceded it, and of the "effect of framework and
        burlesque upon one another...." Suggests that Shamela is
        more than an attack on Pamela but that Fielding uses it to
        criticize the "social, religious, and artistic spoilage" of the
        day.

1024   SHEPPERSON, ARCHIBALD BOLLING.
        The Novel in Motley: A History of the Burlesque Novel in
        English. Cambridge: Harvard Univ. Press, 1936; rpt. New
        York: Octagon Books, 1967.

        Contains a general evaluation of Shamela as burlesque (pp.
        20-28) and of Joseph Andrews (pp. 28-30) emphasizing for
        the latter the realistic aspects.

1025   WATT, IAN.
        "Shamela." Introduction to An Apology for the Life of Mrs.
        Shamela Andrews. In Augustan Reprint Society, No. 57 (Los
        Angeles: William A. Clark Memorial Library, 1956), pp.
        1-11. Rpt. in [898], pp. 45-51.

        Explanatory of some basic matters, such as the source of
        the pseudonymous author, Mr. Conny Keyber, and the reasons
        for the dedicatory letter and the second of the "Letters to
        the Editor"; considers Fielding's main intentions in writing
        the parody: to attack those "who had puffed Pamela as a
        book likely to promote the cause of virtue and religion" and
        to attack "Richardson's interpretation of his heroine's char-
        acter."

1026   WOOD, CARL.
        "Shamela's Subtle Satire: Fielding's Characterization of Mrs.
        Jewkes and Mrs. Jervis." ELN 13 (1976): 266-270.

        Fielding's penetrating insight into the ambiguities in Rich-
        ardson's portrayal of the two housekeepers in the two rape
        scenes in Pamela indicates that Shamela was more than a
        "hurried, careless production." Fielding carefully moves
        plot material from one scene to the other, reversing Richard-
        son's moral evaluations of the two women, thus skillfully
        satirizing Richardson's ambiguities in his "supposedly mirror
        opposite characters."

See also: 1046, 2513, 2529

Joseph Andrews

1027   BATTESTIN, MARTIN C.
        "Fielding's Revisions of Joseph Andrews." SB 16 (1963):
        81-117.

        Argues that "Fielding's own hand was at work in much,
        though certainly not all, of the 'revising and correcting' of
        the third and fourth, as well as of the second, editions."
        The revisions included aspects of style, scene, structure,
        and characterization.

1028   "Lord Hervey's Role in Joseph Andrews." PQ 42 (1963):
        226-241.

        Investigates the role of Hervey in the novel as one of the
        most absurd and contemptible figures, Beau Didapper.

1029   "Fielding's Changing Politics and Joseph Andrews." PQ 39
        (1960): 39-55.

        An interpretation of Fielding's reasons for interrupting
        his work on Joseph Andrews to write The Opposition: A
        Vision in defense of Walpole when, politically, Fielding had
        always been opposed to Walpole.

1030   The Moral Basis of Fielding's Art: A Study of "Joseph An-
        drews." Middletown, Conn.: Wesleyan Univ. Press, 1959.

        Seeks to identify the major themes of Joseph Andrews and
        to "view the ethics of the novel in the related contexts of
        seventeenth- and eighteenth-century latitudinarian Christianity
        and of Fielding's own morality which, in its emphasis upon
        good nature and charity, ultimately derives from such Low
        Church divines as Isaac Barrow, John Tillotson, Samuel Clarke,
        and Benjamin Hoadly." Argues that the novel is not formless
        and disunified, that the "structure of Joseph Andrews ... in-
        cluding the so-called digression of Mr. Wilson, was quite
        carefully designed--given substance and shape by Fielding's
        Christian ethic and by the principle of what he liked to call
        'that Epic Regularity.' "

1031   BROOKS, DOUGLAS.
        "Abraham Adams and Parson Trulliber: The Meaning of
        Joseph Andrews, Book II, Chapter 14." MLR 63 (1968): 794-
        801.

        Discusses Homeric echoes in Joseph Andrews--how Fielding

used the Odyssey as an overriding structural metaphor and
what he really meant by "Comic Epic-Poem in Prose"; shows
parallel between Odysseus' visit to Eumaeus and Adams's call
on Parson Trulliber.

1032   "The Interpolated Tales in Joseph Andrews Again." MP 65
        (1968): 208-213.

        Discusses the relationship of "The Unfortunate Jilt" and
        "The History of Two Friends" to the novel as a whole and
        concludes that these two tales are really an integral part of
        the novel.

1033   CAUTHEN, I. B., JR.
        "Fielding's Digressions in Joseph Andrews." CE 17 (1956):
        379-382.

        Maintains that the three digressions serve an artistic pur-
        pose in the novel--that "they are closely related to Fielding's
        aesthetic of the novel, the exposure of affectation that arises
        from vanity or hypocrisy," and that "by their inclusion Field-
        ing has doubled his emphasis on his theme--the laying bare
        of the only true source of the ridiculous."

1034   COLEY, WILLIAM B.
        "Fielding, Hogarth, and Three Italian Masters." MLQ 24
        (1963): 386-391.

        Discusses Fielding's reference to Hogarth, Amegoni, Ver-
        onese, and Caracci in Joseph Andrews.

1035   DONOVAN, ROBERT ALAN.
        "Joseph Andrews as Parody." In The Shaping Vision: Im-
        agination in the English Novel from Defoe to Dickens (Ithaca,
        N.Y.: Cornell Univ. Press, 1966), pp. 68-88.

        Suggests that Fielding in Joseph Andrews ironically adopts
        Pamela's moral vision while refashioning the events; there-
        fore Joseph Andrews is a comic novel capable of standing
        alone, yet continuously enriched by its relation to Pamela,
        a relation that develops into an "extraordinarily subtle and
        far-reaching commentary of Richardson's ethical assumptions."
        Also argues that Fielding maintains his objective of satirizing
        Pamela through the entire novel and emphasizes the disparity
        between his own moral vision and that of Richardson even in
        the central forty-one chapters.

1036   DRISKELL, LEON V.

"Maritornes and Slipslop: Delusion and Dramatic Irony in Cervantes and Fielding." <u>KPAB</u> (1977): 15-23.

Discusses the relationship between Cervantes's Martornes and Mrs. Slipslop, suggesting that the latter satisfied realistic expectations and the requirements of myth and illusion: "Like Maritornes, whose physical and moral characteristics she shares, Slipslop is indisputably funny without ceasing ... to mean." She supports Fielding's development of the theme of illusion and reality.

1037   "Interpolated Tales in Joseph Andrews and Don Quixote: The Dramatic Method as Instruction." <u>SAB</u> 33, No. 3 (1968): 5-8.

Argues that "the tales are essentially dramatic in function, and their circumstances of narration are more important than their content. Admitting thematic similarities in the three tales, one must yet insist upon their patterned relationship to other events and the similarities of circumstance under which they are told."

1038   DULCK, JEAN.
<u>Henry Fielding: Joseph Andrews</u>. Paris: Librairie Armand Colin, 1970.

Discusses the structure and styles (dramatic, epic, and burlesque) of <u>Joseph Andrews</u>, and analyzes Fielding's treatment of character, social problems, and moral evil.

1039   EHRENPREIS, IRVIN.
"Fielding's Use of Fiction: The Autonomy of <u>Joseph Andrews</u>." In <u>Twelve Original Essays on Great English Novels</u>, ed. Charles Shapiro (Detroit: Wayne State Univ. Press, 1960), pp. 23-41.

Discusses the ironies, unmaskings, conflicts, and reversals that lurk behind the pattern of the novel: "instead of an organic or cumulative plot of suspense, the structure of [Joseph Andrews] depends upon small oscillations of emotion which gather ... into massive waves of reversals."

1040   EVANS, JAMES E.
"Fielding's Lady Booby and Fénelon's Calypso." <u>Studies in the Novel</u> 8 (1976): 210-213.

A comparison of the two characters to show that "[b]ecause of their similar motives, vacillating between lust and indignation, reflected in similar actions and speeches," Field-

ing had Fénelon's Calypso in mind when he created Lady
Booby.

1041   FREEDMAN, WILLIAM.
        "Joseph Andrews: Fielding's Garden of the Perverse." TSL
        16 (1971): 35-45.

        Discusses Fielding's "bestiary" in Joseph Andrews; the
        concept of good nature implies the existence of ill nature and
        the perverse, of such characters as Mrs. Slipslop (a cow),
        Beau Didapper (a bird), Mrs. Tow-wouse (a dragon), and Par-
        son Trulliber (a pig).

1042   "Joseph Andrews: Clothing and Concretization of Character."
        Discourse 4 (1961): 304-310.

        Discusses Fielding's exploitation of "the dubious convention
        that clothes make the man." "In keeping with the aesthetic
        doctrine of example rather than precept, Fielding saw more
        in the use of clothing than merely a means by which to dem-
        onstrate the disparity between appearance and reality, de-
        tecting also its infinite possibilities for character revelation
        in all its ramifications."

1043   GOLDBERG, HOMER.
        The Art of Joseph Andrews.   Chicago: Univ. Chicago Press,
        1969.

        Studies Joseph Andrews's constructional art by exploring the
        characteristics of the continental comic romances that were
        Fielding's models; argues that Fielding's ethical concerns
        must be related to his controlling artistic aim of constructing
        a comic fiction of a special kind.   Joseph Andrews's distinctive
        achievements are analyzed by examining the "ways in which
        [Fielding] adapted and reshaped particular materials and de-
        vices, and by comparing his practices with those of his pred-
        ecessors."

1044   "The Interpolated Stories in Joseph Andrews or 'The History
        of the World in General' Satirically Revised." MP 63 (1966):
        295-310.

        Suggests that "The complex 'indebtedness' of Fielding's
        episodes to the goatherd's tale, the adventure of 'the Knight
        of the Green Coat,' and, especially, 'The Curious Imperti-
        nent' reveals how deeply embedded Don Quixote was in his
        thinking.   The ingenuity with which he adapted these hints
        and reworked these materials to the service of his own ends
        shows how much more analytic and imaginative he had become

in his 'copying' of Cervantes since the youthful adaptation of
Don Quixote in England. "

1045   HARTWIG, ROBERT J.
        "Pharsamon and Joseph Andrews. " TSLL 14 (1972): 45-52.

        Points out similarities in narrative and comic technique
        between Marivaux's Pharsamon and Joseph Andrews and con-
        cludes that this work may have been more influential on Field-
        ing than La Vie de Marianne or Le Paysan parvenu.

1046   HORNAT, JAROSLAV.
        "Pamela, Shamela and Joseph Andrews. " Casopis pro Moderní
        Filologii, 1959.   (In Czech with English summary)

        In comparing Shamela and Joseph Andrews, the author dis-
        cerns "similar components and values," and is especially
        concerned with similar religious and moral issues; argues
        that, though the travels of Joseph, Fanny, and Adams push
        the parody of the first part into the background, the thought
        of Pamela and Richardson's moral code seem to pervade the
        entire novel.   The denouement is more logically a part of
        the central plot than has usually been supposed.

1047   ISER, WOLFGANG.
        "The Role of the Reader in Fielding's Joseph Andrews and
        Tom Jones. " In English Studies Today, 5th Series (Papers
        Read at the Eighth Conference of the International Association
        of University Professors of English, held at Istanbul, 1971),
        ed. Sencer Tonguc (Istanbul: Matbaesi, 1973), pp. 289-325.
        Rpt. in The Implied Reader: Patterns of Communication in
        Prose Fiction from Bunyan to Beckett (Baltimore: Johns Hop-
        kins Univ. Press, 1974), pp. 29-56.

        Argues that the full meaning of the novels cannot be brought
        out unless the reader's participation is actively engaged; the
        reader must not only be willing to be persuaded but must also
        undergo a transformation into an image created by the author:
        "The reader must be made to feel for himself the new mean-
        ing of the novel. " The imagination of the reader must be
        stimulated by allusions and suggestions in the written text that
        will enable it to conjure up what the text does not reveal.

1048   JORDAN, ROBERT M.
        "The Limits of Illusion: Faulkner, Fielding, and Chaucer. "
        Criticism 2 (1960): 278-305.

        Discusses "how deeply the penchant for paradox and for
        unification of sensibility has affected both our fiction and our

critical assumptions about fiction" and points out that "in
Joseph Andrews, although Fielding moves continually back and
forth between the world he is making and the world he lives
in, he never confuses the two, but rather emphasizes the
partition between them. "

1049   LENTA, M.
       "From Pamela to Joseph Andrews: An Investigation of the
       Relationship between Two Originals. " ESA 23 (1980): 63-74.

       A consideration of the links between the new literary form
       (a comic epic in prose) of Joseph Andrews and older forms,
       such as the periodical essay, classical literature of the past,
       and stage comedy. Fielding chose to link Joseph Andrews to
       Pamela with names and plot references and he made use of
       many possible character presentations which he had perceived
       in Pamela. His determination to identify the author's voice
       resulted in immense differences in structure and in tone be-
       tween the two novels. Adams, Joseph, and Fanny, "all fig-
       ures of real innocence and goodness ... embody both a criti-
       cism of Pamela and assertions about the nature of innocence. "

1050   McDOWELL, ALFRED.
       "Fielding's Rendering of Speech in Joseph Andrews and Tom
       Jones. " Language & Style 6 (1973): 83-96.

       A study of the various methods by which Fielding presents
       speeches that are not strictly either indirect or direct dis-
       course. The author analyzes a number of passages from the
       two novels to indicate that "much of the time when Fielding
       appears to be telling, he is subtly and economically drama-
       tizing or showing, by using some variety of free indirect
       speech. "

1051   MACK, MAYNARD.
       "Introduction" to Joseph Andrews. New York: Holt, Rine-
       hart & Winston, 1948), pp. vii-xvi. Rpt. in [898] as "Joseph
       Andrews and Pamela, " pp. 52-58.

       A comparison of Joseph Andrews and Pamela, in the matter
       of moral criticism, and the contrast between comic and tragic
       plot; also considers the influence on Joseph Andrews of Cer-
       vantes and Fielding's dramatic training.

1052   OLSEN, FLEMMING.
       "Notes on the Structure of Joseph Andrews. " ES 50 (1969):
       340-351.

       Deals with 1) the main themes of the book, 2) the way in

which Fielding introduces and handles his characters, and
3) the compositional build-up, both of the book as a whole
and of the individual chapters.

1053   PALMER, E. T.
        "Fielding's Joseph Andrews: A Comic Epic in Prose." ES
        52 (1971): 331-339.

        Examines the epic and comic aspects of the novel, and
        concludes that "The latitudinarian background gives it a firm
        moral basis; Fielding's understanding of the epic convention
        helps, among other things, to impose unity on his moral anal-
        ysis, and his comic conception enables him to change the focus
        continually so that his heroes' weaknesses and limitations are
        exposed as well as their opponents' vices and follies."

1054   PAULSON, RONALD.
        "Models and Paradigms: Joseph Andrews, Hogarth's Good
        Samaritan, and Fénelon's Télémaque." MLN 91 (1976): 1186-
        1207.

        Joseph Andrews is a typological novel, one which evokes
        models for action that "trap" the characters in the novel and
        the author's models for writing the novel. Joseph Andrews
        begins with Fielding's literary models, Richardson's Pamela,
        and Colley Cibber's Colley Cibber and ends with Joseph's re-
        fusal to make himself into a literary model. Several ex-
        amples are paradigmatic for the author: the parable of the
        Good Samaritan lurks behind the episode of Joseph, the rob-
        bers, and the coach full of Pharisees and Levites with its
        one good Samaritan--Hogarth's The Good Samaritan functions
        as the moral paradigm of Joseph Andrews. For Joseph's
        travels Fielding found a precise model in Fénelon's Télémaque,
        which describes a son's search for his father and his return
        home, educated by his adventures.

1055   REID, B. L.
        "Utmost Merriment, Strictest Decency: Joseph Andrews."
        SR 75 (1967): 559-584. Rpt. in [154], pp. 52-77.

        Analyzes several crucial metaphors whose intersecting
        creates dramatic tension: a horizontal journey metaphor that
        involves both a physical progress and a secular quest, com-
        plicated by moral meanings, a "comic Pilgrim's Progress,
        concurrently reverent and gay: utmost merriment corrected
        by the strictest decency"; and against the running horizontal
        metaphor of the journey Fielding counterpoints a vertical
        metaphor, a social order that "both connects and divides
        'high people and low people'" and embodies the theme of vanity
        and affectation.

1056   SABOR, PETER.
       "Joseph Andrews and Pamela." BJECS 1 (1978): 169-181.

            The view that Joseph Andrews began as another parody of
       Pamela, but ended with a life of its own centered on Parson
       Adams, has generally been discredited; a more fruitful ap-
       proach suggests that Fielding was not imitating Richardson's
       morality or artistry, but creating a fiction that was Pamela's
       antithesis, a demonstration of how a novel should be written.
       The contrast between the two works, in structure, organiza-
       tion, intention, comments on the contemporary drama, and
       the character of Pamela, extends throughout Joseph Andrews:
       Fielding's novel provides a searching critique of Pamela's
       shortcomings while representing a new type of comic fiction.

1057   SIMON, IRENE.
       "Early Themes of Prose Fiction: Congreve and Fielding."
       In [36], pp. 19-36.

            Compares Congreve's Incognita with Fielding's Joseph An-
       drews. Concludes that "Fielding's theory of comic prose epic
       is the foundation of his formal realism, and Joseph Andrews
       is a 'just imitation of nature' which produces 'a more rational
       and useful pleasure.' Congreve's characters wear masks or
       other men's clothes as at a masquerade; Fielding's only wear
       the masks of their vanities and hypocrisies, or of their sim-
       plicity, as men do in life."

1058   SPACKS, PATRICIA MEYER.
       "The Dangerous Age." ECS 11 (1978): 417-438.

            Concerned with the growth and developing awareness of
       sexuality in eighteenth-century youth, especially Joseph An-
       drews and Clarissa Harlowe: "Fielding for comic purposes,
       Richardson for tragic, imagine youthful protagonists who di-
       verge from the norm in precisely that aspect of character in
       actuality considered to define their time of life: for them,
       consistently, judgment controls sexuality (although they can
       and do make mistakes of judgment)." Surveys the social con-
       text in which adolescence developed, and compares eighteenth-
       century attitudes with twentieth-century ones: whereas today
       youth is glorified and worshipped, in the eighteenth century
       nothing one reads suggests that adolescence is a desirable
       state of life. The Vicar of Wakefield deals with young people
       largely in a punitive way: no sooner do they experience any
       form of pleasure than punishment quickly follows.

1059   "Some Reflections on Satire." Genre 1 (1968): 22-30.

            Argues that the satiric effect of Joseph Andrews is more

complex than most critics have assumed, that the novel evokes considerably more than a comic response in the reader; in fact, the satiric intention provokes two responses, "uneasiness, the response to recognition of one's own flaws ... and complacency, the response to the evil of others." Suggests that Joseph Andrews's "total structure makes a satiric network which involves the reader, forces him to self-examination in the privacy of his closet, however different he may be in all obvious respects from Joseph and Parson Adams at one extreme, from Beau Didapper at the other."

1060   SPILKA, MARK.
        "Fielding and the Epic Impulse." Criticism 11 (1969): 68-77.

        Argues that, even though human concerns in Joseph Andrews exist on a reduced scale, Fielding and all succeeding novelists actually worked on a larger scale than traditional epic narrative allowed, that they connect with epic by their extension of epic scale and variety to traditional social, personal, and domestic life: "My position is that the epic world is capacious, grand, sublime, precisely because it is small...."

1061   "Comic Resolution in Fielding's Joseph Andrews." CE 15 (1953): 11-19. Rpt. in [53], pp. 78-91; [898], pp. 59-68.

        Argues that the escapades at Booby Hall are an integral part of the scheme of the novel, and not mere comic diversions; they involve all the major characters and both aspects of the main theme, the lust-chastity theme: in the night adventures at Booby Hall, Fielding uses condensed, violent action to stand his book on its head, shake out all the themes and passions, and resolve them through warmhearted laughter.

1062   TAVE, STUART M.
        The Amiable Humorist: A Study in the Comic Theory and Criticism of the Eighteenth and Early Nineteenth Centuries. Chicago: Univ. of Chicago Press, 1960.

        Traces the historical changes in the concept of humor from the Renaissance theory that humor was an aberration requiring satiric attack to a belief that the best comic works present amiable originals who arouse delight, sympathy, and innocent mirth. Parson Adams becomes an example of the "amiable humorist," no longer designed for contempt and ridicule on the Restoration model, but for affection and respect.

1063   TAYLOR, DICK, JR.
        "Joseph as Hero in Joseph Andrews." TSE 7 (1957): 91-109.

Analyzes the singing theme in Book II, Chapter 12, and
the threads of plot and theme which Fielding develops out of
the scene. Traces Fielding's development of Joseph's character in relation to Parson Adams and shows how he emerges
as a strong character.

1064   WEINBROT, HOWARD D.
       "Chastity and Interpolation: Two Aspects of Joseph Andrews."
       JEGP 69 (1970): 14-31.

Seeks to clarify two central aspects of the novel: Fielding's attitude toward Joseph's tenuous virginity, and the function of the interpolated tales; argues that Joseph is not so
comic as he is often thought to be--Fielding does not ridicule
Joseph's defense of his virginity--and that the novel makes
some serious points about truth and morality, primarily observable in the change of time and action during the interpolated tales. Concludes that the interpolations provide an
alternative to the world of a benevolent God and a benevolent
narrator.

1065   WIESENFARTH, JOSEPH.
       " 'High' People and 'Low' in Joseph Andrews: A Study of
       Structure and Style." CLAJ 16 (1973): 357-365.

Suggests that "Fielding turns the social ladder upside down
and makes his lowest people socially (Abraham, Joseph, and
Fanny) his highest people morally. He carries out this moral
revolution in a structure that is reductive and in a style that
is often ridiculous." Concludes that Fielding, having structurally and stylistically destroyed every value that Pamela
stood for, "kills the first daughter of Richardson's imagination with a last deadly shot in the last phrase of the last sentence of his novel: Joseph will not 'be prevailed on by any
booksellers, or their authors, to make his appearance in
"high-life." ' "

1066   WRIGHT, ANDREW.
       "Joseph Andrews, Mask and Feast." EIC 13 (1963): 209-
       221. Rpt. in [997].

A discussion of how Fielding uses art to idealize morality
and how his "artistic motive is festive rather than lenten,
ideal rather than hortatory...." In "Joseph Andrews the narrator masquerading as an author is the player who by his
opening fanfares as well as by his preliminary gambits and
interruptions reminds us that what he is telling is a story,
that what he fabricates is for all its fidelity to nature ultimately and deliberately faithless to mere fact, that what he
is offering is not a guide to life but the transfiguration of
life which is his art."

See also: 901, 902, 903, 904, 912, 914, 917, 918, 927, 930, 932,
    934, 948, 949, 952, 953, 954, 955, 977, 986, 991, 1024, 1148,
    1724, 2500

Jonathan Wild

1067   DIGEON, AURELIEN.
       "Jonathan Wild." From [924], pp. 96-128. Rpt. in [898],
       pp. 69-80.

       A general survey, considering such matters as the histori-
       cal original, the nature of Fielding's parody, and the dramatic
       structure of the novel; argues that Fielding's aim is "to re-
       ject reality when it proves a hindrance, to add to it at need,
       to be more true than nature." Emphasizes that Fielding
       idealizes Wild in order to lift "him out of the crapulous me-
       diocrity of the real man ... to give more weight and univer-
       sality to his example."

1068   DIRCKS, RICHARD J.
       "The Perils of Heartfree: A Sociological Review of Fielding's
       Adaptation of Dramatic Convention." TSLL 8 (1966): 5-13.

       An examination of the techniques that Fielding uses to focus
       attention on the problems of the poor; in order to shift em-
       phasis in Jonathan Wild away from an attack on Walpole to
       the social effects of crime and poverty, Fielding adopted artis-
       tic devices used in the drama of sensibility.

1069   EVANS, DAVID L.
       "The Theme of Liberty in Jonathan Wild." PLL 3 (1967):
       302-313.

       Argues that the thematic unity of Jonathan Wild is more
       apparent if we emphasize the theme of liberty rather than
       that of the greatness-goodness contrast: it is the "opposition
       between moral imprisonment and moral freedom, or between
       a real as opposed to a false conception of social and moral
       freedom."

1070   FARRELL, WILLIAM J.
       "The Mock-Heroic Form of Jonathan Wild." MP 63 (1966):
       216-226.

       Discusses Fielding's use of the long-inherited rhetorical
       and structural devices of panegyric biography as the form
       into which he cast his material. Shows how Fielding is able
       to satirize Wild in a mock-heroic manner but also is able to
       link him with other greats in history whose lives are presented

in a similar fashion. By recognizing this relationship, we
can more fully "appreciate the artistic tightness and full complexity of Fielding's satire."

1071   HATFIELD, GLENN W.
"Puffs and Pollitricks: Jonathan Wild and the Political Corruption of Language." PQ 46 (1967): 248-267. Rpt. in
[936], pp. 89-108.

Discusses Fielding's war on political rhetoric and his view
of politics as a threat to language. "The distinction in Jonathan Wild between 'greatness' and 'goodness' is not a cynical
acquiescence in the political corruption of language but a way
of resisting it by showing how ironically empty a moral term
can be when it is separated from one of its essential ideas."

1072   HOPKINS, ROBERT H.
"Language and Comic Play in Fielding's Jonathan Wild."
Criticism 8 (1966): 213-228.

An analysis of language in the novel to show how "Fielding
makes inert superlatives and dead metaphors operative and
thereby purges and purifies language." Shows how the comic
verbal pattern in the novel of the "lock-and-key" passages
builds up to a climax, and how the "world of Jonathan Wild
offers either raw bestiality and obscentity or a fastidious
asceticism and prudery."

1073   IRWIN, WILLIAM ROBERT.
The Making of Jonathan Wild: A Study in the Literary Method
of Henry Fielding. New York: Columbia Univ. Press, 1941;
Hamden, Conn. : Archon, 1966.

A critical analysis which is a "synthesis of ... biographical and historical, ethical, and literary" background which
produced Jonathan Wild. Shows how Jonathan Wild is the
personification of general evil and as such illustrates the conflict between greatness and goodness.

1074   KISHLER, THOMAS C.
"Heartfree's Function in Jonathan Wild." SNL 1 (1964): 32-
34.

Argues that "Heartfree's dramatic function is to make
more concrete the other half of the central dichotomy between
greatness and goodness, which is introduced but not fully developed in the first book." As the opposite of Wild, he must
represent decency, goodness, and humanity in the abstract,
just as Wild personified the idea of true greatness.

1075   PRESTON, JOHN.
       "The Ironic Mode: A Comparison of Jonathan Wild and The
       Beggar's Opera." EIC 16 (1966): 268-280.

       Examines the differences in the handling of irony. For
       Fielding "irony is a stylistic device, a means of clarification,
       even of simplification: he uses it to consolidate and reas-
       sure." Gay, on the other hand, uses irony "as a means of
       articulating and organizing his knowledge of life."

1076   RAWSON, C. J.
       "Fielding's 'Good' Merchant: The Problem of Heartfree in
       Jonathan Wild (with comments on other 'Good' Characters
       in Fielding)." MP 69 (1972): 292-313.

       Heartfree and his family seem to be the novel's main fail-
       ure, and perhaps the characterization of Heartfree was the
       victim of the "oppressively simplifying demands of the ironic
       scheme"; Fielding's defense of the "good" tradesman is under-
       mined by a note of sentimental gravity.

1077   "The Hero as Clown: Jonathan Wild, Felix Krull, and Others."
       In [9], pp. 17-52. Rpt. and expanded in [965], pp. 101-146.

       Suggests that the "central uncertainty" of Jonathan Wild is
       caused by "Fielding's failure to embody his mock-heroic in
       a live, coherent, and self-sustaining fable"; the mock-heroic
       is largely set in motion by "verbal insistence." Also dis-
       cusses Wild as part of a "not unamiable tradition of clowning
       roguery," and concludes that the comic spirit partly takes
       some of the sting out of Wild's viciousness.

1078   RINEHART, HOLLIS.
       "Fielding's Chapter 'Of Proverbs' (Jonathan Wild [1743], Book
       2, Chapter 12): Sources, Allusions, and Interpretation."
       MP 77 (1980): 291-296.

       Chapter 12, which appeared in the first version of Jonathan
       Wild, is a satire on Bacon's Advancement of Learning and on
       a popular joke book, Joe Miller's Jests, from which Fielding
       drew twelve proverbs as part of his parody of Bacon. Field-
       ing chose to parody the Advancement of Learning partly be-
       cause he took exception to Bacon's advice that men should
       practice hypocrisy for the sake of worldly self-interest and
       partly because he had recently read David Mallet's Life of
       Francis Bacon, in which he found several themes pertinent
       to those of Jonathan Wild. In 1754 Fielding omitted this chap-
       ter, as well as one other, from the revised version of Jona-
       than Wild, probably not for political reasons but rather from
       the desire to unify and condense his novel by omitting largely
       irrelevant material.

1079   "The Role of Walpole in Fielding's Jonathan Wild." ESC 5
        (1979): 420-431.

        Disagrees with the idea that Fielding was attacking Wal-
        pole, and asserts that "the attempt to read Walpole into the
        work has produced serious distortions in interpretation, par-
        ticularly in regard to three important areas: (1) the meaning
        of the term 'Greatness'; (2) the political message; and (3) the
        role of Laetitia Snap." Fielding uses Jonathan Wild as an
        example in his attack upon Greatness by means of an analogy
        between a Great Man and a thief, and although certain refer-
        ences may be to Walpole, there is nothing in the portrait of
        Wild that particularizes Walpole or any other individual.

1080   SHEA, BERNARD.
        "Machiavelli and Fielding's Jonathan Wild." PMLA 72 (1957):
        55-73.

        Argues that "Jonathan Wild is at once an imitation, a parody,
        and a criticism of Machiavelli"; that there are resemblances
        involving parts of the Prince and Discourses on the First Ten
        Books of Titus Livius, and many parallels in content, struc-
        ture, and diction with the Life of Castruccio Castracani of
        Lucca.

1081   SMITH, RAYMOND.
        "The Ironic Structure of Fielding's Jonathan Wild." BSUF
        6, No. 3 (1965): 3-9.

        Argues that what Jonathan Wild, Tom Jones, and Amelia
        have in common is the "author's use of the classical device
        of the eiron, the character who appears to be inferior to his
        antagonist, the alazon, but in the course of the struggle, or
        agon, is proven to be really superior." Jonathan Wild is
        interpreted as a struggle between the benevolent man and the
        self-interested man.

1082   SMITH, ROBERT A.
        "The 'Great Man' Motif in Jonathan Wild and The Beggar's
        Opera." CLAJ 2 (1959): 183-184.

        Contrasts Fielding's and Gay's differing methods of pre-
        senting the "great man" theme; both set up the same basic
        thesis, that ambition will destroy the "great man." Fielding
        used a loosely constructed, biographical prose narrative and
        depended extensively on contrast to present his theme, where-
        as Gay employed a musical medium and presented the "great
        man" motif by spreading evil among Peachum, Lockit, and
        Macheath, and refrained from arranging any sort of punish-
        ment for his characters.

1083   WELLS, JOHN EDWIN.
       "Fielding's Political Purpose in Jonathan Wild." PMLA 28
       (1913): 1-55.

       An early attempt to analyze the political satire in Jonathan
       Wild: "At practically every point of prominence when the
       matter concerns Wild, occur comment and application that
       are made by deliberate statement or by implication to point
       to persons in authority, particularly to those of political ac-
       tivity--to conquerors sometimes, but commonly to statesmen
       or ministers of state.... Wild is made active in passages
       ostentatiously political in their significance, when no such
       activity or significance properly belongs to Wild or to the
       position in life of Wild as he is presented in the surface-
       story proper." Shows that the matter concerning Wild and
       his gang is largely political satire aimed at Walpole.

1084   WENDT, ALLAN.
       "The Moral Allegory in Jonathan Wild." ELH 24 (1957):
       306-320.

       Moral allegory involves conscious reference to limitations
       of Heartfree's passive goodness; examines his character in
       light of eighteenth-century ethical thought. Concludes that
       Heartfree lacks the quality that Wild has in excess, just as
       Wild lacks Heartfree's basic disposition to benevolence--Heart-
       free, therefore, possesses "the disposition without the active
       qualities for doing good"; whereas Wild's qualities--courage,
       ambition, energy--if balanced with Heartfree's benevolence
       would constitute virtue.

See also: 917, 925, 941, 949, 952, 965, 999

                              Tom Jones

1085   ALLOTT, MIRIAM.
       "A Note on Fielding's Mr. Square." MLR 56 (1961): 69-72.

       Argues against identifying Square with Salisbury deist,
       Thomas Chubb. In "Tom Jones ... Fielding epitomizes the
       main arguments in the deist controversy ... and he seeks,
       through the positive and salutary human values of his story,
       to combat the aridity and moral confusion which the depres-
       sing controversy left in its wake." In this design Square's role
       is more complex than a simple identification with Chubb would
       suggest.

1086   ALTER, ROBERT.
       "The Picaroon Domesticated." In Rogue's Progress: Studies

in the Picaresque Novel (Cambridge: Harvard Univ. Press,
1964), pp. 80-105.

    Discusses Fielding's use of the picaresque and the fact
that Tom Jones, although it has elements of the picaresque,
is a different type of novel. Tom is by no means a rogue
but a character of impeccable moral principles and Fielding's
ironic treatment of virtue differs from the picaroon's irony.

1087   ANDERSON, HOWARD.
    "Answers to the Author of Clarissa: Theme and Narrative
    Technique in Tom Jones and Tristram Shandy." PQ 51 (1972):
    859-873.

    Shows how Fielding and Sterne reject "the costly self-
reliance of Richardson's heroine by developing narrative
techniques that establish the possibility and indeed the necessity of mutual trust." Both authors "insist at the start that
we acknowledge the presence of a narrator" and foster "trust"
by demanding "directly the reader's reliance upon the narrator to help him correctly comprehend the experience in
which he is participating." The new and conscious patterns
of personal relationships are in direct response to the "tragic
self-reliance of Clarissa Harlowe."

1088   BAKER, SHERIDAN, ed.
    Henry Fielding: Tom Jones (Norton Critical Edition). New
    York: W. W. Norton & Co. , 1973.

    Contains an authoritative text, backgrounds and sources,
and criticism.

1089   BAKER, SHERIDAN.
    "Bridget Allworthy: The Creative Pressures of Fielding's
    Plot." PMASAL 52 (1966): 345-356. Rpt. in [1088], pp.
    906-916.

    Distinguishing between "plot" (the story) and "plotting"
(selection, disclosure, concealment), the author analyzes
Bridget as a "supreme example of how plot generates character, as the nearly fabulous story strains against the neces-
sities of plotting a realistic mystery and a moral education."

1090   BATTESTIN, MARTIN C. , ed.
    " 'Tom Jones': The Argument of Design." In [42], pp. 289-
    319. Rpt. in [68], pp. 141-163.

    Argues that the special triumph of Tom Jones is as a work
of art: "the form of the novel--its symmetry of design; the

artful contrivance of its plot; the intrusive, omniscient narrator; and that final, miraculous resolution of every compli-
cation--is the expression and emblem of its author's coherent,
Christian vision of life." Specifically concerned with the doctrine of Providence and the argument of the book's design,
Tom Jones becomes the symbol of Fielding's universe.

1091   "Fielding's Definition of Wisdom: Some Functions of Ambi-
        guity and Emblem in Tom Jones." ELH 35 (1968): 188-217.
        Rpt. in [68], pp. 164-192; [1088], pp. 817-843.

        Deals with "the substance and the form of the novel's most
        important theme, the definition of Wisdom," arguing that al-
        legory, ambiguity, and emblem function together to define
        that theme. First half of article discusses "Prudence: The
        Function of Ambiguity" and second half deals with the function
        of emblem in general, and with Sophia as emblem in particu-
        lar. Concludes that Tom Jones has a "quasi-allegorical"
        dimension in that Fielding renders the Platonic idea of Virtue
        or speculative wisdom as associated with Sophia Western.

1092   Twentieth Century Interpretations of "Tom Jones": A Collec-
        tion of Critical Essays. Englewood Cliffs, N. J.: Prentice-
        Hall, 1968.

1093   "Tom Jones and 'His Egyptian Majesty': Fielding's Parable
        of Government." PMLA 82 (1967): 68-77.

        "The account of the gypsy king's enlightened despotism,
        together with Fielding's interpolated denunciation of absolu-
        tism, establishes not only a moral, but a specifically politi-
        cal frame of reference: namely, the question of the relative
        virtues of an absolute, as opposed to a limited monarchy."
        Concludes that "The significance of [this] episode lies ... in
        the paradoxical representation of an alien band of fortune-
        tellers and thieves as a utopian society, eminently happy in
        its civil and political institutions."

1094   "Osborne's 'Tom Jones': Adapting a Classic." VQR 42 (1966):
        378-393. Rpt. in [1102], pp. 193-208.

        Regards the Osborne and Richardson adaptation as "one
        of the most successful and imaginative ... in the brief his-
        tory of film"; but emphasizes that the film lacks the "moral
        seriousness" of the novel. Discusses authorial intrusion in
        novel and film, the use of type characters, the cinematic
        treatment of the scene at Upton, and the artistic qualities of
        the film.

1095   BLISS, MICHAEL.
        "Fielding's Bill of Fare in Tom Jones." ELH 30 (1963):
        236-243.

        A discussion of Fielding's "Bill of Fare" metaphor to show
        that there are "two major and related thematic strains in
        Tom Jones. One is ethical and is carried ... by the nar-
        rative. The other is esthetic and is ... the subject of the
        'subplot' of the introductory chapters. Thus while the nar-
        rative is most obviously concerned with mutuality (as love)
        and the 'subplot' most obviously concerned with perception
        (as creation and criticism) it is in their interpenetration that
        the point of the novel lurks: that mutuality and perception,
        ethics and esthetics, are mutually interdependent."

1096   BOOTH, WAYNE C.
        " 'Fielding' in Tom Jones." In The Rhetoric of Fiction (Chi-
        cago: Univ. Chicago Press, 1961), pp. 215-218. Rpt. in
        [1088], pp. 893-896; [1092], pp. 94-96.

        Discusses the effect of the implied author's character on
        our reactions to the novel as a whole; suggests that the nar-
        rator creates a distinct interest in the "story" of his rela-
        tionship with the reader, and that the account of the growing
        intimacy between the narrator and the reader has a plot of
        its own, separate from that of Tom and Sophia.

1097   BROWN, HOMER OBED.
        "Tom Jones: The 'Bastard' of History." Boundary 7 (1979):
        201-233.

        Considers the problem of Tom's bastardy, that in law he
        cannot inherit Allworthy's estate--he "cannot be heir to any
        one, neither can he have heirs," he is "kin of nobody, and
        has no ancestor from whom an inheritable blood can be de-
        rived." This legal fact raises the issue of a basic pattern
        of genealogical disturbance, without apparent narrative or
        thematic necessity--the genealogical aberration of incest: the
        problem is that "if Tom derives from no one, incest could
        never be a problem." The pattern of genealogical disturbance
        is placed in relation to the 1745 Jacobite Rebellion as the
        context in which Fielding places Tom Jones: "Even a cursory
        glance at the late Stuart succession and some of the large
        events of English History suggests almost comic parallels with
        the plot of the novel."

1098   CARVER, WAYNE.
        "The Worlds of Tom and Tristram." WHR 12 (1958): 67-74.

        A comparison of Tom Jones and Tristram Shandy as comic

novels. Sees the world of Tom Jones as a "common-sensical, work-a-day world that we all move in with more or less assurance" and the world of Tristram as "frangible" where the reader moves with apprehension.

1099   CLEARY, THOMAS R.
"Fielding: Style for an Age of Sensibility." In Trans. of the Samuel Johnson Society of the Northwest, Vol. 6 (Calgary: Samuel Johnson Soc. of the N.W., 1973): 91-96.

Disputes Northrop Frye's description of Tom Jones as a "product" novel and his equation of author and narrator; and ascribes the novel's special quality to its style, a "lengthy, forthrightly asymmetrical, loosely organized adaptation of the 'loose period' employed by such seventeenth century favorites of Fielding's as Montaigne ... Sir Thomas Browne and Sir William Temple."

1100   "Jacobitism in Tom Jones: The Basis for an Hypothesis." PQ 52 (1973): 239-251.

Argues that "related inconsistencies in the development of the political background and the political characters in the novel," especially the violation of chronology by the introduction of the "Forty-Five," indicates that Fielding may have done a partial revision of the novel "after its main action had been elaborated." Also traces relationship between anti-Jacobite passages in the central books and Fielding's editorship of the Jacobite's Journal.

1101   COMBS, WILLIAM W.
"The Return to Paradise Hall: An Essay on Tom Jones." SAQ 67 (1968): 419-436.

Shows how "The movement in Tom Jones from youthful bliss to misfortune to a reconciliation possible only because of errors which ended the initial bliss follows the traditional pattern of the paradoxical 'fortunate fall.'" Analyzes the conflict between Nature and Fortune and their influence on the actions of the characters.

1102   COMPTON, NEIL, ed.
Henry Fielding: 'Tom Jones': A Casebook. London: Macmillan, 1970.

1103   COOKE, ARTHUR L.
"Henry Fielding and the Writers of Heroic Romance." PMLA 62 (1947): 984-994.

Cites the similarities between Fielding and the writers of
heroic romance, especially Mlle. de Scudéry, and concludes
that, although Fielding "enunciated principles which were in
many respects almost identical," there is little resemblance
between Tom Jones and The Great Cyrus because of the difference in concept of such words as "probability," "unity,"
and "morality."

1104   CRANE, R. S.
        "The Concept of Plot and the Plot of Tom Jones." In Critics
        and Criticism Ancient and Modern (Chicago: Univ. Chicago
        Press, 1952), pp. 616-647; in abridged edition, 1957, pp.
        62-93.

        Argues that plot cannot be abstracted from the moral quali-
        ties of the characters and from the operations of their thoughts;
        that "the plot of any novel or drama is the particular tem-
        poral synthesis effected by the writer of the elements of ac-
        tion, character, and thought that constitute the matter of his
        invention." Any analysis of plot must therefore include all
        three of the elements or causes of which the plot is the syn-
        thesis. Crane sees the formal principle that makes the sys-
        tem work--that constitutes the "working or power" of Tom
        Jones--as the comic form of the novel.

1105   "The Plot of Tom Jones." Jour. of General Education 4
        (1950): 112-130. Rpt. in [1088], pp. 844-869; [1092], pp.
        68-93; [53], pp. 92-130.

        An early version of above article.

1106   DeBLOIS, PETER.
        "Ulysses at Upton: A Consideration of the Comic Effect of
        Fielding's Mock-Heroic Style in Tom Jones." Thoth 11, no.
        2 (1972): 3-8.

        Argues that the more subtle and comic effect may be found
        in the reader's capacity to laugh at Language itself, because
        it is exhilarating to hear it in "deliciously foreign contexts,"
        such as in the "wine and blood-spattered fields of the rhetori-
        cal Inn at Upton."

1107   EHRENPREIS, IRVIN.
        Fielding: Tom Jones (Studies in English Literature, No. 23).
        London: Edward Arnold, 1964.

        A brief but perceptive and critically acute introduction to
        Tom Jones, emphasizing such topics as "Story," "Doctrine,"
        "Meaning and Form," and "Comedy."

1108   EK, GRETE.
        "Glory, Jest, and Riddle: The Masque of Tom Jones in Lon-
        don. " ES 60 (1979): 148-158.

            Analyzes problems relating to the presentation of character
        within a narrative structure, not as general issues, but as a
        subject arising from one specific textual problem: the per-
        formance of Tom in the first half of the London narrative.
        Two interlocking narratives, which end at the same point
        (XV, viii and ix), present Tom in morally incompatible roles,
        as reprobate and champion of virtue respectively.   The per-
        formances possess a "referential dimension" given by Tom,
        based on the thesis that they are heroic poses with an inter-
        nal structure deriving from an archetype (Hercules).   Also,
        the character/mask is seen as a "crossroads" of technical
        and thematic interests.

1109   EMPSON, WILLIAM.
        "Tom Jones. " KR 20 (1958): 217-249.   Rpt. in [1088], pp.
        869-893; [1102], pp. 139-172; [1092], pp. 33-55; [898], pp.
        123-145.

            Defends Fielding against triviality and asserts that he "set
        out to preach a doctrine ... and said so, a high-minded
        though perhaps abstruse one": the secret message, accord-
        ing to Empson, relates to the doctrine of mutuality of im-
        pulse: "If good by nature, you can imagine other people's
        feelings so directly that you have an impulse to act on them
        as if they were your own; and this is the source of your
        greatest pleasures as well as of your only genuinely unselfish
        actions. " Shows how Fielding uses "double irony" to convey
        his moral doctrine, and examines the structure of ethical
        thought in Tom Jones.   Through the use of double irony,
        Fielding shows various codes of morals in operation without
        explicitly judging between them.

1110   FOLKENFLIK, ROBERT.
        "Tom Jones, the Gypsies, and the Masquerade. " UTQ 44
        (1975): 224-237.

            Shows how the contrast between the gypsy episode, in the
        last book of the road sequence, and the masquerade episode,
        in the first book of the city sequence, "sums up and sym-
        bolizes what the novel has been telling us throughout. " Con-
        cludes that "In terms of the plot, the gypsy episode may seem
        to be a digression; in terms of the knowledge which Tom ...
        must have at the conclusion of the novel, it is necessary. "

1111   GOLDKNOPF, DAVID.
        "The Failure of Plot in Tom Jones. " Criticism 11 (1969):

262-274. Rpt. with revisions in The Life of the Novel (Chicago: Univ. Chicago Press, 1972), pp. 125-142; in [1088], pp. 792-804.

Argues that the plot of Tom Jones is inadequate to support the embellishments of authorial commentary because it is not "inspirited by symbolism or fortified by sociological insight"; the perfect plot is not enough, for it offers by itself very little human significance.

1112   GREENE, J. LEE.
"Fielding's Gypsy Episode and Sancho Panza's Governorship." SAB 39, No. 2 (1974): 117-121.

Suggests that part of Fielding's purpose in the gypsy episode is to examine his own political ideals and part to employ his general technique of contrasts in order to emphasize some of the novel's major motifs; and concludes that "by implicitly forcing the reader to reconsider the justice and deliberation of Allworthy's judgments, the gypsy episode stresses not merely the fallibility of human nature, but also its potential for achieving right reason nobility regardless of social or political dress."

1113   GUTHRIE, WILLIAM B.
"The Comic Celebrant of Life in Tom Jones." TSL 19 (1974) 91-105.

Argues that "Fielding's satire and his moral intent in Tom Jones are controlled by his comic spirit which expresses an affirmation of the life-force." The main purpose of the novel, therefore, is not to teach Tom prudence or to punish him; it is to celebrate humanity and affirm the life-spirit.

1114   HAHN, H. GEORGE.
"Main Lines of Criticism of Fielding's Tom Jones, 1900-1978." BSM 10 (1980): 8-35.

Surveys the criticism of Tom Jones topically: " ... design (including work on the digressions), the narrator and narrative technique, characterization, and irony and language." Sees the trend in contemporary work to be more interpretative study than research, taking "a linear view of Fielding, the view of the historian but with the emphasis of the critic." Recent books are primarily contextual studies refusing to separate Fielding from his times, and they see in Fielding a tension--between teaching and entertaining, between the "law" of satire and the "justice" of the novel, between the primacy of action and that of narration, and between the demands of Fielding's times and the demands of his art. Recent criticism, however, does not assail "the perfect design" of the plot.

1115   HARRISON, BERNARD.
       Henry Fielding's Tom Jones: The Novelist as Moral Philoso-
       pher.   London: Sussex Univ. Press, 1975.

       A defense of Fielding against the charge that he is philo-
       sophically naïve and simple-minded, that he blurred the dis-
       tinction between the will and the passions, between principle
       and impulse; argues that "[i]f to know what a man is is to know
       what he wants--what he takes pleasure in--then it is no good
       allowing him, as Richardson does Pamela, to indulge in puta-
       tively self-revelatory monologue.... there is such a thing as
       self-deceit ... men edit their consciousness in order to re-
       main ignorant of their real goals.   What a man wants shows
       in what he does and what he says and more especially ... in
       the tension between what he says and the circumstances in
       which he says it.   That is why the action of Fielding's novel
       takes place in the public world--in the spaces between men--
       and not in the private inner world of consciousness."

1116   HATFIELD, GLENN W.
       "The Serpent and the Dove: Fielding's Irony and the Pru-
       dence Theme of Tom Jones."   MP 65 (1967):   17-32.   Rpt.
       in [936], pp. 179-196.

       Discusses Fielding's attempt in Tom Jones to "reclaim
       the 'proper and original' moral sense of 'prudence.'"   Where-
       as Tom and the other characters in the novel suffer from
       "imprudence," Sophia functions as a model of "true prudence."
       Fielding's irony does not illuminate the dangers of "prudence,"
       as many critics have noted, but rather it is an attempt to
       reclaim the word from the corruptions of language.

1117   HERMAN, GEORGE.
       "Fielding Defends Allworthy."   Iowa English Yearbook 10
       (1965):   64-70.

       Fielding's artistic problem, in the portrayal of Allworthy,
       is how to interest us in a morally good man who makes ser-
       ious errors of judgment, yet whom we are not led to blame
       for defects of character and intelligence.   To solve that prob-
       lem Fielding devotes great effort to protecting Allworthy from
       our criticism.

1118   HILLES, FREDERICK W.
       "Art and Artifice in Tom Jones."   In [36], pp. 91-110; rpt.
       in [1088], pp. 916-932.

       Sees the form or design of Tom Jones as shaped like a
       Palladian mansion; the plan reflects the same mathematical
       exactitude as John Wood's plan for Prior Park, the home of
       Fielding's patron, Ralph Allen.

1119   HOOKER, EDWARD N.
       "Humour in the Age of Pope." HLQ 11 (1948): 361-385.

       Records the changes in the concept of humor during the
       first half of the century, showing how it took form in Tris-
       tram Shandy and Tom Jones. Addresses the problem of Tom
       Jones himself, who often is thought of as outside the comic
       scope of the novel and therefore destructive of its unity of
       tone; but the author suggests that Fielding probably viewed
       him as a humorist whose strong passions often lead him into
       difficulties that provoke our laughter. Tom is a passionate
       individualist.

1120   HUTCHENS, ELEANOR N.
       "O Attic Shape! The Cornering of Square." In [32], pp. 37-
       44.

       Analyzes the geometry of Tom Jones: the middle of Molly's
       room, to which Tom propels Square when the philosopher is
       discovered crouching "among other female Utensils," is the
       "only place allowing the full extension of humanity" and a
       "natural freedom from the systems man constructs to trap
       and define goodness, then uses to give plausible housing to
       badness." The geometry of wrong possesses a linear per-
       fection that is incessantly mocked in Tom Jones, as in the
       "black hypocrisy of prudent Blifil"; the good man possesses
       a natural, asymmetrical character; Allworthy in his Gothic
       house is beyond geometry.

1121   Irony in Tom Jones. Birmingham: Univ. Alabama Press,
       1965.

       A study of verbal irony in Tom Jones of an oblique kind:
       "not the well-recognized device of using a word to signify its
       direct opposite, but the subtler one of making the literal
       meaning fit the context while the connotative significance clashes
       with it." Provides a new and inclusive definition of irony as
       the "sport of bringing about a conclusion by indicating its op-
       posite." Incorporates [1122] and [1123].

1122   "Verbal Irony in Tom Jones." PMLA 77 (1962): 46-50.
       Incorporated into [1121], Chapters 4 and 6.

       A detailed analysis of the different types of irony to show
       that the realism, satire, and plot of Tom Jones "keep their
       unified brilliance through being governed by an ironic style
       that forms as important a contribution to the English novel
       as any Fielding made."

1123   " 'Prudence' in Tom Jones: A Study of Connotative Irony."
        PQ 39 (1960): 496-507. Rpt. in [1121], pp. 101-118.

        An analysis of Fielding's unfavorable use of "prudence,"
        which Hutchens calls "connotative irony," shows that "the
        two prudence themes, positive and negative, in Tom Jones
        may be regarded ... as one theme given dual treatment."
        The desirability of prudence, Fielding "teaches directly, by
        straightforward exposition and illustration; its dangers and
        limitations he illuminates obliquely through connotative irony."

1124   IYENGAR, K. R. SRINIVASA.
        "Fielding's Tom Jones." Jour. of the Univ. of Bombay 8
        (1939): 29-44.

        Discusses the special merits of the novel as well as its
        alleged defects; emphasizes Fielding's characterization, and
        suggests that Tom Jones is essentially a character novel.

1125   JOHNSON, MAURICE.
        "The Device of Sophia's Muff in Tom Jones." MLN 74 (1959):
        685-690. Rpt. and revised in [947], pp. 129-137.

        Traces Fielding's use of the muff as a symbol of love
        between Sophia and Tom, and shows how it is "vital in a
        series of crucial actions, as a minute wheel that sets the
        great wheels of the novel in motion."

1126   KAPLAN, FRED.
        "Fielding's Novel About Novels: The 'Prefaces' and the 'Plot'
        of Tom Jones." SEL 13 (1973): 535-549.

        An analysis of the "prefaces" shows how they are an in-
        tegral part of the novel, and how "they present a developed
        sequence of ideas on the nature of art and the relationship
        between art, artist, and audience," always furthering the
        progression of the plot.

1127   KEARNEY, ANTHONY.
        "Tom Jones and the Forty-Five." ArielE 4, ii (1973): 68-
        78.

        Sees Tom Jones as the comic working out of the anxieties
        that disturbed Fielding between 1745 and 1749; argues that he
        had the rebellion very much in the forefront of his mind as
        he wrote, and that after Tom's expulsion from Paradise Hall
        it becomes one of the main themes.

1128   KNIGHT, CHARLES A.
        "Tom Jones: The Meaning of the 'Main Design.'"   Genre 12
        (1979):   379-399.

        Argues that Tom Jones consists of a multiplicity of themes
        and patterns that ought not to be reduced to simplistic read-
        ings: " ... readings of Tom Jones as a providential or cos-
        mic order comically rendered tend to reduce the complex
        clusters of meaning implicit in the main design to a single
        enveloping meaning...."   The author shows how Fielding es-
        tablishes and makes convincing a multiplicity of meanings
        without vagueness or contradiction.   The novel's rococo rich-
        ness of meaning is illustrated by a specific analysis of the
        "interchangeability" inherent in the general theme of politics.

1129   "Multiple Structures and the Unity of Tom Jones."   Criticism
        14 (1972):   227-242.

        Examines the novel's coherence, particularly in Books VII
        through XII, by developing the "notion of multiple structures
        in the arrangement of events," and identifies four distinguish-
        able patterns: 1) a linear pattern of causal sequence, 2) a
        non-linear pattern of causation, 3) a symmetrical pattern of
        narration, and 4) a symmetrical pattern of corresponding
        events.

1130   LAVIN, HENRY ST. C.
        "Rhetoric and Realism in Tom Jones."   Univ. Rev. 32 (1965)
        19-25.

        "The need to make ... [his] characters either comic or
        exemplary, or at once both, has led Fielding to sacrifice cer-
        tain elements of realism to his purposes."   The article ex-
        amines one aspect of this sacrifice: diction and rhetoric, as
        exemplified by three main characters, Allworthy, Tom, and
        Sophia, concluding that their speech is largely unrealistic.

1131   LEAVIS, F. R.
        "Tom Jones and 'The Great Tradition': A Negative View."
        In [1092], pp. 16-18.   From The Great Tradition: George
        Eliot, Henry James, Joseph Conrad (London: Chatto & Win-
        dus, 1948; New York: New York Univ. Press, 1963), pp.
        2-4.

        The classic statement against Fielding, that "he hasn't the
        kind of classical distinction we are ... invited to credit him
        with.   He is important ... because he leads to Jane Austen,
        to appreciate whose distinction is to feel that life isn't long
        enough to permit of one's giving much time to Fielding...."
        Denigrates the perfect plot of Tom Jones: "There can't be

subtlety of organization without richer matter to organize,
and subtler interests, than Fielding has to offer. "

1132   LOCKWOOD, THOMAS.
        "Matter and Reflection in Tom Jones. "   ELH 45 (1978):   226-
        235.

        Abandoning efforts to find fictional unity as the special
        quality of Tom Jones, the author suggests that the novel's
        unique character lies in the relationship between its matter
        and its reflection; the immediate model, therefore, for Field-
        ing's "talkative" book is the eighteenth-century periodical es-
        say. Fielding revitalizes the essayist's role within a new
        kind of essay, "organized by means of a long and complicated
        story, an imaginary history, but communicated through the
        presence of an author who retains the essayist's privilege of
        talking freely in his own person. " The story material has
        almost no independent existence, since the "matter," absorbed
        and transformed, serves largely as subject matter for "re-
        flection. "

1133   LOOMIS, ROGER S.
        "Tom Jones and Tom-mania. "   SR 27 (1919):   478-495.

        Discusses some of Fielding's failures in characterization
        and plot, and some of the medieval aspects of his attitude
        toward women, yet concludes that in many of his ideas he
        was a reformer and praises Tom Jones as a foreshadowing
        of the naturalistic novel.

1134   LYNCH, JAMES J.
        "Structural Techniques in Tom Jones.   ZAA 7 (1959):   5-16.
        Rpt. in Stil und Formprobleme in der Literatur, ed. Paul
        Böckmann. Vorträge des VII. Kongresses der Internationalen
        Vereinigung für Moderne Sprachen und Literaturen in Heidel-
        burg. (Heidelburg: Carl Winter, 1959), pp. 238-243.

        Argues that Fielding employs two kinds of structural tech-
        niques to achieve formal organization: first, he uses plot
        division, temporal and spatial verisimilitude, and parallelism
        to control the plot: they appear continuously throughout the
        narrative; second, he uses such devices as intended reappear-
        ances, the undisclosed motive, and the "blurred sequence" to
        manage small details: they appear intermittently.

1135   McCULLOUGH, BRUCE.
        "The Novel of Manners--Henry Fielding: Tom Jones. " In
        [133], pp. 42-57.

Conventionally suggests that Tom Jones reveals the tendency of the age to think in abstractions by emphasizing a general picture of mankind rather than a study of individual lives; the characters are types, with typical reactions: Tom becomes a "ward, a pupil, a companion, a young man on the highroad. He is, in fact, eager and impulsive youth plunging forward with rash impetuosity into the perils of life"; and Fielding's main purpose is not the development of character but the depiction of manners, so that his chief concern is with what his characters are, not with what they do. Also discusses the famous plot of Tom Jones.

1136   McKENZIE, ALAN T.
        "The Processes of Discovery in Tom Jones." DR 54 (1974-75): 720-740.

        Analyzes the various types of discovery in Tom Jones: "Fielding's characters, the naïve and the sagacious, make too few or too many discoveries. The entanglements multiply until Providence lends a hand."

1137   McKILLOP, A. D.
        "Some Recent Views of Tom Jones." CE 21 (1959): 17-22.

        "A brief survey, with summarizing and comparative comment" on works by Booth, Crane, McKillop, Sherburn, Van Ghent, and Watt and their attempts "to reduce the importance of the epic formula for Fielding's work."

1138   McNAMARA, SUSAN P.
        "Mirrors of Fiction Within Tom Jones: The Paradox of Self-Reference." ECS 12 (1979): 372-390.

        Concerned with the nature of the reality depicted in Tom Jones, suggesting that the things which persuade us of the reality of Fielding's characters are, paradoxically, their fictions; storytelling and fiction-making are an essential part of the world of the novel. Tom Jones emphasizes that the reality of things and fiction are not identifiably separate and contrasting elements, that fictions are not framed off from reality. Tom Jones is "a world composed of multiple, mirroring layers of fiction; a self-enclosed, paradoxical structure, this world illuminates not only the relation of fiction and reality but also Fielding's deepest understanding of the metaphor of the glass to which he repeatedly likens his fiction."

1139   MAFUD HAYE, HILDA.
        "Sátira e ironía Cómica en Tom Jones." NRP 6 (1977): 11-23.

1140   MANDEL, JEROME.
        "The Man of the Hill and Mrs. Fitzpatrick: Character and
        Narrative Technique in Tom Jones." PLL 5 (1969): 26-38.

        Examines "Fielding's narrative techniques in the two tales,
        especially to the extent that they reveal the character of the
        speaker, and [shows] how those narrative techniques parody
        aspects of Fielding's own." Also considers the similarities
        of the two tales and their connection with the rest of the novel.

1141   MERRETT, ROBERT JAMES.
        "Empiricism and Judgement in Fielding's Tom Jones." ArielE
        11, iii (1980): 3-21.

        Fielding introduced empirical ideas, derived from his re-
        action to John Locke, into his narrative commentary for ser-
        ious and comic purposes because he wanted the reader to
        learn from the novel. "The entertaining ways in which he
        connects empiricism and judgment show that not only was he
        aware of the dangers of being didactic but also his doctrine
        of prudence depends upon the extent to which empirical ideas
        should inform literature and life."

1142   MILLER, HENRY KNIGHT.
        Henry Fielding's TOM JONES and the Romance Tradition.
        (ELS 6) Victoria, Canada: Univ. Victoria Press, 1976.

        Argues that "Tom Jones is a comic Romance, a comic
        Epic in prose, unique and incomparable, and that it is thor-
        oughly in the epic-romance tradition. Its affinities are with
        Ariosto and Cervantes, Amadis de Gaule and Sidney's Ar-
        cadia...." Discusses the novel's structure, setting, char-
        acter, theme, and style in relation to the romance tradition.
        Because Fielding thought of Tom Jones as a romance, he
        used "the vast composite 'pool' of narrative possibilities, the
        rich fund of motifs, characters, episodes, themes, and struc-
        tural forms that the Romance tradition--epic, prose fiction,
        and verse narrative--offered."

1143   "The 'Digressive' Tales in Fielding's Tom Jones and the Per-
        spective of Romance." PQ 54 (1975): 258-274.

        Discusses the dimensions which the tale of the Man of the
        Hill and Mrs. Fitzpatrick's story gain from the perspective
        of the romance tradition. The thematic involvement and
        counterpoint of these two digressions are "superb instances
        of Fielding's power ... to generate complex and far-reaching
        moral drama as well as delicious laughter from the play and
        tension between the contingent and the ultimate, the disordered
        and the ordered, the lustful and the loving, 'prudence' and

<u>prudentia</u>, experience and innocence, the merely 'actual' and
the certainly 'real.' "

1144   "The Voices of Henry Fielding: Style in <u>Tom Jones.</u>" In
[42], pp. 262-288.

Concerned with the problem of "Fielding" as a character
in his own romance, and not as a persona but as the historical person, Henry Fielding; argues that "what he narrates ...
can be conceived under the aspect of two quite different ...
modes: as a statement or predication made by the historical
Henry Fielding, which is then ... capable of being construed
as part of his intellectual biography; but also as a calculated
element of a total structure of fictive predications, assertions,
and representations." Specific purpose is to consider some
of the voices that Fielding the narrator-character uses to
convey "force and vivacity" to his comic fiction and to embody
meaning through language and style.

1145   "Some Functions of Rhetoric in <u>Tom Jones.</u>" <u>PQ</u> 45 (1966):
209-235.

A discussion of the composition of <u>Tom Jones</u> from a rhetorical strandpoint. "In the very habits, mannerisms, devices, or strategies which came naturally to Fielding ... in
the habits of style that mirrored, and were part of, his fictional cosmos, he invited the same kind of response from
his reader that larger and more patent structural principles,
involving the play between a universal order and a contingent
order, would also ask."

1146   MILLER, SUSAN.
"Eighteenth-Century Play and the Game of <u>Tom Jones.</u>" In
[32], pp. 83-93.

Discusses the importance of play in the early eighteenth
century, especially its relevance for understanding the role
of play in <u>Tom Jones</u>: plot, characters, setting, and narrative are all influenced by actual or metaphoric games. Tom
is an archetypal quest hero who must win through to a knowledge of his identity and to possession of Sophia, who is the
prize of wisdom. Fielding uses metaphoric games as a means
of describing Tom's growth from the status of a foundling to
that of a responsible member of the game-playing gentry.
When Tom finally wins Sophia's hand, he has in effect agreed
to stop playing games (dalliance with Molly, Mrs. Waters,
and Lady Bellaston) and to enter adult life.

1147   MURRAY, PETER B.

"Summer, Winter, Spring, and Autumn in Tom Jones." MLN
76 (1961): 324-326.

A brief analysis of seasonal symbolism through the surnames and imagery of the novel. The pattern of relationships between characters is based on their association with
Nature's seasons.

1148   PALMER, E. TAIWO.
        "Fielding's Tom Jones Reconsidered." English 20 (1971):
        45-50.

As compared to Joseph Andrews, Tom Jones reflects a
new sense of danger and insecurity, with the result that Fielding seeks to demonstrate his theme by using a basic Christian myth: "He takes the reader to the world of Genesis or
of Milton's Paradise Lost, with its dominant themes of temptation and fall, repentance, redemption, and eventual reha-
bilitation." Fielding therefore "holds out the Christian hope
of pardon and of eventual victory over the forces of evil.
The novel is thus a triumphant affirmation of man's inherent
goodness and his potential for benevolence and virtue...."

1149   "Irony in 'Tom Jones.'" MLR 66 (1971): 497-510.

A detailed analysis of various passages in Tom Jones to
illustrate the tremendous variety of Fielding's irony and its
effectiveness. Shows how "Fielding uses the technique of
double irony to manipulate the reader's responses to his hero,"
and that his skillful use of irony is crucial to the novel.

1150   PARK, WILLIAM.
        "Ironist and Moralist: The Two Readers of Tom Jones."
        Enl. E. 5, iii/iv (1974): 43-48; enlarged and rpt. in SECC
        8 (1979): 233-242.

Considers the relationship between the plot of Tom Jones
and a providential design, and argues that the plot is one
double irony: "Obviously Fielding wanted it both ways. He
did indeed wish to be a natural historian, but he also believed
in Providence. Double irony was one of his means of reconciling wish and belief." As narrator, Fielding frequently appears to be appealing directly to the realist and laughing at
the moralist--this is the first irony; but then, as order and
happiness begin to emerge out of a random world, as Tom's
fortunes are reversed, the comic action contradicts this particular viewpoint, and reveals the second irony, that Fortune
is Providence improperly understood: the realist who believed that human affairs are governed by chance and Fortune
is revealed to be as "literal-minded" as his moralistic counterpart.

1151   "Tom and Oedipus." HSL 7 (1975): 207-215.

Tom is a comic Oedipus, accused of desiring the death
of his "father" Allworthy and imprisoned for murdering Mr.
Fitzpatrick, whose "wife" is his alleged mother. Incest helps
Tom to attain "prudence" and "wisdom": when Tom, at his
lowest point in the novel, thinks he has committed incest, he
achieves his greatest wisdom.

1152   PARKER, A. A.
"Fielding and the Structure of Don Quixote." Bull. Hispanic
Std. 33 (1956): 1-16.

Deals with the dissimilarity of technique between Don
Quixote and Tom Jones and argues that Don Quixote has a
much more "closely-knit structure" giving the novel an artistic whole that Tom Jones does not have because of its "episodic regularity."

1153   PAULSON, RONALD.
"Fielding in Tom Jones: The Historian, the Poet, and the
Mythologist." In [28], pp. 175-187.

Emphasizes the similarity of interests, the one historical
and the other literary, between The Jacobite's Journal and
Tom Jones; false history is seen as the subject of both works,
and the narrator of Tom Jones functions as a historian who
seeks to separate the true from the false. Paulson considers
the effect of the Abbé Banier's Mythology and Fables of the
Ancients on Fielding, especially the relationship between Banier's euhemerism and the travesty mode Fielding had practiced in the 1730s, and suggests that Banier provided him
with the distinction between poet, historian, and mythologist.

1154   POWERS, LYALL H.
"Tom Jones and Jacob de la Vallée." PMASAL 47 (1962):
659-667. Rpt. in [1088], pp. 896-904.

A comparison of Marivaux's Le Paysan parvenu (1735) and
Tom Jones; one similarity emphasized is the humanistic ethic
by which both authors handle the question of good and evil
as it affects their heroes: "Fielding's benevolent treatment
of Tom Jones is much like Marivaux's conception of Jacob
as an honnête homme."

1155   PRESTON, JOHN.
"Tom Jones and the 'Pursuit of True Judgment.'" ELH 33
(1966): 315-326. Revised and rpt. in [151], pp. 114-132.

Argues that Tom Jones "is about judgment, and the understanding necessary for good judgment," and that "the moral
sense is located, in the analysis and evaluation of diverse
judgments." Examines Tom's character and his moral sense
and shows how Fielding uses Tom to set an example of what
is right for the other characters.

1156   "Plot as Irony: The Reader's Role in Tom Jones." ELH
        35 (1968): 365-380. Rev. and rpt. in [151], pp. 94-113;
        rpt. in [1088], pp. 804-817; [1102], pp. 243-262.

        Examines the two "faces" of the plot--one in which the
        plot is like life and the reader does not know what is ahead
        of him, and the other, one in which, on second reading, the
        reader knows all the answers--and concludes that it is "this
        dual response which secures the ironic structure of the plot."
        Fielding, by means of the plot, has been able "to create a
        reader wise enough to create the book he reads." The plot,
        furthermore, is seen less as an assertion of Augustan ration-
        ality than a recognition of the confusion and irrationality in-
        herent in life: "It is in fact a vehicle for what is self-con-
        tradictory, what is emotionally as well as intellectually con-
        fusing in human experience."

1157   PRICE, JOHN VALDIMIR.
        "Sex and the Foundling Boy: The Problem in Tom Jones."
        REL 8, No. 4 (1967): 42-52.

        Argues that Tom's sexual behavior is perfectly consistent
        with Fielding's artistry in the novel, and examines this be-
        havior "in light of its ironic context and Fielding's choice of
        language for making moral observations."

1158   RAWSON, C. J.
        "Professor Empson's Tom Jones." N&Q, N.S. 6 (1959):
        400-404. Rpt. in [1102], pp. 173-181.

        Argues that Empson's essay, on the matter of Tom's sex-
        ual morals, suffers from a "misleading supererogation of
        critical method," that it mistakenly suggests that the "main
        doctrinal points are made by means of an essentially evasive
        irony rather than by what is often an emphatic explicitness."

1159   ROSCOE, ADRIAN A.
        "Fielding and the Problem of Allworthy." TSLL 7 (1965):
        169-172.

        Although Allworthy often seems too virtuous and morally
        superhuman, Fielding always reduces the squire's apparent

moral perfection to human proportions, because Allworthy
and his mistakes are central to the theme that the social
world and its legal system are defective.

1160   RØSTVIG, MAREN-SOFIE.
"Tom Jones and the Choice of Hercules." In Fair Forms:
Essays in English Literature from Spenser to Jane Austen,
ed. Maren-Sofie Røstvig (Totowa, N. J.: Rowman & Littlefield, 1975), pp. 147-177.

Tom Jones is an eighteenth-century version of the Choice
of Hercules, which Fielding derived to a large extent from
Shaftesbury's and Hogarth's treatment of the theme. At the
end of the novel Tom has chosen Sophia's higher beauty, the
sincere love of which guarantees his faithful adherence to the
path of virtue: " ... whoever separates virtue from pleasure
in this life does so because the humanist version of the Choice
of Hercules has ceased to carry conviction. Fielding seems
... to have grasped the true inwardness of this choice and
to have succeeded in conveying it to his readers through a
mode of writing indebted to the joco-serious tradition so popular in the Renaissance."

1161   RUTHVEN, K. K.
"Fielding, Square, and the Fitness of Things." ECS 5 (1971):
243-255.

Examines ways in which Tom Jones reaches "beyond the
banalities of Christian benevolism," especially in the presentation of the philosopher Square and his relationship to the
"anti-deistical polemics" of Samuel Clarke.

1162   SCHNEIDER, DANIEL J.
"Sources of Comic Pleasure in Tom Jones." Conn. Rev. 1
(1967): 51-65.

Analyzes several sources of comic pleasures in Tom Jones
as "an embodiment of fundamental life-affirming and life-
denying impulses in our natures." Offers a new definition
of comedy which seems implicit in Tom Jones.

1163   SCHONHORN, MANUEL.
"Heroic Allusion in Tom Jones: Hamlet and the Temptations
of Jesus." Studies in the Novel 6 (1974): 218-227.

When Tom watches the performance of Hamlet in London,
the reader is expected to realize that Tom embodies Hamlet's
most important quality for the eighteenth century: filial piety.
Tom also represents Jesus, in his forty days in the wilder-

ness away from Paradise Hall and in his three temptations
with Molly, Jenny, and Lady Bellaston.

1164   "Fielding's Digressive-Parodic Artistry: <u>Tom Jones</u> and The
        Man of the Hill." <u>TSLL</u> 10 (1968): 207-<u>214</u>.

   Argues in defense of the novel's artistic unity that, though
the Man of the Hill's career is similar to Tom's, it obviously
diverges from the subsequent development of Fielding's good-
natured hero; and that the "confrontation between the Old Man
of the Hill and young Tom at this mid-point in the novel parallels, though in parodic form, a father-son sequence at the
pivotal center" of Virgil's <u>Aeneid</u>.

1165   SHESGREEN, SEAN.
        "The Moral Function of Thwackum, Square, and Allworthy."
        <u>Studies in the Novel</u> 2 (1970): 159-167.

   Finds the origin and significance of these characters in the
ethical thought of Fielding himself, especially in "Essay on
the Knowledge of the Characters of Men." From the latter
Fielding defines benevolence according to three possible reasons likely to motivate virtuous conduct: 1) sympathy, 2) philosophic love of virtue, and 3) inducements of religion; of the
three motives, sympathy alone "is the only true fountainhead
of benevolence." Using that definition as a guide, Fielding
dramatically presents the three motivations in the three figures
of Thwackum, Square, and Allworthy: "Each figure is a dramatization or an incarnation of one of the motives...."

1166   SOLOMON, STANLEY J.
        "Fielding's Presentational Mode in <u>Tom Jones</u>." <u>CEA</u> 31,
        No. 4 (1969): 12-13.

   Fielding faced a perplexing technical problem in developing
the character of Tom: how was he to depict convincingly the
inner life of a character in a comic novel told from an external point of view? Concludes that "[e]ven without access
to the interior monologue and other techniques of the modern
novel which directly present man's inner life, Fielding was
able to develop a presentational mode employing an indirect
method of suggesting character psychology.... Fielding was
able to capture the vitality of Tom's inner life from the external disparity between what the hero says and what he does."

1167   STITZEL, JUDITH G.
        "Blifil and Henry Fielding's Conception of Evil." <u>W. Va.</u>
        <u>Univ. Phil. Papers</u> 17 (1970): 16-24.

Analyzes Blifil's character and the nature of the evil that
he displays, and concludes that the "unnatural cohabitation of
temperate appetites and perverse attraction in Blifil's breast
is a sign of a more comprehensive unnaturalness. It is a
sign of a pervasive evil which operates at the root of life."

1168   STUMPF, THOMAS A.
       "Tom Jones from the Outside." In The Classic British Novel,
       eds. Howard M. Harper, Jr. and Charles Edge (Athens, Ga.:
       Univ. Georgia Press, 1972), pp. 3-21.

       Analyzes Fielding's "anti-psychologism," his reluctance to
       probe into the motives and to enter into the minds of his
       characters; he adheres to that "kind of realism that places
       true knowledge in the proper appraisal of the objects outside
       us rather than in a delicate ... self-consciousness."

1169   TILLYARD, E. M. W.
       "Tom Jones." In The Epic Strain in the English Novel (Lon-
       don: Chatto & Windus, 1958), pp. 51-58.

       Argues that Tom Jones fails of the epic effect because it
       lacks two of the three epic qualities that define the genre:
       it does not possess a "sustained intensity" and a "heroic im-
       pression" but does display a "communal or choric quality" in
       the sense that it "is the England of the time." Sees Tom as
       the "knight-errant of romance and fairy-tale who wins his
       love after banishment, many adventures, and much misunder-
       standing."

1170   VAN GHENT, DOROTHY.
       "On Tom Jones." In The English Novel: Form and Function
       (New York: Rinehart, 1953), pp. 65-81; rpt. Harper Torch-
       book, 1961.

       Looks at Tom Jones from the standpoint of " ... why in-
       tricate plot should have such importance, as an element of
       structure ... [and] what significance, what meaningful char-
       acter, is given to the Tom Jones world by its intricacy of
       action." Sees "Tom Jones as a complex architectural figure,
       a Palladian palace ... immensely variegated ... elegant and
       suavely intelligent in its details...." Relates the design of
       the novel to the comic themes of "Nature" and "Fortune."

1171   VOPAT, JAMES B.
       "Narrative Technique in Tom Jones: The Balance of Art and
       Nature." JNT 4 (1974): 144-154.

       Argues that Paradise Hall and its landscape represents as-

pects of the theme of control and that the function of art is
to limit nature so that it is meaningful; therefore, "Fielding's
basic narrative strategy ... is to restate the dimensions of
Paradise Hall both in terms of Tom's adventures and in terms
of the actual form of the novel. Specifically, the pattern of
Tom Jones' adventures reveals the necessity of applying artful restrictions to natural impulses...."

1172   WARREN, LELAND E.
        "Fielding's Problem and Ours: Allworthy and Authority in
        Tom Jones. " ELWIU 5 (1978): 15-25.

        "By examining Allworthy's role in the novel and Fielding's
        attitude toward [him], we can see that the work is not only
        about the impossibility of making certain judgment; it is also
        about the common need to make and act upon judgments even
        when the acts conflict with one's best feelings and endanger
        the justice one holds as a primary ideal. " As an authority
        figure who in trying to do the best always brings about the
        worst, Allworthy endures failures which "show that no human
        system can do justice to the complexity of human affairs and
        that the best of systems will distort and even subvert the
        ideal vision of its makers. " Worthy men must, however,
        support that system.

1173   WATT, IAN.
        "Fielding as Novelist: Tom Jones. " In [183], pp. 260-289.
        Rpt. in [898], pp. 98-122; sections ii and iv in [1092], pp.
        19-32.

        Tom Jones and Clarissa are sufficiently similar in theme
        to provide parallel scenes which afford a concrete illustration
        of the differences in method between Fielding and Richardson:
        Fielding's method, for example, is essentially comic, where-
        as Richardson's method is intended to produce a "complete
        identification with the consciousness of Clarissa. " Considers
        also Fielding's handling of the plot in Tom Jones as it re-
        flects his social, moral, and literary outlook, and argues
        that there is "an absolute connection ... between the treat-
        ment of plot and of character. Plot has priority, and it is
        therefore plot which must contain the elements of complica-
        tion and development. " The importance of plot is in inverse
        proportion to that of character. Concludes that Fielding de-
        parts from the canons of formal realism, to such an extent,
        in fact, that his failure to convey moral significance through
        character and action alone emphasizes that his technique was
        unable to "supplement its realism of presentation with a real-
        ism of assessment. "

1174   WEISGERBER, JEAN

"Nouvelle lecture d'un livre ancien: L'Espace dans l'Historie de Tom Jones, enfant trouvé." CREL i (1975): 69-86.

Discusses the central image of the "home," with its implications of the important role of social gatherings, the middle position of Allworthy's house between "high" and "low," the rejection of solitude, separation, and confinement, and the superiority of country life to town life; and analyzes such "spatial polarities" as cold/warm and light/dark to reveal "to what extent the narrator bends the logic of events to an intellectual order."

1175   WESS, ROBERT V.
"The Probable and the Marvelous in Tom Jones." MP 68 (1970): 32-45.

Examines the rules for probability which Fielding followed in Tom Jones and the connections between incidents to show that "the incidents, the characters involved in the incidents, and the moral thought reflected in the actions of the characters are all synthesized into one beautifully self-contained whole that fulfills the reader's hopes in a marvelous and most memorable way."

See also: 358, 787, 898, 901, 902, 903, 904, 911, 912, 914, 917, 918, 920, 923, 928, 929, 930, 934, 938, 941, 948, 949, 953, 954, 957, 961, 977, 981, 986, 997, 999, 1047, 1050, 1081, 1087, 1194, 1559, 2588, 2705, 2733, 2744, 2746, 2903, 3006

Amelia

1176   AMORY, HUGH.
"Magistrate or Censor? The Problem of Authority in Fielding's Later Writings." SEL 12 (1972): 503-518.

Argues that Dr. Harrison in Amelia is a fictive censor and a spokesman for Fielding's social ideals. Because a clergyman's function is close to that of a censor, Dr. Harrison can propose more radical solutions to social abuses than could Fielding in his role as a magistrate: "That society refuses to recognize either the 'invisible and incorporeal' nature of Harrison's authority ... or the utilitarian necessity for Fielding's 'palliatives' is a burlesque demonstration of the effects of luxury."

1177   BAKER, SHERIDAN.
"Fielding's Amelia and the Materials of Romance." PQ 41 (1962): 437-449.

The conflict between the romance elements in Amelia and realism lures Fielding into the pious self-deceptions of sentimentalism. Argues that, in spite of Fielding's desire to write a realistic novel, he could not break away from the old, improbable romantic framework.

1178   BATTESTIN, MARTIN C.
"The Problem of Amelia: Hume, Barrow, and the Conversion of Captain Booth." ELH 41 (1974): 613-648.

An attempt to answer two puzzling questions which Amelia poses by showing the influence on Fielding of Hume's Essays Concerning Human Understanding. The two questions are: what "prompted Fielding during the three years that separate Tom Jones from Amelia, to choose as a protagonist ... a man whose particular spiritual predicament would dramatize the clash of opposing philosophies within his society ... between scepticism and the new passional psychology on the one hand, and, on the other hand, the tradition of Christian humanism?"; What, during the same period, might have led him to modify so radically the form of comic narrative he had perfected in Tom Jones in favor of a darker, more sentimental mode?"

1179   BEVAN, C. H. K.
"The Unity of Fielding's Amelia." RMS 14 (1970): 90-110.

Seeks to demonstrate that the moral psychology of Mandeville is refuted and replaced by one more consistent with benevolist ideas; that Fielding has succeeded in organizing a union of moral vision and representational techniques; that much of Amelia's rhetorical force derives from the range of its conflicts; and, finally, that the partial failure of the novel as a work of art is caused by certain inconsistencies of technique and intention, but that Fielding has succeeded in stating and organically cohering the intentions referred to in his Dedication and the first chapter.

1180   BLOCH, TUVIA.
"Amelia and Booth's Doctrine of the Passions." SEL 13 (1973): 461-473.

Illustrates how Fielding uses Booth's doctrine of the passions in Amelia deriving from it "his emphases and strategies in character portrayal." He first brings out the good nature of the character and then follows with "the blameworthy or vicious behavior into which the character is impelled by overriding passion."

1181 "The Prosecution of the Maidservant in Amelia." ELN 6 (1969): 269-271.

Booth's justification for the prosecution of the servant, Betty, found at the end of Chapter V, Book XI, coincides with Fielding's view of punishment for criminals.

1182 EAVES, T. C. DUNCAN.
"Amelia and Clarissa." In [32], pp. 95-110.

Suggests that if Fielding wished to create a new Clarissa and to move his readers as effectively as Richardson had done, he failed: Amelia is too perfect, and her trials are external rather than internal, so that the reader never enters her mind as he does that of Clarissa. Only once, when she doubts the faithfulness of Booth, does she experience any internal conflict. Amelia's "dismal scenes" are never "touching" because Fielding never permits the reader to enter the minds of his characters, and they tend to be related too objectively and too briefly, without sufficient emotional intensity to engage the reader's involvement.

1183 FOLKENFLIK, ROBERT.
"Purpose and Narration in Fielding's Amelia." Novel 7 (1974): 168-174.

Discusses Fielding's allusions to Othello in the second half of Amelia to show how "these verbal and structural parallels form an allusive counterplot which suggests the tragic possibilities inherent in Fielding's comic plot."

1184 HAGSTRUM, JEAN H.
"Henry Fielding and 'Amelia.'" In [111], pp. 178-185.

Examines Fielding's "buoyant sexuality" and his hatred of hypocrisy, coyness, "socially generated hatred of the male sex as monsters, and all manner of similar sexual fears and hesitations ... the full-bodied ecstasies which his good characters are capable of feeling have something of robust sexual energy and adventuresome animality about them." Equally important in Fielding's attitude toward sex is a refining sensibility or tenderness, so that Tom Jones, for instance, illustrates the vigorous masculine and delicately feminine qualities of Fielding's hero. Amelia is a masterpiece of English sensibility, developing goodness against antithetical evil--love against strong social forces, healthy domestic love against "cancerous social evil." It develops the theme of love and lust, of faithful love and loyal marriage opposed to adulterous love, innocence opposed to guilt.

1185   HASSALL, ANTHONY J.
       "Fielding's Amelia: Dramatic and Authorial Narration. "
       Novel 5 (1972):   225-233.

       Argues that Amelia is a failure because Fielding unsuccess-
       fully mixes his "narrative methods" and reduces his authorial
       method to a point where it does not function as a unifying
       force.

1186   HUNTER, J. PAUL.
       "The Lesson of Amelia. " In [15], pp. 157-182.

       A defense of Amelia against conventional charges--its dull-
       ness, intricately contrived plot, sentimentality, lack of irony,
       moral simplicity, and lack of satiric focus--which emphasizes
       its similarities to the two earlier books.   Amelia differs from
       them in its didactic strategies, thereby ceasing to be "open-
       ended"--i. e. , allowing the reader to make his own moral de-
       cisions.

1187   KNIGHT, CHARLES A.
       "The Narrative Structure of Fielding's Amelia. "   ArielE 11,
       i (1980):   31-46.

       Discusses the narrative structure of the novel with its in-
       tervening narrator and discontinuity of movement to prove
       that Amelia is a successful novel and that its success is due
       to the structure which "is consonant with its overriding sa-
       tiric and ethical concerns. "   Fielding uses this "narrative
       approach and structure to develop a powerful analysis of the
       nature and effect of institutionalized evil in eighteenth-century
       society" and in so doing has written a novel "ranking almost
       with Clarissa in the intensity of its social and moral analysis. "

1188   LePAGE, PETER V.
       "The Prison and the Dark Beauty of Amelia. "   Criticism 9
       (1967):   337-354.

       Discusses the prison, the "black flower," as "the deter-
       minant of tone in the novel and the unifying scene and symbol";
       also shows how Fielding achieved the mimetic and symmetri-
       cal plot and how the characters enact more symbolic, even
       allegorical, roles in Amelia than in the earlier novels.

1189   LOFTIS, JOHN E.
       "Imitation in the Novel: Fielding's Amelia. "   RMMLA Bull.
       31 (1977):   214-229.

       Compares parallels of characters and events in Amelia

and Virgil's Aeneid and shows how against a "backdrop of
epic values and expectations, Fielding explores ... the moral
relationships among the individual, the family, and the society. "

1190   LONGMIRE, SAMUEL E.
        "Booth's Conversion in Amelia. " SAB 40, No. 4 (1975): 12-
        17.

        Defends Booth's conversion at the end of Amelia, by sug-
        gesting that "we can understand more fully Booth's religious
        experience and Fielding's artistic intentions by looking at
        Isaac Barrow's views on the nature of conversion and belief";
        and argues that the sermons Booth reads in proof of Chris-
        tianity make clear the implications of his conversion as well
        as the problems Fielding had to solve in portraying it suc-
        cessfully.

1191   "Amelia as a Comic Action. " TSL 17 (1972): 67-79.

        Defends the frequently criticized comic ending as consis-
        tent with the expectations that the novel raises; Fielding de-
        velops three narrative patterns that support the comic resolu-
        tion: 1) the representation of Booth's arrests; 2) the treat-
        ment of the hindering characters; and 3) the characterization
        of Booth.

1192   NATHAN, SABINE.
        "The Anticipation of Nineteenth Century Ideological Trends
        in Fielding's Amelia. " ZAA 6 (1958): 382-409.

        A Marxist attempt to define the "bourgeois" qualities in
        Amelia.

1193   OAKMAN, ROBERT L.
        "The Character of the Hero: A Key to Fielding's Amelia. "
        SEL 16 (1976): 473-489.

        Captain Booth is an overburdened hero who has a number
        of narrative functions--"husband and father, spokesman for
        the author, representative of a bad philosophy of life, and
        victim of a corrupt society. " Once Booth has fulfilled all
        his narrative functions, enabling Fielding to make his points
        about men, society, and philosophy, Fielding is forced to
        manipulate the ending of the novel by focusing his narrative
        attention on Amelia and calling on Dr. Harrison to resolve
        the story with a happy ending.

1194   OSLAND, DIANNE.
        "Fielding's Amelia: Problem Child or Problem Reader?"
        JNT 10 (1980): 56-67.

        Presents pros and cons for arguing that Amelia is an in-
tellectually demanding novel or that it suffers from dullness,
by comparing it with Tom Jones. In Amelia there are no
real tensions in the conflict because "the philosophy being
advocated denies that there is anything of importance happen-
ing about which to worry, and because the complexity of moral
issues is always hypothetical" and therefore the reader never
becomes involved enough to feel any sense of responsibility
or moral consequence. Tom Jones, on the other hand, involves the reader emotionally and he becomes as much on
trial as Tom is. Fielding tends to isolate the reader from
both Booth and Amelia by the use of the reserved "I," and
his dedication to "the exposure of the most glaring evils"
creates a serious tone which has led to the charge of "dullness."

1195   PALMER, EUSTACE.
        "Amelia--The Decline of Fielding's Art." EIC 21 (1971):
        135-151.

        Argues that Fielding was not completely in control of his
material in Amelia, that "faults of taste and defects of structure and plot point to a certain lack of grip on the events of
the novel," and "that the novel's texture is defective in verbal complexity, richness and variety...." Discusses his use
of the literary analogue.

1196   POSTON, CHARLES D.
        "The Novel as 'Exemplum': A Study of Fielding's Amelia."
        W. Va. Univ. Phil. Papers 18 (1971): 23-29.

        Suggests that Amelia is a consistent artistic work and that
it does not evidence a decline in Fielding's artistic achievement; compares Booth's life with that of Wilson and the Man
of the Hill, and suggests that it represents a methodical presentation of a moral lesson.

1197   POWERS, LYALL H.
        "The Influence of the Aeneid on Fielding's Amelia." MLN
        71 (1956): 330-336.

        Attempts to answer why Fielding chose the Aeneid as his
model for Amelia and why he deviated from his model at the
conclusion of Amelia. Concludes that Fielding wished to create
a modern Christian hero, and so he emphasizes Booth's con-

version to Christianity through his reading of Borrow's sermons.   Therefore the conclusion of Amelia presents us with
"a peculiarly Christian triumph. "

1198   RADER, RALPH W.
       "Ralph Cudworth and Fielding's Amelia. "   MLN 71 (1956):
       336-338.

          Shows a close parallel between Cudworth's True Intellectual
       System of the Universe and Captain Booth's religious beliefs
       as described in Amelia.

1199   RAWSON, C. J.
       "Nature's Dance of Death, Part 2: Fielding's Amelia. "   ECS
       3 (1970): 491-522.

          Argues that the "complexities and ambiguities" of Amelia
       are "a (partly deliberate) rendering of a larger struggle be-
       tween Fielding's rage for order and the senseless brutality
       of fact; and that they produce major and somewhat unique
       strengths, as well as weaknesses, in the novel. "

1200   RIBBLE, FREDERICK G.
       "The Constitution of the Mind and the Concept of Emotion in
       Fielding's Amelia. "   PQ 56 (1977): 104-122.

          Concerned with Fielding's philosophy of mind and how
       he "went soft" in Amelia.   Since Fielding based his account
       of emotion on the assumption that emotion may be regarded
       as a kind of sensation, Ribble begins by examining some of the
       sources of this assumption and their influence on Fielding.
       Then he examines in some detail how Fielding assimilated
       emotion to sensation in Amelia to produce characters "who
       are supposed to feel very intensely, to feel with a violence
       he knows he could never match, but who perform rather less
       because of that feeling. "   Amelia then is an "attempt to imi-
       tate more seriously a kind of domestic pathos, but also ... a
       serious ... attempt to deal explicitly with certain psychologi-
       cal theories, and to integrate them into a work of art. "

1201   ROTHSTEIN, ERIC.
       "Amelia. " In Systems of Order and Inquiry in Later Eighteenth-
       Century Fiction.   (Berkeley & Los Angeles: Univ. Calif.
       Press, 1975), pp. 154-207.

          According to the author, his thesis is simple: "that radi-
       cal similarities of method inform five major works of later
       eighteenth-century fiction, works that appear, and are, mark-
       edly different.   In all five novels, form--pattern, design,

order--is keyed to a concern with epistemological inquiry
that is as broad and as narrow as is suggested by Pope's
'The proper study of Mankind is Man.' Moreover, the formal procedures cohere as a system; so do the epistemological
ones; hence my terms 'system of order' and 'system of inquiry.' Finally, the systems of the five novels closely resemble each other." The five novels analyzed are Rasselas,
Tristram Shandy, Humphry Clinker, Amelia, and Caleb Williams. In Amelia, Fielding makes the "hiddenness of thought,
and therefore of motive," a major epistemological concern;
he returns to a theatrical mode in which outward action, objective reality, "flat" characters, unreliable speakers, and
economy of playing time create a "realistic" version of what
goes on in real life when what we see is all that we can
know.

1202   SHERBO, ARTHUR.
       "The Time-Scheme in Amelia." BUSE 4 (1960): 223-228.

       Suggests that Fielding observes a time-scheme more exact
       than the one in Tom Jones, and that the events of Amelia oc-
       cur in 1750, not in 1734 as suggested by Cross.

1203   SHERBURN, GEORGE.
       "Fielding's Amelia: an Interpretation." ELH 3 (1936): 1-
       14. Rpt. in [7], pp. 266-280; [898], pp. 146-157.

       Sees Amelia as resembling the Aeneid in its structure, its
       organizing themes, and its pictures of domesticity. Analyzes
       the character of Booth and his late conversion, and suggests
       the public theme of the novel--the corruption of the aristoc-
       racy.

1204   SPACKS, PATRICIA MEYER.
       "Laws of Time: Fielding and Boswell." In [166], pp. 264-
       299.

       As Boswell and Fielding grow older they face increasing
       doubts about the value of one's selfhood; they speculate about
       the extent to which the separate personality can survive the
       pressures of time and society. Amelia and Boswell's jour-
       nals collected under the title of Boswell for the Defence "dram-
       atize the increasing tensions of the effort to preserve self-
       hood in maturity." Both works demonstrate the painful need
       for "self-assertion in the face of unopposable forces, the ap-
       parently random distribution of success and failure, and the
       ways in which the sense of self weakens and its literary rendi-
       tions become increasingly complex."

1205   STEPHENS, JOHN C., JR.
        "The Verge of the Court and the Arrest for Debt in Field-
        ing's Amelia." MLN 63 (1948): 104-109.

             Explains for the modern reader "two facets of the system,
        the institution of 'the verge of the court' and the procedure
        for having a debtor seized," and concludes that Amelia had
        little effect on public sentiment regarding prison reform.

1206   THOMAS, D. S.
        "Fortune and the Passions in Fielding's Amelia." MLR 60
        (1965): 176-187.

             Discusses Fielding's use of Fortune, especially in connec-
        tion with his use of the psychology of the passions in Amelia.

1207   TOWERS, A. R.
        "Amelia and the State of Matrimony." RES 5 (1954): 144-
        157.

             Main purpose is to show that the picture of marriage in
        Amelia was in accord with the "best and most widely approved
        authorities on marital conduct"; Amelia stands for the ideal
        wife and Booth as a potentially worthy husband, even though
        Fielding implies that marriage cannot be conducted strictly
        according to the rules--Amelia is a woman as well as an
        ideal.

1208   WENDT, ALLAN.
        "The Naked Virtue of Amelia." ELH 27 (1960): 131-148.

             A study based on the observation that "to Fielding the
        heroine was the principal figure, the ethical center of the
        novel." In Amelia, Fielding studies the symbol of virtue it-
        self, "and tries to make his most serious moral comment,
        in terms of his contemporary society, about the nature of the
        forces that draw men to virtue." Amelia is tested both as
        a real woman and as a symbol; she passes the first test but
        fails the second. "This is the shape of Fielding's final moral
        position: the naked beauty of virtue is a necessary but not
        a sufficient motive to ethically satisfactory actions."

1209   WOLFF, CYNTHIA GRIFFIN.
        "Fielding's Amelia: Private Virtue and Public Good." TSLL
        10 (1968): 37-55.

             Intends to present a coherent analysis of the novel that
        will allow us to understand Fielding's intentions in writing
        it; and attempts to "explain the precise source of the novel's

failures so that the disturbing sense of the work's ambiguity may be either dispelled or explained. " That source is found in Fielding's failure to establish a "significant and workable connection ... between private good and public morality. "

1210   WYNNE, EDITH J.
        "Latitudinarian Philosophy in Fielding's Amelia. "   PMPA 4
        (1979):   33-38.

        Dr. Harrison is always in conflict with Amelia's husband, Booth: "Their conflict is a key to the function of religion in Amelia in which two differing ethical beliefs are brought into juxtaposition. " Dr. Harrison is prudent, wise, and good-natured, whereas Booth, who is a Hobbesian skeptic, sees only the best or worst in others since he believes that all men act from their passions and not from motives of love or virtue.   Booth himself needs to achieve a reformation-- how it is achieved and how effective it is forms the heart of the religious theme.   Booth's conversion comes as the result of Barrow's sermons, from which he derives a rational proof of Christian belief: "His conversion follows the method of the Cambridge Platonists and of the Latitudinarians; appeals to reason, not merely to the emotions, were exercised by them. . . . "

See also: 906, 918, 930, 954, 955, 965, 977, 986, 1081, 1724, 2600

General Studies

1211 AMES, DIANNE S.
"Gay's Trivia and the Art of Allusion." SP 75 (1978): 199-222.

Gay emulated in Trivia Virgil's Georgics, and in other ways he may be seen as ranking among the "most sophisticated and most accomplished exemplars of neoclassical allusiveness." His imitations are generally the Latin setpieces most often "flogged" by schoolboys and scribblers; he revives "the hackneyed themes and set-pieces of the poetry of his era, especially those drawn from the ancients because they were the most tired of all, and he numerizes, that is, makes wonderful, the most pedestrian subjects and events."

1212 ARMENS, SVEN M.
John Gay, Social Critic. New York: King's Crown Press, Columbia Univ. , 1954.

A critical analysis of Gay's work, the structural scope and variety of Gay's usage of pastoral forms, and an investigation of the serious elements in his poetry to try "to determine what he thought about in his serious moments and what he was genuinely serious about."

1213 BATTESTIN, MARTIN.
"Menalcas' Song: The Meaning of Art and Artifice in Gay's Poetry." JEGP 65 (1966): 662-679. Rpt. in [68], pp. 119-140.

An analysis of Trivia reveals that "Gay's verse has precisely that 'third dimension,' that 'prismatic depth,' which it had been said to lack." Gay believes that "art must order, refine, simplify" and Trivia stands "as a kind of extended parable of the relation between actuality and art."

1214 BRONSON, BERTRAND H.
"The True Proportions of Gay's Acis and Galatea." PMLA 80 (1965): 325-331. Rpt. in [76], pp. 45-59.

Argues that "Gay provided Handel with an almost ideal pastoral libretto," that together they created a "masterpiece" in the English pastoral tradition, and that it can only be fully appreciated " 'as a pastoral opera,' words and music inseparably united."

1215   "The Beggar's Opera." In Studies in the Comic (Univ. Calif. Publications in English, Vol. 8, No. 2, 1941), pp. 197-231; rpt. Norwood Editions, 1975, pp. 47-81. Rpt. in [1248], pp. 80-87; [76], pp. 60-90; [7], pp. 14-49.

Discusses the qualities that have made The Beggar's Opera popular--its music, and the musical controversies of the time; its lyrics; and its vivid characters. The final lesson of Gay's satire is that "the world is all alike."

1216   BROWN, WALLACE CABLE.
"Gay's Mastery of the Heroic Couplet." PMLA 61 (1946): 114-125. Rpt. as "Gay: Pope's Alter Ego" in [81], pp. 45-66.

Argues that Gay's achievement in the heroic couplet is technically skillful and excellent and that he excels as a satirist.

1217   BURGESS, C. F.
"Political Satire: John Gay's The Beggar's Opera." Midwest Quart. 6 (1965): 265-276.

Explains the allegorical satire and gives an account of the origin and historical circumstances of Gay's opera; discusses a generally neglected aspect of the political satire in the relationship of Peachum and Macheath--the overall political situation in England under the Whig ministry, and provides an historical background to explain the most effective sally against Walpole, the reference in Act I, Sc. iii to Robin of Bagshot.

1218   "The Ambivalent Point of View in John Gay's Trivia." Cithara 4 (1964): 53-65.

Argues that Gay's best work is "characterized by an ambivalent view of his material, a union of both satiric and sympathetic response." Trivia, for example, contains similar shifts: it begins as satire--of Gay's persona, of Gay himself, and of London; yet Gay becomes interested in his descriptions of walking the streets, so that the poem is also a "useful guide to the city."

1219   "The Genesis of The Beggar's Opera." Cithara 2 (1962): 6-
       12.

       Argues that Gay was not so dependent on his friends as
       critics have commonly supposed, that, in fact, "Gay's in-
       debtedness to Swift has been seriously exaggerated"; The Beg-
       gar's Opera was "the product solely of Gay's creative talent."
       Instead of the opera's being the result of a chance remark
       of Swift's, it can be proved that it evolved slowly in Gay's
       mind for several years--"the result of a sequence of events
       and ideas which animated the author, lay dormant for a time,
       and finally fused to produce The Beggar's Opera as we know
       it."

1220   CHALKER, JOHN.
       "John Gay: 'Rural Sports' and 'Trivia.'" In [87], pp. 141-
       179.

       Studies the Virgilian influence on Gay's Rural Sports, an
       influence that was more purely literary and more complex
       in its mingling of different elements than it was, for example,
       in Thomson; and suggests that the 1720 version places the
       Virgilian elements in a "framework which has a closer struc-
       tural relationship than the earlier version [1713] to the Geor-
       gics." Concludes that "when Gay called Rural Sports 'a Geor-
       gic' he had in mind not only Virgil, but the post-classical
       tradition of hunting poetry that had already freely adapted
       the Virgilian model to its own purposes." Further Virgilian
       and Juvenalian influences are found in Trivia, in which it is
       "Gay's remarkable ability to fuse literary experience with
       day-to-day actualities" that gives the poem its special tone.

1221   DONALDSON, IAN.
       " 'A Double Capacity': The Beggar's Opera." In The World
       Upside-Down: Comedy from Jonson to Fielding (Oxford:
       Clarendon Press, 1970), pp. 159-182. Rpt. in [1248], pp.
       65-80.

       Concerned with the ironic revolution of images, with the
       "double capacity" of Gay's irony in The Beggar's Opera, des-
       cribing the "way in which Gay's own irony works, saying one
       thing and implying another, shaping a double picture of Peach-
       um and (in turn) of every other character in the play"; argues
       furthermore, that it is characteristic of Gay's irony to main-
       tain that somewhere there must be a kind, honest person:
       " ... Gay keeps suggesting possible exceptions to the general
       rule of bourgeois possessiveness and self-interest, possible
       avenues of romantic freedom and escape, possible evidence
       of a primitive honesty; only regretfully, ironically, to dismiss
       such possibilities, to shut off the avenues and to reject the
       evidence as we approach more nearly."

1222   ELLIS, WILLIAM D. , JR.
        "Thomas D'Urfey, the Pope-Philips Quarrel, and The Shep-
        herd's Week. " PMLA 74 (1959): 203-212.

        Describes the use made of D'Urfey as an object of ridicule
        by the Scriblerians and their associates, and suggests that
        D'Urfey and his rustic ballads had far more to do with the
        Pope-Philips controversy over the Englishing of the classical
        ecologue than is usually supposed.   Ellis further suggests
        the possibility that Gay may have pretended to copy D'Urfey
        in order not only to burlesque the pastorals of Philips, but
        also to warn all writers of pastoral not based on classical
        models, "Learn hence for D'Urfey's rules a just esteem;/To
        copy mere nature is to copy him. "

1223   EMPSON, WILLIAM.
        "The Beggar's Opera: Mock-Pastoral as the Cult of Inde-
        pendence. "   In Some Versions of Pastoral (New York: New
        Directions, 1974), pp. 195-252.   Rpt. abridged in [1248], pp.
        15-41.

        Looks at the combination of "heroic and pastoral before
        they are parodied" in The Beggar's Opera to show what sort
        of humor this comic mixture can convey.   Discusses the
        double irony of the play.

1224   ERSKINE-HILL, HOWARD.
        "The Significance of Gay's Drama. "   In English Drama: Forms
        and Development: Essays in Honour of Muriel Clara Brad-
        brook, Marie Axton and Raymond Williams, eds.   (Cambridge:
        Cambridge Univ. Press, 1977), pp. 142-163.

        Emphasizes the relation of Gay's other drama to The Beg-
        gar's Opera, and seeks to "convey to the reader the experi-
        mental combination of forms, idioms and attitudes, and the
        humour and humanity, to be found in most of Gay's work for
        the theatre. "   Agrees with Bertrand Bronson that Gay is less
        interested in laughing Italian opera out of existence than in
        demonstrating its strong appeal to his imagination.   After
        the publication of Polly (1729), Gay moved away from an ex-
        perimental, formally self-questioning drama toward a plain,
        moral drama.   His drama, on the one hand, seems fin-de-
        siècle, the amused, sophisticated parody of the great masters;
        on the other hand, it is experimental and innovative, with a
        "modernistic indeterminacy" about it that links it with the
        twentieth-century work of, say, Brecht.

1225   FORSGREN, ADINA.
        John Gay: Poet "of a Lower Order. "   Vol. II: Comments
        on His Urban and Narrative Poetry.   Stockholm: Natur och
        Kultur, 1971.

Based on a discrimination of the "kinds" of poetry, this
study interprets Gay as leaving the world of Rural Sports,
to maintain his independence, for the Whig-oriented world of
Trivia with its implied criticism of social ills; he examines
that environment by providing "realistic ... answers to [the
contrived and formal] sublimity" emphasized by the Whig poets
and critics whose support of the heroic ideal was hardly consistent with their realistic approach to economic, social, and
political problems. Provides material on the sources of Gay'
ideas, contemporary modes of political thought, and the symbolic role of luxury; and concludes with a section on "Some
General Features" that seeks to discover Gay's personal attitude toward the opposing world of urban and rural convention.

1226   "Lofty Genii and Low Ghosts. Vision Poems and John Gay's
       'True Story of an Apparition.'" Studia Neophilologica 40
       (1968): 197-215.

       Interprets poem as a Scriblerian answer to "high-flown
       Whig visions with guardian angels" that praised the Glorious
       Revolution and the Hanoverian succession; contains much in-
       formation about contemporary opinions on dreams and visions.

1227   "Gay Among the Defenders of the Faith." Studia Neophilologica
       38 (1966): 301-313.

       Background study dealing with "A Contemplation on Night"
       and "A Thought on Eternity" as reflecting the religious ideals
       of the age; in these two contemplative poems, Gay champions
       orthodox religion (in this respect he is similar to Swift), though
       his religion is affected by the nonconformist influences on
       his childhood.

1228   John Gay: Poet "of a Lower Order.": Comments on His
       Rural Peoms and Other Early Writings. Stockholm: Natur
       och Kultur, 1964.

       A historical survey of Gay's early works considered as
       typical of his mature writings, and of Wine and the rural
       poems written on special occasions, as well as of some gen-
       eral features of the latter. Considers, specifically, the
       "poet's rural characters in their relationship to current con-
       ventions as well as the modes of imitation employed, whether
       idealization or the copying of nature ... "; other elements of
       Gay's poetry treated include the "non-heroic Kinds and sub-
       ject matter as opposed to heroic, the imitation of models with
       its 'laborious Art' and its decorating of themes as opposed
       to more 'original composition' supposedly relying on genius
       and inspiration rather than on learning...."

1229   "Some Complimentary Epistles by John Gay." Studia Neo-
        philologica 36 (1964): 82-100.

        Describes several of Gay's complimentary epistles, suggest-
        ing that they are more realistic than the Horation models Gay
        imitated; Gay alters neoclassical method in favor of a fairly
        modern psychological approach.

1230   FULLER, JOHN.
        "Cibber, The Rehearsal at Gotham, and the Suppression of
        Polly." RES 13 (1962): 125-134.

        A record of "some hitherto unnoticed material relating to
        the contemporary belief that Colley Cibber had a hand in the
        suppression, and [an examination of] Gay's posthumous farce
        'The Rehearsal at Gotham', for its bearing on the matter."

1231   GAYE, PHOEBE FENWICK.
        John Gay: His Place in the Eighteenth Century. London:
        Collins, 1938; rpt. Freeport, N.Y.: Books for Libraries
        Press, 1972.

        A rather unreliable biography which tends to portray Gay
        as lazy, irresponsible, and a fool; also tends to depreciate
        his writings.

1232   GRAHAM, EDWIN.
        "John Gay's Second Series, the Craftsman in Fable." PLL
        5 (1969): 17-25.

        Shows how Gay's Fables, read in the context of his life
        and of Opposition satire, were aimed at the vice and corrup-
        tion of Prime Minister Walpole.

1233   HEUSTON, EDWARD.
        "Gay's Trivia and the What D'Ye Call It." Scriblerian 5
        (1972): 39-42.

        Suggests that both the motto offered by Gay in his Advertise-
        ment for Trivia and the poem's epigraph " ... indicate that
        Trivia is Gay's ironic answer to those who disputed his claim
        to be the author of the play."

1234   HÖHNE, HORST.
        "John Gay's Beggar's Opera and Polly." ZAA 13 (1965):
        232-260; 341-359.

        Philosophical and aesthetic analysis and discussion of the

irony, wit, satire and humor in Polly and The Beggar's Opera.

1235   IRVING, WILLIAM H.
       John Gay, Favorite of the Wits.   Durham, N. C. :   Duke Univ.
       Press, 1940; rpt. New York: Russell & Russell, 1962.

       A sympathetic biography of Gay plus interpretations of his
       works in relation to his experience and with reference to con-
       temporary literary fashions.

1236   KLEIN, J. T.
       "Satire in a New Key: The Dramatic Function of the Lyrics
       of The Beggar's Opera."   Mich. A. 9 (1977):   313-321.

       A systematic study of the dramatic function of the lyrics
       in Gay's ballad opera which helps us to understand the com-
       plexity of his characterization.   The similes and metaphors
       which dominate the lyrics "form three thematic patterns:
       (1) sexual exploitation and sexual-financial calculations of hu-
       man value, (2) comparable social, political and legal calcula-
       tions and (3) most frequently, an attack on the stock senti-
       ments of opera and romantic-heroic drama."   The lyrics'
       function is to maintain an equilibrium between "a deadly ser-
       ious mood and one of light-hearted theatrics," because each
       character has a "lyric" portrait which differs from that por-
       trayed in the dialogue.

1237   KURTZ, ERIC.
       "The Shepherd as Gamester: Musical Mock-Pastoral in The
       Beggar's Opera."   In [1248], pp. 52-55.

       Argues that "The Beggar's Opera is not so much an attack
       on Italian absurdities as it is an independent reassertion of
       a native tradition of musical drama which characteristically
       exposes its own artifices and tests them by incorporating
       mock-pastoral formulas into the larger pastoral genre."

1238   LEWIS, PETER ELFED.
       "The Uncertainty Principle in The Beggar's Opera."   DUJ
       72 (1980):   143-146.

       The Beggar's Opera is difficult to classify because it shifts
       its ground from one mode to another.   We can both laugh and
       sympathize with his characters, there is sustained tension be-
       tween romance and realism, his ironic method of burlesque
       lends itself to both social and political satire, and the lang-
       uage is unreliable; it is this restless uncertainty that gives
       the play a modernity and connects it with the modernist and
       avant-garde art of the twentieth century.

1239   John Gay: The Beggar's Opera (Studies in English Literature,
       61). London: E. Arnold, 1976.

       A brief appraisal that emphasizes the diverse and contra-
       dictory strands in the opera: it is both opera and anti-opera,
       romance and anti-romance, a comedy of low life and a roman-
       tic comedy, as well as political satire both topical and gen-
       eral: "the elements move in tandem so that when a character
       sings a song he may be contributing to the burlesque of Italian
       opera and to the political satire or romance, as well as to
       Gay's revolutionary conception of ballad opera."

1240   "Dramatic Burlesque in Three Hours After Marriage." DUJ
       33 (1972): 232-239.

       Undertakes to explain the play as a "deliberately exagger-
       ated burlesque version of the typical intrigue plot," and ar-
       gues that the burlesque is theatrical rather than literary,
       present in the action and not in the language. The dramatic
       burlesque is chiefly directed against the over-elaborate in-
       trigue plots, full of improbable actions and discoveries, that
       neglect genuine wit and real comic invention.

1241   "John Gay's Achilles: The Burlesque Element." ArielE 3,
       i, (1972): 17-28.

       In spite of the fact that Achilles does not have the pre-
       cision of The What D'Ye Call It or The Beggar's Opera, it
       does not deserve to be ignored as it has been by most critics.
       In a few excellent scenes, it "does extend the criticism to
       be found in [Gay's] earlier satirical plays of the current dra-
       matic forms and theatrical fashions that struck him as ab-
       surd and that violated the Augustan aesthetic values he treas-
       ured."

1242   "Another Look at John Gay's The Mohocks." MLR 63 (1968):
       790-793.

       Suggests that even in The Mohocks, Gay's first play, "there
       are traces of the ironic and satirical devices that Gay used
       with such subtlety and sophistication in The Beggar's Opera";
       for example, Gay may have intended burlesquing Dennis's
       rules and Augustan tragedy--Lewis refers to the "magnificent,
       although admittedly unsustained, burlesque of contemporary
       tragedy in the opening scene," a scene that also burlesques
       the content and style of Paradise Lost. In The Mohocks Gay
       used mock-heroic for the first time: the opening speeches,
       employing the stilted rhetoric of Augustan tragedy to describe
       "low" subject-matter, expose the "stiff, declamatory, self-
       consciously sonorous and grandiloquent verse of Augustan trag-
       edy to ridicule."

1243   "Gay's Burlesque Method in The What D'Ye Call It." DUJ
       29 (1967): 13-25.

       An analysis of Gay's "totally ironic method" and of his
       departures from the burlesque method of Buckingham's The
       Rehearsal in his satire of Restoration and Augustan tragedy;
       suggests that "Gay's problem is to ensure that his mock-play
       sufficiently exaggerates the ludicrous characteristics of Augus-
       tan drama for it to be apprehended as satirical burlesque,
       even by an audience accustomed to pathetic tragedy and sen-
       timental comedy." Gay overcomes that difficulty by abandon-
       ing Buckingham's heroic characters and milieu: "he substi-
       tutes a humble pastoral setting and a collection of 'low' char-
       acters, such as servants and soldiers, for the usual court
       and city locales and aristocratic and well-to-do society of
       Augustan drama."

1244   LOFTIS, JOHN.
       "The Displacement of the Restoration Tradition, 1728-1737."
       In Comedy and Society from Congreve to Fielding (Stanford,
       Calif.: Stanford Univ. Press, 1959), pp. 101-110.

       Emphasizes the change heralded by The Beggar's Opera
       (1728): through most of the first three decades of the eigh-
       teenth century, comedies abound with stock characters and
       plot relationships derived from the Restoration; they are so-
       cially and politically complacent; but, after the appearance of
       The Beggar's Opera, comedies frequently "depart radically
       from the older pattern of the love chase, often including so-
       cial commentary rather than love intrigue as their chief re-
       source." Considers specifically The Beggar's Opera and
       Polly and their imitators; their themes of rusticity and of
       corruption in both high and low life; and notes that The Beg-
       gar's Opera contains a hint of criticism of English hierarchi-
       cal society.

1245   McINTOSH, WILLIAM A.
       "Handel, Walpole, and Gay: The Aims of The Beggar's
       Opera." ECS 7 (1974): 415-433.

       Discusses "events and attitudes that occasioned The Beg-
       gar's Opera" and suggests "a cautious view of the political
       satire ... [and] that the dominant force ... is its profes-
       sional and social satire, and that its function is essentially
       didactic."

1246   MOSS, HAROLD GENE.
       "The Beggar's Opera as Christian Satire." In [1248], pp.
       55-64.

Argues thesis that "Gay represents life as a fleeting dream ... structured to satirize man's folly and vice from a timeless, Christian perspective."

1247   NOBLE, YVONNE.
"Introduction: The Beggar's Opera in Its Own Time." In [1248], pp. 1-14.

Relates the satire in Gay's opera to events in London in the 1720s.

1248   NOBLE, YVONNE, ed.
Twentieth Century Interpretations of The Beggar's Opera: A Collection of Critical Essays. Englewood Cliffs, N. J.: Prentice-Hall, 1975.

1249   REES, JOHN O. JR.
" 'A Great Man in Distress': Macheath as Hercules." Univ. Calif. Std. , Series in Lang. & Lit. 10 (1966): 73-77.

Refers to Macheath's dilemma in III, xi, and suggests that it is similar to the classical allegory of Hercules choosing between virtue and vice.

1250   REYNOLDS, RICHARD.
"Three Hours After Marriage: Love on Stage." ECLife 1 (1974): 19-20.

Brief discussion of a poetic tradition coupling the names of Dennis and Gildon, culminating in Three Hours After Marriage by Gay, Pope, and Arbuthnot: Sir Tremendous Longinus (John Dennis) and Phoebe Clinket (Gildon) exchange words that, by their double meaning and their breathless quality, suggest the act of love: "By coupling Dennis with a flatterer who uses the words of Gildon, in a dialogue which echoes the china scene [Wycherley's The Country Wife], the authors extend the interplay of the passionate critic and the fawning playwright to a logical conclusion."

1251   ROGERS, PAT.
"Satiric Allusions in John Gay's Welcome to Mr. Pope." PLL 10 (1974): 427-432.

Cites possible reason why the poem, written in 1720, was not printed until 1776: because it was a sharp political satire on King George.

1252   SCHULTZ, WILLIAM E.
        Gay's 'Beggar's Opera': Its Content, History and Influence.
        New Haven: Yale Univ. Press, 1923.

        A comprehensive study of The Beggar's Opera--its back-
        ground, early productions, its stage history in each century,
        its place in operatic history, the sources for its ballads, and
        subsequent ballad operas; also includes an account of the play
        as social and political satire, and as a literary burlesque,
        as well as a discussion of its morality.

1253   SHERBO, ARTHUR.
        "John Gay: Lightweight or Heavyweight?"   Scriblerian 8
        (1975): 4-8.

        A review of the recent literature on John Gay, dividing
        the critics into those who regard him mainly as a writer of
        burlesque and jeux d'esprit, and those who claim to find in
        his work moral and political high seriousness.

1254   "Virgil, Dryden, Gay, and Matters Trivial."   PMLA 85
        (1970): 1063-1071.

        An analysis of Gay's diction in Trivia and his indebted-
        ness to Dryden's translation of Virgil.   "When one adds an
        occasional clear echo of the Bible or Milton, all intended to
        enhance the mock-dignity of his poem, there can be no doubt
        of Gay's poetic competence."

1255   SHERBURN, GEORGE.
        "The Fortunes and Misfortunes of Three Hours after Mar-
        riage."   MP 24 (1926): 91-109.

        Presents an account of the various pamphlet attacks on
        the play and attempts to explain the reasons for its failure;
        concludes that it was not recognized at first as a failure but
        was withdrawn after the seventh performance mainly because
        of the "tide of malice and party" (Pope) that developed against
        it.   Identifies the objects of Gay's satire.

1256   SHERWIN, JUDITH J.
        " 'The World is Mean and Man Uncouth....' "   VQR 35 (1959):
        258-270.

        Compares The Beggar's Opera and The Threepenny Opera
        noting the similarities in story but differences in mood and
        theme.

1257   SILLARS, S. J.
       "Musical Iconography in The Beggar's Opera?"   BJECS 1
       (1978): 182-185.

          Gay uses the technique of "musical iconography" to show
       the connection between sexual and political corruption, and
       once this connection is made, he turns the words into "a
       scathing denunciation of allegiances made by inane politicians
       who are free to indulge their personal whims with no sense
       of responsibility."

1258   SPACKS, PATRICIA MEYER.
       John Gay. New York: Twayne, 1965.

          A detailed critical analysis of Gay's achievement with sub-
       ject, genre, and technique and an attempt to trace his de-
       velopment chronologically through his literary production.
       Examines both Gay's perceptions and the forms in which he
       embodied them.

1259   "John Gay: A Satirist's Progress."   EIC 14 (1964): 156-
       170.

          Traces Gay's satiric technique in his epistles, eclogues,
       and fables; suggests that the voice of the poet is predominantly
       that of the ingénu or the naïf, so that his satires are strangely
       unconvincing: Gay too often comes to approve that which he
       is satirizing and "because of his own lively sense of pleasur-
       able involvement in the general irrationality cannot be bitter
       or fierce."

1260   STROUP, THOMAS B.
       "Gay's Mohocks and Milton."   JEGP 46 (1947): 164-167.

          Points out the Miltonic influence on the thought and style
       of the play, in order to demonstrate that Gay was attacking
       Milton at the moment when Milton's reputation was beginning
       to grow as a result of the enthusiastic criticism of Dennis
       and Addison.

1261   SUTHERLAND, JAMES.
       "John Gay."   In [17], pp. 201-214.   Rpt. in [18], pp. 130-
       143.

          A general appraisal of Gay's "delicate and sophisticated"
       craftsmanship and of his poetry "on its own terms" rather
       than allowing our critical judgments to be influenced by the
       character of the poet; emphasizes the contrast in Gay between
       the natural and the artificial.

1262   SWAEN, A. E. H.
       "The Airs and Tunes of John Gay's Polly." Anglia 60 (1936):
       403-422.

       Attempts to explain the references to the then-popular
       tunes by listing the sources of as many tunes as possible,
       occasionally quoting the first stanza or other characteristic
       lines.

1263   TROWBRIDGE, HOYT.
       "Pope, Gay, and The Shepherd's Week." MLQ 5 (1944): 79-
       88. Rpt. in [122], pp. 124-134.

       Agrees with Pope's account (in a letter to John Caryll,
       8 June, 1714) that Gay's purpose in writing The Shepherd's
       Week was primarily to burlesque Ambrose Philips and that
       the poem itself, in direct verbal parody and in its adoption
       of a style and manner modeled on those of Philips', provides
       internal evidence of that intention.

1264   WARNER, OLIVER.
       John Gay. (WTW) London: Longmans, 1964.

       A brief, general survey that includes comments about Gay's
       life, his early poems and occasional verse, the plays The
       Beggar's Opera, Polly, and Achilles.

1265   WEISSTEIN, ULRICH.
       "Brecht's Victorian Version of Gay: Imitation and Originality
       in the Dreigroschenoper." Comp. Lit. 7 (1970): 314-335.

       Compares Gay's Beggar's Opera, with its topical political
       satire seeking to demonstrate that English high and low society
       were both corrupt, with the universal satire of Brecht's ver-
       sion; Brecht makes few references to the contemporary Ger-
       man situation, being mainly concerned with showing that the
       "bourgeois is a robber, just as the robber is a bourgeois."

See also: 1075, 1082

General Studies

1266   ARTHOS, JOHN.
"The Prose of Goldsmith."   Mich. Quart. Rev. 1 (1962):
51-55.

     Establishes Goldsmith as the master of prose style--his
doctrine: "Let us, instead of writing finely, try to write
naturally."

1267   BROWN, WALLACE C.
"Goldsmith: The Didactic Lyric." In [81], pp. 142-160.

     An analysis of Goldsmith's use of the heroic couplet in
The Deserted Village, The Traveller, and four of his Epil-
ogues reveals that it is "in the realm of tone and movement
that Goldsmith contributes most memorably to the heroic
couplet"; suggests that " ... the couplets, which are in the
best sense didactic, are expanded by the music into lyric
territory...."

1268   DANZIGER, MARLIES K.
Oliver Goldsmith and Richard Brinsley Sheridan (World Dramatists). New York: Ungar, 1978.

     After a general survey of Goldsmith, Sheridan, and their
world, the author provides a detailed analysis of each writer's
chief plays, emphasizing style, plot, characterization, and
stage history. Concludes that Goldsmith was essentially conservative, sympathizing with an older generation, whereas
Sheridan was an irreverent, questioning spirit, sympathizing
with the young.

1269   DUSSINGER, JOHN A.
"Oliver Goldsmith, Citizen of the World."   SVEC 55 (1967):
445-461.

     Goldsmith seeks an identity as a citizen of the world; in-
tellectual cosmopolitanism is his ideal. Considers the influence of Locke on Goldsmith and the latter's acquaintance
with the scientific and philosophical knowledge of the age.

1270   FERGUSON, OLIVER W.
        "Goldsmith." <u>SAQ</u> 66 (1967): 465-472.

        A general appraisal of Goldsmith both as a writer and a
        man, emphasizing his distinctive qualities of style.

1271   GALLAWAY, W. F., Jr.
        "The Sentimentalism of Goldsmith." <u>PMLA</u> 48 (1933): 1167-
        1181.

        Analyzes the attitude of Goldsmith toward man as actor in
        the events of ordinary life in an attempt to determine whether
        or not Goldsmith was a sentimentalist.   Examines aspects of
        sentimentalism in the <u>Vicar of Wakefield</u>, <u>The Good-Natured
        Man</u>, <u>Citizen of the World</u>, and <u>The Deserted Village</u>.

1272   GOLDEN, MORRIS.
        "The Family-Wanderer Theme in Goldsmith." <u>ELH</u> 25 (1958):
        181-193.

        Discusses the pervasive theme of Goldsmith's works--the
        contrast between the family circle and the wandering son who
        leaves it--to show how "unconsciously, it constantly fills his
        mind."   Goldsmith moves from "a pathetic urge to return to
        the safety of childhood ... to the realization that his past
        exists only as an ideal memory and the awareness that man
        must face alone the chaos of the unknown present and future."

1273   HAYDON, FRANCES M.
        "Oliver Goldsmith as a Biographer." <u>SAQ</u> 39 (1940): 50-57.

        Goldsmith's qualifications for the role of biographer; his
        acceptance of modern theories of biography.   A general dis-
        cussion.

1274   HELGERSON, RICHARD.
        "The Two Worlds of Oliver Goldsmith." <u>SEL</u> 13 (1973): 516-
        534.

        Shows that "much of the irony of the work that Goldsmith
        produced during the first decade of his literary career arises
        from the opposition of two worlds: the static world of the
        village home that he and many of his heroes left behind and
        the active urban world to which they were drawn."   Each
        world came from Goldsmith's own experience and he deftly
        plays one against the other showing his "artistic control" and
        his "ironic and often comic mastery of his materials."

1275   HOPKINS, ROBERT H.
       The True Genius of Oliver Goldsmith.   Baltimore: The Johns
       Hopkins Press, 1969.

       A critical reading of Goldsmith that seeks to present a
       different view of Goldsmith than the one usually contained in
       literary histories: Hopkins sees him as "a master of comic
       satire and refined irony," and at other times as "a lesser
       master of the craft of persuasion." Goldsmith is not a sen-
       timentalist but a writer "committed to a conservative view
       of the fallibility of human nature and of literature as a species
       of virtue." Discusses The Traveller, largely ignores The
       Deserted Village and the plays, but includes a close explica-
       tion of The Vicar of Wakefield.

1276   JEFFARES, A. NORMAN.
       "Goldsmith: The Good Natured Man."   Hermathena 119 (1975):
       5-19.

       A biographical study of Goldsmith's prose and poetry re-
       vealing his good nature.

1277   Oliver Goldsmith.   (WTW) London: Longmans, 1959.

       A brief but rewarding survey of Goldsmith's life and of
       his writings--the novel, the poems, the plays, and the essays.

1278   KIRK, CLARA M.
       Oliver Goldsmith.   New York: Twayne, 1967.

       A Survey of Goldsmith's major writings that attempts,
       among other things, to relate his writings to his life because
       "both the triumph and the failure of [his] writing grew from
       the triumph and the failure of his life."

1279   LOUGHLIN, RICHARD L.
       "Laugh and Grow Wise with Oliver Goldsmith."   Costerus 6
       (1972): 59-92.

       "An overview of Goldsmith's contributions to gaiety and
       sanity"--his versatility as a writer and his philosophy of
       comedy.

1280   LOVEJOY, ARTHUR O.
       "Goldsmith and the Chain of Being."   JHI 7 (1946): 91-98.

       Seeks to refute Winifred Lynskey's assertion [1281] that

Goldsmith's Animated Nature gave the chain of being conception a "practical" and "literal" application to natural history; suggests, in fact, that such an undertaking was intrinsically impossible.

1281   LYNSKEY, WINIFRED.
        "Goldsmith and the Chain of Being." JHI 6 (1945): 363-374.

        Lynskey, noting that Goldsmith's History of the Earth and Animated Nature is undeservedly dismissed in Lovejoy's The Great Chain of Being, presents this work as Goldsmith's unique concept of the chain of being, suggesting that Goldsmith not only included the philosophical implications of the chain, but "actually created a living chain of being": "Animated Nature is not merely a natural history grouped according to the Chain of Being. It actually becomes the Chain of Being."

1282   LYTTON SELLS, A.
        Oliver Goldsmith: His Life and Works. London: Allen & Unwin; New York: Barnes & Noble, 1974.

        Criticism and plot summaries.

1283   McADAM, EDWARD L.
        "Goldsmith, the Good-Natured Man." In [27], pp. 41-47.

        Analyzes the character of Goldsmith and emphasizes as its essential element the desire to dominate; and considers the problem of luxury vs. frugality in Goldsmith's own life.

1284   McCRACKEN, DAVID.
        "Goldsmith and the 'Natural Revolution of Things.'" JEGP 78 (1979): 33-48.

        Goldsmith's theory of cyclical movements in history provided "a structure for his view of the past, present, and future, and a foundation for his 'stock' ideas on such things as wealth, luxury and the middle class." This theory, present in all his writings, was an assumption, not a debatable idea, but even though he assumed dynamic cycles of history, he longed for "a perpetual Auburn of simplicity and happiness."

1285   MAY, JAMES E.
        "Goldsmith's Theory of Composition: my heart dictates the whole.'" PLL 15 (1979): 418-421.

        Since Goldsmith defended extemporaneous composition in

preaching and wrote his own prose in a "first draft, best draft" manner, he probably held a theory of composition "far closer to what was to become the nineteenth and twentieth century's trust in the creative faculties, or talent, than to Ben Johnson's [sic] and to the Renaissance humanists' trust in study and imitation, in art."

1286   MURRAY, CHRISTOPHER.
"The Operation of Generosity and Justice in the Writings of Oliver Goldsmith." CJIS 6, i (1980): 23-35.

A survey of Goldsmith's writings showing how he used "the dialectic of generosity and justice in order to express and contain political and aesthetic ideas." Goldsmith's work may be defined as that of a comic artist and much of the "formal interplay of generosity and justice" relates to the lack of order in his own life. In his work "felicity reigns supreme" and his struggle for perfection "was a struggle to bring into harmony the impulses of generosity and justice."

1287   PITMAN, JAMES HALL.
Goldsmith's Animated Nature (Yale Studies in English 66). New Haven: Yale Univ. Press, 1924. Rpt. Hamden, Conn.: Archon Books, 1972.

A study of Goldsmith using Animated Nature as a tool; discusses details of publication, the sources, Goldsmith's manner and method in Animated Nature, and his relation to his age.

1288   QUINTANA, RICARDO.
"Oliver Goldsmith, Ironist to the Georgians." In [6], pp. 297-310.

Emphasizes Goldsmith's ironies of style, literary execution, and thought and vision, and provides analyses of The Citizen of the World, The Vicar of Wakefield, and She Stoops to Conquer.

1289   Oliver Goldsmith: A Georgian Study. New York: Macmillan, 1967.

A biographical and critical study.

1290   REYNOLDS, W. VAUGHAN.
"Goldsmith's Critical Outlook." RES 14 (1938): 155-172.

An evaluation of Goldsmith's critical principles: "He shared

the general opinions of the Augustan critics, but his judgment
was guided by common sense, honesty, and courage.... His
attitude to rules was on the whole distrustful...."

1291   SEITZ, R. W.
       "Some of Goldsmith's Second Thoughts on English History."
       MP 35 (1938): 279-288.

       A comparison of Goldsmith's political views in History of
       England, in a series of letters from a nobleman to his son
       (1764) and in its expansion into History of England, from the
       earliest times to the death of George II (1771); concludes that
       his earlier zeal as a social reformer and as a supporter of
       the throne seems to have altered in the History (1771) into
       "rancor against the Whig party and a truculent vindication of
       the Tories."

1292   "The Irish Background of Goldsmith's Social and Political
       Thought."   PMLA 52 (1937):   405-411.

       Suggests that Goldsmith "[h]aving found his utopia, osten-
       sibly situated in England, but actually existing ... only in
       his imagination, proceeded ... to build around it a social
       and political philosophy made up mostly of impressions ac-
       quired in Ireland."   The substance of his social and political
       thinking is the result of his having remained an Irishman; he
       firmly believed "that society was made for man and not man
       for society."

1293   WARDLE, RALPH M.
       Oliver Goldsmith.   Lawrence: Univ. Kansas Press, 1957;
       London: Constable, 1958.

       An outstanding biography, the definitive life of Goldsmith.

1294   WINCHCOMBE, GEORGE.
       Oliver Goldsmith and the Moonrakers.   London: Thab Pub-
       lications, 1972.

       Includes chapters on The Vicar of Wakefield and The De-
       serted Village, and reprints in appendices several items from
       the Universal Magazine of July to December, 1762, which are
       attributed to Goldsmith.

See also: 2690, 3183

Plays

1295   FERGUSON, OLIVER W.
        "Antisentimentalism in Goldsmith's The Good Natur'd Man:
        The Limits of Parody." In The Dress of Words: Essays on
        Restoration and Eighteenth Century Literature in Honor of
        Richmond P. Bond, Robert B. White, Jr., ed. (Lawrence:
        Univ. Kansas Libraries [Library Series, 42], 1978), pp. 105-
        116.

        Does not see The Good Natur'd Man as a satire on senti-
        mental comedy or as a parody but rather as "a conventional
        specimen of English comedy in the third quarter of the eigh-
        teenth century."

1296   HEILMAN, ROBERT B.
        "The Sentimentalism of Goldsmith's Good Natured Man." In
        Studies for William A. Read. A Miscellany Presented by
        Some of His Colleagues and Friends, ed. by Nathaniel M.
        Caffee & Thomas A. Kirby (Baton Rouge: La. State Univ.
        Press, 1940), pp. 237-253.

        Argues that the play, though possessing "elements of sen-
        timentalism," is primarily comic satire intended to ridicule
        sentimentalism. A detailed examination.

1297   HUME, ROBERT D.
        "Goldsmith and Sheridan and the Supposed Revolution of 'Laugh-
        ing' Against 'Sentimental' Comedy." In [33], pp. 237-276.

        Cautions against accepting the critical commonplace that
        Goldsmith and Sheridan rebelled against "sentimental" comedy
        and tried to revive "laughing" comedy. In fact, "sentimental"
        comedy was not the dominant mode in the third quarter of the
        century; it did not drive legitimate humor from the stage;
        and both dramatists inherited a thriving comic tradition that
        existed full-blown around them.

1298   JEFFARES, A. NORMAN.
        A Critical Commentary of Goldsmith's "She Stoops to Con-
        quer." London: Macmillan, 1966.

        A brief point-by-point critical exposition, touching on the
        author's life, the contemporary stage, the plot, the charac-
        ters, and the significance of the play.

1299   McCARTHY, B. EUGENE.
        "The Theme of Liberty in She Stoops to Conquer." Univ.
        Windsor Rev. 7 (1971): 1-8.

Detailed examination of the construction of the play to refute the assumption that it is the product of careless construction or indifference to skilled integration of each character,
situation, and idea--a discussion of the complexity of the play
and its theme of liberty.

1300   QUINTANA, RICARDO.
"Goldsmith's Achievement as Dramatist." UTQ 34 (1965):
159-177.

Close examination of the exact nature of his work as a
playwright, and history of his connection with dramatic affairs; also an examination of the plays and the place they
occupy in the life of Goldsmith. Discusses four major Georgian conventions that form the background to Goldsmith's
plays, and the extent to which those plays may be considered
Georgian.

1301   "Oliver Goldsmith as a Critic of the Drama." SEL 5 (1965):
435-454.

Goldsmith's scattered critical comments on the drama provide a background against which his own plays can be more
strongly appraised; he had a theory of comedy, a "truly sophisticated poetic of the drama," that was more subtle than
that of any of his contemporaries.

1302   RODWAY, ALLAN.
"Goldsmith and Sheridan: Satirists of Sentiment." In [25],
65-72.

Argues that Goldsmith and Sheridan's "anti-sentimental
plays must seem, to anyone familiar with the Restoration
mode they purported to revive, to be themselves affected by
the usurping Genteel or Sentimental mode they purported to
attack."

1303   SMITH, JOHN HARRINGTON.
"Tony Lumpkin and the Country Booby Type in Antecedent
English Comedy." PMLA 58 (1943): 1038-1049.

Gives parallels between She Stoops to Conquer and The
Lancashire Witches, The Tender Husband, The Wild Gallant,
George Dandin, Woman's Wit, and The Lottery.

1304   STYAN, J. L.
"Goldsmith's Comic Skills." Costerus 9 (1973): 195-217.

An analysis of The Grumbler, and a summary of Goldsmith's comments on drama; followed by an examination of
his practice.

1305   TUCKER, HERBERT F. , JR.
        "Goldsmith's Comic Monster." SEL 19 (1979): 493-499.

        Goldsmith's exploitation of "lowness" in She Stoops to Con-
        quer manifests itself in the character of Tony Lumpkin, a
        domesticated monster, whose irrepressible vitality is respon-
        sible for the comic action of the play.   Portrayed as both a
        low lout and a comic character clamoring for love and rec-
        ognition, Tony can be compared to Shakespeare's Caliban.

See also: 1271, 1288

                        The Vicar of Wakefield

1306   ADELSTEIN, MICHAEL E.
        "Duality of Theme in The Vicar of Wakefield." CE 22 (1961):
        315-321.

        Argues that Goldsmith changed his theme from prudence
        to fortitude in the course of writing the novel, and that in
        this process the "central character was transformed from an
        innocent simpleton to a courageous, resolute hero."

1307   BACKMAN, SVEN.
        This Singular Tale: A Study of "The Vicar of Wakefield" and
        Its Literary Background (Lund Studies in English 49).   Lund:
        C. W. K. Gleerup, 1971.

        Attempts to describe and analyze the relationship between
        Goldsmith's novel and the literary traditions out of which it
        grew: that of the novel, of the periodical essay, and of the
        drama.

1308   BATAILLE, ROBERT A.
        "City and Country in The Vicar of Wakefield." ECLife 3
        (1977): 112 - 114.

        Goldsmith presents a much more rounded and realistic
        view of country life in The Vicar than in The Deserted Village
        and also manages to avoid its oversimplified moral view of
        the city.   He portrays the country as being not quite as idyl-
        lic and the city as not quite as wicked as eighteenth-century

pastorals were prone to do; the setting then becomes as complex as character and theme. Sir William Thornhill provides the focus for the analysis of the city-country setting because he is as much at home in one as in the other.

1309   BLIGH, JOHN.
"Neglected Aspects of The Vicar of Wakefield." DR 56 (1976): 103-111.

The happy ending to the novel, made possible by the Vicar's superstitious views on marriage, obscures Goldsmith's commentary on political and social issues. The novel is compared to the Book of Job for its general pattern, to Tess of the d'Urbervilles for its sexual morality, and to Caleb Williams for its social and political message.

1310   DAHL, CURTIS.
"Patterns of Disguise in The Vicar of Wakefield." ELH 25 (1958): 90-104.

A thematic analysis of the novel to defend its artistic structure. It shows not only "the relevance to each other and to the whole of the seemingly extraneous and digressive elements," but also focuses into a "coherent pattern many of the apparently disconnected elements of the Primrose story."

1311   DURANT, DAVID.
"The Vicar of Wakefield and the Sentimental Novel." SEL 17 (1977): 477-491.

The narrator possesses a narrative style derived from the sentimental novel, yet The Vicar is not sentimental in effect because of its narrative stance. The novel demonstrates the "impracticality of a life of principle in a fallen world.... Moreover, [it] demonstrates a direct correspondence between the ill success of principle in life and the impotency of the sentimental style in fiction." The reality of experience defeats the Vicar, and that defeat evokes a positive theme: The Vicar proves that personal experience teaches the individual, whereas abstract moral instruction does not; the sentimental mode fails to instruct effectively because it assumes that literature teaches by precept and examples.

1312   DUSSINGER, JOHN.
"The Vicar of Wakefield: A 'Sickly Sensibility' and the Rewards of Fortune." In [98], pp. 148-172.

The flaws in The Vicar may be owing to its romance form: the narrative attempts to show that fundamental changes of

event take place within the mind of Dr. Primrose. If Goldsmith does not entirely succeed in that attempt, it is partly
from "having stumbled into a narrative form that required a
greater projection of self in discourse than he could afford."
Dr. Primrose's sentimentalism is described as a "sickly sensibility," discrediting him in the adult world of economic com-
petition and weakening him in mind and body; when disaster
seems inevitable, Providence rescues him by changing him
into a wise father and priest.

1313   EMSLIE, MACDONALD.
        Goldsmith: "The Vicar of Wakefield" (Studies in English,
        No. 9).   London: Edward Arnold, 1963.

        An evaluative study of The Vicar of Wakefield that concen-
        trates on themes and essential qualities: on, for instance,
        nature and society, rural virtue, the morality of the heart,
        sentiment and the sentimental, the language, and the action.

1314   FERGUSON, OLIVER W.
        "Dr. Primrose and Goldsmith's Clerical Ideal." PQ 54 (1975):
        323-332.

        Even though Goldsmith departs somewhat from his usual
        stereotype of the good clergyman by adding a comic dimen-
        sion to Dr. Primrose's character, he is able to combine the
        clerical stereotype with the amiable humorist in the same
        personality.

1315   GOLDEN, MORRIS.
        "Goldsmith, The Vicar of Wakefield, and the Periodicals."
        JEGP 76 (1977):   525-536.

        Suggests that "the magazines and papers illuminate the
        subjects, themes, conditions, and fashions of the time that
        come one way or another into the novel; elements of Gold-
        smith's own personal background, orientation, and recurrent
        concerns; literary echoes, of Goldsmith's material and that
        of others; and the implications about his practices and reputa-
        tion...." Goldsmith subjected the traditional romance plot
        to the daily world of magazines and newspapers, fully aware
        of the absurdity of both in a doubleness of vision natural to
        his age.

1316   "The Time of Writing of The Vicar of Wakefield." BNYPL
        65 (1961):   442-450.

        Believes that the novel was the subject of steady work from
        about 1759 to the fall of 1762, with some probable touching
        up in 1763.

1317   "Image Frequency and the Split in The Vicar of Wakefield."
        BNYPL 63 (1959): 473-477.

        If "image frequency in the prose is a clear index to the
        amount of work expended by Goldsmith, he wrote the first
        27 chapters carefully ... the last 5 chapters seem to have
        been thrown off in haste."

1318   GREEN, MARY ELIZABETH.
        "Oliver Goldsmith and the Wisdom of the World." SP 77
        (1980): 202-212.

        Discusses treatment of the theme of frugality as the basis
        of true generosity; frugality has replaced justice as the car-
        dinal virtue.   In The Vicar of Wakefield, however, the Vicar
        learns that frugality and hard work do not alone assure suc-
        cess in life; only religion will serve.   Faith insists that God
        will never abandon the righteous, while hope sustains that faith
        when it is most threatened by the harsh realities of life: The
        Vicar--and the reader--learns that there is something more
        important than the world and all its wisdom.

1319   GRUDIS, PAUL J.
        "The Narrator and The Vicar of Wakefield."   Essays in Li-
        terature (Denver) 1, i (1973):   51-66.

        An examination of the Vicar's character to determine the
        response which Goldsmith intends to evoke; concludes that
        Dr. Primrose has enough virtues to be a basically sympa-
        thetic character, that the vicar as narrator is not identical
        to the vicar as central character, and that Primrose is trans-
        formed from an almost comic character into a man who would
        be capable of tragedy if he had lived in a tragic world.

1320   HOPKINS, ROBERT H.
        "Matrimony in The Vicar of Wakefield and the Marriage Act
        of 1753."   SP 74 (1977):   322-339.

        The Parliamentary debates over the Marriage Act of 1753
        and Goldsmith's attitude toward it play a major role in his
        use of matrimony as a major theme.   In spite of the Act,
        the rich do marry the poor, and the Burchell-Sophia marriage
        represents "Goldsmith's ideal of union between the aristocracy
        and the middle class" and his "ideal vision of love being the
        primary motive for marriage"; it is not a contrived marriage
        merely for the sake of resolving the plot.

1321   "Social Stratification and the Obsequious Curve: Goldsmith
        and Rowlandson."   In [8], pp. 55-71.

Argues that social stratification and obsequiousness are important themes in The Vicar of Wakefield; that Rowlandson in his illustrations to the novel "responded intuitively to Goldsmith's deep concern with the changing relationships between classes in a society increasingly dominated by extremes of wealth and poverty." Concludes that all the characters are stripped of their genteel pretensions while Dr. Primrose is in prison and brought back to moral reality.

1322   HUNTING, ROBERT.
        "The Poems in The Vicar of Wakefield." Criticism 15 (1973): 234-241.

Suggests that a useful way to get into the method and meaning of the novel is by a close study of its poetry, and argues for keeping the "patterns of disguise" as a key to interpretation: "Illusion, throughout The Vicar, has an appeal which reality lacks."

1323   JAARSMA, RICHARD J.
        "Satiric Intent in The Vicar of Wakefield." Std. in Short Fiction 5 (1968): 331-341.

Discusses theme, structure, and satiric intent of the novel and examines Goldsmith's attitude toward sentimentality. Comments that the novel, treated as satire, "reveals a countless series of dimensions not otherwise discoverable."

1324   JEFFERSON, D. W.
        "Observations on The Vicar of Wakefield." Cambridge Jour. 3 (1950): 621-628.

A critical analysis of Goldsmith's treatment of the vicar's misfortunes showing how his use of language deliberately reduces their emotional effect.

1325   LEHMANN, JAMES H.
        "The Vicar of Wakefield: Goldsmith's Sublime, Oriental Job." ELH 46 (1979): 97-121.

The vicar partly follows the path of the biblical Job in that he learns the lesson which was the common reading of Job in the period of The Vicar's composition, namely, the doctrine of equal providence--although the dealings of Providence are unequal in this life, the sufferings of good men will be abundantly recompensed in the next life. But the Job-analogy, Lehmann suggests, is not taken too seriously since Goldsmith plays with the biblical story; the "[b]iblical paradigm is often invoked only to be toyed with" because the exegetical tradition was undergoing changes in the eighteenth century. Lehmann

suggests that a moral development exists that closely corresponds to a movement toward the attainment of the sublime:
the Job-figure moves from an ironic condition to one that
sublimely transcends irony through love and humility.   Primrose becomes a Job-figure because he attains the sublime by
ignoring appearances and accepting a "natural and passionate
love of his family and his fellow man. "

1326   McDONALD, DANIEL.
        "The Vicar of Wakefield: A Paradox. " CLAJ 10 (1966):
        23-33.

        Argues that, if the novel is read to express a profound
        moral truth, one faces the fact that Goldsmith did not seem
        to take it seriously: "He develops the theme so obviously
        that the story lacks verisimilitude; he concludes the story so
        festively that the theme is contradicted; and he reveals ele-
        ments in the Vicar which impair his status as a moral guide. "

1327   PRIVATEER, PAUL C.
        "Goldsmith's Vicar of Wakefield: The Reunion of the Alien-
        ated Artist. " Enl. E. 6, i (1975): 27-36.

        Offers a reassessment of Thornbill's historical and nar-
        rative significance by suggesting that he is a "multi-dimen-
        sional character of greater complexity that [sic] the conven-
        tional deus ex machina interpretation admits. "   The composite
        characterization of Thornhill-Burchell may be a representa-
        tive union of two complementary Enlightenment sensibilities:
        as a member of the landed gentry, Thornhill uses the know-
        ledge he gained as Burchell, the artist, to support his pri-
        mary role as the novel's controlling voice and source of au-
        thority.   His artistic sensibility reinforces his authority and
        gives him the moral insight to perceive and control the chaos
        always threatening The Vicar's fictional world.   Finally, in
        the composite character Goldsmith unites an artistic and im-
        aginative vision of human society with a rationalistic and le-
        galistic view.

1328   ROTHSTEIN, ERIC and HOWARD D. WEINBROT.
        "The Vicar of Wakefield, Mr. Wilmot, and the 'Whistonean
        Controversy. ' " PQ 55 (1976): 225-240.

        Examines the text and its thematic functions in an attempt
        to explain why Dr. Primrose left his "elegant house" and
        "thirty-five pounds a year" for a farm and "fifteen pounds a
        year," and shows that he does this "through 'making over'
        his living and disputing with Wilmot. " Goldsmith then uses
        these two points to develop "a pair of motifs, one having to
        do with law and its relationship to personal principles, the

other having to do with Whiston and his practice of 'primitive
Christianity. ' "

1329   SHROFF, HOMAI J.
        " 'The Heart Rather than the Head. ' " In [163], pp. 192-
        235.

        Discusses the idealization of the simple warm-hearted
        man as portrayed by the Vicar and Thornhill.   Also discus-
        ses Sterne's similar portrayal of Uncle Toby and some of
        Mackenzie's characters.   Goldsmith's purpose is to present
        the Vicar as a good and noble person struggling against ad-
        versity, but at times he seems to "be torn between his de-
        sire to criticise the Vicar's naïveté, imprudence, irrespon-
        sible optimism and sermonizing garrulity, and the desire to
        admire unstinting generosity, courageous optimism and simple
        trust in God and man. "

See also: 927, 1058, 1271, 1275, 1288, 1294

                        The Deserted Village

1330   BELL, HOWARD J. , JR.
        "The Deserted Village and Goldsmith's Social Doctrines. "
        PMLA 59 (1944): 747-772.

        A reexamination of the poem as a social doctrine in an
        attempt to answer three questions: 1) what was Goldsmith's
        message; 2) how completely does the poem express his actual
        convictions; and 3) what inspired him to consider the condi-
        tion he was describing as not merely unfortunate but fatal to
        the health of a nation?

1331   DAVIE, DONALD.
        "The Deserted Village: Poem as Virtual History. " 20th
        Cent. 156 (1954): 161-174.

        Takes issue with Suzanne Langer, in Feeling and Form,
        that both "The Deserted Village" and Blake's "The Echoing
        Green" are "created virtual histories. " Davie interprets
        Goldsmith's poem as expressing the rhythm of fruition, gen-
        eration succeeding generation, as frail and vulnerable, and
        concludes that " 'The Deserted Village' is a virtual history
        like 'The Echoing Green, ' and a symbol articulated more
        closely and intricately than Blake's. "

1332   EVERSOLE, RICHARD.

"The Oratorical Design of The Deserted Village." ELN 4
(1966): 99-104.

Argues that the oratorical pattern is composed of the traditional seven parts in their usual order, and concludes that
the blatant sentimentalism is actually a "harmonious assimilation of the principles of classical subjective rhetoric and
the new premise of the association of ideas."

1333   FIELDING, K. J.
       "The Deserted Village and Sir Robert Walpole." English 12
       (1959): 130-132.

       Poem refers to enclosure acts used to evict peasants to
       build Houghton Hall.

1334   GOLDEN, MORRIS.
       "The Broken Dream of The Deserted Village." L & P 9
       (1959): 41-44.

       Explication in terms of "a symbolic picture of the dis-
       integration of the author's dream world of childhood inno-
       cence."

1335   GOLDSTEIN, LAURENCE.
       "The Deserted Village: The Politics of Nostalgia." In [107],
       pp. 95-113.

       The theme of homesickness or nostalgia in Goldsmith:
       where Johnson deprecated homesickness, Goldsmith continually
       sought the shades of the dead. His finest narratives acquire
       their form and emotion from an imaginative revisitation of
       a patriarchal home; he is the "type of a displaced artist whose
       life at the inns of the world turns his imagination toward the
       archetype of return." Discusses The Traveller, The De-
       serted Village, and various miscellaneous essays, emphasiz-
       ing especially Goldsmith's attitude toward the commercial
       spirit, the luxury of the age, and the expansion of the Em-
       pire.

1336   HAHN, H. GEORGE.
       " 'Auburn' in Goldsmith's The Deserted Village: Possible
       Gallic Overtones?" CLAJ 22 (1978): 147-150.

       "Auburn" may or may not be Lissoy in Ireland, but it
       serves as an emblem of a once-idyllic place now forever
       abandoned that could also function as a contrast to the "hor-
       rific implications" of life in the city and in America. Au-
       burn embodies Goldsmith's theme of depopulation; this article

suggests that Goldsmith, to augment that theme, chose the
name Auburn for "its rich and subtle merging of Gallic sound
and sense."

1337   JAARSMA, RICHARD J.
        "Ethics in the Wasteland: Image and Structure in Goldsmith's
        The Deserted Village." TSLL 13 (1971): 447-459.

        Rejects the views that Goldsmith's poem is either a cri
        de coeur or a statement of his social beliefs, in favor of
        the larger idea that it is an independent artistic structure.
        The main theme is luxuria, and the poem is based on the
        structural principle of symbolic contrasts.

1338   MAHONEY, ROBERT.
        "Lyrical Antithesis: The Moral Style of The Deserted Vil-
        lage." ArielE 8, ii (1977): 33-47.

        Gives examples of lyrical antithesis in the poem to show
        the variety of forms it takes to intensify the conflict between
        simplicity and luxury. Argues that the lyrical elements em-
        ployed by Goldsmith fit the moral dimensions of his "argu-
        ment for the traditional values which Auburn represents and
        which luxury threatens." There is a connection between "a
        style thus balanced and the culmination of that argument in
        the ... address to Poetry, envisioned among the 'rural vir-
        tues' leaving England for exile." The poem's metaphorical
        quality enhances Goldsmith's "sense of personal devastation,
        both as a nostalgic man and ... as a poet."

1339   MINER, EARL.
        "The Making of The Deserted Village." HLQ 22 (1959): 125-
        141.

        Examines Goldsmith's ideas "in their proper historical and
        literary contexts ... to show how these ideas have been made
        into poetry." Emphasizes the complex thought and structure
        of The Deserted Village and also the fact that it is a very
        simple work of art to show that it "combines real complexity
        with real simplicity." The historical context is Tory and the
        literary context consists of a redefinition of the pastoral elegy.

1340   MONTAGUE, JOHN.
        "The Sentimental Prophecy: A Study of The Deserted Village."
        Dolmen Miscellany of Irish Writing 1 (1962): 62-79.

        Argues that The Deserted Village is a song of exile from
        Lissoy and a protest against the Enclosure Acts and the new
        commercial oligarchy; but it also represents Goldsmith's final

vision of the general decay that had always haunted him. The poem dramatizes the ravages of opulence by emphasizing its effect upon rural life, and the fall of Auburn is seen as the fall of a whole social order.

1341 QUINTANA, RICARDO.
"The Deserted Village: Its Logical and Rhetorical Elements."
CE (1964): 204-214.

An analysis of the compositional and artistic qualities of the poem concluding that The Deserted Village is much more emotional that his other poems, perhaps because of Goldsmith's rhetorical strategy.

1342 SCHWEGEL, DOUGLAS M.
"The American Couplets in The Deserted Village."   Georgia
Rev. 16 (1962): 148-153.

An analysis of the American lines, and an account of Goldsmith's interest in and knowledge of Georgia and General Oglethorpe.

1343 STORM, LEO F.
"Literary Convention in Goldsmith's Deserted Village." HLQ
33 (1970): 243-256.

Maintains that Goldsmith's debt to the classics was large, and attempts to "show that the social 'doctrines' and the 'sentiment' of the poem do not so much reflect the ideas and personal feelings of the author as they do the conventional, standardized themes of the eighteenth-century 'kinds' Goldsmith was imitating" and that "Goldsmith developed from his standardized material a remarkable and dramatic restatement of the Augustan aesthetic of order."

1344 TILLYARD, E. M. W.
"The Two-Village-Greens."   In Poetry Direct and Oblique
(London: Chatto & Windus, 1934), pp. 11-15; revised & reset, 1945.

Goldsmith's picture of Auburn in The Deserted Village is an example of the "poetry of direct statement: it is to some degree concerned with what the words state as well as with what they imply"; whereas Blake's "Echoing Green" in Songs of Innocence is as "nearly perfect an example of poetical obliquity as can be found" because it is concerned not solely with birds, old and young folks, and village greens, but with an idea--the idea that there is a virtue in desire satisfied.

1345   TINKER, CHAUNCEY BREWSTER.
        "Figures in a Dream." YR 17 (1928): 670-689.

        A discussion of The Deserted Village and Goldsmith's suc-
        cess as a poet.

1346   WENZEL, MICHAEL J.
        "Re-populating The Deserted Village." RMMLA Bull. 28
        (1974): 18-25.

        The "filter of sensibility" through which the poem is pre-
        sented demonstrates "that textual and individuating factors ...
        play a crucial role in the effect of the poem and that, by
        threatening its logical progress, actually assist in making the
        poem's assertions more acceptable." Also suggests that the
        "poem has a purpose beyond the criticism of the effects of
        a particular social policy. Auburn has been repopulated
        through the power of poetry...."

1347   WILLS, JACK C.
        "The Narrator of The Deserted Village: A Reconsideration."
        W. Va. Univ. Phil. Papers 22 (1975): 21-28.

        Discusses the role of the narrator, who is not entirely re-
        liable, and suggests that the narrator is the primary device
        through which the author universalizes his themes; maintains
        that what Goldsmith does with the themes of mutability, ro-
        manticizing of the past, isolation, and pride through the use
        of the narrator establishes him as "an individual and unique
        genius."

1348   "The Deserted Village, Ecclesiastes, and the Enlightenment."
        Enl. E. 4, iii/iv (1973): 15-19.

        Deals with parallelism of theme and tone in The Deserted
        Village and the Book of Ecclesiastes, especially with pessim-
        ism and isolation, and one pattern of imagery, that of light-
        ness and darkness, providing us "with an especially useful
        example of the paradox of the darkness of the Enlightenment."

See also: 1267, 1271, 1275, 1294, 1522, 1954

                        Other Poems

1349   FERGUSON, OLIVER W.
        "Goldsmith's 'Retaliation.' " SAQ 70 (1971): 149-160.

Provides an account of the genesis of the poem, emphasizing Goldsmith's deeply personal relationships with some of his most intimate friends.

1350   FONG, DAVID.
        "Johnson, Goldsmith, and The Traveller." New Rambler (Jour. of the Johnson Society). Autumn 1971: 23-30.

Attempts to explain the intellectual, moral, and psychological reasons Johnson thought so highly of the poem.

1351   JAARSMA, RICHARD J.
        "Satire, Theme, and Structure in The Traveller." TSL 16 (1971): 47-65.

The Traveller is a Juvenalian satire organized as a "Johnsonian journey through human society and a consequent examination of the relationship of the individual human soul to the collective demands of society." Discusses the relationship between theme and technique, and suggests that Goldsmith's technique of "thesis-antithesis" in describing the life that his journey reveals is similar to the ironic reversals in the writings of the Augustan humanists.

1352   LONSDALE, ROGER.
        " 'A Garden, and a Grave': The Poetry of Oliver Goldsmith." In [38], pp. 3-30.

Extended analyses of The Traveller and The Deserted Village, emphasizing especially the autobiographical elements in the poems in opposition to those critics who insist that their rhetorical nature precludes identifying the "I" with Goldsmith himself. The author concludes that The Traveller intends to emphasize the "self-dramatization of the poet" and, "inverting the recent 'rhetorical' approach," insists that "its philosophical and political content should be read as no more than a rhetorical device for winning respect and sympathy for the poet."

1353   STORM, LEO.
        "Conventional Ethics in Goldsmith's The Traveller." SEL 17 (1977): 463-476.

Concerned with his structure of ideas rather than with stress on feeling; seeks to discover the source of his ideas and what gave them shape and authority, by illustrating the "way Goldsmith worked into his description of European cultures and the theme of 'liberty' ... the archaistic political cosmology associated with John Denham's Cooper's Hill, and

the parallel philosophy of the Great Chain of Being to construct his ethical commentary on social happiness. " The
poem's flaw is that Goldsmith lost this ethical theme in the
presentation of his descriptive materials; his ethics are over-
whelmed by his charming personal presence and delightful
descriptions.

Miscellaneous Prose

1354   BOOTH, WAYNE C.
        " 'The Self-Portraiture of Genius': The Citizen of the World
        and Critical Method." MP 73, iv, part 2 (1976): S85-S96.

        Argues that the critic ought not to ignore, in evaluating
        a collection of essays made into a book, the rhetorical values
        of pleasure and utility (for the reader) and variety and genius
        (in the author), in his search for organic unities: "Though
        the rhetorical critics of Goldsmith's time disappoint us by
        their generality, never accounting fully for the genius and
        variety they praise, their interest in such qualities can re-
        mind us that there is after all a genuine 'art of the miscel-
        laneous. ' "

1355   DUSSINGER, JOHN A.
        "Philanthropy and the Selfish Reader in Goldsmith's Life of
        Nash. " SBHT 19 (1978): 197-207.

        Goldsmith's attempt to present Nash as a benevolent man,
        though often foolish, creates a rhetorical ambiguity for the
        reader as he views both the subject and the biographer. The
        biography "guards against sentimental indulgence and oppro-
        brious judgment alike while upholding Nash's innate benevolence
        for the reader to admire if not to imitate. "

1356   FERGUSON, OLIVER W.
        "The Materials of History: Goldsmith's Life of Nash. " PMLA
        80 (1965): 372-386.

        Concerned with the sources of the Life of Nash as well as
        with new details of Nash's affairs during his last years. In-
        cludes much new information about George Scott, the man
        who provided Goldsmith with Nash's papers.

1357   JAARSMA, RICHARD J.
        "Biography as Tragedy: Fictive Skill in Oliver Goldsmith's
        The Life of Richard Nash, Esq. JNT 1 (1971): 15-29.

        Argues that The Life of Nash "is a highly structured,

technically brilliant work of literature, equal in its style and attention to form and meaning to the works which have over-shadowed it. " The greatness of the Life lies not in its stated theme, but in the development of that theme through a species of near-symbolism.

1358   LYNSKEY, WINIFRED.
"Goldsmith and the Warfare in Nature." PQ 23 (1944): 333-342.

A discussion of Goldsmith's optimistic views toward sur-vival in nature as reflected in his Animated Nature.

1359   PATRICK, MICHAEL D.
"Oliver Goldsmith's Citizen of the World: A Rational Accom-modation of Human Existence." Enl. E. 2 (1971): 82-90.

Treats Citizen of the World as "a popularized and simpli-fied presentation of the eighteenth century conception of rea-son." The eighteenth century departs from the seventeenth in thinking of reason not as a static body of knowledge but as a dynamic force which man should use to attain the hu-mane ideas of rational truth, moral virtue, order, and beauty.

1360   SMITH, HAMILTON JEWETT.
Goldsmith's The Citizen of the World: A Study (Yale Studies in English, 71). New Haven: Yale Univ. Press, 1926.

"The correct dates and original order of appearance of all the essays are given accurately for the first time ... hitherto scattered facts have been assembled and much new material presented ... I treat, especially, the circumstances which led to the printing of the essays, the history of their publica-tion and that of the subsequent edition of The Citizen of the World, the Oriental influences and background, and the literary relations and sources. "

See also: 1271, 1288

Collected Studies

1361 DOWNEY, JAMES and BEN JONES, eds.
Fearful Joy: Papers from the Thomas Gray Bicentenary Conference at Carleton University. Montreal: McGill-Queen's Univ. Press, 1974.

General Studies

1362 BELL, CHARLES FRANCIS.
"Thomas Gray and the Fine Arts." E & S 30 (1944): 50-81.

A study of Gray's views and accomplishments in music, painting, prints, architecture, and gardening, as well as letters.

1363 BLAND, D. S.
"Gray and the Spirit of Romanticism." Cambridge Jour. 2 (1948): 169-180.

Argues that Gray's poetry was remarkable only for "its comparative excellence in an age of mediocrity" and that it was excellent only when he wrote as an Augustan, not as a Romantic.

1364 CECIL, LORD DAVID.
Two Quiet Lives: Dorothy Osborne, Thomas Gray. London: Constable; Indianapolis: Bobbs-Merrill Co. , 1948.

Lord David Cecil chooses Dorothy Osborne and Thomas Gray to study as personalities, attracted to them by "some unusual fineness of nature; an eye for the truth, depth, and delicacy of feeling, the presence to be detected in them of a strong and beautiful inner life."

1365 CHAPIN, CHESTER F.
"The Values of Allegorical Personification: Collins and Gray." In [88], pp. 68-80.

Allegorical descriptions in eighteenth-century verse often
have a "static" rather than a "mobile" effect; they decorate
rather than animate the verse in which they appear. But
Collins and Gray often display a literary tact that gives substantial value to their allegorical figures, especially when
their abstractions function as metaphor; even more importantly,
their most successful personifications are those that come
vibrantly alive, as in Collins's Ode to Evening. Gray employs personification as a rhetorical device: the personifications in the Elegy are dramatic rather than pictorial.

1366   DOHERTY, F.
       "The Two Voices of Gray." EIC 13 (1963): 222-230.

       "Gray's language, though distinctive, is used in two ways,
       outward-directed and largely impersonal and self-directed
       and partly personal, prosaic and poetic. "

1367   EVANS, B. IFOR.
       "Thomas Gray and William Blake." In Tradition and Roman-
       ticism: Studies in English Poetry from Chaucer to W. B.
       Yeats (London: Methuen, 1940), pp. 99-108.

       "The contrast between Gray and Blake is a contrast in
       the conception of poetry and its function" and not, as some-
       times assumed, the difference between a "pre-romantic" and
       a "complete romantic. "

1368   GOLDEN, MORRIS.
       Thomas Gray. New York: Twayne, 1964.

       This study of Gray has two main aims: to give the reader
       as much information as he needs for the study of Gray's
       poetry, and to examine freshly all of the poems as litera-
       ture. In the section, "Gray, the man," liberal quotations
       from Gray's letters are used as keys to his personality.

1369   GREENE, DONALD.
       "The Proper Language of Poetry: Gray, Johnson, and Others. "
       In [1361], pp. 85-102.

       Influences that fashioned eighteenth-century diction, and
       the argument between Johnson and Gray: "Johnson's view ...
       has seldom been accorded the importance ... it merits. "
       Wordsworth's and Johnson's similarities are emphasized.

1370   GRIFFIN, DUSTIN.
       "Gray's Audiences. " EIC 28 (1978): 208-215.

Gray's poems reflect his preoccupation with audience and his alienation from it. He presents an audience that he cannot reach, one that cannot hear or understand. This alienation is prevalent in his early poems, especially the Sonnet on the death of West and the Eton College Ode. Some of his poems, however, have an imagined audience, the "kindred spirit" as in the Elegy and The Bard.

1371   GRIFFIN, M. H.
       "Thomas Gray, Classical Augustan." Classical Jour. 36 (1941): 473-482.

       The origins of Gray's work are researched and the influence of Horace noted. Gray is established (as the title indicates) as a classicist, but with a faint prediction of romanticism in his later works.

1372   GUILHAMET, LEON M.
       "Imitation and Originality in the Poems of Thomas Gray." In [34], pp. 33-52.

       Considers Gray's use of imitation and his originality from the perspective given by Plato in Book III of the Republic.

1373   HAGSTRUM, JEAN H.
       "Gray's Sensibility." In [1361], pp. 6-19.

       Discusses Gray's melancholy, and suggests that sensibility struggles with stoicism, as though "disciplined virtue had to be applied like a cold compress to the burning brow of sensibility." Deals with friendships with Bonstetten, Walpole, and West.

1374   "Thomas Gray." In [112], pp. 287-314.

       Discusses Gray's knowledge of the fine arts, especially "the Roman masters of the sixteenth century and the Bolognese masters of the seventeenth," and analyzes the pictorial elements of his poetry.

1375   HERTZ, NEIL H.
       "Poetry in an Age of Prose: Arnold and Gray." In [11], pp. 57-75.

       Arnold's image of Gray as the "lonely poet" of the Romantic age may be a little distorted, as he tries to make Gray into a figure of his own time; however, Gray's Augustan poetry does become colored with a prophetic Romanticism.

1376   JACK, IAN.
       "Gray in His Letters." In [1361], pp. 20-36.

       Gray's letters are more revealing of his life than are Gib-
       bon's Memoirs or Mark Pattison's Memoirs.   Discusses how
       Gray's letters, their style and tone, reveal the "pattern" of
       his life.

1377   JOHNSTON, ARTHUR.
       "Thomas Gray: Our Daring Bard." In [1361], pp. 50-65.

       Traces development of Gray's work as a whole, especially
       poems written between June 1742 and June 1750 as compared
       to his earlier and later work and discusses his boldness as
       a poet--the risks he took with his mind and imagination--as
       recognized by Fuseli, Blake, and Johnson.

1378   JONES, WILLIAM POWELL.
       "Johnson and Gray: A Study in Literary Antagonism." MP
       56 (1959): 243-253.

       Jones takes the position that the two poets were basically
       opposite in temperament, environment, and attitude toward
       writing as a profession.   Johnson was big, loud, slovenly,
       and blustering; Gray was relatively aristocratic, almost dainty.
       Their similarities (poor health, melancholy, indolence) did
       not help the situation.

1379   "Mute Inglorious Gray." Emory Univ. Quart. 11 (1955): 199-
       207.

       Mainly a biographical study showing that Gray's character
       was expressed in his poetry by his conciseness and accuracy
       of phrase.

1380   Thomas Gray, Scholar: The True Tragedy of an Eighteenth-
       Century Gentleman.   Cambridge: Harvard Univ. Press, 1937;
       rpt. New York: Russell & Russell, 1966.

       Attempts to "give a complete account of Gray's learning
       and a critical estimate of its importance in his life."

1381   "The Vogue of Natural History in England, 1750-1770." Annals
       of Science 2 (1937): 345-352.

       The upsurge of interest in natural history in the last half
       of the eighteenth century is explored for its influence on liter-
       ature, particularly the writing of Thomas Gray.

1382   KETTON-CREMER, ROBERT W.
       "The Poet Who Spoke Out: The Letters of Thomas Gray."
       In [1], pp. 148-164.

       Maintains that Gray's letters are among the classics of
       eighteenth-century literature; that his "thoughts were so ex-
       ceedingly good, and so purely his own."

1383   Thomas Gray. (WTW) London: Longmans, 1958.

       A brief biographical account with special attention paid to
       the literary excellence of Gray's letters.

1384   Thomas Gray: A Biography. Cambridge: Cambridge Univ.
       Press, 1955.

       A biography, with special emphasis on the Elegy and the
       Pindaric Odes, but not much in the way of criticism.

1385   LONSDALE, ROGER.
       The Poetry of Thomas Gray: Versions of the Self (Chatterton
       Lecture on an English Poet, British Academy). London: Ox-
       ford Univ. Press, 1973.

       Interprets the poem as a process of self-dramatization;
       deals with the "self" created by the poem, emphasizing the
       complexity of the relationship between Gray and the poetic
       "self." Believes that Gray is talking about himself at the
       end of the Elegy.

1386   LYTTON SELLS, A. L.
       Thomas Gray: His Life and Works. London: Allen & Un-
       win, 1980.

       First part of the book deals with Gray's life; the second
       part with his literary output--poems, translations, and letters
       --and also with Gray as scholar, critic, and student. In-
       cludes an appendix, "Gray's Poetic Diction" by Iris Lytton
       Sells.

1387   MacDONALD, ALASTAIR.
       "Thomas Gray: An Uncommitted Life." HAB 13 (1962-63):
       13-25.

       An essay on Gray's rather tragic life and how his poetry
       reflects it; why "his appeal, both in his lifetime and since,
       is the appeal of the solitary."

1388   MACKERNESS, E. D.
        "The Progress of an Italophile: Thomas Gray and Music."
        Italian Studies 12 (1957): 99-109.

        An attempt to "ascertain the quality of Gray's musical in-
        terests and to relate them to a few of his other preoccupa-
        tions."

1389   MACLEAN, KENNETH.
        "The Distant Way: Imagination and Image in Gray's Poetry."
        In [1361], pp. 136-145.

        Discusses the metaphor of water in Gray's writing, his
        use of the "way," of colour, and of architectural forms, and
        his influence on Wordsworth.

1390   MANDEL, ELI.
        "Theories of Voice in Eighteenth-Century Poetry: Thomas
        Gray and Christopher Smart." In [1361], pp. 103-118.

        Compares Smart's "Song to David" and Jubilate Agno with
        Gray's Pindaric Odes, and especially considers the signifi-
        cance of Gray's and Smart's metaphoric identification of music
        and poetry. Sees as Gray's characteristic note the sense of
        loss.

1391   MARTIN, ROGER.
        Essai sur Thomas Gray. London: Oxford Univ. Press; Paris
        Les Presses Universitaires de France, 1934.

        An extensive and critical study. A study of Gray's per-
        sonality, treating of his moral and physical character, his
        feelings, his intellectual activity, and his poetry.

1392   SCHLÜTER, KURT.
        "Wordsworth als Kritiker von Grays poetische Diktion." Neo-
        philologus 42 (1958): 216-222.

        Wordsworth's opinion is warped perhaps by the age in which
        he lived. Schlüter wants not so much to rescue Gray from a
        misjudgment as to awaken the reader to an appreciation of
        Gray's own individual poetic diction and his innate artistic
        worth.

1393   SNYDER, ROBERT LANCE.
        "The Epistolary Melancholy of Thomas Gray." Biography 2
        (1979): 125-140.

Concerned with the tension in Gray's letters between brooding introspection and a more sanguine interest in events of the public world, but especially concerned with the former--" "... an effort to comprehend the nature of the melancholy involved and to interpret it as a variant mode of eighteenth-century sensibility." The thesis is that Gray's depression is closely linked to his cultural inheritance and to his perception of his age's dominant values: "... if he did experience the culture of his time as being fragmented and self-negating ... then his melancholic absorption with himself is implicitly a criticism of his age."

1394   SPACKS, PATRICIA M.
        "Statement and Artifice in Thomas Gray." SEL 5 (1965): 519-532. Rpt. in [167], pp. 90-103.

        Examines Gray for evidence of sincerity and simplicity, qualities which he is commonly considered to lack. Sees Augustan rhetorical devices throughout his poetry, but defends them: as they are contrasted with passages of relatively undecorated language, the result, Spacks says, is good craftsmanship. Gray demonstrates his "extraordinary skill at playing off highly controlled rhetoric against simple, direct statement."

1395   STARR, HERBERT W.
        Gray as a Literary Critic. Philadelphia: Univ. Pa. Press, 1941; rpt. Folcroft, Pa.: Folcroft Library Editions, 1974.

        Although Gray's direct influence has been slight, "his extraordinary talents, his learning, his tolerance, and his excellent taste in themselves rank him as one of the finest critics of his day." Based on the literary criticism of the letters and prose essays, Starr's book sketches in the critical milieu in which Gray worked and the nature of the materials on which his research depends, and attempts to clarify the theories and principles of Gray's literary criticism and to suggest its resemblance to the criticism of his contemporaries.

1396   STEELE, JAMES.
        "Thomas Gray and the Season for Triumph." In [1361], pp. 198-240.

        Argues that Gray did not withdraw from the world, but was "very much a part of the rentier stratum of the capitalist ruling class in England ... public matters are ... as much a part of Gray's poetry as his subjective feelings and words." Concerned with Gray's relationship to world of politics, business, and empire.

1397   STEUERT, DOM HILARY.
       "Two Augustan Studies. I. Thomas Gray."   Dublin Rev. 216
       (1945): 61-67.

           Explication of Arnold's criticism of Gray in terms of Ar-
       nold's conception of "soul," and defines Gray's affinities with
       the Augustan tradition.

1398   SWEARINGEN, JAMES E.
       "Johnson's 'Life of Gray.'"   TSLL 14 (1972): 283-302.

           A defense of Johnson's attack on Gray's poetry which is
       apart from his personal dislike.   "From the perspective of
       the twentieth century it is more appropriate to give credit
       both to the critic for his integrity and to the assumptions
       that equipped him to feel so accurately the directions English
       poetry was taking than to censure him for being unfair."

1399   TILLOTSON, GEOFFREY.
       "On Gray's Letters." In Essays in Criticism and Research
       (Cambridge: Cambridge Univ. Press, 1942; rpt. Hamden,
       Conn.: Archon Books, 1967): pp. 117-123.

           Discusses Gray's letters written during his travels as ex-
       amples of "perfect informal prose."

1400   VIVANTE, LEON.
       "The Concept of a Creative Principle in the Poems of Collins
       and Gray." CLS 8 (1942): 12-17.

           Discusses simplicity as the principle of beauty in Collins,
       and the importance of inspiration in Gray's conception of
       poetry. Gray's poems reflect a beauty deriving from "the
       essential, radically ontological character of the truths" in
       his life and thought.

1401   WHALLEY, GEORGE.
       "Thomas Gray: A Quiet Hellenist." In [1361], pp. 146-171.

           Discusses Gray's manner of reading Greek literature and
       the quality of his sensibility, and concludes that he was not
       a classical scholar in the sense that Porson or Bentley were.
       Considers Gray's Pindaric Odes.

See also: 517, 1809, 1842, 1962, 2035, 3183

The Elegy

1402   ADEN, JOHN M.
        "An Artless Tale?" SR 85 (1977): 697-701.

    Gray's Elegy is a classical poem, in both theme and exe-
cution; it is full of classical and neo-classical motifs: e. g. ,
memento mori, retirement, a suggestion of the ars vivendi
and beatus ille, and an unromantic version of secretum iter:
the idea that the rural life defeats the world's demands and
applause. The ancestry of the Elegy can be traced back to
Virgil and Horace. The classical case is argued principally
from the standpoint of art or technique, especially the way
in which architectonics illustrates the Elegy's classical attitude and design.

1403   BATESON, F. W.
        "Gray's Elegy Reconsidered. " In English Poetry: A Critical
        Introduction (London: Longmans, Green, 1950), pp. 127-135.

    Discusses the Elegy as a very personal document, so much
so that the original ending was deleted after about a year of
keeping the poem "in storage," and the last fifty-two lines of
the present version added. These late-born lines are seen
as an attempt to depersonalize the poem.

1404   BERRY, FRANCIS.
        "The Sound of Personification in Gray's 'Elegy. ' " EIC 12
        (1962): 442-445.

    Defends Gray's Elegy against the unfavorable criticism of
Wordsworth and others in the matter of personification.

1405   BRADY, FRANK.
        "Structure and Meaning in Gray's Elegy. " In [26], pp. 177-
        189.

    Explores the changes made in the Elegy between the first
draft and the final version, and the reasons for making them.
Shows the structural relationships of such characters as the
Swain, the Rustics, and the Narrator, and suggests that through
them the Elegy "thematically makes a number of interrelated
assertions. " Concludes that in "revising the poem Gray did
not just tack on two discordant and rather inexplicable sketches
of the Narrator to a meditation in the lives of rich and poor;
instead, the transformed poem involves three major contrasts,
in which the opening and closing ones resemble in some ways
the outside panels of a triptych. "

1406   BRONSON, BERTRAND H.
       "On a Special Decorum in Gray's Elegy." In [26], pp. 171-
       176; rpt. in [76], pp. 153-158.

       Considers a special decorum in the Elegy in which " 'mod-
       eration and temperance' display themselves 'with the very
       image of a generous soul' "; refers specifically to the de-
       corum of Gray's handling of the poem's "inescapable egocen-
       tricity."

1407   BROOKS, CLEANTH.
       "Gray's Storied Urn." In The Well Wrought Urn: Studies in
       The Structure of Poetry (New York: Reynal & Hitchcock,
       1947), pp. 96-113; rpt. in [1430], pp. 23-32.

       An extended analysis of the Elegy--personifications, allu-
       sions, irony, contrasts, structure--and the relationship of
       the epitaph to the " 'shapeless sculpture' of the churchyard
       and ... the 'storied urn' of the abbey church."

1408   CARPER, THOMAS R.
       "Gray's Personal Elegy." SEL 17 (1977): 451-462.

       Argues that both the Eton MS version of the Elegy and the
       published version are intensely personal.   Carper examines
       the background of images and interests prominent in the Elegy,
       and demonstrates that Gray habitually portrayed himself in his
       earlier poetry as a "contemplative man behaving in the man-
       ner of a pastoral poet." Other subjects personal to Gray in
       the Elegy are the poet's emphasis on family and the contrast
       between the humble and the highly placed; also Gray works
       toward a poem that will represent an alleviation of those sub-
       jects.

1409   CHIASSON, ELIAS.
       "The Courtly Lady in Gray's Elegy." PMPA 3 (1978): 39-
       49.

       Concerned with the interpretation of the third line of the
       Epitaph and the meanings given by various critics to "Fair
       Science frowned not ... " Ellis [1414]; Sutherland [1433]). Sug-
       gests that "[t]he traditional difficulty in the poem can be re-
       solved by finding within the poem itself some framework with-
       in which the absence of the frown of Science can be thought
       of as a real deprivation," and that the place to look for this
       framework is in the "courtly love" tradition. Gray metaphor-
       ically connects the love of learning to courtly love--the image
       of Science or Knowledge as a courtly lady--and in so doing
       is able "to end the poem in such a way as to resolve the ma-
       jor tensions within it." This interpretation frowns upon tak-
       ing not frowned to mean smiled.

1410   COSGROVE, BRIAN.
        " 'Ev'n in our ashes live their wonted fires': Privation and
        Affirmation in Gray's Elegy." English 29 (1980): 117-130.

        A reading of the Elegy which shows an analogy between the
        situation of the villagers and that of the poet--in many ways
        their condition is a reflection of his own; they were deprived
        of life, Gray of vitality. Explores recurrent imagery, re-
        flects on the meanings of "low" and "lowly," and emphasizes
        "the organic interrelatedness of some of [the poem's] key-
        imagery ... to refute the critical suggestion ... that the
        Elegy is 'defective' in its 'want of plan.' "

1411   COX, STEPHEN D.
        "Contexts of Significance: Thomas Gray." In [93], pp. 82-
        98.

        Suggests that the Elegy expresses the belief that the in-
        dividual self is significant even when it lacks the visible
        signs of significance--wealth, power, or social position; that
        the self gains recognition from the "tenacity of its desires."
        All of Gray's poems display his lifelong hesitation about how
        to evaluate the self; he was unable to accept an external con-
        text of significance that would compensate the self for its
        limitations.

1412   CRANE, R. S.
        "Gray's Elegy and Lycidas." MLN 38 (1924): 183-184.

        Notes the influence of Milton on such poets as Gray and
        Collins, whose poetry may be seen looking back toward Mil-
        ton or forward toward Romanticism. The Elegy by Gray and
        Ode to Evening by Collins are seen as reflecting the tone of
        Lycidas, as well as that of Milton's early short poems.

1413   DYSON, A. E.
        "The Ambivalence of Gray's Elegy." EIC 7 (1957): 257-261.
        Rpt. [1430], pp. 83-87.

        Dyson brings out the apparent contradiction in the Elegy:
        the simple life is celebrated as peaceful and desirable in the
        nostalgic pastoral tradition, but yet the "rude forefathers"
        are presented as victims, to whom so many avenues of life
        are closed. Gray himself is seen as the subject of the "Epi-
        taph."

1414   ELLIS, FRANK H.
        "Gray's Elegy: The Biographical Problem in Literary Criti-
        cism." PMLA 66 (1951): 971-1008. Rpt. in [1430], pp. 51-
        75.

A protest against the widely held view that just as the poet's life and experiences illuminate his poetry, so his poetry will illuminate his biographical experience. Ellis says this is false, that "biographical experiences can no more be reconstructed from a poem than the poem (if it were lost) could be reconstructed from the experiences." Gray's <u>Elegy</u> is chosen to demonstrate this theory, and the author then argues that by a "shift in the antecedent of a pronoun, Gray wrote himself out of his poem," achieving total anonymity; he further suggests that the "thee" of l. 93 refers to a stone-cutter-Poet and "these lines" of l. 94 to the "uncouth rhymes" composed by the Stonecutter.

1415 EMPSON, WILLIAM.
      <u>Some Versions of Pastoral</u>.   London: Chatto & Windus, 1935.

      Includes a brief discussion of social attitudes and "latent political ideas" in the <u>Elegy</u>; suggests that "the truism of the reflections in the churchyard, the universality and impersonality this gives to the style, claim as if by comparison that we ought to accept the injustice of society as we do the inevitability of death."

1416 FISHER, J.
      "Shenstone, Gray, and the 'Moral Elegy.'"   <u>MP</u> 34 (1937):
      273-294.

      Considers the contribution made by the relatively unknown Shenstone to the development of the elegy.   Shows that Shenstone's 26 <u>Elegies</u> were circulating in manuscript form before Gray's <u>Elegy</u> was published; discusses implication: 1) both Shenstone and Gray almost contemporaneously "moralized" the elegy; 2) Gray's <u>Elegy</u> and Shenstone's <u>Elegies</u> display an unmistakable general resemblance in "moral cast"; and 3) although Gray's <u>Elegy</u> appeared thirteen years before Shenstone's <u>Elegies</u>, the latter's influence upon the elegy was at work much earlier than Gray's.

1417 "James Hammond and the Quatrain of Gray's <u>Elegy</u>."   <u>MP</u>
      32 (1935): 301-310.

      Defines the position of James Hammond in the development of the elegy as an art form, pointing out that Gray was not the only poet involved.   Hammond was first to choose the quatrain for this kind of work and to develop it into "our English elegiac stanza."

1418 GARROD, H. W.

"Note on the Composition of Gray's Elegy. In [54], pp. 111-116.

Examines correspondence between Walpole and the Rev. William Morris and argues that Gray began the Elegy in 1742, even though it was not finished until 1750.

1419   GLAZIER, LYLE.
"Gray's Elegy: 'The Skull Beneath the Skin.'" UKCR 19 (1953): 174-180. Rpt. in [1430], pp. 33-40.

A detailed analysis of the theme that all men--both rich and poor--are subject to death; insists that Gray's generalization about death is the true subject of the poem, and that his balancing of privileged and underprivileged is only an illustration, carried to its social limits, of that generalization.

1420   HARTOG, CURT.
"Psychic Resolution in Gray's 'Elegy.'" L & P 25 (1975): 5-16.

The author focuses on the psychological interaction between reader and text in order to understand the unconscious shifts that occur in the poem, especially in the conclusion, and argues that Gray's Elegy, unlike Lycidas, has an ending that fails to achieve a resolution, aesthetically or psychologically.

1421   JACK, IAN.
"Gray's Elegy Reconsidered." In [26], pp. 139-169. Rpt. abridged in [1430], pp. 88-108.

Seeks to establish the probable date of composition and the original intention of the poem. Analyzes the metrics and diction, and suggests even that the use of present participles gives the lines a "static, pictorial quality."

1422   JONES, MYRDDIN.
"Gray, Jaques, and the Man-of-Feeling." RES 25 (1974): 39-48.

The "Jaques" referred to is a character in As You Like It, who "... lay along/Under an oak, whose antique root peeps out/Upon the brook that brawls along this wood"; chief purpose of the article is to "consider the appeal of the character to other writers, artists, and critics of the earlier period." The closing stanzas of the Elegy are interpreted in the light of this allusion, suggesting that Jaques becomes an image of a man of feeling "outside the pale of the fashionable, 'successful,' insensitive world."

1423   KUIST, JAMES M.
       "The Conclusion of Gray's Elegy." SAQ 70 (1971): 203-214.

       Discusses the significance and the effect of Gray's use of
       sentiment.

1424   LOGSDON, RICHARD.
       "Gray's 'Elegy': The Structure and the Poet." Essays in
       Literature (Denver) 2, No. 1 (1973): 1-19.

       Defines the structural principle as the "movement in the
       poet's mind from an emotional affinity with the graveyard
       dead to an imagined union in death with them," and then dis-
       cusses the relationship of the arguments to the poem's cen-
       tral activity; a close reading.

1425   NEWMAN, W. M.
       "When Curfew Tolled the Knell." National Rev. 127 (1946):
       244-248. Rpt. [1430], pp. 17-22.

       Using meteorological evidence to prove that the Elegy was
       written in August 1746 as a result of the trials and execu-
       tions of Jacobite Lords and that it was finished in Stoke,
       August 18.

1426   PECKHAM, MORSE.
       "Gray's 'Epitaph' Revisited." MLN 71 (1956): 409-411.
       Rpt. in [1430], pp. 76-78.

       Comments on the structure of the last part of the Elegy;
       suggests that the Spokesman imagines the "Friend" of l.
       124 to have written the "Epitaph," and that the poem is a
       dramatic monologue.

1427   REED, AMY LOUISE.
       The Background of Gray's Elegy: A Study in the Taste for
       Melancholy Poetry, 1700-1751. New York: Columbia Univ.
       Press, 1924.

       The poetry of melancholy is followed, from the prose def-
       inition of melancholy in 1621 to its "perfection of form,"
       Gray's Elegy, 1751.

1428   ROBERTS, MARK.
       "A Note on Gray's Elegy." ES 39 (1958): 251-256.

       Discusses the interpretation of a central section of the
       Elegy, which the author identifies as the best part, the what-
       might-have-been stanzas.

1429   SHEPARD, ODELL.
        "A Youth to Fortune and to Fame Unknown." MP 20 (1923):
        347-373.

        Intelligent study of the structure of Gray's Elegy, including
        such questions as the relation of the second part to the first,
        and whether the young poet of Part II is intended as a con-
        crete example of that unacknowledged merit with which Part
        I deals in its major subdivision; such problems cannot be
        successfully undertaken until we can establish the identity of
        the "Youth to Fortune and to Fame Unknown." Shepard ar-
        gues that this youth is Richard West, and that the Elegy there-
        fore takes its place with Lycides and Thyrsis, elegies that
        mingle general reflection with personal grief.

1430   STARR, HERBERT W. , ED.
        Twentieth-Century Interpretations of Gray's "Elegy": A Col-
        lection of Critical Essays. Englewood Cliffs, N. J. : Prentice-
        Hall, 1968.

1431   " 'A Youth to Fortune and to Fame Unknown': A Re-estima-
        tion." JEGP 48 (1949): 97-107. Rpt. in [1430], pp. 41-50.

        Argues against Professor Odell Shepard's theory that the
        Epitaph at the end of the Elegy was originally written to
        commemorate Gray's dead friend, Richard West; suggests in-
        stead that the Youth refers to a fictitious village poet who
        had commemorated the "unhonoured Dead."

1432   SUGG, RICHARD P.
        "The Importance of Voice: Gray's Elegy." TSL 19 (1974):
        115-120.

        Emphasizes the importance of poetic voice in man's quest
        for immortality; suggests that though the poet dies, the poetic
        voice he created can survive to speak his Epitaph: the im-
        mortality of poetry is affirmed when the voice of the poem
        separates itself from the speaker and addresses him as "thee"
        in line 93. The Elegy is Gray's own epitaph.

1433   SUTHERLAND, JOHN.
        "The Stonecutter in Gray's 'Elegy.' " MP 55 (1957): 11-13.
        Rpt. in [1430], pp. 79-81.

        Refutes the popular theory that the epitaph in Gray's Elegy
        refers to the "stonecutter-poet" of the twentieth and twenty-
        first stanzas. Sutherland argues that the narrator is the sub-
        ject of the epitaph, and that he is an educated young gentle-
        man, not an unlettered stonecutter.

1434   TRACY, CLARENCE.
        " 'Melancholy Mark'd Him for Her Own: Thomas Gray Two
        Hundred Years Afterwards." Proceedings and Transactions
        of the Royal Society of Canada 9 (1971): 313-325. Rpt. in
        [1361], pp. 37-49.

        Explores the differing meanings of the Elegy for the eigh-
        teenth and the nineteenth centuries; then offers a third inter-
        pretation from the perspective of 200 years: " ... earlier
        readers responded to the poem with their imagination and
        hearts whereas we respond with out heads and our blue pen-
        cils. "

1435   WAGMAN, STEPHEN.
        "Myth and the Commonplace in Gray's Elegy." Enl. E. 5,
        iii/iv (1974): 7-13.

        Concerned primarily with the themes of the Elegy, espe-
        cially with the theme of a pastoral vision of life, "the poetic
        hope ... of peace and joy and freedom from the cares of the
        world. " Yet Gray is not by nature a mythic poet, though the
        mythic impulse reemerges as a sentimental philosophy that
        charmed even Dr. Johnson. The pain of waste and failure,
        the tragedy of unfulfilled lives, is so overwhelming that Gray
        seeks to protect both himself and us from painful thoughts by
        clothing them in the "worn and polished words that give the
        horrors of the commonplace a familiar and unthreatening
        face. "

1436   WATSON, GEORGE.
        "The Voice of Gray." Crit. Quart. 19, iv (1977): 51-57.

        Gray's use of the active and passive voice in the Elegy is
        full of grammatical uncertainties and shows that he was a
        "passionate pedant with language. "

1437   WATSON-SMYTH, PETER.
        "The Origins of the Elegy." ArielE 1, No. 4 (1970): 39-47.

        Argues that Gray began writing the Elegy in August, 1737,
        at Cant's Hill, Burnham, the home of his aunt, Ann Rogers;
        that the Churchyard is that of St. Peter's, Burnham, and that
        the "Youth" is Gray himself, a youth of nineteen or twenty,
        and the "Friend" is Walpole. The poem then becomes an
        epitaph on his youth and his first love.

1438   WEINBROT, HOWARD D.
        "Gray's Elegy: A Poem of Moral Choice and Resolution. "
        SEL 18 (1978): 537-551.

An analysis of setting, character, and poetic language to show that the Elegy "is concerned not with a choice of life or death, but a choice of eternity." A close examination of the poem's seven principal parts reveals that it ends as an elegy "for a man who learns to accept and praise his limited world and its people" and who hopes "to be accepted and praised in the limitless world of God and His people." Gray's poet, therefore, finds that the "paths of moral choice lead beyond the grave."

1439   WRIGHT, GEORGE T.
         "Stillness and the Argument of Gray's Elegy." MP 74 (1977): 381-389.

Suggests that Gray's concern over the ending of his poem, which caused him to substitute the fourteen stanzas following line 72 for the original four, was because the original ending wasn't consistent with his argument about the nature and meaning of epitaphs. In his revised ending, he makes his point that we all, even the poor, need epitaphs by which to be remembered, and that "No matter how modest ... an epitaph works against the stillness to which all human action and achievement are in time reduced."

1440   "Eliot Written in a Country Churchyard: The Elegy and Four Quartets." ELH 43 (1976): 227-243.

Argues that internal evidence suggests that a "possible base from which Eliot evolved Four Quartets is the Elegy Written in a Country Churchyard." The Quartets seem to cover the same material as the Elegy but with more subtle and refined feeling for religious and philosophical implications. Much of Eliot's imagery echoes that of Gray; in both poems the important measurement is that of time, not distance, and both are set in country landscapes remote from the pressures of city life with speaker-poets expressing "melancholy reflections on the relation of the dead to the living, of the past ... to the present, of time to eternity, and of himself to his world."

The Odes and Other Poems

1441   BACHE, WILLIAM B.
         "Gray's 'Sonnet: On the Death of Richard West.'" CEA 31, No. 2 (1968-69): 12.

An interpretive paraphrase of the sonnet, emphasizing the central tension between Gray and nature, between the speaker and nature, between man and nature, including secondary ten-

sions--"this man's anguish and the joys of nature; this man
and happier men; this man's mourning and nature's morning."

1442   ELLIS, FRANK H.
       "Gray's Eton College Ode: The Problem of Tone." PLL 5
       (1969): 130-138.

           Suggests that the tone of the Ode is mixed, that there are
       elements which are not serious.   This "mixed tone enables
       the poem to confront for a moment the real desolations of
       manhood, without hope and yet not without humor."

1443   FOLADARE, JOSEPH.
       "Gray's 'Frail Memorial' to West." PMLA 75 (1960): 61-
       65. Rpt. in [1430], pp. 112-114.

           Careful analysis and exposition of Gray's Sonnet on the
       Death of Richard West are intended to rescue the poem from
       the lowly place allotted to it by nineteenth-century criticism.
       The influence of Virgil, of the pastoral tradition, and espe-
       cially of Milton is discussed.

1444   FRY, PAUL H.
       "Thomas Gray's Feather'd Cincture." In The Poet's Calling
       in the English Ode (New Haven: Yale Univ. Press, 1980),
       pp. 63-96.

           Gray's odes explore an unvarying personal theme, the iso-
       lation of the speaker.   Suggests that Gray's verbal artifice
       embroiders an empty circle; that is, his writing, in drawing
       interest to itself, gains a density that more effectively ex-
       presses meaning than does a naturalistic diction that allows
       meaning to escape through its own transparency.

1445   GILMORE, THOMAS B., JR.
       "Allusion and Melancholy in Gray's Ode on a Distant Prospect
       of Eton College." PLL 15 (1979): 52-58.

           The reader's awareness of the "depth and strength of the
       poet's melancholy is increased if he also grasps the signifi-
       cance of three of the major contexts--Comus, the Crenaeus
       passage in Statius, and Aeneid 6--to which Gray alludes."
       Gray's allusions, especially to Comus and Aeneid 6, increase
       the "unified effect and desolate melancholy" of the Ode.   The
       mock heroic functions almost literally; Gray shows that fea-
       tures of epic poetry, such as divine protection of the hero,
       do not operate in the fallen world of reality.

1446   HINNANT, CHARLES H.
"Changing Perspectives on the Past: The Reception of Thomas
Gray's The Bard." Clio 3 (1974): 315-329.

Suggests that many of the contemporary complaints concerning "The Bard" arose from the eighteenth-century readers'
lack of familiarity with medieval chronicles.   Both Gray and
his readers viewed history as the story of liberty, so that the
significance of the bard's prophecy is deepened by the fact
that he embodies patriotic virtue; both the minstrel's indictment of Edward's massacre of the bards and Gray's effort to
revive the historical myths of earlier times were not clearly
understood by contemporary readers.

1447   HUNT, JOHN DIXON.
"The Landscape of the Bard." In [121], pp. 145-195.

Gray's The Bard expresses an area of cultural history
that seemed to be a new and exciting source of ideas and
images that were, specifically, a challenge to the Augustan
art of gardening.   Gray was able to understand the meanings
of landscape gardens, but disliked their artificial structures,
preferring instead an alternative landscape of sublime mountain scenery; from that source Gray and his followers derived
a vocabulary of images that seemed to reflect a more traditional "British" imagination.

1448   JOHNSTON, ARTHUR.
Thomas Gray and "The Bard." Cardiff: Univ. Wales Press,
1966.

A close examination of the poem shows that the Bard is
Man learning to understand and cope with existence.   Gray's
inspiration in a little known incident of Welsh history is revealed, and his achievement, first among English poets, of
"reproducing a sense of historical period" is emphasized.

1449   "Gray's Use of the Gorchest y Beirdd in 'The Bard.'" MLR
59 (1964): 335-338.

"Gorchest y Beirdd" or "excellence of the Bards," a tricky
fifteenth-century invention in Welsh prosody, is compared to
Gray's double cadence passages in the Bard.

1450   "Gray's 'The Triumphs of Owen.'" RES 11 (1960): 275-285.

The sources of The Triumphs of Owen researched, giving
due credit to the Welsh scholar, Evan Evans.

1451   JONES, WILLIAM POWELL.
       "The Contemporary Reception of Gray's Odes." MP 28 (1930):
       61-82.

            Reasons why the reading public was interested in whatever
       Gray wrote and why, even though readers did not quite under-
       stand the exalted imagination, the elaborate metrical scheme,
       and the historical allusions in the Odes, they were popular.

1452   LYLES, ALBERT M.
       "Historical Perspective in Gray's Eton College Ode." TSE 9
       (1964): 57-61.

            The poem is rich in allusions, the key one being to Izaak
       Walton's Life of Sir Henry Wotton. The historical sequence
       of Gray's poem parallels Walton's Life: "It is through attain-
       ing the historical perspective ... that the reader understands
       Gray's Eton College Ode."

1453   MELL, DONALD C., Jr.
       "Form as Meaning in Augustan Elegy: A Reading of Thomas
       Gray's 'Sonnet on the Death of Richard West.'" PLL 4
       (1968): 131-143.

            Emphasizes the allusory mode of this sonnet and suggests
       that the reader needs to be familiar with the world of Milton's
       Eden to fully appreciate the Sonnet on the Death of Richard
       West. Structure and techniques are discussed. The poem
       is commended as close to the ideal Augustan, "one in which
       maximum tension has resulted from a struggle of contraries
       of many kinds."

1454   MOORE, JUDITH K.
       "Thomas Gray's 'Sonnet on the Death of Richard West': The
       Circumstances and the Diction." TSL 19 (1974): 107-113.

            Considers the circumstances of the poem's composition,
       its language, and its place in a literary and biographical mi-
       lieu; insists that the language deliberately echoes and modu-
       lates the language of Gray's earlier poem, "Noon-tide."

1455   PATTISON, ROBERT.
       "Gray's 'Ode on the Death of a Favourite Cat': A Rational-
       ist's Aesthetic." UTQ 49 (1979): 156-165.

            The Ode is firmly rooted in the dominant aesthetic of Gray's
       time, rationalism; it displays several characteristics of that
       aesthetic: an "eighteenth-century rationalist's love of accur-
       acy and detail, a Renaissance gentleman's manipulation of

classical sources, and a lambent wit playing over the whole
surface of the work." The Ode also displays an eighteenth-
century economy in the application of meaning that facilitates
the development of the poem's primary meaning--the "ration-
alistic description of the mind at work upon itself and the
world of external appearances...."

1456   SPACKS, PATRICIA M.
        "Thomas Gray: Action and Image." In [167], pp. 90-118.

        Artifice, diction, and rhetoric in "Ode on the Spring,"
        "Ode on a Distant Prospect of Eton College," "Sonnet on the
        Death of Richard West," and in the two Great Odes.

1457   " 'Artful Strife': Conflict in Gray's Poetry." PMLA 81
        (1966): 63-69. Rpt. in [167], Chap. V, pp. 103-118.

        A discussion of poetic technique as seen in The Progress
        of Poesy and The Bard. Emphasizes Gray's weaknesses as
        craftsman, particularly in his use of antithesis and inversion,
        and his way of setting the stage for conflict and then avoiding
        the dramatization of that conflict "by escape into the conven-
        tion of image rather than action as central to a poem." Con-
        cludes that Gray's odes, with their emphasis on the pictorial,
        did not allow expression of his interest in conflict as a theme;
        "his sense of poetry as process, as a record of creative ac-
        tivity, could not be fully implemented through primary reli-
        ance on imagery."

1458   STARR, HERBERT W.
        "Gray's Craftsmanship." JEGP 45 (1946): 415-429.

        A study of Gray's revisions in the Elegy, The Progress
        of Poesy, and The Bard.

1459   TILLOTSON, GEOFFREY.
        "Gray's 'Ode on the Spring' "; "Gray's 'Ode on the Death of
        a Favourite Cat....' " In [174], pp. 204-215; 216-223.

        I. "Gray's 'Ode on the Spring'": a discussion of the phrase,
        "purple year," from Virgil to Dryden and Pope, and of other
        borrowings especially from Milton; a close analysis of the
        poem, concentrating on the diction. II. "Gray's 'Ode on the
        Death of a Favourite Cat, Drowned in a Tub of Gold Fishes' ":
        interprets the poem as a "mock-ballad" and discusses John-
        son's criticisms of the poem and the reasons for them.

1460   VERNON, P. F.

"The Structure of Gray's Early Poems." <u>EIC</u> 15 (1965): 381-393.

Says that Gray was unique in the early eighteenth century "in the way he frames the whole structural pattern of his poems around a main symbol."

See also: 503, <u>2253</u>

Collected Studies

1461 BOULTON, JAMES T. , ed.
Johnson: The Critical Heritage. New York: Barnes & Noble, 1971.

1462 GREENE, DONALD J. , ed.
Samuel Johnson: A Collection of Critical Essays. Englewood Cliffs, N. J. : Prentice-Hall, 1965.

1463 HILLES, FREDERICK W. , ed.
New Light on Dr. Johnson: Essays on the Occasion of His 250th Birthday. New Haven: Yale Univ. Press, 1959.

1464 LASCELLES, MARY, ed.
Johnson, Boswell and Their Circle: Essays Presented to Lawrence Fitzroy Powell.... Oxford: Clarendon Press, 1965.

1465 WAHBA, MAGDI, ed.
Johnsonian Studies, including a Bibliography of Johnsonian Studies, 1950-60, compiled by James L. Clifford & Donald J. Greene. Cairo, 1962. Distributed by Oxford Univ. Press.

General Studies

1466 ALKON, PAUL K.
Samuel Johnson and Moral Discipline. Evanston, Ill. : Northwestern Univ. Press, 1967.

Examines chiefly the Rambler, the Adventurer, the Idler, and Rasselas in relation to their intellectual milieu; and analyzes "the controlling assumptions of Johnson's moral writings in order to show the nature of those assumptions and how they are related to a few important but neglected or misunderstood aspects of their intellectual backgrounds. " Discusses Johnson's view of human nature and the ways in which the mind works; the relationship between Johnson and Locke in order to prove that Johnson was not opposed to a naturalistic description of human nature; his views on the consequences, causes, and cures of self-delusion; the way in which his accomplishment as a moral psychologist is shaped by his re-

ligious convictions; and, finally, the reasons why writings
that are deeply religious tend not to be dreary.

1467   AUSTIN, M. N.
        "The Classical Learning of Samuel Johnson." In [10], pp.
        285-306.

        Deals with Johnson's own classical education, with his
        Latin learning, with his knowledge of Greek, and with some
        of his comments on his favorite authors and his opinions on
        classical studies.

1468   BABBITT, IRVING.
        "Dr. Johnson and Imagination." Southwest Rev. 13 (1927):
        25-35. Rpt. in On Being Creative and Other Essays (Boston:
        Houghton Mifflin, 1932), pp. 80-96.

        Johnson has the neoclassic distrust of imagination as a
        sort of Lorelei which can lead the unwary down to the white
        water of error; but, on the other hand, he did not distrust
        it because, as with Descartes and Spinoza, he had an over-
        whelming faith in abstract reason.

1469   BACH, BERT C.
        "Johnson's Concept of Wit." Cithara 11, No. 2 (May 1972):
        33-39.

        In Johnson's view the earlier eighteenth-century concept
        of wit as the ability to see relationships, or patterns of re-
        lationship, between apparently unrelated phenomena must be
        refined by the restrictions he puts on it: that the new per-
        ception arises from a new application of accumulated know-
        ledge, and that the new insight or perception be able to meet
        the test of reason.   Understandably Bach has checked John-
        son's Dictionary for a definition of wit and he notes an omis-
        sion--that wit is not defined as repartee or verbal clever-
        ness, a meaning which was popular even in Johnson's time,
        but one which he rejected for the older sense of the word.

1470   BAKER, CARLOS.
        "The Cham on Horseback." VQR 26 (1950): 76-90.

        Marshals evidence from Johnson's own writings, as opposed
        to the comments of others, to show that Johnson did indeed
        appreciate natural beauty and conveyed the feeling of it ef-
        fectively.   The insensitivity recorded about him comes from
        moments when he was ill, tired, and desperately uncomfort-
        able.

1471   BALDERSTON, KATHARINE C.
        "Johnson's Vile Melancholy." In [27], pp. 3-14.

            Johnson's melancholia viewed from a twentieth-century
        standpoint, with emphasis on his relationship to Mrs. Thrale;
        suggests that his neurotic fantasies were erotic in nature,
        assuming a masochistic form, and that they led him to abase
        himself before Mrs. Thrale--hence, the veiled references to
        padlocks, fetters, and whippings.

1472   BASNEY, LIONEL.
        "Johnson and Religious Evidence: A Note on the 'Wonderful
        Experience.'" ECLife 3 (1977): 89-91.

            Discusses Johnson's sudden improvement in health in Feb-
        ruary 1784--an experience which he regarded as divine inter-
        vention giving him a degree of confidence in his standing with
        God. This religious experience "appears to have moderated
        Johnson's lifelong scepticism about supernatural events" and
        was "a completion ... of his intellectual and spiritual pilgrim-
        age."

1473   " 'Ah ha!--Sam Johnson!--I see thee!': Johnson's Ironic
        Roles." SAQ 75 (1976): 198-211.

            Johnson's flair for role-playing changes our image of him
        "as an essentially defensive character." His ability to direct
        irony at both himself and at the ridiculous side of an other-
        wise serious subject are evident in his writing. "Playing
        roles, either explicitly dramatic or merely stylistic, Johnson
        was on the attack, not the defensive, exploring rather than
        merely preserving, always trying to extend his experience
        and his basis for judgment further into society."

1474   "Johnson on Metaphysical Poetry and Semantic Change." SBHT
        16 (1975): 235-244.

            Suggests that Johnson's ideas about language and semantic
        change may illuminate his discussion of metaphysical poetry
        and help explain what Johnson saw as the broader intellectual
        reasons for the metaphysicals' aesthetic shortcomings.

1475   BATE, WALTER JACKSON.
        The Achievement of Samuel Johnson. New York: Oxford
        Univ. Press, 1955.

            An expanded essay on the theme of its title with emphasis
        on Johnson's writing, especially on that which is concerned

with human experience. A second aim of the book is to relate the discussion of his writing to the more directly personal aspects of Johnson. Includes a final chapter on criticism.

1476   BATTERSBY, JAMES L.
       "Johnson's Negative Capability: Remarks on Omissions from the Canon." PLL 16 (1980): 151-160.

       Takes exception to Paul Fussell's reasoning as to why Johnson never wrote a novel, a stage comedy, a Pindaric Ode, or a pastoral. Argues "that the absence of examples of these types cannot be explained by appealing to Johnson's conceptions of them as genres, since all four, as differentiated 'generically' by Johnson, can be represented by works satisfying the general conditions of pleasure, truth, and novelty (or variety)."

1477   BLOOM, EDWARD A.
       " 'As Fly Stings to a Stately Horse': Johnson Under Satiric Attack." MLS 9, iii (1979): 137-149.

       Places Johnson within a humanistic tradition that gave him both "shield and weapon" against satiric attack; describes him as a critic who is also victim, as a man "deliberating on satire in a setting of empiric and formal evidence." Reason usually prevailed when he found himself under abusive attack, and he exercised restraint: "The best defense ... demands a semblance of dignified indifference." At the lowest level Johnson is characterized as a "freak, pontificating and gross"; at the highest level, he is an "idiosyncratic marvel, the object of awed amusement.... At any level ... he stands philosophically aloof, taller than his critics, who even in the act of mockery or malice tacitly verify his eminence."

1478   "Johnson's 'Divided Self.' " UTQ 31 (1961): 42-53.

       Deals with Johnson's conviction of sin and fear of damnation, in contrast to his otherwise gregarious and outgoing personality. Touches on the psychological problems of puritanism and their contribution to the neurotic elements of Johnson's personality.

1479   Samuel Johnson in Grub Street (Brown Univ. Studies, 21). Providence, R. I.: Brown Univ. Press, 1957.

       Describes Johnson's Grub Street career in some detail, emphasizing especially his responsibilities as editorial advisor: he was in particular responsible for widening the range

of material used in the journals he worked for. Shows how
Johnson's journalistic work extended and deepened his knowledge of men and public affairs.

1480   "Johnson on a Free Press: a Study in Liberty and Subordina-
       tion. " ELH 16 (1949): 251-271.

       Examines Johnson's attitude toward freedom of the press
       and analyzes Johnson's general political views--his insistence
       on authority and his fear of irresponsible and selfish groups.

1481   BOGEL, FREDRIC V.
       "The Rhetoric of Substantiality: Johnson and the Later Eigh-
       teenth Century. " ECS 12 (1979): 457-480.

       Argues that Johnson acknowledges and insists upon the fact
       that the "distinction between the divine and the earthly spheres
       corresponds (whether by nature or convention) to that between
       the metaphysical and the substantial modes of apprehension. "
       Johnson usually presents the heavenly and earthly orders as
       distinct but not entirely discontinuous, so as to subordinate
       earth to heaven and to value each according to the manner
       appropriate to it. Johnson insists, in other words, that there
       is a kind of truth other than the metaphysical, a truth that
       must be respected even though it is limited and imperfect,
       though real.

1482   BRACK, O. M. , JR.
       "The Death of Samuel Johnson and the Ars Moriendi Tradi-
       tion. " Cithara 20, i (1980): 3-15.

       Looks at the "art of dying well" tradition and related liter-
       ary motifs in the works of such authors as Addison and Rich-
       ardson, and the way in which biographers handled the details
       of Johnson's death. Lacking details of his death and needing
       to suppress or explain away any aspects of Johnson's character
       which might detract from his stature as a moral hero, they
       drew upon the ars moriendi tradition.

1483   BROADHEAD, GLENN J.
       "Samuel Johnson and the Rhetoric of Conversation. " SEL 20
       (1980): 461-474.

       An important fact about Johnson's essays is that they re-
       flect a traditional "rhetoric" of conversation that goes back
       to Cicero's De Officiis. Since the eighteenth century exhibited
       a compulsive interest in the "proprieties and elegancies of
       familiar discourse, " it is not surprising that the world of
       Johnson's essays should be populated by a "host of personae

and characters whose vices, vanities, and foibles are reflected
specifically in conversational gaucheries and errors, or in
futile attempts to 'shine' in company." Johnson's essays,
remarkable for the various observations which he refers to
as the "laws of conversation," involve two main norms, subordination and mutuality, a recognition of the interdependence
of man and man.

1484   BRODERICK, JAMES H.
        "Dr. Johnson's Impossible Doubts." SAQ 56 (1957): 217-223.

        Johnson's sermon on the Mercy of God presents arguments
        why belief in God's mercy is <u>necessary</u> to man's sanity. They
        are also a description, singularly sympathetic, of a man who
        does not really believe in Divine Mercy. This statement gives
        us the basic cause of Johnson's intense suffering over guilt,
        sin, and his own chances of salvation. He always kept his
        sanity, however, and in his last year finally came to faith in
        Divine Grace.

1485   BRONSON, BERTRAND H.
        <u>Johnson and Boswell; three essays by Bertrand H. Bronson.</u>
        Berkeley: Univ. Calif. Press, 1944. Rpt. as <u>Johnson Agon-</u>
        <u>istes and Other Essays.</u> Berkeley: Univ. Calif. Press, 1965.

        Includes <u>Johnson Agonistes</u>, an account of Johnson's battles
        and struggles with his world and with himself. These are
        made severe by the opposition of two forces within his per-
        sonality: the conservatism of intellectual attitude and the
        ebullient, aggressive temperament. Also <u>Boswell's Boswell</u>
        [278] and <u>Johnson's Irene</u> [1654].

1486   "The Double Tradition of Dr. Johnson." <u>ELH</u> 18 (1951): 90-
        106. Rpt. in [18], pp. 285-299.

        Contrasts the present critical judgment of Johnson's status
        as man of letters with the lasting popular conception that his
        enduring fame depends on his personality and conversational
        power as depicted by Boswell.

1487   BROWN, STUART GERRY.
        "Dr. Johnson and the Old Order." <u>Marxist Quarterly</u> 1 (1937):
        418-430. Rpt. in [1462], pp. 158-171.

        Argues against the idealist interpretation of Johnson as the
        typical Englishman and ideal man of letters, by examining
        his writings on the problem of evil; asserts that these writings
        frequently reveal a Johnson who is not conservative, because
        "they tend to cast doubt upon the sanctity of classical philos-

ophy and Christian theology and foreshadow the open revolt
which came a few years after his death."

1488   BROWN, WALLACE CABLE.
        "Johnson as Poet." MLQ 8 (1947): 53-64. Rpt. in [81],
        Chap. III.

        While admitting that Johnson is greater in prose than in
        poetry, Brown argues that Johnson is one of the masters of
        the heroic couplet form because of the "dynamic interplays
        of thought, feeling, and music."

1489   CAIRNES, WILLIAM T.
        "The Religion of Dr. Johnson." In The Religion of Dr. John-
        son and Other Essays (London: Oxford Univ. Press, 1946),
        pp. 1-23.

        Upholds Johnson's Christianity firmly and unequivocally.

1490   CAMPBELL, HILBERT H.
        "Shiels and Johnson: Biographers of Thomson." SEL 12
        (1972): 535-544.

        This article is primarily concerned with two biographies
        of James Thomson: one done by Johnson as part of his Lives
        (1779-81) and one done by Robert Shiels, compiler of Cibber's
        Lives (1753). Gives evidence that Shiels was personally ac-
        quainted with Thomson and had more information. Campbell
        does not want to "sacrifice Shiels completely on the altar of
        Johnson mainly because one is assumed to be a hack of no
        consequence, and the other a great critic with a large store
        of literary knowledge." Concludes that Johnson borrowed
        heavily from Shiels.

1491   CHAPIN, CHESTER F.
        "Johnson and Pascal." In [40], pp. 3-16.

        The influence of Pascal upon Johnson, who partly admires
        the Pensées for their emphasis on the "concrete, historical
        proofs of revelation" and partly for their "psychological argu-
        ment for the existence of God and the supernatural."

1492   The Religious Thought of Samuel Johnson. Ann Arbor: Univ.
        Mich. Press, 1968.

        A careful survey of all information relating to Johnson's
        religious thinking, going through not only his writing and con-
        versation but even the books which he read in early life that
        could have influenced him.

1493   "Samuel Johnson's Earliest Instruction in Religion." PMASAL
        52 (1966): 357-368.

        Chapin assigns very little significance to Johnson's religious
        conditioning as received from his parents.   He did receive in-
        struction, certainly, but in a Christianity so basic, tailored
        for the very young, that it fits any Protestant denomination.
        He did, however, commit to memory large sections of the
        Book of Common Prayer, and was exposed to Allestree's
        Whole Duty of Man.

1494   "Samuel Johnson's Religious Development." SEL 4 (1964):
        457-474.

        Discusses the religious experience Johnson went through in
        February, 1784.   Suddenly obtaining extraordinary relief from
        a dangerous illness, Johnson felt that a near-miracle had oc-
        curred.   Before this Johnson's rationalism had steered him
        away from the mystic element in Christianity.   Now he adds
        to the rational Anglicanism of his time "a new and vivid sense
        of the saving power of Christ...."

1495   "Johnson, Rousseau, and Religion. TSLL 2 (1960): 95-102.

        Johnson despised Rousseau more for his radical social
        theories and reforming zeal than for his religion.   His re-
        mark in 1766 bracketing Rousseau with Voltaire has been
        responsible for the myth that he took Rousseau to be in ac-
        cord with Hume and Voltaire in religion.   Johnson knew bet-
        ter than that, although he did not approve of Rousseau's heter-
        odoxy either.

1495A   "Personification as a Figure of Rhetoric."   In [88], pp. 98-
        115.

        Uses Johnson as an example to demonstrate that the best
        didactic verse employs prosopopoeia as more than an "empty
        abstraction," and that a variety of means lend the abstraction
        concrete force.   In his personifications "thought works basic-
        ally through the image; as in metaphor, one finds a close
        and significant interaction between image and idea."

1496   CHAPMAN, R. W. , ed.
        The Letters of Samuel Johnson, with Mrs. Thrale's Genuine
        Letters to Him.   Oxford: Clarendon Press, 1952.

        This collection is of sufficiently late date to contain the
        letters from the two "finds" at Malahide and one at Fetter-
        cairn.   Invaluable for the student of Johnson the Man.

1497   CLIFFORD, JAMES L.
        Dictionary Johnson: Samuel Johnson's Middle Years.   New
        York: McGraw-Hill, 1979.

        Surveys Johnson's life and works for the years 1749 to
        1763, years that represented a fifth of Johnson's life but that
        occupy only about a tenth of the space in Boswell's biography.
        The author has "tried to put into narrative form what is known
        about Johnson's middle years--not only how and with whom
        he spent his days and the sequence of events, but his reac-
        tions to them--evidence of the ambiguity of his feelings toward
        his wife and mother, his failure to conquer bad habits or to
        obtain financial security, and his fears of insanity."

1498   "Some Problems of Johnson's Obscure Middle Years."   In
        [1464], pp. 99-110.

        The fourteen years before Johnson met Boswell are the
        ones most lacking in evidence of his personal life.   Though
        he was eminent at the time, there are fewer personal letters
        and other records to go by.   Clifford discusses what little
        there is, including even items in contemporary newspapers.
        Of interest to biographers.

1499   Young Samuel Johnson.   London: Heinemann; New York:
        McGraw-Hill, 1955.

        A factual, scholarly account of Johnson from his boyhood
        to 1749, when he had just published The Vanity of Human
        Wishes; includes much new information.

1500   CLIFFORD, JAMES L. and DONALD J. GREENE.
        Samuel Johnson: A Survey and Bibliography of Critical Stud-
        ies.   Minneapolis: Univ. Minn. Press, 1970.

        This recognized tool for Johnsonians is especially valuable
        for the many interesting criticisms of Johnson from works in
        which his name does not appear on the title page, or even
        in a chapter heading.   Over 4,000 items covering publications
        through 1968; also contains entries from Johnson's lifetime
        to 1887.

1501   CORMICAN, JOHN D.
        "Samuel Johnson's Struggle with His Personality as Revealed
        in His Prayers."   BSUF 15, No. 3 (1974), pp. 19-25.

        Analyzes Johnson's prayers in order to suggest that his
        struggle with sin emphasized for him that reason seldom pre-
        vailed in his life; that his inability to repress sin and his

awareness of his religious doubts made him fear death. Before he died, however, he achieved a "leap to faith" that allowed him to accept himself and the limitations placed on
reason by the human condition.

1502   CURLEY, THOMAS M.
"Johnson and London: In Search of a City's Civility." JRUL
38 (1976): 7-22.

Johnson's writings reveal "a complex and representative
response to London that combined a lifelong respect for the
traditional rural values of the British countryside with a grow
ing admiration of his modern industrialized society." It was
his interest in London that caused him to investigate savage
and civilized ways of life and eventually to tour Scotland and
return with the comment that "the noblest prospect which a
Scotchman ever sees is the high road that leads him to London."

1503   Samuel Johnson and the Age of Travel. Athens: Univ. Georgia
Press, 1976.

Explores Johnson's "life and literary achievement in terms
of the geographical movements and travel themes of his day."
An examination of Johnson's varied interests in travel must
also include a discussion of his literary career and of the
revolutionary developments in eighteenth-century exploration.

1504   CURTIS, LEWIS P. and HERMAN W. , LIEBERT.
Esto Perpetua: The Club of Dr. Johnson and His Friends,
1764-1784. Hamden, Conn.: Archon Books, 1963.

The nature of the English intellectual aristocracy in the
eighteenth century, and specifically The Club as a brilliant
manifestation of the power of the human mind.

1505   DAMROSCH, LEOPOLD, JR.
"Samuel Johnson and Reader-Response Criticism." ECent.
21 (1980): 91-108.

Johnson considered in the context of reader-response criticism; he often appeals to the "common reader," and all of
his criticism is predicated on the lively response of readers
to literary works. But he is less interested in the "pheno-
menology or structure of reading than in the interpretations
and evaluations that actual readers make." The difference
between Johnson and any modern theorist is that he sees
literature as both cognitive and affective, telling the truth
about reality; whereas modern critics would be "likely to agree

with Iser that 'no literary text relates to contingent reality
as such, but to models or concepts of reality.' " Johnson's
value is that he reminds us that we do, in fact, act as though
reality exists and we can recognize it when we perceive it.

1506   DAVIES, GODFREY.
       "Dr. Johnson on History." HLQ 12 (1948): 1-22.

       "Here, the main effort has been to assemble a fair sample
       of Dr. Johnson's comments on history and on historians, and
       the few explanations suggested for his attitude should be re-
       garded as no more than tentative." Johnson's writings, re-
       ported conversations, and memoirs of his friends are culled
       to find his attitude on history.

1507   DAVIES, R. T.
       "Samuel Johnson, James Boswell, and the Romantic." In
       Literature of the Romantic Period, 1750-1850. R. T. Davies
       and B. G. Beatty, eds. (Liverpool: Liverpool Univ. Press;
       New York: Barnes & Noble, 1976), pp. 1-18.

       An exploratory essay that considers some of the senses of
       the word romantic that appear in the writings of Johnson and
       Boswell; suggests that Johnson was aware that he was often
       deficient in appropriate feelings. If The Vanity of Human
       Wishes is his most romantic work, then Rasselas is his most
       unromantic. When Johnson is thrilled and excited by roman-
       tic scenery, he immediately attempts to "pull the swelling
       spirit down" by resorting to generalities and abstractions;
       his appeal is always to truth, and always he preferred un-
       romantic realism to the "fine fabling" of Gothic romances.

1508   DAVIS, BERTRAM H.
       Johnson Before Boswell: A Study of Sir John Hawkins' "Life
       of Samuel Johnson." New Haven: Yale Univ. Press, 1960.

       Refutes verdict that Hawkins' work is unreliable and vin-
       dictive and argues that many of the so-called digressions are
       relevant.

1509   DELAUNE, HENRY M.
       "Johnson and the Matter of Imitation." XUS 3 (1964): 103-
       122.

       A discussion of Johnson's views on imitation showing how
       he was caught in the middle of the change from neoclassicism
       to romanticism and how he met these changes with an open
       critical mind.

1510   DONALDSON, IAN.
       "The Satirists' London." EIC 25 (1975): 101-122.

       Since a background of recognizable London streets, parks,
       and houses lend to Augustan satire persuasive force, and
       tend to convince the reader of the truth of its propositions,
       the author examines "some of the problems which flow from
       this notion of apparent 'truth'; problems which ... are not
       unique to Augustan city satire." The evidence clearly sug-
       gests that satirists, and poets in general, will often suppress,
       distort, and manipulate the "facts" when they describe the
       city.

1511   DOWNES, RACKSTRAW.
       "Johnson's Theory of Language." REL 3, iv (1962): 29-41.

       It has been said that in the Dictionary Johnson's philosopher
       is Locke, indicated by two quotations of Johnson on words:
       "words are but the signs of ideas," and "words are but the
       images of things." Language is dependent upon the exact ob-
       servation of reality. Many of Johnson's principles, such as
       the general-over-particular, are taken up without arriving at
       a concise statement of his theory of language.

1512   EBERWEIN, ROBERT.
       "Samuel Johnson, George Cheyne, and the 'Cone of Being.' "
       JHI 36 (1975): 153-158.

       Discusses the "strategy employed by Johnson in his attack
       on the chain of being" and points out "the significance of his
       use of ... Cheyne's Philosophical Principles of Religion, Nat-
       ural and Revealed." Concludes that it is "Johnson rather
       than Cheyne who has reduced 'everything to mathematical
       images' in his attempt to undermine the chain of being."

1513   EDINGER, WILLIAM.
       Samuel Johnson and Poetic Style. Chicago: Univ. Chicago
       Press, 1977.

       Reconstructs the premises of some of Johnson's more ob-
       scure critical opinions and makes his principles and his prac-
       tice illuminate each other by looking for a connection between
       them through stylistic analysis. To recover Johnson's stand-
       ards for poetic style is largely an effort to recover the neo-
       classical connotations of terms like "nature" and "simplicity":
       "The task, then, is to make Johnson and his age illuminate
       each other--to describe a significant portion of [his] critical
       achievement in terms of his success or failure in dealing with
       the issues bequeathed him by his tradition. ... "

1514   EINBOND, BERNARD L.
       Samuel Johnson's Allegory (De Proprietatibus Litterarum,
       Series Practica, 24). The Hague: Mouton, 1971.

           Argues that much of "Johnson's imaginative prose is in
       the form of allegory or contains elements of allegory"; and
       also treats of "Johnson on Allegory" and "The Vision of The-
       odore."

1515   ELIOT, T. S.
       "Johnson as Critic and Poet." In On Poetry and Poets (Lon-
       don: Faber, 1957), pp. 184-222.

           Deals primarily with Johnson as a critic; sees the criticism
       as possessing two values: 1) it makes us more conscious of
       our own limitations, and increases our understanding of the
       world in which we now live; and 2) it may help us recover
       some of the criteria of judgment which have all but disap-
       peared from the criticism of poetry.

1516   EMDEN, CECIL S.
       "Dr. Johnson and Imagery." RES, N. S. , 1 (1950): 23-38.

           Discusses Johnson's appreciation of simile; his discrimina-
       tion, including scruples against using rhetorical tricks in a
       moral essay; the materials of his imagery; his proficiency,
       with a comparison of his ability in conversation and in writing;
       and his self-disclosure in similes and metaphors.

1517   "Rhythmical Features in Dr. Johnson's Prose." RES 25
       (1949): 38-54.

           Examines Johnson's prose, notably the endings of essays,
       for their metrical style. "Study of rhythmical features is
       ... interesting in a famous author who is even better known
       as a talker." Emden feels that the famous dinner guest would
       hold forth in sonorously rolling periods or in tripping stac-
       cato notes, according to the meanings of his discourse, as
       he did in his writing.

1518   ENGELL, JAMES
       "Johnson on Novelty and Originality." MP 75 (1978): 273-
       279.

           Discusses the qualities of a work of literature that impart
       pleasure and insure survival: Johnson insists that good writ-
       ing must be fresh, but that "novelty" can be dangerous, es-
       pecially to a moralist, whose strongest allegiance is to those

truths that can never be "novel." Poetic originality, Johnson
was the first to say clearly, no longer "depended on the description of a previously unnoticed image or quality in the
natural world. Originality now meant the ability to reflect
the inner drama and process of a mind charged with feeling
as it descries the value and the elusive truths of experience."

1519   FLEEMAN, J. D.
        "Dr. Johnson and Henry Thrale, M. P." In [1464], pp. 170-
        189.

        Details Johnson's assistance to Thrale in his campaigns
        for election to Parliament.

1520   FOLKENFLIK, ROBERT.
        "Johnson's Art of Anecdote." In [45], pp. 171-181.

        Deals with isolated Johnsonian anecdotes and his analytical
        skill. Maintains that judging by Boswellian standards is the
        greatest obstacle to understanding Johnson's anecdotes.

1521   FONG, DAVID.
        "Macaulay and Johnson." UTQ 40 (1970): 27-40.

        Reexamines Macaulay's immature and prejudicial review
        of Crocker's edition of the Life of Samuel Johnson (1831) and
        shows how his attitude toward Johnson changes as his histori-
        cal, critical, and psychological relationships with him mature.

1522   FRASER, G. S.
        "Johnson and Goldsmith: The Mid-Augustan Norm." E & S
        23 (1970): 51-70.

        A comparison of Goldsmith and Johnson as representing
        most of the modes and forms that were fashionable in the
        middle and later eighteenth century. Goldsmith excels in
        softness and sweetness, Johnson in strength; Johnson is seen
        as writing an eighteenth-century version of seventeenth-century
        "strong" lines, "packing each line with complex and some-
        times difficult sense." Juxtaposes passages from The De-
        serted Village and London and The Vanity of Human Wishes.

1523   FUSSELL, PAUL.
        Samuel Johnson and the Life of Writing. New York: Har-
        court Brace, 1971.

        Examines "Johnson's behavior as a writer" considering
        "especially his 'manner of proceeding,'" and sets "forth some

of the conceptions about writing that governed Johnson's achievement," so that we may better "understand the quality of that
achievement. "

1524   "A Note on Samuel Johnson and the Rise of Accentual Pro-
        sodic Theory. " PQ 33 (1954): 431-433.

        Johnson is revealed as a man who can change with the
        times, responding to criticism of earlier editions of the dic-
        tionary by making a note in the fourth edition whereby he
        relaxes his hard-and-fast stand upon a point of prosody.

1525   GOLDEN, MORRIS.
        "Johnson's Characters: 'The Stubborn Choice. ' "   Mid-Hudson
        Lang. Stds. 1 (1978): 63-80.

        Examines Johnson's characters and their search for hap-
        piness in their particular environment. "For Johnson the
        centrally human activity is choice, the expression of the mind's
        psychological and moral energies. All of his characters,
        therefore, are fixed as anticipating choice, choosing, or ex-
        emplifying the consequences of choice. " Humanity is doomed
        to face the problems of choice for which "Johnson finds no
        sane alternative. "

1526   GREENE, DONALD J.
        Samuel Johnson. New York: Twayne, 1970.

        An introduction to the life and work of Samuel Johnson,
        the chief concern being to "introduce the reader to the fas-
        cinating variety, the intellectual stimulation, the continual
        freshness, and the rare artistry of his writings. " Greene
        discusses six of Johnson's "important critical attitudes," em-
        piricism, psychology, mimesis, morality, contemporaneity
        of language and originality, and an insistence upon the con-
        crete rather than the vaguely abstract.

1527   " 'Pictures to the Mind': Johnson and Imagery. " In [1464],
        pp. 137-158.

        Johnson's use of metaphor explored and commended. Ex-
        amples of concrete imagery cited to answer the criticisms of
        Johnson's abstractions.

1528   "The Development of the Johnson Canon. " In [13], pp. 407-
        427.

        "One purpose of this article is to place the list of John-

son's writings furnished by Boswell in its proper perspective
in the history of the Johnson canon ... to help keep Boswell's
dead hand from inhibiting the urgent work of investigating
pieces attributed to Johnson by others." Also shows how
greatly our picture of Johnson has changed from one period
to another.

1529   "Samuel Johnson and 'Natural Law.'" Jour. of British Stud-
       ies 2 (1963): 59-75.

       Examines the assumption, encountered in some recent dis-
       cussions, that a belief in "natural law" is central to Samuel
       Johnson's political, social, and general moral thinking. Re-
       futes this view.

1530   The Politics of Samuel Johnson.   New Haven: Yale Univ.
       Press, 1960.

       Examines Johnson's writings, rejecting the concept of
       Johnson as a blind conservative, and the ancient definition
       of an eighteenth-century Tory as just such a conservative.
       Argues that Johnson's rationalism was stronger than his tra-
       ditionalism, that he was more concerned with the present
       than with the romantic past. Greene tries to present facts
       with a minimum of theorizing or interpretation, in the hope
       that enough factual material will be made available to dis-
       sipate the old Johnson myth without creating a new one.

1531   GRIFFIN, DUSTIN.
       "Johnson's Funeral Writings." ELH 41 (1974): 192-211.

       A study of Johnson as a writer and critic of epitaph and
       elegy; shows that he was interested in generic criticism, but
       was not bound by "generic prescriptions."

1532   HAGSTRUM, J. H.
       "The Nature of Dr. Johnson's Rationalism." ELH 17 (1950):
       191-205. Rpt. in [7], pp. 88-103.

       Describes what is "traditionally rationalistic and humanistic
       in Johnson's conception of reason"; discusses the "vitally sig-
       nificant empirical strains in his criticism, to clarify the ...
       relationship ... between the empirical and rational faculties";
       and calls "attention to his perception that the reason was not
       only a restraining, normalizing force but was instinct with
       positive energy of its own."

1533   "Johnson's Conception of the Beautiful, the Pathetic, and the
       Sublime." PMLA 64 (1949): 134-157.

Minutely examines Johnson's definitions of three terms,
beautiful, pathetic, and sublime, and his concepts of them as
illustrated in his writings.

1534   "On Dr. Johnson's Fear of Death." ELH 14 (1947): 308-
319.

Hagstrum analyzes Johnson's fear of death in its relation
to his religious position and shows that it is an integral part
of a fairly consistent pattern of belief and emotion.

1535   HARDY, J. P.
Samuel Johnson: A Critical Study.   London: Routledge &
Kegan Paul, 1979.

A critical biography that emphasizes Johnson's humanity
and independence, the originality of his thought, and the variety of his literary production.

1536   HARDY, JOHN.
"Hope and Fear in Johnson." EIC 26 (1976): 285-299.

Compares Johnson's attitude toward life and death as shown
in Rasselas and The Vanity of Human Wishes.   Johnson's impulse, like that of Rasselas, "was to extend his interest out-
wards and meet life fully.   Yet this could also, as in The
Vanity of Human Wishes, make him painfully conscious of
the miseries of the world--the very miseries which Rasselas
professedly set out to see, but did not really see."

1537   HART, FRANCIS R.
"Johnson as Philosophic Traveler: The Perfecting of an
Idea." ELH 36 (1969): 679-695.

Presents Johnson as a philosophical traveler, one " ... re-
flectively intent on the fixing of exact attention and its modes
... a running contrast between the relative but immediate impression and the exacting 'philosophical' computation." Shows
how "Johnson's lifelong concern with the acts of perception
and of fixing 'distinct ideas' is typical of him and central to
the meaning and motive of his Journey to the Western Islands."

1538   HOLTZ, WILLIAM.
"Samuel Johnson and the Abominable Fancy." Cithara 18,
ii (1979):   29-47.

"The Abominable Fancy," Soame Jenyns's system of "cosmic egoism" that sought to justify social injustice, cosmic

evil, and theological damnation, is used to suggest Johnson's
attitude toward death and the after-life; the structure of his
attack on Jenyns becomes a model of his thought in which
logic, experience, and moral passion combine to demolish
the conception of the Chain of Being. Concludes that Johnson
loathed Jenyns's account of human suffering because it "offered a seductively rational sanction to his own irrational
fears, and in its metaphorical identification of the human condition with the bestial, it bodied forth ... the worst of all
possible worlds, truly a vision of Hell."

1539   HOOVER, BENJAMIN B.
       Samuel Johnson's Parliamentary Reporting: Debates in the
       Senate of Lilliput. Berkeley: Univ. Calif. Press, 1953.

          Discusses Johnson and Parliamentary reporting in the
       eighteenth century, the history of the Debates until the pres-
       ent, a comparison of the debates with the corresponding re-
       port in the London Magazine, and the literary qualities of the
       debates.

1540   HYDE, DONALD F. and MARY HYDE.
       "Johnson and Journals." The New Colophon: A Book-Collec-
       tors' Miscellany, Vol. 3 (New York: Duschnes Crawford,
       Inc., 1950): 165-197.

          Considers such topics as Johnson's theory of a journal,
       its contents, the manner of keeping it, and its purposes; his
       influence on others; his own strenuous efforts to keep a jour-
       nal; and the identification of journals supposedly burnt by
       Johnson before his death, and of those that survived the con-
       flagration. Suggests that there were "three records kept by
       Johnson, one of which was destroyed, and the remaining two,
       largely so. They are one major diary in two volumes, most
       of the French Journal, and thirty-two (thirty-eight?) pages of
       the Account."

1541   IRWIN, GEORGE.
       Samuel Johnson: A Personality in Conflict. Auckland: Auck-
       land Univ. Press; London: Oxford Univ. Press, 1971.

          Applies modern psychoanalytic theory to Johnson's emo-
       tional life--his childhood, his disorders of the 1760s, and his
       relationship with Mrs. Thrale--in an attempt to analyze his
       sexual, religious, and social preoccupations.

1542   JACK, IAN.
       "The 'Choice of Life' in Johnson and Matthew Prior." JEGP
       49 (1950): 523-530.

Cites many similarities to prove that Johnson was influenced by the content, the philosophical approach, and the style of Solomon.

1543   JEMIELITY, THOMAS.
"Dr. Johnson and the Uses of Travel." PQ 51 (1972): 448-459.

Marshals evidence to show that Johnson augmented the information he had gained in his own travels by extensive use of travel literature, and by requesting traveling friends to take special note of things he was interested in. Goes on to investigate the bases for his interest in foreign lands.

1544   KETTON-CREMER, R. W.
"Johnson and the Countryside." In [1464], pp. 65-75.

In the eighteenth century even an avowed town man saw a lot of the country and could be, like Johnson, very knowledgeable about it. Instances of Johnson's knowledge and interest are set forth, concluding with that beautiful sentence which he addressed to Langton, "I shall delight to hear the ocean roar or see the stars twinkle, in the company of men to whom nature does not spread her volumes or utter her voice in vain."

1545   KNOBLAUCH, CYRIL H.
"Samuel Johnson and the Composing Process." ECS 13 (1980): 243-262.

Johnson's views on writing as expressed in his Rambler and Adventurer essays. His skepticism about both the writing process and the product stems from the intellectual thought of the age--the rise of empiricism--which distrusted writing and questioned the value of books.

1546   KRUTCH, JOSEPH WOOD.
Samuel Johnson. New York: H. Holt & Co., 1944.

Undertakes to give us "a large inclusive book which would ... give the general reader a running account of Johnson's life, character, and work as they appear in the light of contemporary knowledge and contemporary judgment." The experts on Johnson, he says, know better than to undertake such a thing, which is why he undertook to write a book about Johnson for the layman.

1547   LEAVIS, F. R.

"Johnson and Augustanism" and "Johnson as Poet." In The Common Pursuit (London: Chatto & Windus, Ltd., 1952), pp. 97-120.

The first title above is a review of Joseph Wood Krutch's book, Samuel Johnson, on the whole favorable. Wherever Leavis feels that Krutch is insufficient, he moves to fill us in. "Johnson as Poet" takes satisfaction from the belated inclusion of Johnson's poems in the Oxford English Texts. Though currently (1952) unpopular, Johnson's poetry is great as "a poetry of statement, exposition, and reflection."

1548   "Dr. Johnson." KR 8 (1946): 637-657.

A reexamination of Johnson's whole achievement in the light of Joseph Wood Krutch's biography.

1549   McADAM, E. L., JR.
Dr. Johnson and the English Law. Syracuse, N.Y.: Syracuse Univ. Press, 1951.

Details the lifelong and keen interest in the law shown by Johnson, who once told Boswell he would have had a career in law if his father could have afforded it. Johnson once said "the law is the last result of human wisdom acting upon human experience for the benefit of the public." An in-depth study of Johnson's collaboration with Robert Chambers in the preparation of Chambers' Vinerian lectures.

1550   McCUTCHEON, ROGER P.
"Samuel Johnson: 1709-1959." TSL 6 (1961): 109-117.

Discusses the hills and valleys" of Johnson's prestige from his own generation through the years when his fame took little account of his writings, but rested on his powers as conversationalist (according to Boswell), to the resurgence of interest in Samuel Johnson (not necessarily as presented by Boswell) and his writings.

1551   McGLYNN, PAUL D.
"Samuel Johnson and the Illusions of Popular Culture." MLS 10, iii (1980): 29-35.

Johnson was intensely aware of and interested in popular culture: "he was remarkably cognizant of the wide range of such culture and never scornful of it. He scorned only the misperception of it or the undifferentiated equation of it with pursuits more essential to human existence." Popular culture sweetened life, and was supplied by God as an alleviation to the pains of existence.

1552   McINTOSH, CAREY.
       The Choice of Life: Samuel Johnson and the World of Fic-
       tion. New Haven: Yale Univ. Press, 1973.

       Examines Johnson's narrative writings, especially three
       of the most popular genres in fiction (satire, oriental tale,
       and allegory), analyzing them for his achievements "in terms
       of prose style, irony, vivid pictorialisms and dark pessimism."
       Also discusses the "choice of life" as a central theme, and
       devotes a chapter to an analysis of Rasselas.

1553   "Johnson's Debate with Stoicism." ELH 33 (1966): 327-336.

       Deals with Johnson's moral thinking and the extent to which
       Stoic attitudes and principles contributed to it, especially as
       expressed in his moral essays and in Rasselas, and shows
       that " ... the general temper of his moral thought is Stoic,
       in limited but important ways." He cannot accept "apathy"
       and "self-sufficiency" and " ... as moralist is less concerned
       with 'interpersonal relations' than with individual well-being,
       less interested in social ethics than in individual values."

1554   McNULTY, JOHN BARD.
       "The Critic Who Knew What He Wanted." CE 9 (1948): 299-
       303.

       Refutes stereotype of Johnson as only an eccentric user of
       ultra-Latinate language. Presents him as a refreshingly posi-
       tive, witty, and incisive critic.

1555   MAST, DANIEL DEE.
       "Philosophical Speculatists: Representatives of the Age of
       Enlightenment." Enl. E. 2 (1971): 23-29.

       Johnson's treatment of the searcher in pure science, like
       his attitude to the artist-inventor in Rasselas, is interesting
       because it is sympathetic even in its rejection of their values.
       He defends the speculatists against those who condemn them
       for not producing useful knowledge. "The folly of projection
       is very seldom the folly of a fool"--which may be taken to
       mean that he sees the essential creativity of many projectors
       (experimenters). The story of the philosopher in Rasselas,
       however, shows his essential skepticism; he is one of the
       first "mad scientists" of literature.

1556   MIDDENDORF, JOHN H.
       "Johnson on Wealth and Commerce." In [1464], pp. 47-64.

       Johnson's thoughts on economics, the role of government
       in guaranteeing quality of life, and the dangers which accom-

pany consumption of wealth show "the full range of possible
responses, from the disengaged to the passionately involved."
Johnson's pragmatism operates to help him live with attitudes
and opinions which are sometimes contradictory.

1557 MINER, EARL ROY.
"Dr. Johnson, Mandeville, and 'Publick Benefits.'" HLQ
21 (1958): 159-166.

Miner emphasizes the basic philosophical and religious
bases for Johnson's economic theory which prevented him
from going along with Shaftesbury's optimistic faith in goodness of man, to say nothing of Mandeville's happily conscience-
free system of letting "private vices" contribute to the public
good. He sometimes defends luxury as a Tory might be expected to do, but Johnson the moralist insists that "the happiness of society depends on virtue."

1558 MOORE, JOHN ROBERT.
"Johnson as Poet." Boston Public Library Quarterly 2 (1950):
156-166.

Evidence of the lack of understanding of Johnson as poet
is impressively demonstrated, followed by the defense of his
poetry.

1559 MOORE, ROBERT E.
"Dr. Johnson on Fielding and Richardson." PMLA 66 (1951):
162-181.

Suggests "that Fielding's opinions on literature are constantly and consistently reflected in Johnson, and that Fielding's novels are in large measure splendid illustrations of
many of Johnson's deeply-felt principles, better illustrations
by far than the novels of Richardson" even though Johnson
always praised Richardson and condemned Fielding. Compares Johnson's conception of a great novel in the 4th Rambler
with Fielding's ideas as expressed in Book IX of Tom Jones.

1560 MORGAN, EDWIN.
" 'Strong Lines' and Strong Minds: Reflections on the Prose
of Browne and Johnson." Cambridge Jour. 4 (1950-51): 481-
491.

Defines the prose style of "strong lines" as found in the
writings of Johnson and of Sir Thomas Browne. Browne's
"sumptuous writing", an elevated style admired by Johnson
but too flamboyant for his own personality, is yet reflected
in Johnson's more restrained style.

1561   NICHOL SMITH, DAVID, R. W. CHAPMAN, and L. F.
       POWELL.
       Johnson and Boswell Revised by Themselves and Others.
       London: Oxford Univ. Press, 1928.

       Three essays on Johnson's revision of his own works,
       Boswell's "revises" for the Life of Johnson, and the forth-
       coming new edition of Hill's Boswell. All three deal with
       textual variations between editions, author's notes to printers,
       proof sheets, lists of alterations compiled by scholars, etc.
       Johnson himself believed in continuing to take care of and
       keep an interest in works already published, making changes
       between printings.

1562   NORTH, RICHARD.
       "The Religion of Dr. Johnson." Hibbert Jour. 56 (1957):
       42-46.

       Johnson's well-known fear of death is attributed to his
       "Christian orthodoxy" and his inability to determine whether
       or not he would qualify for salvation. The choice of the Es-
       tablished Church and the absolute acceptance of its teachings,
       North suggests, is dictated by Johnson's "deference to mass-
       opinion."

1563   PETERSON, R. G.
       "Samuel Johnson at War with the Classics." ECS 9 (1975):
       69-86.

       Unlike other writers of his time, Johnson was not fond of
       the classics, and when he did use them, he eliminated every-
       thing which had no moral significance. Even though London
       and The Vanity of Human Wishes are both imitations of the
       classics, they are not really classical because of the way in
       which they perceive and represent reality. Johnson was able
       to use the classics better than anyone in England, but he did
       not have "a pure and classical taste" because "he did not spin
       any of the usual dreams of antiquity...."

1564   PIPER, WILLIAM BOWMAN.
       "Samuel Johnson as an Exemplary Critic." TSLL 20 (1978):
       457-473.

       In the debate between structuralist and non-structuralist
       critic, the need is not for further theoretical refinement--
       "a new spasm of abstraction"--but for a convincing and en-
       lightening example, such as we find in Johnson's critical con-
       duct. The critic who studies Johnson's practice comes to
       understand exactly what criticism can actually accomplish:
       "Only the Johnsonian critic, who locates his personal exper-

iences and judgments in the changing but continuous fabric
of society and conceives of his own discourse as one voice
in the great cultural exchange, can consider his public contribution as an essential aspect of his labors. "

1565   PRESTON, THOMAS R.
        "Samuel Johnson--A Religious Misanthrope. " In [152], pp.
        121-143.

        Johnson was a living embodiment of benevolent misanthropy,
        yet at the same time he believed that men were more inclined
        to evil than to good.   Johnson is himself the benevolent mis-
        anthropic satirist behind the satiric spokesman in the Vanity
        of Human Wishes and the narrator of Rasselas.   Johnson's
        misanthropic vision of the world is intended to "increase vir-
        tue" and to make us think on a future state, though it is not
        intended to deprive us of the good things of this life or to re-
        ject mankind.   The religious aspects of that vision can be
        found in nearly all of his works, but are revealed most com-
        pletely in the satiric apologue, Rasselas, a novel that follows
        the basic pattern of the inexperienced man of feeling entering
        the world of experience.

1566   PYLES, THOMAS.
        "The Romantic Side of Dr. Johnson. "   ELH 11 (1944):   192-
        212.

        Shows Johnson as a rebel within the neoclassicist tradition.
        He dislikes pastorals, mythology, and some neoclassic "rules,"
        feeling that "Reason's rules" should take precedence over such
        hallowed observances as the unities, the necessity of five
        acts to every play, etc.

1567   QUINLAN, MAURICE J.
        Samuel Johnson: A Layman's Religion.   Madison: Univ.
        Wisc. Press, 1964.

        An examination of various aspects of Johnson's faith, and
        the motives for his attitudes and behavior.   Discusses John-
        son's concern with salvation, his sermon-writing activities
        and theological views, his devotion to the principles of charity,
        his conflict with God and death, and his position as an Eng-
        lish Churchman.

1568   RADNER, JOHN B.
        "Samuel Johnson, The Deceptive Imagination, and Sympathy. "
        SBHT 16, (1974):   23-46.

        Johnson's cure for envy, for wasteful dreaming and mad-

ness, and for vain hopes and fears was based partly on the
fact that "he saw that imaginative projection, properly directed,
is the chief basis for the intelligent, ready sympathy that is
a major source of happiness and goodness."

1569   RAMAGE, JOHN D.
        "The Politics of Samuel Johnson: A Reconsideration." SBHT
        15 (1974): 221-240.

        Argues against Donald Greene's view that Johnson was "one
        of the most effectual propagators of democracy in the eigh-
        teenth century"; rather, Johnson after the 1730s and '40s be-
        came disenchanted with democratic principles and became in-
        creasingly authoritarian.

1570   REYNOLDS, W. VAUGHAN.
        "The Reception of Johnson's Prose Style." RES 11 (1935):
        145-162.

        Johnson's detractors, Macaulay, Campbell, Colman, Chur-
        chill, John Callander, Robert Burrowes, and notably Horace
        Walpole, claimed that Johnson's "love of Latinisms and hard
        words forced him into a pompous, obscure and affected style;
        his attempts to attain the sublime introduced licentious con-
        structions into his work; and in seeking rhythm he had only
        achieved monotonous parallelisms and disjointed harmonies."
        His admirers, Mrs. Piozzi, Joseph Towers, Hawkins, Mur-
        phy, Robert Anderson, Alexander Chalmers, and Nathan Drake,
        claimed that "[h]e was precise, both in the choice and the
        use of his terms and he never indulged in empty verbiage.
        If he was fond of Latinisms, he was always careful to form
        them on English analogies.... To this purity and clearness
        was added an unremitting care for the harmony and dignity
        of his construction," producing "a style remarkable for its
        elegance and strength."

1571   RICHMAN, JORDAN.
        "Johnson as Swiftian Satirist." UDR 7, ii (1971): 21-28.

        Argues that Johnson is a Swiftian satirist in manner and
        spirit; compares passages from both authors that express
        similar attitudes toward satire and ridicule, and concludes
        that Johnson is a Swiftian satirist because of his "grim humor,
        sense of evil, fast pace and sense of physical action, shifts of
        tone, and energetic delivery."

1572   ROBERTS, SYDNEY CASTLE.
        Doctor Johnson and Others. Cambridge: Cambridge Univ.
        Press, 1958.

Four essays on Johnson--as moralist, churchman, and biographer, and Johnson's views of the imagination--and an essay on Gray.

1573   Samuel Johnson. London: Longmans, 1954.

A fresh introduction to the study of Johnson as a man of letters, plus a select bibliography.

1574   ROGERS, DONALD O.
"Samuel Johnson's Concept of the Imagination." SCB 33 (1973): 213-218.

Analyzes the ways in which Johnson conceived the imagination to function in a work of literature, and emphasizes two important but neglected functions, the "generalizing" function and the "moral" function. Imlac declared that the poet, rising "to general and transcendental truths ... must write as the interpreter of nature and the legislator of mankind"; this article argues that "the former function is accomplished through the generalizing imagination, while the latter function depends upon the moral imagination." But Johnson insisted that the moral imagination should predominate over and guide the generalizing imagination.

1575   SACHS, ARIEH.
Passionate Intelligence: Imagination and Reason in the Work of Samuel Johnson. Baltimore: Johns Hopkins Press, 1967.

Evaluates Johnson's thought as seen in his work, rather than the works themselves. Talks about the thematic unity observable in the periodical papers, The Vanity of Human Wishes, and Rasselas, and presents a penetrating account of the structure of Rasselas in terms of the recurrent clashes between escapist illusion and stubborn reality. Study concludes that "Johnson's entire exposé of man's delusions and fallacies--in philosophy, in morals, in art, in day-to-day life--is reducible to his basic definition of man as a creature who seeks out many subtle ways of forgetting the unpleasant fact that he is destined to die."

1576   SCHWARTZ, RICHARD B.
Samuel Johnson and the Problem of Evil. Madison: Univ. Wisc. Press, 1975.

Examines Johnson's philosophy with the hope "that an examination of one contribution to the dialectic of controversy will add to our understanding ... but my chief aim is to add to our understanding of the thought and art of Samuel Johnson."

Analyzes Johnson's review of Soame Jenyns's <u>Free Enquiry</u> <u>into the Nature and Origins of Evil</u> (1757) in which he gathers together his thoughts on the problem of evil.

1577   <u>Samuel Johnson and the New Science.</u>   Madison: Univ. Wisc. Press, 1971.

Refutes a popular opinion, nurtured by reading nineteenth-century commentators and by "a careful avoidance of the reading of Johnson's works," that Samuel Johnson disliked science and had little use for it.   He <u>does</u> dislike hypotheses backed only by argument, without hard evidence.   Schwartz describes Johnson's defense of science against the various attacks of the satirists, and defines Johnson's basic position as Baconian.

1578   SELDEN, RAMAN. "The 18th Century Juvenal: Dr. Johnson and Churchill." In [159], pp. 153-175.

Describes the historical situation after 1740 when many writers were "allowing Longinian rhetoric to colour their theories and even to modify their practice in a direction which favoured the Juvenalian manner in satire." Johnson, especially in his imitations of Juvenal, illustrates this tendency; he is a religious satirist because he raises a rational, plain style by infusing it with a "Christian emotional depth." Churchill, on the other hand, represents the final breakdown of the neoclassical principle in his pre-Romantic experimentation.

1579   SHACKLETON, ROBERT. "Johnson and the Enlightenment."   In [1464], pp. 76-92.

Johnson is still identified as a conservative, in religious matters particularly; but as a rationalist his close ties with the early enlightenment are shown.   "He believed in the spread of knowledge.   He accepted the empiricism of Locke.   He leaned to utilitarianism in politics.   His natural bent of mind was sceptical.   In all these respects he was at one with Voltaire and with Diderot."

1580   SIEBERT, DONALD T. , JR. "Johnson and Hume on Miracles."   <u>JHI</u> 36 (1975): 543-547.

Argues that Johnson, in his treatment of Hume's essay "Of Miracles," did not blindly reject Hume's reasoning, though generally antagonistic to him.   Johnson's efforts to resist Hume's skepticism were largely ineffectual.

1581   STAUFFER, DONALD A.
        "Samuel Johnson." In [168], pp. 386-402.

        Johnson's view of biography as objective reporting rather
        than panegyric had a salutary effect on the state of the art.
        His statements of biographical credo from the Rambler and
        the Idler are outlined.

1582   STERNBACH, ROBERT.
        "Pascal and Dr. Johnson on Immortality." JHI 39 (1978):
        483-489.

        Argues that an important connecting link between Pascal
        and Johnson, and an important avenue of Pascal's influence
        on the eighteenth century, may be found in the belief that
        every religious choice, for a rational man, must be a wager:
        " ... it can be shown that Johnson was impressed by Pas-
        cal's famous argument of the 'wager,' as it was transmitted
        to him, in substance, in the writings of several seventeenth-
        century English divines, whose sermons he had been marking
        to illustrate certain words in his Dictionary of the English
        Language."

1583   TAYLOR, DONALD S.
        "Triangulating Sensibilities: Johnson, the Metaphysicals, and
        Us." Trans. Samuel Johnson Society of the Northwest 7
        (1974): 19-43.

        Argues that Johnson's definition of metaphysical poetry,
        since it accurately measures the distances between two sen-
        sibilities different from our own, can help us to "locate our-
        selves by a sort of triangulation in the now relative geography
        of taste."

1584   TRACY, CLARENCE R.
        Johnson and the Common Reader. Hamilton, Ont.: McMaster
        Univ. Press, 1976: Rpt. Dalhousie Rev. 57 (1977): 405-423.

        In both his writings and conversation Johnson favored and
        took pride in the growth of the reading public. He was aware,
        however, that authors faced a new problem, that of identify-
        ing the exact audience to which they must address their works;
        the audience that he identified was that of the common reader,
        which consisted of mankind in miniature, but stripped of all
        particular details and superficial differences, leaving a basic
        man reduced to the level on which all men's minds work
        alike.

1585   "Democritus Arise! A Study of Dr. Johnson's Humor." YR
        39 (1950): 294-310.

"Mirth with thought behind it, laughter with motive, and the smile of the wise man: these are the ingredients of Johnson's humor and make up no bad definition of it. ..." Absolves Johnson of the cruel and almost vicious humor practised by some satirists. Also suggests that Imlac's discussion of poetry should not be taken too seriously; Imlac and Johnson are not necessarily the same.

1586   "Johnson and the Art of Anecdote." UTQ 15 (1945): 86-93.

Boswell's Johnson differs from the neoclassic ideal of the general over the particular, delivering to us a vast accumulation of details and specifics. Similarly Johnson as a biographer made some use of anecdotes. But his expressed principles triumph again when he turns away from his source materials to generalize with "shrewd and sympathetic understanding." Johnson's work as a biographer shows the conflicting tendencies of biography, which can swing in the direction of science and its factual material, or of art in the biographer's analysis of his subject.

1587   UPHAUS, ROBERT W.
"Johnson's Equipoise and the State of Man." In [180], pp. 89-107.

Johnson, like Richardson and Fielding, accepts as fact the fallen nature of man, but in The Life of Savage and Rasselas he refuses to accept Richardson's Christian rigor and Fielding's "sudden conversions." He believes in the possibility of acting virtuously in an imperfect world and that the state of religious belief surpasses the "affective possibilities" of imaginative literature. In The Life of Savage and especially in Rasselas, Johnson "accommodates his sense of 'equipoise' to the uncertainties of human life"; in the former, we are asked to balance good against evil, virtue against vice, whereas in the latter's conclusion we find the experience of equipoise pushed almost to the breaking point--we are asked to accept distinctions between competing acts of virtue, none of which can possess more than a temporary stability.

1588   VESTERMAN, WILLIAM.
The Stylistic Life of Samuel Johnson.   New Brunswick, N. J. : Rutgers Univ. Press, 1977.

"After describing the general pattern of critical reaction to Johnson and what I see as some of the bases for it in the differences between Johnson's written and spoken styles, I wish ... to express my sense of the changing and growing artistic consciousness created for a reader by the activity of Johnson's style within particular works in the course of his career." Each chapter alternates between studies of a major

work at a particular point in Johnson's career and studies of
several works that illustrate a form or theme extending through
different phases of that career. The living relation of Johnson
to his language, the extent of his control over it, is the main
interest of the book.

1589   VOITLE, ROBERT.
       "Stoicism and Samuel Johnson." In [47], pp. 107-127.

       "Looks at evidence available and systematically considers
       in what senses, or to what extent, if any, Johnson can be
       termed a Stoic." Though Johnson's traits of character in-
       clude some of the more admirable characteristics of Stoicism,
       there is much more to this ancient philosophy that the Chris-
       tian Johnson would have to (and did) reject.

1590   Samuel Johnson the Moralist.   Cambridge: Harvard Univ.
       Press, 1961.

       Seeks to outline a "comprehensive view of Johnson's moral
       notions"; the first two chapters relate Johnson's rationalism
       to Lockean empiricism, and suggest that he applied the "fac-
       ulty much as the moralists of the Renaissance did." Chap-
       ters III-V are concerned with Johnson's concept of righteous-
       ness, which is equated with altruism or "conduct toward
       others, ... dealing with everything from domestic relations
       to the individual's relation with 'the great community of man-
       kind.'" Chapter VI defines his practical ethic, emphasizing
       that for Johnson "it is the end achieved which governs the
       morality of an action, not the character from which it pro-
       ceeds or the sense of duty behind it"; and the last chapter
       relates Johnson's morality to his religious beliefs, arguing
       that behind his moral writings lies a fundamental religious
       impetus.

1591   WAIN, JOHN.
       Samuel Johnson: A Biography.   London: Macmillan, 1974.

       Present-day treatment of Johnson, " ... addressed to the
       intelligent general reader," refuting the prevailing stereotype
       of him as an "arch-conservative." This picture results, Wain
       says, from seeing Johnson through the eyes of Boswell, "a
       sentimental-romantic Tory of a very different stripe." Wain
       cites Johnson's interest in social justice and his opposition
       to colonialism, the slave trade and "every form of exploita-
       tion" to present him as a more sympathetic figure. Because
       of his position " ... to see [Johnson's] life from the inside,"
       Wain states that "[t]he literary and social situation that John-
       son knew in its early days, I know in its twilight."

1592   WARD, JOHN CHAPMAN.
       "Johnson's Conversation. <u>SEL</u> 12 (1972): 519-533.

       What has sometimes been considered rudeness on John-
       son's part, interrupting, contradicting, and holding the con-
       versational floor, is explained by the picture of Johnson as
       performer which was uppermost in his mind and in that of
       his listeners. Apparently Boswell sometimes set up these
       soirées, arranging that certain subjects should come up.
       Johnson, while not consciously aware of these machinations,
       knew it was up to him to put on a show.

1593   WEITZMAN, ARTHUR J.
       "Dr. Johnson's Philurbanism." In <u>Aeolian Harps: Essays</u>
       <u>in Literature in Honor of Maurice Browning Cramer</u>, Donna
       G. and Douglas C. Fricke, eds. (Bowling Green, Ohio:
       Bowling Green Univ. Press, 1976), pp. 95-109.

       Although Johnson's love of London can hardly be questioned,
       his theories seem to be ambivalent; in <u>London</u>, he expressed
       the views of the anti-urbanists and attacked the city's luxury
       which he thought was destroying the moral fibre and integrity
       of the nation, but later in his <u>Adventurer</u> and <u>Rambler</u> es-
       says, he defends the city. While seeing the evil in London's
       growth, he could reconcile the commercial domination "and its
       fearful consequences with the ancient urban ideal of the cultiva-
       tion of arts and leisure." London was "a community which of-
       fered hope to every range of human talent."

1594   WELLINGTON, CHARMAINE.
       "Dr. Johnson's Attitude Towards the Education of Women."
       <u>New Rambler</u> 18 (1977): 49-58.

       Johnson favored intellectual and liberally educated women.
       This attitude is evident in <u>Journey to the Western Islands</u>
       when he discovers Miss Maclean of Mull, in <u>Rasselas</u> when he
       condemns female shallowness, and in <u>Rambler</u> 75 where he
       comments on the weaknesses of women's education.

1595   WILTSHIRE, JOHN.
       "Pains and Remedies: An Aspect of the Work of Samuel
       Johnson." <u>CR</u> 21 (1979): 3-10.

       Discusses the influence on Johnson's work of his obsessive
       preoccupation with the body's pain and suffering: when con-
       fronted by physical suffering, Johnson wrote with "unusual
       agility, pungency and passion." He tends to relate physical
       and mental disease so frequently that the analogy between the
       moralist and the doctor seems to be Johnson's most prevail-
       ing metaphor: the habitual identification of body and mind
       becomes the primary act of his moral imagination.

1596   "Dr. Johnson's Seriousness." CR 10 (1967): 63-73.

Johnson's strength as a moralist comes from the restatement of those truths about which men need to be reminded and from his questioning whether wisdom can "arm the heart against calamity." This question is central in Rasselas: Johnson is disturbed to perceive that the intellect's growth actually causes the problems it might solve. The greatness of his work comes from the agitation of his mind (imagination) and the breadth of his experience, together forming an essential sanity.

1596A   WIMSATT, W. K.
Philosophick Words: A Study of Style and Meaning in the "Rambler" and "Dictionary" of Samuel Johnson. New Haven: Yale Univ. , 1948.

Emphasizes connection between biography, linguistic history, and stylistic criticism in estimating Johnson's achievement. A study of "hard" words (the vocabulary of science or physical philosophy) during the 17th and 18th centuries, of which Johnson's Dictionary and prose writings are classic examples.

1596B   The Prose Style of Samuel Johnson. New Haven: Yale Univ. , 1941. Rpt. Hamden, Conn. : Archon, 1972.

Emphasizes on Johnson's theory of style in a "rich collection" of his statements on theory of composition, a system that relates to Johnson's actual practice. Also describes characteristics of his style and relates them to a general science of verbal style. Wimsatt seeks general conclusions about style as a medium of expression and explores the mind from which that expression came. Two chapters deal with historical considerations, the antecedents of Johnson's style, and its effects on later writers.

1597   YOUNGREN, WILLIAM.
"Dr. Johnson, Joseph Warton, and the 'Theory of Particularity.'" Dispositio 4 (1979): 163-188.

A comparison of Johnson's theory of poetry and that of Joseph Warton in the Essay on Pope. Discusses both writers' views on generality and particularity, primarily in reference to Pope's works, and concludes that their values and standards were virtually identical and that they applied them with very similar results. Also looks at the changes that took place in English criticism and aesthetics between 1660 and 1800.

See also: 79, 182, 227, 269, 285, 289, 303, 335, 368, 487, 973, 1369, 1378, 1924, 2690, 3202

The Life of Savage

1598   ALKON, PAUL K.

"The Intention and Reception of Johnson's Life of Savage."
MP 72 (1974): 139-150.

Attempts to apply Wolfgang Iser's theory of indeterminacy,
that "any text's form, meaning, and intention are most clearly
reflected not by the words on its pages, but in the responses
it elicits from readers," to Johnson's Life of Savage. How
Johnson's work was read is surveyed in a number of encyclo-
pedias and biographical dictionaries written between 1753 and
1831, and especially by the response elicited in 1841 by Charles
Whitehead's novel, Richard Savage: A Romance of Real Life.

1599   BOYCE, BENJAMIN.
        "Johnson's Life of Savage and Its Literary Background."   SP
        53 (1956): 576-598.

        Examines Johnson's narrative in the light of the other stor-
        ies of Richard Savage and relates it to the traditions of "crim-
        inal biography": notices how the biographical details accumu-
        late and the characterizations of the two main figures change.

1600   COHEN, MICHAEL M.
        "The Enchained Heart and the Puzzled Biographer: Johnson's
        Life of Savage." New Rambler 18 (1977): 33-40.

        Speculates on Johnson's treatment of Savage and his ideas on
        biography (Rambler No. 60 and Idler essay on biography) and sug-
        gests that his approach influences later biographies and imagina-
        tive literature, and is a good illustration of "the idea that any
        man's life makes a useful subject for the form." Suggests that
        Johnson refrains from judging Savage "not only because Savage is
        unique in his experience, but also because some deeply held be-
        lief of his own about the nature of man and his progress through
        the world is challenged by Savage's behaviour."

1601   DAVIDSON, VIRGINIA SPENCER.
        "Johnson's Life of Savage: The Transformation of a Genre."
        In Studies in Biography, Daniel Aaron, ed. (Cambridge: Har-
        vard Univ. Press, 1978), pp. 57-72.

        Johnson transmutes the facts of Savage's career into a
        genuinely tragic action and he himself functions as a choric
        voice: "Johnson exhibits the richly various responses avail-
        able to the chorus in an almost rhythmic regularity, accom-
        modating to himself typical choric patterns of omniscience,
        severity, compassion, caution, and regret." By taking biog-
        raphy beyond its merely commemorative function and demon-
        strating the complex nature of his subject, Johnson created
        a mimetic relationship between biography and actual human
        nature, and thus proved that biography, like poetry, could
        aspire to be more philosophical than history.

1602   DUSSINGER, JOHN A.
       "Style and Intention in Johnson's Life of Savage." ELH 37
       (1970): 564-580. Rpt. and rev. in [98], pp. 127-147.

       Comments that the Life of Savage is constructed like a
       Greek tragedy or medieval morality play, and that Johnson's
       conception of social order gives shape to it, showing Savage's
       "circular life" as the turning of Boethius's Wheel of Fortune.
       Johnson's intensely psychological view of the mother-son con-
       flict anticipates Freud; it also reflects "the deepest anxieties
       of the seventeenth and eighteenth centuries ... the individual's
       sense of discontinuity." Other themes concern the treatment
       of Savage as the son who is "part of a larger victimization
       of the male by a Circean feminism" and the implication that
       he is a "life-long child prone to fantasies of unfulfilled ex-
       pectation and at times even to narcissistic dreams of aliena-
       tion"; therefore, the narrator's norms of Christian Stoicism
       cannot provide the moral freedom necessary for the individual
       struggling for personal identity.

1603   ELLIS, FRANK H.
       "Johnson and Savage: Two Failed Tragedies and a Failed
       Tragic Hero." In [38], pp. 337-346.

       Discusses the relationship between Johnson and Savage, and
       analyzes the defects that made The Tragedy of Sir Thomas Over-
       bury and Irene: A Tragedy both "failed tragedies." Suggests
       Johnson's An Account of the Life of Mr. Richard Savage is actu-
       ally a scenario for a play, with Savage its "failed tragic hero."

1604   FLEEMAN, J. D.
       "The Making of Johnson's Life of Savage, 1744." Library 22
       (1967): 346-352.

       Bibliographical; analysis of the earliest editions and their
       differences.

1605   GROSS, GLORIA SYBIL.
       "Samuel Johnson's Case History of Richard Savage." HSL
       12 (1980): 39-47.

       Johnson's analysis of Savage's anti-social behavior and the
       reasons behind it is a superb illustration "of his lifelong study
       of psychodynamics and problems in human relationships." The
       Life is an analytic history of Savage's illness, which closely
       resembled Johnson's own in terms of Oedipal and masochistic
       conflicts. The outcome of Savage's feelings of persecution,
       rage, and self-abuse is that he is unable to deal with the
       problems of real life. Johnson has written "a deliberate and
       accurate record of psychopathology ... with the insight of
       [modern] professional clinical studies."

1606 MANER, MARTIN W.
      "Satire and Sympathy in Johnson's Life of Savage." Genre 8
      (1975): 107-118.

      Discusses how Johnson's narrative techniques function to
      make The Life of Savage a great biography and to create a
      dynamic conflict of emotions within the reader.

1607 MISENHEIMER, JAMES B., JR.
      "Samuel Johnson's Life of Savage: A Survey." The New
      Rambler 10, ser. C (Spring 1971): 18-26.

      A favorable report on this biography which is so often dis-
      missed as biased. Speculates on how and why Johnson wrote
      such a superb biography about a man so controversial as
      Savage. Concludes that "Johnson's genius may be said to
      have produced a kind of tour de force of the biographical art,"
      so much so that the reader today can almost hear Johnson saying,
      "If we owe regard to the memory of the dead, there is yet more
      respect to be paid to knowledge, to virtue and to truth."

1608 UPHAUS, ROBERT W.
      "The 'Equipoise' of Johnson's Life of Savage." SBHT 17
      (1976): 43-54. Incorporated into [180], pp. 89-107.

      Concerned with how the "symbolic force" of the Life of
      Savage accepts the "reader's ability to see Savage as an em-
      bodiment of a set of characteristics, but it depends ... on
      the reader's willingness to participate, by an act of imagina-
      tion, in the experiences of Savage's life as Johnson presents
      them." The "symbolic force" derives from Johnson's insis-
      tence on the psychological correspondences between his vision
      of Savage and the reader's own experiences and observations.
      The main assumption is that Savage's life at essential points
      links up with the reader's life as well. Since Johnson believed
      that equipoise represented the general state of mankind, he
      expects the reader to distinguish between the peculiarly individ-
      ual and the basic human experience of Savage's life.

1609 VESTERMAN, WILLIAM.
      "Johnson and The Life of Savage." ELH 36 (1969): 659-678.

      Johnson writes an apologetic biography of a man whom he
      likes but cannot altogether admire, so that his failure to live
      up to the requirement of fidelity results in a confusion of in-
      tention. In this his practice is at odds with his theory that
      all that is needed of a biographer is a "judicious and faithful
      narrative." But his essential honesty and sense of duty are
      finally stronger than his sympathy as a friend; thus The Life
      of Savage fulfills Johnson's requirements for biography. John-
      son's ambivalence toward Savage--his alternating between

moral condemnation and sympathetic understanding--finds corresponding reversals of attitude within the Life; e. g. , in
Steele's at first supporting Savage and then withdrawing that
support.   Concludes that Johnson resisted the melodrama inherent in his material--"he refuses to betray either Savage
or himself. "

See also: 1587, 1802, 1822, 2746

Poems

1610   ADLER, JACOB H.
       "Notes on the Prosody of The Vanity of Human Wishes. "
       Std. in Lit. Imag. 5, No. 2 (1972): 101-117.

       Compares Johnson's stated views on prosody with his prac-
       tice as seen in The Vanity of Human Wishes.   Also, his pros-
       ody is compared throughout with that of Pope.

1611   AMIS, GEORGE T.
       "The Style of The Vanity of Human Wishes. "   MLQ 35 (1974):
       16-29.

       A discussion of tone and control, particularly as they re-
       late to larger patterns of meaning in the poem.   Johnson's
       style cooperates "in generating a voice magisterial and au-
       thoritative, controlled and detached," and the power of the
       poem is due to "courageous manliness. "

1612   BATE, W. JACKSON.
       "Johnson and Satire Manqué. " In [6], pp. 145-160.

       The Vanity of Human Wishes is identified as the prototype
       of "Satire Manqué"--a satire more in sorrow than in anger.
       " 'Satire manqué' could also be described as a carrying further
       of satire into meditative reflection. "

1613   BLOOM, EDWARD A.
       "The Vanity of Human Wishes: Reason's Images. "   EIC 15
       (1965):   181-192.

       This essay was written to "strengthen the recent case for
       a critical re-evaluation," in the light of modern criticism's
       discovery of the "essential originality" of The Vanity of Human
       Wishes.   Bloom does this by a comprehensive analysis of the
       poem's recurrent images, stressing that "the order of the
       ideas" is "closely related to the sequence of the visual
       images. "

1614   BLOOM, EDWARD A. and LILLIAN D. BLOOM.
        "Johnson's London and its Juvenalian Texts." HLQ 34 (1970):
        1-23; continued as "Johnson's London and the Tools of Scholar-
        ship," HLQ 34 (1971): 115-139.

        First article examines Juvenalian editions to prove which
        Johnson used for London, and concludes that "he recreated
        his Latin text from memory" with deletions and deviations,
        and that his "understanding of the Third Satire was guided by
        a study of the Schrevelius edition of 1684." Second article
        discusses Johnson's translation of Juvenal and how his erudi-
        tion contributed to London's effectiveness "as an English poem."

1615   "Johnson's 'Mournful Narrative': The Rhetoric of 'London.'"
        In [6], pp. 107-144.

        The primary concern of the article is the powers of per-
        suasion, through applying the principles of rhetoric to the
        writing of satire, which Johnson admired in Juvenal and strove
        to emulate. Defends Johnson's translation of Juvenal in Lon-
        don.

1616   BOYD, D. V.
        "Vanity and Vacuity: A Reading of Johnson's Verse Satires."
        ELH 39 (1972): 387-403.

        What makes Johnson's satires fail as satire? Boyd says
        the subversive element is "the sympathetic imagination";
        Johnson is trapped by "ontological insecurity," that is, he
        sees mankind trapped in the flux between Pascal's two infini-
        ties, so that "[i]n the presence of the ultimate perspective
        of being and nothingness, the finite and the infinite, those
        finer distinctions and discriminations which are the normal
        business of satire tend to fade into oblivion.... In the onto-
        logical context of the two infinities, the follies of man lose
        half their foolishness." Concludes that satire reveals the
        "vanity" of human life, but its "vacuity" can only be trans-
        cended by religion.

1617   BROWN, STUART GERRY.
        "Dr. Johnson, Poetry, and Imagination." Neophilologus 22
        (1938): 203-207.

        Johnson was a neoclassic critic who was concerned more
        with style and matters of morals than with the higher function
        of poetic imagination.

1618   BROWN, WALLACE C.
        "Johnson: 'Pathos in Isolation.'" MLQ 8 (1947): 53-64.
        Rpt. in [81], pp. 67-86.

Although as a poet Johnson is generally overlooked, his mastery of the heroic couplet makes The Vanity of Human Wishes one of the greatest poems in English literature.

1619   EMSLIE, MACDONALD.
       "Johnson's Satires and the 'Proper Wit of Poetry.' "   Cambridge Jour. 7 (1954): 347-360.

       Relates Johnson's "proper wit of poetry" to the poetic methods of Pope.   Johnson follows Pope in subordinating the metaphorical images to other devices, such as "antithesis, and the building up of complex parallels."

1620   GIFFORD, HENRY.
       "The Vanity of Human Wishes."   RES 6 (1955):   157-165.

       Emphasizes differences between The Vanity of Human Wishes and Juvenal's Tenth Satire and shows that Johnson's work differs radically in imagery, tone, and subject-matter from the original.   Suggests that The Vanity of Human Wishes is colored by Johnson's feeling, and his philosophy of life is both more sombre and more kindly than Juvenal's.

1621   GOLDBERG, S. L.
       "Augustanism and the Tragic."   CR 17 (1974):   21-37.

       Argues against Leavis's thesis that the eighteenth century was incapable of attaining the tragic by analyzing The Vanity of Human Wishes; concludes that the importance of Augustan poetry is that "at its best it can be exploratory and creative enough to find the tragic realities ... within them."

1622   GRANT, DOUGLAS.
       "Samuel Johnson: Satire and Satirists."   New Rambler 3, Ser. C (June 1967): 5-17.

       Discusses the movement in eighteenth-century satire away from personalities to focus attack upon the works of the author as exemplified by Johnson's London and The Vanity of Human Wishes; contrasted with the personal but more powerful satire of Dryden, Pope, and Churchill.

1623   HARDY, JOHN.
       "Johnson's London: The Country Versus the City."   In [10], pp. 251-268.   Rpt. with revisions in Reinterpretations: Essays on Poems by Milton, Pope and Johnson (London: Routledge & Kegan Paul, 1971), pp. 103-123.

A reconsideration of London that "enables us to view in a new light its structure and theme." Resolves some apparent contradictions in the politically-oriented contrasting of city and country, and suggests that the corruption of the city is imaginatively linked with the current political scene.

1624   HART, EDWARD L.
"Johnson's Affirmation of Faith through the Vehicle of Time in The Vanity of Human Wishes." C & L 28, iii (1979): 41-49.

Johnson uses the present tense to suspend time--to provide tension. The present is held in a state of tension between the past and the future and is always "the seed of what will be." His strategy of suspending time in the present is the principal means by which Johnson asserts his religious faith. "A past tense of belief in God and of following him yields, through the present tense of causation, a future tense of happiness.... Happiness is made according to the law of cause and effect implicit in the time formula around which the poem is built."

1625   HILLES, FREDERICK W.
"Johnson's Poetic Fire." In [26], pp. 67-77.

A defense and analysis of The Vanity of Human Wishes: the poem does have personal emotion, it does betray artistic control, it does say something old in a fresh and original way. It reflects Johnson's "clear vision, betrays his strong feelings (controlled though they are) and displays brilliantly the eloquence, the powerful manner of expression for which he was to become famous."

1626   HORNE, COLIN J.
"The Opening of 'The Vanity of Human Wishes': Johnson's Observation and the Elevated Manner." AUMLA 49 (1978): 5-21.

The opening couplet, as well as the entire first stanza, effectively establishes the quality of the ensuing poem by its blend of elevation and precision in concept and style. Appearing first in Pope and partaking of the nature of the epic, a prophetic strain acquires its authentic voice for the eighteenth century in The Vanity of Human Wishes. The opening lines are functional in three aspects: "as an anticipation of the rest of the poem, as a concentrated resumé of a long tradition of philosophical and religious poetry, and as an enquiry conducted in accordance with the epistemology of the new age of scientific observation."

1627   KRIEGER, MURRAY.
        "Samuel Johnson: The 'Extensive View' of Mankind and the
        Cost of Acceptance." In The Classic Vision: The Retreat
        from Extremity in Modern Literature (Baltimore: Johns Hop-
        kins Press, 1971), pp. 125-145.

        Sees The Vanity of Human Wishes as the model of the pe-
        riod style of the mid-eighteenth century: "it is a splendid,
        if not unique, example of how that style can be exploited with
        a self-consciousness and a consistency that verge on perfec-
        tion.... And, clearly, the end to which ... these qualities
        [are] so successfully adaptable is one created by Johnson's
        adherence to his classic vision, his special cherishing of blood-
        less abstractions." It is that cherishing of abstractions that
        buys Johnson the placidity of temperament he needs.

1628   KUPERSMITH, WILLIAM.
        " 'More Like an Orator Than a Philosopher': Rhetorical
        Structure in The Vanity of Human Wishes." SP 72 (1975):
        454-472.

        A comparison of Johnson's poem with Juvenal's Tenth Sat-
        ire, arguing that, in spite of minor differences between the
        two poems, "Johnson not only derived from Juvenal the gen-
        eral arrangement of his poem, but also imitated, although
        not always in exactly the same order, the elements of each
        of Juvenal's sections which describe the consequences of each
        'specious pray'r.' " Concludes that critics are correct in
        denying logical structure or organic form in The Vanity of
        Human Wishes, but that, on the other hand, it is not a simple
        enumeration or "farrago"; the poem has "rhetorical struc-
        ture" because its scheme of organization, pattern, or arrange-
        ment does, in fact, derive from Classical rhetoric.

1629   "Declamatory Grandeur: Johnson and Juvenal." Arion 9
        (1970): 52-72.

        Kupersmith approaches apology for his article when he
        says: "Excessive stylistic analysis may begin to sound like
        the Grammarian's Funeral, but ... if close analysis of style
        leads critics to take seriously Juvenal's influence on John-
        son's poetic technique, the effort will have been worthwhile."
        Johnson's elevated style in his imitations of Juvenal, London
        and The Vanity of Human Wishes, is minutely examined, com-
        pared with the Juvenalian originals and with Dryden's elevated
        or epic style, and the conclusion made that Johnson went to
        great lengths to present the "declamatory grandeur" that Dry-
        den had failed to achieve.

1630   LIPKING, LAWRENCE.
        "Learning to Read Johnson: The Vision of Theodore and The

Vanity of Human Wishes." ELH 43 (1976): 517-537.

Emphasizes the importance, in relation to Johnson's spiritual biography and his other works, of "The Vision of Theodore": "All that it teaches us--the central importance of education, the view of life as a heroic journey, the Christian applications of Prodicus and Cebes, the power of habit in the author's mind, and the ambivalent attitude toward vision itself--informs his later work." "Theodore" was Johnson's model, and he followed that model when he wrote The Vanity of Human Wishes. Like Theodore, the narrator experiences melancholy visions, from which he awakes to face the truth: Theodore finds himself back on the lower slopes of his mountain, whereas the reader of the Vanity learns to abandon his wishes.

1631   MacANDREW, ELIZABETH.
"Life in the Maze: Johnson's Use of Chiasmus in The Vanity of Human Wishes." Studies in 18th Cent. Culture 9 (1980): 517-527.

Johnson's extended use of chiasmus in four key passages (ll., 5-10, 343-48; 31-6, 326-40) is "an important means of making us experience the futility of the world-confined view which, concluding that all human endeavors are inevitably defeated, decides that all aspirations are vain." An analysis of the chiastic arrangement in these lines indicates that Johnson wants us "to face the futility of aspirations which have a worldly direction." Then in lines 355-56, 360, and 366, he uses chiasmus again "to express the fervor of true hope and the calm which replaces fear in the mind which trusts in God." In the final couplet of the poem he says that it is "within the mind that the happiness is made--i. e. , created--which the mind cannot find by itself in the world outside itself."

1632   McGLYNN, PAUL D.
"Rhetoric as Metaphor in The Vanity of Human Wishes." SEL 15 (1975): 473-482.

Suggests that a close relationship exists between Johnson's elementary rhetorical structure and his broad philosophical structure, and that the "nature of this particular kind of poetry is, at least by analogy, the nature of that philosophy."

1633   MOODY, A. D.
"The Creative Critic: Johnson's Revisions of London and The Vanity of Human Wishes." RES 22 (1971): 137-150.

Manuscripts of some of Johnson's works still exist, and support the statements he made that he would compose as many as fifty lines of poetry and keep them in his mind be-

fore putting anything on paper, and that then a good bit of
revision occurred on that same copy. Later and more considerable revisions, concerning the philosophic and moral nature of the content, were often done after the first publication.

1634   "Johnson's Poems: Textual and Critical Readings." Library,
        5th ser., 26 (1971): 22-38.

        Takes exception to the decisions made by the editors of
        Oxford English Texts and the Yale editions in accepting "new"
        readings of portions of London and The Vanity of Human
        Wishes. Moody is not convinced by the evidence which sug-
        gests that the changes were made to agree with an annotated
        copy of the 1789 edition of Johnson's Poetical Works, believed
        to be altered according to notes made by Johnson.

1635   NEEDHAM, J. D.
        "The Vanity of Human Wishes as Tragic Poetry." AUMLA 46
        (1976): 206-219.

        A critical analysis of the "tragic irony" of the poem argu-
        ing that "Johnson ... exhibits a typically Augustan incapacity
        for creating tragic poetry." Largely based on F. R. Leavis's
        discussion of tragic poetry in his "Tragedy and the 'Medium.'
        Discusses Johnson's rhythms, sound patterns, and tone, and
        states "that the poem's 'complexity' resides in that interplay
        of insight and feeling" found in tragedy.

1636   NICHOL SMITH, DAVID.
        "The Heroic Couplet--Johnson." In [141], pp. 31-55; 2nd.
        ed. 1960, rpt. 1964.

        Praises The Vanity of Human Wishes as an example of
        Johnson's mastery of the heroic couplet; admitting his recog-
        nized faults in poetry--that his proper language is prose, that
        he is "not a very good starter" since he is inclined to weak
        opening lines--Nichol Smith argues that the poem is more
        moving and pathetic than the prose version of the same theme,
        Rasselas. Defends Johnson in Vanity as a "master of pathos"
        and insists that the abstractions are justified by the occasion;
        further defends his ear for the music of poetry: "Johnson's
        ear was very sensitive to what he calls 'collisions of conson-
        ants' and in particular to the sibilant"; concludes by analyzing
        Johnson's criticism of Lycidas.

1637   O'FLAHERTY, P. A.
        "The Art of Johnson's London." In [35], pp. 77-89.

Seeks to "reaffirm the artistry and integrity of London,
and in addition to propose a modification of the widely held
view of satire as 'conscious exaggeration.' " The emotion
exhibited is genuine; Johnson turns the Third Satire into a
political poem, concentrating and heightening the emotional
impact of Juvenal's poem by changing Umbricius into a character for whom we can feel great sympathy and by focusing
the satiric attack on the Walpole administration rather than,
as in Juvenal, leaving the object of satire vague and general.

1638   O'FLAHERTY, PATRICK.
"The Rambler's Rebuff to Juvenal: Johnson's Pessimism Reconsidered." ES 51 (1970): 517-527.

Refutes view of Nichol Smith and others that The Vanity of
Human Wishes represents Johnson's personal beliefs. It is
after all an "Imitation" of Juvenal; and O'Flaherty discusses
Juvenalian aphorisms in the poem and discovers them to be
oversimplified statements on human life.

1639   Johnson as Satirist: A New Look at The Vanity of Human
Wishes." ELH 34 (1967): 78-91.

Argues that Johnson is unable to maintain strong satire to
achieve his original object, the close imitation of Juvenal,
and that The Vanity of Human Wishes fails because it wanders
from its purpose. The poem is finally judged a failure because "Johnson ... adopts the pose of the cynical, bitter satirist, rather than allowing his generous feeling unfettered expression."

1640   OLSON, ROBERT C.
"Democritus Laughs for Samuel Johnson: A Plain Reading of
The Vanity of Human Wishes." McNR 25 (1978-79): 65-74.

Johnson's poem is not "an aborted Juvenalian satire" as
many see it but rather a moral essay in verse in which he is
appealing to the common sense of the reader. Johnson's tone
is both "wary and encouraging" rather than satiric, and his
skillful use of rhetoric enforces the moral strength of the
poem. Because Johnson is unable to be scornful of man, he
has to call on Democritus to do it for him.

1641   PARKIN, REBECCA.
"The Journey Down the Great Scale Reflected in Two Neo-
classical Elegies." Enl. E. 1 (1970): 197-204.

Theorizes how Dryden's "To the Memory of Mr. Oldham"
and Johnson's "On the Death of Dr. Robert Levet" reflect the
movement downward in civilized values.

1642 RICKS, C. B.
      "Wolsey in The Vanity of Human Wishes." MLN 73 (1958):
      563-568.

         Ricks cites numerous attacks on Sir Robert Walpole which
      bracket him with Cardinal Wolsey, who in turn was repeatedly
      compared to Sejanus, an infamous leader in the reign of Ti-
      berius.   Sejanus was satirized by Juvenal; thus begins the
      chain of associations.   Suggestion is made that when Johnson
      writes "Wolsey" he may also be thinking of Walpole.

1643 SELDEN, R.
      "Dr. Johnson and Juvenal: A Problem in Critical Method."
      Comp. Lit. 22 (1970): 289-302.

         Maintains that The Vanity of Human Wishes is a complete
      recreation in which Johnson heightens the Augustan plain style,
      replaces irony with pathos, and adds an infusion of Christian
      ethics to the stoic passages of Juvenal.   "Study of the poem
      as an imitation not only can provide a fuller understanding of
      his individual voice, but also ... can confirm established
      readings of the larger literary continuum."

1644 SITTER, JOHN E.
      "To The Vanity of Human Wishes through the 1740's." SP
      74 (1977): 445-464.

         An attempt to explain the difference between Johnson's
      voice in London and The Vanity of Human Wishes as being
      largely due to the shifts in English poetry which occurred
      during those years which separated the two poems.   A com-
      parison of The Vanity of Human Wishes with five shifts which
      occurred in poetry during the 1740's--from Epistle to Ode,
      from Persona to Personification, from Clarity to Obscurity,
      from Conversationalist to Solitary, and from Aggression to
      Solace--suggests the difference in voice from that of London.

1645 TUCKER, SUSIE I. and HENRY GIFFORD.
      "Johnson's Poetic Imagination." RES 8 (1957): 241-248.

         Discusses the use of metaphor in The Vanity of Human
      Wishes, and shows that despite Boswell's comment to the con-
      trary, Johnson's poetry contains a wealth of imagery.   Not-
      able figures are those of birds of prey or of disease, both
      seen as enemies of man; time is represented as flowing water.
      " ... The pleasure of Johnson's poetry is mainly imparted
      by the images, which give general truth a most moving per-
      sonal ring."

1646 TUTT, RALPH.

"Johnson on Pastoral Poetry." Serif 4 (Sept. 1967): 12-
16.

Takes up Johnson's objections to pastoral poetry and sifts
them to arrive at the core: "In its purest sense ... the
pastoral represents the kind of escapism which Johnson scorns
persistently ... one readily understands his antipathy to pastoral conventions."

1647   VALES, ROBERT L.
       "A Reading of the Basic Images in The Vanity of Human
       Wishes." Enl. E. 3 (1972): 106-112.

An examination of the imagery pattern stresses that Johnson is using and contrasting two basic images, one temporal,
one permanent, to lead the reader to the poem's optimistic
conclusion.

1648   WEINBROT, HOWARD D.
       "No 'Mock Debate': Questions and Answers in The Vanity of
       Human Wishes." MLQ 41 (1980): 248-267.

The author examines the Vanity's different questions in
order to see how they help the reader "to move from frantic
worldly to calming celestial wisdom." Johnson uses questions
to aid the speaker in enlarging both the dramatis personae
and the historical and chronological sweep of the poem; he
questions the reader in order to involve him in a vocal dialogue. Johnson "allows us to try on different psychological
roles (the harsh, the sympathetic), as well as choices of life
(the statesman, scholar, hero), to see the weaknesses in
each, and to enter into the poem ourselves...."

1649   "Johnson's London and Juvenal's Third Satire: The Country
       as 'Ironic' Norm." MP 73, iv, part 2 (1976): S56-S65.

Argues against the view that London fails as an imitation
because Johnson was unable to perceive Horace's ironic attitude toward the country. The modern critic, it is argued,
should try to read Horace as Johnson and the eighteenth century read him, and their reading was apparently non-ironic.
Four criteria are established to suggest that Horace was not
ironic toward the country in the Third Satire: 1) in his other
satires he was consistently favorable to the country; 2) lines
229 and 231 are not jokes: the 100 Pythagoreans and mastery
of a single lizard in the country must be contrasted with the
100 dinnertime dependents and metaphorical enslavement in
Rome; 3) English, Latin, and French commentators, transla-
tors, and imitators for over 200 years have regarded the
country as a norm that is not ironically undercut; and 4) Johnson, sensitive to irony in 1738, was not likely to have missed

ironic overtones if they were present in Horace.   Johnson,
in other words, clearly regarded Horace's praise of the country as positive and non-ironic.

1650   WHITE, IAN.
        "The Vanity of Human Wishes."   Crit. Quart. 6 (1972): 115-
        125.

        Points out the contrasts in theme and language between
        The Vanity of Human Wishes and Rasselas.

1651   WIESENTHAL, ALAN J.
        "On the Literary Value of Samuel Johnson's Latin Verse."
        HumLov 28 (1979): 294-301.

        Although Johnson's Latin verse is not always successful,
        it is impressive for the way in which it contributes to a liv-
        ing tradition by reorganizing the poetic strategies of its sources.
        For example, Johnson effects two changes in the Latin
        funeral elegy: he makes it more public than it was in the
        hands of Catullus, and the address has been shifted away
        from the loved one to all those who are grieving for him.

1652   WILKINSON, R. T.
        "Johnson's London: The Ironic Framework."   CP 4, i (1971):
        27-33.

        An analysis of the complexity of the poem--its structure,
        its execution, and its conception--shows that it is "not only
        London ... that is being satirized through Thales' invective,
        but Thales as well.   One is being satirized by means of the
        other."   Discusses the role of the narrator as satirist.

1653   WILSON, GAYLE EDWARD.
        "Poet and Moralist: Dr. Johnson's Elegiac Art and 'On the
        Death of Dr. Robert Levet.'" Enl. E. 4 (1973): 29-38.

        Answers the question of how Johnson as "a neo-classicist
        writing to please a classically oriented audience, ... [and]
        as a Christian moralist seeking to enhance Christian virtue,"
        wrote a commemorative poem to a person of Levet's obscur-
        ity.   Analyzes the exordium, the divisio, and the conclusio to
        show the effectiveness of the poem "based on the structure
        and topics of an epedeictic oration."

See also: 1488, 1513, 1536, 1558, 1563, 1565, 1575, 1593, 1711,
        1906

Irene

1654   BRONSON, BERTRAND H.
"Johnson's Irene." In [1485], pp. 431-468.

Details history of the Irene story from oral tradition through
various written versions, showing how the character of Irene
develops.   Examines Johnson's first draft and follows it to
the published text of Irene.   Continues with an analysis of
the "private content" of this Irene for biographical illumination and an evaluation of it as "artifact."

1655   CLAYTON, PHILIP T.
"Samuel Johnson's Irene: 'An Elaborate Curiosity.'" TSL
19 (1974): 121-135.

Seeks to demonstrate how carefully Johnson followed the
rules in Irene and that, "looked at as a neoclassical tragedy,
the play has Irene for its heroine, not Aspasia, as Bronson
suggests." Aspasia functions as an immutable standard by
which to judge Irene's tragic fall.

1656   MORAN, BERNA.
"The Irene Story and Dr. Johnson's Sources." MLN 71 (1956):
87-91.

Shows that Johnson used a number of sources for this play,
rather than basing it entirely on Knolles's Historie of the
Turks (1603) as had been previously thought.   The anonymous
tale Irene (1664) can be traced in it by the additional characters and plotting.

1657   NICHOL SMITH, DAVID.
Samuel Johnson's "Irene." Oxford: Clarendon Press, 1929.

"This simple tale of lust and cruelty became in [Johnson's]
hands a drama of the struggle between virtue and weakness."
Comparisons of his story with earlier versions bring out in
strong relief the characteristic moral quality of Johnson's
work, especially in the way in which he converts a story of
senseless cruelty into a study of temptation.   Also considers
the facts concerning Irene's composition and performance.

1658   WAINGROW, MARSHALL.
"The Mighty Moral of Irene." In [26], pp. 79-92.

Irene is not a simple character, but contains within her-

self the mixtures of idealistic and self-serving motives which
Johnson sees in all humanity. Johnson's lesson is that ill-
gotten security and power will not be worth the price, that
the sinner will have to pay though the Almighty--or the Kar-
mic force--may use human injustice as the instrument of Divine or poetic justice.

Periodical Essays

1659 BLOOM, EDWARD A.
"Symbolic Names in Johnson's Periodical Essays." MLQ 13
(1952): 333-352.

A technical examination of Johnson's theory and practice
in the use of symbolic names, especially in the Rambler;
argues that "[t]he metaphorical significance of names ... is
not a mere literary idiosyncrasy, but a solidly grounded lin-
guistic-philosophical concept with a literary application." Considers also the well-known attitudes and prejudices shown in
the periodical essays, relating them to the names: Misargyrus,
"money-hater," for instance.

1660 BRADFORD, C. B.
"Johnson's Revision of the Rambler." RES 15 (1939): 302-
314.

Presents the facts disclosed by a systematic collation of
the original and revised texts of the Rambler, partly to illustrate Johnson's method of composition. Attempts to establish the text of the Rambler, studies characteristic changes,
and summarizes the results of this investigation. Concludes
that the "man who wrote so hastily was later careful to de-
lete, elaborate, and correct."

1661 BULLOUGH, GEOFFREY.
"Johnson the Essayist." New Rambler 5, ser. C. (June
1968): 16-33.

A survey of specific Rambler and Adventurer essays showing Johnson's ability to relate his topics to his fundamental
principles of religion, morals, manners and literary work;
also points out how the Idler essays differ from the Rambler,
not only in length but also in content.

1662 CORDER, JIM W.
"Ethical Argument and Rambler No. 154." Quart. Jour.
Speech 54 (1968): 352-356. Rpt. in Der Englischen Essay
Analysen, Horst Weber, ed. (Darmstadt: Wissenchaftliche
Buchgesellschaft, 1975), pp. 170-177.

Shows how persuasiveness is achieved by Johnson in ethical argument--a form in which "hard evidence" can seldom be used to prove or disprove. "How, then, may discourse create trust, how give assertions weight and relevance?" Rambler No. 154 is analyzed to suggest that its persuasiveness depends upon the transformation of voice to create trust.

1663   DAMROSCH, LEOPOLD, JR.
        "Johnson's Manner of Proceeding in the Rambler." ELH 40
        (1973): 70-89.

Concentrates on Rambler 1 and 2 and 155 to show two rhetorical modes used by Johnson to encourage a rigorous "critical" thinking on the part of his audience. The first mode is one of "dismantling of commonplaces, which exposes all their weaknesses before reassembling them into a positive statement; the second is a mode of amplification, almost of meditation, which surrounds a subject with reflections that enlarge our understanding but do not advance an argument." Shows how Johnson combines these two modes in a single essay.

1664   EDINGER, WILLIAM C.
        "The Background of Adventurer 95: Johnson, Voltaire, Dubos."
        MP 78 (1980): 14-37.

Describes Johnson's relation to a critical dispute between Voltaire and Dubos over the choice between conservative and liberal critical principles; helps to determine his "place and role in the movement of eighteenth-century critical thought and also to clarify important features of his distinctive critical achievement." Johnson's position as stated in Adventurer 95 and The Preface to Shakespeare is one which "mediates between the conceptualism of Neo-Aristotelian and Horatian tradition and the empiricism of Dubos."

1665   ELDER, A. T.
        "Thematic Patterning and Development in Johnson's Essays."
        SP 62 (1965): 610-632.

Undertakes to "define the themes comprehensively, to classify the essays according to themes, to examine the development of the themes ... [and] seek an underlying thematic pattern within the essays of the Rambler, the Adventurer and Idler."

1666   "Irony and Humour in the Rambler." UTQ 30 (1960): 57-71.

Examines the lighter aspects of the Rambler and argues that, even though the periodical is heavy reading and full of gloom, "Johnson's sense of the irony of human existence enables him to regard with wry humour not only the weaknesses of Mr. Rambler but also the futile efforts of his fellows to attain their desires."

1667   GREENE, DONALD.
       "Samuel Johnson, Journalist." HAB 27 (1976): 441-457.
       Rpt. in [5], pp. 87-101.

       Emphasizes the "extent, variety, and quality" of Johnson's journalistic career, including the history of his association with the Gentlemen's Magazine and the Literary Magazine, an account of the Idler and Rambler series of essays, and an analysis of his theories of journalism; suggests that Johnson was the first modern journalist, that, in fact, "Johnson is a great journalist, in the sense that Macaulay, Bertrand Russell, H. L. Mencken, and George Orwell ... are great journalists: writers intensely dedicated to the education of as many of the general public as are educable...."

1668   KNIGHT, CHARLES A.
       "The Writer as Hero in Johnson's Periodical Essays." PLL 13 (1977): 238-250.

       Concerned with such questions as, what characteristics of the periodical essay were appropriate to Johnson's literary and philosophical interests? For what literary purpose did he use the periodical form? Concludes that Johnson discarded the periodical eidolon for the more "universal image of the writer as moral hero, struggling against the inner monsters of vanity, illusion, and frustrated ambition in order to achieve his social function as a moral teacher," and he therefore redefined "both the scope and the nature of the periodical essay in a way that engages the reader in a particularly powerful exemplification of the nature of man as a moral being."

1669   KOPER, PETER T.
       "Samuel Johnson's Rhetorical Stance in The Rambler." Style 12 (1978): 23-34.

       An analysis of Johnson's prose in the Rambler essays and in particular his use of pronouns in Rambler No. 76; views his "style as an aspect of his rhetoric, that is, as a tool being used by a moralist in an argument." Also attempts to reconcile the views of William K. Wimsatt (The Prose Style of Samuel Johnson) who thinks Johnson's style is abstract and generalized, and Walter Jackson Bate (The Achievement of Samuel Johnson), who sees in Johnson a "continual concreteness." The resolution to such debates and the explanation of the power of the Rambler essays as moral argument lie in the grammatical features of Johnson's style.

1670   LEED, JACOB.
        "Patronage in the Rambler." SBHT 14 (1972): 5-21.

        The Rambler papers written between 1750 and 1752 con-
        tain Johnson's fullest comments on patronage which are not
        always antagonistic. "Johnson creates for his culture the
        image of a strong and independent professional writer."

1671   McGLYNN, PAUL D.
        "Johnsonian Prose and the Musical Baroque." SHR 13 (1979):
        209-214.

        Argues that "the characteristics of late Baroque music pro-
        vide both useful analogies and a lexicon of terms for approach-
        ing the formidable topic of Samuel Johnson's prose style."
        Uses Idler #103 as example.

1672   MISENHEIMER, JAMES B., JR.
        "Dr. Johnson on Prose Fiction." New Rambler 4, ser. C
        (1968): 12-18.

        By analyzing Rambler 4, the author suggests that Johnson
        valued the "new genre" of prose fiction as a vehicle for moral
        instruction only; he took little interest in the techniques in-
        volved.

1673   "Dr. Johnson on the Essay." New Rambler 18, ser. B (1966):
        13-17.

        Johnson assigns great importance to the essay, which may
        affect men's minds on serious subjects as it gains readers
        by its attractiveness as a relatively short piece entertainingly
        written. Its flexibility, which gives it unusual advantages,
        also imposes a responsibility on the writer to use it for sig-
        nificant and moral purposes.

1674   O'FLAHERTY, PATRICK.
        "Towards an Understanding of Johnson's Rambler." SEL 18
        (1978): 523-536.

        Johnson's purpose in writing the Rambler essays was to
        give men knowledge that he thought was most important for
        them to have. His essays show us the process of his think-
        ing rather than the results, and acknowledge "the complexity
        of leading a moral life and of the difficulty of containing that
        complexity within neatly ordered sequences of ideas." John-
        son's perception "of man's moral life ... is generally ... of
        something threatened from within and without and maintained
        only be perpetual vigilance."

1675   "Johnson's Idler: The Equipment of a Satirist." ELH 37
        (1970): 211-225.

        Johnson's emergence as a satirist is made possible by the
        stance of amused detachment assumed by the persona of the
        Idler. This satirical ability is well demonstrated but not sus-
        tained; it is weakened by his habit of seeing all sides of a
        question. "What we see in the Idler is Johnson reaching be-
        yond satire to a new form, a form which could accommodate
        both irony and love."

1676   OLSON, ROBERT C.
        "Rambler Mottoes from Horace's Odes: Consciousness of
        Impending Death." CF 33 (1979): 57-70.

        Examines nine mottoes from Horace which Johnson uses
        in his Rambler essays "to determine whether [he] uses [the
        motto] as an appropriate text for an essay, whether he re-
        veals an awareness of the context of the motto in his essay,
        and whether the tenor of his remarks bears resemblance to
        the spirit of the Horatian Ode he utilizes."

1677   POWELL, L. F.
        "Johnson's Part in the Adventurer." RES 3 (1927): 420-429.

        New information on the literary and financial history of
        the paper, including evidence that Johnson wrote the four
        papers subscribed "Misargyrus" (Nos. 34, 41, 53, 62) which
        Boswell, Malone, and Hill did not accept as his.

1678   REWA, MICHAEL.
        "Aspects of Rhetoric in Johnson's 'Professedly Serious' Ram-
        bler Essays." Quart. Jour. Speech 56 (1970): 75-84.

        Johnson, the essayist, specifically in the Rambler, is pre-
        sented in the light of his early training at Lichfield Grammar
        School, the grounding in the Latin classics through to the
        basic neo-classic writer's purpose to "teach and delight."

1679   RIELY, JOHN CABELL.
        "The Pattern of Imagery in Johnson's Periodical Essays."
        ECS 3 (1970): 384-397.

        Riely shows Johnson as a "creative writer" in the sense
        of a craftsman. He analyzes Johnson's use of image and
        metaphor as deliberate technique, then moves to a considera-
        tion of what the choices of image can tell us about Johnson:
        "The pattern of the images which predominate in the essays
        reveals the paradox underlying his obsession with personal

struggle and 'with the pain of being a man' "; the essential
images--of emptiness, sinking, slavery, defeat, sickness--
depict Johnson's "dark description of the journey of life."

1680   SCHWARTZ, RICHARD B.
        "Johnson's 'Mr. Rambler' and the Periodical Tradition."
        Genre 7 (1974): 196-204.

        Discusses the question of the Rambler's relatively unde-
        veloped eidolon.

1681   SMITTEN, JEFFREY R.
        "Johnson and the Sin of Sloth." Renascence 30 (1977): 3-18.

        Johnson regarded sloth as a "vice which strikes at the
        foundation of all Christian virtue and for this reason is one
        of his most profound concerns." He is concerned in the
        Rambler and Idler essays not only with those who are alone
        and have nothing to do but also with those who do not want
        to do anything. Seductive daydreams are a part of a larger
        psychological process. Johnson's understanding of that proc-
        ess is close to that of modern psychologists, but is controlled
        and limited by his acceptance of Christian doctrine; his analy-
        sis of sloth is clearly linked to the traditional view that sloth
        consists of neglect of religious duties.

1682   WOODRUFF, JAMES F.
        "Johnson's Idler and the Anatomy of Idleness." ESC 6 (1980):
        22-38.

        Johnson's Idler, although possessing the variety character-
        istic of the eighteenth-century periodical essay, emphasizes
        the theme of idleness--"a theme which not only pervades this
        work but determines its ultimate character, his own attitude
        to it, and the form towards which it moves." The character
        "Mr. Idler" is largely a symbolic figure who "can be appro-
        priately addressed by those who are themselves idlers or who
        are agitated by the sight of idleness in the world around
        them." Tracing the theme of idleness throughout the essays
        establishes Johnson conclusively as a Menippean satirist.

1683   "The Allusions in Johnson's Idler No. 40." MP 76 (1979):
        380-389.

        Although Johnson's concern with advertising shows parallels
        with Addison's Tatler No. 224, Johnson is more concerned
        with the rhetorical and moral implications of advertising, and
        he "introduces such currently fashionable topics as the sub-
        lime in a way which, though facetious, is also curiously ser-
        ious."

See also: 1466, 1545, 1553, 1559, 1581, 1593, 1744

The "Dictionary"

1684   BRAUDY, LEO.
"Lexicography and Biography in the Preface to Johnson's
Dictionary." SEL 10 (1970): 551-556.

The Preface seems quite different according to whether the
the evaluation is made by a biographer or by a linguistic historian.   But "Johnson seems to have fused the scholarly and
personal elements with extraordinary power.... It is Johnson's double sense of the creative authority of the Dictionary
and the human weakness of its creator that gives his preface
its compelling power."

1685   GRIFFITH, PHILIP MAHONE.
"Dr. Johnson's 'Diction of Common Life' and Swift's Directions to Servants." In [3053], pp. 10-30.

Discusses Johnson's use in his Dictionary of Swift's Directions to Servants; lists all words for which Johnson used
Swift as illustration.

1686   HANSEN, DAVID A.
"Redefinitions of Style, 1600-1800." In [1709], pp. 95-116.

Establishes the variable meanings of style in the eighteenth
century, determines the extent to which the term did undergo
a change in meaning, and suggests possible relations between
the dominant trends in prose style and the definition of style
in references of the time.

1687   JACKSON, H. J.
"Johnson and Burton: The Anatomy of Melancholy and the
Dictionary of the English Language." ESC 5 (1979): 36-48.

Fifteen words in the Dictionary are illustrated by quotations
from the Anatomy, lending support to the belief that "Johnson
was attentive to Burton's ideas and observations upon human
life; that he considered Burton's work to be morally sound;
and that he looked upon the Anatomy as therapeutic in cases
of melancholy 'which,' as Hawkins remarked in 1787, 'the
public now too well knows was the disease of his mind.' "

1688   KEAST, WILLIAM R.
"The Two Clarissas in Johnson's Dictionary." SP 54 (1957):
429-439.

Keast discovers a mystery, the great number of quotations from Richardson's Clarissa which appear in the Dictionary. He finds a solution--"a busy lexicographer's dream--a thesauras of quotations from Clarissa: 'An Ample Collection of Such of the Moral and Instructive Sentiments interspersed throughout the Work, as may be presumed to be of General Use and Service,' appended to Volume VII of the fourth edition of Clarissa, 1751." Johnson derived the majority of his quotations from the source rather than from the novel itself.

1689   "Johnson's Plan of a Dictionary: A Textual Crux." PQ 33 (1954): 341-347.

Keast reconstructs what must have happened as Johnson revised and proofread the Plan of a Dictionary. Finding an apparent duplication, Keast suggests that three paragraphs were rewritten, but that the printer printed these along with the first-draft paragraphs which he should have discarded.

1690   "Some Emendations in Johnson's Preface to the Dictionary." RES 4 (1953): 52-57.

Keast is concerned not with obvious errors but those "of the more insidious type which make a kind of sense, enough to beguile the reader into acquiescence, but not the sense the author intended."

1691   "The Preface to A Dictionary of the English Language: Johnson's Revision and the Establishment of the Text." SB 5 (1952-53): 129-146.

Studies of revisions of Johnson's other writings have given a picture of his process of arriving at the final version, but for The Preface to A Dictionary these studies have an additional value in establishing the true text. There are two sets of revisions, and a question as to which variants are by Johnson.

1692   KNOBLAUCH, C. H.
"Coherence Betrayed: Samuel Johnson and the 'Prose of the World.'" Boundary 7 (1979): 235-260.

Johnson attempts to resolve the epistemological crisis of the eighteenth century, the dissociation of mind and world, language and its referents, which empiricism had provoked. The Dictionary represents an effort to "recover the signifying capacity of language in a culture whose peculiar malevolence had been to pervert and trivialize the Word." Because confidence in the power of writing and in the authority of texts had been shaken, Johnson struggled to maintain the purity of the English language and to regain the classical ideal of the "stability of truth"; he sought to bring language under his authority.

1693   KOLB, GWIN J. and RUTH A. KOLB.
       "The Selection and Uses of the Illustrative Quotations in Dr. Johnson's Dictionary." In [1709], pp. 61-72.

       A study of Johnson's "selection, treatment, and ultimate use" of illustrative quotations; concludes that Johnson's achievement merits enhanced respect and admiration.

1694   KOLB, GWIN J.
       "Establishing the Text of Dr. Johnson's 'Plan of a Dictionary of the English Language.'" In [6], pp. 81-87.

       Details the textual sources of the Plan available to the modern student: rough draft ("Short Scheme"), fair copy, demonstrably used as printer's copy, and two editions: the first with an address to Chesterfield, and the second without. Leads to a choice of the first editions, with certain changes taken from the second, as definitive.

1695   KOLB, GWIN J. and JAMES H. SLEDD.
       "Johnson's Dictionary and Lexicographical Tradition." MP 50 (1953): 171-194.

       The authors give Johnson full credit for his monumental achievement but, without intending to belittle, they reevaluate it in the light of twentieth-century advances in linguistics and philology. The result is that the place of Johnson's Dictionary is reduced as the perspective widens. It is identified as a great compilation rather than a creative work. Evidence is cited to show that its influence on language has been overestimated.

1696   McCRACKEN, DAVID.
       "The Drudgery of Defining: Johnson's Debt to Bailey's Dictionarium Britannicum." MP 66 (1969): 338-341.

       Hawkins reports that as Johnson assembled definitions for his dictionary he put these slips of paper in the proper alphabetical pages of his copy of Bailey, and thus the skeleton of his own dictionary developed. Johnson's specific debt to Bailey was small since he copied very few definitions verbatim. "But his general debt ... is immeasurable" because in etymologies and techniques of lexicography, as well as in word lists, Bailey provided an invaluable base.

1697   MACDONALD, ANGUS.
       "Johnson as Lexicographer. "   Univ. of Edinburgh Jour. 8
       (1936): 17-23.

           Assesses favorably Johnson's qualifications as lexicographer
       and his finished product, the Dictionary. A few tolerant chuck-
       les are sounded for the few evidences of bias shown, as in
       the definitions of "Whig" and "Tory. "

1698   NAGASHIMA, DAISUKE.
       "An Historical Assessment of Johnson's Dictionary (II). "
       Anglica 6, No. 4 (1968): 20-34.

           Compares the word lists in the C section of Johnson's and
       Bailey's dictionaries, to the credit of Johnson as an elimina-
       tor of excess verbiage as well as a keeper of the language.
       In this and in the treatment of such traditional features as
       "dictionary words" Johnson is present as "a man of meticulous
       discretion, not a dogmatic bigot as popular fancy is fond of
       making him. "

1699   "An Historical Assessment of Johnson's Dictionary (I). "
       Anglica 6 (1966): 161-200.

           Nagashima submits that English dictionaries, up to and
       including Bailey, had been encyclopedic in nature, deficient
       or lacking in any emphasis on philology.   Johnson, therefore,
       checked and rechanneled the flow of English lexicography by
       modeling his work on that of the French Academy and produc-
       ing a philologically oriented dictionary of the English language.
       The author seeks to refute the position of Starnes, Noyes,
       and others that Johnson is just one in a chain of lexicographers.

1700   "Johnson's Dictionary Reconsidered. "   Studies in English Lit-
       erature (Tokyo): 41 (1964): 35-57.

           Attempts " ... to set the Dictionary in a more proper his-
       torical perspective, which will lead us to a revision, in some
       degree, of the hitherto generally received standard view on
       the development of the English dictionary. "

1701   NOYES, GERTRUDE E.
       "The Critical Reception of Johnson's Dictionary in the Latter
       Eighteenth Century. " MP 52 (1955): 175-191.

           The author aims to give a "general view of the notice taken
       of the Dictionary in the first fifty years of its existence, under
       the following topics: (I) reviews in magazines; (II) criticisms

included in early lives of Johnson; (III) special works devoted largely or wholly to the Dictionary; (IV) comments by succeeding lexicographers; and (V) references by other writers on linguistic topics." Concludes that "Johnson is his own best critic and that there is not a true shortcoming pointed out by his rivals or a worthy ideal envisioned which he had not himself conceived and eloquently expressed in his preface." He was more realistic than his critics in measuring how far such ideals could be attained.

1702   READ, ALLEN W.
"The Contemporary Quotations in Johnson's Dictionary." ELH 2 (1935): 246-251.

Johnson in his definitions resisted using quotations from writers of his own day, untested by time; therefore, the list as given here is small and manageable. Even this limited use of contemporaries advances the historical principle in lexicography, as it recognizes that a quotation, even from a "mean source," may be important in showing the history of a word.

1703   RYPINS, STANLEY.
"Johnson's Dictionary Reviewed by his Contemporaries." PQ 4 (1925): 281-286.

Considers the longer and more general reviews, rather than the nit-picking of the funny-story types who delighted in selecting an item for ridicule. Comments by Adam Smith, Maxwell, Adelung, Horne-Tooke, and Webster.

1704   SAN JUAN, EPIFANIO, JR.
"The Actual and the Ideal in the Making of Samuel Johnson's Dictionary." UTQ 34 (1965): 146-158.

Shows Johnson as both a realist and an idealist: a realist in acknowledging the value of experience, and an idealist in desiring a perfection of correct and elegant style.

1705   SHERBO, ARTHUR.
"Dr. Johnson's Revision of his Dictionary." PQ 31 (1952): 372-382.

Sherbo conducts his analysis of Johnson's preparation of the second edition by careful comparison of one section as seen in each edition, the "M" section. He finds about 700 changes, and concludes that Johnson's editorial work was thorough, careful, and methodical. It was done during a period of emotional depression, and was a steadying influence upon the writer.

1706   SLEDD, JAMES H. and GWIN J. KOLB.
        Dr. Johnson's Dictionary: Essays in the Biography of a Book.
        Chicago: Univ. Chicago Press, 1955.

        Sledd details the building of the Dictionary from its incep-
        tion, giving a chronological table of events, an account of the
        influence of Chesterfield, and an evaluation of Johnson in lex-
        icographical tradition. Here Johnson holds his own pretty
        well in spite of attacks from Webster whose American brand
        of scholarship shows weaknesses.

1707   TILLOTSON, GEOFFREY.
        "Johnson's Dictionary." In [174], pp. 224-228.

        Johnson is revealed in two pieces of writing connected
        with the Dictionary, the Plan and the Preface, which provide
        balance to Boswell's accounts of Johnson, the witty conversa-
        tionalist. Johnson's masterful understanding of his responsi-
        bility to the language shows him as anything but a "harmless
        drudge."

1708   WEINBROT, HOWARD D.
        "Samuel Johnson's Plan and Preface to The Dictionary: The
        Growth of a Lexicographer's Mind." In [1709], pp. 73-94.

        Contrasts the Plan with the later Preface, suggesting that
        in the latter Johnson rejects the Plan and many of his earlier
        conceptions of language.

1709   WEINBROT, HOWARD D. , ed.
        New Aspects of Lexicography. Carbondale: Univ. So. Ill.
        Press, 1972.

1710   WIMSATT, W. K. , JR. and MARGARET H. WIMSATT.
        "Self-Quotations and Anonymous Quotations in Johnson's Dic-
        tionary." ELH 15 (1948): 60-68.

        Quotations as indicated in the title are listed, misquotations
        and inaccuracies pointed out, and differences in the editions
        are discussed. Suggests that much needs to be done to clear
        up textual mysteries.

Rasselas

1711   ADEN, JOHN M.
        "Rasselas and The Vanity of Human Wishes." Criticism 3
        (1961): 295-303.

Considers Rasselas a repudiation of the pessimism and
melancholy of the poem rather than a prose statement of it.

1712   BAKER, SHERIDAN.
"Rasselas: Psychological Irony and Romance." PQ 45 (1966):
249-261.

Examines Johnson's use of irony in his exposition of the
futility and the dangers of daydreaming.

1713   BRINTON, GEORGE.
"Rasselas and the Problem of Evil." PLL 8 (1972): 92-96.

As Johnson confronts the problem of evil and why it is
permitted by a beneficent Deity, he tries to strike the right
balance between comedy and tragedy, hope and despair.   In
his effort to make the reader accept unhappiness and pin his
hopes on life after death, he runs the risk of going too far,
Candide style, and causing his readers to doubt God.

1714   BROADHEAD, GLENN J.
"The Journey and the Stream: Space and Time Imagery in
Johnson's Rasselas." Explor 8 (1980): 15-24.

A view of Rasselas as travel literature.   Spatial and temporal images characterize Johnson's thought, and he uses the
image of the stream as a major element in the tale.   He
uses the long journey which Rasselas makes "as a means of
forcing his hero into acquaintance with a variety of persons
and ideas" but what saves the book from "inconsequence" is
his use of the stream image--a "conventional image for conversation, for social intercourse, [which] also serves to maintain the spatial and temporal scale appropriate to an essentially asocial journey into knowledge....   Life is a journey
of discovery, a journey is like a stream, a stream is like
conversation, conversation is an emblem of life."

1715   BUTTERICK, GEORGE F.
"The Comedy of Johnson's Rasselas." In Studies in the Hu-
manities 2: i, ed. William F. Grayburn (Bloomington: Univ.
Ind. Press, 1971), pp. 25-31.

Argues that the essential quality of Rasselas is comic irony,
though the danger is that the reader will see only the comic
satire: "Rasselas' tale is actually and curiously quite modern
in effect, and takes on the coloration of the black comedy of
recent literature, or at least the suspended air of Waiting
for Godot.   The comedy of Rasselas is, in fact, almost in
spite of itself, very much a tragi-comedy like Waiting for
Godot...."

1716   EVERSOLE, RICHARD.
        "Imlac and the Poets of Persia and Arabia." PQ 58 (1979):
        155-170.

            Perhaps it has been a mistake for critics to have assumed
        that Johnson took sides with or against Imlac: both Imlac
        and Rasselas speak in Chapter X without the author observing
        their minds or commenting on their ideas.   Since Johnson
        associates Imlac with the poets of Persia and Arabia, Chap-
        ter X contains sufficient Oriental material to raise "doubts
        about conflating Imlac's attitudes and principles with those
        in Johnson's own declared range of critical activity"; the first
        half of Chapter X tells us more about the eighteenth century's
        understanding of Eastern poetry than about Johnson's critical
        theory.   Imlac's "dissertation upon poetry," in the second
        half of the chapter, is "an extension of his distinct fictional
        identity as an Eastern poet." Chapter X, finally, is impor-
        tant in the structure of the whole book as the principal state-
        ment concerning the choice of a life: Rasselas wants to ap-
        proach life as he would a text.

1717   FOLKENFLIK, ROBERT.
        "The Tulip and Its Streaks: Contexts of Rasselas X." ArielE
        9, ii (1978): 57-71.

            Seeks to "establish what Johnson thought with more exact-
        ness, and the historical place of this dissertation on poetry
        should emerge from such an examination" of Chapter X.   The
        Life of Thomson, however, sets the limits of particularity
        that Johnson was willing to allow: the "enumeration of cir-
        cumstantial varieties" within a "wide expanse of general views."
        It is because Imlac is so frequently Johnson's mouthpiece that
        Johnson undercuts him in Chapter X: it is "at once a last
        statement of the Renaissance conception of the poet and a
        critique of it."

1718   FULTON, HENRY L.
        "Theme and Structure in Rasselas." Mich. A. 1 (1969): 75-
        80.

            Takes the position that the theme of Rasselas is determined
        by the structure or pattern of events.   These events show
        him as unteachable to the end, clinging to his preconceived
        ideas.

1719   GABA, PHYLLIS.
        " 'A Succession of Amusements': the Moralization in Rasselas
        of Locke's Account of Time." ECS 10 (1977): 451-463.

            Locke's theory of time which "furnishes us with the idea
        of succession'" and gives us the "foundation for our conception

of duration (and of eternity)" underlies a great deal of Johnson's work and "provides much of the conceptual framework
of Rasselas." In that novel he constantly emphasizes the importance of "succession" and "duration" to life in the Happy
Valley and to Rasselas's decision to return to Abyssinia.

1720   GROSS, GLORIA SYBIL.
        "Sanity, Madness and the Family in Samuel Johnson's Rasselas." Psycul R 1 (1977): 152-160.

        Portrays Johnson as a pioneer in social psychiatry, anticipating family process and child outcome theorists by 200
        years, when he "engages the characters of Rasselas in situations that exposit inchoate theories of social psychiatry," and
        compares his insights into marriage and family relationships
        as portrayed by Rasselas and his sister, Nekayah, with those
        of modern-day studies of schizophrenia. Johnson also probes
        the impact of family dynamics on personality disorders in
        his diagnosis of Rasselas's malady.

1721   HANSEN, MARLENE R.
        "Rasselas, Milton, and Humanism." ES 60 (1979): 14-22.

        Finds a significant source for Johnson's description of the
        Happy Valley in Milton's account of Eden in Book IV of Paradise Lost, and suggests that a consideration of the similarities and differences between the two works will help to define
        the nature of Johnson's humanism: the author considers
        "several ... nodes of resemblance and their relation to the
        broadly humanistic theme of human nature and its duties in
        life." Rasselas argues the dual nature of man, but the opposition is not the traditional one between angel and beast,
        flesh and spirit, but between "the aspirations and convictions
        of Adam and the absurdity and anguish of Satan."

1722   HARTLEY, LODWICK.
        "Johnson, Reynolds, and the Notorious Streaks of the Tulip
        Again." ECS 8 (1975): 329-336.

        Argues that "Imlac's assumption ... of a stance that is in
        specifics closer to Johnson's good friend Reynolds than to
        Johnson himself is, even though ironic only in a gentle fashion, an additional reason that an argument for the identity of
        Imlac and Johnson throughout the chapter [ten] is too restrictive for acceptance."

1723   HILLES, FREDERICK W.
        "Rasselas, an 'Uninstructive Tale.'" In [1464], pp. 111-
        121.

Defends Rasselas against the principal accusations made against it, pointing out to its detractors that it has been reprinted on an average of three times a year since its first appearance.

1724   HILLIARD, RAYMOND F.
"Desire and the Structure of Eighteenth-Century Fiction."
Studies in 18th Cent. Culture 9 (1980): 357-370.

The author surveys the "structural similarities among several types of eighteenth-century fiction--the prose satire, the novel of manners, the Gothic romance, and so on--with a view to argue that the similarities reveal a widespread conception of desire," defined loosely as "an appetite of the imagination." Desire is often equated with sexual passion, but its more subtle meaning concerns the attempt to enlarge the boundaries of the self. Hilliard's comments are restricted to the relationship between desire and fictional structure. Such books as Rasselas, Clarissa, Amelia, Joseph Andrews, Gulliver's Travels, and The Monk are discussed.

1725   HOVEY, RICHARD B.
"Dr. Samuel Johnson, Psychiatrist." MLQ 15 (1954): 321-325.

A "modern" attempt to diagnose Johnson's melancholy. Argues that Johnson's mad astronomer in Rasselas is really Johnson himself.

1726   JONES, EMRYS.
"The Artistic Form of Rasselas." RES 18 (1967): 387-401.

Rasselas is usually seen as either a gloomy moral work or as a kind of comic narrative. Less noticed are similarities to Tristram Shandy. Both novels might be called "philosophical fiction," but more importantly both Johnson and Sterne were enemies of rigid theoretical systems. Johnson's sense of the multifariousness of life shows in the tripartite structure of Rasselas; this structure "exhibits the breakdown of untested theory in the face of actual experience."

1727   JOOST, NICHOLAS.
"Whispers of Fancy; or, The Meaning of Rasselas." Modern Age 1 (1957): 166-173.

Rasselas considered as a moral and religious novel: on the symbolic or allegorical level, as a Freudian preconscious dream revelatory of its author, on the moral level, and in a Christian context.

1728   KALLICH, MARTIN.
        "Samuel Johnson's Principles of Criticism and Imlac's 'Dissertation upon Poetry.'" Jour. of Aesthetics & Art Criticism 25 (1966): 71-82.

        Johnson and Imlac "represent the past. They may be considered the last important exemplars of neoclassical theory in England." Argues that a close reading of chapter 10 indicates that it systematically "summarizes Johnson's critical theory, blending Platonic (mimesis and idea) into Aristotelian (nature, pity and terror) notions and producing a succinct restatement of the traditional theory of literature in the eighteenth century."

1729   KAUL, R. K.
        "The Philosopher of Nature in Rasselas XXII." Indian Jour. of English Studies 3 (1962): 116-120.

        Argues that the philosopher is not Rousseau, and "although the philosopher of nature's prenouncements echo the views of three schools of philosophy, the connecting link, if we wish to look for it, is Shaftesbury."

1730   KEENER, FREDERICK M.
        "Conflict and Declamation in Rasselas." In [50], pp. 157-181.

        Analyzes the trinitarian assumption, that the views of Imlac, the narrator, and Johnson are roughly identical, and seeks to illuminate Imlac's relation to both the narrator and to Rasselas. Although Imlac has said, in Chapter XXX, that the characters have neglected to live, the author argues that, on the contrary, "they have seriously become engaged not just in life but also in conflict, with each other.... The main characters' disagreement, anger, and estrangement from each other deserves recognition." In spite of conflict, however, Rasselas at the end needs Imlac's guidance, so that something, after all, is concluded.

1731   KENNEY, WILLIAM.
        "Rasselas and the Theme of Diversification." PQ 38 (1959): 84-89.

        Interprets the tale as showing that while happiness can never be solid or permanent, a man's best chance of attaining some measure of it is to "diversify his activities in such a way that both satiety and its consequent withdrawal into an unhealthy solitude can be avoided." The main incidents develop the theme of controlled diversification and the return to the Happy Valley at the end provides that "union of the

novel with the familiar" which has been the chief lesson of
the prince's travels. Kenney's interpretation leaves the story
pretty tame, a picture of the moral life with few risks and
little of either comedy or tragedy. This tameness would
seem to arise from a confusion--or a fusion--of the concept
of happiness and security.

1732   "Johnson's Rasselas After Two Centuries." BUSE 3 (1957):
        88-96.

        Rasselas is regaining the good opinion of critics after be-
        ing condemned by the disciples of romantic individualism
        throughout the nineteenth century. Its somber pessimism is
        now accepted and its humor appreciated.

1733   KOLB, GWIN J.
        "Rousseau and the Background of the 'Life Led According to
        Nature' in Chapter 22 of Rasselas." MP 73 iv, part 2 (1976):
        S66-S73.

        Contends that, in the absence of persuasive evidence, Rous-
        seau's Discourses must be rejected as sources of any part
        of the philosopher's conversation in Chapter 22, and that the
        material from which Johnson derived the "conversation must
        be sought not in the works of a single person but rather in
        the pronouncements of heterogeneous writers, probably both
        classical and modern English (especially), who expounded the
        persistent but often ill-defined 'law of nature' and kindred
        philosophical, religious, and ethical ideas and whose modes
        of thought and/or expression lent themselves to ambiguity and
        ridicule. "

1734   "The Intellectual Background of the Discourse on the Soul in
        Rasselas. " PQ 54 (1975): 357-369.

        Investigates the probable antecedents of the notions regard-
        ing the soul advanced by Imlac and others, in Chapter XLVIII,
        and details the resemblances between discrete passages and
        statements in earlier works.

1735   "The 'Paradise' in Abyssinia and the 'Happy Valley' in Ras-
        selas. " MP 56 (1958): 10-16.

        Asks the question, why does Johnson prefer fancy to fact
        in Rasselas? Is it because he is presenting a moral tale
        and finds that this is the most effective way to make his point?
        Shangri-La, Eden, or Happy Valley settings are commonly
        used as backgrounds for a state of "lasting bliss. " Thus,
        this is an effective setting for man's unhappiness.

1736   "The Use of Stoical Doctrines in Rasselas, Chapter XVIII."
        MLN 68 (1953): 439-447.

        Relates Chapter XVIII to ideas on Stoicism current in John-
        son's time. Passages in Seneca, in Senault's Use of Pas-
        sions, Epictetus, and Le Grand's Man Without Passion, among
        others, are given as probable sources for the ideas of the
        "Sage" character in Johnson's Rasselas.

1737   "The Structure of Rasselas."   PMLA 66 (1951): 698-717.

        Contends that Johnson was not writing an oriental tale but
        merely adopted certain of its traits in order to impress his
        ideas of the vanity of belief in "permanent earthly happiness."
        The critic who looks at Rasselas as following the form of
        Arabian Nights necessarily gets a bad impression of its form.
        Kolb says Rasselas is an apologue.   The story of the prince
        is "a device for presenting certain notions about happiness...."
        In this perspective Rasselas is vindicated or acquitted of the
        criticism of inadequate form.

1738   "Johnson's 'Dissertation on Flying' and John Wilkins' Mathe-
        matical Magick."   MP 47 (1949): 24-31.

        Lines up parallels and derivative passages sufficient to
        show that this chapter in Rasselas, concerned with flying,
        owes something quite clearly to the earlier work by John
        Wilkins, Mathematical Magick: or the Wonders that May be
        Performed by Mechanical Geometry.

1739   LANDA, LOUIS A.
        "Johnson's Feathered Man: 'A Dissertation on the Art of
        Flying' Considered." In [6], pp. 161-178. Rpt. in [129],
        pp. 160-177.

        An examination of Chapter VI of Rasselas, in the light of
        Johnson's lifelong opinion that man had no reason to learn
        how to fly.   The "artist" becomes an emblem of aspiring
        and prideful man, and therefore supports one of the main
        themes of the work, that man does not know his true nature
        or relationship to the world he lives in.   The chapter can
        also be read as part of the great eighteenth-century contro-
        versy between moral philosophers and natural philosophers,
        between the opposing values of the humanist and the scientist;
        it is an affirmation that man, not nature, is the proper study
        of mankind.

1740   LASCELLES, MARY.
        "Rasselas: A Rejoinder." RES 21 (1970): 49-56.

Lascelles answers the critics who have published since
1951 by reaffirming her original views: that Johnson undertook Rasselas as a sort of therapy for his grief, and that it
was effective; that though its tone is ironic it was not intended
to satirize the "oriental tale" genre as such; and that one
statement made by the book is that, although imagination is
necessary to insight, it is a dangerous substance.

1741   "Rasselas Reconsidered." E & S 4 (1951): 37-52.

An attempt to see Rasselas afresh and to present it as a
book into which Johnson "has written himself," to express
some of his deepest convictions in a form popular at the time
but to which he conforms only insofar as it suits his purpose,
narrative not being his main object.

1742   LEYBURN, ELLEN DOUGLASS.
        " 'No Romantick Absurdities or Incredible Fictions': The
        Relation of Johnson's Rasselas to Lobo's Voyage to Abys-
        sinia." PMLA 70 (1955): 1059-1067.

Leyburn's title indicates the reason for Johnson's attraction
to Lobo's travel story, for he found more fact than wild fantasy in it. She makes an interesting point about Johnson's
use of this source for Rasselas, in his departure from it in
changing the bleak mountainous prison of the princes to the
"Happy Valley": "Johnson's development in the story of Seged
[Rambler, 204 & 205] of the impossibility of compulsory enjoyment could have led his imagination on ... " to the theme
of unhappiness in an earthly paradise in Rasselas. Lobo did
present a picture of an idyllic region, though unconnected
with the imprisonment of the princes; in a creative act Johnson combined them. Concludes that "[w]hy Lobo's account
of Abyssinia would have appealed to [Johnson] in the first
place is clear enough in ... the report it presents of hard-
ship endured, human nature examined, and credulity rebuked."

1743   LINK, FREDERICK M.
        "Rasselas and the Quest for Happiness." BUSE 3 (1957):
        121-123.

"Johnson's ... concern with morality and ethics rather
than with metaphysics" and his acceptance of Christian doctrine "determine the point of view he takes toward happiness
in Rasselas."

1744   LOCKHARD, DONALD M.
        " 'The Fourth Son of the Mighty Emperor': The Ethiopian
        Background of Johnson's Rasselas." PMLA 78 (1963): 516-
        528.

Convincingly demonstrates that Johnson's Ethiopian materials probably came from nine particular works on Ethiopia published before 1759, that these materials served for both Rasselas and Rambler essays 204 and 205, and that this research "must have been in progress and may even have been completed "before 29 February 1752," publication date of Rambler 204, thus significantly modifying the traditional view of the composition of Rasselas.

1745   LOMBARDO, AGOSTINO.
"The Importance of Imlac." Trans. Barbara Arnett Melchiori. In [1764], pp. 31-49.

Emphasizes the numerous functions performed by Imlac: he is Johnson's spokesman, the guide of Rasselas, an independent character, and the "means by which irony can be thrown on Rasselas and on his quest"; concludes that it is Imlac, not Rasselas, who represents the "portrait of man."

1746   MARGOLIS, JOHN D.
"Pekuah and the Theme of Imprisonment in Johnson's Rasselas." ES 53 (1972): 339-343.

Rasselas is throughout governed by the radical metaphor of imprisonment: "In Pekuah's resignation to her imprisonment by the Arabs, she demonstrates her tacit understanding of the lesson that Rasselas learns only during his journey." Pekuah, therefore, serves as a moral exemplum of Johnson's ideal of human behavior, stressing particularly the necessity of man's resignation to the human condition; she represents the natural impulse toward resigned obedience.

1747   MONIE, WILLIS J.
"Samuel Johnson's Contribution to the Novel." New Rambler 17 (1976): 39-44.

Discusses Johnson's theories about what constitutes a novel, and how he attempted to put these theories into practice with Rasselas, perhaps the first philosophical novel. Johnson has attempted in Rasselas "to combine his moral philosophy with a realistic plot ... carefully conceived to include a total picture of various types of mankind" and characters which, although different, contribute "to our total understanding of Johnson's picture of reality."

1748   MOORE, JOHN ROBERT.
"Rasselas and the Early Travelers to Abyssinia." MLQ 15 (1954): 36-41.

When Johnson described the Happy Valley he was drawing
on the accounts not only of Lobo but also of various other
available narratives of Jesuit explorers, such as Father Fran-
cisco Alverez' Narrative of the Portuguese Embassy to Abyssinia during the years 1520-1527. Moore speculates on this
at some length because most accounts of the detention area
of the princes depict it as a bleak mountain-top area rather
than a paradise.

1749   O'FLAHERTY, PATRICK.
        "Dr. Johnson as Equivocator: The Meaning of Rasselas."
        MLQ 31 (1970): 195-208.

        Rasselas dramatizes the uncertainty and fear which char-
        acterize Johnson's perception of Christianity. "What we wit-
        ness in Rasselas is a kind of catharsis: a purgation of sor-
        row in absurd comedy, and of doubt in a grimly deterministic
        philosophy of life which is revealed, on close analysis, as
        equivocation." Johnson, at the time of writing Rasselas, is
        still having intellectual problems in accepting Christianity.

1750   PAGLIARO, HAROLD E.
        "Structural Patterns of Control in Rasselas." In [40], pp.
        208-229.

        Attempts to find the novel's meaning in the interplay of
        various rhetorical elements. Johnson's narrator presents a
        series of contrasting pairs--Imlac-Rasselas, detail-generaliza-
        tion, quest-withdrawal, time-eternity.

1751   PARKE, CATHERINE N.
        "Imlac and Autobiography." In [50], pp. 183-198.

        Emphasizes that "Johnson's thinking about the first-person
        form of biography helps us better to read Imlac's story of
        himself." The story one man writes of another man and the
        story he tells of himself are not differentiated for Johnson, with
        one significant exception, the difference in their probable
        truthfulness--an autobiographer knows more about himself than
        a biographer can ever know about another man. Imlac's auto-
        biography in Rasselas, therefore, gains in importance in the
        light of that belief, as well as a result of the further belief
        that autobiography is valuable for delight and moral instruc-
        tion.

1752   PRESTON, THOMAS R.
        "The Biblical Context of Johnson's Rasselas." PMLA 84
        (1969): 274-281. Partly rpt. in [152], Chap. 5.

Argues that "Rasselas ... is ... actually designed to re-
call both the Preacher's futile quest for perfect happiness
and the meaning of that quest as the 'reformed' school interpreted it"--i. e. , the "reformed" school, which included most
eighteenth-century divines, argued that Ecclesiastes does not
teach us to despise the pleasures of this world but to enjoy
them, a modern view that contradicted the "traditional" school
that believed the Preacher's futile search for perfect happiness
teaches man to despise this world and to look for happiness
in the next world.   The purpose of the article is "to show,
first, that Rasselas is informed with a complex of images,
sentiments, and ideas drawn from Bishop [Simon] Patrick's
paraphrase and annotations, and, second, that the thematic
structure ... follows the thematic structure attributed to Ecclesiastes by the 'reformed' school"; concludes that Rasselas
teaches man, not to reject the pleasures of life, but to direct
his hopes to eternity because no state or condition of life can
provide the perfect happiness he desires: " ... after choosing
eternity, man can and should then partake of the limited goods
of this world. "

1753   PROBYN, CLIVE T.
       "Johnson, James Harris, and the Logic of Happiness. "   MLR
       73 (1978):   256-266.

       In spite of Johnson's "ideological antagonism" to Harris's
       attempt to revive classical philosophy, there is a relation-
       ship, though complex, between Rasselas and Harris's Dialogue
       on happiness.   The similarities deal with the chosen life
       being the life of nature; the achievement of happiness; and the
       poet as legislator.

1754   REED, KENNETH T.
       " 'This Tasteless Tranquility': A Freudian Note on Johnson's
       Rasselas. "   L & P 19 (1969):   61-62.

       Writing at the time of his mother's last illness, Johnson
       produced a story which can be interpreted à la Freud and
       found to conform to a classic pattern: life in the womb (Happy
       Valley), emergence from it, the life struggle, return to pas-
       sive acceptance paralleling that of old age--but no return to
       the valley which represents the womb.

1755   ROTHSTEIN, ERIC.
       "Rasselas. "   In Systems of Order and Inquiry in Later Eight-
       eenth-Century Fiction (Berkeley & Los Angeles: Univ. Calif.
       Press, 1975), pp. 23-61.

       Based on analyses of Rasselas, Tristram Shandy, Humphry
       Clinker, Amelia, and Caleb Williams, this work is mainly

concerned with suggesting that certain formal and epistemological procedures cohere as a system: two procedures used to
analyze the rich texture of Rasselas are "modification" and
"analogy," especially in connection with the chapters about
the Happy Valley. Rothstein also considers the formal structure of the novel, dividing it into seven groups of approxi-
mately seven chapters each, and analyzes two sections (chapters 30-44) in detail; and concludes that the principle of unity
and variety is maintained: "Analogy, often in the form of
incremental repetition, supplies conceptual unity because the
answer to the question is the same in such various but overlapping ways. Modification, since the answer is never what
Rasselas wants, leads to empirical breadth."

1756   SCHWARTZ, RICHARD B.
        "Johnson's Philosopher of Nature; Rasselas, Chapter 22."
        MP 74 (1976): 196-200.

        The philosopher of nature, in Chapter 22, speaks common-
places, but the search for objects of attack is less important
than the search for norms. Johnson's source for the issues
raised by the philosopher may be found in a passage from
Soame Jenyns's Free Enquiry, and a probable source for
Jenyns's comments can be found in the Reverend John Gay's
Concerning the Fundamental Principle of Virtue or Morality,
a work that combines associationism and utilitarianism.

1757   SCOUTEN, ARTHUR H.
        "Dr. Johnson and Imlac." ECS 6 (1973): 506-508.

        Suggests that Imlac's remarks in Chapter 10 of Rasselas
are not an idealized or model definition of the eighteenth-
century poet, but functions as an integral part of the theme
of the impossibility of finding happiness in any secular profession.

1758   SHERBURN, GEORGE.
        "Rasselas Returns--To What?" PQ 38 (1959): 383-384.

        The travellers return to "Abissinia" but are forever barred
from the Happy Valley. Seeks to refute the interpretation of
William Kenney and others that the novel ends with the characters snugly ensconced in their original haven. This could
not be, given Johnson's beliefs, personality, and the message
of the novel; Rasselas ends in complete frustration.

1759   SIEBERT, DONALD T., JR.
        "The Reliability of Imlac." ECS 7 (1974): 350-352.

A reply to Scouten (above) which argues that Johnson does not always indicate mistaken ideas by using the " 'injunctions each and all, together with the auxiliary verb must,' " and that therefore Imlac's views on poetry should be taken as generally those of Johnson himself: Johnson merely regards Imlac's inspiring oration as "simply too beautiful, too dogmatic, and too self-centered a statement to stand by itself, unqualified by Democritean laughter."

1760   TILLOTSON, GEOFFREY.
       "Imlac and the Business of a Poet." In [2], pp. 296-314.

Imlac as a persona contains some of the traits of Johnson himself. Though Imlac finds that it is not in him, after all, to be a poet, he presents the ideal poet as Johnson sees him; perhaps as Johnson sees himself. Among the requirements for a poet are: first, learning, an Augustan requirement destined to diminish in importance in romanticism and again after the moderns; second, the poet must have a special vision. Tillotson develops this from Imlac's words: "Whatever is beautiful, and whatever is dreadful, must be familiar to his imagination; he must be conversant with all that is awfully vast or elegantly little."

1761   "Rasselas." In [174], pp. 229-248.

A general discussion of the themes of Rasselas, and the facts of composition and publication. Also deals with thematic relationships with earlier works of Johnson.

1762   "Time in Rasselas." In [1764] pp. 97-103; [174] pp. 249-255.

Argues that "time is seen as a prime condition governing human life--indeed as the prime condition, for the worth of human life is to be measured ... by how time has been used."

1763   " 'Rasselas' and the 'Persian Tales.' " In Essays in Criticism and Research (Cambridge: Cambridge Univ. Press, 1942, pp. 111-116; rpt. Hamden, Conn.: Archon Books, 1967).

Shows similarities between Rasselas and the Persian Tales and suggests that Johnson improved his version by improving "the darkness in the scepticism and [making] it cover everything, the framework and all the stories inside it...."

1764   WAHBA, MAGDI, ed.
       Bicentenary Essays on "Rasselas" (Cairo Studies in English).
       Cairo: S. O. P. Press, 1959.

A collection of essays on Rasselas, ranging from serious scholarship and criticism to unsubstantiated guesses and personal remarks.

1765   "A Note on the Manner of Concluding in Rasselas." In [1764], pp. 105-110.

Argues that the final chapter in Rasselas "fulfills a number of purposes inherent in the very fabric of the narrative."

1766   WALKER, ROBERT G.
Eighteenth-Century Arguments for Immortality in Johnson's RASSELAS. (ELS 9) Victoria, B. C.: Univ. of Victoria, 1977.

Rasselas "can be understood most fully ... if regarded in the context of eighteenth-century philosophical discussions on the nature of the human soul. [The] opening chapters trace the main directions of these discussions involving philosophers and poets, deists and Christians, from 1690 to 1759; the second half of this study is a close critical reading of Rasselas based on this context." With the appearance of Locke's Essay concerning Human Understanding the metaphysical proof of immortality was discredited, and Christian apologists were forced to formulate two other arguments, the moral argument and the argument from desire. The author seeks to "indicate what caused the metaphysical argument, and to a lesser extent the moral argument, to lose effectiveness, and why rather suddenly in the middle of the eighteenth century the argument from desire became the main support for a belief in life after death."

1767   WASSERMAN, E. R.
"Johnson's Rasselas: Implicit Contexts." JEGP 74 (1975): 1-25.

This article proposes that "there are ... presiding narrative patterns [which] the eighteenth-century reader would have brought to the apologue as formal expectations and as implicit norms ... to generate a significance beyond the limits of the explicit text." An example is the educational-journey or Odyssey plot in which there is an outward journey so that there may be a return at a higher and more secure level of wisdom and happiness.

1768   WEINBROT, HOWARD D.
"The Reader, the General, and the Particular: Johnson and Imlac in Chapter Ten of Rasselas." ECS 5 (1971): 80-96.

Johnson has Imlac describe "the poet" generally, but exalting him above Johnson's own rather pedestrian definition of a poet. "Awareness of the larger function of chapter ten ... in Rasselas also indicates that Imlac is an actor in a scene which Johnson directs, and thus portrays the poet's occupation as a possible choice of life." Concludes that a "minority of Imlac's critical principles ... are wholly Johnson's, he would have misgivings about several others, and clearly disagree with two. Johnson does use Imlac to epitomize his own views of normative generality: this is based upon the empirical, particular, and sensational, embodies the species, which is ... hardly universal or ideal, and is intended to evoke the original 'conformable to it.' "

1769   WEITZMAN, ARTHUR J.
"More Light on Rasselas: the Background of the Egyptian Episodes." PQ 48 (1969): 42-58.

Weitzman shows that a very great deal of reading on Egypt and the Ottoman Empire is reflected in Rasselas, and that one might "regard with skepticism Boswell's assertion that Rasselas was composed 'in the evenings of one week.' "

1770   WHITE, IAN.
"On Rasselas." Crit. Quart. 6 (1972): 6-31.

A philosophical analysis dealing with Johnson's true meaning of "happy valley" and "choice of life."

1771   WHITLEY, ALVIN.
"The Comedy of 'Rasselas.' " ELH 23 (1956): 48-70.

Rasselas is presented by Whitley as a "satire on the illusioned view of life, using as its method dramatic irony and having ... a dramatic frame narrative [with an] overall plan and method and ... various subdivisions." Argues that Rasselas is not a loose collection of polite essays, but is "carefully and subtly planned and executed, not lyric but dramatic, not solemn but satiric and ironic"; that Rasselas is not mainly a positive statement of Johnson's philosophy, but a satiric exposé of philosophical errors; that it is primarily a satiric comedy unfolding itself in a "dramatic context which has been largely ignored"; and that its moral is not merely the vanity of all human endeavors but concerns the contrast between two views of life, one of which is explicitly condemned by dramatic irony, and the other of which is implicitly upheld.

1772   WIMSATT, W. K.
"In Praise of Rasselas: Four Notes (Converging)." In [36], pp. 111-136.

Wimsatt's "Praise of Rasselas" comes across as rather
faint praise. In section (i) he isolates episodes in the story
which seem to have occurred to the author later and were
then inserted into the story line. The evidence for this is
found in discrepancies in the plot of an admittedly hastily
written book. Section (ii) discusses the loose and episodic
structure, and section (iii) takes up the means Johnson uses
to try to produce an exotic, oriental coloring in his description of a place and way of life that he has not seen. Section
(iv) discusses genre without definitely classifying Rasselas,
compares the book to a series of Ramblers, and--finally--
commends Johnson for his subtle self-mocking humor.

See also: 740, 1466, 1536, 1552, 1553, 1555, 1565, 1575, 1587,
    1594, 1596, 1650, 1802

The Edition of Shakespeare

1773   CARNOCHAN, W. B.
       "Johnsonian Metaphor and the 'Adamant of Shakespeare.' "
       SEL 10 (1970): 541-549.

       "The passage in the Preface to Shakespeare that builds
       up to and closes with 'the adamant of Shakespeare' depends
       on a dialectical process of reconciliation ... dualisms are
       overcome as the distinction between primary and secondary
       qualities is effaced. In the adamant, representing unity,
       permanence, and the affective powers of art, the synthesis
       becomes explicit and complete."

1774   EASTMAN, ARTHUR M.
       "In Defense of Dr. Johnson." Shakespeare Quart. 8 (1957):
       493-500.

       Eastman warmly and ably defends Samuel Johnson against
       the charge of plagiarism and worse--"an eighteenth-century
       Iago" is the picture painted by Sherbo, he says. Eastman's
       examination of the evidence disposes of most of it, and at-
       tributes Johnson's remaining lapses to his habits of irregular
       and uneven work.

1775   "Johnson's Shakespeare and the Laity: A Textual Study."
       PMLA 65 (1950): 1112-1121.

       Eastman lists three reasons why "Johnson's text fell":
       1) cautious and limited emendation when emendation was pop-
       ular; 2) failure to collate fully; and 3) the appearance soon
       afterward of Capell's and Steevens's editions, as well as
       competition from the cheap reprints of Theobald and Hanmer.

After giving the above reasons for the limited popularity of
Johnson's presentation of Shakespeare's text, Eastman praises
Johnson for cleaning up the confusions of previous editions,
especially in weeding out a lot of redundant punctuation.

1776   "The Texts from Which Johnson Printed His Shakespeare."
        JEGP 49 (1950): 182-191.

        A study of the relationship of Johnson's edition of Shake-
        speare to the two previous editions which are held to be his
        main sources, the Warburton and the Theobald editions.   Mi-
        nute examination of texts, and criticism of Johnson for lack
        of attention to detail.

1777   EDDY, DONALD D.
        "Samuel Johnson's Editions of Shakespeare (1765)."   PBSA
        56 (1962):   428-444.

        A study to supply the necessary differentiations in a bib-
        liographical account of all the editions of Johnson's Shakespeare
        published in 1765.

1778   FLEISCHMANN, WOLFGANG B.
        "Shakespeare, Johnson, and the Dramatic 'Unities of Time
        and Place.' "   In [47], pp. 128-134.

        Attempts to explore "Johnson's view of Shakespeare's dis-
        regard of the rules in the light of other insights Johnson
        voiced specifically about Shakespeare" and to relate "John-
        son's reflections on Shakespeare and the unities to a larger
        intellectual framework concerned with the concepts of time
        in literature, as such."

1779   GARDNER, HELEN.
        "Johnson on Shakespeare."   New Rambler 17, ser. B (1965):
        2-12.

        Johnson's criticism, contained mostly in the Preface to
        his edition, is valuable for 1) his powerful mastery of sum-
        mary, 2) the insights of a professional writer, and 3) his
        perspective as a moralist.

1780   HARDY, JOHN.
        "The 'Poet of Nature' and Self Knowledge: One Aspect of
        Johnson's Moral Reading of Shakespeare."   UTQ 36 (1967):
        141-160.

        Johnson, who demanded moral value even from entertain-

ment, may have decried Shakespeare's "lack of moral purpose" but he gave high marks to his insights into human nature and to the wisdom to be gained from a study of it.

1781 HARRISON, CHARLES T.
      "Common Sense as Approach." SR 79 (1971): 1-10.

      Concentrates on Johnson's criticism of Shakespeare, accept-
ing it as a touchstone of sanity; concludes that "[n]ot the least
attraction of Johnson's writing about Shakespeare is its intel-
ligibility. Johnson's appeal is to the world of men and women,
superior and inferior, who love and kill and marry and fight:
the world we know, rather than a verbal universe that may
elude us forever."

1782 KRIEGER, MURRAY.
      "Fiction, Nature, and Literary Kinds in Johnson's Criticism
      of Shakespeare." ECS 4 (1971): 184-198. Rpt. in Poetic
      Presence and Illusion: Essays in Critical History and Theory
      (Baltimore: Johns Hopkins Univ. Press, 1979), pp. 55-69.

      Examines three of Johnson's central claims in his "Pre-
face", emphasizing the ways in which they tend to disagree
with one another: 1) "Nothing can please many, and please
long, but just representations of general nature"; 2) Johnson
refers to our common experience as a "chaos of mingled purposes and casualties," an apparent contradiction of the first
principle; and 3) Johnson's defense of Shakespeare's neglect
of the unities. The first claim seems "exclusively dedicated
to an existentially blind unity"; the second seems chaotically
dedicated to variety; and the third seems to look forward to
the organicistic call for unity in variety and for a discordia
concors.

1783 LILL, JAMES.
      "Some Semi-Apocryphal Additions to Johnson's Notes on Ham-
      let." SAQ 78 (1979): 333-341.

      Begins with "questioning why Johnson did not recognize the
kindred concerns he shares with Hamlet and thus did not sym-
pathize with Hamlet's dilemma" in his Proposals for an Edition of Shakespeare and ends with questioning "why Johnson
did not respond more vigorously to the dangerous posturing
and speculation of Shakespeare's hero." Many of his comments in his Rambler essays and as recorded by Boswell in
the Life could well have been a part of his comment as editor
of Shakespeare.

1784 MIDDENDORF, JOHN H.

"Ideas vs. Words: Johnson, Locke, and the Edition of Shakespeare." In [40], pp. 249-272.

Johnson did not read Shakespeare's plays solely as ethical poems and ignored them as dramatic presentations; between "the crowded stage and the solitary editor was the intermediating world of idea explored by Locke."

1785   SHERBO, ARTHUR.
Samuel Johnson, Editor of Shakespeare.   With an Essay on "The Adventurer" (Illinois Std. in Lang. & Lit., Vol 42). Urbana: Univ. Ill. Press, 1956.   See also [1774].

A detailed study of the origin and progress of Johnson's edition of Shakespeare and the relationship with Johnson's editorial labors on his Dictionary.   Concentrates specifically on a detailed analysis of Johnson's 3600 notes, in the editions of 1765, 1773, and 1778, and gives evidence of Johnson's debt in the Preface, General Observations, and Notes, to earlier editors and commentators.   Includes interesting random notes on Johnson's opinion of Shakespeare, as well as a series of detailed appendices for further study of Johnson's likes and dislikes, and feelings about characters in Shakespeare.

1786   SIEBERT, DONALD T., JR.
"The Scholar as Satirist: Johnson's Edition of Shakespeare." SEL 15 (1975): 483-503.

A study of the rhetoric of the Preface from the standpoint that it is primarily a defense of scholarship and criticism and of Johnson's position as scholar-critic.

1787   STOCK, R. D.
Samuel Johnson and Neo-Classical Dramatic Theory: The Intellectual Context of the Preface to Shakespeare.   Lincoln: Univ. Nebr. Press, 1973.

After examining the several critical attitudes toward Shakespeare by which Johnson may have been influenced, the author concludes that Johnson's opinions were generally orthodox.

1788   TROWBRIDGE, HOYT.
"Scattered Atoms of Probability."   ECS 5 (1971): 1-38.

Discusses Johnson's Preface to Shakespeare as an example of probable reasoning in humanistic thought.   An understanding of probabilistic reasoning "might illuminate the actual processes of thought in many fields during the eighteenth century ... explaining why those writers reasoned as they did."

The author first summarizes the theoretical basis of the subject in Book IV of Locke's An Essay concerning Human Understanding (1690), and then proceeds to a practical analysis of
Johnson's Preface, in which Johnson adapts this mode of reasoning to the solution of problems in cultural history, textual
scholarship, and literary criticism.

A Journey to the Western Islands of Scotland

1789   CURLEY, THOMAS M.
        "Johnson and the Geographical Revolution: A Journey to the
        Western Islands of Scotland. " SBHT 17 (1976): 180-198.

        Concerned with Johnson's Journey as a representative
        travel work from an age of travel and discovery, but one
        that is based on enlightened principles of investigation.   He
        succeeded in pursuing a moral study of the people of Scotland
        with a scientific precision that was to change his attitude
        toward the Hebrides.

1790   "Philosophic Art and Travel in the Highlands: Johnson's A
        Journey to the Western Islands of Scotland. " Explor 2 (1974):
        8-23.

        Suggests that the Journey to the Western Islands of Scot-
        land was a "skilful blend of philosophic art and travel and
        magnificently documented the intellectual process of a great
        mind coming to grips with an unknown moral environment. "
        The theme is similar to that of Rasselas, a traveler's dis-
        illusionment with foreign manners as his preconceptions con-
        flict with the realities encountered abroad; the Journey is a
        twofold triumph of art and travel, incorporating the moral
        themes of Johnson's travel tales and the conventional format
        of contemporary travel books.

1791   HAMILTON, HARLAN W.
        "Samuel Johnson's Appeal to Nature. " WHR 21 (1967): 339-345.

        Gives many instances of Johnson's attention to detail, with
        some rebukes to others who have published misinformation--
        such as Loch Ness is twelve miles wide--by failing to check
        even cursorily.   Digresses somewhat from nature per se,
        showing rather that Johnson carefully considered the particu-
        lar as well as the general.

1792   HART, JEFFREY.
        "Johnson's A Journey to the Western Islands: History as Art. "
        EIC 10 (1960): 44-59.   See also Donald J. Greene, "John-
        sonian Critics. " Ibid. : 476-480, and Sherbo [1806]: 382-396.

Argues that the Journey has three major themes: the destruction of pre-Reformation Christian culture, the disintegration of contemporary Highland culture, and the rise of the middle-class, progressive culture, toward the "values of which Johnson maintains an ambivalent attitude." Sees the book as a "highly-wrought work of art, possessing a complex organization. Its themes ... are interwoven, contrasted, counterpointed, and modulated; its greatness derives largely from its manner of organization."

1793 JEMIELITY, THOMAS.
" 'More in Notions than Facts': Samuel Johnson's Journey to the Western Islands." DR 49 (1969): 319-330.

Presents Johnson's account of his trip to the Hebrides as "a generalized presentation of an entire society, an analysis of the principles underlying it, and an examination of the basic questions associated with it in the public mind." Examines those characteristics that enhance the Journey's philosophical, moral, and reflective nature.

1794 JENKINS, RALPH E.
" 'And I Travelled After Him': Johnson and Pennant in Scotland." TSLL 14 (1972): 445-462.

Pennant traveled in Scotland and wrote about it before Johnson did. He was neither philosopher nor artist; but for a strictly travel book, Johnson himself admits that Pennant excels in wealth and detail of observation. Jenkins examines Johnson's debt to Pennant, and notes that his writing in the Journey was often shaped "by his desire to avoid direct comparison" with Pennant.

1795 KAUL, R. K.
"A Journey to the Western Isles Reconsidered." EIC 13 (1963): 341-350.

Suggests that Johnson is merely reacting to Scotland as being less civilized than his England. He believes in civilization and its refining influence, in division of labor, brain supervising brawn, and industrialization, so that it is not necessary to search for deeper motives to explain anything negative in his report on Scotland.

1796 LASCELLES, MARY.
"Some Reflections on Johnson's Hebridean Journey." New Rambler (June 1961): 2-13.

Praises Johnson's organized structure of the Journey, with

its balance of narrative and reflection. Assesses, too, the
influence of the Hebridean journey upon Johnson.

1797   McLAREN, MORAY.
        The Highland Jaunt; a Study of James Boswell and Samuel
        Johnson Upon Their Highland and Hebridean Tour of 1773.
        New York: W. Sloan & Assoc. , 1955.

        An account of McLaren's journey through the Highlands
        covering the same ground as Boswell and Johnson, filling in
        details of the scenery and the changes which have taken place.
        Succeeds in making Boswell and Johnson appear almost as
        his companions.

1798   MEIER, T. K.
        "Johnson and Boswell: On the Survival of Culture. "   Aberdeen
        Univ. Rev. 47 (1978): 329-333.

        Johnson and Boswell possessed fundamentally different
        opinions about culture and society that can be analyzed from
        an economic, a psychological, or an ethical point of view.
        Johnson's interest in Scotland was in its institutions, history,
        and topography, and he is chiefly interested in tracing the
        development of institutions and customs to their origin.   Bos-
        well, on the other hand, was interested in people, in particu-
        lar their personalities, their actions, and their conversations;
        he was interested in the present, with little concern for the
        future, and to him history was composed of individuals, not
        of groups of men: "Johnson generalizes, and Boswell par-
        ticularizes: Johnson seeks unity, while Boswell explores di-
        versity. "

1799   "Johnson in the Highlands. "   FMLS 12 (1976): 189-193.

        Takes issue with Patrick O'Flaherty's [1801] contention
        that Johnson's prejudices and biases toward the Scots, his
        English nationalism, his "class prejudice" against the "lower
        orders," and his "anti-pastoral, anti-rural viewpoint" made
        it difficult for him to be objective in the Journey to the West-
        ern Islands of Scotland.   The Journey is an "extraordinarily
        complex" work which should be read for its "richness and
        diversity" instead of its limitations.

1800   "Pattern in Johnson's A Journey to the Western Island. "   SSL
        5 (1968): 185-193.

        Argues that because Johnson gave a general impression of
        Scotland, he produced a work of art as well as a travel ac-
        count.

1801   O'FLAHERTY, PATRICK.
       "Johnson in the Hebrides: Philosopher Becalmed." SBHT
       13 (1971): 1986-2001.   Comment by Arthur Sherbo, Ibid.,
       pp. 2119-2227; response, pp. 2229-2233.

          "We ... discover that [Johnson] is not to be taken seriously
       as an analyst of Highland and Hebridean problems." Many
       instances are cited of his extreme prejudice against the Scots
       and his lack of understanding of their problems.

1802   PARKE, CATHERINE N.
       "Love, Accuracy, and the Power of an Object: Finding the
       Conclusion in A Journey to the Western Islands." Biography
       3 (1980): 105-120.

          Johnson's theory of biography is that it is like the first
       half of life when we learn by collecting knowledge in the form
       of images; the second half of life should be concerned with
       the joint activities of autobiography and teaching, when man
       distributes his knowledge by taking significant details from
       his earlier collected images.   Johnson follows this scheme
       in most of his writings--The Life of Savage represents in-
       complete learning, a failed autobiography; Rasselas is con-
       cerned with learning to teach; and the Journey supplies John-
       son with new images to collect, while recording these impres-
       sions gives him an opportunity to teach.

1803   PRESTON, THOMAS R.
       "Homeric Allusion in A Journey to the Western Islands of
       Scotland." ECS 5 (1972): 545-558.

          Johnson thinks of the Gaelic-speaking Scots as being in
       that state of cultural evolution in which the ancient Greeks
       found themselves in the times of which Homer sings.   This
       analogy, easier for the Augustans than for us to see and ac-
       cept, runs throughout Johnson's analysis and counsel to the
       Highlanders.

1804   SAVAGE, GEORGE H.
       " 'Roving among the Hebrides': The Odyssey of Samuel John-
       son." SEL 17 (1977): 493-501.

          An important element in Johnson's Journey to the Western
       Islands is "the careful--almost subliminal--construction of the
       sense of misty distance and indeterminate time." Johnson
       uses Scotland as a metaphor: it is an island, isolated from
       the sea, static and uncultivated; but it is also the sea, a
       "sea of nearly unrelieved emptiness within which, without
       continual effort of the will, man will disappear."

1805   SCHWARTZ, RICHARD B.
        "Johnson's Journey." JEGP 69 (1970): 292-303.

        Contends that the prevailing view of the Journey as a stand-
        ard travelogue, expressed by Sherbo and others, needs ampli-
        fication. It can teach us a lot about Johnson: "the empirical
        temperament ... dynamic struggle for knowledge ... humility
        and consciousness of limitations--all are apparent...."

1806   SHERBO, ARTHUR.
        "Johnson's Intent in the Journey to the Western Islands of
        Scotland." EIC 16 (1966): 382-396.

        Sherbo finds that Johnson refined the travel-book genre by
        enriching his accounts of actual happenings with thoughtful
        comment. The reporter-traveler becomes the philosophical
        traveler. But he does not read into the Journey the historical
        or sociological significance perceived by Jeffrey Hart [1792]
        who, says Sherbo, attempts a new reading of the work by
        discovering irony and tragedy where they do not exist.

1807   SIEBERT, DONALD T., JR.
        "Johnson as Satirical Traveler: A Journey to the Western
        Islands of Scotland." TSL 19 (1974): 137-147.

        Sees A Journey as consisting of a number of ironies, all
        of which make up the fabric of the book's satirical under-
        structure. Johnson, an open-minded and open-eyed foreign
        traveler, sees things as they are because "he sees them with-
        out the blinders of theoretical expectation, national interests,
        or simply familiarity itself."

1808   TRACY, CLARENCE.
        "Johnson's Journey to the Western Islands of Scotland: A Re-
        consideration." SVEC 58 (1967): 1593-1606.

        Johnson, the townsman, is evaluated in his attitudes toward
        the country. His open mind and capacity to learn are com-
        mended. Tracy further indicates that the stereotype of John-
        son as super-Tory has caused misreadings of the Journey.
        His interest in the socioeconomic welfare of the Scots is
        clearly indicated.

See also: 316, 1537, 1594

Literary Criticism and the "Lives of the Poets"

1809   ALBERTINI, VIRGIL.
       "Samuel Johnson's Life of Gray." Missouri English Bull. 25
       (1969): 8-12.

            Johnson's "standards for judging poetry were such that ...
       he could not like and commend Gray's poetry."

1810   ALKON, PAUL K.
       "Johnson's Concept of Admiration." PQ 48 (1969): 59-81.

            Starts with the neo-classical theories of admiration and
       then considers Johnson's use of admiration as a critical term;
       with these in mind, he then takes up Johnson's case against
       Paradise Lost.

1811   BASNEY, LIONEL.
       " 'Lucidus Ordo': Johnson and Generality." ECS 5 (1971):
       39-57.

            To Johnson the organizing generality is the sine qua non
       under which the particular can make sense. Without it one
       has only the mishmash of particularities--chaos. Literature
       is the interaction of particular and general because a "particu-
       larized generality" fits the mind's cognitive capacity; there-
       fore, "Johnson's insistence on generality ... far from de-
       flecting attention from the sensory particulars of art, actually
       focuses on them. Choosing his particulars from the pleni-
       tude of experience is the poet's crucial task."

1812   BATTERSBY, JAMES L.
       Rational Praise and Natural Lamentation: Johnson, LYCIDAS,
       and Principles of Criticism. Rutherford, N.J.: Farleigh
       Dickinson Univ. Press, 1980.

            Analyzes Johnson's critical thought and suggests the rela-
       tion between practical judgment and critical principle; the
       first section discusses the cognitive and interpretive deficien-
       cies of four recent Johnsonian critics--Oliver Sigworth, Paul
       Fussell, Arieh Sachs, and Murray Krieger--and the second
       is chiefly concerned with the coherent body of principles and
       assumptions governing Johnson's practical, critical judgment.

1813   "Patterns of Significant Action in the 'Life of Addison.' "
       Genre 2 (1969): 28-42.

            Goes beyond the accepted analysis of the structure of John-

son's _Lives_ as generally being divided into three sections:
biographical history, character sketch, and critical analysis
of the poet's writings.   Concentrates "on those structural
parts which, in various ways, bridge the lines of sectional
demarcation. "

1814   BELL, VEREEN M.
        "Johnson's Milton Criticism in Context. "   _ES_ 49 (1968):   127-
        132.

        Johnson "often seems to have been responsive less to Mil-
        ton's poetry than to his critics. "   Since Johnson had defended
        Pope against derogatory criticism, he felt called upon to sound
        a note of deflating criticism in the age's adulation of Milton;
        but ironically, some of Johnson's more critical remarks seem
        to have derived from three of the critics in the Milton quarrel
        whom Johnson probably regarded as opponents--Addison, John
        Dennis, and Thomas Newton.

1815   BOOTH, MARK W.
        "Proportion and Value in Johnson's _Lives of the Poets_. "   _SAB_
        43, i (1978):   49-57.

        Although the "longest _Lives_ are those of poets to whom
        Johnson means to give most prominence in a historical view
        of the period ... this is not the same ... as saying that the
        scale of short to long is in his view the scale of worst to
        best poet. "   In other words, Milton does not necessarily meas-
        ure less than two thirds of Pope because _Milton_ is less than
        two thirds the length of _Pope_.   For Johnson's purpose, to
        construct a history of modern English poetry, Dryden and
        Pope are the most important poets in the "main road of con-
        tinuous development, of teaching and learning," with Milton
        off to the side: Milton was not an educative force, though
        Johnson admits that he constructed the "second greatest achieve-
        ment of the human mind. "

1816   "Johnson's Critical Judgments in the _Lives of the Poets_. "
        SEL 16 (1976):   505-515.

        Johnson's criticism may be more easily understood by
        examining the form it takes in the _Lives_.   His practice of
        pronouncing approval or disapproval on poets, poems, and
        details of poetry suggests that he desires to control the pub-
        lic's responses to English literature by emphasizing the edu-
        cative power of both good and bad examples.   Usually the
        terms of praise and dispraise are nonspecific, and seldom
        say more than whether the example succeeds or fails; they
        do not make clear the standard of judgment, but only the
        judgment itself.

1817   BOYCE, BENJAMIN.
       "Samuel Johnson's Criticism of Pope in the 'Life of Pope.'"
       RES 5 (1954): 37-46.

       Examines paragraph by paragraph Johnson's criticism of
       Pope and compares it with other critics, such as Addison,
       Dennis, and Warburton.   Concludes that Johnson was not as
       original or as superior as is generally supposed and that
       "Johnson did not imitate so much as he attempted to adjudi-
       cate; he was often writing a critique of the critics."

1818   BRINK, J. R.
       "Johnson and Milton."   SEL 20 (1980):   493-503.

       Although Johnson could not agree with Milton on politics
       or religion, his assessment of Milton as an author is more
       favorable than most critics acknowledge.   As a literary biog-
       rapher, Johnson saw himself as a "guardian of public taste
       and morals" and therefore his duty was "not only to weigh
       Milton's weaknesses and strengths, but also to instruct his
       audience and promote piety...."

1819   BROWN, JOSEPH E.
       Critical Opinions of Samuel Johnson.   Princeton, N. J. : Prince-
       ton Univ. Press, 1926; rpt. New York: Russell & Russell,
       1961.

       This work aims to preserve as much as possible by actual
       quotation, not merely the kernel of thought, but that Johnson-
       ian vigor of expression which is perhaps at its best in his
       critical writings.   A 54-page introduction analyzes Johnson's
       attitudes as they affect his criticism.

1820   BURKE, JOHN J. , JR.
       "Excellence in Biography: Rambler No. 60 and Johnson's
       Early Biographies."   SAB 44, ii (1979):   14-34.

       The author examines "Johnson's theoretical views on biog-
       raphy, particularly those in Rambler No. 60, in relation to
       his own practice during the years before it.   The relation-
       ship between the two is complex and sometimes confusing,
       but it throws considerable light on both, because ... Rambler
       No. 60 is in large part Johnson's response to his own earlier
       practice."   It is both a criticism and a vindication of that
       practice.

1821   DAMROSCH, LEOPOLD, JR.
       The Uses of Johnson's Criticism.   Charlottesville: Univ.
       Press of Va. , 1976.

Damrosch seeks "to look at what Johnson can tell us about actual authors and works, and beyond that about the relation between literature and life." Concerned with the criticism not as a body of doctrine and adjudications but as a way of reading in which the reader shares. The book's polemical theme is that Johnson's greatness as critic consists of his resistance to abstract theory and his attempt to make the critic and scholar understandable to the common reader.

1822   Samuel Johnson and the Tragic Sense. Princeton, N. J. : Princeton Univ. Press, 1972.

Two purposes stated are "first, to argue that although the tragedies of the period were indeed bad, intelligent people were still capable of genuine appreciation of earlier tragedies; and second, to explore the nature and limitations of the tragic sense as it appears in a specific writer, Samuel Johnson." Comments that Johnson's "Life of Savage ... in its way is a true tragedy, but muted by a characteristic blend of compassion and clear-sightedness" and suggests that it may be used to measure the failure of Irene because in the play "Johnson did not (for whatever reason) draw upon the deep understanding of the tragic in human life which he was developing during this period and which found moving expression in the Life of Savage."

1823   DARBISHIRE, HELEN.
        Milton's "Paradise Lost." London: Oxford Univ. Press, 1951.

Defends Milton against the "change in literary fashion: Donne and the metaphysicals are in, Milton and the Romantics are out." Darbishire allows more virtue in Johnson's and Bentley's criticisms than in those of Moderns like Eliot and Herbert Read, but still maintains that they cannot mask the greatness of Milton.

1824   DeMARIA, ROBERT, JR.
        "Johnson's Form of Evaluation." SEL 19 (1979): 501-514.

Johnson mainly rewrites Dryden's fundamental definition, that dramatic poetry represents: "A just and lively image of human nature, representing its passions and humours, and the changes of fortune to which it is subject, for the delight and instruction of mankind." Johnson's critical evaluations reveal two opposing tendencies: they move either in the direction of formality and uniformity or toward representing "each particular literary experience in a particular, ad hoc critical act." Johnson usually describes a particular work, and does not attempt a general definition; but at the same time he seems to be either moving toward or away from Dryden's definition of dramatic poetry. As a result of these antagonistic tendencies, Johnson's criticism is varied yet similar.

1825 EDINGER, WILLIAM.
"Johnson on Conceit: The Limits of Particularity." ELH
39 (1972): 597-619.

A detailed study of Johnson on metaphor, extended metaphor, and conceits. Johnson demands "complete correspondence" between vehicle and tenor of "extended images," and like many critics and poets of the time, he visualizes these images in great detail. Quotes other critics.

1826 EVANS, BERGEN.
"Dr. Johnson's Theory of Biography." RES 10 (1934): 301-310.

Johnson valued biography over fiction or history because it afforded many lessons applicable to the private lives of its readers. He took a very personal interest in Boswell's projected work and groomed him in all his own theories of the art, which are here detailed.

1827 FOGLE, RICHARD HARTER.
"Johnson and Coleridge on Milton." Bucknell Rev. 14 (1966): 26-32.

Discusses Johnson's opinion of Milton, which was highly unfavorable although he praised Paradise Lost, with that of Coleridge, who thought Milton great and Johnson "one vile antithesis."

1828 FOLKENFLIK, ROBERT.
Samuel Johnson, Biographer. Ithaca, N. Y.: Cornell Univ. Press, 1978.

A reassessment of Johnson's work as a biographer that describes the principles and the sensibility underlying his biographies as well as the nature of his achievement: "In order to see that achievement whole and in relation to the biographies and biographical theory of his day, [Folkenflik attempts] to focus on the Lives of the Poets, and, to a lesser degree, on his earlier biographies in the context of the totality of his thought, and to show how his conception of man determines their nature."

1829 GREENE, DONALD.

"The Term 'Conceit' in Johnson's Literary Criticism." In [58], pp. 337-351.

Johnson did not define "metaphysical conceit" in the "Life of Cowley"; he nowhere mentions "conceit" in the famous passage referring to wit as a kind of discordia concors. Neither did he equate "conceit" with "metaphorical language"; the word meant to him something opposed to imagery, "sentiment," or "inferences," implying an act of conscious cerebration; "for Johnson ... a conceit may take the form of word-play pure and simple (false wit), or of playing with both the (weakened) metaphorical sense of a word and its literal sense (mixed wit)...." Johnson, therefore, was not responsible for the definition of "metaphysical conceit" as "extended metaphor" or "elaborate image."

1830   HAGSTRUM, JEAN H.
        Samuel Johnson's Literary Criticism. Minneapolis: Univ.
        Minn. Press, 1952; London: Oxford Univ. Press, 1953.
        New edition, Chicago: Univ. Chicago Press, 1967 (Includes
        "Studies of Johnson's Literary Criticism Since 1952.")

Attempts to "get behind the particular critical occasion to the underlying principle," seeking at the same time to be faithful to the "complex richness" and variety of Johnson's mind. Considers such topics as "Experience and Reason," "The Theory of Criticism," "Nature," "Pleasure," "The Beautiful, the Pathetic, and the Sublime," and "True Wit"; concludes that Johnson's "demand that literature express both the familiar and the unfamiliar is perhaps his most basic aesthetic requirement," and that his best criticism derives from the tentative and skeptical cast of his mind.

1831   HART, EDWARD.
        "Some new Sources of Johnson's Lives." PMLA 65 (1950):
        1088-1111.

Nichols's contribution of source material for Lives of the Poets is documented, not to detract from Johnson's reputation but as "an addition to the already large stature of Nichols as the literary biographer of the eighteenth century."

1832   HAVENS, RAYMOND D.
        "Johnson's Distrust of the Imagination." ELH 10 (1948): 243-255.

Johnson distrusts imagination because of its ability to blur the line between fact and fantasy, because he associated it with threatening change and novelty, and with the whole world of the fictitious. He uses the word "imagination" somewhat

differently than most, ascribing to it al least six closely related functions, but never assigning to it the profoundly important role which Blake, Coleridge, and Wordsworth attributed to it because of its creative or unifying power; nor does
he suggest that it is a means of acquiring truth.   Johnson
feared the imagination because it was the day-dreaming faculty
--a means to escape from reality and avoid actions.

1833   INGHAM, PATRICIA.
        "Dr. Johnson's 'Elegance.'"   RES 19 (1968): 271-278.

        A report on intensive reasearch into Johnson's use of the
        words elegant and elegance, in various editions of the Dic-
        tionary.   Comparisons made to the usage of Joseph Priestly
        and other writers of the times.

1834   JOHNSTON, SHIRLEY WHITE.
        "The Unfurious Critic: Samuel Johnson's Attitude toward
        Contemporaries."   MP 77 (1979): 18-25.

        We should not take too seriously Johnson's "criticism"
        contained in his conversation, especially that of Fielding and
        Richardson: "Johnson's public silence on both Fielding and
        Richardson was deliberate and in keeping with a principle of
        his criticism that has been ignored.   Johnson believed that
        because no man can evaluate objectively the time in which
        he lives he should not as a critic assess the literary work
        of contemporaries."

1835   KALLICH, MARTIN.
        "The Association of Ideas in Samuel Johnson's Criticism."
        MLN 69 (1954): 170-176.

        Discusses the extent to which Johnson uses the "association of
        ideas" in his works, especially in the popular meaning of "con-
        nexion of ideas," and points out those that contain it. "Johnson
        adopts Locke's interpretation ... and in his literary criticism
        he applies it best ... to the non-classical concept of decorum,
        especially the propriety of diction and subject-matter."

1836   KEAST, WILLIAM R.
        "The Theoretical Foundations of Johnson's Criticism."   In
        Critics and Criticism Ancient and Modern, ed. R. S. Crane
        (Chicago: Univ. Chicago Press, 1952), pp. 389-407; rpt. in
        abridged ed. , Phoenix Books, 1957, pp. 169-187.

        Refutes the popular view that Johnson had no theoretical
        foundation for his criticism and no reasoned view of litera-
        ture; that his literary judgments are founded on sensibility

and taste, and not on an elaborated system of principles.
Brings up much evidence to support his statement that Johnson's criticism derives "from positions capable of formula-
tion, of confirmation or revision....."; and suggests that
Johnson's attack on eighteenth-century critical principles derived partly from a perception that the poet's imagination was
(in Johnson's words) "unsusceptible of limitations, and impa-
tient of restraint" and that Nature also is unlimited in its
possibilities.   Argues, finally, that for Johnson the literary
process consists of four elements--author, work, nature, and
audience--of which the first and last are primary; and that,
since the satisfaction of pleasure is the aim of literature and
the "first principle of critical reasoning," the author is primary in creating those conditions of pleasure.

1837   "Johnson's Criticism of the Metaphysical Poets." ELH 17
        (1950): 59-70. Rpt. in [18], pp. 300-309.

        Johnson measures the metaphysicals and finds them wanting
by application of criteria which he uses in judging literature
of all kinds.   Shows Johnson's "mingling of critical sagacity
and wrongheadedness."   He is given great credit for his analysis of metaphysical wit, and even his lack of appreciation for
the "beauties" of Donne is defended by asserting that only a
handful of Donne's poems, from none of which Johnson quotes,
are valuable for the modern reader.   Keast basically upholds
Johnson's criticism in spite of admitted faults: "For he forces
upon our attention a concern for the ultimate effects and values
of literature--its power to interest and move our emotions."

1838   KELLY, RICHARD.
        "Johnson Among the Sheep." SEL 8 (1968): 475-485.

        Johnson's attitude toward the pastoral form, as shown in
his dicussion of Lycidas, is shaped by the value he sets upon
reality and experience, with the corresponding negative value
of escapism through fancy and imagination.   "For him a poem
must reflect man's experience in a real world, be guided by
reason more than imagination, be written out of sincere emotions, be moral, original, and broad enough in its scope so
as to offer a variety of subjects.   A refutation of his judgments upon the pastoral might show that Johnson is not always a perfect critic, but an examination of his critical tenets
indicate that he is not a perfect fool."

1839   KORSHIN, PAUL J.
        "Johnson and Swift: A Study in the Genesis of Literary Opin-
        ion." PQ 48 (1969): 464-478.

        Swift's views on the total depravity of human nature went

so far beyond Johnson's acceptance of the standard doctrine
of original sin as to make Swift appear to Johnson ethically
and intellectually conservative.   "On the other hand, ...
Swift's satire often implies a strong attack upon the established order, particularly, in the case of A Tale of a Tub,
upon established religion. ..."   In this respect, Swift is too
radical and iconoclastic for Johnson.   "Thus it can be plau-
sibly argued that Johnson was both attracted and repelled by
Swift."   The end result is that Johnson is unfair in his Life
of Swift, dismissing Swift's works as unworthy of any extended
comment.

1840   LEAVIS, F. R.
       "Johnson as Critic."   Scrutiny 12 (1944):   187-204.   Rpt. in
       [1462], pp. 70-88.

       Johnson is portrayed as a "qualified critic," "a powerful
       and distinguished mind operating at first hand upon literature."
       His limitations, as for instance his negative attitude toward
       blank verse, are seen as the conditioning effect of the sen-
       sibility of the age and of the literary tradition to which he
       owed allegiance; but those limitations had positive correla-
       tives.   Emphasizes, for instance, Johnson's inability to ap-
       preciate Shakespeare's poetry, and therefore the dramatic or-
       ganization of the plays; he "cannot appreciate the ways in
       which ... all works of art act their moral judgments."

1841   LONGAKER, JOHN MARK.
       "Johnson's Lives of the Poets."   In English Biography of the
       Eighteenth Century (Philadelphia: Univ. Pa. Press, 1931),
       pp. 314-406; rpt. New York: Octagon Books, 1971.

       A critical and historical account of Johnson's Lives, em-
       phasizing the skill of the author's treatment and the histori-
       cal significance of his method.

1842   LUCAS, F. L.
       "Johnson's Bête Grise."   New Rambler (June 1960):   15-28.

       Examines the mutual dislike which existed between Johnson
       and Gray, and finds fundamental differences.   Defends Gray
       from Johnson's evaluations in his Life of Gray.

1843   McADAM, EDWARD L., JR.
       "Johnson's Lives of Sarpi, Blake, and Drake."   PMLA 48
       (1943):   466-476.

       Attempts to analyze the three lives in relation to their
       sources to learn how Johnson worked at writing biographies;

seeks in particular to find out "what sources he went to, what material he used and omitted, what additions he made, and what precisely was the result." The conclusion is that Johnson relied on a single volume as the main source, tending to omit factual details but adding occasional facts from other narratives, and inserting many Johnsonian generalizations and interpretive comments.

1844   McCARTHY, WILLIAM.
        "The Moral Art of Johnson's Lives." SEL 17 (1977): 503-517.

        The Lives is almost a religious work, with Johnson approaching his task with a moralist's dedication. The subjects of his biographies are "tampered with," in order to emphasize their moral relevance; they illustrate certain traditional themes, such as the theme of misspent talents which is central to the Lives. Johnson's themes are few, but they are the "moral gestures" of the brief life, and they illustrate his imaginative use of pre-existing materials.

1845   MAYS, MORLEY J.
        "Johnson and Blair on Addison's Prose Style." SP 39 (1942): 638-649.

        Johnson considered Addison a model writer of prose, and constantly recommended the reading of Addison to aspiring writers. He characterizes Addison's style as midway between the elevated and the plain, a mixed or middle style. Blair says of Addison, "of ... the highest, most correct, most ornamented degree of the simple manner, Mr. Addison is ... the perfect example."

1846   MISENHEIMER, JAMES B. , JR.
        "Dr. Johnson's Concept of Literary Fiction." MLR 62 (1967): 598-605.

        Concludes that Johnson has a twentieth-century concern for credibility in fiction. He disapproved of unrealistic fiction and approved of fiction "grounded soundly in man--his frailties, his strengths, his accomplishments, his aspirations."

1847   PERKINS, DAVID.
        "Johnson on Wit and Metaphysical Poetry." ELH 20 (1953): 200-217.

        Very useful and convincing analysis of "the background of Johnson's favorable approach to qualities--such as 'wit' and 'novelty' in the use of imagery and language--that are now

commonly associated with the 'metaphysical' style...." In
his criticism of poetry of any period, style, or genre, Johnson was against stock devices.

1848   REYNOLDS, W. VAUGHAN.
       "Johnson's Opinions on Prose Style." RES 9 (1933): 433-
       446.

          Johnson had a greater love of native idiom and native dic-
       tion than he has been given credit for; he did, however, favor
       many words of Latin origin and classical formation, and he
       took a stand for clarity and waged bitter war on obscurity.
       He liked what he called elegance of style, and felt that the
       style should be suited to the theme.

1849   ROGERS, PAT.
       "Johnson's Lives of the Poets and the Biographic Dictionaries."
       RES 31 (1980): 149-171.

          Considers the Lives in relation to the available biographi-
       cal sources, especially attempting to assess the work in the
       context of "collective biography" as represented by such works
       as Biographia Britannica. The study is confined to the bio-
       graphical section of the Lives and disregards the four major
       works, those of Milton, Dryden, Swift, and Pope. The re-
       maining 47 lives establish the norm of Johnson's performance
       --"in particular they exhibit his characteristic relation to
       previous biography as the larger studies do not." Concludes
       that a great deal of Johnson's labor was devoted to close
       paraphrase, varied by the substitution of elegant variations;
       he generally went to a good single life if one existed, but
       he also consulted the dictionaries: often they were all that
       existed in the public domain.

1850   SACHS, ARIEH.
       "Generality and Particularity in Johnson's Thought." SEL 5
       (1965): 491-511.

          Relates Imlac's dictum on poetry, that "the business of a
       poet is to examine, not the individual, but the species," to
       his thinking on moral and religious issues. The association
       of imagination (unreason), the faculty that leads to error,
       with the particular and reason, the faculty that leads to truth,
       with the general is central to Johnson's sense of values.
       Johnson continually balances the general and the particular,
       so that the limiting effects of Imagination become positive
       when regulated by the wider view of Reason: "The particular
       fulfills a positive function in true poetry so long as it re-
       mains subservient to the initial conception of a whole." John-
       son feels that "the human tragedy lay in the insufficiency of

all things limited and ephemeral to a hunger limitless and infinite," and insists that poetry must go "beyond the bounds
of the narrow, the detailed, and the particular."

1851   SANSOM, E. STEVE.
        "The Language of Humanism: Modes of Argument and Self-
        Authentication in the Literary Criticism of Johnson and Ar-
        nold." (In 4 parts). Enl. E. 4, ii (1973): 9-24; iii/iv: 20-
        35; 5, i (1974): 34-47; ii: 18-25.

        "By examining each writer's modes of ethical argument,
        his methods of viewing literature, and the substance of his
        literary criticism, a comparison of both critics' roles in
        humanistic criticism can be formulated. Parts I and II ex-
        plore modes of ethical argument in both Johnson's and Ar-
        nold's critical essays, while Part III is a comparison of both
        writers' methods and theories of literary criticism. These
        three parts unite in Part IV to show that the several modes
        of ethical argument previously discussed are, in essence, a
        form of humanistic argument."

1852   SCHWARTZ, RICHARD B.
        "Dr. Johnson and the Satiric Reaction to Science." SBHT 11
        (1969): 1336-1347.

        Concludes that Johnson's general interest in all learning,
        and his special interest in science, caused him to reject as
        invalid the attacks of the Tory satirists.

1853   TARBET, DAVID W.
        "Lockean 'Intuition' and Johnson's Characterization of Aesthe-
        tic Response." ECS 5 (1971): 58-79.

        Locke seemed uncomfortable with the pleasure of immedi-
        ate, intuitive perception of beauty, warning that there may
        be no "labour of thought to examine what truth or reason
        there is in it." But Johnson, as a creative artist, was more
        interested in aesthetics and was able to "build a coherent aes-
        thetic approach to literature on the foundations of Locke's
        empiricism."

1854   TATE, ALLEN.
        "Johnson on the Metaphysicals." KR 11 (1949): 379-394.
        Rpt. in [1462], pp. 89-101.

        Tate feels that Johnson was so steeped in the neo-classic
        style that it gave him a complacency or provincialism detri-
        mental to his judgment of other styles. He thinks that John-
        son lacked the critical terms and the philosophical temper for
        the estimation of poetry outside of his period style.

1855   TURNAGE, MAXINE.
        "Samuel Johnson's Criticism of the Works of Edmund Spen-
        ser." SEL 10 (1970): 557-567.

            Ascribes Johnson's adverse criticism of Spenser to his
        dislike of the pastoral convention and to his use of Spenser's
        early works as a source of obsolete and archaic words for
        the Dictionary; from that experience Johnson developed a dis-
        satisfaction with Spenser's linguistic curiosities.

1856   WARNCKE, WAYNE.
        "Samuel Johnson on Swift: The Life of Swift and Johnson's
        Predecessors in Swiftian Biography." Jour. of British Stud-
        ies 7 (1968): 56-64.

            Argues that Johnson's prejudice against Swift accounts for
        his antagonism but that it was the moral purpose of the biog-
        raphy that made it so vindictive.

1857   WATKINS, W. B. C.
        Johnson and English Poetry Before 1660.   Princeton, N.J.:
        Princeton Univ. Press, 1936; rpt. New York: Gordian Press,
        1965.

            Johnson's knowledge of English poetry before 1660, derived
        from the Dictionary, the notes to Shakespeare, and other works.
        Presents matter on "Eighteenth Century libraries and John-
        son's manner of reading" and on the sources used for the
        Dictionary.

1858   WEINSHEIMER, JOEL C.
        "The Value of Failure: Johnson on Critical Displeasure."
        SHR 11 (1977): 243-251.

            Discusses Johnson's literary criticism. "By constantly
        balancing the faults of an author against his beauties Johnson
        is able to measure and express the gradations of pleasure
        much more accurately and thus achieves a more vigorous,
        credible, precise, and honestly humble assessment of the
        works he examines than is now apparently possible." Sug-
        gests that critics today would do well to imitate Johnson in
        his eagerness to detect faults and register disapproval.

1859   WENDORF, RICHARD.
        "The Making of Johnson's 'Life of Collins.'" PBSA 74 (1980):
        95-115.

            "An examination of the making of the 'Life of Collins'
        raises issues that are of some importance in our estimate

of Johnson as a biographer, as a proofreader, and as a re-
viser of his own work. ... A collation of the various versions ... suggests ... that in revising his early sketch of
Collins for the later portrait, Johnson worked from a corrupt text that restricted his access to important biographical
information. "

1860   WESLING, DONALD.
        "An Ideal of Greatness: Ethical Implications in Johnson's
        Critical Vocabulary. " UTQ 34 (1965): 133-145.

        Johnson's ideal for a man of letters contains two basic
        demands: that he possess a fine mind applying its force and
        comprehension of nature to literature, and that he exercise
        an absolute moral integrity, capable of rising to the general
        and writing "as the interpreter of nature, and the legislator
        of mankind. " Article explores Johnson's "critical demand
        for vigorous intellection and a manly moral seriousness which
        interpenetrate to reinforce one another"--Johnson's ideal of
        greatness--by examining several of his key critical terms.

1861   WILES, R. M.
        "Samuel Johnson's Response to Beauty. " SBHT 13 (1972):
        2067-2082.

        Through an examination of Johnson's use of the words
        "beauty" and "beautiful," Wiles is able to demonstrate that
        Johnson was well aware of the beauty to be found around
        him. Although Johnson did not develop a highly sophisticated
        aesthetic system, he did possess the ability to respond to
        beauty in a practical and empirical manner.

1862   WRIGHT, JOHN W.
        "Samuel Johnson and Traditional Methodology. " PMLA 86
        (1971): 40-50.

        Demonstrates Johnson's awareness of traditional metho-
        dology, as defined by Newton and Plato, and of the distinc-
        tions between principle, opinion, and experience. Points out
        that in many of the most memorable passages in John-
        son's criticism he is "analyzing received opinion," and com-
        ments on Johnson's analysis of language and definition.

See also: 318, 1398, 1515, 1559, 3694

Miscellaneous

1863   GRAY, JAMES.
       Johnson's Sermons: A Study.   Oxford: Clarendon Press,
       1972.

       Johnson's sermons are examined for structure, sources,
       content, and style.   The relationship with John Taylor is ex-
       plored and the influence of the nonconformist Baxter is an-
       alyzed.

1864   QUINLAN, MAURICE J.
       "The Reaction to Dr. Johnson's Prayers and Meditations."
       JEGP 52 (1953):   125-139.

       The posthumous publication of Prayers and Meditations,
       with its open and vulnerable insights into Johnson's private
       life, acted as ammunition to those who were inclined to at-
       tack his character.   The Rev. George Strahan, who had at-
       tended the dying Johnson, was censured vigorously.   Augus-
       tans were embarrassed by the unseemly revelation of his
       physical symptoms.   Some were worried about the damage
       to Johnson's reputation as a Christian.

1865   REYNOLDS, RICHARD R.
       "Johnson's Life of Boerhaave in Perspective."   YES 5 (1975):
       115-129.

       Examines Johnson's use of the funeral oration by Boer-
       haave's close friend, Albert Schultens, and shows that John-
       son used it to fill in gaps left by Boerhaave's autobiographi-
       cal notes which he used extensively.   However, the powers
       of Johnson's "own mind are constantly evident; his reflections
       on Boerhaave in particular and humanity in general, and his
       concise, vigorous phrases, enrich the narrative and make it
       art."

1866   SIEBENSCHUH, WILLIAM R.
       "On the Locus of Faith in Johnson's Sermons."   SBHT 17
       (1976):   103-117.

       Johnson's sermons "are important human documents with
       biographical as well as theological significance.   Contradic-
       tions in the methods of argument and tensions in the style
       mirror and help to illuminate some of the most central facts
       about [his] compulsive and uneasy relationship to orthodoxy
       and can give us a better sense of the locus of his faith and
       the nature of his struggles."

Collected Studies

1867   BARNARD, JOHN, ed.
Pope: The Critical Heritage.   London: Routledge & Kegan
Paul, 1973.

1868   CLIFFORD, JAMES L. and LOUIS A. LANDA, eds.   Pope
and his Contemporaries: Essays Presented to George Sherburn.   Oxford: Clarendon Press, 1949.

1869   DIXON, PETER, ed.
Alexander Pope: Writers and Their Background.   Athens:
Ohio Univ. Press, 1972.

1869A   ERSKINE-HILL, HOWARD and ANNE SMITH, eds.
The Art of Alexander Pope.   London: Vision Press; New
York: Barnes & Noble, 1979.

1870   GUERINOT, JOSEPH V., ed.
Twentieth Century Views.   Englewood Cliffs, N.J.: Prentice-
Hall, 1972.

1871   MACK, MAYNARD and JAMES A. WINN, eds.
Pope: Recent Essays by Several Hands (Essential Articles
Series).   Hamden, Conn.: Shoe String Press (Archon), 1980.

1872   MACK, MAYNARD, ed.
Essential Articles for the Study of Alexander Pope.   Hamden,
Conn.: Archon Books, 1964, 2nd. ed., 1968.   London: F.
Cass, 1964.

1873   O'NEILL, JUDITH, ed.
Critics on Pope.   Coral Gables: Univ. Fla. Press, 1968.

General Studies

1874   ADAMS, PERCY G.
"Pope's Concern with Assonance."   TSLL 9 (1968): 493-502.
Rev. and rpt. as "Music Resembles Poetry: The Auditory
Appeal of Pope's Meter" in [61], pp. 87-117.

Adams seeks to "demonstrate that Pope's assonance ... is perhaps as important as any of his sound effects and that the manuscripts of his poems prove not only that he labored to achieve assonance but that he was apparently more concerned with it than he was with alliteration." Pope is a master of assonance: "His poems attest to his concern for 'sweet and pleasing' numbers used for 'printing the image'...."

1875 ADEN, JOHN M.
Pope's Once and Future Kings: Satire and Politics in the Early Career. Knoxville: Univ. Tenn. Press, 1978.

This study emphasizes the unity of Pope's career in satire and politics, with politics as the predominant partner. Since for the Augustans politics partly meant religious controversy, the author first sketches the penal history of English Catholicism, arguing that the disabilities under which English Catholics lived led Pope to be a satirist and a Tory; he also examines the question of Pope's commitment to his religion as well as his early reading and imitation of religious and political satire, and finally discusses Pope's work from the beginning to 1728.

1876 "Pope and the Receit to Make a Satire." SNL 5 (1967): 25-33.

Pope's theory of satire as related to his theory of human nature, in which, though reason provides the standard, passion is the motive force. By attacking the person and the specific crime, satire supports reason by forcing the change from self-love to social love.

1877 "Pope and Politics: 'The Farce of State.'" In [1869], pp. 172-199.

Letters and poems of Pope as they relate to political events of the age; discusses Catholicism, Tory wit, patriotism, and Walpole, and their influence on Pope.

1878 ADLER, JACOB H.
The Reach of Art: A Study in the Prosody of Alexander Pope. Gainesville: Univ. Fla. Press, 1964.

A traditional analysis of Pope's prosody, describing characteristic features; the poems are studied chronologically to show how Pope changed his style with his material.

1879 "Balance in Pope's Essays." ES 43 (1962): 457-467.

An examination of balance as a method in An Essay on Criticism and An Essay on Man; its causes and effects, and its relationship to other rhetorical and prosodic techniques.

1880   "Pope and the Rules of Prosody." PMLA 76 (1961): 218-226.

Examines "the rules laid down in Pope's letter on prosody and the critical statements upon prosody to be found elsewhere in his works"; compares "Pope's views with the general critical opinion of the century concerning prosody"; and compares "both with Pope's actual practice throughout his career." Concludes that Pope frequently violates his own rules; that he objects to the rules more often than he praises them.

1881   AKSTENS, THOMAS.
"Pope and Bolingbroke on 'Examples': An Echo of the Letters on History in Pope's Correspondence." PQ 52 (1973): 232-238.

Pope's opinions on the usefulness of history as a resource for the poetic satirist; his use of contemporary figures as examples of corruption and historical figures as lessons in morality.

1882   ALLEN, ROBERT J.
"Pope and the Sister Arts." In [1868], pp. 78-88.

Pope's use of the sister arts, primarily painting, in his imagery.

1883   ALTENBERND, A. LYNN.
"On Pope's 'Horticultural Romanticism.'" JEGP 54 (1955): 470-477. In [1872], pp. 122-131.

Considers Pope's theory and practice as a gardener against the background of English gardening and argues that they are not a romantic contradiction to the prevailing neo-classicism of his poetry.

1884   ALTICK, RICHARD D.
"Mr. Pope Expands his Grotto." PQ 21 (1942): 427-430.

Letters between Thomas Edwards, Pope's successor as "ruler of Twickenham," and Richard Owen Cambridge relating to Cambridge's donation of geological specimens for Pope's grotto.

1885   ATKINS, G. DOUGLAS.
"Pope and Deism: A New Analysis." HLQ 35 (1972): 257-278. Rpt. in [1871], pp. 392-415.

Analyzes evidence as to whether Pope was a deist and decides that he wasn't.

1886   AUDEN, W. H.
"Alexander Pope." EIC 1 (1951): 208-224. Also in From Anne to Victoria, ed. Bonamy Dobrée, (New York: Scribner's, 1937); [1872], pp. 22-37; [1870], pp. 15-29.

Relates Pope to the age in which he lived as the reason for his success as a poet in spite of his personal character and his limitations as a poet. An important revaluation that emphasizes the beauties and variety of his verse: his images are from contemporary life and he can be as direct as any poet when he chooses.

1887   AUDRA, E.
L'Influence française dans l'oeuvre de Pope. Paris: Champion, 1931.

Pope's knowledge of French literature and his relationships with French men of letters arising from the controversy over Essay on Man; his use of French sources in The Rape of the Lock and Eloisa to Abelard and of French ideas in Essay on Man and the Moral Essays.

1888   AULT, NORMAN.
New Light on Pope, with Some Additions to His Poetry Hitherto Unknown. London: Methuen, 1949.

A collection of essays, largely biographical and bibliographical, which provides several variant texts of minor poems, and makes a number of questionable attributions.

1889   "Pope and the Miscellanies." Nineteenth Century 116 (1934): 566-580.

Discusses the reasons for Pope's life-long disparagement of the miscellanies. Argues that he was the real editor and compiler of "Lintot's Miscellany."

1890   BATESON, F. W. and MAX BLUESTONE.

"Pun and Metaphor and Pope." <u>EIC</u> 9 (1959): 437-443.

I.   A reply to Aubrey Williams's "Submerged Metaphor in Pope," <u>EIC</u> 9 (1959): 197-201, and to Max Bluestone's "The Suppressed Metaphor in Pope," <u>EIC</u> 8 (1958): 347-354. Mr. Bateson supports Mr. Bluestone's contention that Pope employs suppressed metaphors.

II. Max Bluestone's reply to Aubrey Williams's strictures on Mr. Bluestone's original essay.

1891   BEAUMONT, CHARLES.
"Pope and the Palladians." <u>TSLL</u> 17 (1975): 461-479.

A discussion of Palladian architecture and Pope's references to it in his poems and letters.

1892   BISHOP, CARTER R.
"General Themes in Pope's Satires." <u>W. Va. Univ. Bull:</u>
<u>Phil. Papers</u> 6 (1949): 54-68.

Discusses Pope's satirical attacks on topics of current interest--literary patronage, the indigent and mediocre poet, decadent drama, schools, politics, and the moneyed classes.

1893   BLUESTONE, MAX.
"The Suppressed Metaphor in Pope." <u>EIC</u> 10 (1960): 114-116.

An answer to Aubrey Williams's comment in <u>EIC</u> 9 (1959): 197-201.

1894   "The Suppressed Metaphor in Pope." <u>EIC</u> 8 (1958): 347-354.

An analysis of an extended metaphor equating language and clothes in <u>An Essay on Criticism</u> (II, 305-336), indicating the ways in which Pope manages to suppress the metaphor. The process seems to suggest that Pope sees metaphor essentially as ornament.

1895   BOGEL, FREDRIC V.
<u>Acts of Knowledge: Pope's Later Poems.</u>   Lewisburg, Pa.:
<u>Bucknell Univ. Press, 1981.</u>

A study of structure and meaning in Pope's later poems, in particular the way in which structure and meaning express the central theme of knowledge. Argues that "Pope is as much concerned with the discovery of values as with values themselves, as much concerned with the problem of knowing the world rightly as with the need to value it rightly, and thus as much a poet of knowledge as a poet of morality. "

1896 BOND, DONALD F.
"Pope's Contributions to the Spectator." MLQ 5 (1944): 69-78.

Lists the definitely known contributions of Pope to the Spec tator, and instances numerous parallels between the Spectator and Pope's later work in order to cast doubt on Norman Ault' attribution [in The Prose Works of Alexander Pope, ed. Norman Ault (Oxford, 1936)] of seven additional essays to Pope.

1897 BOYCE, BENJAMIN.
"The Poet and the Postmaster: The Friendship of Alexander Pope and Ralph Allen." PQ 45 (1966): 114-122.

Friendship between the two men began in 1735 and lasted until Pope's death.

1898 "Mr. Pope, in Bath, Improves the Design of his Grotto."
In [13], pp. 143-153.

Pope's visit to Bath in November 1739 and his acquaintance with Dr. William Oliver and Rev. William Borlase gave him many new ideas for developing his grotto.

1899 The Character Sketches in Pope's Poems. Durham, N.C.: Duke Univ. Press, 1962.

Considers Pope's theory and practice in the traditional use of the character-sketch in verse satire; La Bruyère's influence is analyzed in detail.

1900 BRACHER, FREDERICK.
"Pope's Grotto: The Maze of Fancy." HLQ 12 (1949): 141-162. Rpt. in [1872], pp. 97-121.

Discusses what Pope's grotto was like, how it compared with traditional grottos of the eighteenth century, and what it reveals of his taste and personality.

1901 BROWER, REUBEN A.
"Dryden and the 'Invention' of Pope." In [13], pp. 211-233.

Explores some of the ways in which Dryden's poetry from

about 1685 until his death anticipated Pope in Horatian style, the pastoral and the descriptive modes, and the style described as "poetry of retirement."

1902   Alexander Pope: The Poetry of Allusion.   Oxford: Clarendon Press, 1959.   Rpt. , 1968.

A study of the European and English poetic tradition, especially that of Homer and the Roman poets, in order to emphasize the "poetic character and design" of the poems.

1903   "An Allusion to Europe: Dryden and Poetic Tradition." ELH 19 (1952):   38-48.   Rpt. in [1902], pp. 1-14; [1872], pp. 132-145.

Pope's indebtedness to Dryden, especially for the allusive mode: " 'allusive irony' is a more adequate term than 'mock-heroic' for Dryden's satirical mode."

1904   BROWNELL, MORRIS R.
Alexander Pope & the Arts of Georgian England.   Oxford: Clarendon Press, 1978.

Attempts to give a "comprehensive account of Pope's career as a virtuoso in its biographical and art-historical context. It amounts to a history of the arts of the Georgian period in the light of Pope's career." The book's purpose is to refute the notion that Pope was a dilettante in painting, unresponsive to landscape, a trifler in his grotto, and ignorant of architecture and music. It claims that Pope, the major poet of the age, was "endowed with an aesthetic sensibility of his own."

1905   BRUCKMANN, PATRICIA.
"Allusions to Pope." UTQ 33 (1964): 227-232.

Discussion and criticism of works on Pope by Reuben A. Brower, Benjamin Boyce, and Earl Wasserman, and of the Twickenham Edition edited by E. Audra and Aubrey Williams.

1906   BUDICK, SANFORD.
"The Demythological Mode in Augustan Verse." ELH 37 (1970): 389-414.

The demythological mode--i. e. , the demythologizing of one myth in order to proclaim another in classical and biblical literature when a public voice is required to speak out on matters of public concern--is an essential part of the Augustan poet's authority.

1907   BUTT, JOHN A.
        Pope, Dickens and Others: Essays and Addresses.   Edin-
        burgh: Edinburgh Univ. Press, 1969.

        Includes: "Imitation of Horace in English Poetry," "Sci-
        ence and Man in Eighteenth-Century Poetry," and "Pope and
        the Opposition to Walpole's Government."

1908   "Pope and the Opposition to Walpole's Government." In [1907]
        pp. 111-126.

        Illustrates how Pope expressed his moral objections to
        Walpole's government in his poetry.

1909   "Pope: The Man and the Poet." In [12], pp. 69-79; [1871],
        pp. 1-14; abridged in [1873], pp. 32-36.

        Discusses the blending of the artifact and the real in Pope's
        satires and gives examples of Pope's exceptional career.

1910   "Pope Seen Through his Letters." The Listener, June 20,
        1957. Rpt. in [18], pp. 62-67.

        Pope's decision to publish some of his letters was an ef-
        fort to change peoples' view of his moral character.

1911   "The Inspiration of Pope's Poetry." In [54], pp. 65-79.

        An essay on how to understand and appreciate Pope's po-
        etry. Concludes " ... that the three inspirations of Pope's
        work, the inspirations drawn from fancy, morality, and
        books ... " not only exist separately in his poetry but also
        as a blend of all three.

1912   CALLAN, NORMAN.
        "Pope and the Classics." In [1869], pp. 230-249.

        Pope's development as a classical poet and the relation-
        ship of his poems to the classical originals.

1913   CARRUTH, HAYDEN.
        "Three Notes on the Versewriting of Alexander Pope." MQR
        15 (1976): 371-381.

        Makes three points about Pope's versification: 1) he used
        apostrophes, not to make an elision, but for various and in-
        consistent reasons, sometimes for metrical effects, some-

times for rhetorical effects, and sometimes for stylistic or orthographic convenience; 2) he faced the problem of how to justify a line in which a weak syllable falls in a normally accented position by using "extended patterns, whole paragraphs of shifting accents, in which successive lines work forward and backward against one another"; and 3) he sought to attain the couplet's "true qualities"--poise, sharpness, a certain elegance, and, most important of all, naturalness, which includes freedom from padding.

1914   CASE, ARTHUR E.
        "Pope, Addison, and the 'Atticus' Lines." MP 33 (1935): 187-193.

        Discusses the relations between Pope and Addison during the last three years of the latter's life; argues that Gildon had no connection with A True Character of Mr. Pope, which aroused Pope's animosity toward Addison: the latter did not hire Gildon to attack Pope.

1915   CHAPIN, CHESTER F.
        "Alexander Pope: Erasmian Catholic." ECS 6 (1973): 411-430.

        Maintains that Pope did not wish merely to "appear" a Catholic, he sincerely believed he "was" one, and that his opinions were in general accord with those of Erasmus; the harmony between his religious views and the life he led is evident in Essay on Man and the Dunciad written with a serious moral purpose.

1916   "The Inherent Values of Eighteenth-Century Personification: Pope." In [88], pp. 116-130.

        An analysis of Pope's use of allegorical personification in The Rape of the Lock and the Dunciad IV. Emphasizes "the peculiar advantages which attach to the use of allegorical figures in satire, and ... provides an opportunity to examine the personified abstraction ... as it appears in relation to the total structure and content of the poem." Pope, finally, illustrates a positive feeling for abstraction that is found in the best neo-classical verse.

1917   CHURCHILL, R. C.
        "The Enduring Element in Pope." Dublin Rev., Oct. 1944: 160-170.

        A survey of Pope's reputation, and an analysis of his dramatic quality and of his immense concern for humanity as the "enduring elements" in the poetry. Emphasis on the portraits.

1918 CLARK, DONALD B.
Alexander Pope. New York: Twayne, 1967.

A useful survey of Pope's poetic career, emphasizing interpretation and criticism, and arguing especially that the poet's vision of harmony through variety--the friendly strife --gives unity to his whole work.

1919 COHEN, RALPH.
"Pope's Meanings and the Strategies of Interrelation." CREL 4 (1976): 68-92; rpt. in [44], pp. 101-130.

Explains Pope's poetry as composite: "The ideas of interrelation ... are those which explain Pope's manner of relating poetry to society, to his self-conscious processes of composition, to his artistic and didactic procedures of diction and rhetoric, and to his principles of connection." Argues for a reinterpretation of Augustan poetry based on the premise that "these poems are combinations of parts associatively connected to achieve particularized generic ends," and discusses the problem of meaning and the question of the significance of reader expectations to an understanding of Pope's work.

1920 COWLER, ROSEMARY.
"Shadow and Substance: A Discussion of Pope's Correspondence." In [1], pp. 34-48.

Pope as a letter writer and the literary implications of his concern for publication.

1921 CRAWFORD, CHARLOTTE E.
"What was Pope's Debt to Edward Young?" ELH 13 (1946): 157-167.

On indebtedness of Pope's epistolary satire to Young's The Universal Passion; parallel passages show extent to which both authors expressed their common social, intellectual, and literary milieu in their poetry.

1922 CRUTTWELL, PATRICK.
"Alexander Pope in the Augustan World." Cent. Rev. 10 (1966): 13-36.

Pope's endeavors to "please" and to "instruct": "his fanat-

ical devotion to his art by which he never ceased to strengthen
and purify the medium he used", and his "constant search
for what he believed to be the best elements of the society
he lived in, his praising of those elements and his denounc-
ing of their rivals...."

1923   "Pope and his Church." HR 13 (1960): 392-405.

Discusses Pope's relationship to the Catholic Church and
questions why his works virtually exclude any reference to
his faith.

1924   CUNNINGHAM, SANDY.
        "Bedlam and Parnassus: Eighteenth Century Reflections."
        E&S 24 (1971): 36-55.

The importance of the theme of madness and folly, as a
contrast to Augustan rationality and stability, in the work of
Pope, Swift, and Johnson.   Pope is seen as rationally skeptical about the accomplishments of rationality.   Caught off-
guard, the rational Augustan finds himself in Bedlam.

1925   CURTIS, PENELOPE.
        "Pope the Good Augustan." MCR 7 (1964): 34-48.

Argues, by concentrating on the satires, that the assumption of Pope's Augustanism must be questioned; that strain
and fragmentation are more central to his achievement than
any orthodox conception of "Order."

1926   DEARING, VINTON A.
        "Pope, Theobald, and Wycherley's Posthumous Works." PMLA
        68 (1953): 223-236.

Consideration of first volume of Posthumous Works calls
into question authenticity of some of Wycherley's poems as
published by Theobald; discusses the use of Pope's private
correspondence with Wycherley in the second volume.

1927   DIXON, PETER.
        " 'Talking Upon Paper':   Pope and Eighteenth-Century Con-
        versation." ES 46 (1965): 36-44.

Discusses the conversational qualities of Pope's verse:
his avoidance of expletives and his skillful use of asides;
gives an historical account of the various definitions of raillery, and of the increasing importance of the concept of delicacy, and concludes with examples from Pope's work.

1928   DOBREE, BONAMY.
        Alexander Pope. London: Sylvan Press, 1951; New York:
        Philosophical Library, 1952.

        A short biography of Pope, necessarily emphasizing his
        quarrels and friendships, with brief comments on the poetry.

1929   DOUGLAS, LLOYD.
        "A Severe Animadversion on Bossu." PMLA 62 (1947): 690-
        706.

        Denies truth of Joseph Warton's assertion that Pope wrote
        his "Receipt to make an epic poem" (Peri Bathous 15) in
        ridicule of Le Bossu; asserts that Blackmore was the chief
        target.

1930   DURHAM, WILLARD H.
        "Pope as Poet." In Essays in Criticism, 2nd. ser. (Berke-
        ley: Univ. of Calif. Press, 1934), pp. 93-110.

        Investigates the question raised by Warton in 1756--was
        Pope a good poet and is the reader of Pope's poetry treated
        to a poetic experience?

1931   EASTMAN, ARTHUR M.
        "The Quality of Mercy: A Reply to Pope's Apologists."
        PMASAL 43 (1957 meeting; pub. 1958): 335-342.

        Examines the way in which, to justify Pope's satire, apolo-
        gists have defended uncritically the doctrine that his satire
        is fictional to the exclusion of its factual basis: "Pope's sat-
        ire tends to incarnate its universals in particulars that are
        partly real." The dramatic Alexander Pope wears at times
        a character that does not quite fit: his respect for virtue is
        flawed by vanity and the absence of mercy.

1932   EDWARDS, THOMAS R. , JR.
        "Visible Poetry: Pope and Modern Criticism." In Twentieth-
        Century Literature in Retrospect, ed. Reuben A. Brower.
        Harvard English Studies, 2 (Cambridge, Mass. : Harvard Uni-
        versity Press, 1971), pp. 299-321.

        Using Epistle II of the Essay on Man as an example, sug-
        gests that "Pope's perspective on his own 'civilization,' what
        Arnold meant by prose and reason, was in its own way no
        less questioning and skeptical than Arnold's perspective on
        his, or ours on our own"; analyzes Pope's relation to his
        own poetic art and suggests that our age understands the ex-
        pressiveness of Pope's poetic "prose" and the issues at play
        beneath the surface of his "reason."

1933   This Dark Estate: A Reading of Pope (Perspectives in Criti-
        cism, 11). Berkeley & Los Angeles: Univ. of Calif. Press,
        1963.

            A short survey of Pope's poetic career, excluding the Ho-
        meric translations, which argues that the Augustan synthesis
        between the "dark estate" of the real world and the ideal
        world of the imagination in the early poems gives way, in
        the later poems, to a "grotesque" style in which that balance
        is weakened by powerful feelings that no longer can be con-
        tained within the Augustan forms.

1934   "The Colors of Fancy: An Image Cluster in Pope." MLN
        73 (1958): 485-489.

            Locates in the whole of Pope's works the repeated use of
        an image of the transient colors of clouds to suggest the im-
        permanent and delusive nature of the fancy.

1935   EFFROSS, SUSI H.
        "The Influence of Alexander Pope in Eighteenth-Century Spain."
        SP 63 (1966): 78-92.

            Argues that Pope's influence in Spain was greater than
        E. Allison Peers allows, that his influence depended not only
        on his "neo-classical" and philosophic poems but also on
        Eloisa to Abelard, and that Spanish interest in Pope was
        largely the result of his popularity in France.

1936   EHRENPREIS, IRVIN.
        "Pope: Bipolar Implication." In [99], pp. 83-111.

            Argues that Pope's methods of satirical implication gain
        strength from the contrast between style and meaning, and
        that patterns of sound and rhythm in which he embodied nu-
        ances of implication found a place inside the parallels and
        antitheses of phrase and clause. Pope establishes two orders
        of satirical implication--one, conventionally didactic, is in-
        volved with explicit meaning; the other, boldly subversive,
        has a different center from the explicit meaning, which it
        uses as a screen or code. This contrast between thematic
        and topical meanings represents the bipolarity of Pope's im-
        plications.

1937   "The Style of Sound: The Literary Value of Pope's Versifi-
        cation." In [42], pp. 232-246.

            Using versification as a guide, concludes that "Pope com-
        posed his greatest works when he invented a comprehensive

structure that could hold--without contradictions or incongruities--the whole range of his expressive devices. "

1938 ERSKINE-HILL, HOWARD.
The Social Milieu of Alexander Pope. New Haven: Yale
Univ. Press, 1975.

"A study of Pope's society, and of the social poetry which, as a member of that society, Pope produced. " Concentrates on six of Pope's contemporaries: John Kyrle, John Caryll, Peter Walter, Lord Digby, Sir John Blunt, and Ralph Allen and traces their influence on Pope's poetry.

1939 FEDER, LILLIAN.
"Sermo or Satire: Pope's Definition of His Art. " In [2], pp. 140-155.

Pope's defense of his own art, although to a large extent a defense of the Horatian image of satire, created a new type of English satire. His departures from Horace are as significant as his borrowings in the formation of his own satiric persona.

1940 FRASER, DONALD.
"Pope and the Idea of Fame. " In [1869], pp. 286-310.

Looks at Pope's poetry in relation to his attitude toward fame and friendship and his efforts to commemorate his friends in spite of his attitude of the inadequacy of fame to compensate for isolation during life and separation by death.

1941 FRASER, G. S.
Alexander Pope. London: Routledge & Kegan Paul, 1978.

Written for the lover of poetry rather than for the scholar, this critical study discusses the collected Works of 1717, the Homeric translations, An Essay on Man, the Epistles to Several Persons, The Dunciad, and the Imitations of Horace. Argues that Pope's aristocratic tastes make him seem more like a survivor from the Restoration than a precursor of middle-class culture. Because his satires reflect his admirations and hatreds so violently, and therefore lack coolness, they are perhaps great poems rather than great satires in any conventional sense.

1942 GASSMAN, BYRON.
"The Augustan Nightmare. " In "The Need Beyond Reason" and Other Essays: College of Humanities Centennial Lec-

tures 1975-76 (Provo, Utah: Brigham Young Univ. Press, 1976), pp. 27-45.

The main characteristic of Augustan literature, principally embodied in the poetry of Pope, is a tone of frustration and weariness with the incorrigible follies and vices of the human race. The Augustan vision contains a note of terror that the comprehensible universe is disintegrating into chaos, that madness is the only sane course to follow. The Augustans created some of the most vivid nightmares in all literature to emphasize the apparent destruction of their ideal world and man's violation of cosmic decorum.

1943   GOLDBERG, S. L.
        "Integrity and Life in Pope's Poetry." In [8], pp. 185-207; Rpt. [1871], pp. 15-44.

Emphasizes Pope's "dramatic" power, in the sense that he came to "represent" the world as the embodiment of its ideal possibilities of self-awareness and self-criticism. Pope came to realize that to create an objective world was also to create and to define himself; he realized that the "relevant kind of impersonality to seek in his work is that manifested in the greatest dramatic 'masterpieces'--an integrity and plenitude of dramatic and personal realisation."

1944   "Alexander Pope." MCR 7 (1964): 49-65. Rpt. as "Alexander Pope: The Creative Poet." In [1873], pp. 37-53.

Discusses Pope's insight into the world in which he lived and how his poetry revealed his feelings, his ideas, his values, and his role as a poet in this world.

1945   GOLDSTEIN, MALCOLM.
        Pope and the Augustan Stage. Stanford, Cal.: Stanford Univ. Press, 1958.

A study of Pope's theatrical relationships, emphasizing especially the importance which the theatre had for Pope and demonstrating the appeal of early eighteenth-century drama to a man of taste and intelligence.

1946   GOONERATNE, YASMINE.
        Alexander Pope. Cambridge: Cambridge Univ. Press, 1976.

An introductory study that concentrates on Pope's works, with great attention to concrete details; the poetry is allowed to defend itself. Intended for new readers of Pope.

1947   GORDON, I. R. F.
       A Preface to Pope.   London: Longman, 1976.

       A general and introductory survey of Pope's life and work,
       and the social, literary, artistic, and intellectual context in
       which he lived.

1948   GREENE, DONALD J.
       "Dramatic Texture in Pope." In [26], pp. 31-53.

       Attempts to show how a sensitive, subtle, and accurate
       reading of Pope's poems is enhanced when individual parts
       of the poem are seen in the context of the poem as a whole.

1949   GRESS, ELSA.
       "The Culmination of Formalism in English Literature: Alex-
       ander Pope as Critic." OL 2 (1944-45): 293-301.

       In An Essay on Criticism, the prefaces to Homer and
       Shakespeare, and the Dunciad, Pope displays "his acute criti-
       cal eye, his sense of form, and his feeling of poetic values";
       his activities as an artist and as a critic are difficult to dis-
       tinguish from each other.

1950   GRIFFIN, DUSTIN H.
       Alexander Pope: The Poet in the Poems.   Princeton, N. J. :
       Princeton Univ. Press, 1978.

       Pope's projection of self-images in his poems; Part I deals
       with "Pope the Man" and Part II with the poems, always em-
       phasizing the ways in which they can be interpreted as self-
       expressive. He examines poems from the entire range of
       Pope's career in which the historical Pope or a narrator is
       prominent, but with no extended discussions of The Rape of
       the Lock, Eloisa to Abelard, or the Moral Essays; the book
       is not, therefore, a comprehensive analysis of Pope's poetry,
       but a reading from one particular point of view.

1951   GURR, ELIZABETH.
       Pope (Writers & Critics Series).   Edinburgh: Oliver & Boyd,
       1971.

       An introduction to Pope; popular and general.

1952   HAGSTRUM, JEAN H.
       "Verbal and Visual Caricature in The Age of Dryden, Swift,
       and Pope." In [55], pp. 173-195.

Discusses the art of satire in relation to the visual arts, emblematic caricature, and portrait caricature as portrayed by Dryden, Swift, and Pope.

1953   HALSBAND, ROBERT.
"Two New Letters from Lady Mary Wortley Montagu to Alexander Pope." PQ 29 (1950): 349-352.

Two letters, dating between 1722 and 1726, show that their friendship lasted longer than previously thought and provide new clues to their relationship.

1954   HANSEN, MARLENE R.
"Some Female Images in Eighteenth Century Rural Poetry." In [16], pp. 181-195.

Studies the personification of the Country in the poetry of Pope, Crabbe, Goldsmith, and Cowper, and the contrasting personification of the Town.   Pope uses two female personifications in Epilogue to the Satires and The Dunciad, Virtue and Vice, and "the symbols of the Whore and the Virgin operate at various levels and play an important part in the contemporary manifestation of the eternal antipathy between town and country" in The Deserted Village, The Village, and The Task.

1955   HARDY, JOHN.
"Stockdale's Defence of Pope." RES 18 (1967): 49-54.

Suggests that the defense of Pope's poetry from Joseph Warton's charge, in his Essay on Pope, that Pope was not "at the head of his profession," came largely from Percival Stockdale's Inquiry into the Nature and Genuine Laws of Poetry; including a Particular Defence of the Writings and Genius of Mr. Pope (1778).

1956   HARTLEY, LODWICK.
"Ambiguity about Mr. Pope." CE 1 (1939): 254-261.

A defense of Pope's poetry.

1957   HOOKER, EDWARD N.
"Pope and Dennis." ELH 7 (1940): 188-198.

Argues that Dennis was not the persecutor of Pope that everyone says he was; that Dennis was so satirized by Pope and his friends that he was driven to critical attacks in response.

1958   HUMPHREYS, A. R.
        "Pope, God, and Man." In [1869], pp. 60-100.

        Aspects of the Augustan Age and Pope's attempt to "define
        the world picture, and the social picture of a whole culture
        in its aspirations, policies, arts, and conduct" through poetry
        which was lucid, critical, dramatic, and profound.

1959   HUNT, JOHN DIXON.
        "Gardening, and Poetry, and Pope." Art Quart. 37 (1974):
        1-30.   Expanded and rpt. in [121], pp. 58-104.

        Attempts to answer questions regarding "what part Pope's
        gardening criticism and activity played in his career, and
        how did his contributions" to the development of the English
        landscape garden agree with the needs and instincts of his
        contemporaries by considering why "his most formal state-
        ment on gardening in the Epistle to Burlington" is at the cli-
        max of his Moral Essays, and why he considered that "Gar-
        dening is ... nearer God's own work than Poetry."

1960   HUTCHINGS, W.
        "New Light on Pope?" Crit. Quart. 19, iv (1977): 39-50.

        Takes issue with various critics of Pope (Reeves [2005],
        Rogers [2011], Gordon [1947], Gooneratne [1946], and Erskine-
        Hill [1938]) and suggests that perhaps we would do well to
        read Pope himself instead of so much criticism about him.

1961   JACK, IAN.
        Pope. (WTW) London: Longmans, 1954.

        A short essay that sees Pope as belonging to the same
        tradition as Spenser and Milton, to the "Renaissance tradi-
        tion."

1962   JOHNSTON, ARTHUR.
        " 'The Purple Year' in Pope and Gray." RES 14 (1963):
        389-393.

        Examines the phrase, "the purple year," which Pope de-
        rived from Dryden and Virgil and which Geoffrey Tillotson
        discussed in Augustan Studies (1961), pp. 205-06; the author
        studies the contexts in which "purple" is used by other poets,
        and concludes that the phrase refers to the brilliance of spring
        flowers, and not to the brilliant light of the sun in spring.

1963   JONES, EVAN.
        "Verse, Prose and Pope." MCR 4 (1961): 30-40.

Discussion of the structural character of Pope's couplets within the context of a poem and how it is related to a deprivation of Pope's sensibility; compares Pope and Donne.

1964   JONES, JOHN A.
"The Analogy of Eighteenth Century Music and Poetry: Bach and Pope." Cent. Rev. 21 (1977): 211-235.

The poetry and music of the late-Baroque-Augustan Period share some analogies of form and style, mainly because in the age of Bach and Pope both music rhetoricians and literary critics shared a world view that encouraged similar modes of expression. Pope's form represents late Baroque mind and sensibility which attempted to gain unity and harmony more "by variations of similarity and likeness than by the resolution of difference and contrast."

1965   Pope's Couplet Art. Athens: Ohio Univ. Press, 1969.

A study of the basic features of Pope's couplet--balanced antithesis and parallelism, rhyme, closure, and sentence form--in order to see how they work together to create different modes of expression. Attempts to explain Pope's development as a stylist.

1966   KALMEY, ROBERT P.
" 'The Struggles of Grace and Nature' in the Poems of Alexander Pope." Shippensburg (Pa.) S.C. Rev. Oct. (1968): 3-9.

A review of the harmony of grace and nature as discussed by various philosophers and Pope's theory as expressed in Eloisa to Abelard.

1967   KEENER, FREDERICK M.
An Essay on Pope. New York: Columbia Univ. Press, 1974.

Concentrates on both the life and the work, emphasizing Pope's affinities with the Enlightenment; deals with "total designs," as well as fables and actions, of the major poems, and relates the changes in Pope's poetic voice to the events of his life.

1968   KENNER, HUGH.
"Pope's Reasonable Rhymes." ELH 41 (1974): 74-88. Rpt. in [1871], pp. 63-79.

"Pope's great triumphs of normal and abnormal rhyming remain for us to admire, but no poet we can now foresee

is likely to want to do more in that vein, so alien now is
the intuition of language to which it appealed."

1969   KNIGHT, G. WILSON.
        Laureate of Peace: On the Genius of Alexander Pope.   Lon-
        don: Routledge & Kegan Paul, 1955 (pub. Dec. 1954).   Re-
        issued as The Poetry of Pope: Laureate of Peace, 1965.

        Devoted to the "total contents" of Pope's poetry which the
        author sees as part of a tradition that extends from the New
        Testament to Blake and Nietzsche.   Pope analyzed according
        to the "technique of spatial interpretation."

1970   KNOEPFLMACHER, U. C.
        "Impersonations of Alexander Pope: Current Views Within
        a Nineteenth-Century Perspective."   MLQ 34 (1973):   448-461.

        Review essay considering recent studies by Spacks, Sitter,
        and Russo.

1971   KRUTCH, JOSEPH WOOD.
        "Pope and Our Contemporaries."   In [17], pp. 251-259.

        Presents reasons why Pope is not a popular poet today
        (i. e. , 1949).

1972   LEAVIS, F. R.
        "Pope."   Scrutiny 2 (1933-34):   268-284.   Rpt. in Revaluation
        (London: Chatto & Windus, 1935), pp. 68-91; [1872], pp. 3-21.

        A discussion of Pope's achievements with respect to the
        little attention paid to him by critics; attempts a revaluation,
        emphasizing the Metaphysical influence.

1973   LEEDY, PAUL F.
        "Genres, Criticism and the Significance of Warton's Essay on
        Pope."   JEGP 45 (1946):   140-146.

        Argues that Warton's essay, with its emphasis on the im-
        portance of invention and imagination, represents a sharp
        break with Pope's neoclassicism.

1974   LEVINE, JAY A.
        "The Status of the Verse Epistle Before Pope."   SP 59 (1962):
        658-684.

        A historical study of the theory and practice of the verse

epistle that anticipated and influenced Pope's conception of
the "ethic epistle." The author confines his attention to the
kind of verse epistle that discusses serious subjects of social,
political, or individual conduct in an intimate or middle style.

1975   LEWALSKI, BARBARA K.
        "On Looking into Pope's Milton." EA 27 (1974):   481-500.
        Rev. and rpt. in Milton Stds. 11 (1978):   29-50.

        The author's purpose is to "attempt an overall perspective
        on the relation of these two poets: to see what Pope thought
        of Milton as a poet, and in what ways--stylistic, thematic,
        mythopoeic--he drew upon Milton as a poetic resource."

1976   LEWIS, DAVID E.
        "A Quarrelsome Romance of the Eighteenth Century." DR
        26 (1946):   198-202.

        On Pope's affair with Lady Mary Wortley Montague.

1977   LITZ, FRANCIS E.
        "Pope and Twickenham's Famous Preacher." MLQ 17 (1956):
        204-212.

        The attitudes and indebtedness of Jeremiah Seed to his
        neighbor, Alexander Pope, and especially his use of passages
        from An Essay on Man and An Essay on Criticism.

1978   LOCKWOOD, THOMAS.
        "On the Relationship of Satire and Poetry After Pope." SEL
        14 (1974):   387-402.   Rpt. in [492], pp. 167-182.

        Discusses the question, Was Pope a poet? as well as the
        more general question, What is poetry? as they were argued
        by late eighteenth- and early nineteenth-century writers.   The
        domain of poetry shrank to exclude verse satire, and such
        satire as was written no longer ambitiously dealt with man,
        Dulness, or pride.

1979   LOOMIS, EMERSON ROBERT.
        "The Turning Point in Pope's Reputation: A Dispute Which
        Preceded the Bowles-Byron Controversy." PQ 42 (1963):
        242-248.

        Controversy which began in 1798 between Thomas J. Mathias
        and William Burdom concerning Pope's ideas.

1980   MacCLINTOCK, LANDER.

"Sainte-Beuve and Pope." PMLA 41 (1926): 442-451.

A description of Sainte-Beuve's essay on Pope, and of the similarities and differences between their doctrines of the Ruling Passion. Sainte-Beuve's use of "Pope, Boileau and Horace" as a symbol of the classical ideal.

1981 MacDONALD, W. L.
Pope and His Critics: A Study in Eighteenth-Century Personalities. London: Dent, 1951; Seattle: Univ. Wash. Press, 1951.

Investigates the question how far personalities entered into the criticism of Pope and the extent to of which critical judgement was affected. Discusses taste and criticism in Essay on Criticism, the background of the "wits," and both contemporary and later eighteenth-century biographers of Pope.

1982 MACK, MAYNARD.
"Pope: The Shape of the Man in His Work." YR 67 (1978): 493-516.

Speculates as to the effects of Pope's disability on his life and his writings, especially his Horatian poems and those which deal with women.

1983 The Garden and the City: Retirement and Politics in the Later Poetry of Pope, 1731-1743. Toronto: Univ. Toronto Press, 1969.

Emphasizes biography and literary history in considering Pope's later satires and epistles; Mack argues that a certain emblematic quality in Pope's life at Twickenham represented an "angle of vision" from which he could attack political corruption in the age of Walpole. Discusses Pope as poet, philosopher, and gardener.

1984 "A Poet in His Landscape: Pope at Twickenham." In [26], pp. 3-29.

An account of Pope's house and garden, 1719 to 1744, and what effect they may have had on his poetic imagination.

1985 "Secretum Iter: Some Uses of Retirement Literature in the Poetry of Pope." In [56], pp. 207-243.

Examines passages from Pope's poems, especially those of the thirties, to show how the retirement theme moves always under the surface of his consciousness.

1986   " 'The Shadowy Cave': Some Speculations on a Twickenham
        Grotto. " In [13], pp. 69-88.

        A study of the nature and use of garden, countryside, and
        landscape themes in Pope's poetry using his famous grotto
        as the main focal point.

1987   "On Reading Pope. " CE 7 (1946): 263-273. Rpt. as "1946:
        On Reading Pope, " CE 22 (1960) : 99-107.

        A close analysis of two passages in Windsor-Forest to
        illustrate how to read Pope by adjusting our apprehension of
        a poem's interior organization with various external facts,
        feelings, beliefs, values--what Mack calls the poem's "ma-
        trix. " Suggests that much of Pope's significance derives
        from the conflict between an opening vista and the immediate
        subject.

1988   "The Muse of Satire. " YR 41 (1951): 80-92. Rpt. in [7],
        pp. 218-231; [48], pp. 190-201; abridged in [1873], pp. 84-
        91.

        An essay, drawing its illustrations from Pope, especially
        from his formal satires, that makes the distinction between
        the historical Alexander Pope and the dramatic Alexander
        Pope in order to show how Pope's satiric persona affects the
        qualities of the hero, the ingenue, and the vir bonus to achieve
        comic ends.

1989   " 'Wit and Poetry and Pope': Some Observations on his Im-
        agery. " In [1868], pp. 20-40; rpt. in [18], pp. 21-41.

        Supports the argument that Pope's kind of poetry is a
        "poetry of statement" and discusses some of the aspects of
        reconciliation between qualities of poetry and prose that af-
        fect Pope's imagery.

1990   "Letters of Pope to Atterbury in the Tower. " RES 21 (1945):
        117-125.

        A letter attributed to the Duke of Wharton, a staunch de-
        fender of Atterbury, upon examination proves to be a com-
        posite of two letters written by Pope; speculates how Wharton
        obtained these letters.

1991   MASON, H. A.
        "Nature in Pope and Homer, I: Similes of Inanimate Nature. "
        CQ 5 (1970): 3-24. II. "Similes of Animal Nature. " CQ
        5 (1970): 134-159.

"Pope had the keenest eye for large and small natural effects, and ... he considered possession of a similar eye one
of Homer's greatest gifts." If Pope's translations "annihilated"
inanimate nature, it was "in order to construct something
greater, a Nature that formed a unity with Human Nature."
The second part of the article argues that Pope has "converted
Homer's animal nature to pastoral."

1992   MILLER, JOHN H.
"Pope and the Principle of Reconciliation." TSLL 9 (1967):
185-192.

Pope's efforts to harmonize and reconcile various critical
ideas and religious differences are especially evident in the
Essay on Criticism and The Rape of the Lock.

1993   MONK, SAMUEL HOLT.
"A Grace Beyond the Reach of Art." JHI 5 (1944): 131-150.
Rpt. in [1872], pp. 38-62.

Traces the history of "grace" as a critical term to show
that Pope knew the technical language of criticism and aesthetics when he first used the term in the Essay on Criticism.

1994   NICHOL SMITH, DAVID.
"Pope--Poetic Diction." In [141], pp. 9-30.

Poetry of the eighteenth century and Pope's contributions;
emphasizes that what we today call "poetic diction" perfectly
expresses Pope's meaning and intention, and that his "conventional" diction probably in his own day had the charm of
novelty. Sees Pope as one of the great masters of the familiar style, which is illustrated by the portrait of Atticus.

1995   NICOLSON, MARJORIE HOPE and G. S. ROUSSEAU.
"This Long Disease, My Life": Alexander Pope and the Sci-
ences. Princeton, N.J.: Princeton Univ. Press, 1968.

A study of Pope's health and of his scientific interests:
medicine, astronomy, and geology.

1996   PARKIN, REBECCA PRICE.
"Alexander Pope's Use of Biblical and Ecclesiastical Allusions."
SVEC 57 (1967): 1183-1216.

The brilliance of rhetorical strategems with which Pope
uses Judaeo-Christian material is a tribute to his craftsmanship. Article deals with Messiah, Essay on Man, Eloisa to
Abelard, Rape of the Lock, and the Dunciad.

1997   The Poetic Workmanship of Alexander Pope.   Minneapolis:
        Univ. Minn. Press, 1955.

        A study of such poetic devices as implied dramatic speaker,
        irony, tension, antithesis, paradox, narrative, and metaphor
        in order to demonstrate the close relationship between morality
        and poetic technique.

1998   "The Quality of Alexander Pope's Humor." CE 14 (1953):
        197-202.

        The uses of humor, especially in the Essay on Criticism,
        to sweeten the instruction and to enforce brevity; also the
        contrasting modes of humor in the Essay on Man, The Rape
        of the Lock, Dialogue I of the Epilogue to the Satires, and
        The Dunciad.

1999   "Tension in Alexander Pope's Poetry." UKCR 19 (1953):
        169-173. Rpt. in [1872], 1st edition, pp. 291-296.

        Pope achieves tension in his poetry by transforming the
        mock-epic tension between low subject and high style into a
        three-way tension pointing back to epic seriousness, through
        reference to particular people and events by name, and by
        making syntax or meaning fight against form.

2000   "Alexander Pope's Use of the Implied Dramatic Speaker."
        CE 11 (1949): 137-141.

        Examination of major poems shows that Pope used the de-
        vice of the implied dramatic speaker and "though the use
        varied with the theme and approach adopted for a particular
        poem, it always conduces to a ... greater dramatic tension and
        ... enlarges the possibilities of compression in ideas and
        phrasing ... contributing toward that epigrammatism which
        is so salient a feature of Pope's style."

2001   PAULSON, RONALD.
        "Satire, Poetry, and Pope." In [14], pp. 55-106. Rpt. in
        part in [1871], pp. 45-62.

        An analysis of Pope's satires suggesting they take two
        general forms: one is an emblematic, allegorical, allusive
        anti-Pollio vision of chaos and disorder, and the second be-
        gins with the pastoral Alexis whose tone is never quite lost,
        supporting the strong tendency toward apologia in which the
        satirist defends himself and at the same time produces satire,
        and concludes with the Horatian sermon in which Pope con-
        verses with somebody. Pope's strategy is to take something
        known and metamorphose or restore it.

2002   PIPER, WILLIAM B.
        "The Conversational Poetry of Pope." <u>SEL</u> 10 (1970): 505-524.

           Beginning with <u>An Essay on Criticism</u> and ending with <u>Epilogue to the Satires,</u> Pope's poems are tremendously lively essays in conversation, and tremendously dynamic exercises in common sense, and show his "remarkably deepening sense of the problems and perils involved in rendering serious public topics in a broadly ingratiating way" so that society could be convinced to agree and approve.

2003   PROBYN, CLIVE T.
        "Pope's Bestiary: The Iconography of Deviance." In [1869A], pp. 212-230.

           Pope's animal imagery is unusual: "animal homologues are a habitual element in [his] rhetoric of satiric contempt, vital realizations of [his] imagination, a feature of both style and subject, at times an inseparable amalgam of tenor and vehicle, a way of looking at the world and of man's part in it." Suggests that Pope's "poetic bestiary" may well be the supreme moral achievement of his imagination.

2004   RAWLINSON, DAVID H.
        "Pope and Addison on Classical Greatness." <u>Wascana Rev.</u> 2, No. 2 (1967): 69-74.

           A comparison of Pope's and Addison's prose: Pope's is ordered and neat and animated, Addison's is fashionable but the movement is feebler and the phrasing facile.

2005   REEVES, JAMES.
        <u>The Reputation and Writings of Alexander Pope.</u>   London: Heinemann; New York: Barnes & Noble, 1976.

           Written not for the uncritical devotee but for the general reader concerned with poetic values, and written out of a conviction that Pope's poems have been overvalued in the present century. In Part II, dealing with the poetry, the author attempts to show the reader what he enjoys.

2006   REICHARD, HUGO M.
        "The Independence of Pope as a Political Satirist." <u>JEGP</u> 54 (1955): 309-317.

           Although Pope has been linked, as a political satirist, with the Patriot Opposition in his criticism of the business men and the aristocracy, he concentrates on "vice," not as a so-

cial philosophy of the middle class but as the ethic of an up-
per class that has lost the virtues of a landed aristocracy.

2007   RIELY, JOHN and W. K. WIMSATT.
        "A Supplement to The Portraits of Alexander Pope." In [58],
        pp. 123-164.

        Intended to serve as a guide to the iconography of Pope
        and as biography of Pope, to the extent that portraiture can
        enlarge our understanding of both the man and his works.
        This supplement consists mainly of new entries describing
        portraits that were not in Wimsatt's 1965 volume [2051] or
        that were mentioned only in Appendix 2 as "Unexplained Al-
        lusions to Pope Portraits."

2008   RIVERS, ISABEL.
        The Poetry of Conservatism, 1600-1745: A Study of Poets
        and Public Affairs from Jonson to Pope.   Cambridge: Cam-
        bridge Univ. Press, 1973.

        Pope seen as a poet reflecting a conservative view of so-
        ciety; he comes to distrust his role of national poet, finally
        becoming more interested in his role as a private individual.
        The theme of discordia concors in Windsor-Forest.

2009   ROBERTS, MICHAEL.
        "Pope and English Classicism." Poetry Rev. (May-June,
        1930): 161-170.

        T. E. Hulme's definition of classicism as applied to Pope,
        and a discussion of Miss Sitwell's defense of Alexander Pope
        [2028].

2010   ROGERS, PAT.
        "Pope's Rambles." In [28], pp. 107-118.

        Pope was especially fond of taking a "ramble" (his pre-
        ferred term), though the word usually appears in his letters
        in a slightly disparaging tone.   He possessed one prime char-
        acteristic that made him a perfect traveller--he had a con-
        noisseur's interest in contemporary architecture, and his
        fondness for "romantic" moods anticipated the mid-century
        taste for "evocative twilight scenery and Gothic (not yet truly
        Gothick) appurtenances."

2011   An Introduction to Pope. London: Methuen, 1975.

        Attempts to take note of the latest research; after two

chapters on Pope's historical situation and his art, six chapters are devoted to the major poems; followed by chapters
on his prose and his relationship to his age.

2012   "Pope and the Social Scene." In [1869], pp. 101-142.

Discusses eighteenth-century England and Pope's relationship with four social groups who influenced his writing--the
peer and landowner group, the Country Gentlemen, profes-
sional men, and women; examines poems dedicated to individuals in those groups.

2013   "Pope and the Syntax of Satire." In Literary English Since
Shakespeare, ed. G. Watson (New York: Oxford Univ. Press,
1970), pp. 236-265.

Concerned with Pope's poetic technique; attempts to present
the first part of a "grammar" of his work. Pope, of course,
used the obvious devices of Augustan poetics, as well as exploiting a number of its effects; in particular, Pope and the
Augustans found that "closed syntax" was well suited to their
poetic purposes, especially in aiding them to achieve "that
coherence they habitually sought--that variety of precision
which takes the form of knowing when you are moving from
one thing to the next, and knowing too in what direction that
move takes you."

2014   ROGERS, ROBERT W.
.The Major Satires of Alexander Pope (Illinois Studies in Language and Literature, vol. 40). Urbana: Univ. Ill. Press,
1955.

A discussion of what Pope was trying to say in the Dunciad, the Ethic Epistles, and the Imitations of Horace, and
of the ethical assumptions on which they were based. Considers the nature of his satiric achievement and the origin
of each poem.

2015   "Notes on Alexander Pope's Early Education." SAQ 70 (1971):
236-247.

Limited educational opportunities made Pope a self-taught
poet.

2016   ROOT, ROBERT K.
"Pope's Contributions to the Lintot Miscellanies of 1712 and
1714." ELH 7 (1940): 265-271.

An analysis of Lintot's Miscellanies relative to Pope's contributions of about one-third of the contents suggests that perhaps the dates Pope gives for publication of some of his poems
are correct and not erroneous as some critics believe.

2017   The Poetical Career of Alexander Pope.   Princeton, N. J. :
        Princeton Univ. Press, 1938.

        A series of essays on Pope's poetry, attempting a reap-
        praisal for the 1930s; considers the Canons of Poetic Art
        and the importance of the Heroic Couplet, and then proceeds
        to a detailed analysis of individual poems.   Discusses wit,
        judgment, and invention.

2018   ROUSSEAU, G. S.
        "On Reading Pope." In [1869], pp. 1-59.

        A bibliographic study.

2019   RUSSO, JOHN PAUL.
        Alexander Pope: Tradition and Identity.   Cambridge: Har-
        vard Univ. Press, 1972.

        A survey of Pope's literary career, in which the author
        emphasizes the theme that Pope sought to develop his own
        identity through the study of the classical and English poetic
        tradition.

2020   RYLEY, ROBERT M.
        "Warburton, Warton, and Ruffhead's Life of Pope." PLL 4
        (1968): 51-62.

        Demonstrates that a great deal more of Ruffhead's opinions
        and stylistic mannerisms, and much less of Warburton's, re-
        mains in the Life of Pope than most scholars have assumed;
        but the general reply to Warton's criticism of Pope represents
        Warburton's own opinions.

2021   SAMBROOK, JAMES.
        "Pope and the Visual Arts." In [1869], pp. 143-171.

        Deals with Pope's taste in painting, sculpture, architecture,
        and gardening; his grotto; and the relationship between art
        and nature in his poetry; illustrations.

2022   SELDEN, RAMAN.
        "The 18th-Century Horace: Pope and Swift." In [159], pp.
        119-152.

Concerned with the revival of the Horatian tradition, especially in the coterie surrounding George Granville "the polite"; this "coterie cultivated refinement and correctness in diction and prosody, and consolidated the development of a rigorously plain-style classicism." Swift, in spite of his low-style realism and philosophical bitterness, is regarded as essentially a Horatian poet. Edward Young, in his Love of Fame, tried to be a public scourge and a man of feeling, but failed to gain success in either role. Pope's success is defined as the perfecting of the "plain-style Horatian voice," while Swift is praised for extending the "scope of the autobiographical Horatian voice by multiplying points of view and by introducing an existential bitterness into the Horation candour."

2023   SHERBURN, GEORGE.
"Pope and 'The Great Shew of Nature.'" In [31], pp. 306-315.

Concerned with the shaping influence that physical science had upon Pope's art.

2024   "Pope at Work." In [54], pp. 49-64.

Notes from Joseph Spence taken in the spring of 1730 relative to a study of the working manuscripts of some of Pope's poems and the manner in which he put his ideas on paper.

2025   The Early Career of Alexander Pope, 1688-1727. Oxford: Clarendon Press, 1934; rpt. 1968.

A fully documented narrative of Pope's early life; indispensable.

2026   SIGWORTH, OLIVER F.
"Alexander Pope: Renaissance and Modern Poet." Ariz. Quart. 31 (1975): 249-264.

An informal discussion of Pope as a "modern" because he was "the first major poet truly alienated from the power structure of his society."

2027   SIMON, IRENE.
"Pope and the Fragility of Beauty." Revue des Langues Vivantes 24 (1958): 377-394.

Insists that Pope was not complacent, but had in fact a strong feeling for the transitory nature of things.

2028   SITWELL, EDITH.
        Alexander Pope. London: Faber & Faber, 1930.

        A poet's appreciation of another poet, and a strong de-
        fense of Pope's character.

2029   SPACKS, PATRICIA M.
        "Pope's Satiric Use of Nature." Std. in Lit. Imag. 5 (1972):
        39-52.

        Looks at a number of Pope's poems to show how he uses
        the "attractive aspects of nature for complex satiric purposes,"
        and how he concerns himself "with the ways in which human
        modes of action affect our understanding of natural process."
        To look at nature through Pope's eyes, "the reader sees true
        and false juxtaposed, and sees how--and at what cost--they
        can be separated," and to "focus on nature in the ways Pope
        does is an emphatic technique of rooting satire in the real."

2030   An Argument of Images: The Poetry of Alexander Pope.
        Cambridge: Harvard Univ. Press, 1971.

        Analyzes Pope's imagery as representing principles of
        aesthetic control, and distinguishes three kinds of imagery
        controlled by wit, perception, and judgment in, respectively,
        Essay on Criticism, Essay on Man, and the Dunciad. Also
        discusses the methods of expressing through imagery the prob-
        lem of ethical control, concentrating on three areas of ref-
        erence: imagery of character, imagery that directly alludes
        to or defines standards and limits, and imagery of madness.

2031   "The Search for Sincerity." CE 29 (1968): 591-602.

        A discussion of "poetic sincerity" and its use by Pope,
        Donne, and Eliot.

2032   STEVENSON, SAMUEL W.
        " 'Romantic' Tendencies in Pope." ELH 1 (1934): 126-155.

        Traces the continuance of Pope's youthful romantic inter-
        ests in his later works; regards those interests as real, not
        superficial.

2033   SUTHERLAND, W. O. S., JR.
        "Object to Symbol." In [173], pp. 25-80.

        Discusses The Rape of the Lock, Absalom and Achitophel,
        Hudibras, and Epistle to Dr. Arbuthnot from the standpoint

that their values and aesthetics are more important than their
origins or milieu.

2034   SYPHER, WYLIE.
       "Arabesque in Verse (Reconsiderations III)." KR 7 (1945):
       456-466.

       A critical consideration of Pope's poetry in light of Fiske
       Kimball's book on The Creation of the Rococo.

2035   TILLOTSON, GEOFFREY.
       "The Methods of Description in Eighteenth-and Nineteenth-Century
       Poetry." In [13], pp. 235-238.

       Two syntactical methods of description: that of Milton,
       Thomson, and Pope contrasted with that of Gray and the nine-
       teenth century.

2036   "Pope and the Common Reader." SR 66 (1958): 44-78.

       A discussion of Pope's language and versification, and of
       his use of invention and imagination in the "making" of poetry,
       especially as they affected his desire to appeal to the com-
       mon reader.

2037   Pope and Human Nature.   Oxford: Clarendon Press, 1958.

       On Pope's subject matter, dealing with such topics as con-
       cepts of human nature and man's place in the scale of being,
       man and his feelings, the meaning of "Truth" to Pope and
       the relation of particular to general truth, and the relation
       of the beautiful to Nature; the final chapters consider the ex-
       tent to which Pope's work agrees with or departs from those
       central ideas.

2038   "Alexander Pope, I and II." In Essays in Criticism and Re-
       search (Cambridge: Cambridge Univ. Press, 1942; rpt. Ham-
       den, Conn., Archon Books, 1967), pp. 86-104.

       A discussion of Pope's ability as a poet: how his sense
       of beauty was so closely and continuously allied to his sense
       of human values, and how he allowed the age in which he
       lived to dictate what poems he should write.

2039   On the Poetry of Pope.   Oxford: Clarendon Press, 1938;
       2nd ed., 1950.

Considers such topics as Pope's diction, the concept of correctness, nature, "stratification" (layer upon layer of complex meaning, partly derived from phrasal echoes of earlier poets), and Pope's description.

2040   TOBIN, JAMES E.
"Alexander Pope and Classical Tradition." Quart. Bull. Polish Inst. 3 (1945): 343-354.

Pope and Horace as craftsmen.

2041   TORCHIANA, DONALD T.
"Brutus: Pope's Last Hero." JEGP 61 (1962): 853-867. Rpt. in [1872], pp. 705-723.

Relates the general scheme of Brutus to Pope's opposition to Walpole, to the third epistle of the Essay on Man, and to the fourth book of the 1743 Dunciad. Concludes that the Essay on Man celebrates man's precarious glory, that the Dunciad mocks his precipitous ruin, and that Brutus suggests the means for his redemption or restoration.

2042   TRICKETT, RACHEL.
The Honest Muse: A Study in Augustan Verse.   Oxford: Clarendon Press, 1967.

Concerned with the "attitudes and assumptions" underlying the poetry of Dryden, Pope, and Johnson; discusses the "three main forms" of poetry inherited by the Augustans--satire, panegyric, and elegy--and analyzes the structure, tone, and imagery of individual poems.   Also presents some common ideas in Restoration poetry which were prominent in the Augustan period.

2043   WARREN, AUSTIN.
"The Mask of Pope." SR 54 (1946): 19-33. Revised as "Alexander Pope" and rpt. in Rage for Order (Ann Arbor: Univ. Mich. Press, 1948; rpt. as Ann Arbor Paperback, 1959), pp. 37-51; rpt. in [1872], pp. 58-96.

Pope as a neo-classical poet; The Rape of the Lock and the Dunciad his burlesque masterpieces.   His development proceeded from the "elegantly decorative to the richly--even the grotesquely--expressive."

2044   Alexander Pope as Critic and Humanist (Princeton Studies in English, No. 1).   Princeton, N.J.: Princeton Univ. Press, 1929; Gloucester, Mass.: Peter Smith, 1963.

Surveys Pope's critical works--Essay on Criticism, commentary on Homer, the edition of Shakespeare, and the Dunciad--summarizes his poetic theory, and discusses his knowledge of classical, continental, and English literature.

2045   WASSERMAN, EARL R.
"The Return of the Enjambed Couplet." ELH 7 (1940): 239-252.

Surveys the more significant events and their causes in the revival of the emjambed couplet before Leigh Hunt.

2046   WELLINGTON, JAMES E.
"Pope and Charity." PQ 46 (1967): 225-235.

Pope's view of charity as expressed in the Epistle to Bathurst, Essay on Man, and the Odyssey shows that his attitude is essentially biblical and that he was not as indifferent to human suffering as he has been accused of being.

2047   WILLIAMS, AUBREY.
"Alexander Pope's 'Knack' at Versifying." In ... All These to Teach: Essays in honor of C. A. Robertson, ed. Robert A. Bryan, et al. (Gainesville: Univ. Fla. Press, 1965), pp. 171-179.

A study of Pope's poetic strategies, especially his "knack" of concealing art by an apparent "easiness, a natural inevitability of thought and movement" that has lead many readers to suppose that that which appears easy cannot be good or profound.   Illustrates briefly some of the metrical variety in Pope's verses.

2048   "Submerged Metaphor in Pope." EIC 9 (1959): 197-201; see also 437-439 and 440-443.

A reply to Max Bluestone's essay, "The Suppressed Metaphor in Pope," [1894].   Williams denies that the passage from An Essay on Criticism II, 305-336, displays imagery that is either suppressed or "otiose," and rejects Bluestone's argument that Pope sees metaphor "essentially as ornament."

2049   WILLIAMS, KATHLEEN.
"The Moralized Song: Some Renaissance Themes in Pope." ELH 41 (1974): 578-601.

Spenser's influence on Pope, especially in Windsor-Forest and An Essay on Man.

2050   WIMSATT, W. K., JR.
        "An Image in Pope." In [26], pp. 55-65.

        Relationship among six portraits of Pope painted between
        1742 and 1800.

2051   The Portraits of Alexander Pope. New Haven: Yale Univ.
        Press, 1965.

        A catalogue raisonné of all known portraits of Pope, with
        more than 200 illustrations, supporting the "importance to
        him of having an adequate image of himself made public, and
        his apparently persistent efforts toward that end."

2052   "Rhetoric and Poems: the Example of Pope." In English
        Institute Essays, ed. D. A. Robertson (New York: Columbia
        Univ. Press, 1949). Rpt. in The Verbal Icon: Studies in the
        Meaning of Poetry (Lexington: Univ. Ky. Press, 1954), pp.
        169-185.

        The relationship between theory and poems and the way in
        which Pope makes extensive and varied use of literary theory
        as poetic material.

2053   "One Relation of Rhyme to Reason: Alexander Pope." MLQ
        5 (1944): 323-338. Rpt. in [1872], pp. 63-84; The Verbal
        Icon: Studies in the Meaning of Poetry (Lexington: Univ.
        Ky. Press, 1954), pp. 153-166; [7], pp. 304-320.

        A discussion of rhyme as it "makes variation against the
        parallels of verse," and of the "sameness of the rhyme sound
        as a binding force" when applied to English rhyme, especially
        to the neoclassical rhyme of Pope. Verse gives to poetry a
        quality of the concrete and particular, largely because its
        alogical character imposes upon the meaning a counter-pattern.

2054   WINSLOW, ANN.
        "Re-evaluation of Pope's Treatment of Nature." Univ. Wyo.
        Publ. 4, No. 2 (1938): 21-43.

        An analysis of Pope's poetry, primarily Windsor-Forest,
        with respect to his use of nature images in an attempt to
        show that Pope had much in common with the Romantics and
        that the difference was one of technique; Pope believed that
        "each phase of nature, including man, had its own prescribed
        place in the universe."

2055   WOODMAN, TOM.
        "Pope and the Polite." EIC 28 (1978): 19-37.

Pope's poetic career as seen in terms of his dialogue with the tradition of "politeness." Pope was able to write in the "sublime mode" but still incorporate wit and skepticism into his work; he could be both comic and serious, and he was capable of "both using and transcending the themes and techniques of the polite mode."

2056   WYLD, H. C.
"Observations on Pope's Versification." MLR 25 (1930): 274-285.

Considers the chief means by which Pope obtains infinite variety of movement in the couplet. Emphasizes the importance of speed.

See also: 243, 498, 967, 990, 1597, 1817, 3063, 3141

Pastorals

2057   BATTESTIN, MARTIN C.
"The Transforming Power: Nature and Art in Pope's Pastorals." ECS 2 (1969): 183-204. Rpt. in [1871], pp. 80-105.

Discusses Pope's vision of the Golden Age in which the poet's words and numbers have the transforming power to remind us of the identity of Art and Nature that once existed in Eden. Art is the sole means of re-creating the Golden Age; it is only through the idealizing powers of the poetic imagination that a return to Nature can be effected: that is the paradox of the pastoral.

2058   BOIRE, GARY A.
"The Context of Allusion and Pope's 'Winter' Pastoral." CP 10, i, (1977): 79-84.

The Pastorals contain Pope's first attempt to create a symbiotic relationship between allusion and context: "Pope reforms the traditional eclogue and infuses it with a highly personal, highly particularized poetic voice." The poem, a "threnodic diatribe" on the failure of true Wit and the death of the poetic principle, represents Pope's criticism of contemporary culture and his view that it was disintegrating before the rise of cultural Dulness. "Winter", therefore, is an early attempt to expose the horrors of Dulness.

2059   DURANT, DAVID S.
"Man and Nature in Alexander Pope's Pastorals." SEL 11 (1971): 469-485.

Pope, in his Pastorals, develops a theory of the relationship between nature and art, proceeding from "Spring," in
which art reflects nature, to the final "Winter" where nature
becomes subservient to the poet and is used merely to depict
man: the study of man through man replaces the study of
man through nature.

2060   FINEMAN, DANIEL A.
       "The Motivation of Pope's Guardian 40."   MLN 67 (1952):
       24-28.

       The traditional explanation of Pope's motive for writing
       Guardian 40, that he was angered by the conspiracy of silence
       against his pastorals by members of Addison's literary coterie,
       is disputed: Pope was mentioned in Guardian 30, but it was
       the equivocal nature of the reference that provoked Pope into
       writing No. 40.

2061   JUSSEL, RICHARD.
       "Time and Pope's 'Pastorals.' "   PVR 8 (1980): 65-68.

       Shows how Pope structures the argument of the "Pastorals"
       in time to create "his major antithesis: Art and Nature exist
       in time but are not subject to its destruction."

2062   MELCHIORI, GIORGIO.
       "Pope in Arcady: The Theme of Et in Arcadia ego in his
       Pastorals."   Eng. Misc. 14 (1963):   83-93.   Rpt. in [1872],
       pp. 149-158.

       The theme of death in the Pastorals: the sense of the
       human condition, from Pope's youthful work to his most adult,
       adds a further dimension of greatness.

2063   PROVOST, FOSTER.
       "Pope's Pastorals: An Exercise in Poetical Technique."
       In Contributions to the Humanities, 1954 (Louisiana State
       Univ. Studies: Humanities Series, No. 5.   Baton Rouge: La.
       State Univ. Press, 1954), pp. 25-37.

       Pope's techniques of versification and total poetic effect in
       his pastoral eclogues are experimental and the basis of his
       later works.

2064   ROGERS, PAT.
       "Rhythm and Recoil in Pope's Pastorals."   ECS 14 (1980):
       1-17.

Analyzes some of the repetitive effects in the Pastorals and indicates what they seem to be doing. Pope intends to reenact the natural cycle: the "rowling Year," the cause of human life, and the progress of the day: "The elaborate symmetries and echoes ... are a way of rendering cyclical events; the surges and diminuendos in the expressive medium relate to troughs and crests of human life as we experience it as a temporal process." Concludes that Pope was in close contact with the doctrine and techniques of the Renaissance than he was later in his career.

An Essay on Criticism

2065   ADEN, JOHN M.
       "The Doctrinal Design of An Essay on Criticism."   CE 22
       (1961): 311-315.

       Pope's concern is with what art is and how it is to be at-
       tained (by the poet) and appreciated (by the critic); art has
       its beginning and its end in nature.

2066   " 'First Follow Nature': Strategy and Stratification in An Es-
       say on Criticism." JEGP 55 (1956): 604-617.

       Discusses how Pope masses, in "First Follow Nature,"
       devices of rhetoric, antithesis (tension), rhythm, ambiguity,
       allusion, imagery, and symbolism, but refrains from these
       devices in the "grace beyond the reach of art" passage.

2067   ATKINS, G. DOUGLAS.
       "Poetic Strategies in An Essay on Criticism, Lines 201-559."
       SAB 44, iv (1979): 43-47.

       The poetic continuity that Pope imposes on the "least ad-
       mired section" of the poem possesses an organizing principle
       in the "parts-whole problem": it "functions as an important
       device to unify the section and to connect with major themes,
       and it also allows Pope to exhibit the wit and judgment he
       has earlier called for in the critic"--that is the central mora
       concern of the Essay.

2068   BENSON, JAMES D.
       "Confusion in An Essay on Criticism and The Dunciad." Enl.
       E. 3 (1972): 3-6.

       Pope's denunciation of critics and the differences in the
       poetic purposes of the two poems.

2069   BOGUE, RONALD L.
        "The Meaning of 'Grace' in Pope's Aesthetic." PMLA 94
        (1979): 434-448.

        Suggests what Pope meant by grace by showing "that the
        usual notion of grace renders Pope's aesthetic incoherent;
        that [his] remarks on grace can be seen as an important and
        harmonious aspect of his poetic theory stated in An Essay on
        Criticism; that [his] appreciation of Homer, the prime ex-
        emplar of grace, is compatible with his basic poetic theory;
        and that grace arises from the proper imitation of Nature,
        which [he] regards as the basic principle underlying all artis-
        tic creation."

2070   CAMERON, J. M.
        "Mr. Tillotson and Mr. Pope." Dublin Rev. 233 (1959):
        153-170. Rpt. in The Night Battle (Baltimore: Helicon Press,
        1962); abridged as "Pope's Use of 'Nature' " in [1873], pp.
        54-62.

        Examines An Essay on Criticism to show that "Pope is
        not relying upon the concept of nature as defined by Tillotson
        (2037); and that Pope uses the ambiguities of the concept--
        ambiguities which arise out of its complex history--in order
        to frame, not a critical argument in any way to be compared
        with the critical work of Aristotle or Johnson or Coleridge,
        but a poem capable of evoking an attitude to criticism and to
        the subject-matter of criticism."

2071   DeLISLE, HAROLD F.
        "Structure in Part I of Pope's Essay on Criticism." ELN 1
        (1963): 14-17.

        "A simplified outline of the structure reveals that Pope
        framed Part I of the Essay in accordance with the traditional
        divisions of a classical oration which is appropriate to argu-
        mentation."

2072   EMPSON, WILLIAM.
        "Wit in the Essay on Criticism." HR 2 (1950): 559-577.
        Rpt. in Structure of Complex Words (London: Chatto & Win-
        dus, 1951), pp. 84-100; [1872], 208-226.

        Analysis and history of the word "wit" and how the struc-
        ture of its meaning is built up by Pope through repeated use
        in the Essay.

2073   FENNER, ARTHUR.

"The Unity of Pope's Essay on Criticism." PQ 39 (1960): 435-446. In [1872], 227-241.

Attempts to prove that the Essay on Criticism is a "rather admirably unified poem": it possesses transitions between couplets and paragraphs, and a thematic movement between sections, with the controlling idea of pride brooding over the entire poem.

2074   FISHER, ALAN S.
"Cheerful Noonday, 'Gloomy' Twilight: Pope's Essay on Criticism." PQ 51 (1972): 832-844.

Suggests the implications for Pope's critical thought of two analogies found in the Essay on Criticism: the relation of criticism, first, to politics, and second, to religion. Concludes that Pope's triple equation of religion, politics, and criticism represents a universality that regards all activities of the human spirit as one--that is the fundamental creed of Pope's "group," and goes far towards explaining their "gloom.

2075   FOGLE, RICHARD H.
"Metaphors of Organic Unity in Pope's Essay on Criticism." TSE 13 (1963): 51-58.

Discussion of Romantic organicism (Coleridge) and Pope's use of extended metaphors that contained many of the characteristic marks of organicist doctrine.

2076   GRIFFITH, R. H.
"Early Warburton? or Late Warburton?" Univ. of Texas Studies in English (1940): pp. 123-131.

Traces variants in a passage of the Essay on Criticism to Warburton's meddling.

2077   HAMM, VICTOR M.
"Pope and Malebranche: A Note on the Essay on Criticism, Part II." PQ 24 (1945): 65-70.

Suggests that the "spirit and method of Malebranche's inquiry are reflected in Pope's enumeration and illustration of the obstacles to critical judgment"; compares Part Two of the Essay with Part Two of Book II of the Recherche by Malebranche.

2078   HOOKER, EDWARD NILES.
"Pope on Wit: The Essay on Criticism." In [31], pp. 225-

246. Rpt. in [18], pp. 42-61; [1873], pp. 63-76; [1872], pp.
185-207.

Addresses itself to three questions: 1) why does Pope
lavish space and attention on wit rather than on taste? 2) what
were the controversies at the time Pope was writing the poem
that caused him to take a stand and how is that stand established in the Essay? and 3) what body of contemporary thought
was available to him and how did it illumine the direction
and implications of his thinking?

2079   HOTCH, RIPLEY.
        "Pope Surveys His Kingdom: An Essay on Criticism." SEL
        13 (1973): 474-487.

Shows how the Essay is designed to show Pope's qualifica-
tions for his position as heir to the throne of poetry--his
taste, learning, judgment, truth, candor, and tact.

2080   ISLES, DUNCAN.
        "Pope and Criticism." In [1869], pp. 250-285.

A survey of the nature and particular emphases of Pope's
literary criticism from the beginning, which included An Essay on Criticism, through the 1711-to-1729 period when his
activities as a literary theorist and practical critic were at
their height, to the great satires and imitations of the 1730s.

2081   KALLICH, MARTIN.
        "Image and Theme in Pope's Essay on Criticism." BSUF
        8, no. 3 (1967): 54-60.

Describes Pope's poetic imagination and the unifying function of images in the Essay.

2082   "Pegasus on the Seesaw: Balance and Antithesis in Pope's
        Essay on Criticism." TSL 12 (1967): 57-68.

A rhetorical analysis of the way in which Pope uses antithesis to express the theme, and to impart imaginative unity
and intensity to An Essay on Criticism. Balanced images
suggest the need for balance and design in art.

2083   LOTSPEICH, C. M.
        "The Metrical Technique of Pope's Illustrative Couplets."
        JEGP 26 (1927): 471-474.

An interpretation of lines 364-73 of Essay on Criticism,

illustrating Pope's principle that in good poetry the sound
must seem an echo to the sense.

2084   MARKS, EMERSON R.
       "Pope on Poetry and the Poet." Criticism 12 (1970): 271-
       280.

       Discusses Pope in light of Matthew Arnold's criticism that
       since Pope's poetry was "conceived and composed" in the wits
       rather than in the soul, it was not genuine poetry, with the
       opinion of Sainte-Beuve that Pope was a classical poet by vo-
       cation and by inborn originality.

2085   MORRIS, DAVID B.
       "Civilized Reading: The Act of Judgment in An Essay on Cri-
       ticism." In [1869A], pp. 15-39.

       Morris proposes an unfashionable interpretation, that "An
       Essay on Criticism is an original and significant document
       in the history of critical theory," emphasizing in particular
       that Pope thought deeply and seriously about the problems
       and nature of literary criticism.   The Essay represents a
       major effort to place English criticism on the foundation of
       a coherent theory.

2086   PARK, DOUGLAS B.
       " 'At Once the Source, and End': Nature's Defining Pattern
       in An Essay on Criticism." PMLA 90 (1975): 861-873.

       Discusses how "Pope's poetry transforms and unifies the
       apparent commonplaces that are the raw material of An Es-
       say on Criticism." At the center of Pope's vision of art and
       criticism is "an image of Nature, created by explicit imagery"
       and unobtrusive puns. "From this image, analogical patterns
       of meaning radiate out into the poem, appearing and reappear-
       ing in different forms and contexts ... suffusing and helping
       to unify the whole."

2087   PETTIT, HENRY.
       "Apposite Metaphor in Pope's Essay on Criticism." BA 35
       (1961): 225-230.

       Concludes that "the imagery is fully effective only at an
       intellectual level" and "that taken altogether the images form
       a pattern which not only accentuates the theme but aids in its
       statement." Examines the watch, light, and prism-glass im-
       ages in Part II.

2088   RAMSEY, PAUL.

"The Watch of Judgment: Relativism and An Essay on Criticism." In [2], pp. 128-139.

Explores some of the real and apparent discrepencies in
technique and doctrine--flatness of style, conflict of intentions, contradictions on subject of Reason--and argues in particular that the judgments in the poem are not relativistic;
that Pope is an aesthetic absolutist.

2089   REICHARD, HUGO M.
"Pope's Exacting Course in Criticism." SAQ 75 (1976): 470-
482.

A discussion of the Essay on Criticism as instruction in
the art of criticism in which Pope appears to be talking to
non-specialists while at the same time being "insidiously rigorous." That rigor is necessary for the sake of the poem's
point and unity, its place in Pope's oeuvre, and its range of
appeal. Modern readers can find in the Essay "some of the
most dramatic and artful teaching since Socrates."

2090   SANDERS, CHARLES.
" 'First Follow Nature': An Annotation." ES 49 (1968): 289-
302.

Suggests that Pope's famous injunction illustrates the Horatian rhetorical-cautionary tradition, as codified by Vida and
Boileau; and that Pope, following Vida through Mulgrave and
Roscommon, used "Nature" in the sense of the mean or con-
cord between reason and imagination, between judgment and
wit.

2091   SPACKS, PATRICIA M.
"Imagery and Method in An Essay on Criticism." PMLA 85
(1970): 97-106. Rpt. in [1871], pp. 106-130.

The method of the poem "is to demonstrate how wit can
operate, through imagery, as both controlling and creative
power." Argues that Pope sought to enlarge the function of
imagery and to supply a logic of metaphor in order to achieve
an organic unity that would demonstrate the power of wit to
organize as well as to decorate a didactic theme.

2092   STEIN, WILLIAM BYSSHE.
"Pope's 'An Essay on Criticism': The Play of Sophia." Bucknell Rev. 13, iii (1965): 75-86.

Pope's adroit manipulation of light imagery and his equation
of Sophia and "true wit."

2093   WEATHERSBY, HARRELL.
       "An Analysis of Pope's An Essay on Criticism and Thomson's
       'Winter' as Examples of Burke's Concepts of the Beautiful
       and the Sublime." SoQ 10 (1972): 375-383.

       Examines the antithetical nature of the two terms, in order
       to "elucidate a microcosmic view of the larger struggle out
       of which issued a major break in the aesthetic continuity" that
       goes back to the Greeks; analyzes An Essay on Criticism as
       an example of the neoclassical idea of the Beautiful and Thom-
       son's "Winter" as an example of the Sublime.

See also: 243, 1879, 1894, 1949, 1981, 1992, 1993, 1998, 2030, 2044,
    2048

                         Windsor-Forest

2094   CLEMENTS, FRANCES M.
       "Lansdowne, Pope, and the Unity of Windsor-Forest." MLQ
       33 (1972): 44-53.

       Argues that Windsor-Forest achieves unity not only by the
       fusion of scenic, moral, and political correspondences, but
       also by using Lord Lansdowne as a unifying figure of a poet
       who is better able than Pope himself to describe in Part 2
       (ll. 219-434) the future glories of Britain that will follow
       from the Peace of Utrecht.

2095   HAUSER, DAVID R.
       "Pope's Lodona and the Uses of Mythology." SEL 6 (1966):
       465-482.

       Explores the manner in which Pope absorbs and reshapes
       traditional materials for his own purposes in Windsor-Forest.

2096   HEUSTON, EDWARD.
       "Windsor-Forest and Guardian 40." RES 29 (1978): 160-
       168.

       The significance of Windsor-Forest is that the closing lines
       comment on the reception of Pope's pastorals and apparently
       provoked a witty rejoinder by Tickell in his Guardian essays.
       He taunts Pope in Guardian 30, a fact that influenced Guardian
       40 in two important ways. Pope takes over the taunt's stra-
       tegy of mocking praise: Pope praises the poems of Philips
       and damns his own--for ridiculous reasons; and he singles
       out Addison for ridicule, as well as Tickell and Philips.

2097   KIEHL, JAMES M.
        "Windsor-Forest as Epical Counterpart." Thoth 7 (1966):
        53-67.

        Windsor-Forest, when viewed as a epical innovation, ac-
        quires the meaning it lacks when viewed as a pastoral georgic,
        or topographical poem.

2098   MARSHALL, W. GERALD.
        "Pope's Windsor-Forest as Providential History." TSL 24
        (1979): 82-93.

        To show the influence of providential visions of history on
        the poem, the following contextual and artistic elements are
        explored: "sermons and other writings contemporary to the
        Treaty of Utrecht which envision the treaty as a direct mani-
        festation of Providence and as an occasion to view all of
        British history as being under divine guidance; the poem's
        temporal perspective; its system of retributive justice; images
        of growth, pregnancy, and fruition; and ... its use of com-
        merce as symbol of providential direction for the historical
        process."

2099   MILLER, RACHEL A.
        "Regal Hunting: Dryden's Influence on Windsor-Forest."
        ECS 13 (1979-80): 169-188.

        Pope is deeply indebted to Dryden's Fables for Windsor-
        Forest's imaginative design and satiric technique. Both "con-
        demn William III, tyranny, and imperialist warfare through
        the hunt, both celebrate Stuart succession and peace, and
        both attempt to direct the nation toward art and trade." Some
        of the significant parallels are: "the governing symbol of
        concordia discors, the image of the hunter hunted, and the
        reliance on Ovidian myth."

2100   MOORE, JOHN ROBERT.
        "Windsor Forest and William III." MLN 66 (1951): 451-454.
        Rpt. in [1872], pp. 242-246.

        Discusses the use of Tory propaganda in the poem.

2101   MORRIS, DAVID B.
        "Virgilian Attitudes in Pope's Windsor-Forest." TSLL 15
        (1973): 231-250. Rpt. in [1871], pp. 131-158.

        Pope's imitation of Virgil consists in such general attitudes
        as a permanent loyalty to the civilized and civilizing ideals
        of "humanitas" rather than in "verbal echoes and structural
        similarities."

2102   ROGERS, PAT.
        "Windsor-Forest, Britannia, and River Poetry." SP 77 (1980)
        283-299.

        We can better understand Windsor-Forest if we recognize
        its roots in the Renaissance river-poem De Connubio Tamae
        et Isis which was used by Camden in his Britannia.   In ad-
        dition to numerous verbal parallels, there is a striking identity
        of purpose.   Both poets "focus their nationalistic and patri-
        otic themes in a local image," the River Thames.   When
        Father Thames enters Windsor-Forest, "the generic motifs
        of river-poetry become more prominent."

2103   "Time and Space in Windsor-Forest." In [1869A], pp. 40-
        51.

        Insists that the elements that make up Windsor-Forest are
        blended in such a way as to create particular imaginative ef-
        fects: by alternating time and place, landscape and retrospec-
        tion, Pope uses the device of displacement to make "a richer
        and more resonant statement." The meaning "expands in two
        related but separate dimensions ... time passes but the scene
        remains the same; or the scene changes but the golden age
        is renewed, and so on." The shifting patterns of like and un-
        like features give Windsor-Forest its special quality.

2104   "Trade and Dominion: Annus Mirabilis and Windsor-Forest."
        DUJ 59 (1976): 14-20.

        Argues that Annus Mirabilis was a "strong and direct" in-
        fluence on Windsor-Forest and that the similarities extend
        from verbal echoes to a close identity in rhetorical aim. The
        influence is of the most straightforward kind: Annus Mirablis
        "is not a passive analogue, feebly paraphrased here and there
        it is an important source of key ideas and images for Windsor
        Forest."

2105   " 'The Enamelled Ground': The Language of Heraldry and
        Natural Description in Windsor-Forest." Studia Neophilologica
        45 (1973): 356-371. Rpt. in [1871], pp. 159-176.

        "The iconographic descriptions in the poem are not those
        of landscape painting: they lie within the metaphor of heraldry
        which Pope, knowingly or unknowingly, adopted."

2106   VARNEY, A. J.
        "The Composition of Pope's Windsor-Forest." DUJ 36 (1975):
        57-67.

While allowing for the thematic unity of the poem, the author seeks to vindicate Pope's account of its composition, in substance if not in matters of exact dating, and to show that it is more of a patchwork than is generally allowed.

2107   WASSERMAN, EARL R.
        The Subtler Language. Baltimore: Johns Hopkins Univ. Press, 1959. Rpt. 1968.

        Chapter IV: "Pope: Windsor-Forest." The theme of concordia discors is evoked by the symbol of the forest, with the three hunts forming a unit with a possible political center.

See also: 1906, 1987, 2008, 2049, 2054

                            The Rape of the Lock

2108   BABB, LAURENCE.
        "The Cave of Spleen." RES 12 (1936): 165-176.

        The Augustan meaning and connotation of the Cave of Spleen passage in The Rape of the Lock; examines various Tudor and Stuart treatises on melancholy, and describes the characteristics of the disorder.

2109   BARKER, ROSALIND.
        "A Note on Belinda's 'Sev'nfold Fence.'" W & L 3 (1975): 39.

        Belinda's "sev'nfold Fence" in The Rape of the Lock refers not only to the shield of Ajax in the Iliad, but also to Antony's mention of the same shield in Shakespeare's Antony and Cleopatra, a reference that provides a love/war context that makes "Belinda's ultimate susceptibility to sexual love the more inevitable."

2110   BEYETTE, KENT.
        "Milton and Pope's The Rape of the Lock." SEL 16 (1976): 421-436.

        The moral judgment in the poem is controlled by Miltonic allusion. Pope's sylphs are indebted to Milton's angels, and their mission is "to establish perspectives on the central action--they are most important in understanding Pope's attitude toward Belinda, before and after her 'fall,'" which "implies far more than ... her chastity, and she violates

more, too, than the standards of 'taste.' She violates the
true character of woman. "

2111   BROOKS, CLEANTH.
        "The Case of Miss Arabella Fermor: a Re-examination. "
        SR 51 (1943): 505-524. Rpt. in The Well Wrought Urn:
        Studies in the Structure of Poetry (New York: Reynal &
        Hitchcock, 1947), pp. 74-95; in [1870], pp. 93-110; [2135],
        pp. 135-153; [2166], pp. 21-37; [1872], pp. 247-265.

        The epic framework of The Rape of the Lock and the char-
        acter of Belinda--a goddess or a frivolous tease? Also dis-
        cusses Pope's attitude toward Belinda, metaphoric patterns,
        the role of the sylphs, sexual implications, the importance of
        the chastity theme.

2112   BROWER, REUBEN A.
        "Am'rous Causes. " In [1902], pp. 142-162. Rpt. in [2166],
        52-68; [2135], 180-200.

        Discusses Pope's reliance on Dryden and the heroic tradi-
        tion in his composition of The Rape of the Lock.

2113   BROWN, JACK R.
        "It's All in the Cards: Pope's Game of Ombre in The Rape
        of the Lock. " W. Va. Assoc. Coll. Eng. Teachers News
        Bull. 1, no. 2 (1955): 16-21.

        An explanation of the game of Ombre, and of how the lines
        "serve Pope's purposes in the poem as a whole and illustrate
        certain principles of eighteenth century poetry. "

2114   CASE, ARTHUR E.
        "The Game of Ombre in The Rape of the Lock. " In Studies
        in English, Department of English, the Univ. of Texas, 1944
        (Austin: Univ. Texas, 1945), pp. 191-196.

        An attempt to clarify issues about the game raised by
        Tillotson and Morrah and by Bateson by analyzing the content
        of the hands and the manner in which the cards were played.

2115   CLEVER, GLENN.
        "The Narrative Effectiveness of Pope's The Rape of the Lock
        and The Dunciad. " JNT 1 (1971): 122-134.

        Especially concerned with The Rape of the Lock (The Dun-
        ciad's narrative is less effective); the author emphasizes the
        progressive nature of the narrative which develops such dis-

tancing devices as epic parallel, couplet antithesis, and static characters; as a progress poem, The Rape of the Lock exhibits three aspects of mock-heroic: the heroic ideal, the mockery of that ideal, and the real.

2116   COHEN, MURRAY.
"Versions of the Lock: Readers of 'The Rape of the Lock.' "
ELH 43 (1976): 53-73.

The poem's subject is the "nature of meaning, and its method is a careful discrimination among ways of reading." An analysis of the concluding stanzas "should give us insight into how the poem works and why it has been read in the ways that it has." The problem of right reading is the problem of how one interprets words and what is the proper relationship between words, ideas, and things. Right reading involves a metaphoric sense which perceives analogy without succumbling to "object identification ... or ... to symbolic reification"; it lets us "see that the poem is what it makes us do as readers--to recognize difference, distance, and the dangers of self-deception. "

2117   COHEN, RALPH.
"The Reversal of Gender in The Rape of the Lock. " SAB 37, no. 4 (1972): 54-60.

Discusses the reversal of sex roles among the men and women, and the way in which that reversal is mirrored in the poem's mythological machinery: the inversion matches the mock-epic form.

2118   "Transformation in The Rape of the Lock. " ECS 2 (1969): 205-224.

Discusses natural or normal change and unnatural or artificial change in The Rape of the Lock; various kinds of transformation are seen as the primary method of development in the poem, whose composition is also realized through transformation. Also analyzes the relation of language and rhetoric to social forms.

2119   COOK, RICHARD I.
"Garth's Dispensary and Pope's Rape of the Lock. " CLAJ 6 (1962): 107-116.

Emphasizes, not the similarities, but the differences between The Dispensary and The Rape of the Lock, especially in the natures of the subjects. "With a purpose at once less solemn and less restricted than Garth's, Pope is able to direct

his satire at an entire society, while Garth is limited to satire directed at a specific moral issue."

2120   CORNELIA, MARIE.
       "The Rape of the Lock and the Romance Tradition." Conn.
       Rev. 8 (1974): 84-89.

       Explains the "satiric use made by Pope of some elements
       of the amour courteois as it came down to him from the
       troubadours and the Roman de la Rose through the Petrarchan
       and Elizabethan sonneteers."

2121   CUNNINGHAM, J. S.
       "An Introduction to The Rape of the Lock." From The Rape
       of the Lock, ed. J. S. Cunningham (Oxford: Clarendon Press,
       1966). Rpt. in [2135], pp. 244-263.

       A general survey of The Rape of the Lock as mock-epic.

2122   Pope: The Rape of the Lock (Studies in Eng. Lit., No. 2).
       London: E. Arnold; Great Neck, N. Y.: Barron's Educational
       Series, 1961. Introductory section rpt. in [2166], pp. 15-20.

       Discusses the mock-heroic tradition as it relates to the
       social satire; a detailed analysis.

2123   CUNNINGHAM, WILLIAM F., JR.
       "The Narrator of The Rape of the Lock." In Literary Studies:
       Essays in Memory of Francis A. Drumm, ed. John H. Doren-
       kamp (Worcester, Mass.: College of the Holy Cross, 1973),
       pp. 134-142.

       Suggests that readers of the poem should "respond to the
       varieties of audience (within and without the poem) who are
       addressed; the shifting tones, points-of-view, and tenses; and
       ultimately, the narrator's view of himself as poet-muse whose
       vision creates life in art."

2124   DELANEY, SHEILA.
       "Sex and Politics in Pope's Rape of the Lock." ESC 1 (1975):
       46-61. Rpt. in Weapons of Criticism: Marxism in America
       and the Literary Tradition, Norman Rudich, ed. (Palo Alto:
       Ramparts Press, 1976), pp. 173-190.

       The politics of the Rape of the Lock is expressed in two
       ways: in the sexual attitudes of the characters, and in the
       narrator's comments: "In criticizing Belinda and the Baron,
       Pope criticizes the social class which behaves politically as

they do personally." The Baron's "theft" constituted a breach
of class trust, just as his "class existed, in a sense, by
theft. Their wealth ... was the fruit of theft on a national
scale."

2125   DYSON, A. E. and JULIAN LOVELOCK.
       "In Spite of All Her Art: Pope's 'The Rape of the Lock.'"
       Critical Survey 5 (1971): 197-210.

       Discusses the curious interactions of tone and imagery us-
       ing Belinda's toilette as chief point of reference.

2126   FAIRER, DAVID.
       "Imagination in The Rape of the Lock." EIC 29 (1979): 53-
       74.

       For the Augustans, the demands of "truth" required that
       the findings of the imagination must be submitted to the ra-
       tional faculty for verification. In The Rape of the Lock, truth
       does make its demands of the imagination: "The tension be-
       tween these two elements lies behind the clash of personali-
       ties within the poem, making it at several levels a drama of
       the mind." The poem treats the imagination as a "glorious,
       amoral, irresponsible and alluring thing, a paradoxical clus-
       ter of adjectives as apt for Belinda as for the sylphs"--it is
       that parallel between heroine and mythology that the author
       explores in this article, especially the allegorical elements,
       and offers an interpretation that joins the poem's imaginative
       world with an evaluation of its human concerns.

2127   FERNS, JON.
       "Neo-Classical Structure: The Rape of the Lock and Pride
       and Prejudice." Queen's Quarterly 75 (1968): 685-690.

       " ... Both Pope and Jane Austen explore the division be-
       tween rational morality and unregenerate human nature. How-
       ever, what is finally of interest is the way in which both au-
       thors are prepared to dramatize their beliefs in order, rea-
       son, and moral proportion through the medium of balanced
       and symmetrically organized literary structures."

2128   FOLKENFLIK, ROBERT.
       "Metamorphosis in The Rape of the Lock." ArielE 5, no. 2
       (1974): 27-36.

       Argues that metamorphosis "on the one hand seems to imply
       a conservation of matter--beautiful things merely change into
       different beautiful things ... on the other hand we have per-
       manent transformations: the vase shattered, the lock cut ...

virginity lost, beauty gone, death.... Metamorphosis has
been central to Belinda's life without her being conscious of
it. Clarissa tries to make her aware that metamorphosis
... must be seen as external to human consciousness."

2129   FROST, WILLIAM.
"The Rape of the Lock and Pope's Homer. MLQ 8 (1947):
342-354. Rpt. in [1872], pp. 266-283.

Suggests how certain passages in The Rape of the Lock
seem to mimic passages in Pope's own translation of Homer.

2130   GOSSELINK, R. N.
"The 'Dissolving Antithesis': Technique in The Rape of the
Lock." HAB 24 (1973): 191-196.

Analyzes those antitheses that "produce a double thrust of
irony: 1) the irony of the opposition of values in the ideal
heroic world and in the real world of mannered social action,
and 2) the antithesis dissolving into a further irony. A proper
understanding of the social and literary milieu of Pope's time
shows that the antitheses between Bibles and billet-doux,
counsel and tea, and prayers and masquerade dissolve to
prove more apparent than real."

2131   GRENANDER, M. E.
"Pope, Virgil, and Belinda's Star-Spangled Lock." MLS 10,
i (1979-80): 26-31.

In the "stellification" passage of The Rape of the Lock,
Pope makes a claim for Belinda's immortality as well as
for his own. He creates an equation: "just as Dido is still
remembered because Virgil made her immortal in the Aeneid,
so Belinda will be remembered because he will make her immortal in his epic." Dido is immortal because of echoes of
the Aeneid in Pope's poem; Belinda is immortal because we
today are reading The Rape of the Lock.

2132   GROVE, ROBIN.
"Uniting Airy Substance: The Rape of the Lock 1712-1736."
In [1869A], pp. 52-88.

Concerned with Pope as "poet-critic" of his own work,
with the criticism he practiced on The Rape: his habit of
continual revising suggests, "not in theory but in living practice, the nature of his creative enterprise." The creative
writer and the critic in him were closely allied; in fact,
"much of the most interesting revisions are those where creativity, as we watch, renews itself by repossessing and re-
shaping what it has already made."

2133   HARDY, J. P.
        "The Rape of the Lock." In Reinterpretations: Essays on
        Poems by Milton, Pope, and Johnson (London: Routledge &
        Kegan Paul, 1971), pp. 50-80.

        Argues that Belinda, in The Rape of the Lock, is a more
        ambiguous character than generally allowed; though she may
        be coquettish, she also does not deny the claims of love with
        the Baron.

2134   HOFFMAN, ARTHUR W.
        "Spenser and The Rape of the Lock." PQ 49 (1970): 530-
        546.

        Spenserian parallels in The Rape of the Lock involving
        major conventional actions, imagery and symbolism as well
        as phrasal analogues; importance and significance.   Concludes
        that they are more significantly present in the poem than
        previously supposed, and that "the Spenserian presence sig-
        nificantly affects many problems" in the poem's interpretation.

2135   HUNT, JOHN DIXON. , ed.
        Pope: The Rape of the Lock: A Casebook.   London: Mac-
        millan, 1968.

2136   HUNTLEY, FRANK L.
        "How Really to Play the Game of Ombre in Pope's Rape of
        the Lock." ECLife 4 (1978): 104-106.

        Relates Pope's game of Ombre with his "panoply of fairy-
        like sprites, with the obvious sexual war that is going on,
        and with the popular associations of particular cards from
        ancient cartomancy," then replays the game having Belinda
        bid Hearts instead of Spades.   Had she bid Hearts, which
        are lucky for women, she would have won effortlessly and
        we would have had no plot; instead she uses her head instead
        of her feminine intuition and bids Spades, which are daring
        and unlucky.

2137   HYMAN, STANLEY E.
        "The Rape of the Lock." HR 13 (1960): 406-412.   Rpt. in
        Poetry and Criticism: Four Revolutions in Literary Taste
        (New York: Atheneum, 1961), pp. 85-95.

        Suggests various interpretations of the poem; describes it
        mainly as "one vast comic symbolic defloration."

2138   JACK, IAN.
        " 'The True Raillery. ' "   Cairo Std. in Eng. (1960): 9-23.

Finds that Pope's satire in The Rape of the Lock and the Dunciad are examples of "true raillery" in that both poems teach as well as attack.

2139 "A Complex Mock-Heroic: The Rape of the Lock." In [123], pp. 77-96. Rpt. in [2166], pp. 38-51; abridged in [1873], pp. 77-79.

Discusses how Pope used elements of the mock-heroic mixed with elements of the Rosicrucian doctrine to make the poem an outstanding satire on immoderate female pride.

2140 JACKSON, JAMES L.
"Pope's The Rape of the Lock Considered as a Five-Act Epic." PMLA 65 (1950): 1283-1287.

Taking a hint from Joseph Warton, the author suggests that Pope, when he expanded the 1712 version of The Rape of the Lock for the 1714 edition, may have used the five-part structure of Elizabethan drama for the organization of his mock-epic.

2141 KING, JAMES and BERNADETTE LYNN.
"The Metamorphoses in English eighteenth-century mythological handbooks and translations with an exemplum, Pope's The Rape of the Lock." SVEC 185 (1980): 131-179.

A study of handbooks and translations suggests that during the first half of the eighteenth century a renewed interest in Ovid's Metamorphoses developed. A good example of the influence of the moralized Ovidian tradition may be found in the early poetry of Pope, especially in the 1714 version of The Rape: "We will show that Pope used 'metamorphoses' as solutions to the problems presented in Winter and Windsor-Forest and that Pope's employment of such resolutions crowns his efforts in The Rape of the Lock [sic]." His use of that tradition "betrays a darker and more sombre vision than that with which he is usually credited."

2142 KINSLEY, WILLIAM.
"Ombre Replayed." ESC 4 (1978): 255-263.

An analysis of the card game in The Rape of the Lock, which "forms the symbolic centre of the poem, the focal point of all its themes and images," and of its significance in relation to the poem as a whole. The poem "may be described as the war between the sexes or the war of love ... and the game reflects this ... on several levels. Socially, cards and other games have a very practical Eton-like role to play

in the war: they provide a setting in which potential marriage
partners can meet each other socially and get acquainted."
The game becomes a duel between Belinda and the Baron,
"a trivial and superficial activity of the beaux and belles" presented "in the most heroic, high-sounding language that we
find anywhere in the poem."

2143   KNIGHT, G. WILSON.
       "Drama and Epic in The Rape of the Lock." In [2135], pp.
       105-116.   Rpt. from The Burning Oracle (London, 1939) and
       Laureate of Peace: On the Genius of Alexander Pope (Lon-
       don: Routledge & Kegan Paul, 1955).

       Describes the epic and dramatic qualities of the poem,
       and especially emphasizes the sensuous and erotic quality of
       the verse.

2144   KRIEGER, MURRAY.
       "The Cosmetic Cosmos of 'The Rape of the Lock.'" In The
       Classic Vision: The Retreat from Extremity in Modern Liter-
       ature (Baltimore: Johns Hopkins Press, 1971), pp. 105-124.

       Argues that Pope playfully evades the neoclassical genres
       even as he indulges them and that he half converts the mock-
       epic in The Rape of the Lock to a "new genre of pastoral-
       epic fabricated for the occasion."   Concludes that, "Fearful
       of body ... , in love with abstractions that escaped its limits,
       its ugliness, its time-ridden destiny, Pope had to oppose
       Clarissa, if only by the frailty of that ravished and resur-
       rected lock, metonymic symbol of the wispy world of appear-
       ance, the cosmetic powers."

2145   "The 'Frail China Jar' and the Rude Hand of Chaos." Cent.
       Rev. of Arts & Sciences 5 (1961): 176-194. Rpt. in The
       Play and Place of Criticism (Baltimore: Johns Hopkins Press,
       1967), pp. 53-68; in [1872], pp. 301-319; [2135], pp. 201-219.

       Contrasts the aesthetic world of innocence and purity in
       The Rape of the Lock with the horrifying vision of reality
       in the Dunciad.

2146   KROITOR, HARRY P. and BETTY JANE PROCTOR.
       "The Ridiculous: Elevation and Diminution in Pope's The Rape of
       the Lock." Enl. E. 10 (1979): 85-101.

       Examines the theory of "the ridiculous" as defined by Pope
       and his contemporaries, Fielding and Corbyn Morris, and its
       application in The Rape of the Lock to show that "Pope in-
       tended to evoke in his readers more than a sense of the comic

... that he intended to create in the poem a predominant
sense of the ridiculous by 'using a vast force to lift a feather.'"
Therefore "an important key to effect ... is the interplay of
implied comparisons in subject and style and the overlapping
of elevation and diminution...."

2147   KROLL, BARRY M.
       "The Relationship of the Supernatural Machinery to Humoral
       Doctrine in The Rape of the Lock (1714)." Thoth 14 (1974):
       45-50.

       Considers the psychology of "humors" and the effect on
       the unifying theme of the poem.   Believes that Pope "satirizes
       Belinda's affectation, her 'humors,' to cure them with affec-
       tionate laughter."

2148   LANDA, LOUIS A.
       "Pope's Belinda, the General Emporie of the World, and the
       Wondrous Worm." SAQ 70 (1971): 215-235. Rpt. in [129],
       pp. 178-198; [1871], pp. 177-200.

       Relates Belinda, the embodiment of luxury, to the economic
       expansion and to the mercantilist doctrines of the day; Belinda
       at her toilette suggests the theme of England as a world em-
       porium, a theme that would "generate in a contemporary
       reader responses appealing to the geographical imagination
       and related to the romantic image of an England made mag-
       nificent by maritime activity."

2149   LAUTER, PAUL.
       "Belinda's Date." CE 20 (1959): 164-166.

       Attempting to overcome the unsophistication of modern
       students, the author interprets The Rape of the Lock as not
       too distant from their world of the "date": he uses Geoffrey
       Gorer's account of the ritual of dating to explain the game
       of love between Belinda and the Baron, and concludes that
       the poem is not the history of an attempted seduction and its
       consequences.

2150   McKEE, JOHN B.
       "The 'Outside World' and the Game of Omber in Pope's The
       Rape of the Lock: An Experiment in the Use of Evolutionary
       Evidence." CP 9, ii (1976): 47-52.

       Argues that Pope did not, as suggested by Cleanth Brooks,
       introduce the jury-men into Canto III as a way of emphasizing
       the triviality of Belinda's world by contrast with the real world
       outside; on the contrary, the activities of Belinda and the Baron

can be looked upon as significantly less trivial than those of
the outside world.   The game of ombre has an undercurrent
of sexuality that suggests a serious battle between the sexes,
with one result being the possibility that Belinda, if she loses
the game, will become a bride and a woman: " ... in terms
of real life consequences, the activities at Hampton can therefore be quite as important as, and perhaps more genuinely
useful to society than, the activities of the careless judges
and jury-men. "

2151   McMANMON, JOHN J.
"Phalli non Erecti, Feminae non Fecundatae, et Entia Neutra. "
Antig. Rev. 2, no. 2 (1971): 63-72.

Discusses sexual identity of the men, women, and deities
in The Rape of the Lock.

2152   MACK, MAYNARD.
"Mock-Heroic in The Rape of the Lock. " In [2135], pp. 154-
157; from Introduction to The Augustans, ed. Maynard Mack (New
York: Prentice-Hall, 1950; 2nd. ed. 1961), pp. 20-34.

Discusses parodies of epic convention, and the various
levels of complexity in the action.

2153   MARESCA, THOMAS E.
"Pope. " In [137], pp. 79-131.

The Rape of the Lock aligns itself to the epic through its
manner: its content is trivial, and exists separately from
its form.   The Dunciad, on the other hand, emphasizes epic
matter.   The Rape's structure is episodic, with little in the
way of formal plot; the structure is essentially reflexive:
"Ultimately, it mirrors itself ... the real nature of the mock
epic ... lies in the enclosure of everything by epic. "   The
Dunciad has as its center of interest the gradual revelation
of its hero's identity and mission; Pope employs Cartesian
physics to provide him with the "sustaining myth or metaphor
he needed to depict in orthodox epic form the complete inversion of orthodox epic subject matter. "

2154   "Language and Body in Augustan Poetic. "   ELH 37 (1970):
374-388.

The ability of language to reflect and to affect reality is
discussed relative to Belinda in Rape of the Lock, and as
also employed by Dryden, Swift, Fielding, and Sterne.

2155   MARTIN, L. C.

"Lucretius and The Rape of the Lock." RES 20 (1944): 299-303.

Influence of Book IV of the De Rerum Natura on Pope when he wrote The Rape of the Lock.

2156   MEYERS, JEFFREY.
"The Personality of Belinda's Baron: Pope's 'The Rape of the Lock.'" Amer. Imago 26 (1969): 71-77.

A psychological analysis of the Baron's conduct and behavior toward Belinda.

2157   NICHOLSON, C. E.
"A World of Artefacts: The Rape of the Lock as Social History." L & H 5 (1979): 183-193.

Argues that in the 1714 version of The Rape the "story itself has changed and that the thin thread of the incident between Lord Petrie and Arabella Fermor is woven into a complex design in which the youthful poet undertakes a light-hearted but nonetheless profound and far-reaching examination" of contemporary English society. Suggests further that the poem "provides a poetic grammar for the process whereby relations between people acquire the characteristics of being relations between things, a process during which commodities acquire an autonomy which conceals their true nature."

2158   PARKIN, REBECCA PRICE.
"Mythopoeic Activity in The Rape of the Lock." ELH 21 (1954): 30-38. Rpt. in [2166], pp. 85-92.

An analysis of the function and characteristics of divinity in The Rape of the Lock, especially that which surrounds Belinda.

2159   PRESTON, JOHN.
" 'Th' Informing Soul': Creative Irony in The Rape of the Lock." DUJ 27 (1966): 125-130.

Pope's irony has two dominant aspects: one, closely related to mock-heroic, is Pope's way of defining his relationship to the social world, and the other is the satirical aspect by which Pope exposes the inner contradictions of that world.

2160   PRICE, MARTIN.
"The Problem of Scale: The Game of Art." In [2135], pp. 237-243 (extracted from 153).

Looks at Belinda's world which is " ... a world of triviality measured against the epic scale ... [and] also a world of grace and delicacy, a second-best world, but not at all a contemptible one."

2161   QUINSEY, K. M.
"From Moving Toyshop to Cave of Spleen: The Depth of Satire in The Rape of the Lock." ArielE 11, ii (1980): 3-22.

Argues that "The 'little unguarded Follies' of Arabella and her sex become part of a searing psychological study of the contemporary coquette, which itself moves out into a depth of social criticism anticipating the satires to come; and almost from its beginning the poem is pervaded by growing hints of the chaos which will end The Dunciad."

2162   QUINTANA, RICARDO.
"The Rape of the Lock as a Comedy of Continuity." REL 7, no. 2 (1966): 9-19.

Analyzes The Rape of the Lock from the point of view of transformation and continuity, a pattern reflecting an intellectual way of playing with the concepts of dissimilarity and resemblance as a form of wit. Related rhetorical patterns include the list or collection and anaphora.

2163   REICHARD, HUGO M.
"The Love Affair in Pope's Rape of the Lock." PMLA 69 (1954): 887-902. In [2135], pp. 158-179.

Sees the amour as a series of maneuvers that makes the plot a contest of wiles between an uninhibited philanderer and an invincible flirt.

2164   ROGERS, PAT.
"Faery Lore and 'The Rape of the Lock.'" RES 25 (1974): 25-38.

Argues that "gnomes are as important as the sylphs in the design; that Pope writes in a tradition of rustic 'faery' lore, involving Shakespeare, Spenser, Drayton, and others; and that the work of William Draper--notably Dryades--has a perceptible relevance to the additions Pope made."

2165   "Wit and Grammar in The Rape of the Lock." JEGP 72 (1973): 17-31.

Examination of syntax and vocabulary in several passages

shows that Pope's use of "syntactical forms give body to witty
poetic statements, and provide the source of wit in other
elements of the poem. "

2166   ROUSSEAU, G. S.
        Twentieth-Century Interpretations of "The Rape of the Lock. "
        Englewood Cliffs: N. J. : Prentice-Hall, 1969.

2167   RUDAT, WOLFGANG E. H.
        "Pope's 'Agreeable Power of Self-Amusement' and the Separate
        Narrative in The Rape of the Lock. " Wascana Rev. 13, ii
        (1979): 89-97.

        The study "is on the one hand a 'psychoanalysis' of per-
        sonalities in Pope's poem, and on the other a psychological
        study of the poet himself ... [this] inquiry [is] an attempt
        to reconstruct what may have gone through Pope's mind as
        he was composing The Rape. " Suggests that the poem pos-
        sesses a new level of existence, a level the author calls
        "separate narrative" in contrast to a "poetry of allusion";
        this separate narrative was not necessarily intended to be
        understood by Pope's contemporaries, so that it becomes an
        "in-joke," written for the "in-crowd. " The author attempts
        to explicate that "separate narrative," emphasizing in partic-
        ular its sexual implications.

2168   "Pope's Sermo Polysemus: The Virgilian Tradition in The
        Rape of the Lock. " Orbis Literarum 34 (1979): 99-112.

        Considers the importance of several contexts that are al-
        luded to in the poem.   Since Pope and his contemporaries
        read Virgil along with the commentaries written by the "Man-
        tuan's exegetists," the author also attempts to demonstrate
        how "Pope makes allusively operative in his own poem ob-
        servations made by two of the 'received' Virgilian commenta-
        tors. " Also attempts to demonstrate that "the device of 'a
        phrase capable of carrying many connotations' ... is used by
        Pope throughout his poem so that one line or phrase, by al-
        luding to many different contexts, 'can carry many connota-
        tions' to the point of becoming audaciously polysemous. "

2169   "Another Look at the Limits of Allusion: Pope's Rape of the
        Lock and the Virgilian Tradition. " DUJ 71 (1978): 27-34.

        Shows "that in defining The Rape of the Lock's mode of
        existence we may have to go even beyond Wasserman's her-
        meneutics when we consider the relevances of allusive contexts. "
        In particular, attempts "to demonstrate how Pope employs
        Virgillian allusions for the purpose of bawdy. "

2170 "Pope's Clarissa, the Trojan Horse, and Swift's Houyhnhnms."
      FMLS 13 (1977): 6-11.

          Clarissa's speech in The Rape in which she tries to bring
      Belinda to reason is related to Virgil's Second Aeneid as is
      her presentation of the fatal engine to the Baron.   This in-
      terpretation suggests that Pope was trying to confuse and
      challenge the reader in much the same manner as Swift does
      with Gulliver and the Houyhnhnms.   When Pope alludes to
      the Trojan Horse in Clarissa's speech, "he is giving us a
      subtle warning comparable to Swift's references to the Wooden
      Horse."

2171 "Allusive Technique in Pope's Early Rota Virgilii Poetry."
      Antike & Abendland 22 (1976): 70-99.

          Pope is satirizing phallic hubris and also punishing Belinda
      for her vaginal hubris.

2172 "Shakespeare and Virgil Parodied: The Rape of Lucrece in the
      Light of Pope's Rape of the Lock." ECLife 2 (1976): 98-102.

          " ... Shakespeare's description of the rape of Lucrece in
      the terms of the conquest of Troy is a 'received interpreta-
      tion' of the fall of Ilium, and when Pope alludes to Virgil's
      description of the conquest ... he is ... including in his alu-
      sive [sic] ambience what Shakespeare had made of the legend
      of Troy.   Using the shared Virgilian context as a link, Pope
      reinforces the association between The Rape of the Lock and
      The Rape of Lucrece with the latter's lock-and-gate imagery."
      Pope employs the principle of "mutual commerce" to corrupt
      "The Rape of Lucrece into a rape of locks and latches."   He
      describes "the gates, doors, and locks in Shakespeare's poem
      ... as though they were human: each lock 'retires his ward,'
      and the portal is 'unwilling.' "

2173 "The 'Mutual Commerce' in The Rape of the Lock: Pope and
      the Virgilian Tradition." EA 29 (1976): 534-544.

          Demonstrates how Pope "in the 'sermo polysemus' of 'The
      Rape of the Lock' ... not only follows the referential paths
      laid out by the foremost Virgilian commentator [Servius] but
      actually makes the latter's exegesis allusively operative ...
      and thus transmogrifies the epic into a physiological mock-
      epic" which "fiercely satirizes a representative of the 'enor-
      mous engrossers of manhood.' "   This redefinition of The
      Rape suggests that the English literature of the eighteenth
      century "possesses the breadth and sexual exuberance that
      characterizes classical literature--and it expresses its own
      exuberance by the very manner in which it uses the classics."

2174   "Belinda's 'Painted Vessel': Allusive Technique in The Rape
        of the Lock. " TSL 19 (1974): 49-55.

        Considers the allusive associations connected with the pic-
        ture of the "painted Vessel" gliding down the Thames; it is
        a parody of Shakespeare's description of Cleopatra's barge,
        wherein the ship becomes the woman's body.

2175   SCHMIEL, ROBERT.
        "The 'Impossible' in Pope's Rape of the Lock." HAB 29
        (1978): 147-150.

        Discusses an example of an adynaton in Pope's The Rape
        of the Lock, IV, 117-120, and suggests that it is close to
        Oldham's Prologue to Satires Upon the Jesuits, ll. 38-50;
        another adynaton occurs at the end of The Rape when Be-
        linda's lock takes its place in heaven, an apotheosis anticipated
        by the passage near the end of Canto IV and by another pas-
        sage (Canto III, 161ff.) in which Pope is clearly thinking of
        the adynaton but describes the possible, not the impossible.

2176   SCRUGGS, CHARLES.
        " 'Well Our Pow'r to Use': The Meaning of Clarissa's Speech
        in The Rape of the Lock. " TSL 25 (1980): 84-93.

        Clarissa's speech to Belinda is comic parody of Sarpedon's
        speech to Glaucus in the Iliad in that she tries to reconcile
        Belinda to life rather than to death.   Pope emphasizes old
        age and disease as enemies of beauty, and Clarissa tries to
        tell Belinda that once her beauty fades her life will be dif-
        ferent, but that she has the resources within herself to face
        the ruthlessness of nature.   By acquiring wisdom and good
        humor, she will have the courage to face the future.   Clar-
        issa is "offering Belinda a chance to have a character ...
        [and] to become human in a society which would deny her
        humanity. "

2177   SEIDEL, MICHAEL.
        "Things Unborn: Pope's The Rape of the Lock and The Dun-
        ciad. " In [158], pp. 226-249.

        Suggests that The Rape of the Lock is a poem of reunion
        for a marriage that did not take place; The Dunciad is a suc-
        cession poem for a kingdom that should not exist.   For The
        Rape the satiric principle concerns denial: the idea of rape
        violates hope of renewed union.   In The Dunciad the action
        affects the structures of satiric inheritance, and "irony trans-
        forms the birth of the hero into a misconception, a generic
        narrative parody in all senses. "   Cibber must get rid of his
        own progeny (his books) before he can succeed as the progeny

of his mother; he buries his head in her lap, evoking a kind
of death, a descent to a visionary hell.

2178   SENA, JOHN F.
        " 'The Wide Circumference Around': The Context of Belinda's
        Petticoat in The Rape of the Lock.   PLL 16 (1980): 260-267.

        If we look at the social, economic, and moral implications
        of the petticoat in Pope's time in order to more fully under-
        stand his allusions to it, we see that Belinda's petticoat sym-
        bolizes far more than the heroic shield from the Iliad or the
        Aeneid; it was also a fashionable and foolish garment "that
        called into question the moral integrity and sexual purity of
        its unmarried wearer" which coincides with Pope's attitude
        toward Belinda's morality.

2179   "Belinda's Hysteria: The Medical Context of The Rape of the
        Lock." ECLife 5, iv (1979): 29-42.

        The hysterical fit which Belinda experiences after the Baron
        cuts her lock is "a realistic depiction of a fashionable eighteenth-
        century malady which reflects not only Pope's knowledge of
        contemporary medicine but his ability to employ medical theor-
        ies for characterization and satiric purposes." In addition
        to adding richness to Belinda's character, Pope also uses her
        hysteria for satiric purposes: to attack the hypocrisy of
        women who use sickness to achieve selfish objectives, to sug-
        gest the frailty and weakness of human nature, to attack pride,
        and to undermine the entire world of Hampton Court.

2180   TOLIVER, HAROLD.
        "The Augustan Balance of Nature and Art in 'The Rape of the
        Lock.' " CP 1, no. 1 (1968): 58-69.

        The balance between art and nature in The Rape of the
        Lock--a fusing of the aristocratic boudoir with the natural
        garden.

2181   TRIMBLE, JOHN.
        "Clarissa's Role in The Rape of the Lock." TSLL 15 (1974):
        673-691.

        Sees Clarissa, not as an unimpeachable character, a wis-
        dom figure, but as an inconsistent and elusive character sub-
        ject to Pope's irony, yet remaining his surrogate: she is
        essentially a prude, in whom "sublimity and meanness, right-
        eousness and self-righteousness, clash head on."

2182   WASSERMAN, EARL R.

"The Limits of Allusion in The Rape of the Lock." JEGP
65 (1966): 425-444. Rpt. in [2166], pp. 69-84. Rpt. in
[1871], pp. 224-246.

A study of the poem as it relates to the classical epic to
determine "whether the text of Pope's allusion acts upon
his poem or whether it also imports its own context."

2183   WILLIAMS, AUBREY.
       "The 'Fall' of China and The Rape of the Lock." PQ 41
       (1962): 412-425. Rpt. in [2135], pp. 220-236; [1872], pp.
       284-300.

       The vessel imagery in The Rape of the Lock, and other
       eighteenth-century works, and its allusions to chastity; sug-
       gests the paradoxical nature of Pope's concern over the loss
       of perfection and the marring of beauty.

2184   WIMSATT, W. K., JR.
       "Belinda Ludens: Strife and Play in The Rape of the Lock."
       New Literary History 4 (1973): 357-374. Rpt. in [1871], pp.
       201-223.

       A discussion of the card game as a "microcosm of the
       whole poem, a brilliant epitome of the combat between the
       sexes which is the theme of the whole" and of the relation-
       ship to the tradition of epic games. An expansion of Wim-
       satt's earlier essay [2185].

2185   "The Game of Ombre in The Rape of the Lock." RES 1
       (1950): 136-143.

       Attempts to show to what extent the technicalities of Ombre
       --both the transpired facts and the possibilities so far as they
       affect the drama of the heroine's skill and fortune--get into
       Pope's poem; the game is a "microcosm of the whole poem...."

See also: 1887, 1906, 1916, 1992, 1996, 1998, 2033, 2043, 2338,
       2344, 3248

                        Eloisa to Abelard
                              and
            Elegy to the Memory of an Unfortunate Lady

2186   ACKERMAN, STEPHEN J.
       "The Vocation of Pope's Eloisa." SEL 19 (1979): 445-457.

In order "to understand Pope's success in portraying Eloisa,
we must appreciate his harmonizing of her metamorphosis
with Catholic theology, as seen in his references to the workings of the Paraclete." As a result, Pope uses couplets to
provide "a framework of order within which her passions are
contained, and to which they must be reconciled." Thus
Eloisa's "ungoverned passions" are controlled by the limits
of the heroic couplets, allowing Pope to comment upon her
psychological predicament--the conflict between her weak nature and her religious vocation.

2187   ANDERSON, DAVID L.
        "Abélard and Héloïse: Eighteenth-Century Motif." SVEC
        84 (1971): 7-51.

        Includes discussion of Pope's version of the story and of
        his imitators.

2188   BRUCKMANN, PATRICIA CARR.
        " 'Religious Hope and Resignation': The Process of 'Eloisa
        to Abelard.' " ESC 3 (1977): 153-163.

        A reading of the poem that regards the final lines as the
        most critical part: Abelard's and Eloisa's fate does not leave
        one dejected, for Eloisa has come to accept her death and
        that of Abelard, and realizes that their passion is not ended
        by death, but is translated into legend and history. The final
        response is that of the future bard who will sing of their
        sorrows--and sing them well. It is essential, given the ar-
        gument of the poem, that the singer should have experienced
        deprivation before he can overcome his own melancholy and
        write a poetical epistle.

2189   FAIRER, DAVID.
        "Milton's Lady and Pope's Eloisa." Southern Rev. (Adelaide)
        12 (1979): 209-226.

        Eloisa to Abelard is a poem about the working of the im-
        agination, revealing a "deeply Miltonic concern with the right
        and wrong ways of seeing." An important theme determines
        the tone and structure of the poem, and gives to the hero-
        ine's fantasies a moral urgency: the theme, namely, of
        Eloisa's struggle to draw her imagination away from enslave-
        ment to physical passion and melancholy and redirect it toward
        divine contemplation. Milton handled this theme in "L'Al-
        legro," "Il Penseroso," and the Mask; Pope consciously as-
        sociates his poem with these Miltonic fictions. Concludes
        that Eloisa does achieve some sort of salvation, for she fin-
        ally gains the right kind of vision.

2190   FOSTER, EDWARD E.
        "Rhetorical Control in Pope's Eloisa to Abelard." TSL 13
        (1968): 63-74.

        Discusses Pope's use and control of the original letters
        between Abelard and Eloisa, his omissions, his rearrange-
        ment, and his weaving of emotional elements into a struc-
        tured, artistic unity.

2191   GILLIE, CHRISTOPHER.
        "Alexander Pope: 'Elegy to the Memory of an Unfortunate
        Lady.'" In Interpretations: Essays on Twelve English
        Poems, ed. John Wain (London: Routledge & Kegan Paul,
        1955), pp. 75-85.

        Discusses Pope's ethical attitude toward the tragedy of the
        lady.

2192   HAGSTRUM, JEAN H.
        "Eloisa: 'Breathings of the Heart.'" In [111], pp. 121-132.

        Eloisa is seen as belonging to the eighteenth-century "cur-
        rent of eros and sensibility that was transforming English
        mentality and manners"; she stands, with Marianna Alcoforado
        and Dido, as almost a mythic heroine in the pantheon of mod-
        ern love.   The poem represents a high point in the develop-
        ment of sensibilité and Pope's finest example of "Romantick"
        feeling: emotion and sensibility are powerfully present, es-
        pecially since there may be some identification between Pope
        and Abelard and between Lady Mary Wortley Montagu and
        Eloisa.   Sexual passion, which was increasingly recognized
        as the basis of love and marriage, becomes the main subject
        of the poem.

2193   JACK, IAN.
        "The Elegy as Exorcism: Pope's 'Verses to the Memory of
        an Unfortunate Lady.'" In [28], pp. 69-83; rpt. in [1871],
        pp. 266-284.

        Considers the various theories as to the identity of the
        Unfortunate Lady.   Pope's Elegy was written according to a
        plan, perhaps suggested by the discussion of the funeral elegy
        in Scaliger's Poetics; an even more likely source and influ-
        ence might be Joseph Trapp's Praelectiones Poeticae, in which
        Trapp concludes that Death and Love are the two chief sub-
        jects of Elegy.   The center of Pope's poem is a rite of exor-
        cism that provides the structure for the first 68 lines, which
        are divided into five verse-paragraphs; analyzed in that way,
        the poem must have contained as part of its plan a "variation
        of tone and tempo as one movement of thought and emotion
        succeeds another."

2194   JEFFREY, DAVID K.
        "A 'Strange Itch in the Flesh of a Nun': The Dramatic Move-
        ment and the Imagery of Pope's 'Eloisa to Abelard.'"   BSUF
        16, no. 4 (1975): 28-35.

        Argues against rhetorical criticism of the poem and for
        the dramatic elements of conflict, struggle, and ultimate
        change.   It is through Eloisa's "dramatic struggles, under-
        lined by the metaphorical and linguistic structures," that she
        is gradually redeemed.

2195   KALMEY, ROBERT P.
        "Rhetoric, Language, and Structure in Eloisa to Abelard."
        ECS 5 (1971-72): 315-318 (with a "Reply" by Murray Krieger,
        pp. 318-320).

        Argues against Krieger's statement [2197] that rhetoric is
        separate from language in the poem--argues that poem re-
        futes the false existential dichotomy of "love and religion."

2196   "Pope's Eloisa to Abelard and 'Those Celebrated Letters.'"
        PQ 47 (1968): 164-178. Rpt. in [1871], pp. 247-265.

        Seeks to explain the basic Christian fabric of the poem in
        an effort to learn how Pope creates, out of a collection of
        old letters, a new poem with its own meaning.   Evaluates
        the influence of John Hughes' translation of the Letters on
        Pope's treatment of Eloisa's grief and suffering.

2197   KRIEGER, MURRAY.
        " 'Eloisa to Abelard'--The Escape From Body or the Embrace
        of Body." ECS 3 (1969): 28-47. Rpt. in The Classic Vision:
        The Retreat from Extremity in Modern Literature (Baltimore:
        Johns Hopkins Press, 1971), pp. 83-103.

        Considers "Eloisa to Abelard" as a serious religious con-
        flict between the sensual and the ascetic; evaluates the rhetor-
        ical structure of the poem.   Sees Abelard as like God in his
        relation to Eloisa.

2198   KROPF, C. R.
        "What Really Happens in 'Eloisa to Abelard' "?   SAB 41, ii
        (1976): 43-49.

        Accepting Murray Krieger's position that rejects an inter-
        pretation of the poem as a debate and insists that a "blurring"
        exists between the two poles of Abelard and God, Kropf sug-
        gests that nothing "happens" in Eloisa in the sense that the
        "poem dramatizes or is even supposed to dramatize a decision-
        making process."   Instead he suggests that Eloisa is essen-

tially a study of a state of mind: "The poem does not depict
Eloisa's choosing between alternatives; it depicts her inability
to do so and the agony that that inability causes her."

2199   MANDEL, BARRETT J.
        "Pope's 'Eloisa to Abelard.'"   TSLL 9 (1967): 57-68.

        Compares analyses of poem by O Hehir and by Brower and
        in his own analysis justifies the view that Eloisa's love for
        Abelard is stronger than her religious sense, and that nature
        and passion touch her more deeply and lastingly than grace
        and virtue.

2200   MELL, DONALD C., JR.
        "Pope's Idea of the Imagination and the Design of 'Elegy to
        the Memory of an Unfortunate Lady.'"   MLQ 29 (1968): 395-
        406.

        "The extended story of the Unfortunate Lady is Pope's
        metaphor for the moral urgencies and attendant pathos of the
        experience of time, and the poem is his affirmation of life
        and beauty through the act of elegizing and the creation of
        order through poetic form"; the relationship between art and
        time, the ideal and the real.

2201   MORRIS, DAVID B.
        " 'The Visionary Maid': Tragic Passion and Redemptive Sym-
        pathy in Pope's 'Eloisa to Abelard.'"   MLQ 34 (1973): 247-
        271.

        A detailed study of the aesthetic, ethical, and moral ob-
        jections to the poem.

2202   O HEHIR, BRENDAN P.
        "Virtue and Passion: The Dialectic of Eloisa to Abelard."
        TSLL 2 (1960): 219-232. Rpt. in [1872], pp. 333-349.

        A study of Pope's deliberate and conscious handling of
        "pathetic fallacy" and "romantic" language which traces Eloisa's
        emotional state from its beginning of passionate frenzy to its
        end and her final acceptance of Christ.

2203   PARKS, A. FRANKLIN.
        "Pope's Eloisa to Abelard: Spirituality and Time."   CP 12,
        i (1979): 3-11.

        Argues that Eloisa does succeed in replacing Abelard with
        God, that the ending of the poem contains a transcendence of

passion and time, even though the spiritual union that she attains encompasses rather than eliminates erotic experience. Eloisa is permitted a transcendence of the death to which her passion for Abelard would have ultimately led her.

2204   PETTIT, HENRY.
"Pope's Eloisa to Abelard: An Interpretation." Univ. Colo. Studies, Series in Lang. & Lit., no. 4 (1953): 67-74. Rpt. in [1872], pp. 320-332.

Studies the poem's philosophical temper and structure as well as the character of the heroine by exploring the impact of Cartesian dualism upon her. Argues that "Eloisa's struggle is not satisfactorily stated as a conflict between grace and nature," and concludes that Pope saw in Eloisa a woman capable of emotionally transcending the gulf into which a "casual and hasty acceptance of Cartesian metaphysics threatened to plunge mankind."

2205   QUIVEY, JAMES.
"Pope's Eloisa to Abelard: A Study in Irony." In Studies in the Humanities 2, ii, William F. Grayburn, ed. (Indiana: University of Pennsylvania, 1971), pp. 14-22.

Looks at the highly ironic nature of the poem and considers the possible effects of this irony upon the problem of interpretation.

2206   TILLOTSON, GEOFFREY.
"Lady Mary Wortley Montague and Pope's Elegy to the Memory of an Unfortunate Lady." RES 12 (1936): 401-412.

Analysis of a letter written by Pope in 1735 to prove that the Elegy was written about Lady Mary long before her death.

2207   TROWBRIDGE, HOYT.
"Pope's Eloisa and the Heroides of Ovid." In [45], pp. 11-34. Rpt. in [178], pp. 135-153.

Uses an eighteenth-century interpretation of the Heroides as a basis for analyzing the artistic intention of Pope in Eloisa; an attempt to read the poem in the spirit in which Pope wrote it.

2208   WEINBROT, HOWARD D.
"Pope's 'Elegy to the Memory of an Unfortunate Lady.'" MLQ 32 (1971): 255-267.

Argues that the speaker, not the lady, is the important
person in the poem: that Pope tries to show the disturbed
state of mind of the bereaved poet whose excessive passion
constantly leads him to condemn himself and others--that to
understand the poem we should focus on the speaker and his
remarks.

2209   WINN, JAMES A.
       "Pope Plays the Rake: His Letters to Ladies and the Making
       of the Eloisa." In [1869A], pp. 89-118.

       Explores the similarity of phrasing and attitude that indi-
       cates a significant relationship between Pope's love-letters
       and Eloisa to Abelard; where Pope dreamed and fantasized
       in his letters to Lady Mary and Martha Blount, dramatically
       creating a persona, he used similar tools in creating the per-
       sona of the writer of the love-epistle Eloisa.

See also: 1887, 1966, 1996

                          An Essay on Man

2210   BARBEAU, ANNE T.
       "The Wild and the Garden: A Double Focus on Reality in
       Pope's An Essay on Man." TSL 22 (1977): 73-84.

       A double view of reality, which the author calls the "Wild
       and the Garden," is suggested by Pope at the beginning of
       the Essay (I:6-8), and provides the theme for the first three
       Epistles. "In Epistle I the Wild and the Garden views are
       not reconciled, yet neither cancels the other; in the next two
       epistles the individual, the society, and finally Nature be-
       come gardens within the Wild, until, in Epistle IV, a new
       separation occurs between Wild and Garden, the true scale
       of happiness being shown to be outside of Nature." It is "an
       extended allusion to our first Parents transplanted from the
       Garden of Eden to the Wilderness of this World."

2211   BEAUMONT, CHARLES.
       "The Rising and Falling Metaphor in Pope's An Essay on Man."
       Style 1 (1967): 121-130.

       The metaphor of those who "blindly creep" or "sightless
       soar," thereby violating their position on the Great Chain of
       Being, is used by Pope to attack those men who fail to follow
       Nature's path; it is the central metaphoric axis of the poem.

2212   BOYCE, BENJAMIN.

"Baroque into Satire: Pope's Frontispiece for the 'Essay on Man.' " Criticism 4 (1962): 14-27.

Frontispiece of the 1745 edition of the Essay as related to Capriccio-pictures and tomb-pictures, and Pope's message as portrayed in the illustrations.

2213 BRETT, R. L.
"Pope's Essay on Man." In Reason and Imagination: A Study of Form and Meaning in Four Poems (New York: Oxford Univ. Press, for the University of Hull, 1960), pp. 51-77.

How the thought of the age influenced not only the content of the Essay but also its form and verbal pattern.

2214 CAMERON, J. M.
"Doctrinal to an Age: Notes Towards a Revaluation of Pope's Essay on Man." Dublin Rev. 225 (1951): 54-67. Rpt. in The Night Battle: Essays (London: Burns & Oates, 1962), pp. 150-168; and [1872], pp. 353-369.

Argues that the unfavorable judgments of the poem are in part misconceived, "that if we expect of the poem a system of ethics and a cosmic scheme notable for their internal coherence and capable of being derived from plausible first principles, we are likely to be disappointed." As compared with Hooker, whose attitude is serious, Pope reveals a "certain lightness, almost jauntiness, indicating some complacency in our contemplation of the maze."

2215 FABIAN, BERNARD.
"Pope and Lucretius: Observations on 'An Essay on Man.' "
MLR 74 (1979): 524-537.

The interpretation of the Essay as an Horatian epistle presents difficulties; it "is an allusive poem, though not obviously so. It is not ... an allusion to Horace but to Lucretius ... it must be read against a background that is larger than Horace, though it includes him." The Essay attempts to restore, for a mechanistic age, the unity of the macrocosm and the microcosm; it is an anti-Lucretian poem in that Pope sought a modern counterpart to the only Latin poem that presented a consistent philosophical exposition of man's place in the universe.

2216 "Zum literarischen Hintergrund des Essay on Man: Eine Notiz zu Pope und Lukrez." In Studien zur englischen und amerikanischen Sprache und Literatur: Festschrift für Helmut Papajewski (KBAA 10), Paul G. Buchloh, Inge Leimberg, & Herbert Rauter, eds. (Neumünster: Wachholtz, 1974), pp.

176-187. Rpt. [1871] as "On the Literary Background of the Essay on Man: A Note on Pope and Lucretius, Kenneth Larson, tr. , pp. 416-427.

Discusses the relationship between the first epistle of The Essay on Man and Lucretius's De Rerum Natura to show that "the poem as a whole is a historically significant representation of Lucretius in the way Pope's translations of the Greek epics are a representation of Homer. "

2217   FRENCH, DAVID P.
"Pope, Milton, and the Essay on Man. " Bucknell Rev. 16 (1968): 103-111.

Argues that An Essay on Man is partly both a response and a challenge to Milton's Paradise Lost. Sees affinity in intention and differences in method.

2218   GEDALOF, ALLAN J.
"The Implicit Mock-Heroic in Pope's Essay on Man. " Genre 13 (1980): 187-201.

The Essay on Man alternates between idealism and fallen reality, thus forcing man to see that, whatever his aspirations and potential, he is the mock-hero of the universe. Pope presents images of God and man, one unattainable and the other unacceptable: "while man aspires to Godhead or perfection ... his base nature, measured against the ideal standards implicit in the [mock-heroic] form, drags him down to earth. " Concludes that two central concepts emerge from a study of Essay on Man: man will try to rise above his assigned place through folly and pride, and God or nature will correct and limit him.

2219   GOLDEN, MORRIS.
"Life Style and Literary Style: An Essay on Man. " MLS 9, iii (1979): 29-36.

Suggests that the poem's purpose is to provide an acceptable organization for the life styles generally in effect in 1729-34; that "irrespective of whatever influenced An Essay on Man and its precise contemporaries ... they were concerned with quite the same things, that Pope is often in the poem the spokesman for the intellectual life style of the early 1730's. " Concludes that the "personal part, though submerged, provides motive energy, underlying passion; intellectual fashions contribute subjects, manner, and most profoundly ... anonymity--an avenue toward universality. "

2220   GOLDGAR, BERTRAND A.

"Pope's Theory of the Passions: The Background of Epistle
II of the Essay on Man." PQ 41 (1962): 730-743.

Background of ethical and psychological attitudes toward
the passions, and the relationship to Pope's concepts.

2221   GRABES, HERBERT.
"Die Rhetorische Struktur von Popes Essay on Man." Anglia
84 (1966): 353-387.

Analyzes the "formal unity" of the poem.

2222   HOWARD, LEON.
"The American Revolt Against Pope." SP 49 (1952): 48-65.

Evidence against a widespread and general revolt against
the ideas contained in An Essay on Man.

2223   HUGHES, R. E.
"Pope's Essay on Man: The Rhetorical Structure of Epistle
I." MLN 70 (1955): 177-181. Rpt. in [1872], pp. 370-374.

The second, third, and fourth epistles are all built on the
rhetorical structure of the first, and each contains a logical
extension of the argument first stated in the opening epistle.

2224   KALLICH, MARTIN.
Heav'n's First Law: Rhetoric and Order in Pope's "Essay
on Man." DeKalb, Ill.: Northern Ill. Univ. Press, 1967.

Discusses important doctrinal terms in the Essay, two
"focal" images, the use of antithesis, and the poem's imagery.

2225   "The Conversation and the Frame of Love: Images of Unity
in Pope's Essay on Man." PLL 2 (1966): 21-37.

Pope achieves coherence and synthesis in the Essay through
a careful selection and deliberate development of a pattern of
imagery, expecially the images of conversation and nature.

2226   "Unity and Dialectic: The Structural Role of Antithesis in
Pope's Essay on Man." PLL 1 (1965): 109-124.

Argues that Pope structures the thought of each epistle
around large governing antitheses; he concludes the thought
of each by a dynamic synthesis that reconciles major conflicts, thereby sounding a positive note of hope and affirmation.

2227   LAIRD, JOHN.
       "Pope's Essay on Man." RES 20 (1944): 286-298. Rpt. in
       Philosophical Incursions Into English Literature (Cambridge:
       Cambridge Univ. Press, 1946), pp. 34-51.

       Discussion of the four epistles in the Essay relative to
       comment by Leslie Stephen, "though often brilliant ... has
       never passed for logical"; discussion of the philosophy of Pope
       versus Bolingbroke shows that "Bolingbroke was the master
       and Pope but the pupil who 'turned the tuneful art.' "

2228   LAWLOR, NANCY K.
       "Pope's Essay on Man: Oblique Light for a False Mirror."
       MLQ 28 (1967): 305-316.

       Pope's moral philosophy, Christian or Deistic, as related
       to eighteenth-century religious thought; argues that the Essay
       on Man seeks to reconcile natural with revealed religion, and
       that the thought of the poem is essentially Thomist.

2229   LERANBAUM, MIRIAM.
       Alexander Pope's OPUS MAGNUM, 1729-44. Oxford: Claren-
       don Press, 1977.

       A description and analysis of the evidence concerning the
       "nature and scope of the ethic system that Pope planned to
       erect upon the foundation of the Essay on Man...." The au-
       thor's aim has been to "gather, present, and evaluate all the
       available evidence pertaining to the origin and persistence of
       the plan from 1729 until Pope's death in 1744" and "to ex-
       amine the eight completed epistles as inter-related parts of
       the larger scheme in order to suggest some possible ways
       in which our understanding and appreciation of them can be
       enriched by seeing them in this perspective." Chapter I
       evaluates all the non-poetic evidence from 1729 to 1735, Chap-
       ters II to V offer interpretations of An Essay on Man and the
       individual Moral Essays that suggest the evolution of the poems
       in relation to the larger project, and Chapters VI to VIII con-
       sider the fluctuating fortunes of the ethic scheme after 1735.

2230   LITZ, FRANCIS E.
       "Pope's Use of Derham." JEGP 60 (1961): 65-74.

       Provides evidence that Pope used passages from Derham's
       Physico-Theology and Astro-Theology in his Essay on Man,
       and analyzes his techniques of converting science into rhetoric
       and poetry.

2231   NIERENBERG, EDWIN.

"Pope and God at Twickenham." <u>Personalist</u> 44 (1963): 472-489.

Pope's orthodoxy and views of immortality; looks at <u>An Essay on Man</u> from standpoint that it was Pope's most complete statement "of the need to establish a creative equilibrium between man and God, reason and passion, fate and free will."

2232   POLLARD, ARTHUR.
"Five Poets on Religion: Dryden, Pope, and Young." <u>Church Quart. Rev.</u> 160 (1959): 352-362.

Examines the contrast between reason and enthusiasm in the poetry of Dryden, Pope, Young, Cowper, and Blake, in order to discover the nature of religious response in the eighteenth century; specifically, considers the question of Christian orthodoxy in the <u>Essay on Man.</u>

2233   PRIESTLEY, F. E. L.
"Order, Union, Full Consent of Things!" <u>UTQ</u> 42 (1972): 1-13.

The persistent underlying theme of <u>Essay on Man</u> is God's Providence, functioning as an aspect of God's love. Pope inspects man, society, and the physical world in order to discover the principles of that divine order.

2234   "Pope and the Great Chain of Being." In [37], pp. 213-228.

Argues that, since the theory of the great chain is essentially ontological and <u>a priori</u>, it is <u>not</u> the dominant theme of Epistle I in the <u>Essay on Man;</u> and that Pope rejects "its system of ontological logic, its certainty of demonstration, its confident elucidation of how the Divine mind and powers operate."

2235   RANSOM, HARRY.
"Riddle of the World." <u>SR</u> 46 (1938): 306-311.

On the possibility of Pope's indebtedness to, and misunderstanding of, Pascal, and the question of whether Pope borrowed from Pascal in the <u>Essay on Man.</u>

2236   ROGERS, ROBERT W.
"Critiques on the <u>Essay on Man</u> in France and Germany, 1736-1755." <u>ELH</u> 15 (1948): 176-193.

Ignoring the aesthetic qualities of the <u>Essay on Man,</u> Continental theologians severely attacked the poem's heterodox arguments, and the philosophes looked upon Pope as one of themselves.

2237   SHACKLETON, ROBERT.
        "Pope's Essay on Man and the French Enlightenment." In [9], pp. 1-15.

        The reception of the Essay on Man in France; Pope regarded as a disciple of the Enlightenment, and therefore attacked as a subverter of society and religion.

2238   SHERBURN, GEORGE.
        "Two Notes on the Essay on Man." PQ 12 (1933): 402-403.

        Important note on The Universal Prayer, and one arguing that Bolingbroke's "Fragments" were not used by Pope in writing the Essay on Man.

2239   SIMON, IRENE.
        " 'An Essay on Man' III, 109-146. A Footnote." ES 50 (1969): 93-98.

        Pope's ethics, his doctrine of self-love, as a reinstatement of passion that allows him to avoid the extremes of the lawless individualism of modern Epicureans and the reliance on natural benevolence of Shaftesbury. Pope seen as a Christian Stoic.

2240   SUTHERLAND, JOHN.
        "Wit, Reason, Vision and 'An Essay on Man.' " MLQ 30 (1969): 356-369.

        Argues that the images and paradoxes in the Essay constitute a more important part of the total meaning than is commonly supposed; that some of the images imply a vision of man and his world that Pope could not have communicated in the more abstract language of judgment. Describes a few "nameless graces" and concludes that Pope, by using Locke's despised language of wit, creates true poems, not versified philosophic arguments.

2241   TROY, FREDERICK S.
        "Pope's Images of Man." Mass. Rev. 1 (1961): 359-384.

        Analysis of the Essay on Man to show that in this work Pope radically departs from his traditional position as a classical moralist and satirist; concentrates on his treatment of the idea of the law of nature.

2242   TUVESON, ERNEST.
        "An Essay on Man and 'The Way of Ideas.'"   ELH 26 (1959):
        368-386.   Comment by Robert Marsh, PQ 39 (1960): 349-
        351; reply by Tuveson, PQ 40 (1961):   262-269.

            Suggests, not entirely convincingly, that Pope's method in
        An Essay on Man was influenced by the "new" epistemology
        of Locke.

2243   VAREY, SIMON.
        "Rhetoric and An Essay on Man."   In [1869A], pp. 132-143.

            A significant relationship exists between the Essay and
        Pope's Horatian poems, especially in Pope's development of
        a rhetorical speaking voice, provoking the question--who nar-
        rates the poem, and whom is he addressing?   Pope employs
        his rhetoric to emphasize the poet's intellectual superiority
        to those whom he satirizes, an idea central to the theme of
        universal order and the poet's conception of himself standing
        above other men.   The Essay, therefore, is a necessary link
        between the satires that preceded it and those that followed:
        Pope's traditional rhetoric elevates him in the public's es-
        teem in order to prepare for the acceptance of his later sat-
        ires.

2244   WHITE, DOUGLAS H.
        Pope and the Context of Controversy: The Manipulation of
        Ideas in "An Essay on Man."   Chicago: Univ. Chicago Press,
        1970.

            Describes the intellectual climate necessary for an under-
        standing of some of Pope's important ideas, and relates his
        use of those ideas and issues to contemporary interpretations
        which controversialists put upon them.

2245   ZOELLNER, ROBERT H.
        "Poetic Cosmology in Pope's An Essay on Man."   CE 19
        (1958):   157-162.

            Analyzes the four main ideas of Epistle I in terms of struc-
        ture (informing ideas) and texture (ideas not convertible into
        a prose paraphrase):   the concepts of the Chain and the Sphere,
        and of Balance and Paradox.

See also: 1879, 1887, 1941, 1996, 1998, 2030, 2041, 2046, 2049,
    2398, 3691, 3698

Epistles to Several Persons

2246   ALPERS, PAUL J.
"Pope's To Bathurst and the Mandevillian State." ELH 25
(1958): 23-42. Rpt. in [1872], pp. 476-500.

Discusses the influence of The Fable of the Bees on To
Bathurst, and argues that Pope fundamentally disagrees with
Mandeville's conception of the state as an end in itself, and
is not committed to Mandevillian harmony as an explanation
of social order.   Also examines the poem as a moral criticism of contemporary society: private virtues are public
virtues.

2247   AULT, NORMAN.
"Pope and Addison." RES 17 (1941): 428-451. Rpt. in
[1888], pp. 101-127; [1872], pp. 501-532.

Traces the history of the "Atticus" lines and their relation
to the Epistle to Addison and reexamines the facts in the light
of new evidence.

2248   BRADY, FRANK.
"The History and Structure of Pope's To a Lady." SEL
9 (1969): 439-462.

Traces history of the "deathbed" edition of Pope's Epistles
to Several Persons and attempts to show that "To a Lady"
was given its final form by Warburton; discusses textural
changes made in the poem during Pope's lifetime.

2249   BUTT, JOHN A.
" 'A Master Key to Popery.' " In [1868], pp. 41-57.

Discusses and reprints the prose manuscript "A Master
Key to Popery" found in the papers of the Earl of Burlington
with evidence that this manuscript, which is a defense against
criticism of the Epistle to Burlington, was written by Pope
himself and not by William Cleland.

2250   CARRETTA, VINCENT.
"Pope's Epistle to Bathurst and the South Sea Bubble." JEGP
77 (1978): 212-231.

Why did Pope in this Epistle address an Opposition peer
of easy morals? The evidence suggests strongly that Pope
probably expected the first readers to interpret the poem as
an "occasional party piece" intended to open the Parliamentary

session of 1733 in which Bathurst led the attack on the Ministry: "Pope knew Bathurst was going to lead the fight over the South Sea directors, and ... he emphasizes the corruption and fraud of Ward, Bond, and Blunt ... to recapitulate the Opposition triumphs of the previous session, as well as to prepare the public for the offensive to come."

2251   DAVIDOW, LAWRENCE LEE.
"Pope's Verse Epistles: Friendship and the Private Sphere of Life." HLQ 40 (1977): 151-170.

Emphasizes three points "with regard to the theme of friendship and its relation in Pope to the epistolary form: first, that friendship plays a role of central importance in Pope's poetry, his letters, and in what one may call his 'self-image'; second, that friendship symbolizes, in a virtually syndechdochial [sic] way, the values which Pope attributes to the private sphere of life; and third, that the verse epistle serves as a natural medium for espousing friendship and the virtues of the private sphere." The theme of friendship plays an important role in the Epistle to Dr. Arbuthnot.

2252   EDWARDS, THOMAS R., JR.
" 'Reconcil'd Extremes': Pope's Epistle to Bathurst." EIC 11 (1961): 290-308.

A thematic analysis of the Epistle to Bathurst as an exposure of the growing confusion between worldly wealth and moral value.

2253   EHRENPREIS, IRVIN.
"The Cistern and the Fountain: Art and Reality in Pope and Gray." In [2], pp. 156-175. Rpt. in [1870], pp. 111-123; [1871], pp. 502-526.

Compares Pope's Epistle to a Lady with Gray's The Bard and similar poems by Pope and Edward Young; considers poem in terms of the arrangement of parts and patterns of images and how it depends on allusions to reality.

2254   ERIKSEN, ROY T.
" 'The Last Image of That Troubled Heap': From Chaos to Coherence in Pope's Epistle to Cobham." Studia Neophilologica 52 (1980): 299-310.

Pope's compositional technique shows that he "has given to the section on the ruling passion (ll. 174-265) a balanced conceptual and textual form, which contrasts significantly with the linear form of the preceding paragraphs, at the same time that it indicates that the concept of the ruling passion solves the problem of how to reconcile apparent inconsistencies in human behaviour." Our understanding of the poem's thematic movement depends on our ability to identify Pope's preplanned structure and our awareness of "the ghostly presence" of the seven deadly sins in the conclusion and of the way in which Cobham's entry overcomes them.

2255   ERSKINE-HILL, HOWARD.
"Heirs of Vitruvius: Pope and the Idea of Architecture."
In [1869A], pp. 144-156.

Erskine-Hill considers the meaning of architecture in the Augustan Age, bearing in mind "the comprehensive ancient and Renaissance significance of architecture, the interaction between the metaphor of building and the activity of building, and the architectural analogue as formative of poetic structure." Architecture becomes a symbol of order and civilization, the Epistle to Burlington appearing last in the sequence so that we may see the four epistles as a complete poem which "takes us through the darkness of men's hearts and deeds to bring us out into the redemptive light ... " of a new civilized age.

2256   "Pope and the Financial Revolution." In [1869], pp. 200-229.

A consideration of John Blunt's life in relation to the Epistle to Bathurst.

2257   FEINGOLD, RICHARD.
"The Good Society and the Bucolic Mode: Virgil and Pope."
In [102], pp. 19-49.

Discusses the vision that concludes the Epistle to Burlington, a vision which answers an implicit question: "under what conditions are the works of empire and of power and politics good works and not the result of aggressive greed, luxury, and corruption?" How does this vision of nature dominated and controlled by man exist without clashing with the earlier description of nature guiding and commanding man and his works?

2258   FOX, CHRISTOPHER.
" 'Gone as Soon as Found': Pope's 'Epistle to Cobham' and the Death-Day as Moment of Truth." SEL 20 (1980): 431-448.

The concluding death scenes play a significant role, and their function "rests, specifically, in Pope's poetic use of the classical-Montaignean tradition of the death-day as moment of truth, not only to support his theory of the ruling passion but to suggest, as well, a time-honored answer to the problem of knowledge he has posed throughout" the poem.   Pope prepares for these final scenes, which are essential to the main design of the poem, by suggesting "that every man, paradoxically, is 'gone as soon as found.' "

2259   GIBSON, WILLIAM A.
"Three Principles of Renaissance Architectural Theory in Pope's Epistle to Burlington." SEL 11 (1971):   487-505. Rpt. in [1871], pp. 352-371.

Argues that Pope derived his aesthetic norms largely from humanist architectural theory and that Vitruvius's rule of "decor" provides most of the poem's specific key tenets.   It requires uniformity of style and a correspondence between the form and function of a building.   A builder who observes the rules, thereby imitating cosmic design, can achieve "Magnificence": Timon's Villa is the antithesis of "Magnificence."

2260   HENRY, AVRIL and PETER DIXON.
"Pope and the Architects: A Note on the Epistle to Burlington." ES 51 (1970): 437-441.

Discusses the influence of Burlington, Inigo Jones, and Palladio on Pope's architectural ideas in Epistle to Burlington.

2261   MAHAFFEY, KATHLEEN.
"Timon's Villa: Walpole's Houghton." TSLL 9 (1967): 193-222. Rpt. in [1871], pp. 315-351.

Well-argued; critical reading of Pope's Epistle to Burlington and "Master Key to Popery" in an effort to prove that Timon was in reality Sir Robert Walpole and that the villa was based on Houghton Hall.

2262   MAISON, MARGARET.
"Pope and Two Learned Nymphs." RES 29 (1978): 405-414.

Attempts to identify several unclarified references and unknown nymphs" in Of the Characters of Women.

2263   MARSTELLER, DANIEL F.
"Some Informal Remarks on Pope's Epistle to Bathurst and the Satire of Sir Robert Walpole." Bull. W. Va. Assoc. of Coll. Eng. Teachers 1, i (1974): 11-19.

Discusses Pope's politics in relation to Sir Robert Walpole in 1733 when the Epistle was published. He refers to Walpole as Satan and "By concentrating almost exclusively on political corruption in the early stages of the work, by naming known friends and consorts of the Prime Minister, and by returning to the theme of corruption through financial and political advancement in his concluding partrait, [he] lays the blame for the state of England squarely at the door of ... Walpole."

2264   MARTIN, PETER E.
"The Garden and Pope's Vision of Order in the 'Epistle to Burlington.'"   DUJ 34 (1973): 248-259.

Implications of the garden as metaphor for order.

2265   NUSSBAUM, FELICITY A.
"Pope's 'To a Lady' and the Eighteenth-Century Woman."
PQ 54 (1975): 444-456.

Expands the meaning of the poem by placing Martha Blount, the ideal woman, in the context of eighteenth-century attitudes toward women.

2266   OSBORN, JAMES M.
"Pope, the 'Apollo of the Arts,' and His Countess."   In [55], pp. 101-143.

Traces relationship between Pope, Lord Burlington, and Dorothy Savile, Countess of Burlington, showing the Burlingtons' influence upon Pope's writings.

2267   PARKIN, REBECCA PRICE.
"The Role of Time in Alexander Pope's Epistle to a Lady."
ELH 32 (1965): 490-501. Rpt. in [1872], pp. 406-419; [1871], pp. 486-501.

Argues that Pope maintains simultaneously two interpenetrating paradoxes--one regarding time and the other regarding ethics--and therefore achieves nearly perfect adaptation of poetic means to subject.

2268   ROTHMAN, IRVING N.
"The Quincunx in Pope's Moral Aesthetics."   PQ 55 (1976): 374-388.

Pope uses the quincunx as a "symbol of order, variety, perspective, design, color, and relatedness," and as an al-

ternative to the rigid horizontal and vertical lines of the formal Renaissance garden. In the Epistle to Burlington, Pope
exposes Timon's Villa as large, expensive, and lacking in
taste because of the rigid style of planting. In the First Satire of the Second Book of Horace, his friend, Lord Peter-
borough, stands as the antithesis of Timon: he is "possessed
of the genius of 'invention' ... the exemplar of judgment,
taste, and morality...."

2269   SCHAFER, ROBERT G.
        "Cannons no Canon: Pope's Epistle to Burlington." PMASAL
        45 (1959 meeting; publ. 1960): 403-410.

        Discusses the "accumulated irrelevancies" that identify
        Timon's Villa with Cannons and suggests that Pope's main
        intention is to present an aesthetic theory that will both at-
        tempt to raise the standards of taste and call attention to
        some current aberrations in the application of existing stand-
        ards.

2270   SCHMITZ, R. M.
        "Peterborough's and Pope's Nymphs: Pope at Work." PQ
        48 (1969): 192-200.

        Pope's method of self-plagiarism: three courtly nymphs
        in a poetic charade inspired by Lord Peterborough's Chloe
        (on Mrs. Howard) are reworked several years later in a frag-
        ment, Sylvia (in Miscellany, 1727), most of which reappears
        eight years later in Epistle to a Lady: Of the Characters of
        Women to form the larger part of the characters of Calypso
        and Narcissa.

2271   SHERBURN, GEORGE.
        " 'Timon's Villa' and Cannons." HLB 8 (1935): 131-152.

        Traces the course of events preceding and following the
        publication of the poem and the relationships between Pope,
        the Duke of Chandos, and various friends in an effort to de-
        termine whether the poem was an attack on the Duke or
        whether Pope was falsely accused.

2272   SITTER, JOHN E.
        "The Argument of Pope's Epistle to Cobham." SEL 17 (1977):
        435-449. Rpt. [1871], pp. 469-485.

        A defense of the Epistle by looking closely at its argument.
        "Cobham" is the generalized "you" of the epistle, and there-
        fore stands for the reader, and to him is assigned an empiri-
        cal argument that would discredit bookish knowledge. Pope

attacks the empiricist's argument, insisting that man's senses are unreliable; that is his most emphatic and important argument in the epistle, not, as commonly supposed, the argument in defense of the ruling passion.

2273   STUMPF, THOMAS A.
"Pope's To Cobham, To a Lady, and the Traditions of Inconstancy." SP 67 (1970): 339-358.

Deals with the tradition of moral philosophy underlying both poems, the phenomenon of inconsistent human behavior, and the extent to which the tradition of inconstancy gives unity to To Cobham and indicates a close relationship between the two poems.

2274   WASSERMAN, EARL R., ed.
Pope's Epistle to Bathurst: A Critical Reading with an Edition of the Manuscripts. Baltimore: Johns Hopkins Press, 1960.

Analyzes the "climate of attitudes" or "tone of voice" which is the most subtle feature of Pope's art, and seeks to prove the skill with which Pope controlled the "satiric and Christian tones" in the poem. Pope integrates the Horatian sermo into the Christian sermon.

See also: 1887, 1941, 1959, 2014, 2046, 2285

Epistle to Dr. Arbuthnot; Satires and Epistles of Horace Imitated;

Satires of Dr. John Donne, Versified; Epilogue to the Satires

2275   ADEN, JOHN M.
"Bethel's Sermon and Pope's Exemplum: Towards a Critique." SEL 9 (1969): 463-470.

An analysis of image and symbol in Pope's satire, and of the relationship between Bethel's sermon and Horace. Concentrates on "two strategic and polar images," that of the Fall (in Bethel's sermon, ll. 37-40), and that of the redemption (in Pope's exemplum, ll. 148-50). Points out some political overtones in the poem.

2276   Something Like Horace: Studies in the Art and Allusion of Pope's Horatian Satires. Nashville, Tenn.: Vanderbilt Univ. Press, 1969.

Considers Pope's satiric methods in the Horatian poems, especially the political allusions and satiric background. Chapters on "The Satiric Adversary" and "The Satiric Prolocutor."

2277   "That Impudent Satire: Pope's 'Sober Advice.'" SP extra series 4 (1967): 88-106, and [47], pp. 88-106; [1871], pp. 527-545.

Argues that the poem Sober Advice should be restored to the study of Pope because of its virtue as satire and its relevance to the moral and satirical vision of the author; examines influences affecting style and method of the poem, and the quality of its wit.

2278   "Pope and the Satiric Adversary." SEL 2 (1962): 267-286. Rpt. with alterations in [2276]. Rpt. in [1870], pp. 158-177; [1872], pp. 607-628.

Use of a rhetorical device, the adversarius, adapted from Horace and Persius, and a discussion of Pope's handling of it in The First Satire of the Second Book of Horace, An Epistle to Dr. Arbuthnot, and the two dialogues of the Epilogue to the Satires.

2279   ATKINS, G. DOUGLAS.
       "Strategy and Purpose in Pope's Sober Advice from Horace.: PLL 15 (1979): 159-174.

Pope's strategy is to emphasize the distance between the poet and the "author" of Sober Advice: "Close attention to that speaker, his language, the nature of his allusions, and the differences between him and Horace reveals the distance and indicates the technical accuracy of Pope's denials of authorship. Such analysis may also indicate that ... rather than an 'attack' upon Pope intended as 'ground bait' for the Epistle to Dr. Arbuthnot, Sober Advice is a complex depiction of Pope's view of the state of classical learning and moral understanding in the 1730's." The poem's purpose and strategy cannot be understood unless we recognize that the imitation of Horace is written by someone other than Pope.

2280   BERLAND, ALWYN.
       "Some Techniques of Fiction in Poetry." EIC 4 (1954): 372-385.

Discusses Epistle to Dr. Arbuthnot and the Dunciad as techniques of dramatic poetry related more to fiction than to drama.

2281 BLOOM, LILLIAN D.
"Pope as Textual Critic: A Bibliographical Study of His Horatian Text." JEGP 47 (1948): 150-155. Rpt. in [1872], pp. 533-544.

Concludes that Pope's Latin text was an eclectic one based largely on Heinsius's edition and occasionally emended by the most substantial of the Bentley variants.

2282 BROSS, ADDISON C.
"Alexander Pope's Revisions of John Donne's Satyres." XUS 5 (1966): 133-152.

An examination of the "stylistic differences" between the two poems based on certain principles which lie behind many of the changes Pope made in Donne's poems: "his propensity to set Donne's material in patterns of climactic sequence, his tendency to arrange material in order of abstract rule and particular instance, his placing metaphors and similes of similar content in close conjunction, and his untangling of complex grammatical structure."

2283 BROWN, WALLACE CABLE.
"Dramatic Tension in Neoclassic Satire." CE 6 (1945): 263-269.

Examines Epistle to Dr. Arbuthnot as an example of controlled patterns of dramatic tension. Also looks at satires of Dryden, Johnson, and Churchill.

2284 CREWE, J. V.
"Sporus: A Reconsideration." Theoria 34 (1970): 51-56.

The Sporus passage in The Epistle to Dr. Arbuthnot interpreted as an example of Swiftian disgust, and analyzed for the sensuous vitality of the imagery. Sporus is seen as a contemporary Satan threatening the ideal Augustan society.

2285 DIXON, PETER.
The World of Pope's Satires: An Introduction to the "Epistles" and "Imitations of Horace." London: Methuen, 1968; rpt. 1973.

Sees Pope's poems as deriving from and reflecting both a world of moral value and the specific world of eighteenth-century society. Considers such topics as the "controversial" technique of satire, the complete gentleman, rural virtue, courtly vice, the standard of friendship, attitudes toward money, and eighteenth-century stoicism.

2286   "The Theme of Friendship in the Epistle to Dr. Arbuthnot."
       ES 44 (1963): 191-197.

       Suggests that Arbuthnot, as a good friend of Pope, serves
       as a satiric standard, guaranteeing Pope's own good char-
       acter; he is a symbol of health to put against the mad and
       diseased writers who besiege the poet.   Analyzes bad and
       dangerous friends: Atticus, Bufo, and Sporus.

2287   DOUGLASS, RICHARD H.
       "More on the Rhetoric and Imagery of Pope's Arbuthnot."
       SEL 13 (1973):   488-502.

       Examines the indirection of Pope's rhetorical technique
       and discusses images of hunger and ingestion as related to
       Pope's own virtues.

2288   EDWARDS, THOMAS R. , JR.
       "Heroic Folly: Pope's Satiric Identity." In [11], pp. 191-
       205.   Rpt. in [1871], pp. 565-584.

       The relationship of Pope to the characters Fr. and P. in
       The Epilogue to the Satires: are they versions of Pope him-
       self or is Pope creating a persona, a mask of rhetoric which
       is not to be identified with the "real" personality of the writer?
       The answer is that the voices are not "real," yet the "mask"
       is not a false face, but an identity quite as "real" as any of
       the poet's other identities; so that "P" is Pope and "Fr." is
       Pope, though not in any precise or literal sense.   Both Fr.
       and P. are versions of Pope himself, and Pope controls both
       voices in a planned imitation of a conversation.

2289   FINEMAN, DANIEL A.
       "The Case of the Lady 'Killed' by Alexander Pope." MPQ
       12 (1951): 137-149.

       Biographical explication of ll. 374-75 of Epistle to Dr.
       Arbuthnot about "Welsted's Lye," that Pope had occasioned
       the death of a lady.   Shows, in fact, that Welsted was making
       malicious jokes at Pope's expense, not charging him with
       murder, and identifies the lady.

2290   GABRINER, PAUL.
       "Pope's 'Virtue' and the Events of 1738." Scripta Hierosoly-
       mitana: Further Studies in English Language & Literature
       25 (1973): 96-119.   Rpt. [1871], pp. 585-611.

       Dialogue I possesses an "unabashed topicality" because in
       May, 1738, the Tory Opposition suffered what appeared to be

a total defeat in its long struggle to overthrow Walpole.   The
author asks, therefore, whether ll. 137-172, the contest between "Vice" and "Virtue," may not be an indirect reference
to the political struggle between Walpole and the Tories, and
concludes that the ending is "to be understood not only in
terms of an inversion of moral values, but more urgently, as
the dramatization of a political debacle. "

2291   GILDENHUYS, FAITH.
        "Conversational Style in Pope's 'Epistle to Dr. Arbuthnot. ' "
        ESC 3 (1977): 401-415.

        Points out some of the important stylistic traits which con-
        tribute to "Pope's emphasis on the necessary interrelationship
        between art and ethics [as] his primary means of generalizing
        the particularity. "   Throughout the poem, Pope uses the in-
        terplay between particularity and generality in his "realism
        of portrayal" and "idealism of the message" and by combining
        the intimacy and realism of the conversational style with the
        rigorous techniques of his rhymed couplet, he "was able to
        turn the particular into a general statement of the human con-
        dition. "

2292   GREANY, H. T.
        "Satiric Masks: Swift and Pope. " SNL 3 (1966): 154-159.

        An analysis of Pope's "masks" in the Epistle to Dr. Arbuth-
        not and a comparison with the different technique used by
        Swift.

2293   GRIFFITH, R. H.
        "Pope's Satiric Portrait of Addison. " Texas Rev. 8 (1923):
        273-284.

        A copy of a contemporary manuscript of Pope's lines on
        Addison with comments upon our knowledge of the circum-
        stances of the quarrel.

2294   HALSBAND, ROBERT.
        "Sporus, or Lord Hervey. " TLS 15 Sept. 1972, pp. 1069-
        1070.

        Traces development of the persona from its beginnings in
        1731 until Pope's apotheosis of it four years later.   Distin-
        guishes between "Sporus-the-image as a brilliant feat of Pope's
        rhetorical and poetic imagination; [and] Lord-Hervey-the-man
        as an accomplished and complex writer, courtier, and politic-
        ian. "

2295   HARDY, J. P.
       "An Epistle to Dr. Arbuthnot." In Reinterpretations: Essays
       on Poems by Milton, Pope and Johnson (London: Routledge
       & Kegan Paul, 1971), pp. 81-102.

           The Epistle to Dr. Arbuthnot has a "skillfully articulated
       structure" in which the virtues of the "poet-speaker" are
       contrasted implicitly with the vices of Bufo, Sporus, and
       Aticus.

2296   HOTCH, RIPLEY.
       "The Dilemma of an Obedient Son: Pope's Epistle to Dr. Ar-
       buthnot." ELWIU 1 (1974): 37-45. Rpt. in [1871], pp. 428-
       443.

           "The Epistle to Dr. Arbuthnot treats the dilemma of a poet
       caught between the fear that he may be (like the fools he sat-
       irizes in the poem) cursed because he writes in a form that
       is useless or harmful, and the fear that the impulse to write
       was itself a curse that his parents may have caused by their
       own sin."

2297   HUGHES, R. E.
       "Pope's Imitations of Horace and the Ethical Focus."   MLN
       71 (1956): 569-574.

           Pope's changes in the Horatian originals, changes which
       reflect an ethical defense of himself and his satire, and which
       redirect Horace's intention so as to give an ethical focus that
       the original did not have.

2298   HUNTER, G. K.
       "The 'Romanticism' of Pope's Horace." EIC 10 (1960): 390-
       404. Rpt. in [1872], pp. 591-606.

           Argues that Pope in his Horatian Imitations is quite un-
       Horatian and presents a different theory of satire that depends
       more on the sensibility of the individual author, and is more
       concerned with the split between individual ideals and social
       realities, than Horace's theory did. Analysis of the "Imita-
       tion of the First Satire of the Second Book" suggests that
       Pope's alterations move Horace's point of view toward a "Ro-
       mantic" position.

2299   HUNTER, J. PAUL.
       "Satiric Apology as Satiric Instance: Pope's Arbuthnot."
       JEGP 68 (1969): 625-647. Rpt. in [1871], pp. 444-468.

           Discusses the strategies Pope uses in his satire, and ana-
       lyzes the poem from three points of view: 1) the artistic

effect of contemporary lampoons; 2) an examination of how
the major metaphors are fused into a satiric vision of poetic
perversion; 3) a genetic examination (through extant manuscripts) of how Arbuthnot grew in Pope's mind.

2300   JACK, IAN.
        "Pope and 'the Weighty Bullion of Dr. Donne's Satires.' "
        PMLA 66 (1951): 1009-1022. Rpt. in [1872], pp. 420-38.

        A study of the scope and nature of the changes which Pope
        made when he imitated two of Donne's Satyres; shows that
        they were both poets of the Renaissance.

2301   KELSALL, MALCOLM.
        "Augustus and Pope." HLQ 39 (1976): 117-131.

        A close look at the opening of the first epistle of the second
        book--to Augustus--the first satire of the second book, and
        the Epilogue to the Satires shows that "a carefully considered
        and ultimately desperate view of Augustan history underlies
        Pope's use of the figure of the princeps."

2302   KEYSER, LESTER J.
        "Alexander Pope's 'Living Examples.' " XUS 8, no. 3 (1969):
        19-27.

        Analyzes the "verbal density" in Pope's portraits of Sporus,
        George II, and Atticus.

2303   KNOEPFLMACHER, U. C.
        "The Poet as Physician: Pope's Epistle to Dr. Arbuthnot."
        MLQ 31 (1970): 440-449.

        Emphasizes that Arbuthnot in the poem was also a fictional
        figure, and analyzes the differences between that figure and
        the one in which Pope presents himself. Argues that the
        mode of the work is closer to Marston than to Horace.

2304   KUPERSMITH, WILLIAM.
        "Pope, Horace, and the Critics: Some Reconsiderations."
        Arion 9 (1970): 205-219.

        Criticism of the critics--Reuben Brower, Thomas Maresca,
        John M. Aden--on Pope's Horatian poems.

2305   LAUREN, BARBARA.
        "Pope's Epistle to Bolingbroke: Satire From the Vantage of
        Retirement." SEL 15 (1975): 419-430.

Disagrees with Thomas Maresca's interpretation of Pope
as a Christian moralist (Pope's Horatian Poems, 1966) and
supports thesis that Pope's concerns in the poem are purely
political, and that his "passionate commitment to satire is
not inconsistent with a retired stance."

2306   LEVINE, JAY A.
"Pope's Epistle to Augustus, Lines 1-30." SEL 7 (1967):
427-451.

Attempts to advance awareness of Pope's irony--through
an analysis of the "whole exordium"; concludes that he believed in the divinity of the ideal king who combined the best
aspects of absolutism and libertarianism, and that "the horror
with which Pope viewed the antithesis of that kingly ideal in
George II brought the To Augustus into being and dictated its
mode of expression in the ironically conflated language of religion, politics, and poetry."

2307   MARESCA, THOMAS E.
Pope's Horatian Poems.   Columbus: Ohio State Univ. Press,
1966.

Seeks to demonstrate that the eighteenth-century conception
of Horace as more Christian than hedonistic is reflected in
Pope's Horatian poems.

2308   "Pope's Defense of Satire: The First Satire of the Second
Book of Horace, Imitated." ELH 31 (1964): 366-394.

Analysis of the poem for literary accomplishment and literary theory; poem affirms validity of "ideal world where God's
creation and man's actions are equally rational and concordant,"
and that "real satire is greeted, not with scorn or fear, but
with appreciative laughter."

2309   MENGEL, ELIAS F., JR.
"Patterns of Imagery in Pope's Arbuthnot." PMLA 69 (1954):
189-197. Rpt. in [1872], pp. 566-576; abridged in [1873],
pp. 92-95.

Five main images--animal, filth, disease, persecution,
virtuous man--are all connected and are so related as to
give to the whole a metaphoric value which helps tie the poem
together.

2310   MOSKOVIT, LEONARD A.
"Pope and the Tradition of the Neo-Classical Imitation."
SEL 8 (1968): 445-462.

Defining two kinds of neo-classical imitation, the transla-
tional and the creative, the author sees Pope's Imitations of
Horace as belonging chiefly to the latter: Pope employs all
the conventional elements of the genre, while exploiting them
in an original way.

2311   "Pope's Purposes in Sober Advice." PQ 44 (1965): 195-199.

Pope's imitation of Horace's Satire I. 2 seems to be an
attempt to make fun of as many people as possible and probably written to amuse himself, his friends, and his readers.

2312   OLSON, ELDER.
        "Rhetoric and the Appreciation of Pope." MP 37 (1939): 13-
        35. Rpt. in Rhetorical Analyses of Literary Works, ed. Ed-
        ward P. J. Corbett (New York: Oxford Univ. Press, 1969),
        pp. 37-53.

Rhetorical devices used by Pope in The Epistle to Dr. Arbuthnot to show that he was a "man of good sense, good moral
character, and good will," and that he was a skillful rhetorician as well as a great poet.

2313   OSBORN, JAMES M.
        "Pope, the Byzantine Empress, and Walpole's Whore." RES
        6 (1955): 372-382. Rpt. in [1872], pp. 577-590.

Discusses Pope's vivid lines on Vice Enthroned in "The
Epilogue to the Satires" from standpoint of a double allusion
to the Empress Theodora and to Robert Walpole's second
wife, Molly Skerrett.

2314   PAULSON, KRISTOFFER F.
        "Rochester and Milton: The Sound, Sense, and Sources of
        Pope's Portraits of Bufo, Atticus, and Sporus in An Epistle
        to Dr. Arbuthnot." PLL 12 (1976): 299-310.

The portrait of Bufo is derived from Rochester's My Lord
All-Pride, and the Atticus picture from the description of
Belial in Paradise Lost. The Sporus portrait derives from
several poems either by Rochester or attributed to him, from
obvious references to Paradise Lost, and from some images
in William Pulteney's A proper reply to a late scurrilous
Libel. The presentation of character is symbolic of the theme
of social and literary corruption, and is especially indebted
to Milton: "Sporus, Atticus, and Bufo are the fallen angels
in the world of literature and art, corrupt in themselves and
the source of corruption in others."

2315   REICHARD, HUGO M.
        "The Drift of Pope's First Epilogue." BUSE 4 (1960): 106-
        113.

            An analysis of Epilogue to the Satires, Dialogue I attempt-
        ing to show "that Vice is so fashioned, by her role in the
        unifying plot of the poem, as to give an acute impression of
        modern society ... she is the upshot of a devious, elliptical,
        but directed conversation."

2316   REVERAND, CEDRIC D. II.
        "Metaphoric Structuring in Pope's 'An Epistle to Dr. Arbuth-
        not.'" Archiv 214 (1977): 328-341.

            Examines a number of metaphors in the poem--sickness,
        madness, persecution, and bestiality--to show "how these
        simultaneously sustained metaphors, and their complex inter-
        actions, help reinforce and define 'Arbuthnot's' themes, es-
        tablish changes in tone, and interrelate different sections of
        the poem." Pope's metaphors move "back and forth repeatedly
        across the poem" helping to establish a spatial interrelation-
        ship of parts.

2317   "Ut pictura poesis, and Pope's 'Satire II, i.'" ECS 9 (1976):
        553-568. Rpt. [1871], pp. 373-391.

            An exploration of Pope's pictorialism and the response it
        demands from the reader contributes to the reader's under-
        standing of individual poems, such as "Satire II, i," the first
        of the Horatian Imitations. If we examine the pictorial ele-
        ments, we can perhaps answer the question--whose point of
        view, Pope's or Fortescue's, prevails in the end? The an-
        swer would seem to be that Pope will not appease the es-
        tablishment, that the poem is not a confession of defeat, but
        a "satirist's forceful, resolute, and convincing proclamation
        against a corrupt establishment; his vision of the ideal com-
        munity, epitomized by his grotto, is not a never-never land,
        but rather a viable alternative."

2318   SCHONHORN, MANUEL.
        "Pope's Epistle to Augustus: Notes Toward a Mythology."
        TSL 16 (1971): 15-33. Rpt. in [1871], pp. 546-564.

            Shows how Pope employed allusions to Astraea and Arthur
        to develop a jaundiced account of the age into a view of the
        dissolution of order.

2319   "The Audacious Contemporaneity of Pope's Epistle to Augus-
        tus." SEL 8 (1968): 431-443.

Suggests that poem is a remarkable political satire on the tension and feudings of the Royal Family, that it is a "topical polemic containing a more personally abusive stratum of allusionary comment and criticism which can be explained by the current political situation at the court of George II."

2320   STACK, FRANK.
"Pope's Epistle to Bolingbroke and Epistle I. i." In [1869A], pp. 169-191.

Considers Epistle to Bolingbroke from one specific point of view, that of the extent and particularity by which it exists as an imitation of Horace; by a detailed analysis of Pope's parallel texts, the author intends "to show how this intriguing poem grows out of its Horatian model, and how as a complete work it compares and contrasts with that epistle." The imitation implies that in 1738 the passions that drive men are greater than the men themselves, and more intensely corrupting.

2321   STEIGER, RICHARD.
"Pope's 'Augustan' Horace." Arethusa 10 (1977): 321-352.

Part I of the paper attempts to interpret the relationship between the English and Latin texts of Pope's imitation of The First Satire of the Second Book of Horace, especially those sections in which the two texts are in substantial agreement. Part II discusses the rhetorical relationship between the two texts.

2322   WEBER, HAROLD.
" 'One who held it in disdain': The Tragic Satirist in Pope's Final Works." Criticism 22 (1980): 25-39.

Argues that in much of the "Epilogue to the Satires" Pope departs from Horace's view of the world, that Pope's tone is substantially different from his tone in the rest of the Imitations, reflecting a shift in his vision of society: in the "Epilogue" Pope abandons the comic pose he had adopted in the Imitations. The world's corruption overwhelms the comic satirist, with his devices of irony and indirection, and forces him to become a tragic satirist. The author, in the second half of his essay, discusses the relationship between the "Epilogue" and The Dunciad, attempting to relate the "tragic resonances" of the "Epilogue" to the poet's final tragic vision in the fourth book of The Dunciad.

2323   "The Comic and Tragic Satirist in Pope's Imitations of Horace." PLL 16 (1980): 65-80.

Pope's treatment of the themes of death, friendship, and retirement reflects both comic and tragic satire and allows the poet to "retain his tragic isolation and bitterness while successfully participating in the human community." Essay attempts to explain how he does this.

2324   WEINBROT, HOWARD D.
"The Conventions of Classical Satire and the Practice of Pope." PQ 59 (1980): 317-337.

Weinbrot focuses on "Pope's three main satiric legacies-- the Roman formal verse satires of Horace, Persius, and Juvenal, and the ways they were perceived both by poets and commentators. [He] hopes to clarify some of the choices before Pope, to indicate the received conventions and reputations of the Roman satirists, and then to suggest how Pope used his inheritance to create his own and greater estate in his imitation of Horace's first satire of the second book." He concludes that Pope turned to Persius and Juvenal because Horace was an inadequate model.

2325   "Such as Sir Robert Would Approve? Answers to Pope's Answer from Horace." MLS 9, iii (1979): 5-14.

Concerned with the dangers of ignoring the contemporary response to Pope's First Satire of the Second Book of Horace Imitated (1733): these dangers are exemplified in the controversy regarding the satirist's real or apparent victory. "The evidence suggests that outrages and indignation, rather than a civilized mea culpa, were the responses to Fortescue, and that reports of the demise of Pope's opponents has been greatly exaggerated." The conclusion is that Pope received more than he gave in the exchange with his adversaries, and that it is probably incorrect to suggest that Pope and his values are victorious at the end of the poem.

2326   "Pope's Epistle to Augustus: The Ironic and the Literal." In [184], pp. 182-217.

Weinbrot offers a revisionist interpretation of To Augustus, rejecting the traditional view that Pope contrasted Horace's honest praise of Augustus with his own ironic praise of George II: "What Pope wishes us to see is not that George Augustus is unlike but shockingly like his Roman namesake; and it is not in Pope's similarity to but difference from Horace that he finds his greatest moral force." Pope becomes the Juvenalian lasher of vice, adopting the pose of the indignant satirist who rejects most of the political standards that Augustus and Horace had come to represent.

2327   WILLIAMS, AUBREY.
       "The 'Angel, Goddess, Montague' of Pope's Sober Advice from
       Horace." MP 71 (1973): 56-58.

           Argues that Pope is referring to Lady Mary Churchill,
       Duchess of Montagu, not to Lady Mary Wortley Montagu.

2328   "Pope and Horace: The Second Epistle of the Second Book."
       In [13], pp. 309-321.

           Pope's departure from Horace's original are measured
       against two contemporary critical accounts of the structure
       and development of Horace's Epistle II ii, in the editions of
       Horace edited by André Dacier and Noël-Etienne Sanadon;
       the purpose is to suggest that when Pope deviates from Hor-
       ace it is chiefly to "create in English a poem with its own
       new unity and design." One important change creates a meta-
       phoric pattern of thievery that controls the main theme of
       the Imitation, the losses brought by Time.

See also: 1906, 1941, 1954, 1998, 2014, 2033, 2268, 3488, 3490, 3543

                            The Dunciad

2329   BATTESTIN, MARTIN C.
       "Pope's Magus in Fielding's Vernoniad: The Satire of Wal-
       pole." PQ 46 (1967): 137-141.

           Pope's reference to "Magus" (Dunciad IV, 515-28) is shown
       to relate to the corrupt practices of Sir Robert Walpole partly
       because the passage demonstrably derives from a similar at-
       tack on Walpole in Fielding's satiric mock-epic, The Ver-
       noniad, 1741.

2330   BROCKBANK, J. PHILIP.
       "The Book of Genesis and the Genesis of Books: The Crea-
       tion of Pope's Dunciad." In [1869A], pp. 192-211.

           The Dunciad is concerned with the "material and spiritual
       conditions under which books are 'created' in Augustan Eng-
       land." Pope's verbal wit and allusory skill serves the meta-
       phor which "makes the creation of fiction analogous to the
       creation of the natural world. Since fiction must ... be dis-
       seminated and marketed, the Book of Genesis gets itself trans-
       posed into a prophecy on the genesis of books."

2331   BROOKS, BENJAMIN GILBERT.
       "Pope's Dunciad." Nineteenth Century 137 (1945): 135-141.

An interpretative study of the poem and review of the
Twickenham Edition edited by Sutherland.

2332   CHAMBERS, JESSIE RHODES.
        "The Episode of Annius and Mummius: Dunciad IV, 347-
        396." PQ 43 (1964): 185-192.

        Suggests that the episode is blasphemous, being a Satanic
        parody of the Incarnation. The purpose of the episode is to
        introduce and place in moral perspective the blasphemy of
        the Dunces in the episodes which follow.

2333   CROWTHER, JOHN W. , JR.
        "Pope's Defense of Theology, Philosophy, and the Arts in
        Dunciad, IV. " In Essays and Studies in Language and Litera-
        ture, ed. Herbert H. Petit (Pittsburgh: Duquesne Univ. Press,
        1964), pp. 133-137.

        Analyzes three passages of Book Four for Pope's satire
        of modern man's debasement of theology and philosophy.

2334   DENEAU, DANIEL P.
        "Pope's 'Iv'ry Gate': The Dunciad, III, 340. " MLN 74 (1959):
        208-211.

        Discusses the significance of dismissing the "Vision" through
        the gate of lies, and suggests that the contradiction with Book
        IV was consciously intended by Pope.

2335   DORRIS, GEORGE E.
        "Scipione Maffei Amid the Dunces. " RES 16 (1965): 288-
        290.

        Amplifies one of Pope's pseudo-scholarly notes to The New
        Dunciad (1742), ll. 201-02, by describing the meeting at Cam-
        bridge of Scipione Maffei and Richard Bentley in August, 1736;
        quotes from the journal of Jean-Francois Séguier, a friend
        of Maffei.

2336   EDWARDS, THOMAS R. , JR.
        "Light and Nature: A Reading of the Dunciad. " PQ 39 (1960):
        447-463. Rpt. in slightly different form in [1933], Chap. 5;
        in [1872], 768-89; and abridged in [1873], pp. 104-111.

        Analyzes the contrast between the ugliness of Dulness and
        the beautiful dignity of human reason; the contrast of Dulness
        with light; the rhetorical situation lying behind the ugliness of
        the poem; and finally suggests that Pope had two opposing ideas
        about the relation of order to anarchy, two myths about man's

role in nature: nature as peaceful and perfect and nature as disorder and conflict.

2337   ERSKINE-HILL, HOWARD.
        The Dunciad (Studies in English Literature). London: Edward Arnold, 1972.

        A close analysis of the poem, with a discussion of sources and analogues.

2338   "The 'New World' of Pope's Dunciad." RMS 6 (1962): 49-67. Rpt. in [1872], pp. 803-824.

        A comparison of the Dunciad and The Rape of the Lock to support thesis that the design of the Dunciad differs from The Rape of the Lock and that they should not be judged on the same pattern--that judged as a mock-heroic on its own merits, the Dunciad's highly original effect is unmarred by major faults.

2339   FAULKNER, THOMAS C. and RHONDA L. BLAIR.
        "The Classical and Mythographic Sources of Pope's Dulness." HLQ 43 (1980): 213-246.

        Analyzes Pope's use of the Magna Mater cult in the Dunciad to show that "the composite figure of the Magna Mater, built up from many goddesses, not only forms the basis of Dulness and her 'cult' but is alluded to throughout the four books of the Dunciad, and that this composite Dulness is extensively based on Renaissance and especially eighteenth-century mythographic works as well as classical sources." By using this composite Magna Mater "as the prototype for his own 'Magna Mater,' Pope has rendered Dulness larger and more terrible than she may at first appear."

2340   FRIEDMAN, ARTHUR.
        "Pope and Deism (The Dunciad, iv. 459-92)." In [1868], pp. 89-95.

        Suggests that "at the end of his literary career Pope was aware of the main issues involved in the deist controversy and that he was able to place himself on the side of orthodoxy in a way that his contemporaries were not likely to misunderstand."

2341   GNEITING, TEONA TONE.
        "Pictorial Imagery and Satiric Inversion in Pope's Dunciad." ECS 8 (1975): 420-430.

Points out that " ... just as the mock-heroic structure of
The Dunciad is a satiric inversion of the epic form, so its
pictorial imagery is a satiric inversion of the great Renaissance art which Pope admired so much. ... Pope was doing
satirically what the Goddess of Dulness would do seriously
should she return once more to power. "

2342   GRIFFITH, R. H.
        "The Dunciad. " PQ 24 (1945): 155-157. Rpt. in [1872],
        pp. 727-729.

        Historical background as to why Pope wrote The Dunciad:
        "He has taken an experience actually lived through and felt
        intensely, and placed it in a framework wherein its meaning-
        fulness transcends its individual importance.   The result he
        named The Dunciad. "

2343   HAUSER, DAVID.
        "Medea's Strain and Hermes' Wand: Pope's Use of Mythology. "
        MLN 76 (1961): 224-229.

        The Hermes and Medea allusions in the Dunciad, IV, 635-
        40, are Janus-like: they are symbols of forces that are de-
        stroying civilized values and also of the very values being
        destroyed.

2344   HIGHET, GILBERT.
        " 'The Dunciad. ' "   MLR 36 (1941): 320-343.

        Analyzes why The Dunciad is a failure as a satiric poem
        and The Rape of the Lock is such a success.

2345   HOPKINS, ROBERT H.
        " 'The Good Old Cause' in Pope, Addison, and Steele. "   RES
        17 (1966): 62-68.

        Pope's use of the phrase "good old cause" in The Dunciad
        as eighteenth-century satire; the change in meaning of the
        phrase in Restoration and early eighteenth-century literature.

2346   HOWARD, WILLIAM J.
        "The Mystery of the Cibberian Dunciad. "   SEL 8 (1968):
        463-474.

        Discusses the structure of the 1743 Dunciad, and especially
        emphasizes the religious element in Book IV: the initiation
        ceremony was influenced by a religious controversy between
        Dr. Conyers Middleton and Richard Challoner on the myster-
        ies of Christianity.

2347   JONES, EMRYS.
       "Pope and Dulness." Proc. of British Acad. 54 (1968): 231-
       263. Rpt. in [1870], pp. 124-157; [1871], pp. 612-651.

           Argues that recent critics of The Dunciad confine them-
       selves to Pope's deliberate artistry and conscious intentions
       and the poem's "intellectual qualities." Stresses Pope's meta-
       phoric energy and thematic ambiguity.

2348   KERNAN, ALVIN B.
       "The Dunciad and the Plot of Satire." SEL 2 (1962): 255-
       266. Rpt. in [1872], pp. 790-802.

           Argues that the action or movement of dulness at the level
       of the single verb, the limited movement, and the individual
       scene is exactly duplicated in the plot of The Dunciad. The
       basic movement is "a complex, not a simple, movement, for
       on first appearance it is heavy, formless, and directionless,
       a vague slipping, oozing movement...."

2349   KINSLEY, WILLIAM.
       "Physico-Demonology in Pope's Dunciad." MLR 70 (1975):
       20-31.

           A study of Pope's characterization of Dulness and the dun-
       ces by an analysis of Book IV, 70-90, of the Dunciad to show
       that Pope's "scientific ideas, interacting with literary allu-
       sions, play a more complex, less straightforward role, akin
       to that of epic poetry in his mock-heroics." Suggests that
       "Pope uses physico-theology in the same way that he uses
       Paradise Lost, Genesis, logos theology, and other European
       cultural landmarks: he postulates it as a positive value threat-
       ened by the dunces with perversion into a immoral gravity,
       a symbol of the love of Dulness, or, in short, a physico-
       demonology."

2350   "Varieties of Infernal Experience: Pope's Dunciad & Dante's
       Inferno." In [22], pp. 281-301.

           Analyzes the metaphor "the Dunciad is Pope's Inferno" and
       concludes that it " ... contains a subordinate assertion: the
       Inferno is also Dante's Dunciad." Gives similarities and dif-
       ferences in the two poems.

2351   "The Dunciad as Mock-Book." HLQ 35 (1971): 29-47. Rpt.
       in [1871], pp. 707-730.

           The Dunciad seen as both a book and a mock-book, a par-
       ody of a book, intentionally mocking such aspects as prefaces,

footnotes, and proof-sheets. Three conceptions of the book influenced Pope's poem: 1) as an incarnation of wisdom and a metonym for learning and culture; 2) as a mirror of nature; and 3) as a symbol of the mental habits fostered by the domination of printing as a means of learning and communication.

2352   KNUTH, DEBORAH J.
"Pope, Handel, and the Dunciad." MLS 10, iii (1980): 22-28.

Provides evidence that Pope's praise of Handel in Book IV of the Dunciad represents his own favorable view, and was not an opinion borrowed from Dr. Arbuthnot.

2353   KROPF, C. R.
"Miscreation: Another Miltonic Allusion in The Dunciad." PLL 10 (1974): 425-427.

Argues that Pope's reference in Dunciad, I, 57 to a "warm Third day" alludes to the warm third day of creation in Paradise Lost (VII, 276-81) and suggests Dulness's power to miscreate, or only half-create, a new cosmic order.

2354   "Education and the Neoplatonic Idea of Wisdom in Pope's Dunciad." TSLL 14 (1973): 593-604.

Argues that Pope sought to avoid the problems that the use of Christian machinery would cause The Dunciad by basing his machinery, and especially Dulness, on Neoplatonic theology. The theme of education proves that Pope's indictment of the dunces goes beyond a simple contempt for their bad writing.

2355   LAWLER, TRAUGOTT.
" 'Wafting Vapours from the Land of Dreams': Virgil's Fourth and Sixth Eclogues and the Dunciad." SEL 14 (1974): 373-386. Rpt. in [1871], pp. 731-748.

Discusses the relationship between Eclogue 4 and Eclogue 6, and argues that both poems are "sources" for The Dunciad and facilitate the interpretation of it.

2356   MENGEL, ELIAS F. , JR.
"The Dunciad Illustrations." ECS 7 (1973-74): 161-178. Rpt. in [1871], pp. 749-773.

A study of seven plates of illustrations reveals that these mock emblems not only satirize the visual aids of Dulness but also "reflect the wit of the poem in such a way as to make the pictures at one with the page."

2357   MORRIS, DAVID B.
        "The Kinship of Madness in Pope's Dunciad." PQ 51 (1972):
        813-831.

        Relationship between Colley Cibber and two stone statues
        of raving and melancholy madness above the gates of Bedlam
        "demonstrates Pope's subtlety and skill in transforming familiar
        satire of hack writers into a powerful moral and psychological
        study of the irrational."

2358   PEAVY, CHARLES D.
        "Pope, Cibber, and the Crown of Dulness." SCB 26 (1966,
        pub. 1967): 17-27.

        Pope elevated Cibber to the throne of the Dunces in his
        1743 version of the Dunciad, replacing Theobald (1728) be-
        cause he felt that Cibber stood for everything which Pope
        felt to be demoralizing in the Augustan Age.

2359   PETERSON, R. G.
        "Renaissance Classicism in Pope's Dunciad." SEL 15 (1975):
        431-445.

        In the Dunciad, Pope stands firmly against the new scholar-
        ship and for the old wisdom. Author traces the Apollonian
        imagery which runs through the poem to show that "when
        Pope went to the classics he went almost as a Renaissance
        man and when he used the classical world he did so in ways
        belonging to the tradition of Renaissance classicism rather
        than to the more modern scientific, archaeologizing, demytho-
        logizing study of Greece and Rome."

2360   RAWSON, C. J.
        "Nature's Dance of Death; Part I: Urbanity and Strain in
        Fielding, Swift and Pope." ECS 3 (1970): 307-338.

        The dance as literary emblem: Pope sees the dance as
        patterned, completing itself with established finality; it stylizes
        and orders the ordinary graceful movements of everyday life.
        Pope, in the Dunciad, is less interested in cosmological and
        metaphysical harmonies than in cultural and social coherences.

2361   REGAN, JOHN V.
        "The Mock-Epic Structure of the Dunciad." SEL 19 (1979):
        459-473.

Even though the Dunciad employs the basic structure of
Virgil's Aeneid, it was not until Book 4 was added and created
patterns of alternation and division in parallel halves that the
poem became a mock-Aeneid in structure. The movement of
the poem "from preparation in the private and public sphere
in Books 1 and 2 to a fulfillment in each of Books 3 and 4"
shows that Cibber's "increasing inaction and degeneration
through three forms of sleep are ... absolutely central to
the main action of the poem, the refounding of the kingdom
of the dull...."

2362   "Orpheus and the Dunciad's Narrator." ECS 9 (1975): 87-
101.

A study of the similarities linking The Dunciad and the
Orphic myth, how the traditional interpretations of Orpheus,
especially as seen in Milton's works, come into play, and
how the motto suggests a reading of the poem different from
the traditional one.

2363   REICHARD, HUGO M.
"Pope's Social Satire: Belles-Lettres and Business." PMLA
67 (1952): 420-434. Rpt. in [1872], pp. 747-767.

Discussion of how Pope associates the spread of bad books
with the dynamics of a commercialized society--how Grub
Street is radically fastened to, and fashioned like, the higher
quarters of Society.

2364   REID, B. L.
"Ordering Chaos--The Dunciad." In [15], pp. 75-96. Rpt.
in [1871], pp. 678-706.

Discusses the poem from the standpoint of whether the
ending and the main body of the poem deserve each other,
and whether the conclusion is a true one, an honest rounding
of a unified design. Maintains that the poem marches "forward, a unity, and the yawn of Dulness does reach upward
and outward to enclose the ends of all four books."

2365   RIVERS, WILLIAM E.
"Pope, The Spectre, and Mr. Busby." ECLife 5, iv (1979):
43-53.

Questions why Pope did not identify the "Spectre" in the
fourth Book of the Dunciad as the headmaster of Westminster
School, Dr. Richard Busby, even though many details pointed
to him; also was Busby worthy of this satire?

2366   ROGAL, SAMUEL J.
        "Pope's Treatment of Colley Cibber." <u>Lock Haven Rev.</u> 8
        (1966): 25-30.

            Maintains that Pope's dislike of the early eighteenth-century
        comic stage, his disrespect for the position of poet laureate,
        and his sadistic delight in attacking persons who wouldn't fight
        back were his main reasons for making Colley Cibber "King
        of the Dunces" in the 1742 version of the <u>Dunciad.</u>

2367   ROGERS, PAT.
        "Pope, Settle, and The Fall of Troy." <u>SEL</u> 15 (1975): 447-
        458.

            Seeks "to recover [Pope's] satiric ground by relating the
        fictive circumstances of 'Settle' as they emerge through the
        poem to the actual life-history of his avatar in this world";
        a defense of the biographical approach to literature, and specif-
        ically a consideration of Settle's role in <u>The Dunciad.</u>

2368   "The Name and Nature of Dulness: Proper Nouns in <u>The
        Dunciad.</u>" <u>Anglia</u> 92 (1974): 79-112.

            Attempts to show how Pope deliberately blurs the status
        of proper nouns "in order to reinforce certain thematic and
        satiric motifs" and how he uses this trick to give imaginative
        density to <u>The Dunciad.</u>

2369   "The Critique of Opera in Pope's <u>Dunciad.</u>" <u>Musical Quarterly</u>
        59 (1973): 15-30.

            Discussion of Pope's use of Italian opera in his attack on
        the "Dulness" in contemporary taste.

2370   ROSENBLUM, MICHAEL.
        "Pope's Illusive Temple of Infamy." In [30], pp. 28-54. Rpt.
        in [1871], pp. 652-677.

            Sees <u>The Dunciad</u> as "primarily a work of art, an artifact,
        something separate from the world," and shows the importance
        of a rhetorical definition of satire. Concerned primarily with
        the idea that Pope's poetic vision becomes an artistic monu-
        ment through rhetoric.

2371   ROUSSEAU, G. S.
        " 'To Thee, Whose Temple is all Space': Varieties of Space
        in <u>The Dunciad.</u>" <u>MLS</u> 9, iii (1979): 37-47.

Pope transformed Newtonian concepts of time and space into something quite non-Newtonian. In The Dunciad, the "form--or intentional defect of form--reflects a new way of thinking about the poetic possibilities of attraction, impulse, energy, and space." The author describes the seven kinds of space found in the poem, and concludes that "the reader's journey into the interior is one of witnessing a terrifying new world of grotesque space, energy, impulse and attraction."

2372   SELLERY, J'NAN M.
"Language and Moral Intelligence in the Enlightenment: Fielding's Plays and Pope's Dunciad." Enl. E. 1 (1970), part I: 17-26; part II, 108-119.

A two-part essay exploring the relationship between the two writers and how they dealt with the central artistic and moral problem of the age. Investigates the "significance of the theater in the aesthetic economy of Pope and Fielding ... and the relationship developing out of this in the Dunciad between the imagery of the ear and the metaphor of the theater." The study reveals "the full range of dramatic qualities inherent in Pope's poem while at the same time revealing a perhaps unsuspected seriousness of theme and treatment in Fielding's farces."

2373   SHEEHAN, DAVID.
"The Movement Inward in Pope's Dunciad." MLS 8, i (1977-78): 33-39.

The purpose of this essay is "to show that the inward movement of the dunces' parade in Book II, and the portrayal of the hero in Books I and III, serve to develop the fundamantal theme of the Dunciad. The poem is primarily about the cause of dulness, and only secondarily about its spread." The evidence for this proposition is adduced from the 1729 Dunciad Variorum, though the argument applies equally to the later version.

2374   SHERBO, ARTHUR.
"No Single Scholiast: Pope's 'The Dunciad.'" MLR 65 (1970): 503-516.

Detailed commentary on some of Pope's language and allusions in The Dunciad and other poems.

2375   SHERBURN, GEORGE.
"The Dunciad, Book IV." In Studies in English, Department of English, the University of Texas, 1944 (Austin: Univ.

Texas Press, 1945): pp. 174-190. Rpt. in [1872], pp. 730-746; abridged in [1873], pp. 112-117.

An analysis and reevaluation of the fourth book as to its intellectual and imaginative qualities--the structure of the book as a whole and the specific quality of individual images. Examines "intellectual content" of lines 138-336 and 459-516.

2376   SIEBERT, DONALD T., JR.
"Cibber and Satan: The Dunciad and Civilization." ECS 10 (1976): 203-221.

Presents the Dunciad as a work of satire and Pope's attitude toward the dunces as one of laughter. Pope is always in control of his characters' actions, whether ludicrous or disgusting; they are presented in a farcical world and "Dulness can be counted on to defeat herself in a great clown show." Suggests that we should read the poem with a smile because, as Johnson once said, "It was worth while being a dunce then."

2377   SITTER, JOHN E.
The Poetry of Pope's Dunciad. Minneapolis: Univ. Minn. Press, 1971.

A study of themes and imagery in the Dunciad, which the author sees as an "anti-epic." Argues that the poem has artistic unity.

2378   SUTHERLAND, JAMES R.
"The Dunciad of 1729." MLR 31 (1936): 347-353.

An early history of the poem, the Gilliver lawsuit in 1729, and the famous 'A. Dob' piracy.

2379   TANNER, TONY.
"Reason and the Grotesque: Pope's Dunciad." Crit. Quart. 7 (1965): 145-160. Rpt. in [1872], pp. 825-844.

How Pope's Dunciad deals with the tensions and paradoxes of the Enlightenment mind and how his attitude changes toward life and time from his earlier works to the grotesque elements found in the Dunciad.

2380   WILLIAMS, AUBREY.
"Pope's Dunciad, A Study of Its Meaning. Baton Rouge: La. State Univ. Press, 1955.

Discusses the ways in which the poem is supported by traditions and attitudes rooted in the medieval and classical past, and emphasizes especially the Virgilian parallel of the progress of Dulness from the City of London to Westminster.

2381   WILLIAMS, ROBERT W.
       "Some Baroque Influences in Pope's Dunciad." BJA 9 (1969): 186-194.

       A discussion of the elements of Baroque art and how they are used in the Dunciad, especially in the character of Dulness.

See also: 1916, 1941, 1949, 1954, 1996, 1998, 2014, 2030, 2041, 2043, 2044, 2068, 2115, 2145, 2153, 2177, 2280, 2323

Translations of Homer

2382   CALLAN, NORMAN.
       "Pope's Iliad: A New Document." RES 4 (1953): 109-121. Rpt. in [1872], pp. 631-648.

       A collection of the proofsheets of the first 8 books of the Iliad illustrates Pope's methods, both as poet and translator.

2383   CLARK, DAVID RIDGLEY.
       "Landscape Painting Effects in Pope's Homer." Jour. of Aesthetics & Art Criticism 22 (1963): 25-28. Rpt. in [1872], pp. 668-674.

       Pope interprets the "pictures" of Homer in a way that links his conception of classical epic with his understanding of contemporary landscape painting by freezing actions into momentarily static pictures, by framing scattered landscape items within single views, and by emphasizing perspective where Homer has neglected to do so.

2384   CROSSLEY, ROBERT.
       "Pope's Iliad: The Commentary and the Translation." PQ 56 (1977): 339-357.

       Pope's commentary on the Iliad has a literary value of its own. Without his extensive notes, his Iliad would be just another poem and not a translation. His penetrating analysis, based on good sense and educated taste, provides "a detailed ... course in problems of literary appreciation and evaluation," and shows the process of how a translator arrives at decisions about his text.

2385   FARNHAM, FERN.
        "Achilles' Shield: Some Observations on Pope's Iliad. " PML/
        84 (1969): 1571-1581.

           Examination of Pope's translation of a passage in Iliad
        XVIII, of manuscript revisions and notes, and of Pope's "ob-
        servations on the Shield of Achilles" in an effort to see more
        clearly Pope's position in the quarrel between the Ancients
        and Moderns; considers some modern ways of interpreting
        the passage based on insights of which Pope was ignorant.

2386   FRASER, GEORGE.
        "Pope and Homer. " In [28], pp. 119-130.

           Since Pope correctly realized that a literal version of
        Homer would not succeed, he employed elegant variation and
        other verbal elaborations to appeal to the modern reader.
        Analyzes one short, self-contained passage from Book XI of
        the Odyssey where Ulysses describes his arrival in the land
        of the Cimmerians, comparing Pope's version with modern
        translations by Pound and Ennis Rees; concludes that Pope's
        Augustan sensibility could not respond to the special fusion
        of wit and grief exemplified by the passage.   That passage
        describes the death of Elpenor; of the three translators, how-
        ever, only Pope makes us become Elpenor.

2387   KNIGHT, DOUGLAS M.
        "The Development of Pope's Iliad Preface: A Study of the
        Manuscript. "   MLQ 16 (1955):   237-246.   Rpt. in [1872], pp.
        649-663.

           A study of Pope's stylistic revisions; suggests that Pope
        creates a speaking voice that is both interpretive and oracular
        and concludes that the finished Preface "presents as a com-
        plex whole the strong sense of a continuing relation between
        Homer and a community of readers, and an equally strong
        sense of the self-contained and absolute nature of great po-
        etry. "

2388   "Pope as a Student of Homer. " Comp. Lit. 4 (1952): 75-
        82.

           The importance for Pope of maintaining a live relationship
        between his own poetry and that of Homer.   The great value
        of Homer lies in the establishment for his own poetry of an
        ironic relation among the heroic norms, those which his own
        society pretends to, and those which it actually lives by; he
        is also important as an embodiment of the heroic ideal and
        as an exemplum for English criticism.

2389   Pope and the Heroic Tradition: A Critical Study of His "Iliad."
        New Haven: Yale Univ. Press, 1951.

        Emphasizes Pope's poetry, discussing his relationship to
        the European epic tradition and the extent to which he derives
        from the tradition of epic writing or from the "possibilities
        of English poetry." Argues that Pope balances two kinds of
        language, abstract and concrete, traditional and contemporary.

2390   MASON, H. A.
        To Homer Through Pope: An Introduction to Homer's Iliad
        and Pope's Translation.   London: Chatto & Windus, 1972.

        Attempts to show that Pope's translation and his notes are
        useful in appreciating Homer's Iliad.

2391   ROSSLYN, FELICITY.
        "Pope on the Subject of Old Age: The Iliad Translation,
        Books XXII-XXIV." In [1869A], pp. 119-131.

        Pope displays great sensitivity toward old men, softening
        Homer's starker and franker language about the burdens of
        old age, emphasizing, for instance, Homer's attempt to save
        Nestor's pride.   Pope always refuses to be as blunt and frank
        as Homer.

2392   SCHWANDT, PAMELA POYNTER.
        "Pope's Transformation of Homer's Similes." SP 76 (1979):
        387-417.

        Some of the particular difficulties that Pope tried to resolve
        in translating Homer's similes are: 1) extraneous details that
        have no functional relation to the narrative; 2) inappropriate,
        strained, or inexact comparisons; 3) repetitious or hyperbolic
        similes; 4) similes containing "low" subject matter; and 5)
        details making up Homer's similes appearing in random order,
        piled one on top of the other without the subordinate conjunc-
        tions that might make the relationship clear.   Concludes that
        Pope was fully aware that the Homeric similes would have
        to undergo a thorough reconstruction to make them acceptable
        to English readers.

2393   WARREN, AUSTIN.
        "A Note on Pope's Preface to Homer." PQ 9 (1930): 210-
        212.

        Influence of Fontenelle on Pope's conception of Homer's
        dialects.

2394   ZIMMERMANN, HANS-JOACHIM.
Alexander Popes Noten zu Homer: Eine Manuskript-und Quell-
enstudie (Studien zum Fortwirken der Antike, 2).   Heidelberg:
Carl Winter, 1966.

Monograph with extensive analysis of Pope's work as a
critic and translator of Homer.

See also: 1941, 1949, 2044, 2046

Pope's "Shakespeare"

2395   BUTT, JOHN A.
Pope's Taste in Shakespeare.   Oxford: University Press for
the Shakespeare Assoc. , 1936.

Analyzes the praise and criticism which appeared in Pope's
edition.

2396   DASH, IRENE.
"The Touch of the Poet. "   MLS 4, No. ii (1974):   59-64.

A defense of Pope's editing of Shakespeare's Works (1725),
especially that of The Winter's Tale, in which one of Pope's
unorthodox techniques, the numerous small scene divisions,
"reveals a unity beneath the seeming diversity, illuminates
obscure areas of text, and suggests the theatrical potential
of the play. "

2397   DIXON, PETER.
"Pope's Shakespeare. "   JEGP 63 (1964):   191-203.

Demonstrates Pope's indebtedness to other neo-classic
critics, from whom he derived his interest in particular
"beauties," and his strong preference for Shakespeare the
satirist: "Pope finds Shakespeare a congenial spirit, almost
an Augustan 'wit. ' "

2398   FRASER, RUSSELL A.
"Pope and Shakespeare. "   SAQ 59 (1960): 88-102.

Discusses theological and philosophical aspects of man and
his relationship to God in Essay on Man and compares them
with Shakespeare's plays.

2399   SEARY, PETER.

"Language Versus Design in Drama: A Background to the
Pope-Theobald Controversy." UTQ 42 (1972): 40-63.

The dispute between Dryden and Thomas Rymer.

2400 SUTHERLAND, JAMES R.
      " 'The Dull Duty of an Editor.' "   RES 21 (1945): 202-215.
      Rpt. in [1872], pp. 675-694.

      Pope's ideas about editors and editing, especially as ex-
      emplified by Theobald, and suggests that his liveliest and
      most complete criticism of contemporary scholarship is found
      in the Dunciad.

See also: 1949, 2044

               Minor Works and Miscellaneous

2401 ADEN, JOHN M.
      " 'The Change of Scepters, and impending Woe': Political
      Allusion in Pope's Statius." PQ 52 (1973): 728-738.   Rev.
      & rpt. in [1875], Chap. 5.

      Compares the Thebaid, a story of civil war and contending
      royal claimants, with Pope's translation, emphasizing that
      out of Statius's poem Pope "distilled a subtle but unmistakable
      commentary on his own time and place"; concludes that "In
      his Statius Pope is doing more than 'preparing to become the
      translator of Homer.' He is preparing to become the imitator
      of Horace."

2402 "Pope's Temple of Fame and 'dark Politicks.' "   PLL 9
      (1973): 138-144.   Rev. & rpt. in [1875], Chap. 5.

      Pope's references to political events of 1714 to 1715 show
      that earlier publication of the poem, 1710, 1711, or 1712, is
      questionable; line analysis shows Pope's political association
      with the Tories.

2403 AULT, NORMAN.
      "Pope and England's arch-poet." RES 19 (1943): 376-385.

      Story of the discovery, or identification, of an anonymous
      poem, "Verses on England's Arch-Poet"; suggests that it rep-
      resents Pope's rebellion against the daily strain of his major
      works, and that it is one of Pope's poems.

2404   "New Light on Pope." <u>RES</u> 18 (1942): 441-447.

Describes the circumstances surrounding the publication of Pope's <u>Version of the First Psalm</u> and proves that Pope was parodying the style of Sternhold and not of David.   The poem was a coffee-house <u>jeu d'esprit</u> not meant for the public.

2405   BLANCHARD, RAE.
       "Pope's 'Ode for Music on St. Cecilia's Day.'" <u>ELH</u> 8 (1941): 143-145.

Provides evidence suggesting that the "Ode," which was published in 1713, was written as early as 1711.

2406   CAWLEY, A. C.
       "Chaucer, Pope, and Fame." <u>REL</u> 3, no. 2 (1962): 9-19.

Differences between Chaucer's "House of Fame" and Pope's "Temple of Fame" compared; divergences attributed to differences of age and century.

2407   ERSKINE-HILL, HOWARD.
       "The Medal Against Time: A Study of Pope's Epistle <u>To Mr. Addison.</u>" <u>JWCI</u> 28 (1965): 274-298.

Discusses the poem's content and form in relation to its intellectual background--du Bellay, Bacon, Petrarch, Addison --in order to define Pope's Augustanism.

2408   FULLER, JOHN.
       "A New Epilogue by Pope?" <u>RES</u> 17 (1966): 409-413.

Evidence that Pope wrote "Epilogue" for the 1730 version of John Gay's comedy, <u>The Wife of Bath</u>.

2409   GOLDGAR, BERTRAND A.
       "Pope and the <u>Grub-Street Journal</u>." <u>MP</u> 74 (1977): 366- 380.

Investigates the problem of Pope's involvement with the Grub-Street Journal--did he begin the paper, and if so, for how long did he remain a part of it?

2410   GRIFFIN, DUSTIN.
       "Revisions in Pope's 'Ode on Solitude.'" <u>MLQ</u> 36 (1975): 369-375.

Analyzes the revision, especially to the first stanza, that
increases the "restraint, understanding, and power" of Pope's
finest lyric.

2411   HALSBAND, ROBERT.
       "Pope, Lady Mary, and the Court Poems (1716)." PMLA 68
       (1953): 237-250.

       Establishes authorship of the eclogues and the reasons
       for Pope's animosity and revenge against Curll for publishing
       them.

2412   HUNTING, ROBERT S.
       "The 'Cura Cuiusdam Anonymi' of Pope's Anthologia." PQ
       31 (1952): 430-432.

       Supports theory that the Anthologia of 1684, of which Pope's
       Anthologia was an enlargement, was written by Thomas Power
       and not by Atterbury [see 2419].

2413   KORKOWSKI, EUGENE.
       "Scriblerus' Sinking Opera: Peri Bathous XIII." L & P 24
       (1974): 80-88.

       In Peri Bathous XIII, Pope and Arbuthnot reduce Scrib-
       lerus' "Project for the Advancement of the Bathos" to the
       level of a bowel movement and suggest that "division of labor"
       is merely a variation of the digestive-eliminative function;
       they use ingenious word-play to parody "modern projectors"
       of naive schemes, but restrict their audience and put self-
       amusement foremost.

2414   MAHAFFEY, KATHLEEN.
       "Pope's 'Artimesia' and 'Phryne' as Personal Satire." RES
       21 (1970): 466-471.

       Identifies Pope's "Artimesia" and "Phryne," two early
       satires, as attacks on two of George I's German mistresses,
       Madam Kielmannsegge, later Countess of Darlington, and
       Ehrengard Melusina Schulenberg, Duchess of Kendal. Some
       analysis of insect imagery in "Phryne."

2415   MARTIN, PETER E.
       "Some Background to the Rhetoric of Blame in Pope's 'Epistle
       to Harley.'" SAB 37, No. 2 (1972): 3-9.

       Pope's rhetoric of praise creates a model of heroism while

at the same time exposing some of Harley's shortcomings through his allusions to classical patterns of retirement.

2416   OSBORN, JAMES M.
"Addison's Tavern Companion and Pope's 'Umbra.'" PQ 42 (1963): 217-225.

Identifies "Umbra" in Pope's poems as Walter Cary, a Buttonian whom Pope found a convenient target for his satirical shafts because of Cary's zeal for the Whig cause and his attachment to Addison.

2417   ROGERS, ROBERT W.
"Alexander Pope's Universal Prayer." JEGP 54 (1955): 612-624. Rpt. in [1872], pp. 375-391.

A look at four transcripts of the Universal Prayer "gives us a reasonably reliable picture of the way in which the poem developed before Pope published it and of the way in which Pope sought to justify himself in the light of criticism of his Essay on Man."

2418   RYLEY, ROBERT M.
"A Note on the Authenticity of Some Lines from Pope." PQ 46 (1967): 417-421.

Supports authenticity of 16 lines at end of "Epistle to Miss Blount, on Her Leaving Town, After the Coronation."

2419   SPARROW, JOHN.
"Pope's Anthologia Again." PQ 33 (1954): 428-431.

Argues against Hunting [2412] that Anthologia more likely written by Atterbury than by Power.

2420   SURTZ, EDWARD L.
"Epithets in Pope's Messiah." PQ 27 (1948): 209-218.

The attitude of the eighteenth century toward epithets and the application of its standards to Pope's Messiah; concludes that the failure of the Messiah is due to the redundancy of Pope's epithets.

2421   THOMAS, W. K.
"His Highness' Dog at Kew." CE 30 (1969): 581-586.

Pope's couplet on His Highness' dog at Kew provides the the opportunity for an urbane and entertaining analysis of satire.

2422   TILLOTSON, GEOFFREY.
       "Pope's 'Epistle to Harley': An Introduction and Analysis."
       In [1868], pp. 58-77. Rpt. in [174], pp. 162-183.

       A "magnificent" poem which expresses the relationship be-
       tween the dead (Thomas Parnell) and the surviving friend (Har-
       ley), and between the author (Pope) and the recipient (Har-
       ley).

2423   WASSERMAN, EARL R.
       "Pope's Ode for Musick."   ELH 28 (1961): 163-186.   In
       [1872], pp. 159-184.

       Defends the structural coherence of the poem and argues
       that the Orpheus does not occupy a disproportionate space in
       relation to St. Cecilia: Orpheus is the center of the poem,
       since Pope's main intention is to relate "man's conduct to
       his spiritual welfare and his future existence, expressed as
       a similar pattern of ascent and descent, triumph and failure."

2424   WINN, JAMES ANDERSON.
       A Window in the Bosom: The Letters of Alexander Pope.
       Hamden, Ct. : Shoe String Press (Archon), 1977.

       By combining historical and analytical methods, the author
       recounts the history of the literary letter in the West and
       the history of Pope's own letters, emphasizing how they came
       to be selected, edited, printed, and sold; Chapters 3, 4, and
       5 discuss the individual characteristics of several specific
       correspondences, chosen to indicate the range and variety of
       Pope's epistolary production.

See also: 1996, 3062

2425 BARRETT, W. P.
"Matthew Prior's _Alma_." _MLR_ 27 (1932): 454-458.

    Establishes a close relationship between Prior and Montaigne.

2426 COX, MARY ELIZABETH.
"Prior's Conversation Poems." _Bull. W. Va. Assoc. of Coll. Eng. Teachers_ 1 (1974): 20-27.

    Looks at some of Prior's conversational poems to show "how enjoyable his lightness, urbanity, and elegance can be"; and also how he deliberately mixed styles and livened up the conventional with the realistic. He knew how "to make mythological characters seem members of Augustan society ... and could just as easily ... apply 'poetic diction' to everyday material."

2427 DOUGHTY, OSWALD.
"The Poet of the 'Familiar Style.'" _ES_ 7 (1925): 5-10.

    Supports Cowper's contention that Prior was a great poet as opposed to Johnson's comment that, as a poet, he was "dull."

2428 EVES, CHARLES KENNETH.
Matthew Prior, Poet and Diplomatist (Columbia Univ. Std. in English & Comparative Literature, No. 144). New York: Columbia Univ. Press, 1939; rpt. 1973.

    A biographical and literary study, but lacking in extended criticism.

2429 EWING, MAJL.
"Musical Settings of Prior's Lyrics in the 18th Century." _ELH_ 10 (1943): 159-171.

    Prior's lyrics lent themselves admirably to the new type of musical setting that had become popular by 1700; they had heavy instrumental accompaniment and were intended for pro-

fessional entertainment. The composers who set Prior's
lyrics to music were chiefly influenced by the sophisticated
Italian style; the musical settings show hardly any trace of
ballad style and popular melody.

2430   FELLOWS, OTIS.
        "Prior's 'Pritty Spanish Conceit.'"   MLN 87, No. 6 (1972):
        3-11.

        Suggests that the source of Prior's "Pritty Spanish Conceit,"
        that the "Mind comes in at our Toes, so goes upward thro
        our Leggs to our Middle, thence to our Heart and Breast,"
        an idea already used early in Alma, may be found in Chap-
        ters XII and XV of the Memoirs of Martinus Scriblerus.

2431   HIGBY, JOHN.
        "Idea and Art in Prior's Dialogues of the Dead."   Enl. E. 5,
        ii (1974):   62-69.

        Generally a survey of the four dialogues, emphasizing the
        contrasting ideas and personalities of the contenders and sug-
        gesting that the connecting theme concerns the verdict that
        "there are no unassailable standards of greatness or know-
        ledge or conscience...." The fourth dialogue goes farther
        by concluding that one's private vision regarding these matters
        is incommunicable and that sanity can be judged only subjec-
        tively.

2432   KETTON-CREMER, R. W.
        Matthew Prior (The Rede Lecture, 1957).   Cambridge: Cam-
        bridge Univ. Press, 1957.

        A general and uncritical consideration of Prior's life and
        literary career, seeing in him " ... perhaps the most Hora-
        tian of all our poets, perfectly attuned to the qualities and
        moods of his master--the grace and ease of versification; the
        gaiety, tolerance, good temper; the sense of the flight of time,
        the uncertainty of human life, the vanity of human wishes."

2433   KLINE, RICHARD B.
        "Matthew Prior and 'Dear Will Nuttley': An Addition to the
        Canon."   PQ 47 (1968):   157-163.

        A newly discovered letter to Prior's friend, Robert Ingram,
        shows that "the portrait of 'Dear Will' is typical of the kind
        of writing that Prior did best, both in poetry and in prose--
        wry, ironical, with a gentle sort of wit, and altogether good-
        natured."

2434   MORTON, RICHARD.
        "Matthew Prior's Dialogues of the Dead." BSUF 8, No. 3
        (1967): 73-78.

        Places Prior's Dialogues in the established tradition of
        dialogue des morts, emphasizing such conventional themes as
        the decay of human fortune and the futility of various kinds
        of pretension. Prior, in the longest poem, adopts the ap-
        proach of the great French moralists, displaying a pair of
        philosophical positions in conflict when he has Montaigne and
        Locke dispute on the great questions of philosophy; and un-
        like other practitioners of the genre, Prior never lets the
        reader forget that the characters are in the realm of the
        dead. Concludes that Prior absorbs what is meaningful from
        the traditional forms of the dialogue des morts and adds in-
        sights of his own; his Dialogues "manifest that sophistication
        which distinguishes all of his work."

2435   ROWER, RONALD.
        "Pastoral Wars: Matthew Prior's Poems to Cloe." BSUF
        19, ii (1978): 39-49.

        Divides the Cloe poems into two groups, those published
        in 1709 and those in 1718 and discusses how "The whole se-
        quence ... concerns itself constantly with the ambiguity of
        the division between the natural and the artificial; and since
        it is a real ambiguity, a real confusion, for the lover as
        well as for his nymph, it never does get resolved." Shows
        the Cloe poems as "impressive examples of Prior's talent
        for depicting with warmth and understanding the intimate,
        somewhat childish, but central concerns of ordinary people,"
        and that "they place over against the ideals through which
        life expresses some of its hopes for itself--ideals of pastoral
        innocence and true love--the emotional subterfuges and ra-
        tionalizations through which people try to reconcile themselves
        to their sense of their own finiteness and impotence."

2436   SPEARS, MONROE K.
        "Matthew Prior's Attitude Toward Natural Science." PMLA
        63 (1948): 485-507.

        An analysis of Prior's attitude toward natural science.
        Examines the character and probable sources of Prior's know-
        ledge of science, and discusses his concern with the mater-
        ialistic and deterministic implications of science, and his
        questioning of certain doctrines important to the prevailing
        reconciliation of science with religion. Also considers "Prior's
        rejection of the whole world-view founded upon science...."

2437   "Matthew Prior's Religion." PQ 27 (1948): 159-180.

Seeks to account for John Wesley's admiration for Prior's poetry, by suggesting that he found in Prior's lighter poems as well as in his devotional pieces a "significance ultimately religious: an intense awareness of what Pascal called 'misère de l'homme sans Dieu,' and an earnest, if unsuccessful search for faith." Specifically the article examines Prior's religious beliefs apart from other aspects of his thought: "The external or formal manifestations of his religion will first be discussed: the question of expediency, the relation of religion to politics as shown in Prior's attitude toward the Dissenters and the Catholics. After a brief consideration of Anglican Fideism ... the religious problems which perplexed him throughout his life will be surveyed, with special reference to the extended discussions of them in the third book of Solomon and in Predestination...."

2438   "Some Ethical Aspects of Matthew Prior's Poetry." SP 45 (1948): 606-629.

"A consideration of Prior's poetry from the point of view of ethics reveals clearly an intellectual as well as a temperamental basis for his characteristic melancholy and pessimism." Attempts to show that "the logical patterns stated in or implied by Prior's verse make it very clear that his melancholy outlook is determined by his whole intellectual position," and relates "the ethical aspect of Prior's thought to the traditions to which it belongs, and to the contemporary milieu." Concludes that "Prior was a resolute pessimist, convinced of man's depravity."

2439   "The Meaning of Matthew Prior's Alma." ELH 13 (1946): 266-290.

Contrary to Dr. Johnson's basic criticism of Alma, that it "seems never to have had a plan," Spears attempts to show that, "seen in relation to its intellectual milieu, [it] does reveal a coherent plan, and a corresponding theme and point as burlesque." Deals with "the contemporary significance of the two opposing theories about the location of the mind which are described at the beginning of Alma," and attempts also to show "that Prior is a consistent exponent of the sceptical philosophy, and that the 'system' of Alma is a characteristic expression of this philosophy."

2440   WRIGHT, H. BUNKER.
        "Ideal Copy and Authoritative Text: The Problem of Prior's Poems on Several Occasions (1718)." MP 49 (1952): 234-241.

The Text of Poems on Several Occasions, published by

Tonson and Barber in 1718, is both an "ideal copy" from the publishers' point of view and an authoritative text representing Prior's own intentions.

2441 "Biographical Allusions in Prior's 'The Mice, a Tale.'" MLN 53 (1938): 498-501.

Shows that, contrary to previous belief, the poem has no reference to Prior's life and that the signature "Matthew" is not Prior's. However, "in the absence of evidence to the contrary, we may continue to suppose that Prior is the author of the verses."

See also: 1542, 2819

Collected Studies

2442 CARROLL, JOHN, ed.
Samuel Richardson: A Collection of Critical Essays (Twentieth Century Views). Englewood Cliffs, N. J.: Prentice-Hall, 1969.

General Studies

2443 BALL, DONALD L.
"Richardson's Resourceful Wordmaking." SAB 41, iv (1976): 56-65.

The purpose of the study is to observe the degree of exactness that Richardson was seeking in his wordmaking, to see the linguistic thinking of a writer who presents the intimate "oral" expression of characters in public, "formal," written form, and to provide a detailed examination of English vocabulary when propriety of language was becoming important just before grammarians began to formulate rules of grammar and usage.

2444 Samuel Richardson's Theory of Fiction. The Hague: Mouton, 1971.

Analyzes and compares Richardson's theory and his practice; divided into three parts: 1) Chapter I presents Richardson's statements of his theory of fiction; 2) Chapters II-V present a detailed analysis of his practice of fiction in his four published novels; and 3) the Conclusion relates his practice to his theory. Provides systematic analyses of four novelistic techniques: narrative structure, epistolary technique, characterization, and presentation of moral doctrine.

2445 BARKER, GERARD A.
"The Complacent Paragon: Exemplary Characterization in Richardson." SEL 9 (1969): 503-519.

Examines the belief in the validity of self-judgment as exemplified by Richardson's characters. "Pamela, Sir Charles Grandison, and eventually Clarissa manifest their virtue through an unhesitant and consistent approval of their own conduct.,.. And, in their self-assurance and sense of superiority, Pamela and Sir Charles resemble their Calvinistic forbears, although faith in one's own goodness has supplanted faith in one's election. Such self-approval, though it weakens his characterizations, constitutes for Richardson a necessary concomitant of virtue, confirming the validity of personal judgment. "

2446   BRADBROOK, FRANK.
"Samuel Richardson. " In From Dryden to Johnson. Pelican Guide to English Literature, IV, ed. Boris Ford (Harmondsworth: Penguin Books, 1957), pp. 293-312.

Attempts to explain the mingled attraction and repugnance that Richardson's novels excite--prolix novels with their "curious mixture of coarseness and distinction"; a general survey that also looks for the causes of Richardson's influence.

2447   BRISSENDEN, R. F.
Samuel Richardson. (WTW) London: Longmans, 1958. Rpt. in [2505], pp. 50-56.

Brief but exciting comments on Richardson's art and outlook; brief chapters on Pamela, Clarissa, and Sir Charles Grandison.

2448   BROPHY, ELIZABETH BERGEN.
Samuel Richardson: The Triumph of Craft. Knoxville: Univ. Tenn. Press, 1974.

An attempt "to formulate Richardson's artistic precepts from an examination of his own statements found in his personal correspondence as well as in the more formal presentations of the prefaces and postscripts to the novels" and to review the novels to see whether his practice "did fulfill his ideas and whether his artistic precepts seem to have been the primary factor responsible for the strengths or weaknesses of the novels. "

2449   BULLEN, JOHN SAMUEL.
Time and Space in the Novels of Samuel Richardson (Monograph Series, 12, ii). Logan: Utah State Univ. Press, 1965.

Concerned not with the relationship between events of the novels and external history, but with the various principles of time and space that Richardson used in creating a fictional world; concludes that time and space blend together in Clarissa as part of a unified dramatic development.

2450   COCKSHUT, A. O. J.
        "Richardson and Fielding." In Man and Woman: A Study of
        Love and the Novel 1740-1940. (New York: Oxford Univ.
        Press, 1978), pp. 32-45.

        Fielding, in his parodic criticism of Pamela, was not suf-
        ficiently subtle in his judgment to allow for the greater com-
        plexity and vulnerability of Pamela's situation over Joseph's:
        her situation is not, as Fielding seems to suppose, as comic
        as Joseph's. Fielding's morality in Tom Jones is comforting,
        because it wrongly suggests that sexual morality can be sep-
        arated from all other kinds of morality. Clarissa is superior
        to Pamela: "it draws a clear distinction, at once subtle,
        firm and flexible between the morality of conscience and the
        morality of the respectable world." Finally, special credit
        is due to Fielding for portraying in Amelia, what most novel-
        ists have ignored, the sexual delights that can be found within
        marriage.

2451   COHEN, RICHARD.
        "The Social-Christian and Christian-Social Doctrines of Samuel
        Richardson." HSL 4 (1972): 136-146.

        Argues that morality in Richardson is subsumed in major
        doctrinal classifications, so that one may "conceive of the
        basic orientation ... toward either the social-Christian or
        the Christian-social doctrines." Clarissa teaches "how to
        die," whereas Pamela and Sir Charles Grandison are directed
        primarily toward "how to live."

2452   COPELAND, EDWARD W.
        "Samuel Richardson and Naive Allegory: Some Beauties of
        the Mixed Metaphor." Novel 4 (1971): 231-239.

        Discusses the stylistic implications of Richardson's attempt
        to combine the mimetic and didactic. Believes that "as Rich-
        ardson's use of figurative language grows increasingly more
        frequent and more ornate, it becomes more an integral part
        of the emotional and psychological effects of his novels."

2453   DAICHES, DAVID.
        "Samuel Richardson." Literary Essays (Edinburgh: Oliver
        & Boyd, 1956), pp. 26-49. Rpt. abridged in [2505], pp. 14-
        25.

        A discussion of Richardson as a novelist and his attempt
        to deal with "basic moral problems imaginatively in a de-
        tailed social context."

2454   DALZIEL, MARGARET.
       "Richardson and Romance." <u>AUMLA</u> 33 (1970): 5-24.

       Richardson's novels "have close affinities with the romances
       he so heartily despised."

2455   DOODY, MARGARET ANNE.
       A Natural Passion: A Study of the Novels of Samuel Richard-
       son. Oxford: Clarendon Press, 1974.

       Literary background, sources, and analogues of the three
       novels discussed in some detail; deals with Pamela as pas-
       toral comedy, the "deathbed" theme of Clarissa, and visual
       images in both Clarissa and Sir Charles Grandison.

2456   DOWNS, BRIAN W.
       Richardson. London: Routledge & Kegan Paul, 1928; rpt.
       New York: Barnes & Noble, 1969.

       Discusses Richardson's life, character, and opinions, and
       analyzes the purpose and artistic qualities of the three novels;
       concludes with an account of sentimentalism and Richardson's
       influence.

2457   DUSSINGER, JOHN A.
       "Richardson's 'Christian Vocation.'" <u>PLL</u> 3 (1967): 3-19.

       Examines Richardson's specific religious attitudes and their
       function in his novels, and suggests that he was concerned
       with the decline of religion as a result of the influence of
       deism and free-thinking. His support of the Church of Eng-
       land was reflected in three aspects of his faith: 1) his em-
       phasis on Old Testament morality; 2) his belief in Christ's
       atonement as a pattern for man; and 3) his belief in God's
       grace as necessary for salvation. "From the evidence of
       his whole career as master printer, editor, compiler, cor-
       respondent, and novelist, Richardson's direct involvement with
       the religious movements of his time appears suggestive and
       any interpretation of his novels from an historical perspective
       needs to take into account the impact of these events."

2458   EAVES, T. C. DUNCAN and BEN D. KIMPEL.
       Samuel Richardson, a Biography. Oxford: Clarendon Press,
       1971.

       A definitive biography that attempts to do three things:
       1) to treat all the problems connected with Richardson's life
       and to interpret the evidence; 2) to present a picture of Rich-
       ardson as a person, giving all details that would reveal his
       personality; and 3) to discuss the intrinsic merit of the novels.

2459   FRANK, FREDERICK S.
        "From Boudoir to Castle Crypt: Richardson and the Gothic
        Novel." Revue des Langues Vivantes 41 (1975): 49-59.

        Richardson as progenitor of the Gothic fashion that developed
        in the last decade of the century: first, he introduces the
        figure of the ruthless erotic criminal; second, Richardsonian
        Gothic disseminates the prototype of the victimized and vio-
        lated female sufferer; and, third, Richardson's novels created
        a self-gratifying Gothic aesthetic which encourages the reader
        to enjoy incidents of pain and sexual barbarity, to admire
        ugliness, and to find beauty in depravity and decay.

2460   GOLDEN, MORRIS.
        "Richardson's Repetitions." PMLA 82 (1967): 64-67.

        Examples of Richardson's use of repetition in Pamela and
        Clarissa--similarity of form and substance, similarity of ma-
        jor situations, similarity of characters--and reasons for these
        repetitions.

2461   Richardson's Characters. Ann Arbor: Univ. Mich. Press,
        1963. Pp. 1-28 rpt. in [2442], pp. 161-180.

        The purpose of this essay is to "examine [Richardson's]
        characters in the light of [his] evident preoccupations, in the
        hope thereby to isolate the qualities of his novels that give
        them life now and make his work important for other than
        historical reasons." Sees character as essentially the urge
        to dominate, and argues that the merit of a character is not
        directly related to the degree of restraint: Lovelace, without
        restraint, is almost completely evil, yet as "Richardson's
        best-realized character" is immensely attractive.

2462   GREENSTEIN, SUSAN.
        "Dear Reader, Dear Friend: Richardson's Readers and the
        Social Response to Character." CE 41 (1980): 524-534.

        Discusses the importance of the social response of readers
        to fictional characters, especially how readers in the eigh-
        teenth century responded to Richardson's novels. Richardson
        was very much aware of the importance of social response
        to character in reading and interpreting, and the reaction of
        his readers and his concern with their reaction created an
        extensive correspondence between reader and novelist unique
        in literary history.

2463   GUILHAMET, LEON M.
        "From Pamela to Grandison: Richardson's Moral Revolution
        in the Novel." In [33], pp. 191-210.

Argues that Richardson's novels are not essentially realistic, but are intended to present characters that are moral exemplars. Richardson's achievement is that he is the first "English novelist to establish a coherent moral ideal well-suited to the imaginative character of his work.... Action and moral are so successfully integrated as to be indistinguishable from one another."

2464   HAGSTRUM, JEAN H.
       "Richardson." In [111], pp. 186-218.

       Explains Richardson's central theme, the relations of women and men, in the three novels, and relates it to the tradition of erotic myth-making: Richardson has created a world in which sexuality, love, and the desire for union in marriage are motives for action.

2465   HORNBEAK, KATHERINE.
       "Richardson's Familiar Letters and the Domestic Conduct Books." Smith College Studies in Modern Languages, 19, No. 2 (1938): 1-50. Rpt. Folcroft Library Editions, 1973.

       Argues that, although in form Richardson's Familiar Letters is a book on letter-writing, in spirit and content it is very closely related to the domestic conduct books.

2466   HUGHES, LEO.
       "Theatrical Convention in Richardson: Some Observations on a Novelist's Technique." In [13], pp. 239-250.

       Examines the method by which Richardson's imagination and observation operated in his novels, especially his use of stylized gestures.

2467   HUMPHREYS, A. R.
       "Richardson's Novels: Words and the 'Movements Within.'"
       E & S, 23 (1970): 34-50.

       Analyzes the style and syntax of Pamela and Clarissa as "acute transmitters of psychological idiosyncrasies." Sees Richardson as dramatizing in the reader's mind a psychological situation through stylistic sophistication, and as potentially more dramatic than Fielding.

2468   KEARNEY, ANTHONY.
       "A Recurrent Motif in Richardson's Novels." Neophilologus 55 (1971): 447-450.

Richardson's novels are related in meaning by a system of repetition; an obvious example is one basic to all three novels: the heroine trapped by circumstances and plot and forced to defend herself against a cunning villain. That situation is given various metaphoric expressions in the novels, the most striking example being "that of the unwary bird threatened by the fowler's snare."

2469   Samuel Richardson. London: Routledge & Kegan Paul; New York: Humanities Press (Profiles in Literature Series), 1968.

Uses extracts to consider five aspects of Richardson's art: the kind of situation that recurs, the way he uses surroundings to create a meaningful "atmosphere" and "setting," his character portrayal, his epistolary technique, and the range and achievement of his novels.

2470   KERMODE, FRANK.
"Richardson and Fielding." Cambridge Jour. 4 (1950): 106-114. Rpt. in [53], pp. 64-77.

A study of "the posthumous antagonisms of Richardson and Fielding" and of the effect of Coleridge's ascribing moral as well as technical superiority to Fielding; defends Richardson by describing Fielding as the moralist of the Good Heart who "evades the only genuinely crucial test that confronts his hero as a moral being, in the whole course of his adventures." Richardson's complexity is genuine, and inheres in his structure--it is a matter of the suggestiveness of event, whereas Fielding's complexity inheres in his texture, a matter merely of verbal suggestiveness; the "complexity" of Tom Jones, therefore, is relatively superficial, that of Clarissa full of moral overtones and tragic significance.

2471   KINKEAD-WEEKES, MARK.
Samuel Richardson: Dramatic Novelist. Ithaca, N.Y.: Cornell Univ. Press, 1973.

An interpretative reading of the three novels, followed by a section on their form. Attempts to "read to the moment" (to paraphrase Richardson on his method), working from "situation to situation, exploring the implications of each in a flexible, changing and complex process" in an effort to establish the quality of Richardson's imagination.

2472   KLOTMAN, PHYLLIS R.
"Sin and Sublimation in the Novels of Samuel Richardson." CLAJ 20 (1977): 365-373.

An analysis of the character of Pamela and of Clarissa
to show their "kind of proportionate or disproportionate blend-
ing between productive ability, perversion and neurosis." The
Puritan fascination with sin and depravity is more artistically
comprehensible in Richardson's characterization of Clarissa
because her psychosexual makeup is similar to her twentieth-
century counterparts.

2473   KONIGSBERG, IRA.
       "The Dramatic Background of Richardson's Plots and Char-
       acters." PMLA 83 (1968): 42-53. Rpt. in [2474], part of
       Chap. 2.

       Discusses the striking similarities between Richardson's
       plots and characters and those of the Restoration and early-
       eighteenth-century dramatists.

2474   Samuel Richardson and the Dramatic Novel.   Lexington: Univ.
       Ky. Press, 1968.

       Argues that "Richardson brought to the English novel sub-
       ject matter and techniques developed in the drama, and that
       it was the resulting integration of these dramatic elements
       with fiction which caused the mutation in genre that is re-
       sponsible for the subsequent course of the English novel."
       Deals with plays that contain the Cinderella myth of Pamela
       and the theme of the heroine's enforced betrothal and rape in
       Clarissa; and argues the influence of the sentimental drama
       on Richardson's novels.

2475   KRUTCH, JOSEPH WOOD.
       "Samuel Richardson." In Five Masters: A Study in the Muta-
       tions of the Novel.   (New York: Jonathan Cape & Harrison
       Smith, 1930), pp. 109-173; rpt. Bloomington: Indiana Univ.
       Press, 1959.

       Commentary on each of Richardson's novels and his place
       in the history of the novel: he was the first "to discover
       how domestic life could be made the subject of improving
       fiction."

2476   LEFEVER, CHARLOTTE.
       "Richardson's Paradoxical Success." PMLA 48 (1933): 856-
       860.

       Maintains that Richardson is far more successful in por-
       traying his women characters realistically than his men, per-
       haps because of his experience as a letter-writer for women.

2477   LEVIN, GERALD.
        Richardson the Novelist: the Psychological Patterns.   Amster-
        dam: Rodopi, 1978.

        Concerned with how Richardson created his characters.
        This psychological approach pays attention to Richardson's
        characters, not to Richardson himself, with special emphasis
        on the "dislocations of character existing at two 'levels' in
        the work--the surface plot and the underlying fantasy...."
        The novels are analyzed according to Freud's theory of mas-
        ochism; also considered are the "sentimental" treatment of
        character and action, the relationship between sentimentality
        and sadism, and the problem of character in fiction in the
        light of those ideas generally.

2478   McKILLOP, ALAN DUGALD.
        "Samuel Richardson."   From [134], Chap. II.   Partially rpt.
        as [2615].

        A general attempt to define the quality and texture of Rich-
        ardson's art, with constant relations with the historical and
        social background emphasized; suggests, among many original
        insights, that Clarissa finally fails to be a great tragedy be-
        cause Richardson fails to reach the "ultimate degree of im-
        aginative concentration."

2479   "Epistolary Technique in Richardson's Novels."   Rice Inst.
        Pamphlet 38.   (1951): 36-54.   Rpt. in [7], pp. 198-217;
        [2442], pp. 139-151.

        Analysis of Richardson's technique, with the conclusion
        that if he "falls short of classic control of his themes, the
        reason may be, not that he was inept or incompetent, but on
        the contrary that his use of the letter form led him in one
        direction toward a specific analysis of the enmeshing com-
        plexities of life, and in another direction toward a heightened
        awareness of the discontinuities and blockages, the frustra-
        tions and loose ends, that seem to make up the plight of man."

2480   Samuel Richardson, Printer and Novelist.   Chapel Hill: Univ.
        N.C. Press, 1936; rpt. Hamden, Conn.: Archon Books,
        1960.

        Centers on the origins, publication, and reception of Rich-
        ardson's three novels as well as on his personality and asso-
        ciations.

2481   MUNRO, JAMES S.
        "Richardson, Marivaux, and the French Romance Tradition."
        MLR 70 (1975): 752-759.

Suggests that Richardson was more influenced by the French romance tradition than by Marivaux because of its interest in the study of nascent love. All three of Richardson's novels use the 'surprise de l'amour' convention which offers him "a stock of analytical techniques, which he uses in their primary role of instruments for studying nascent love, rather than extending their application, as Marivaux had done, to the study of other emotional states."

2482 ROGERS, KATHERINE M.
"Sensitive Feminism vs. Conventional Sympathy: Richardson and Fielding on Women." Novel 9 (1976): 256-270. Rpt. as "Richardson's Empathy with Women" in The Authority of Experience, Arlyn Diamond and Lee R. Edwards, eds. (Amherst: Univ. Mass. Press, 1977), pp. 118-136.

Richardson was a radical feminist by probing "traditional assumptions about male-female relationships: if a woman is not to be regarded as sexual prey, perhaps she exists as a human individual apart from her sexuality; if marriage is to be more than a mercenary contract for the propagation of lawful children, perhaps it should be a partnership between equals." Fielding, on the other hand, accepted the conventions of a male-dominated society, and in the relationship between Booth and Amelia, for instance, emphasized the superiority of the male even though generally he was sympathetic toward women.

2483 SALE, WILLIAM M. , JR.
Samuel Richardson: Master Printer (Cornell Studies in English, Vol. 37). Ithaca, N. Y.: Cornell Univ. Press, 1950.

An extensive study of Richardson's work as a printer and how it affected his life and writings. Identifies all the works that came from his press.

2484 "From Pamela to Clarissa." In [27], pp. 127-138; rpt. in [2442], pp. 39-48; [53], pp. 18-31.

Shows Richardson's concern with "the interpenetration of classes" and how his "fiction rendered the conflicts he saw in his own society." Despite the inadequacy of his technique, we should be able to understand his intent: "He wants us to see that Clarissa is a child of heaven finally removed from the world of the Harlowes and of the Lovelaces" because in this world, Richardson could not "find room in which to fit everything and a place in which everything might fit."

2485 Samuel Richardson: A Bibliographical Record of His Literary

Career with Historical Notes.   New Haven: Yale Univ. Press,
1936; rpt. Hamden, Conn.:   Archon Books, 1969.

Chiefly a bibliographical account of all Richardson's works,
including an introduction that summarizes his career as a
writer and a chronological list of his works and of the books
written in imitation of them.   The book is divided into three
parts: Part I, Novels, Edited Works, Pamphlets, Books
written in Collaboration; Part II, Contributions to Periodicals;
and Part III, Works inspired in whole or in part by the publication of Richardson's novels.

2486   SHERBURN, GEORGE.
        " 'Writing to the Moment':   One Aspect. "   In [13], pp. 201-
        209.   Rpt. in [2442], pp. 152-160.

        Richardson used the technique of 'writing to the moment'
        very effectively.   His naturally strong visual imagination en-
        abled him actually to see the episodes he depicted, but he
        had little interest in environmental detail or objective des-
        cription.

2487   "Samuel Richardson's Novels and the Theatre: A Theory
        Sketched. "   PQ 41 (1962):   325-329.

        Emphasizes the influence of the theatre on Richardson's
        novels, especially on his strong focus on the central plot-
        situation, character types, and vivid, extensive conversation.
        Suggests that Richardson's knowledge of upper-class life comes
        chiefly from the stage.

2488   SHROFF, HOMAI J.
        "The Woman's Gentleman or the Anatomy of the Rake. "   In
        [163], pp. 96-122.

        Discusses Richardson's "persistent inquiry in all his three
        novels concerning the motives and principles that determine
        the conduct and behavior of the ideal gentleman and lady, and
        of their opposites, the frivolous, unregenerate profligates...."
        His "ideal gentleman is, before all things, an ideal husband;
        the gentleman he condemns is the one who traps women in
        his nefarious designs and makes them miserable. "   Mr. B.
        and Lovelace are portrayed as rakes but Sir Charles Grandi-
        son is a perfect gentleman.

2489   SINGER, GODFREY FRANK.
        "Samuel Richardson and his Development of the Epistolary
        Novel. "   In The Epistolary Novel: Its Origin, Development,
        Decline, and Residuary Influence.   (Philadelphia: Univ. Pa.

Press, 1933), Chap. V; rpt. New York: Russell & Russell,
1963.

General comments on and plot summaries of the three
novels; sees Richardson as aiming in Clarissa at "an ultimate
naturalism"; and considers the influences on the epistolary
novel and the advantages of the form to Richardson.

2490   SKILTON, DAVID.
       "Richardson and Fielding." In [165], pp. 19-31.

Richardson introduced into English fiction a realistic treatment of the contemporary world, while at the same time he
represented the ideology of his class and age.   His novels
reflect a fear of sexuality--"a fetishistic devotion to 'purity'
in women, set against an almost demonic sexual drive in the
evil man." Fielding, on the other hand, wrote a highly for-
malized kind of novel, creating "new fictional worlds by traditional formulas of character and action which are the common property of neo-classical culture."

2491   SMIDT, KRISTIAN.
       "Character and Plot in the Novels of Samuel Richardson."
       Crit. Quart. 17 (1975): 155-166.

A study of the various characteristics of Richardson's
achievement--his sense of humor, his belief in the malleabil-
ity of character, his psychological insight, his projecting
character in action--that concludes that his main accomplishment is in uniting plot and character very closely in spite of
the epistolary technique and the enormous quantity of words.

2492   WOLFF, CYNTHIA GRIFFIN.
       Samuel Richardson and the Eighteenth-Century Puritan Char-
       acter.   Hamden, Conn.: Archon, 1972.

Examines Richardson's novels for his conception of character, his literary devices for rendering character, and the
sources of both.   Sees him as a psychological novelist, with
a special genius for capturing the "dynamics of character
under stress: he anatomizes identity by detailing its disintegration" in Clarissa. In Sir Charles Grandison, Richardson
writes the novel of manners.

2493   WRIGHT, TERENCE.
       " 'Metaphors for Reality': Mind and Object and the Problem
       of Form in the Early Novel." DUJ 38 (1977): 239-248.

The relationship between Man and his world in novels is

essentially empirical. This article traces the "emergence of
metaphoric structures from this empirical approach to reality
by examining the relationship between mind and object" in
Robinson Crusoe, Clarissa, Sir Charles Grandison, and Tristram Shandy. The process by which the novelist transmutes
imitation into realism constitutes a first principle for a "poetic" of the novel--"poetic" in the sense that the process is
a "metaphorization" of reality.

2494   ZIRKER, MALVIN R. , JR.
        "Richardson's Correspondence: The Personal Letter as Pri-
        vate Experience." In [1], pp. 71-91.

        Discusses Richardson's commitment to the letter form and
        states that his personal letters were relatively uninteresting
        as compared to those used in his epistolary novels.

See also: 376, 681, 686, 723, 724, 908, 909, 959, 973, 991, 1559,

                            Pamela

2495   ALLENTUCK, MARCIA EPSTEIN.
        "Narration and Illustration: The Problem of Richardson's
        Pamela." PQ 51 (1972): 874-886.

        An analysis of Plates I and II in the later editions of Pam-
        ela to illustrate seminal passages in the novel. These illus-
        trations (29) "neither elaborate nor extend the inward life of
        the novel, but they do afford important evidence for [Richard-
        son's] fictive intentions on the conscious level."

2496   BALL, DONALD L.
        "Pamela II: A Primary Link in Richardson's Development as
        a Novelist." MP 65 (1968): 334-342.

        Demonstrates "the importance of Pamela II to Richardson's
        growth as a novelist by showing in some detail just how he
        developed his narrative, characterization, and epistolary tech-
        niques in Pamela II beyond those in Pamela I and then ap-
        plied these improved techniques in Clarissa and Grandison."
        Shows how he broadened and refined his narrative technique
        by exercising his skill in the timing and spacing of narrative
        events, and by improving his ability in the drawing of scenes.
        He also widens the scope of his characterization and develops
        new methods of presenting character; concludes that Pamela II
        played a major role in the development of Richardson's tech-
        nique in Clarissa.

2497   BELL, MICHAEL D.
       "Pamela's Wedding and the Marriage of the Lamb." PQ 49
       (1970): 100-112.

       Maintains that Pamela "owes at least some of its power
       to a kind of religious substructure" and that the "theological
       connotations of the novel's language and situation permit Rich-
       ardson to tap for his own secular purposes the strongly emo-
       tional religious current of his day." The romantic love ele-
       ment, which made the novel so popular, was based on an
       anxiety which plagued English society in the 1740s--the anxiet
       of eternal damnation.

2498   BREDSDORFF, THOMAS.
       "Whatever Happened to Women's Lust?" In [16], pp. 175-
       180.

       Examines the disappearance of women's lust with the novel,
       Pamela. Attempts to answer the questions: How does Pam-
       ela remain virtuous in spite of the many attempts made on
       her virtue? How does she, reared under the feudalism of
       Lady B, react to and overcome the economic materialism of
       Mr. B?

2499   BRISSENDEN, R. F.
       "Pamela." In [2505], pp. 50-56; rpt. from [2447], pp. 12-
       21.

       Argues that it is the "confused but angry concern with so-
       cial injustice" displayed in Pamela that made it popular in
       its day, and still readable today.

2500   BROOKS, DOUGLAS.
       "Richardson's Pamela and Fielding's Joseph Andrews." EIC
       17 (1967): 158-168.

       Argues that "in writing Joseph Andrews Fielding was, in
       fact, rewriting Pamela in his own mode. In its structural
       symmetry, its comic approach to the psychological, its theme
       ... indeed, in all respects--Fielding's novel stands as a sym
       bol of Augustanism, opposed to Pamela, the real voice of
       the future."

2501   BRUCKMANN, PATRICIA C.
       "The Settings in Pamela." In Trans. of the Samuel Johnson
       Society of the Northwest, 6 (Calgary: Samuel Johnson Soc.
       of the N.W., 1973): 1-10.

       Pamela grows in experience "by moving from B's peaceful

house in Bedfordshire, a version of pastoral ... to his gothic
mansion in Lincolnshire, an emblem of melancholy, not only in
the rendition of the house, but more critically in terms of
the resonances offered by a study of Lincoln, a county tra-
ditionally associated with dampness, gloom, and gothic activity. "

2502   CHALKER, JOHN.
       " 'Virtue Rewarded': The Sexual Theme in Richardson's
       Pamela. "   Literary Half-Yearly 2 (1961): 58-64.

       A defense of Richardson's morality based on a considera-
       tion of the moral tradition to which he belonged.   Pamela re-
       sists Mr. B. because "she belongs to a Puritan moral tra-
       dition which regards personal inviolability as the great moral
       end and because chastity is, for her, symbolic of personal
       integrity. "

2503   CLARK, JOHN R.
       "Unnoticed Satire: Pamela's Shape and Form. "   Scholia Saty-
       rica 1, No. 1 (1975):   32-37.

       Argues that Pamela is sexually intentional in her pursuit
       of Mr. B, and that he follows a "Descensus, or Downward
       Path" on her body, fully realizing "the plunge and cadence
       of the pursuit down the surfaces of this pseudo-religious wrig-
       gling wench. "

2504   COSTA, RICHARD HAUER.
       "The Epistolary Monitor in Pamela. "   MLQ 31 (1970): 38-
       47.

       Demonstrates that "the epistolary form, as refined by
       Richardson, has an efficacy in Pamela beyond the merits most
       commonly ascribed to it. "   Pamela's letters and journal,
       intercepted and read by Mr. B, play an important role in her
       real escape, her flight from the ruin that awaited her at her
       parents' lower-class home: "They have led to a breaking
       through by a servant girl of the bastions of gentry. "

2505   COWLER, ROSEMARY.
       Twentieth Century Interpretations of Pamela.   Englewood
       Cliffs, N. J. : Prentice-Hall, 1969.

2506   DONOVAN, ROBERT A.
       "The Problem of Pamela, or, Virtue Unrewarded. "   SEL 3
       (1963): 377-395.   Rpt. in The Shaping Vision (Ithaca, N. Y. :
       Cornell Univ. Press, 1966), pp. 47-67.

Examines the novel from the standpoint of "the purely social dilemma which confronts Pamela" and argues that it is
Pamela's response to this social dilemma that gives "integrity to the novel as an artistic structure." Takes exception
to critics who judge the novel solely on moral grounds.

2507   DUSSINGER, JOHN A.
        "What Pamela Knew: An Interpretation." JEGP 69 (1970):
        377-393. In [98], pp. 53-76.

        On the growth of Pamela's character and self-knowledge,
        and her search for identity as a moral agent. Pamela is
        neither "reliable" as a narrator nor a "moral stereotype" as
        a character. She plays various roles, from child to wife of
        Mr. B, so that she might impose order on her subjective ex-
        perience. In the epilogue the novel ends as it began, with a
        completed cycle of experience, the cycle of the daughter's
        growth as a reincarnate mother, reigning in her deceased
        mistress's household in a restored matriarchal order.

2508   EAVES, T. C. DUNCAN and BEN D. KIMPEL.
        "Richardson's Revisions of Pamela." SB 20 (1967): 61-88.

        A study of Richardson's revisions concludes that it is the
        first edition which "is closer to the Pamela whom Richardson
        actually imagined," whereas later editions "try to approach
        the Pamela he thought he should have imagined."

2509   ERICKSON, ROBERT A.
        "Mother Jewkes, Pamela, and the Midwives." ELH 43 (1976)
        500-516.

        This paper shows that "in the Lincolnshire episode of Pam-
        ela ... the antagonism ... between the heroine-victim and
        her 'rough-natur'd Governess,' Mrs. Jewkes ... is a passage
        of considerable power and resonance, and that much of the
        success of the novel itself is owing to Richardson's skillful
        elaboration of the characters of Mrs. Jewkes and Pamela from
        the folklore of midwifery and witchcraft."

2510   FOLKENFLIK, ROBERT.
        "A Room of Pamela's Own." ELH 39 (1972): 585-596.

        Discusses the importance of "place" and privacy in Pamela.
        "There are three kinds of spatialization ... : social hierarchy
        seen in terms of distance, the actual layout of the house,
        and Pamela's body, divided into discrete portions which have
        varying amounts of value. The invasion of one spatial order
        involves the perversion of all, and Pamela's problem is to

create an interior space through the private consciousness
constituted by her writings. "

2511   FORTUNA, JAMES LOUIS, JR.
        The Unsearchable Wisdom of God: A Study of Providence in
        Richardson's Pamela (UFMH 49).   Gainesville: Univ. Press
        of Fla. , 1980.

        The design of Pamela derives from a "fictive mirroring
        of what was considered to be the world order of [Richardson's]
        day--a world order which was Christian, sustained through a
        divine providence both general and particular, and one in which
        the reward of virtue and the punishment of vice were ...
        things believed actually to occur in daily life. " By under-
        standing how providence (the major theme) works in Pamela,
        the reader will realize that the religious elements serve a
        larger purpose: they provide evidence that a divine power is
        perpetually at work in and through man and nature, to nourish
        and reward virtue.

2512   JEFFREY, DAVID K.
        "The Epistolary Format of Pamela and Humphry Clinker. "
        In [32], pp. 145-154.

        The advantage of the epistolary format is that the writer
        exists somewhere between stream of consciousness and emotion
        recollected in tranquillity, so that he remains close to the
        reality of experience, yet is able to react consciously to it;
        the writer of letters is both isolated and unreliable.   Both
        heroines (Pamela and Lydia) define themselves by projecting
        themselves onto paper; the epistolary form, therefore, iso-
        lates both heroines from reality and enables them to create
        their own portraits of themselves.

2513   JENKINS, OWEN.
        "Richardson's Pamela and Fielding's 'Vile Forgeries. ' "   PQ
        44 (1965): 200-210.

        An analysis of Pamela II as a defense of Pamela I against
        Fielding's parody rather than a sequel to it, and of Richard-
        son's supposed offenses against truth and morality in the orig-
        inal Pamela, Fielding's criticism, and Richardson's reply.

2514   KAY, DONALD.
        "Pamela and the Poultry. " SNL 10 (1973): 25-27.

        Concerned with the fowl imagery which Richardson uses to
        heighten the dramatic tension of the plot.

2515   KEARNEY, ANTHONY.
        "Richardson's Pamela: The Aesthetic Case." REL 7, iii
        (1966): 78-90. Rpt. in [2442], pp. 28-38; [2505], pp. 78-
        88.

            Examines the complex relationship between experience and
        the literary product in Pamela. Richardson's problem arises
        from the "two voices" of Pamela, one as "author" and one
        as "character"; the two voices are never successfully fused.

2516   KINKEAD-WEEKES, MARK.
        "Pamela." Introduction to Everyman's Library Edition of
        Pamela. London: J. M. Dent & Sons Ltd. , 1962. Rpt. in
        [2442], pp. 20-27; [2505], pp. 57-63.

            Discusses Richardson's dramatic imagination.

2517   KOVACS, ANNA-MARIA.
        "Pamela's Poverty." Revue des Langues Vivantes 44 (1978):
        3-14.

            Richardson's problems in the development of Pamela's
        character "stem from a complete lack of faith in the very
        possibility of her existence." He could not create both a
        perfect and a poor heroine; therefore much of the conflict
        within Pamela's character is due to Richardson's "ambivalence
        to poverty." When she is no longer poor she becomes ob-
        sequious; it is when her "problems" disappear that she be-
        comes flawed as a character--and exceedingly dull.

2518   KREISSMAN, BERNARD.
        Pamela-Shamela: A Study of the Criticisms, Burlesques,
        Parodies, and Adaptations of Richardson's "Pamela." Lin-
        coln: Univ. Nebr. Press, 1960.

            An entertaining account of the criticism of Pamela, both
        pro and con, during the eighteenth century, and a final chap-
        ter dealing with Upton Sinclair's parody Another Pamela, or
        Virtue Still Rewarded (1950) to illustrate that, even with all
        of Pamela's personal defects replaced by virtues, and all the
        revisions suggested by the criticism included, the Sinclair
        novel is not as great as the original.

2519   LESSER, SIMON O.
        "A Note on 'Pamela.' " CE 14 (1952): 13-17. Rpt. in The
        Whispered Meanings: Selected Essays, ed. Robert Sprich
        and Richard W. Noland (Boston: Univ. Mass. Press, 1977),
        pp. 14-19.

A psychological study which shows the novel to be a Cinderella love story.

2520   LEVIN, GERALD.
"Richardson's Pamela: 'Conflicting Trends.'" Amer. Imago
28 (1971): 319-329. Rpt. in [2477], pp. 29-53.

A psychoanalytic analysis of the masochistic traits of Pamela and Mr. B. "Richardson's ability to disturb the emotional current of the novel in order to follow the turns of fantasy gives credence to Freud's idea that character in the psychological novel may reflect 'conflicting trends' in mental life."

2521   LYLES, ALBERT M.
"Pamela's Trials." CLAJ 8 (1965): 290-292.

Argues that "the characterization of Mr. B as a justice permits Richardson to dramatize climactic scenes of the novel in terms of the legal metaphor of a trial and thus to make more obvious the relationship of both the melodramatic and comic scenes to the theme of virtue rewarded."

2522   McINTOSH, CAREY.
"Pamela's Clothes." ELH 35 (1968): 75-83. Rpt. in [2505],
pp. 89-96.

An analysis of the clothing allusions that constitute a leitmotif in Part I of Pamela. Clothes function as an emblem of social standing and as sexual symbols.

2523   McKILLOP, ALAN D.
"Samuel Richardson: 'Pamela.'" In [2505], pp. 26-32; rpt.
from [134], pp. 51, 55-63.

Discusses Richardson's "enlargement," his "writing to the moment" and use of the letter form in Pamela.

2524   "The Mock-Marriage Device in Pamela." PQ 26 (1947): 285-
288.

Discusses the mock-marriage episode as it related to similar episodes in real life.

2525   MILLER, NANCY K.
"The Rewards of Virtue: Pamela." In The Heroine's Text
(New York: Columbia Univ. Press, 1980), pp. 37-50.

Pamela's problem is to learn how to reconcile love and sexuality. Although the reader can "decipher the text of Pamela's inner conflict, the structure of the novel is dominated by the externalized struggle between Pamela and Mr. B., between virtue and vice." Thematically the novel is divided into two parts: the first is concerned with a daughter's confrontation with aggressive male sexuality, the second by her transformation from daughter to wife and the testing of her marriage as "integrator of sexuality."

2526   MORTON, DONALD E.
"Theme and Structure in Pamela." Studies in the Novel 3 (1971): 242-257.

The qualities of balance, proportion, order, and harmony support the "essentially Puritan theme of 'Virtue Rewarded.'" Concludes that " ... two planes of action, the vertical plane of the social scale and the horizontal plane of spiritual regeneration" and the act of Mr. B's repentance help to make "Pamela's story unfold with the functional beauty of Puritan art."

2527   MUECKE, D. C.
"Beauty and Mr. B." SEL 7 (1967): 467-474.

Compares Pamela to fairy tales, especially Beauty and the Beast, and considers the significance of this resemblance.

2528   NEEDHAM, GWENDOLYN B.
"Richardson's Characterization of Mr. B. and the Double Purpose in Pamela." ECS 3 (1970): 433-474.

A close analysis of the novel reveals that "Richardson gives us a thorough and realistic characterization of Mr. B, in whose successful creation he demonstrates his knowledge of the male psyche and his powers of conscious artistry, both of which are effectively displayed in the ... careful integration of the villain-hero's consistent psychological motivation with his protagonist's role in the plot." It also points out how "an awareness of Mr. B's complete character and role leads to a clearer understanding of Pamela's character and role, to a better appreciation of Richardson's dramatic interplay of their personalities, to a revelation of the author's double purpose, and to a deeper realization of his conscious craftsmanship in constructing a closely integrated plot which achieves both his double purpose and the story's predetermined happy ending."

2529   OLIVIER, THEO.

"Pamela and Shamela: A Reassessment." ESA 17 (1974):
59-70.

Argues that Richardson is an entertaining as well as a
moral writer: "The structure of Pamela suggests a constant
duality of intention toward Mr B.; this indicates that Richardson has woven a tale of suspense that is also amusing and
moralistic." Shamela is considered a slight but amusing piece
of bawdy parody that soon loses sight of Pamela and develops
in the direction of Joseph Andrews.

2530   PARKER, DOROTHY.
        "The Time Scheme of Pamela and the Character of B." TSLL
        11 (1969): 695-704.

        A study of the time scheme in Pamela, reversing it and
        reading the novel backwards, shows that the traditional inter-
        pretation of Mr. B as "absurd or monstrous" is not valid
        and that "the virtue rewarded at the end is not only Pamela's,
        but B's."

2531   PONS, CHRISTIAN.
        Samuel Richardson: Pamela. Paris: Colin, 1970.

        Discusses the sources of Pamela, including the moral and
        literary traditions, the dramatic movement and the structure
        of the novel, its realism, and its ethical and psychological
        aspects.

2532   REID, B. L.
        "Justice to Pamela." HR 9 (1956): 516-533. Rpt. in [154],
        pp. 31-51. Abridged in [2505], pp. 33-41.

        An essay on the artistic achievement of Pamela; "a defence
        against the two commonest and most serious indictments of
        the novel: that it is fatally sentimental and artificial, and
        that its pretentious moralism is vicious and false."

2533   ROUSSEL, ROY.
        "Reflections on the Letter: The Reconciliation of Distance
        and Presence in Pamela." ELH 41 (1974): 375-399.

        In Pamela "the letter incarnates the movement of love and
        defines ... the choices open to [Richardson's] characters"
        and serves "as the resolution of this tension, the agency which
        reconciles distance and presence, the self defined by society
        and the self defined by love."

2534   SHARROCK, ROGER.

"Richardson's Pamela: the Gospel and the Novel." DUJ 27 (1966): 67-74.

Interprets the novel as a Christian work of art: "it is the Christian recognition of individual personality that makes a single human heart worth examining all that closely." Pamela is a new kind of heroine, a common, ordinary person representing common life described in a mean style.

2535   SIEGEL, JUNE SIGLER.
"Lovelace and Rameau's Nephew: Roots of Poetic Amoralism." DidS 19 (1978): 163-174.

Despite their many differences, both Lovelace and the Neveu represent a new type of character in prose fiction possessing three major features which make them different from their predecessors: 1) abnormal energy or intensity of life, 2) dichotomy, and 3) poetic expansion. Both characters "go beyond the pale of 18th-century realism by the power of their violent imaginations. They have a creative life of their own."

2536   SPACKS, PATRICIA MEYER.
"The Sense of Audience: Samuel Richardson, Colley Cibber." In [166], pp. 193-226.

In both Pamela and Cibber's Apology writing is performance and process; both books emphasize writing as pleasure, as control, and as significant action. In Pamela, Richardson suggests the "creation of a life through writing about it, the writing itself literally affecting the course of action...." Pamela uses letters to develop her sense of self and to assert her identity, through the process of communication and dramatization that illustrates the universal nature of writing about the self. She uses her letters, with complete self-awareness, to tell a story, her sense of plot and audience as strong as that of her creator.

2537   STEEVES, HARRISON R.
"Virtue Unrewarded." In [169], pp. 53-87.

A discussion of Pamela and Richardson as a novelist. Looks at "whether [Pamela's] 'morality' is really moral, or despicable; whether Richardson's characters resemble humanity as most of us know it; and whether he writes badly because he didn't know better or because almost nobody wrote well at that time."

2538   STEIN, WILLIAM BYSSHE.
"Pamela: The Narrator as Unself-Conscious Hack." Bucknell Rev. 20 (1972): 39-66.

Discusses Richardson's handling of his chief narrative
voice: Pamela is the spokesman of the people, through whom
he primarily addresses the reader; and he intends that the
"simultaneity of the telling and the penning of the story is devised to present Pamela in the act of writing a novel about
how to write a novel."

2539   TEN HARMSEL, HENRIETTA.
        "The Villain-Hero in Pamela and Pride and Prejudice." CE
        23 (1961): 104-108.

Similarities between the two novels: both plots develop
from the same basic question: Will the "low" heroine catch
the aristocratic hero? And they both emphasize in the rising
action the hero's villainy: " ... for both heroines the whole
social struggle is dramatized in a conflict with a hero who
serves, in a sense, as the villain of the piece."

2540   WATT, IAN.
        "Love and the Novel: Pamela." From [183], pp. 135-173.
        Partially rpt. in [2505], pp. 42-49.

Discusses the unique literary qualities which Pamela brought
into fiction: "a detailed presentation of a personal relationship enriched by a series of developing contrasts between the
ideal and the real, the apparent and the actual, the spiritual
and the physical, the conscious and the unconscious."

2541   WILSON, STUART.
        "Richardson's Pamela: An Interpretation." PMLA 88 (1973):
        79-91.

Argues that Pamela's traumatic experience forms the "soul
of the plot; and as the record of her ordeal unfolds, we witness the development of a carefully designed and formally
proportioned work of fiction, one with the unity, balance, and
symmetry which are essential to the total form of any work
of art."

2542   WOLFF, RENATE C.
        "Pamela as Myth and Dream." Costerus 7 (1973): 223-235.

Interprets Pamela as a "remarkably consistent and revealing dream fantasy." Compares the novel to the Cinderella
story, and suggests that it is the projection of such a dream
as such a girl would fabricate during her hours of toil--a
dreamer who lives out the dream of the Puritan lower middle
class.

See also: 391, 821, 835, 1022, 1023, 1025, 1026, 1035, 1046,
     1049, 1051, 1065, 2447, 2455, 2460, 2464, 2467, 2472, 2474,
     2489, 2492

Clarissa

2543   BABB, HOWARD S.
       "Richardson's Narrative Mode in Clarissa." SEL 16 (1976):
       451-460.

          An analysis of a letter written by Lovelace to John Belford
       to illustrate Richardson's "narrative, dramatic, and stylistic
       art," and "his imaginative power ... in the complexities of
       Lovelace which come alive here, that character who ... exists
       in perpetual conflict, the demands of his rakish code warring
       ceaselessly with his love for Clarissa." Richardson's style--
       the multiplicity of alternatives, the suspense, pressure, and
       irony of shifting episodes--keeps the reader "in agonizing
       tension."

2544   BARKER, GERARD A.
       "Clarissa's 'Command of her Passions': Self-Censorship in
       the Third Edition." SEL 10 (1970): 525-539.

          Argues that Richardson's change in the third edition, to
       eliminate Clarissa's love for Lovelace, also eliminates "much
       of the psychological subtlety of the novel and replace[s] it
       with a banal melodrama of seduction. Clarissa's self-conflict
       becomes attenuated, and undue emphasis is placed on the ex-
       ternal struggle with her male adversary."

2545   BEER, GILLIAN.
       "Richardson, Milton, and the Status of Evil." RES 19 (1968):
       261-270.

          An analysis of the conscious parallels between Clarissa
       and both Comus and Paradise Lost to demonstrate how "Rich-
       ardson evolves an art which gives to the fate of the ordinary
       individual acting within a minutely observed society a grandeur
       of emotion and expression only previously attained in English
       literature by tragic princes or by Milton's epic religious art."

2546   BRAUDY, LEO.
       "Penetration and Impenetrability in Clarissa." In New Ap-
       proaches To Eighteenth-Century Literature, ed. Philip Harth
       (Selected Papers from the English Institute). (New York:
       Columbia Univ. Press, 1974), pp. 177-206.

Explores the social and cultural changes in the eighteenth
century and their effect on the attitudes toward personal identity and relations with other people in Clarissa; deals primarily with the sexual theme of the novel.

2547   BRISSENDEN, R. F.
        "Clarissa: The Sentimental Tragedy." In Virtue in Distress:
        Studies in the Novel of Sentiment from Richardson to Sade
        (New York: Barnes & Noble, 1974), pp. 159-186.

        Discusses the thematic complexity of Clarissa, "its range
        of social and moral significance, and the way in which the
        various elements in the work are brought tegether into a single
        coherent, concentrated action." Concludes that Clarissa's
        "greatness lies in the rigour, the unremitting thoroughness
        and the compassion with which the sentimental ideal is tested
        against the reality of man's nature."

2548   BROWNSTEIN, RACHEL MAYER.
        " 'An Exemplar to Her Sex': Richardson's Clarissa." YR
        67 (1977): 30-47.

        Clarissa's "paradoxical aim is to live up to her own ap-
        pearance" as an exemplar, "beautiful and desirable, ... an
        art object, too good for the real goods of the real world ...
        desired and imitated and beseiged by the world." Given this
        image, she had little choice but to die. The importance of
        the house and clothing as images, as well as her existence
        in her letters, is also discussed.

2549   CARROLL, JOHN
        "Annotating Clarissa." In [4], pp. 49-66.

        Discusses quotations and allusions in Clarissa, and the way
        in which they reveal or influence theme and character; con-
        cludes that Richardson's range of allusions and quotations sug-
        gests that he had sophisticated readers in mind as well as
        the young and the ignorant.

2550   "Richardson at Work: Revisions, Allusions, and Quotations
        in Clarissa." In [9], pp. 53-71.

        A collation of the first, second, and third editions indicates
        the meticulous care with which Richardson revised Clarissa;
        discusses the allusions that help to characterize Lovelace:
        he compares himself to the great conquerors of antiquity, and
        there are many references tying him both to Milton's Satan
        and to events in English and Continental history; frequent de-
        rogatory references to Swift.

2551   "Lovelace as Tragic Hero." UTQ 42 (1972): 14-25.

    Analyzes the novel's motifs--political, military, cosmic, otherworldly, and satanic--as well as Lovelace's good and bad traits. Traces the evolution of Lovelace from a Don Juan to a Tristan who in the end loses his soul as Clarissa saves hers.

2552   CARTER, A. E.
"The Greatest English Novelist (On the Occasion of the Bicentenary of Clarissa, 1748)." UTQ 17 (1948): 390-397.

    Argues that Clarissa is the greatest of Richardson's novels, especially in its powers of characterization and psychological insight; but also emphasizes Richardson's defects: Clarissa, for instance, is more symbol than woman.

2553   COHAN, STEVEN M.
"Clarissa and the Individuation of Character." ELH 43 (1976): 163-183.

    Discusses Richardson's development of the complex characters of Lovelace and Clarissa and examines their responses, " ... for there--in the emotional substance of the narrative ... we see how Richardson individuates character." Shows us how Richardson is able to involve the reader in the conflict just as much as the main characters are involved. Both Clarissa and Lovelace are "struggling to write a different script for themselves. Clarissa wants a 'tragical story' ... while Lovelace sees a 'comedy.' " Both fail.

2554   COPELAND, EDWARD W.
"Allegory and Analogy in Clarissa: The 'Plan' and the 'No-Plan.' " ELH 39 (1972): 254-265.

    Analyzes the effects that "two essentially different figurative strategies--allegory, a tool of rhetoric, and analogy, a form of logic--have on the possible or potential interpretations of the 'meaning' of Clarissa." Suggests that the "Plan" and the "No-Plan" can be seen as moving in two opposing directions: the " 'Plan' ... elevates the story to cosmic significance; and the 'No-Plan' insistently returns all the metaphors, allusions, and symbolic pretensions of the characters to the social and psychological world of the novel."

2555   "Clarissa and Fanny Hill: Sisters in Distress." Studies in the Novel 4 (1972): 343-352.

    A discussion of the nature of conventions shared by Fanny

<u>Hill</u> and Richardson's novels, especially <u>Clarissa</u>, to illustrate
the hermetic nature of sentimental fiction. Similar conventions and techniques suggest a possible source for the erotic
energies of <u>Clarissa</u>, especially its verbal ambiguities describing physical and spiritual passion.

2556   COX, STEPHEN D.
       "Defining the Self: Samuel Richardson's <u>Clarissa.</u>" In [93],
       pp. 59-81.

       Considers <u>Clarissa</u> "one of eighteenth-century literature's
       fullest investigations of the self's attempt to define its identity
       and significance...." At the same time, Richardson's sen-
       sitive analysis of his characters' psychology asserts the com-
       plexity and difficulty in determining the real nature of the
       self.   Concludes that Richardson, by focusing so fixedly on the
       death of Clarissa, converts the tragedy of personality into the
       tragedy of situation, and that for him the concept of sympathy
       can not be the ultimate solution to the problem of the self.

2557   DENTON, RAMONA.
       "Anna Howe and Richardson's Ambivalent Artistry in <u>Clarissa.</u>"
       <u>PQ</u> 58 (1979): 53-62.

       Anna Howe is a major character who affects <u>Clarissa's</u>
       action, structure, narrative point of view, and thematic com-
       plexity, and she supports feminist doctrines that Richardson
       himself might have considered dangerous: Anna rejects the
       traditional role of women in marriage because it threatens
       their autonomy.   Richardson dramatizes in Clarissa's situa-
       tion the very dangers of which Anna writes.

2558   DUSSINGER, JOHN A.
       "<u>Clarissa</u>: the Curse of Intellect." In [98], pp. 77-126.

       The discourse of mind in <u>Clarissa</u> creates a history of the
       self that moves toward death as atonement for the evil in
       human nature; the longing for permanence and perfection is
       really a longing for death.   Dussinger analyzes the unconscious
       process that leads Clarissa to isolation and death, seeking to
       "explore [her] relationship to authority ... to interpret her
       narcissistic fantasy in terms of the topographical symbolism
       of Harlowe Place; and finally, to trace the movement toward
       her death as a final deliverance from the body and from con-
       sciousness of time."

2559   "Richardson's Tragic Muse." <u>PQ</u> 46 (1967): 18-33.

       Emphasizes Richardson's indebtedness to late seventeenth-

century drama for his characterization of Clarissa as a tragic
heroine. Discusses the chastity theme of Clarissa as being
especially relevant to the distressed-heroine tradition, and
asserts that Richardson's real genius was in giving psychological complexity and social relevance to stage conventions.

2560   "Conscience and the Pattern of Christian Perfection in Clar-
       issa." PMLA 81 (1966): 236-245.

       An analysis of the religious theme of Clarissa shows that
       the novel "combines formal realism and moral allegory" and
       sets "forth an ideal pattern of holy living and holy dying which
       derives from the central Christian doctrine of the atonement."

2561   FARRELL, WILLIAM J.
       "The Style and the Action in Clarissa." SEL 3 (1963): 365-
       375. In [2442], pp. 92-101.

       Disagrees with Ian Watt's thesis that Richardson broke with
       "the traditional decorums of prose" and maintains that he used
       them whenever they suited his artistic purpose, as in the case
       of Lovelace, who writes and speaks in a style associated with
       courtly love, and that of Pamela, "who uses the pathetic lang-
       uage of the contemporary 'she-tragedy.' "

2562   GARBER, FREDERICK.
       "Richardson, Rousseau, and the Autonomy of the Elect."
       CRCL 5 (1978): 154-168.

       Compares Clarissa with La Nouvelle Héloïse with regard
       to the heroines' struggle for autonomy of self. In spite of
       the many similarities between the two novels, Rousseau has
       made a world for Julie "which turns the shapes of Clarissa's
       Hell into a paradigmatic but unsteady Eden." Concludes that
       "Richardson and Rousseau built on the same elemental nar-
       rative, a quest for forms of shelter for the self, forms which
       would acknowledge its contextual autonomy. The quest ended
       with a shelter found but with the self no longer there."

2563   GILLIS, CHRISTINA MARSDEN.
       "Private room and public space: the paradox of form in Clar-
       issa." SVEC 176 (1979): 153-168.

       Through the character of Clarissa, Richardson explores
       "enclosed, internalized, highly personalized experience; he
       gives us rooms where doors remain closed, windows curtained,
       where a confined and isolated heroine writes letters for the
       self." These private rooms come under attack when Clarissa
       is raped and the letter writing mode changes to the more pub-

lic or openly rhetorical. The "ordering of space which Richardson ultimately brings to bear in Clarissa is that of the
Palladian house ... [whose] inter-connected, 'thoroughfare'
rooms provided [him] with a model fully commensurate with
his own epistolary craft."

2564   GOLDKNOPF, DAVID.
"The Meaning of the Epistolary Format in Clarissa." In The Life
of the Novel (Chicago: Univ. Chicago Press, 1972), pp. 59-78.

   Discusses Richardson's mastery of the epistolary format
and how that format lends itself to its function: " ... the
sense or 'message' it conveys as a literary phenomenon of
its age." Shows how Richardson's concentration on the inner
life of the characters, through the use of letters, holds the
objective events of the story at a distance. These letters
are " ... the attempt to relieve the banality of [the characters'] inner life, to shape its confusions into a coherent
image, and to project that image as an esthetically processed
wish-fulfillment against the moral chaos of the outer world
--all through the instrument of literacy."

2565   GOPNIK, IRWIN.
A Theory of Style and Richardson's "Clarissa." The Hague:
Mouton, 1970.

   A structural analysis of the novel from a linguistic basis.
"This analysis reveals the esthetic integrity of an extremely
complex but masterfully ordered ironic manipulation of language of which the major structural elements are subtle but
pervasive networks of verbal motifs."

2566   HARVEY, A. D.
"Clarissa and the Puritan Tradition." EIC 28 (1978): 38-51.

   Argues that Clarissa's death is the only alternative because
of the loss of her virginity. Although the Puritan moral code
is at the core of the novel, it has little to do with Clarissa's
death because the Puritans were not particularly concerned
with female virginity. Her "death is partly the ultimate indulgence of eighteenth-century sexual fantasies, and partly the
result of the contradictions implicit in the ... century's reification of female sexuality...."

2567   HILL, CHRISTOPHER.
"Clarissa Harlowe and Her Times." EIC 5 (1955): 315-340.
Rpt. in [2442], pp. 102-123; [53], pp. 32-63.

   Considers "the novel in the light of eighteenth-century economic developments and evolving Puritan attitudes toward society, marriage and the individual."

2568   HILLES, FREDERICK W.
"The Plan of Clarissa."   PQ 45 (1966):   236-248.   Rpt. in
[2442], pp. 80-91.

Argues that Richardson had a plan in writing Clarissa and that that plan reveals a plot that is highly symmetrical and "a mighty maze." Analyzes the constructive art of the novel by breaking it up into roughly equal parts, according to the eight volumes in which it was printed.

2569   JOHNSON, GLEN M.
"Richardson's 'Editor' in Clarissa."   JNT 10 (1980):   99-114.

Richardson's editor, in one sense an alienation device similar to those that appear in twentieth-century drama, provides 429 footnotes, various editorial headnotes and interpolations within and between letters; his intrusions and interpretive comments become an integral part of Clarissa's presentational strategy.   The editor is essential to the tension existing between intellect and emotion, for within the structure of Clarissa he is the ethical norm that maintains the book's unique double vision: he is "reader's friend, spokesman for ethical judgment, source of irony and of dramatic tension...."

2570   KAPLAN, FRED.
" 'Our Short Story': The Narrative Devices of Clarissa."
SEL 11 (1971):   549-562.

Argues that Richardson displays "artistic expertise" in his use of such narrative devices as "flashback, foreshortening, chronological discontinuity, delayed details, editorial summary, abridgement, footnotes, reported dialogue, and multiple point of view" to develop "themes of isolation, discontinuity, the challenge to moral order, and the nature of Christian salvation."

2571   KARL, FREDERICK R.
"Samuel Richardson and Clarissa."   In [126], pp. 99-145.

A close analysis of Clarissa " ... in a medium that involves slow revelations, deceit, disguised intentions, mixed motives--that is, in an epistolary style." Gives proof that Richardson was more successful in using the epistolary style in Clarissa than in Pamela.

2572   KEARNEY, ANTHONY.

Samuel Richardson: Clarissa (Studies in English Literature, No. 55). London: Arnold, 1975.

A general survey that emphasizes design and movement, the voice and style of the characters reflected in the letters, and characterization.

2573   "Clarissa and the Epistolary Form." EIC 16 (1966): 44-56.

Richardson's letter-writing technique does more than narrate the action of Clarissa, it gives coherence and shape to the tragic action: "As Richardson saw it, ... the finest qualities of epistolary expression have an obvious affinity with those of character. Ideally, one expects propriety, frankness, modesty, and, above all, 'ease and simplicity.' These qualities are basic to the business of letter-writing, and by relying on this assumption in the minds of his first readers Richardson was able to use them as criteria for character judgement."

2574   KINKEAD-WEEKES, MARK.
"Clarissa Restored?" RES 10 (1959): 156-171.

Discussion of the changes Richardson made in the various editions of Clarissa due to the reactions and criticism of its earliest readers--changes which were designed to counteract misinterpretations and reinforce moral value. Argues that the third edition is in many ways cruder than the first and that if these changes were made because of the audience's misreading and criticism, then the first edition is the best.

2575   KNIGHT, CHARLES A.
"The Function of Wills in Richardson's Clarissa." TSLL 11 (1969): 1183-1190.

Discusses the role of legacies in the plot and the relationship between characters; demonstrates how Richardson uses the legacies to "anchor both plot and character in social reality." Author is "concerned with social attitudes as they are embodied in the structure of the novel."

2576   KONIGSBERG, IRA.
"The Tragedy of Clarissa." MLQ 27 (1966): 285-298. Rpt. with revisions in [2474], pp. 74-94.

An examination of the character of Clarissa and her behavior in a tragic world reveals that as a heroine she does err and that her calamities are brought about by a special tragic flaw; she is also a victim of tragic irony. "The basic pattern of the novel is not the pattern of tragedy; yet by con-

sciously following the critical rules of his own period, Richardson created a tragic novel and embodied within eight volumes a tragic cosmos."

2577   LANSBURY, CORAL.
       "The Triumph of Clarissa: Richardson's Divine Comedy."
       Thalia (Ottawa) 1, i (1978): 9-17.

       Clarissa's death, far from being a tragedy, is in reality
    a divine marriage in the Celestial City and she is now Queen
    of the Universe.   Through her posthumous letters and her
    Will, Richardson has made Clarissa live and "the tone of the
    novel moves from tragedy to comedy, as her happy ending
    marks the downfall of her enemies." The author uses many
    references to Christian scripture and suggests that perhaps
    the real tragedy of Clarissa lies in her triumph, which none
    of us can share.

2578   LAUREN, BARBARA.
       "Clarissa and The Newgate Calendar (1768): A Perspective
       on the Novel Twenty Years Later." MLS 8, iii (1978): 5-
       11.

       Earlier readers of Clarissa found the subject matter mor-
    bid and the treatment neurotic: it is instructive, therefore,
    to read in the Newgate Calendar the details of a crime very
    similar to that committed by Lovelace and to discover an al-
    most contemporary reaction to it.   The seducer was Lord
    Baltimore, who committed rape upon a young milliner whom
    he kept captive for the purpose.   What chiefly impressed the
    Newgate writer was not the psychological or physical anguish
    that the victim suffered but the extraordinary social abyss
    that separated the noble lord and his victim.

2579   LEIBOWITZ, JUDITH.
       "The Poetics of Salvation in Clarissa, La Nouvelle Héloïse,
       and Die Leiden des jungen Werther." In Proceedings: Pa-
       cific Northwest Conference on Foreign Languages.   Twenty-
       fifth annual meeting, April 19-20, 1974, Eastern Washington
       State College.   Vol. 25, Part 1: Literature and Linguistics,
       ed. Walter C. Kraft.   (Corvallis: Ore. State Univ. Press,
       1974), pp. 242-245.

       Argues that the salvation of self through abnegation changes
    during the eighteenth century to the glorification of an asser-
    tive and passionate self, which is a secularized attitude that
    anticipates the "religion" of the self in the Romantic Age;
    Clarissa gains salvation in Christian terms solely through the
    quality of her feelings.

2580   LEVIN, GERALD.
        "Lovelace's Dream." L & P 20 (1970): 121-127.   Rpt. in
        [2477], pp. 54-86.

        Lovelace's pursuit of Clarissa is the result of a particular
        kind of masochism--moral masochism, in which morality be-
        comes sexualized again and the Oedipus complex becomes ac-
        tive; the Clarissa who lives through the rape is the Oedipal
        mother, and Lovelace is the Oedipal child whom Clarissa
        suckles.   She has become in his imagination a punishing
        mother whose desexualized morbid moralism demands the sac-
        rifice of his erotic life.

2581   McCULLOUGH, BRUCE.
        "The Novel of Sentiment." In [133], pp. 23-41.

        A look at Richardson's novels, especially Clarissa, in com-
        parison to Moll Flanders.   Concludes that Clarissa, although
        called a novel of sentiment, is not particularly sentimental,
        but that it "is a study of violence done to a temperament for-
        mulated upon the moral concepts of a highly sensitive and
        somewhat romanticized Puritan conscience....   It is the cu-
        mulative force of masterly handling of innumerable small de-
        tails that makes the novel what it is.   The connection between
        action and feeling finding dramatic expression in the character
        of Clarissa makes her not just a character but a personality."

2582   MILLER, NANCY K.
        "The Misfortunes of Virtue: I. Clarissa." In The Heroine's
        Text (New York: Columbia Univ. Press, 1980), pp. 83-95.

        An interpretive account of Clarissa's seduction and rape,
        emphasizing that Clarissa is governed by her inability to for-
        get the "singular event that forces her to exist in the world
        as a sexual personality on its terms."   Clarissa wants to
        escape the judgment of this world by a symbolic transforma-
        tion that would dissolve the social and sexual polarization in
        which she is trapped; when she realizes that a secular reso-
        lution is impossible, she has no alternative but to accept
        death.

2583   MOYNIHAN, ROBERT D.
        "Clarissa and the Enlightened Woman as Literary Heroine."
        JHI 36 (1975): 159-166.

        Values and patterns established by Defoe in Religious Court-
        ship are essential to the structure and theme of Clarissa.
        Discusses Clarissa's struggle with "her own moral preroga-
        tives ... in the face of impossible and unreasoning family
        demands."

2584   NAPIER, ELIZABETH R.
        " 'Tremble and Reform': The Inversion of Power in Richard-
        son's Clarissa. " ELH 42 (1975): 214-223.

        An analysis of the power imagery in Clarissa and the shift
        from Lovelace in the beginning of the novel to Clarissa at
        the end. The "usurpation of Lovelace's power has been ac-
        complished through explicit manipulation of image and event
        by the novel's characters. The result is a perfect inversion
        of the novel's formal pattern: the triumphant resolution of
        Clarissa's fictional design. "

2585   NOBLE, YVONNE.
        "Clarissa: Paradise irredeemably Lost. " In Transactions of
        the Fourth International Congress on the Enlightenment, The-
        odore Besterman, pub. (SVEC 154) Oxford: Voltaire Fndtn. ,
        1976, pp. 1529-1545.

        Considers the question of why Richardson was able to real-
        ize the divisive principle of the Fall in his modern local world,
        yet could not follow Milton in proclaiming a life-renewing al-
        ternative. Richardson's conscious intention was to convey to
        his reader the confidence in Christian salvation that Milton's
        poem explicitly confirms, yet his imagination never lets the
        reader's attention go beyond the dead Clarissa. "Whereas
        Eve carries forth her fruitful seed into a significant human
        history, Clarissa's deathbed is sterile; death triumphs, and
        Paradise remains irredeemably lost. "

2586   PALMER, WILLIAM J.
        "Two Dramatists: Lovelace and Richardson in Clarissa. "
        Studies in the Novel 5 (1973): 7-21.

        Lovelace, the "objective correlative" of Richardson's sub-
        conscious mind, establishes dramatic control over Clarissa;
        he expresses the frustrated desires of Richardson's uncon-
        scious: the "desire for dramatic control over other people,
        the desire for self-drmatization, and the obsessive need to
        be acclaimed as an artist. "

2587   PARK, WILLIAM.
        "Clarissa as Tragedy. " SEL 16 (1976): 461-471.

        The meaning of Clarissa may be found in its tragic form,
        not in cultural speculations about Puritan sexual mores or in
        conduct-book lessons to children and parents. From the be-
        ginning, Clarissa is isolated and associated with death, and
        she quickly becomes aware that she is playing a tragic role.
        Several motifs, such as Clarissa's relations with her father
        and that of incest, gain full meaning only when placed in a

tragic context: it is perfectly natural--in tragedy--for hate
and incompatibility to arise between Clarissa and her father.

2588   POOVEY, MARY.
       "Journeys from this World to the Next: The Providential
       Promise in Clarissa and Tom Jones." ELH 43 (1976): 300-
       315.

       Clarissa and Tom Jones are "fictional expressions of the
       Christian epic ... based on the design of providence with its
       attendent promise of reward...." What is important are the
       differences in expressing the relationship between the absolute
       world, which offers the promise, and the temporal world, in
       which it must be earned. Richardson conceives of the two
       realms as contiguous but incompatible, whereas Fielding as-
       sumes that "the absolute can be perceived through temporal
       realities...."

2589   PRESTON, JOHN.
       "Clarissa (i): A Process of Estrangement," "Clarissa (ii):
       A Form of Freedom." In [151], pp. 38-93.

       I.   Analyzes Clarissa as displaying an existential crisis:
       the characters are "all seen at those moments when their
       connections with reality are imperilled, that is when they are
       involved in the process of writing and reading. Thus their
       crisis is the crisis of the novel itself, a crisis of form."
       Considers the relationship of author and reader: the reader
       is expected to sustain the novel, even as he abandons himself
       to it, a fact that explains why we feel the novel leads to ali-
       enation.
       II. Richardson tells the reader that he can grasp the real
       only in the shape of fiction, for "the essence of fiction is that
       it is the whole story"; but Richardson is modern in his notion
       that a "completed action" does not conform to actual exper-
       ience. The "second self" created by the author chooses to
       ally himself very closely with the reader, so that his role
       makes possible the existence of the concept of the "whole
       story"; discusses the role and character of Lovelace, who
       lives a fantasy life, while Clarissa represents real life, and
       is therefore a threat to his world.

2590   PRICE, MARTIN.
       "Clarissa and Lovelace." In [153], pp. 276-284.

       Sees in Clarissa the theme of the divided heart being given
       formal rigor and tragic consequences; analyzes the characters
       of Lovelace and Clarissa, and concludes both that Clarissa is
       not the great Bible of the bourgeoisie and that Clarissa her-
       self, in her defense of her chastity, cannot be interpreted as
       a myth of bourgeois sexual morality.

2591   PRITCHETT, V. S.
        "Clarissa." In The Living Novel (New York: Reynal & Hitch-
        cock, 1947), pp. 24-31.

        A general appreciation of the novel, mainly emphasizing
        character analysis and seeing Richardson as "mad about sex";
        suggests that Richardson's genius consisted of his ability to
        "elevate the inner conflict of the passions and the will to an ab-
        stract level, so that the struggle of Clarissa and Lovelace
        becomes a universal battle-piece."

2592   RABKIN, NORMAN.
        "Clarissa: A Study in the Nature of Convention." ELH 23
        (1956): 204-217.

        Attempts to prove "that the action of Clarissa is the battle
        in man between the free force of instinct born in him, and
        the decorum which he finds it necessary to construct in order
        to live with other men, and that the real purpose of the novel
        is to find the needed balance in this decorum in which animal
        nature and external regulation may counter each other."

2593   RUNTE, ROSEANN.
        "Dying Words: The Vocabulary of Death in Three Eighteenth-
        Century English and French Novels." CRCL 6 (1979): 360-
        368.

        A metaphorical study which compares the deaths of the
        heroines in Clarissa, La Nouvelle Héloïse, and Les Liaisons
        dangereuses.

2594   SACKS, SHELDON.
        "Clarissa and the Tragic Traditions." In [46], pp. 195-221.

        A discussion of poetical justice as a literary concept and
        Richardson's narrative skill in having Clarissa make not only
        "the 'right' ethical choice in each instance but the very one
        designed to raise her virtues in our estimation from mere
        domestic goodness to tragic nobility as it moved her towards
        tragic destruction."

2595   SCHMITZ, ROBERT M.
        "Death and Colonel Morden in Clarissa." SAQ 69 (1970):
        346-353.

        Discusses death symbolism in the novel as exemplified by
        Morden. He is "both 'cousin' to Clarissa and the embodiment
        of death, who resolves all matters, both good and evil, in this
        existence."

2596   SHERBO, ARTHUR.
        "Time and Place in Richardson's Clarissa." BUSE 3 (1957):
        139-146.

            "Part ... of the effect that Richardson is able to create
        and nurture through ... Clarissa can be traced to his delib-
        erate and careful eschewal of precise references to the time
        and place (other than London) when and where his domestic
        tragedy is enacted."

2597   TODD, JANET.
        "Sentimental Friendship: Samuel Richardson's Clarissa (1747-
        48)." In Women's Friendship in Literature (New York: Co-
        lumbia Univ. Press, 1980), pp. 9-68.

            Discusses Clarissa's legacy and her place in the patriarchal
        family as opposed to the female world. She is encircled by
        three groups: within her family she is restricted by father
        and brother, outside by Lovelace; a second group comprises
        women within patriarchy--her mother and sister within, and
        Sinclair and the whores outside; and a third group--outside
        patriarchy--is comprised only of Anna Howe.

2598   TRAUGOTT, JOHN.
        "Clarissa's Richardson: An Essay to Find the Reader." In
        [44], pp. 157-208.

            Attempts to understand what happened in Richardson's im-
        agination, as a man of questionable personality and silly pos-
        tures remakes himself into an artist; tries to get into the
        consciousness of the author, to determine what he did with
        his personality and his history, in order to suggest the aesthe-
        tic importance of his presence in Clarissa. The tragedy oc-
        curs because Lovelace and Clarissa are each playing a game
        in which neither could realize his or her full potential of
        character without the other to "play" against: the "game" re-
        quires that he achieve damnation and she beatitude.

2599   ULMER, GREGORY L.
        "Clarissa and La Nouvelle Héloïse." Comp. Lit. 24 (1972):
        289-308.

            Though admitting Richardson's influence, the author defends
        Rousseau's originality by suggesting that he inverts Richard-
        son--where Richardson begins with a positive premise, but
        ends with an uncompromising model of a pure maiden destroyed,
        Rousseau begins with a moral premise that is negative, but
        provides a positive conclusion, that virtue and life are com-
        patible. His purpose was to provide an alternative to Rich-
        ardson's extremist position. Discusses both novels in terms

of two, inter-related themes: the moral ordeal and the sexual
ordeal; both themes involve duplicity and manipulation, and
the latter especially involves "self-deception in the expression,
repression, or sublimation of unconscious needs and desires."

2600   UPHAUS, ROBERT W.
        " 'Clarissa,' 'Amelia,' and the State of Probation." In [180],
        pp. 71-88.

        Richardson and Fielding attempt to test the reader's under-
        standing of and relation to a "State of Probation." Fielding
        presents the possibility of religious conversion, and eventually
        saves his principal characters as well as his readers. Rich-
        ardson rejects the possibility of Lovelace's conversion be-
        cause it would "falsify the uncompromising tragic severity of
        Clarissa's Christian dying to the world"; his view of human
        nature requires that most of his principal characters, and
        by implication many of his readers, must be abandoned with
        their own limited understanding.

2601   VAN GHENT, DOROTHY.
        "On Clarissa Harlowe." In The English Novel: Form and
        Function (New York: Rinehart, 1953), pp. 45-63; rpt. Har-
        per Torchbook, 1961. Rpt. in [2442], pp. 49-66.

        Discusses the novel as image and myth, seeing in myth
        the explanation for the "strange fact that, though the book
        reflects an essentially perverse psychology, it is nevertheless
        a great and powerful piece of fiction."

2602   "Clarissa and Emma as Phèdre." PR 17 (1950): 820-833.

        Clarissa Harlowe and Madame Bovary are compared as
        versions of love-myth; "the one ingenuously, the other iron-
        ically, give a universal voice to modern idealism, giving
        dramatic form and religious significance to the same given
        mass of aspirations, attitudes, customs, and passions. The
        myth of Clarissa conforms naively to that acquisitive idealism
        that has been morally rationalized by Puritanism and afforded
        religious depth by fear, perverted sexuality, and death-worship."

2603   VAN MARTER, SHIRLEY.
        "Richardson's Debt to Hester Mulso Concerning the Curse in
        Clarissa." PLL 14 (1978): 22-31.

        Hester Mulso, in three letters to Richardson, suggests
        criticisms in his treatment of Mr. Harlowe's curse on Clar-
        issa; Richardson's willingness to make suggested alterations
        emphasizes his sensitivity to contemporary criticism. The
        revisions also indicate how closely he "reexamined the as-

sumptions underlying the emotions, actions, and intentions
of his major characters" when he thought they might be mis-
construed by readers.

2604 "Hidden Virtue: An Unsolved Problem in Clarissa." YES 4
       (1974): 140-148.

       Considers the problem of why Richardson permitted Hick-
       man's hidden virtue, set against Lovelace's hidden vice, to have
       little power to warm a reader; why is Hickman so unattractive?
       The author discusses the revisions and additions by which Rich-
       ardson tried to make him more attractive to women.

2605 WARNER, WILLIAM BEATTY.
       "Proposal and Habitation: The Temporality and Authority of
       Interpretation in and about a Scene of Richardson's Clarissa."
       Boundary 7 (1979): 169-199.

       Proposes "to interpret interpretation in the light of pro-
       posal, to interpret proposals as a type of interpretation," by
       analyzing the central issue in Clarissa--will Clarissa and
       Lovelace marry, and should they?--and one scene--the pro-
       posal scene in which that might have occurred.

2606 Reading "Clarissa": The Struggles of Interpretation. New
       Haven: Yale Univ. Press, 1979.

       A reading of Clarissa "informed and molested by theoreti-
       cal questions addressed in the texts of Nietzsche, Derrida,
       Barthes, and others." It demonstrates "how Clarissa's two
       most characteristic activities--her mimetic narrative and her
       efforts at 'self'-construction--are designed in and for Clar-
       issa's struggle with her family and Lovelace." Part I "in-
       terprets the body of the novel and Part II recounts the inci-
       dents of reading that attempt to comprehend, interpret, de-
       liver, and redeliver the text of Clarissa."

2607 WATT, IAN.
       "Clarissa and Lovelace." From [183], pp. 225-238; in [2442]
       pp. 67-79.

       An analysis of the effects the sexual code, and especially
       the masculine and feminine stereotypes, have on Clarissa's
       and Lovelace's relationship: "the sophistries both conscious
       and unconscious produced by the sexual code ... helped Richard-
       son to produce a pattern of psychological surprise and dis-
       covery...." The excerpt also explores the sexual symbolism
       of the unconscious, especially as it affects the meaning of the
       central action: the rape, when Clarissa is unconscious from

opiates, suggests that the feminine sexual role is one of passive suffering, while the animality of the male can be fulfilled only when the woman's spirit is absent.

2608   WENDT, ALLAN.
       "Clarissa's Coffin. " PQ 39 (1960): 481-495.

       An ethical study of the novel shows it to be Richardson's "most careful analysis of the good life in orthodox terms.... In dramatizing the 'great doctrines of Christianity' Richardson was compelled to emphasize 'self-denial and mortification. ' ... Clarissa is a Christian saint, who by her probationary mortification assures herself of a reward in heaven. "

2609   WILLS, ANTONY A.
       "The World of Clarissa. " Rendezvous 9, No. i-ii (1974): 1-14.

       A critique of Watt's treatment of Clarissa; suggests that "the world of Clarissa is ... an apocalyptic battle between 'his satanic majesty' ... and his spirits in the shapes of men on the one hand, and the City of God on the other...."

2610   WILT, JUDITH.
       "He Could Go No Farther: A Modest Proposal about Lovelace and Clarissa. " PMLA 92 (1977): 19-32.

       Attempts to analyze the rape scene in Clarissa, the relationship between Lovelace and Clarissa, the role of the women of the house, and the meaning of Lovelace's words in a letter to Belford, "I can go no farther. " The circumstances of the rape play a significant role in Richardson's last third of the novel where he is working "desperately to affirm a concrete paradox about Clarissa; that she is breeding life while dying. "

2611   WINNER, ANTHONY.
       "Richardson's Lovelace: Character and Prediction. " TSLL 14 (1972): 53-75.

       Analyzes Clarissa in Christian terms, seeing Clarissa as a "female figuration of Christ" in a fallen world and her year of trial as similar to "that process of refinement souls must undergo in Purgatory. " Lovelace, a "demonic version of the man of feeling," plays Satan to her Job, representing the nemesis of false pride and the "horror of the hell awaiting those who do not repent. "

See also: 696, 725, 787, 835, 840, 1058, 1087, 1173, 1182, 1688, 1724, 2447, 2449, 2455, 2460, 2464, 2467, 2472, 2474, 2478, 2484, 2489, 2492, 2493, 2496, 2779

Sir Charles Grandison

2612   CRABTREE, PAUL R.
"Propriety, Grandison, and the Novel of Manners." MLQ
41 (1980): 151-161.

The novel of manners is indebted to Grandison for an important pattern of the genre, the illumination of character.
Grandison also contributes to the novel of manners a subtle and
pervasive element--the reality of the inner directives of the
characters: " ... it is that the idea of genteel society has some-
how taken possession of the imaginations of all of Grandison's
characters ... breeding a new, universal self-consciousness."

2613   HARRIS, JOCELYN.
"Learning and Genuis in Sir Charles Grandison." Stds. in
the Eighteenth Cent. 4 (1979): 123-146.

In Grandison Richardson uses three characters--Harriet,
Walden, and Sir Hargrave Pollexfen--to present an elaborate
defense of unlearned genius. They were created "primarily
to discuss ... the case for 'natural' or innate genuis against
learning, and by logical extension, the case for the moderns
against the ancients." In the sixth edition, Richardson modi-
fies his attack on the ancients but added "further arguments
for unlearned genius from the equality in natural genius of
women, from the example of Shakespeare, and from the idea
of a Christian inspiration."

2614   LEVIN, GERALD.
"Character and Fantasy in Richardson's Sir Charles Grandison." Conn. Rev. 7 (1973): 93-99. Rpt. in [2477], pp. 87-109.

An analysis of the family romance theme in the novel showing how "it proves to be the fantasy which unites the various
main and subplots in which rescue themes--strongly aggressive in nature--and Oedipal themes dominate."

2615   McKILLOP, ALAN DUGALD.
"On Sir Charles Grandison." From [134], pp. 81-97; in [2442],
pp. 124-138.

Sees in Sir Charles Grandison an ideal gentleman as antitype
to Lovelace and Tom Jones; considers Grandison as a novel of
manners, and concentrates on its plot and characters.

See also: 2447, 2455, 2464, 2489, 2492, 2493, 2496

General Studies

2616 ABBOTT, CHARLES DAVID.
"Christopher Smart's Madness." PMLA 45 (1930): 1014-1022.

Attempts to establish the dates of Smart's madness and of his confinement in an asylum, as biographical background to the Song to David; concludes that he was distinctly mad from January 1756 to September 1762, being first confined privately by his family at home until sometime in 1760, at which time he was put in a mad-house for about two years.

2617 ADAMS, FRANCIS D.
"Wordplay in the D Fragment of Jubilate Agno." PQ 48 (1969) 82-91.

Argues that, as with fragments A, B1, B2 and C, the "D fragment is rich in wordplay--usually bilingual Latin and English, or Greek and English puns--and that this wordplay, though idiosyncratic, frequently can account for the choices Smart makes in linking natural objects and proper names." The wordplay is intended to contribute to the overall meaning of the poem, to demonstrate especially God's presence in the universe; to Smart, the erudite puns and far-fetched relationships seemed an important part of God's unrevealed spiritual order.

2618 Jubilate Agno and the 'Theme of Gratitude.' " PLL 3 (1967): 195-209.

Argues that the theme of gratitude "not only reveals the poem's comprehensive, though unfinished, plan ... it also enables the critic to explain many of the individual verses that in the past seemed fantastic or irrelevant." As primary element in the theme of gratitude, Smart intended to maintain a dual purpose, to "Confess" God's presence and "report" his praise. In Jubilate Agno, " ... each of the two parts individually accomplishes one of the two purposes Smart had set for his verse, and together the parts fulfill his whole intention. A pair of verses say, 'Let God's creatures praise

Him; For His existence is demonstrated by the following example. ' " The "For" verses, therefore, are Smart's attempt
to prove God's presence in the universe, and mainly carry
the theme of gratitude.   Article also suggests that Jubilate
Agno has a careful artistic structure formed through an as-
sociational technique.

2619   "The Seven Pillars of Christopher Smart. "   PLL 1 (1965):
        125-132.

        Attempts to find an explanation for "the seven pillars of
        knowledge" in the Song to David and suggests a new reading
        in which "David is the speaker in the pillar stanzas and each
        of the pillars represents an individual psalm. "   Concludes
        that Smart uses the pillars to suggest three levels of mean-
        ing: not only to describe the seven days but also to link
        David's psalms to the whole of creation and to suggest that
        his singing carries with it an inherent goodness.

2620   AINSWORTH, EDWARD G. and CHARLES E. NOYES.
        Christopher Smart, a Biographical and Critical Study (Univ.
        Missouri Studies, Vol. 18, No. 4).   Columbia: Univ. Mis-
        souri Press, 1943.

        Surveys the life and work of Smart, with the specific in-
        tention of proving that A Song to David is "of a piece with
        his other religious verse--finer, stronger, sweeter, but of
        the same substance"; especially concentrates on "Smart's late
        verse, the religious poetry which had been ignored until re-
        cently, but which constitutes the real message Smart had for
        the world. "   Includes a detailed analysis of the Song to David,
        though quotation often substitutes for critical reading.

2621   ANDERSON, FRANCES E.
        Christopher Smart.   New York: Twayne, 1974.

        The life and work of Christopher Smart, with emphasis on
        the ways in which his ideas, attitudes, and experiences are
        reflected in his poetry; the largest space is devoted to a criti-
        cal evaluation of the poetry, arranged chronologically, with
        special emphasis on Song to David.   Concludes with a survey
        of Smart's reputation.

2622   BEIFUSS, JOHN P.
        "Christopher Smart: Translator of Horace. "   Interpretations
        6 (1974): 24-30.

        Smart's verse translation of Horace, "after a few initial
        bows to accepted theory, was very definitely outside the theory

and the practice of Eighteenth Century translation." Smart
follows Horace thematically, and in an effort to capture Horace's spirit he uses twenty-seven different verse forms. His
translation is essentially paraphrase, but more exact than free;
it is controlled, yet "vivid and fresh in image and diction."

2623   BINYON, LAURENCE.
"The Case of Christopher Smart" (The English Association,
Pamphlet No. 90). London: Oxford Univ. Press, 1934.

General account of Smart, with an extensive analysis of
A Song to David.

2624   BLAYDES, SOPHIA B.
Christopher Smart as a Poet of His Time: A Re-appraisal
(Studies in Eng. Lit. 28). The Hague: Mouton, 1966.

Surveys Smart's life and critical reputation, with the emphasis falling on Jubilate Agno and, especially, on Song to
David, poems that separate Smart from "his time"; includes
a discussion of eighteenth-century poetics and of Smart's
prosodic practice in particular, as well as a chapter on "Enthusiasm."

2625   BOND, WILLIAM H.
"Christopher Smart's Jubilate Agno.   HLB 4 (1950): 39-52.

The author attempts to "reconstruct the design of the poem
from the surviving portions of the holograph manuscript; concludes that Smart "began with the idea of an antiphonal composition, and to this he adhered more or less closely for
about a quarter of the piece.   The poem was written slowly;
its composition extended over at least four years.   Gradually
a change took place ... midway in Fragment B the two halves
drew apart and thereafter their relationship was seldom more
than mathematical."

2626   CHRISTENSEN, ALLAN C.
"Liturgical Order in Smart's Jubilate Agno: a Study of Fragment C."   PLL 6 (1970): 366-373.

Suggests a new way of understanding the relationship between "Let" and "For" verses: "Like the melody line and
accompaniment of an air, the 'For' verses lyrically develop
bold and irregular phrases against the regular, punctuating
beats and simple harmonic progressions of the 'Let' lines."

2627   COSKREN, ROBERT.

"Surname Puns in Fragment D of Smart's Jubilate Agno. "
Studia Neophilologica 52 (1980): 115-118.

An analysis of Smart's use of surnames shows that "this
method ... allowed him to continue--in a new way--his thematic concern with linking the worlds of man and nature; and
it provided a structural apparatus linking Fragment D to earlier fragments. "

2628   DAVIE, DONALD.
       "Christopher Smart: Some Neglected Poems. " ECS 3 (1969):
       242-264.

       An analysis of Smart's translations of the Psalms as
       eighteenth-century devotional poems in their own right and
       of the Hymns and Spiritual Songs of 1765, finding for the latter
       English influences in Pope and Crashaw; and finally discusses
       Smart's translations from Horace and the Preface to them
       that Smart wrote, explaining, or hinting at, his own poetic
       practice. Concludes that whether Smart "writes poems of
       ecstasy and wonder, or poems of a more worldly cast, he
       does not fit into the category that is sometimes called 'pre-
       Romantic'; he is not 'a Romantic precursor,' but wholly a
       poet of the eighteenth century. "

2629   DEARNLEY, MOIRA.
       The Poetry of Christopher Smart.   London: Routledge & Kegan
       Paul, 1968.

       Although ignoring Smart's Horatian translation, the author
       seeks to see his poetry as a coherent whole; she has tried
       to study "the main phases of Smart's poetic activity--the se-
       cular work, the early religious verse, the mad poetry, and
       the religious verse written after madness. [She] examine[s]
       each phase of Smart's work in relation to the literary con-
       ventions of the eighteenth century, and ... [tries] to em-
       phasize the dichotomy between the idiosyncratic aspects of
       his poetry, and its conventional basis in the contemporary
       genres of hymn, Psalm, oratorio, and the rest. "

2630   DENNIS, CHRISTOPHER M.
       "A Structural Conceit in Smart's Song to David. " RES 29
       (1978): 257-266.

       Examines the structural problems and interpretations of
       the poem to show how the harp of David, a "structural con-
       ceit," is "carefully worked into the poem's structure and
       relates perfectly to Smart's personal typology. " Study shows
       that "Smart vies with the 'bless'd pattern' and divides his
       song into three major sections: the thirty-seven stanzas which

precede the 'harp,' the twelve stanzas which make up the
'harp,' and the block of thirty-seven which follows."

2631   DEVLIN, CHRISTOPHER.
        Poor Kit Smart. London: Hart-Davis, 1961.

        Emphasizes the importance of religion in Smart's life and
        work, and seeks especially to analyze his "ideas and impul-
        ses, mystical or maniacal or whatever they were"; the author
        divides his spiritual experience into the three classical cate-
        gories of the Purgative Way, the Illuminative Way, and the
        Unitive Way, in an attempt to explain Smart's urge "to preach
        to others and to assume the guises of an arrogant pseudo-
        prophet." Includes critical analyses.

2632   "Christopher Smart and the Seven Pillars." Month 24 (1960):
        86-98.

        Suggests, in explanation of the meaning of the seven Greek
        letters assigned to the seven days, that "the letters must be
        taken not as letters but as the numbers for which they stood
        in classical Greek" and that "Christ is all the intermediate
        letters (or numbers) between alpha and omega; that is to say,
        the letters or numbers are not symbols of the attributes of
        the Deity ... but aspects or appearances of Christ, the Word
        made Flesh." Concludes that this explanation shows "some
        connection in [Smart's] mind between the day of creation and
        some aspect or appearance of the Redeemer. In every case
        except one (sigma) it shows how the connection could be sym-
        bolized by the Greek letter or number in question."

2633   DILLINGHAM, THOMAS F.
        " 'Blest Light': Christopher Smart's Myth of David." In
        The David Myth in Western Literature, Raymond-Jean Frontair
        and Jan Wojcik, eds. (West Lafayette, Ind.: Purdue Univ.
        Press, 1980), pp. 120-133.

        The myth of David serves as the inspiration of Smart's
        best poetry and it projects a vision of a man whose every
        action becomes poetry and whose poetry is inspired by the
        voice of God: poetry therefore becomes a sacred act of praye:
        or devotion. Smart identifies Orpheus with David, and is
        therefore able to reconcile the classical and Christian tradi-
        tions as well as the opposition between "divine inspiration"
        and "art and nature."

2634   FITZGERALD, ROBERT P.
        "The Form of Christopher Smart's Jubilate Agno." SEL 8
        (1968): 487-499.

Seeks the answer to two related questions that arise from
Smart's nonmetrical lines in a responsive scheme: why did
he use for Jubilate Agno, in contrast to the conventional meters
of all of his published work, a prose line reminiscent of biblical poetry, and why did he write the two kinds of line in
the poem on separate sheets? Concludes that Smart originally
wrote a prose draft of the Let section, intending later to put
it into verse for publication; it is a "public" poem. The For
section, on the other hand, is a personal journal, never intended for publication; it is a "private" poem. He did not,
therefore, write the Let and For lines alternately.

2635   FRIEDMAN, JOHN BLOCK.
       "The Cosmology of Praise: Smart's Jubilate Agno." PMLA
       82 (1967): 250-256.

       Argues that Jubilate Agno celebrates God's goodness to
men and the plenitude of His creation; it is a poem about
man's part in a cosmic hymn. Concludes that "finding the
world view of eighteenth-century England not to his liking ...
Smart set about to construct a new order in which he was
both a participant and a narrator pointing out beauties to the
observer. "The Jubilate Agno is thus at once a personal glor-
ification of God and a portrayal of man's part in the new
world order in which Smart hopes God will eternally be glor-
ified. This poem is, in a certain sense, a prayer, offering
thanksgiving, as the Psalmist had done, under conditions far
from conducive to it. The Jubilate can also be seen as a
choral work modeled upon the song of Orpheus-David, written
for the entire creation in praise of God."

2636   GEDALOF, ALLAN J.
       "Smart's Poetics in Jubilate Agno." ESC 5 (1979): 262-274.

       By an analogy with type-casting Smart suggests that in
writing poetry he is " 'punching' out an 'impression,' which
then forms a mould, a pattern for future images which the
reader will take up. The process of composition ... is not
a pure act of intellect but the much more dynamic and im-
petuous 'punching.' " The mould, into which the poet has
"cast" an image, gives form to the entire poem and to individual lines; the mould is the pattern of the universe itself,
bearing the mark of God, so that both reader and poet are
communicating with the mind of God: " ... external nature,
the mind of the poet, and God all become one...."

2637   GREENE, D. J.
       "Smart, Berkeley, the Scientists and the Poets: A Note on
       Eighteenth-Century Anti-Newtonianism." JHI 14 (1953): 327-
       352.

Illustrates from the work of Smart a complex and subtle
kind of anti-Newtonianism, traces its sources in the writings
of Berkeley, and attempts to determine the relation of science and poetry. Argues that it is Smart, not Blake, who is
the earliest rebel against Newtonian and Lockean "rationalism"; Smart in the 1750s had an attitude toward Newton that
was very like Blake's "Romantic" one. Concludes that one
finds in Smart and Berkeley a similar "interest in the nature of language and a belief in the importance of using it
with all possible accuracy; an intense awareness of the concrete (sensation) and a contempt for the oversimple and il-
logical Cartesian and Lockean hypostasis of the abstraction
'substance'; a feeling that any view of life based on the di-
vorce of the physical world from man's mind is bound to be
pleasureless, and ... immoral; coupled with all this, an attitude toward practical and experimental science that was in
Berkeley at least one of approval, and was in Smart an intense and many-sided interest. "

2638   GRIGSON, GEOFFREY.
        Christopher Smart. (WTW) London: Longmans, 1961.

A brief biographical and critical introduction, stressing in
particular Smart's relationship with the seventeenth-century
religious poets; suggests the importance of "that recurrent
image, of the interaction of the wild and the composed, of
nature and art, of imagination and reason, of the hard gem
of an uncultivated flower and the scythe-shaven grass, which
was to become a structural integrator of Smart's vision. "

2639   HART, EDWARD L.
        "Christopher Smart's Verse Satire. " SNL 6 (1968): 29-34.

Finds satiric touches in most of Smart's poems. The author examines representative passages of satire to determine
what people or situations he chose to attack, and seeks to
discover how interpretation of his use of satire can facilitate
a larger evaluation of his work; evaluates the effectiveness
of Smart's satiric techniques, and analyzes the imagery and
symbolic language in order to find the source in his imagination of his satiric materials.

2640   " 'Christopher Must Slay the Dragon' (A Note on Smart's Sat-
        ire). " L & P 17 (1967): 115-119.

The author is not so much concerned with Smart's relationship to Butler, Dryden, Pope, and Gay as with showing
"how satire functioned personally for Smart in his statement
of hopes for himself in life and how, as hope died, he used
satire to condition himself to the acceptance of failure. " Deals

with such themes in the satires as sexual fulfillment and the
fear of impotence, the accusation that his wife had committed
adultery, and the preoccupation with horns as symbols of potency, especially associated with the adversary. With the
sense that his marriage had failed, Smart increasingly turned
toward religious exaltation as a source of hope.

2641   HARTMAN, GEOFFREY.
        "Christopher Smart's Magnificat: Toward a Theory of Rep-
        resentation." ELH 41 (1974): 429-454. Rpt. in The Fate
        of Reading and Other Essays (Chicago: Univ. Chicago Press,
        1975), pp. 74-98.

            Since there is always some difficulty in presenting our-
        selves, we must fall back on a form of "representation."
        In Jubilate Agno the "magnifi-cat theme expresses ... the
        artist's sense that he is disturbing the 'holy Sabbath' of cre-
        ation by his recreation; that he is trespassing on sacred prop-
        erty or stealing an image of it or even exalting himself as
        a maker--in short, that he is magnifying mankind instead of
        'giving the glory' to God. Smart therefore atones the ex-
        posed, self-conscious self by 'at-one-ing' it with the creature.
        He shows mankind 'presenting' before God the animal creation
        it has exploited. And, in return, he asks that his verse-
        representation be 'represented' before God by a mediator
        who enters the first line of his poem as 'Lord, and Lamb.' "

2642   HAVENS, RAYMOND D.
        "The Structure of Smart's Song to David." RES 14 (1938):
        178-182.

            Suggests that the Song is constructed on one or another
        formal pattern; it is made up of stanzas grouped in threes,
        or sevens or their multiples--the mystic numbers, so that
        the "most romantic poem of its time--ecstatic, sensuous,
        abrupt, and above all strange--was constructed with unusual
        attention to parallelism, formal design, and pattern--to the
        ordered beauty of classic and neo-classic art."

2643   HOPE, A. D.
        "The Apocalypse of Christopher Smart." In [10], pp. 269-
        284.

            Argues that Jubilate Agno "contains in itself the explanation
        of a plan of reform ... so revolutionary, that it amounts to
        an apocalyptic vision. Smart's references to his theory of
        the universe are by no means systematic, as is natural in
        a hymn of praise, but they are sufficient to show that the
        poem itself is based ... on a single fairly coherent theory
        of the universe which must have been elaborated before his

confinement and which he probably continued to hold after his cure, for it appears to some extent in A Song to David and in the Hymns and Psalms."

2644   KUHN, ALBERT J.
"Christopher Smart: The Poet as Patriot of the Lord."   ELH 30 (1963): 121-136.

After 1756 Smart's poetry, particularly the Jubilate Agno, shows his obsession with the idea of messianic mission and martyrdom and his view of himself as the Davidic patriot of the Lord.   He strives to create this status of patriot for him- self in Jubilate Agno by exploiting etymology, traditional re- ligious symbolism and typology, and some bits of his own personal history; at the same time, the work is intended as prophetic poetry.

2645   MACGREGOR, C. P.
"The Origin and Significance of the Let:For Couplet in Smart's Jubilate Agno."   HLB 24 (1976): 180-193.

Suggests "that Smart owed the basic elements of the Let: For couplet to Thomas Hobbes's remarks" about knowledge, and that in the couplet structure of Jubilate Agno, he is both "witness" and "philosopher."   In his experiment with verse- form, Smart shows "his desire to communicate the dependence of the whole range of human knowledge upon Christ."

2646   MERCHANT, W. MOELWYN.
"Patterns of Reference in Smart's Jubilate Agno."   HLB 14 (1960): 20-26.

Considers patterns of verbal wit in the poem that imply a "greater power of the ordering mind than we have customarily ascribed to Christopher Smart.   The whole disorganized poem is traversed by those patterns of allusion, association, and reference, which depend on a wealth of learning, linguistic and traditional."

2647   PARISH, CHARLES.
"Christopher Smart's Knowledge of Hebrew."   SP 58 (1961): 516-532; errata, 59 (1962): 96.

Concludes, from a detailed analysis of Smart's puns in Jubilate Agno, that "there is no doubt about [his] knowledge of Hebrew," and that the poem contains a great deal of wit not yet recognized.

2648   "Christopher Smart's 'Pillars of the Lord.'"   MLQ 24 (1963):
        158-163.

        Attempts to interpret stanzas 31-37 with regard to the let-
        ters depicting the days of Creation based on two conditions;
        " ... Smart's background in Greek and Hebrew, and the let-
        ters in the order in which they stand."   Suggests that, if we
        do take the letters in the order in which they occur, we get
        the word   which exists neither in the Bible nor in the
        Greek language; it suggests a Greek word so strongly that
        one may perhaps assume a mistake on Smart's part: "Smart
        intended to make an acrostic of the word   'I shall
        be hallowed, sanctified':   he is speaking for God as the Cre-
        ator or the glory he is describing, for David as the singer
        of the glory of God the Creator, and for himself as the re-
        creator of the entire tableau."

2649   PARKIN, REBECCA PRICE.
        "Christopher Smart's Sacramental Cat."   TSLL 11 (1969):
        1191-1196.

        Regards Smart's cat, Jeoffry, as a symbol of divine con-
        cern for humble creatures, and relates Jeoffry to man on
        three levels--physical, cultural, and metaphysical; Smart uses
        Jeoffry to "make the familiar seem strange and the strange
        seem familiar."   Jeoffry is an exemplar of Christian char-
        ity; he belongs to the tribe of Tiger, and therefore, some-
        what like Blake's tiger, is a symbol for the mystery of na-
        tural evil.

2650   RIZZO, BETTY W.
        "Christopher Smart's 'Chaucerian' Poems.   Library, 5th ser.
        28 (1973): 124-130.

        Seeks to add one song, "The Precaution," to Smart's "Chau-
        cerian" canon, to explain some of the obscurities of "Chau-
        cer's 'Recantation'"; and provides the text of a third song,
        "The Trial of Chaucer's Ghost," that has never been reprinted.

2651   ROGERS, K. M.
        "The Pillars of the Lord: Some Sources of A Song to David."
        PQ 40 (1961): 525-534.

        A look at the sources from which Smart drew his ideas
        for A Song to David to help clarify some of the obscurity.
        Deals specifically with his account of the Creation in Stanzas
        XXX-XXXVII and his presentation of "the excellence and lustre
        of David's character" in Stanzas IV-XVI.   Concludes that Smart
        drew from the Old and New Testaments, the Talmud and the
        Cabala, Masonic lore and classical ethics, fusing them to-

gether to give not only occasional obscurity but also " ... a
depth and complexity which do justice to its sublime subject."

2652   SALTZ, ROBERT D.
        "Reason in Madness: Christopher Smart's Poetic Develop-
        ment." SHR 4 (1970): 57-68.

        Smart's early religious poems were written with a clearly
        defined poetic of the "sublime" in mind: the five Seaton prize
        poems on the attributes of the Deity (1745-55), for instance,
        were influenced by the traditional language, style, and illus-
        trative material established by such critics as Dennis and
        such poets as Thomson. Henceforth he saw as his mission
        that he would become the English David, the "archetypal sub-
        lime poet"; this development was furthered by the influence
        of Bishop Lowth's Sacred Poetry of the Hebrews, which in-
        duced Smart to adapt his psalmistic vision to forms recog-
        nized as Hebraic, thus freeing him when writing Jubilate Agno
        from the deadening weight of Miltonic diction and syntax.
        Jubilate itself gives evidence of orderly, coherent structure,
        and of a conscious intention to imitate Hebraic prayers in an
        effort to achieve a different kind of sublimity. Also discusses
        Smart's concrete use of language.

2653   SHERBO, ARTHUR.
        Christopher Smart, Scholar of the University.   East Lansing:
        Mich. State Univ. Press, 1967.

        Chiefly biographical, with much new information; discusses
        all of Smart's work, but does not contain much in the way of
        criticism; the historical commentary, however, is extensive.

2654   "Christopher Smart's Three Translations of Horace."   JEGP
        66 (1967): 347-358.

        Demonstrates how Smart drew "on his two prose transla-
        tions as he translated Horace into English verse, for now he
        chose a word or a phrase from the 1756 version and at an-
        other time he went to the revised version. At other times
        he availed himself of both, even within the compass of a line.'
        Concludes that "Smart's final version of Horace's poems is
        couched in fresh, highly idiomatic, and often quite striking
        language."

2655   "Jubilate Agno: The Mind of Christopher Smart."   PMASAL
        45 (1960): 421-425.

        Considers what Smart thought about while confined in the
        asylum, as revealed in Jubilate Agno: love and sex, his wife
        and other women, and his two daughters.

2656   "Christopher Smart, Reader of Obituaries." MLN 71 (1956):
        177-182.

            Argues that Smart, in section D of Jubilate Agno, recorded
        many names because he had come upon them in the "lists of
        births, deaths, marriages, promotions and appointments, ec-
        clesiastical preferments, and bankruptcies" that appeared in
        newspapers and periodicals.

2657   "The Dating and Order of the Fragments of Christopher Smart's
        Jubilate Agno." HLB 10 (1956): 201-207.

            Assuming that Smart wrote from one to three pairs of
        lines per day, the author arrives at 11 March 1759 as a pos-
        sible terminus a quo for the beginning of Jubilate Agno, and
        believes that the poem is a chronological record of Smart's
        confinement from the day he entered the asylum to the day
        he was released.

2658   "The Probable Time of Composition of Christopher Smart's
        Song to David, Psalms, and Hymns and Spiritual Songs."
        JEGP 55 (1956): 41-57.

            Suggests that "the Song, the Psalms, and probably the
        Hymns and Spiritual Songs were largely composed between
        March, 1759, and August 26, 1760, a period earlier than
        any hitherto conjectured." Evidence consists chiefly in ver-
        bal parallels and echoes among the three poems.

2659   "Christopher Smart, Free and Accepted Mason." JEGP 54
        (1955): 664-669.

            Argues that masonic symbolism is present in Jubilate Agno
        and can be used to explain many difficult passages; suggests
        possibility that parts were "conceived and must be interpreted
        on two levels, the literal and the Masonic."

2660   SPACKS, PATRICIA MEYER.
        "Christopher Smart: The Mystique of Vision (1) and (2)."
        In [167], (1), Chap. VI, pp. 119-139; (2), Chap. VII, pp.
        140-164.

            Chapter VI: Seeks to discover Smart's special poetic qual-
        ity; suggests that the most common pattern controlling the
        images in A Song to David is that of comparison and contrast,
        and then discusses the larger relationships and themes as
        well as the language, concluding that "Smart seems in this
        poem to deal directly with ways of seeing."
        Chapter VII: Concerned with Jubilate Agno, the "maddest"
        of Smart's poems, yet "in many respects the most illuminat-

ing: some of the special attitudes toward language and toward
experience which it demonstrates are crucial also in even
Smart's most conventional poetry." Looks at some underlying
principles of Smart's work, including his hymns, which include "the relation between the name and the object named,
the function of language as praise, the connection between the
word and the natural creation...."

2661   SUMMERLIN, CLAUDE W.
        "Christopher Smart's A Song to David: its Influence on Robert
        Browning." Costerus 2 (1972): 185-196.

            Gives an account of Browning's discovery of the Song to
        David, and lists several phrases of Smart's that find an echo
        in Browning's poetry; especially notable is the influence on
        Paracelsus and Sordello.

2662   SUTTON, MAX KEITH.
        "Smart's 'Compleat Cat.'" CE 24 (1963): 302-304.

            "By recording his cat's [Jeoffry] behaviour and character-
        istics, Smart shows how this particular creature exemplifies
        the might and wisdom of the Creator...."

2663   TENNANT, R. C.
        "Christopher Smart and The Whole Duty of Man." ECS 13
        (1979): 63-78.

            Smart's Children's Hymns are more purely expository than
        Hymns and Spiritual Songs and are more closely related to
        their source-texts. This essay considers only two hymns,
        "The Conclusion of the Matter" and "Prayer," which are based
        on a seventeenth-century devotional manual, The Whole Duty
        of Man, perhaps by Richard Allestree.

2664   WALKER, JEANNE MURRAY.
        Jubilate Agno as Psalm." SEL 20 (1980): 449-459.

            Compares the structure of the poem with the structure of
        the biblical psalms. Music plays an important role in the
        formulation of the poem, and it is "through music that the
        public and the private, the present and the future, the ques-
        tion and the answer, are finally merged." The analogies be-
        tween the sound of music and language governed by the "poet's
        will to order ... to defy the alienation and tedium of passing
        time, results in a poem which, like the psalms, draws to-
        gether elements which time has ruptured."

2665   WILLIAMSON, KARINA.

"Smart's Principia: Science and Anti-Science in Jubilate Agno." RES 30 (1979): 409-422.

Smart's knowledge of science "appears shallow, inaccurate, and often out of date"; his indiscriminate assemblage of "facts," acquired from any source, is "unscientific" even by contemporary standards. Therefore, in Jubilate Agno Smart "was clearly not attempting to answer the scientists on their own ground by offering an alternative explanation of phenomena in physical terms, but challenging the materialist foundations on which scientific theory itself was based." The central portion of Jubilate Agno, Smart's "Principia," is a collection of notes mainly derived from St. John's gospel: no coherent system can be constructed from it.

2666   "Christopher Smart in the Songbooks." RES 25 (1974): 410-421.

Study of Smart's songs in the song books, music magazines, and broadsheets of the eighteenth century is important as "evidence of his popularity as a writer of light and ephemeral verse; as a source of textual history; and as an aid to attribution."

2667   "Christopher Smart: Problems of Attribution Reconsidered." The Library, 5th ser., 28 (1973): 116-123.

Considers carefully the nature of the external evidence that can be used to attribute poems to Smart; suggests that works can be regarded as authentic if they carry his "signature, initials or known pseudonym in periodicals for which he had editorial responsibility or to which he was a frequent contributor."

2668   "Christopher Smart's Hymns and Spiritual Songs." PQ 38 (1959): 413-424.

Emphasizes the originality of Smart's hymns by considering them in relation to the conventions of hymn writing in the eighteenth century: a detailed study. Includes a comparison with Smart's contemporaries, stressing the ways in which he differed from them: "Certainly all the evidence suggests that Smart looked upon the writing of hymns as a deliberate exercise of creative skill, and it is in this way that he differs most fundamentally from the evangelical hymn writers of the eighteenth century."

2669   WOOD, FREDERICK T.
"Christopher Smart." Eng. Studien 71 (1936): 191-213.

A general survey of Smart's life and work; praises The Hop-Garden, among the minor poems, which the author tends to denigrate, and reserves most of his praise for the Song to David, "one of the most marvellous nature poems which the eighteenth century has to show before the time of Wordsworth and Coleridge." Judges Smart to be more than a typical minor poet who not frequently enough gave rein to his spontaneity: he had "within him a genius and an imagination potentially poetic in the highest sense, but ... he was hampered by traditional techniques and modes of expression from which he could never break completely free."

See also: 1390

Collected Studies

2670   ROUSSEAU, G. S. and P.-G. BOUCE, eds.
Tobias Smollett: Bicentennial Essays Presented to Lewis M.
Knapp. London: Oxford Univ. Press, 1971.

General Studies

2671   BERTELSEN, LANCE.
"The Smollettian View of Life." Novel 2 (1978): 117-127.

The short episode or scene is the prime structural unit
of Smollett's novels and he uses the physical chain reaction
as the cornerstone of his scene-building. The "Smollettian"
view of life is thus "characterized by an acute consciousness
of the immediate interconnectedness of people and events, and
by a clear emphasis on resulting 'chains' of action and reaction." He views life as a great web in which every person
or activity is linked together with another, and another, and
on and on.

2672   BLOCH, TUVIA.
"Smollett's Quest for Form." MP 65 (1967): 103-113.

An analysis of Ferdinand Count Fathom and Sir Lancelot
Greaves shows that Smollett attempted to emulate Fielding
and that the form of Humphry Clinker resulted from his failure to write "the Fielding type of novel."

2673   BOEGE, FRED W.
Smollett's Reputation as a Novelist (Princeton Studies in Eng-
lish, No. 27). Princeton: Princeton Univ. Press, 1947.
Rpt. New York: Octagon Books, 1969.

A detailed survey of the criticism of Smollett from 1748
to 1940. The treatment is more selective from 1800 on.

2674   BOUCE, PAUL-GABRIEL.

The Novels of Tobias Smollett. Trans. Antonia White in collaboration with the author. London & New York: Longman,
1976.

A slightly abridged version of Les Romans de Smollett:
Etude Critique (Publications de la Sorbonne, Littératures I)
Paris: Didier, 1971. Seeks to discern biographical themes
in Smollett's life, and argues that his personality is not identical with those of his major characters. Insists that the
novels are not strictly picaresque, and that they do possess
a firm structure beneath the apparent discontinuity of the
plots. Further subjects dealt with include Smollett's realism
and his comic structures.

2675   "Smollett's Pseudo-picaresque: A Response to Rousseau's
Smollett and the Picaresque." SBHT 14 (1972): 73-79.

Argues that Rousseau's definition of the picaresque is incomplete, that the picaro is usually illegitimate and of lowly
origins, that he is cheerfully and totally amoral, and that
life (in contrast to Rousseau's view) is not regarded as a
"game." Ferdinand Count Fathom comes closest to the picaro
tradition.

2676   BRUCE, DONALD.
"Smollett and the Sordid Knaves." Cont. Rev. 220 (1972):
133-138.

Discusses Smollett's political opinions as revealed by the
characters in his novels: " ... Smollett disliked both par-
ties, although he disliked the Whigs slightly more than the
Tories."

2677   Radical Doctor Smollett. London: Gollancz, 1964; Boston:
Houghton Mifflin Co. , 1965.

A popular biography that argues that Smollett's voice is
one of outrage and protest against social and political conditions in England, that he is the "first of the great British
reforming novelists." His "artistically concealed purpose"
is to formulate a definition of the nature of man.

2678   BUCK, HOWARD S.
Smollett as Poet. New Haven: Yale Univ. Press, 1927.

A contribution to our understanding not only of Smollett's
admittedly meager poetic achievement, but even of the development of the eighteenth-century novel as a whole; offers some
important biographical details about Smollett's life and proves

Smollett's authorship of some poems, such as the Ode to Independence, about which some questions had been asked; and concludes that Smollett "possessed in some degree that poetical temperament, and used it in his novels.... In his prose fiction ... it was the poet that was in him that is the leaven of the lump."

2679   BUTT, JOHN.
"Smollett's Achievement as a Novelist." In [2670], pp. 9-23.

Smollett's success was due to his ability to represent "familiar scenes in an uncommon and amusing point of view," and to his astute observations of mankind.

2680   COZZA, ANDREA.
Tobias Smollett. Bari, Italy: Adriatica Editrice, 1970.

A survey of the life and works, including Travels Through France and Italy and the minor works. (In Italian)

2681   ELLISON, L. M.
"Elizabethan Drama and the Works of Smollett." PMLA 44 (1929): 842-862.

Supports Thackeray's statement that Smollett draws heavily on his own experiences for his novels but also points out parallels in language, incident, and character between Elizabethan drama and Smollett's novels.

2682   FABEL, ROBIN.
"The Patriotic Briton: Tobias Smollett and English Politics, 1756-1771." ECS 8 (1974): 100-114.

Smollett's political views as expressed in his writing show no political allegiance to any party. Throughout the Seven Years' War, however, he did advocate measures which he thought indispensable to save England, first, from danger posed by the enemy, and, second, from danger of bankruptcy and of internal strife.

2683   FOSTER, JAMES R.
"Smollett and the Atom." PMLA 68 (1953): 1032-1046.

Gives evidence to support Smollett's authorship.

2684   GIDDINGS, ROBERT.
The Tradition of Smollett. London: Methuen, 1967.

An attempt to place Smollett in the context of the picaresque tradition and to evaluate his achievement. Maintains that he "developed the picaresque novel to a level of perfection never equalled again in our language," and that Peregrine Pickle is his masterpiece.

2685 GOLDBERG, M. A.
Smollett and the Scottish School: Studies in Eighteenth-Century Thought. Albuquerque: Univ. New Mexico Press, 1959.

An examination of the five novels against the ideas current amongst the Scottish Common-Sense School. Taking as proved that the eighteenth-century tradition involved conflict between seemingly antithetical concepts, the author examines the antithesis of reason and passion in Roderick Random; art and nature in Ferdinand Count Fathom; imagination and judgment in Peregrine Pickle; benevolence and self-love in Sir Launcelot Greaves, and primitivism and the idea of progress in Humphry Clinker.

2686 GRANT, DAMIAN.
Tobias Smollett: A Study in Style. Manchester, England: Manchester Univ. Press, 1977.

The first part discusses the criteria by which Smollett's work is usually judged: the "first chapter deals with the implications of the argument about Smollett's fidelity to fact, the second with the question of his moral purpose, and the third with the problems surrounding his consciousness of form and artistic intentions generally." In chapters four and five the author discusses language and style, and Smollett's attitude to and employment of both; suggests that Smollett writes in a different linguistic tradition from that of his fellow novelists. Chapters six and seven provide a sustained analysis of Smollett's prose style, which is divided into the comic "style of the circumference" and the passionate "style of the centre." The final chapter presents evidence for Smollett's poetic use of language.

2687 GREENE, DONALD.
"Smollett the Historian: A Reappraisal." In [2670], pp. 25-56.

A rereading of Smollett's History of England in light of today's historiography reveals that it is a greatly underrated work and that it furnishes the intelligent modern reader with ample delight and instruction. Defends work against criticism of poverty of style, intellectual shallowness, and gross partisanship.

2688   HART, FRANCIS R.
        "Limits of the Gothic: The Scottish Example." In [45], pp.
        137-153.

        Looks at the limits of the Gothic tendency by way of study-
        ing the Gothic beginnings of the Scottish novel; examines three
        novelists, Smollett, Scott, and Hogg, whose limits may be
        marked out with the three terms, "grotesque," "historic," and
        "diabolic," and concludes that these three novelists "belong
        in their distinctive--and distinctively Scottish--ways to the
        Gothic tendency in fiction of the late enlightenment."

2689   HUMPHREYS, A. R.
        "Fielding and Smollett." In Pelican Guide to English Litera-
        ture, Vol. IV: From Dryden to Johnson, ed. Boris Ford
        (Harmondsworth: Penguin Books, 1957), pp. 313-332.

        A general discussion of the two authors tracing Smollett's
        career as moving from a tone of ferocity to a spirit of bene-
        volence and good humor in Humphry Clinker; seeks to account
        for Smollett's unpleasant heroes by referring to their origin
        in the tradition of the Spanish picaro.

2690   JEFFERSON, D. W.
        "Speculations on Three Eighteenth-Century Prose Writers."
        In [12], pp. 81-91.

        The Augustan style of Smollett, Goldsmith, and Johnson;
        suggests that "style seems almost to be having a game of its
        own."

2691   JONES, CLAUDE E.
        Smollett Studies (Univ. Calif. Publications in English, Vol. 9,
        No. 2). Berkeley: Univ. Calif. Press, 1942. Rpt. New
        York: Phaeton Press, 1970.

        Deals primarily with Smollett as critic of the navy and
        as writer for the Critical Review.

2692   KAHRL, GEORGE.
        "Smollett as a Caricaturist." In [2670], pp. 169-200.

        A review of the genre of caricature to understand better
        Smollett's use of it in his novels. Discusses his use of car-
        icature as an art form in itself and not as a medium of satire
        in Roderick Random and Peregrine Pickle culminating in the
        perfection of Humphry Clinker.

2693   Tobias Smollett, Traveler-Novelist.   Chicago: Univ. Chicago
        Press, 1945.   Rpt. New York: Octagon Books, 1968.

            Studies the effect that Smollett's travels and his knowledge
        of the literature of travel had on his novels.   Extensive an-
        alyses of each novel--the sources and interpretation, Smol-
        lett's purpose, importance of travel material, composition,
        etc.

2694   KNAPP, LEWIS MANSFIELD.
        Tobias Smollett: Doctor of Men and Manners.   Princeton,
        N. J. :   Princeton Univ. Press, 1949.

            A definitive biography.   Attempts to correct factual and
        interpretative inaccuracies in earlier lives of Smollett; seeks
        "to project a living personality vitalized by facts rather than
        by specious fictions."   Concludes with an account of his con-
        tribution to the English novel.

2695   "Smollett's Early Years in London. "   JEGP 31 (1932):   220-
        227.

            Traces Smollett's residences in London from 1744 to 1750
        as related to his progress as a writer during that time.

2696   KORTE, DONALD M.
        "Smollett's 'Advice' and 'Reproof':   Apprenticeship in Satire. "
        SSL 8 (1971):   239-252.

            Emphasizes that the relationship between Smollett's early
        verse satires, "Advice" and "Reproof," and the novels indi-
        cate the continuity of his work and the important part these
        satires play in his literary development: the satirist of "Ad-
        vice" and "Reproof" and his cynical adversary, the "Friend,"
        appear in the guise of other characters in the novels; numer-
        ous themes and motifs, various satiric butts, and certain
        modes, conventions, and structures such as the exemplum re-
        appear in the novels.

2697   MACK, EDWARD C.
        "Pamela's Step-Daughters: the Heroines of Smollett and Field-
        ing. "   CE 8 (1947):   293-301.

            Compares the heroines in the novels of Smollett and Field-
        ing with respect to the conventional portrayal of the eighteenth-
        century heroine and concludes that Fielding showed more orig-
        inality.

2698   McKILLOP, ALAN DUGALD.
        "Tobias Smollett." In [134], pp. 147-181.

        A general but perceptive account of Smollett's literary
        career, especially concentrating on his characterization, his
        satiric intentions, and the element of the grotesque in his
        fiction; suggests, among many insights, that Smollett uses
        "indignant satire ... as an ethical short-cut, a kind of in-
        verted sentimentalism, with spontaneous indignation instead
        of spontaneous benevolence as the test of virtue...."

2699   MARTZ, LOUIS L.
        The Later Career of Tobias Smollett (Yale Studies in Eng-
        lish, Vol. 97). New Haven: Yale Univ. Press, 1942. Rpt.
        Hamden, Conn.: Archon Books, 1967.

        Attempts to account for changes in style and quality be-
        tween Smollett's early and his later work by examining the
        years of literary drudgery from 1753 to 1766. The later
        creative works are related to the contemporary trend toward
        the classification and synthesis of historical, topographical,
        and scientific facts. Deals with Smollett's methods as com-
        piler and editor, and especially contrasts the qualities of his
        later works with those of the three earlier novels; includes
        a chapter on his later prose style.

2700   MELVILLE, LEWIS.
        The Life and Letters of Tobias Smollett. London: Faber &
        Gwyer, 1926. Rpt. Port Washington, N.Y.: Kennikat Press,
        1966.

        A biographical account of Smollett's life, with brief com-
        ments on the novels.

2701   MOORE, ROBERT E.
        "Hogarth and Smollett." In Hogarth's Literary Relationships
        (Minneapolis: Univ. Minn. Press, 1948), pp. 162-195.

        Discusses Smollett's debt to Hogarth and the larger sub-
        ject of the relationship of the art of the two men. Smollett
        and Hogarth had similar temperaments and they both used
        real figures known to everyone to gain popular success; but
        Smollett is distinguished from both Hogarth and Fielding by
        his use of caricature to vent his spleen.

2702   NIEHUS, EDWARD L.
        "Quixote Figures in the Novels of Smollett." DUJ 71 (1979):
        233-243.

Suggests that Smollett was so fascinated with Don Quixote
that he returned again and again to the Spanish prototype as
a source for different characters and effects; Quixotes became
an integral and complex part of his narrative method, and
Smollett was particularly attracted to them because of the opportunities for caricature and farce that they provided.

2703   OROWITZ, MILTON.
       "Smollett and the Art of Caricature." Spectrum 2 (1958):
       155-167.

       Defining comic caricature as the emphasis of one aspect
       of personality by suppressing all other aspects, the author
       suggests that Smollett's comic caricatures possess one trait
       in common--they are all marked by some degree of unpleas-
       antness; but some caricatures are morally elevated into "char-
       acters" by an unsuspected impulse to generosity, an eighteenth-
       century ethical and ontological issue.   In the creation of the
       other kind of caricature, the non-comic, "Smollett is without
       peer or rival"; his discovery is that "to be a caricature is
       to be less than human."   Concludes that "comic and non-
       comic caricature are for Smollett two modes of unsentimen-
       tally representing the dehumanizing effects of society on men."

2704   PARKER, ALICE.
       "Tobias Smollett and the Law." SP 39 (1942):   545-558.

       Traces Smollett's personal encounters with the law for a
       better understanding of relevant passages in his novels and
       of his character and thought.

2705   PAULSON, RONALD.
       "The Pilgrimage and the Family: Structures in the Novels
       of Fielding and Smollett." In [2670], pp. 57-78.

       Traces the similarities between the characters, Tom Jones
       and Peregrine Pickle, and shows how family relationships
       were becoming the dominant structure of the English novel
       in the latter half of the eighteenth century.

2706   "Satire in the Early Novels of Smollett." JEGP 59 (1960):
       381-402.   Rpt. in [146], part of Chap. 5.

       Investigates the satirical element in Smollett's early novels,
       Roderick Random and Peregrine Pickle, based on the pica-
       resque form.   All his "miniature satires deal with one general
       subject ... 'the selfishness, envy, malice, and base indiffer-
       ence of mankind.'"   The shift between his earlier and later
       novels "represents no break in Smollett's career at all but a

continuation of his search for a satirical vehicle within the
precincts of the then fashionable novel ... his most characteristic concerns were with the nature and technique of satire."

2707   PIPER, WILLIAM BOWMAN.
        "The Large Diffused Picture of Life in Smollett's Early Novels."
        SP 60 (1963): 45-56.

        Discusses the two sets of Smollettian characters--the gro-
        tesque and the heroes--their interrelation to each other, and
        how they were used to expose a world of "folly and fraud, of
        selfish immobile gulls and crafty, rootless rascals."

2708   PRESTON, THOMAS R.
        "Tobias Smollett--A Risible Misanthrope." In [152], pp. 69-
        120.

        In all his novels Smollett tried to harmonize a satiric vi-
        sion of the world with a comic story about the man of feeling,
        a goal that eluded him until Humphry Clinker: "Through the
        concept of benevolent misanthropy dramatized in Matt Bramble,
        Smollett finally achieved his artistic goal, producing one of
        the most brilliant satirists in the benevolent misanthrope tra-
        dition." All of Smollett's novels are surveyed, in order to
        place in perspective the artistic search that ended with Hum-
        phry Clinker.

2709   "The 'Stage Passions' and Smollett's Characterization." SP
        71 (1974): 105-125.

        Studies the influence of the stage on the tableaux-structure
        of many scenes in Smollett's novels and discusses how this
        influence shaped his method of characterization.

2710   PUTNEY, RUFUS D. S.
        "Smollett and Lady Vane's Memoirs." PQ 25 (1946): 120-
        126.

        Analysis of Smollett's style leads the author to conclude
        that Smollett was responsible for Lady Vane's Memoirs: "The
        style of the 'Memoirs' not only displays the major features
        of Smollett's, the compound-complexity of his long sentences,
        the constant use of participial phrases ... the high percentage
        of nouns ... verbs that evoke images of action, and a large
        vocabulary heavily weighted with words of Latin origin, but
        there are also to be found ... two mannerisms characteristic
        of him"; his habit of using two words, wholly or partly syn-
        onymous, where one would suffice, and his use of alliteration
        carried to unusual lengths.

2711   READ, HERBERT.
"Tobias Smollett." In Reason and Romanticism: Essays in
Literary Criticism (London: Faber & Gwyer, 1926; rpt. New
York: Russell & Russell, 1963), pp. 187-205. Rpt. in Col-
lected Essays in Literary Criticism (London: Faber & Faber,
1938; 2nd. ed. 1951), pp. 234-246.

A general account of Smollett's essential qualities, especially of his aesthetic judgment in Travels Through France
and Italy; and specifically an evaluation of his humor and indecency: " ... Smollett was not essentially a humorist, and
... the charge of indecency is, if not meaningless, at least
misleading."

2712   ROSENBLUM, MICHAEL.
"Smollett and the Old Conventions." PQ 55 (1976): 389-402.

Smollett uses the romance sequence of disinheritance, exile,
and restoration in his novels, and "his reworking of romance
conventions ... suggests that ... [he] had to find a way to
use and go beyond the language of fiction that he inherited."
Suggests that Smollett's "affinities with the writers of picaresque have been exaggerated" and that his novels are not
"education novels."

2713   "Smollett as Conservative Satirist." ELH 42 (1975): 556-
579.

A discussion of order and design in the five novels of
Smollett. Author argues that "the encounter between the protagonist and the fallen society is shaped by the images and
themes ... associated with the conservative imagination."
In all five novels "the bad society is essentially the same--
one which recognizes no values and has lost the sense of ob-
ligations and distinctions upon which social class depends."

2714   ROSS, ANGUS.
"The 'Show of Violence' in Smollett's Novels." YES 2 (1972):
118-129.

In the "Smollett World" we see the violence of the eighteenth-
century social scene as a jungle struggle for survival. Discusses the author's rhetorical use of violence and his tactical
use of it, especially in Peregrine Pickle and Ferdinand Count
Fathom.

2715   ROUSSEAU, G. S.
"Beef and Bouillon: A Voice for Tobias Smollett, with comment on his Life, Works, and Modern Critics." BSM 7, i
(1977): 4-56.

A critical essay which focuses on the contents of Smollett's writings--the rawness, cruelty, savagery, crudity, ugliness, and squalor which pervade his novels. An "attempt to misread" Smollett that " ... discards genres and tosses away all historicism and scientific validity ... to demonstrate how an author such as he was could have selected 'beef and bouillon,' or ... 'baroque economics,' as the substance of his fiction. "

2716   "Smollett and Sterne: A Revaluation. " Archiv 208 (1972): 286-297.

A comparison of Sterne and Smollett--why has Sterne always been popular and Smollett not?   Also an attempt to establish Smollett as a valuable contributor to English fiction.

2717   "Smollett and the Picaresque: Some Questions About a Label. " SBHT 12 (1971): 1886-1904.

Argues that Smollett's novels are no more picaresque than the eighteenth century was an "Age of Reason. " The author attempts a definition of the "picaresque" and then applies that definition to the novels.

2718   SEKORA, JOHN.
Luxury: The Concept in Western Thought, Eden to Smollett.
Baltimore: Johns Hopkins Press, 1977.

An historical and literary study of one of the oldest and most powerful traditions in Western literary and intellectual life; Smollett is discussed at length, for "he is probably the last major English writer to accept wholly the classical conception," and three chapters are devoted to "The Attack upon Luxury and the Forms of Humphry Clinker"--that novel because it is the "last major English literary work to be informed by the older sense of luxury. " Discusses theme also in relation to his History, the Critical Review, and the Briton.

2719   SHROFF, HOMAI J.
"Angry Young Gentlemen and 'A Most Risible Misanthrope. ' "
In [163], pp. 161-191.

Discusses Smollett's idea of the gentleman as portrayed by characters in his novels, and argues that his characterization of Roderick Random and Peregrine Pickle antagonizes readers because they do not agree with Smollett's moral appraisal "of the character and behaviour of his young 'gentlemen. ' "

2720 SPECTOR, ROBERT DONALD.
Tobias Smollett. New York: Twayne, 1968.

Attempts a full-scale analysis of Smollett's literary achievement; deals first with the basic values and techniques in the
minor writings that also characterize the novels, and then
offers detailed analyses of each novel. Argues that all five
novels maintained the picaresque form.

2721 STEEVES, HARRISON R.
"Sad Dogs and Saints." In [169], pp. 131-159.

Discusses the theme and structure of Smollett's novels to
show how he handles human nature, and makes a concession
to sentiment by contrasting "the sad dog and the saint." Smollett makes the point that his heroes, who "are not nice, either
by nature or by social conditioning ... could be nicer than
they are, given the right influences; and the best possible influence he conceives as the character and example of a perfect young lady--perfect indeed, even to the most delicate
shades of thought and conduct."

2722 STEVICK, PHILIP.
"Stylistic Energy in the Early Smollett." SP 64 (1967): 712-
719.

An analysis of Smollett's narrative style shows that it is
"in the syntax and rhythm ... that the energy and violence
of his world are conveyed, as well as in his explicit hyper-
boles."

2723 TAYLOR, S. ORTIZ.
"Episodic Structure and the Picaresque Novel." JNT 7 (1977):
218-225.

Suggesting that episodic narrative in picaresque novels is
circular and that within the larger circular structure each
episode is also circular, Taylor identifies three sequential
segments in each episode: 1) the picaro's entry into a new
position in life, 2) an error in judgment or stroke of fate,
and 3) his expulsion from social position. A fourth element,
not considered part of the episode proper, is "time lapse,"
which is "structurally important in delineating, or rendering
discrete the configurations of each episode." These identifying characteristics are illustrated by analyses of Roxana
and Roderick Random.

2724 WARNER, JOHN M.
"The Interpolated Narratives in the Fiction of Fielding and

Smollett: An Epistemological View." Studies in the Novel
5 (1973): 271-283.

Suggests that Smollett's and Fielding's use of the interpolated story is not a simple throwback to earlier modes of
fiction but is a foreshadowing of epistemological concerns expressed more clearly by the Romantics; that Smollett uses
interpolated tales as a means of authenticating the private
histories of his protagonists.

2725   "Smollett's Development as a Novelist." Novel 5 (1972): 148-
161.

A study of Smollett's novels reveals his "struggle to come
to terms with the implications of Lockean epistemology for
both his conception of reality and his novel form"; suggests
that his career began with satire and the picaresque and ended
with the imaginative creation of a world in a unified work of
art, Humphry Clinker.

2726   WEBSTER, GRANT T.
"Smollett's Microcosms: A Satiric Device in the Novel."
SNL 5 (1967): 34-37.

Discusses a structural device similar to the digression,
a kind of digression of humor characters, defined as a "little
world set within the plot of an episodic novel, in which a
number of humor characters are presented and exposed as
frauds." Smollett's microcosm seems to indicate a capacity
for indignation closer to satire than to raillery.

See also: 253, 686, 908, 909, 916, 3183

Roderick Random

2727   ALTER, ROBERT.
"The Picaroon as Fortune's Plaything." In Rogue's Progress:
Studies in the Picaresque Novel (Cambridge: Harvard Univ.
Press, 1964), pp. 58-79; rpt. [53], pp. 131-153.

Considers specifically the "distinctive realism of Roderick
Random, and the connection of this realism with the form of
the book."

2728   BEASLEY, JERRY C.
"Roderick Random: The Picaresque Transformed." Coll. L.
6 (1979): 211-220.

Smollett's novel is not so much a picaresque tale as a
comic work whose concluding chapters emphasize the nature
of his comic vision and the extent of his departures from the
conventions of the picaresque. The ultimate affirmation concerns the existence of a Christian vision of a return to Eden,
an affirmation that rests upon those various a priori assumptions that the picaresque mode seems to deny.

2729   BJORNSON, RICHARD.
       "Victimization and Vindication in Smollett's Roderick Random."
       SSL 13 (1978): 196-210. Rpt. with revisions in The Picares-
       que Hero in European Fiction (Madison: Univ. Wisc. Press,
       1977), pp. 228-245.

           Smollett, in making changes in the "plan" of Lesage's Gil
       Blas, is able "to reconcile sentiment and satire in a narrative
       which is introduced as being more true to life than a romance."
       The novel is constructed around "a nostalgic desire for jus-
       tice and stability in an apparently chaotic world" and Roderick,
       "seeking to express his independence and lust for life, ...
       may commit evil acts, but they are always portrayed as ex-
       cusable on the grounds of momentary blindness or sheer im-
       petuosity." Roderick always triumphs over his enemies and
       in the "happy ending" he is vindicated and his happiness "rep-
       resents a young nobleman's victory over the general wicked-
       ness of the world."

2730   FREDMAN, ALICE GREEN.
       "The Picaresque in Decline: Smollett's First Novel." In
       [40], pp. 189-207.

           Chiefly concerned with modifications of (or decline in) the
       picaresque in Roderick Random, comparing it with Gil Blas:
       Roderick Random is largely motivated by revenge, which is
       quite alien to the picaresque vision; and as a moral satirist
       and disappointed idealist, really belonging to the Sensibility
       School, Smollett turns to abuse, invective, and satire instead
       of to laughter.

2731   JEFFREY, DAVID K.
       "Roderick Random: The Form and Structure of a Romance."
       RBPH 58 (1980): 604-614.

           Uses the elements of romance as set forth by Northrop
       Frye in his The Secular Scripture (Cambridge: Harvard Univ.
       Press, 1976) as a basis for a study of Roderick Random and
       concludes that the form, the structure, and the imagery of
       the novel are those of a classical romance. It is "not a real-
       istic novel, nor does it contain merely 'elements' of romance."
       Smollett "traces his hero's descent from an idyllic world to

a night world and his eventual ascent from hell to Eden,"
and "includes in the work prophetic dreams, witches, metamorphoses, and sea-changes."

2732   KNAPP, LEWIS M.
        "The Naval Scenes in Roderick Random." PMLA 49 (1934):
        593-598.

        Presents evidence to show that Chapters 24-38 were based
        on Smollett's personal experience as surgeon's mate in the
        navy.

2733   McCULLOUGH, BRUCE.
        "The Picaresque Novel: Tobias George Smollett." In [133],
        pp. 58-68.

        Discusses the picaresque elements in Roderick Random and
        compares Smollett's method with that used by Fielding in Tom
        Jones.

2734   MARTZ, LOUIS L.
        "Smollett and the Expedition to Carthagena." PMLA 56 (1941):
        428-446.

        Concludes that Roderick Random is not autobiographical by
        comparing Smollett's account of the expedition with one in
        Compendium of Voyages.

2735   MOSS, HAROLD GENE.
        "The Surgeon's Mate: Tobias Smollett and The Adventures of
        Roderick Random." In Medicine and Literature, Enid Rhodes
        Peschel, ed. (New York: Watson, 1980), pp. 35-38.

        Just as Matthew Bramble's journey to health is the central
        theme of Humphry Clinker, so is Roderick's face-to-face con-
        frontation with death and his lessons in life's values as de-
        tailed in five episodes (Chapters 28-38) central to the theme
        of Roderick Random. These five episodes are significant to
        the organization of the novel and are very likely based on
        Smollett's own experience as a surgeon.

2736   PRATT, T. K.
        "Linguistics, Criticism, and Smollett's Roderick Random."
        UTQ 42 (1972): 26-39.

        An analysis of Smollett's descriptions of Jenny Ramper,
        Issac Rapine, and the Wenzels to prove the value of modern
        linguistics (knowledge of structure) to literary criticism; com-

ments on the formulaic elements of Smollett's vocabulary and grammar.

2737   ROSS, IAN CAMPBELL.
       "Language, Structure and Vision in Smollett's Roderick Random." EA 31 (1978): 52-63.

       Although concerned with the dual importance of both the narrative and thematic structures, this study asserts that it is by means of sustained verbal repetition that Smollett "details his view of a world in disorder and simultaneously gives coherence to his novel." Verbal repetition helps form the reader's attitude toward Roderick and forces him to share in Roderick's experience of moral disorder. Roderick, and hence the reader, become victims of the disorder which characterizes their world.

2738   RUNTE, ROSEANN.
       "Gil Blas and Roderick Random: Food for Thought." FR 50 (1977): 698-705.

       In both novels food acts on three levels and serves at least three purposes: "On the systematic level we find abundant images relating to gastronomy which serve as realistic, comic, or ironic elements in the relation. On a structural level ... the meal [is] both introducer of secondary adventures and marker of time on a macroscopic level ... and on a microscopic level.... On the level of a value system we find gastronomic terms operating as the primary metonyms ... [applying] to very nearly all physical and mental processes described."

2739   SHEINKER, V.
       "Tobias Smollett's Roderick Random." Uchenye Zapiski Murmanskogo Pedinstituta (Trans. of the Murmansk Pedagogical College), 1 (1957): 23-62.

2740   SIMPSON, K. G.
       "Roderick Random and the Tory Dilemma." ScLJ 2, ii (1975): 5-17.

       Smollett fails to maintain consistency in his characterization of Roderick and to substantiate the claims of his preface. Because "Smollett epitomizes the enduring Tory dilemma: how to reconcile material improvement with the preservation of hereditary social hierarchy," the novel cannot be reconciled with the moral scheme which he sets forth in the preface--Instruction, Verisimilitude, and Amusement. The conclusion is exclusively materialistic in its view of human happiness.

2741   STEVICK, PHILIP.
       "Smollett's Picaresque Games." In [2670], pp. 111-130.

       A discussion of picaresque elements in Roderick Random
and Peregrine Pickle to show "Smollett's pivotal position, at
the end of the classic picaresque tradition" and "his ability
to provide us with patterns of game not only peculiar to himself but suggestive of the nature of the genre."

2742   UNDERWOOD, GARY N.
       "Linguistic Realism in Roderick Random." JEGP 69 (1970):
       32-40.

       An analysis and evaluation of Smollett's literary dialects
show his "ability to fuse the real with the comic and make
it one."

2743   WEINSHEIMER, JOEL.
       "Impedance as Value: Roderick Random and Pride and Pre-
       judice." PTL 3 (1978): 139-166.

       Concerned with two questions: whether valuation and inter-
pretation are separable or inseparable activities; and whether
value inheres in the text or is conferred from an extrinsic
source. If value theorists reject the distinction between intrinsic and extrinsic value, then they are committed to a rejection of that between valuation and interpretation: such a
thesis is confirmed by comparing Roderick Random and Pride
and Prejudice, because "interpretation is the value-conferring
activity and the nature of literary value is to be found in the
nature of interpretation."

See also: 2685, 2692, 2706, 2723

Peregrine Pickle

2744   BATES, ROBIN.
       "Smollett's Struggle for a New Mode of Expression." Thalia
       1, iii (1978-79): 25-31.

       Smollett's empirical approach to reality results in both
major weaknesses and major strengths of Peregrine Pickle.
Because he "minutely examined the present," he "achieved
in intensity what he lost in suspense." Suggests that the
novel should be read as "one reads an artist's sketch book,"
not as a unified work of art. Contrasts Peregrine Pickle with
Tom Jones and shows how Smollett's differences with Fielding
are not merely authorial jealousy but part of his own internal
contradictions.

2745   BUCK, HOWARD SWAZEY.
        A Study in Smollett, Chiefly "Peregrine Pickle." New Haven:
        Yale Univ. Press, 1925; Mamaroneck, N. Y.: Paul P. Appel,
        1973.

            Concerned primarily with the revision of Peregrine Pickle,
        the authorship of the Memoirs of a Lady of Quality, and Smol-
        lett's quarrels deriving from the Regicide. Includes a colla-
        tion of the first and second editions.

2746   COLLINS, R. G.
        "The Hidden Bastard: A Question of Illegitimacy in Smollett's
        Peregrine Pickle." PMLA 94 (1979): 91-105.

            The relationship between Mrs. Pickle and her son suggests
        that the many similarities between Peregrine Pickle and Tom
        Jones include the illegitimacy of the two heroes. The fact
        that Smollett never presents Peregrine as illegitimate but
        slyly implants the idea in the reader's mind might be caused
        by fear of being accused of plagiarism. Also discusses the
        parallels with Johnson's Life of Savage.

2747   EVANS, DAVID L.
        "Peregrine Pickle: The Complete Satirist." Studies in the
        Novel 3 (1971): 258-274.

            Approached as a lively and distinctive experiment, Pere-
        grine Pickle turns out to be "fascinating and almost success-
        ful for all its shortcomings"; a discussion of its originality
        and uniqueness. Suggests that Smollett's satire is so per-
        vasive that the "thread of Peregrine's development as ulti-
        mately admirable hero will not hold the weight of the cynical
        vision he serves as satirist"; author is therefore mainly con-
        cerned with the "dynamics of Smollett's experiment" of fusing
        satire with a conventional, romantic plot.

2748   EVANS, JAMES E.
        "Smollett's Verbal Performances in Peregrine Pickle."
        NDEJ 8 (1973): 87-97.

            An analysis of the ways in which stylistic devices further
        Smollett's comic and satiric purposes: double entendre, sex-
        ual innuendo, and comic distortion.

2749   FLANDERS, W. AUSTIN.
        "The Significance of Smollett's Memoirs of a Lady of Quality."
        Genre 8 (1975): 146-164.

            Considers "the qualities of the Memoirs as an autobiography-

confession whose interest is that of fiction" and relates them
"to certain broad patterns of experience in Smollett's fiction
and the early British novel in general."

2750   JEFFREY, DAVID K.
       "Smollett's Irony in Peregrine Pickle." JNT 6 (1976): 137-
       146.

       Attempts to answer the question of why Smollett included
       the "memoirs" of Lady Vane in his novel. Suggests that it
       is "to mark contrasts between her and [Peregrine] and be-
       tween her narration and his own." Although she is flawed in
       the same way as Peregrine, she doesn't develop as he does;
       she lacks the clear-sighted judgment of Peregrine, and "Her
       'Memoirs' thus subvert the purposes of satire and exemplify
       instead that 'true No-meaning' which 'puzzles more than Wit.'"

2751   PUTNEY, RUFUS.
       "The Plan of Peregrine Pickle." PMLA 60 (1945): 1051-
       1065.

       Attempts to show that Peregrine Pickle is not a haphazard
       collection of episodes as most critics claim but that it was
       composed according to a plan, and that it was Smollett's lack
       of dramatic skill that made his novels rambling and disjointed.

2752   ROUSSEAU, G. S.
       "Pineapples, Pregnancy, Pica and Peregrine Pickle." In
       [2670], pp. 79-109.

       A discussion of "how adeptly Smollett used science, par-
       ticularly medical learning, for the purposes of wit," especially
       in his satirical portrayal of Mrs. Pickle's pregnancy, Chap-
       ters V-VI, and her desire for pineapple.

2753   SHEINKER, V.
       "Peregrine Pickle and Some Features of Smollett's Satire."
       Uchenye Zapiski Murmanskogo Pedinstituta (Trans. of the
       Murmansk Pedagogical College), 2 (1958): 179-202.

2754   WEINSHEIMER, JOEL.
       "Defects and Difficulties in Smollett's Peregrine Pickle."
       ArielE 9, iii (1978): 49-62.

       Peregrine Pickle, though praised rather extravagently by
       some recent critics, "misses in three inter-connected areas
       of execution--as a satire, as a comic-picaresque Bildungs-
       roman, and as a combination of the two." Because Peregrine

is a fallible individual, he loses his satiric authority and our attention is diverted from the objects of satire to the satirist. Since Peregrine never manifests significant moral development, he never seems fit for acceptance into society. Finally the two literary types--satire and Bildungsroman--are incompletely blended: the "consequence is that the novel promotes an ultimately equivocating morality...."

See also: 2685, 2692, 2705, 2706, 2710, 2714, 2741

Ferdinand Count Fathom

2755   JEFFREY, DAVID K.
        " 'Ductility and Dissimulation': The Unity of Ferdinand Count Fathom." TSL 23 (1978): 47-60.

        Argues that Ferdinand Count Fathom is "unified by image clusters which reinforce the thematic and structural movement of the work. The primary thematic movement is from appearance to reality...." In order to emphasize that thematic movement the author briefly compares sections of the opening chapters with the last chapter; next, he examines the two major plots to suggest that their developments both parallel one another and intersect at significant places; and finally he analyzes the image clusters that provide the main unifying force to the narrative.

2756   PRESTON, THOMAS R.
        "Disenchanting the Man of Feeling: Smollett's Ferdinand Count Fathom." In [15], pp. 223-239. Rpt. in [152], Chap. 4.

        Argues that "Ferdinand Count Fathom dramatizes the man of feeling in need of disenchantment with the pleasing appearances of the world, in need of acquiring the wisdom of the serpent"; the man of feeling lives in an evil and unfeeling world and suffers from lack of perception. The author uses Fielding as background to prove the Fathom is a problem or thesis novel, and suggests that it has a morality structure, or an allegorical form that represents the eternal struggle between good and evil.

2757   SHEINKER, V.
        "Tobias Smollett's Ferdinand Count Fathom." Uchenye Zapiski Leningradskogo Universiteta (Trans. of Lenigrad Univ.), No. 234 (1957): 3-22.

2758   STRAUSS, ALBRECHT B.

"On Smollett's Language: A Paragraph in Ferdinand Count
Fathom." In Style in Prose Fiction, ed. Harold C. Martin
(English Institute Essays, 1958). (New York: Columbia Univ.
Press, 1959), pp. 25-54.

Analyzes a passage from Chapter 64 to suggest the technique by which Smollett evokes powerful emotions and especially creates the mood of boisterous, farcical humor; offers
a detailed examination of Smollett's diction and concludes that
his language is full of clichés and is both "obviously stylized
and highly conventional": the effect is to generalize the emotions.

2759   THOMAS, JOEL J.
        "Smollett and Ethical Sensibility: Ferdinand Count Fathom."
        SSL 14 (1979): 145-164.

        The contention of this article is that "Smollett's prose
        fiction shows an adherence to the most fundamental dictum of ...
        'philosophical' or 'ethical' sensibility, namely, that our moral
        lives are directed toward the good by our feelings rather than
        our reason." Smollett's ethical sensibility appears in two
        ways: 1) it provides the moral basis of each of his novels;
        2) internal evidence shows that Smollett was influenced by
        current theories of sympathy and the sympathetic imagination
        as they applied to ethics. Ferdinand Count Fathom illustrates
        Smollett's use of ethical sensibility, for it contains perhaps
        the harshest satiric world of all the novels, yet it most clearly
        reveals the "ethics of feeling generally as well as the ethical
        principle of sympathy propounded by Hume."

2760   TREADWELL, T. O.
        "The Two Worlds of Ferdinand Count Fathom." In [2670],
        pp. 131-153.

        Smollett's reaction to criticism of Roderick Random and
        Peregrine Pickle led to his attempt to combine within Fer-
        dinand Count Fathom the didactic techniques of the "novel of
        manners and the novel of nature." The fictional worlds of
        these two novelistic types are irreconcilable and Fathom ends
        in bitterness and pessimism.

See also: 2672, 2685, 2714

                        Sir Launcelot Greaves

2761   ROUSSEAU, G. S. and R. A. HAMBRIDGE.
        " 'On Ministers and Measures': Smollett, Shebbeare, and

the Portrait of Ferret in Sir Launcelot Greaves." EA 32
(1979): 185-191.

Discusses one of Smollett's most interesting charlatans,
Ferret in Sir Launcelot Greaves, and the original from which
he was drawn, Dr. John Shebbeare; describes the relationship between Smollett and Shebbeare, and concludes that Smol-
let attacked Shebbeare because of the latter's public conduct
--"Smollett saw something ... ominous on the English hori-
zon: a debasing turn for the worse in politics."

See also: 2672, 2685

Humphry Clinker

2762 ANDRES, SOPHIA.
      "Tobias Smollett's Satiric Spokesman in Humphry Clinker."
      SSL 13 (1978): 100-110.

      Smollett uses Matthew Bramble as his satiric spokesman
      and through him directs his satire against the evil of indi-
      viduals which he regards as the cause for social evils. Smol
      lett, however, believes that in the country, away from the
      city, there are still people who value social responsibility,
      hospitality, and friendship and through Bramble is constantly
      juxtaposing the advantages of country life with the shortcom-
      ings of city life.

2763 BAKER, SHERIDAN.
      "Humphry Clinker as Comic Romance." PMASAL 46 (1961):
      645-654. Rpt. in [53], pp. 154-164.

      Discusses the comedy of names in Smollett, why Humphry
      is the titular hero, and the three strands of comedy in the
      novel: 1) in Lydia's youthful romance, 2) in Tabitha's spin-
      sterish version of it, and 3) in Clinker's.

2764 BARLOW, SHERYL.
      "The Deception of Bath: Malapropisms in Smollett's Hum-
      phrey [sic] Clinker." Mich. A. 2 (1970): 13-24.

      Sees Smollett not as a gentle humorist but as a keen satir-
      ist making a significant comment on life, and suggests that
      the malapropisms and other anomalies in the letters of Win
      Jenkins and Tabitha Bramble make a significant contribution
      to that statement. Malapropisms contribute to the themes of
      primitivism and progress, and to the living problems of the
      social situation.

2765   BATTEN, CHARLES L., JR.
       "Humphry Clinker and Eighteenth-Century Travel Literature."
       Genre 7 (1974): 392-408.

           Considers Humphry Clinker from the standpoint of "an ex-
       tremely sophisticated fictional reworking of the travel book"
       and despite its "lack of novelistic unity, it has an artistic
       brilliance...."

2766   BOGGS, W. ARTHUR.
       "Dialectical Ingenuity in Humphry Clinker." PLL 1 (1965):
       327-337.

           An analysis of Win Jenkins' speech.

2767   BOUCE, PAUL-G.
       "Les Procédés du comique dans Humphry Clinker." Etudes
       anglaises: Actes du Congrès de Lille, 25 (1966): 53-75.

           Examines several kinds of humor in the novel: slapstick
       and burlesque comedy; caricature and satire; juxtaposition; an-
       tagonistic personalities; mangled orthography. Suggests that
       "cathartic humor" unifies Humphry Clinker and differentiates
       it from Smollett's other novels which are mainly picaresque.

2768   COPELAND, EDWARD.
       "Humphry Clinker: A Comic Pastoral Poem in Prose?" TSLL
       16 (1974): 493-501.

           Describing Humphry Clinker as a "Comic Pastoral Poem
       in Prose," the article examines the "general widening of the
       concept of pastoral during the eighteenth century; second, it
       ... [reviews] Smollett's own experiments with the tradition; fin-
       ally, it [seeks] to place Humphry Clinker in a general line of pas-
       toral literature."

2769   DEMPSEY, I. LINDSAY.
       "The Metamorphosis of Humphry Clinker." New Laurel Re-
       view 4, i-ii (1975): 19-26.

           A general interpretation of Matthew Bramble's spiritual
       quest for purification and love, with Humphry as the agent
       of salvation.

2770   DONOVAN, ROBERT A.
       "Humphry Clinker and the Novelist's Imagination." In The
       Shaping Vision: Imagination in the English Novel from Defoe
       to Dickens (Ithaca, N.Y.: Cornell Univ. Press, 1966), pp.
       118-139.

Finds the imaginative center or animating principle of
Humphry Clinker in growth of the acceptance of the family
relation; all characters participate in a movement by which
their idiosyncrasies "remain as strong as ever, but now they
come into play over a firm substructure of acknowledged responsibility and family unity." Since the characters are independent of the author's purposes, the novel can be regarded
as an "imaginative construct" with an internal principle of
organization; at the center of Smollett's imaginative vision is
the "way in which the raw materials of observation are transformed by the idiosyncrasies of the various observers into
feelings, beliefs, and valuations" which express the individuality
of the five main characters.

2771 DUNN, RICHARD J.
"Humphry Clinker's Humane Humor." TSLL 18 (1976): 229-
239.

After failing in Roderick Random and Peregrine Pickle to
present a convincing picture of his dehumanized world, Smol-
let in Humphry Clinker finally "hits upon an imaginative mean
of employing a more humane humor and more convincingly
dramatizes the tension between men of modest merit and a
vicious world." Humphry Clinker is a humane comedy that
never denies the world's inhumanity; the outside world is as
disagreeable as in the earlier novels, but the "novel presents
it as a world against which the good-natured man may both
rail and admit himself attracted." Humphry Clinker is the
one Smollett novel that successfully illustrates the comic idea
that affection may exist independent of esteem.

2772 EVANS, DAVID L.
"Humphry Clinker: Smollett's Tempered Augustanism." Crit
ticism 9 (1967): 257-274.

Traces one strand of Augustanism--the myth of rural simplicity, retirement, and order--in Humphry Clinker, and considers its opposite, the corrupted rural existence of the gentry.

2773 FOLKENFLIK, ROBERT.
"Self and Society: Comic Union in Humphry Clinker." PQ
53 (1974): 195-204.

The reader's movement in and out of the consciousness of
Smollett's characters "enables us to see their selfhood as
comically limited, and leads us to encompass all their views
in a tolerant and embracing vision which prepares us for the
accommodation of their various views in one social vision of
the good life at the novel's end. This interplay of perspectives within the framework of a broader vision ... gives the
novel its comic vitality."

2774   FRANKE, WOLFGANG.
        "Smollett's Humphry Clinker as a 'Party Novel.'"   SSL 9
        (1971-72): 97-106.

        The author examines various aspects of the novel and con-
        siders their contribution to the total effect of persuasion in
        order to determine the "extent to which Smollett's propagan-
        distic intention functions as a principle of organization."

2775   GASSMAN, BYRON.
        "Humphry Clinker and the Two Kingdoms of George III."
        Criticism 16 (1974): 95-108.

        Smollett's vision of England is both realistic and mythopoeic
        as he presents in Humphry Clinker his ideas of the king and
        kingdom that George III and his England might be or might
        have been.

2776   "The Economy of Humphry Clinker." In [2670], pp. 155-168.

        Argues that Smollett "effectively blended his variegated
        materials and diverse aims by his use of multiple point of
        view" and by so doing "brilliantly and effectively assembled
        the materials and ideas of a lifetime into Humphry Clinker
        to produce one of the enduring delights of English fiction."

2777   "Religious Attitudes in the World of Humphry Clinker." Brig-
        ham Young Univ. Std. 5 (1965): 65-72.

        Smollett's satiric treatment of religion, especially the Meth-
        odist movement, points out the religious elements of English
        Society in the 1760's and relates these elements to the total
        picture of a Society which Smollett thinks in danger of de-
        terioration and tottering on the brink of chaos and anarchy.

2778   "The Briton and Humphry Clinker."   SEL 3 (1963): 397-414.

        Smollett's political ideas and experience, especially in con-
        nection with his editorship of the Briton, are a strong under-
        current in the thought of Humphry Clinker.

2779   GRIFFITH, PHILIP MAHONE.
        "Fire-Scenes in Richardson's Clarissa and Smollett's Humphry
        Clinker: A Study of a Literary Relationship in the Structure
        of the Novel." TSE 11 (1961): 39-51.

        Argues that Smollett possibly "recalled the famous fire-
        scene in Clarissa when he adopted for the only time in his
        novelistic career an epistolary method introduced by and

largely associated with Richardson; [and] utilized the fire-
scenes in Clinker for comic rather than tragic purposes" in
order to ridicule Richardson's "inherently lurid and tediously
lengthened-out incident." Also suggests that the two scenes
in Clinker "serve a definite rhythmical function and thus provide the novel with a sort of balancing structure that may
give the novel form...."

2780   HOPKINS, ROBERT.
       "The Function of the Grotesque in Humphry Clinker." HLQ 32
       (1969): 163-178.

       A redefinition of the term "grotesque" and Smollett's use
       of it within the context of humor. Argues that because Smol-
       lett's use of the grotesque in Humphry Clinker is more inte-
       grated, functional, and profound than in his other works, it
       is his most successful novel.

2781   ISER, WOLFGANG.
       "The Generic Control of the Aesthetic Response: An Examin-
       ation of Smollett's Humphry Clinker." SHR 3 (1969): 243-
       257. Rpt. in The Implied Reader: Patterns of Communica-
       tion in Prose Fiction from Bunyan to Beckett (Baltimore:
       Johns Hopkins Univ. Press, 1974), pp. 57-80.

       An examination of the novel that studies the "aesthetic re-
       sponse brought about by a new combination of significant forms
       which had been developed in eighteenth-century prose fiction."
       Seeks to explore the reactions and expectations of Humphry
       Clinker's readers to a new development in fiction; for Smol-
       lett blends the epistolary novel, the book of travels, and the
       picaresque novel.

2782   KARL, FREDERICK R.
       "Smollett's Humphry Clinker: The Choleric Temper." In
       [126], pp. 183-204.

       Sees Humphry Clinker as reflecting incipient revolt and
       traditional consolidation: whereas Bramble represents the
       traditional values of a golden past, Humphry "represents the
       new spirit of the age, the youthful element moving outside
       the traditional family structure, coming ... naked into the
       world," but eventually returning to the family as Bramble's
       love child. Smollett is a lesser novelist than Fielding and
       Richardson; because, unlike them, he fails to conceptualize
       his material, "particulars remain particulars, not part of an
       author's way of seeing or arranging."

2783   KNAPP, LEWIS M.

"Smollett's Self-Portrait in The Expedition of Humphry Clinker." In [27], pp. 149-158.

Regards Bramble as being in many ways Smollett's exact portrait, and since Jery writes about 50 percent of the letters, the author suggests that Smollett has provided for himself two sources of "varied self-revelation." The article summarizes the biographical facts that can be observed in Humphry Clinker, and suggests the extent to which Smollett's character and social criticism are present.

2784   KORTE, DONALD M.
"Verse Satire and Smollett's Humphry Clinker." SSL 7 (1970): 188-192.

Comparison of a satiric episode in Humphry Clinker involving the Baynards with Pope's targets in his fourth "Moral Essay."

2785   NEMOIANU, VIRGIL.
"The Semantics of Bramble's Hypochondria: A Connection Between Illness and Style in the Eighteenth Century." Clio 9 (1979): 39-51.

Sketches the ways in which disease is integrated into culture, and then uses as a case analysis the example of Matthew Bramble to illustrate the manner in which illness can have a "society-preserving" function.

2786   PANNILL, LINDA.
"Some Patterns of Imagery in Humphry Clinker." Thoth 13, No. 3 (1973): 37-43.

Suggests that Bramble's expedition and cure may be interpreted as his reaction to the absence, and later the presence, of rational order in society and in his own family; an interpretation supported by the imagery of heaven and hell, monsters, music, and animals, the emblems of irrationality.

2787   PARK, WILLIAM.
"Fathers and Sons--Humphry Clinker." L & P 16 (1966): 166-174.

Demonstrates how one of the three quests in the novel, "the mutual discovery of a father and son and the psychological complications attendant upon such an event pervade Humphry Clinker from the very outset, forming a pattern of images and motifs which more than amply prepares the reader for the comical, surprising, and satisfying revelation that Clinker is Bramble's love-begotten child."

2788   PRESTON, THOMAS R.
        "Smollett and the Benevolent Misanthrope Type." PMLA 79
        (1964):   51-57.

        Discusses the literary sources and popularity of the benevo-
        lent misanthrope type of character and how Smollett was suc-
        cessful in creating, in Matt Bramble, a character who could
        "express benevolently and yet virulently the satire he had been
        striving to write in his earlier novels."

2789   PRICE, JOHN VALDIMIR.
        Tobias Smollett: "The Expedition of Humphry Clinker" (Studies
        in English Literature, 51). London: Arnold, 1973.

        A comprehensive analysis of plot, structure, theme, and
        character.

2790   PUZON, BRIDGET, O. S. U.
        "The Hidden Meaning in Humphry Clinker." HLB 24 (1976):
        40-54.

        Sees Humphry Clinker not as a typical eighteenth-century
        novel but as a "Bildungsroman of middle age." It is "the
        record of Matthew Bramble's experience of the journey in
        the middle of life." It is through the experiences he encoun-
        ters on his journey that he will be "unwittingly transformed
        into a renewed person."

2791   REID, B. L.
        "Smollett's Healing Journey." VQR 41 (1965):   549-570.   Rpt.
        in [154], pp. 78-99.

        Traces the action in Humphry Clinker "which moves from
        negative to positive, from passive to active: sickness to
        health, constipation to purgation, irritability to sensitivity,
        anonymity to identity, distance to intimacy, doubt to trust,
        celibacy to marriage, ignorance to knowledge."

2792   ROTHSTEIN, ERIC.
        "Humphry Clinker." In Systems of Order and Inquiry in Later
        Eighteenth-Century Fiction (Berkeley & Los Angeles: Univ.
        Calif. Press, 1975), pp. 109-153.

        Using Humphry Clinker to support a thesis that association-
        ist and epistemological principles govern the eighteenth-century
        novel, the author argues that Smollett in that work makes a
        complex statement possessing conceptual breadth and subtlety,
        which is not inherent in the picaresque, by using a Richard-
        sonian model, the "compound eye," in whose double vision the

authority of the novel lies. Concludes that "Humphry Clinker combines inclusiveness and control, through tying visible order to Bramble's system of inquiry and creating covert order through procedures of inquiry like analogy, modification, and grouping. Incremental repetition of events, surrogate characters, the use of the travelling party as a unit--these techniques of order ... recur here."

2793   ROUSSEAU, G. S.
        "Matt Bramble and the Sulphur Controversy in the XVIIIth Century." JHI 28 (1967): 577-589.

        Explores the medical background, with special emphasis on the opening scenes in the pump room at the Hot Wells, Bristol. Provides information about Dr. Linden whom Smollett bitterly satirized.

2794   SENA, JOHN F.
        "Ancient Designs and Modern Folly: Architecture in The Expedition of Humphry Clinker." HLB 27 (1979): 86-113.

        Matthew Bramble's preoccupation with architecture has a vital moral function in the novel. "Through [his] architectural analyses, Smollett is able to present a general indictment of English society which he saw as vain and proud, as cut off from tradition, as tearing down all hierarchical distinctions-- while asserting the essential virtue and integrity of Scotland." Through Bramble's architectural analyses, Smollett is able to show the contrast "between the old and the new, ... the heroism and virtue of the past and the foolishness and vice of the present." He condemns "contemporary society, not merely in words, but in visible metaphors."

2795   "Smollett's Matthew Bramble and the Tradition of the Physician-Satirist." PLL 11 (1975): 380-396.

        Supports thesis that Bramble is a fictional creation not identical to Smollett, that he is the typical physician-satirist of the eighteenth century portraying vice and corruption as diseases which must be cured. Bramble's journey is both moral and healing and by railing against the evil and immorality in the world, he heals himself.

2796   SIEBERT, DONALD T., JR.
        "The Role of the Senses in Humphry Clinker." Studies in the Novel 6 (1974): 17-26.

        Argues that Smollett counterbalances offensive sensory material by pleasant imagery, that sensory experience is essential to the thematic development of Humphry Clinker: "it is the epistemological basis for most of the serious social and philosophical commentary in the novel." The philosophical basis derives from Locke, so that the basis of Smollett's satire thus consists of an empirical reliance on sensory experience as the source of true knowledge.

2797   WAGONER, MARY.
        "On the Satire in Humphry Clinker." PLL 11 (1966): 109-116.

        Smollett's satire is not that of the picaresque tradition, but closer in mood and intention to that of Swift and Pope. The satiric movement is toward the "norm of easier, more tolerant, more reasonable behavior, a movement away from idiosyncrasy and peculiarity."

2798   WEST, WILLIAM A.
        "Matt Bramble's Journey to Health." TSLL 11 (1969): 1197-1208.

        Argues that Matthew Bramble's journey from illness to health provides Humphry Clinker with its main development. In an effort to understand Matt's development, the article surveys the psychological attitudes of the century and concludes: "By the end of the novel, Matt Bramble ... has discovered the importance of the mind to bodily health and the importance of emotional expression to mental health."

See also: 370, 391, 927, 2512, 2672, 2689, 2692, 2708, 2718, 2725, 2735, 2880

The Travels

2799   RICE, SCOTT B.
        "Smollett's Seventh Travel Letter and the Design of Formal Verse Satire." SEL 16 (1976): 491-503.

        Argues that the main purpose of Smollett's Travels is not to give a literal description of the author's travels in Europe but to write a satire; that the "characterization of the French and later of the Italians, is a deliberate distortion in keeping with the governing satiric scheme, and that this scheme emerges from a deft integration of two uniquely compatible genres --the conventionalized Grand Tour narrative and formal verse satire."

2800   "The Satiric Persona of Smollett's Travels." SSL 10 (1972):
        33-47.

        In achieving his aim of exposing foreign luxury and reaf-
        firming native virtue, Smollett creates as his persona a plain-
        speaking Scotch physician who represents a select dramatiza-
        tion of his own literal characteristics.

2801   "Smollett's Travels and the Genre of Grand Tour Literature."
        Costerus 1 (1972): 207-220.

        Provides background to the style and organization of the
        Travels by describing the educational and didactic goals of
        the Grand Tour.   An extensive survey of Grand Tour litera-
        ture.

2802   SENA, JOHN F.
        "Smollett's Persona and the Melancholic Traveler: An Hy-
        pothesis." ECS 1 (1968): 353-369.

        Argues that "by editing personal letters sent home during
        a tour of the Continent, Smollett created ... a persona which
        exemplified a type of personality well-known in the eighteenth
        century"--a splenetic or melancholic personality.

2803   SPECTOR, ROBERT D.
        "Smollett's Traveler." In [2670], pp. 231-246.

        Presents the view that creating Smollett's persona is the
        main business of the design of the Travels; that Smollett's
        purpose is didactic, and that the over-all design is to con-
        vince the reader "that for all its faults, England offers the
        best prospect for happiness on earth."

See also: 2680, 2711

General Studies

2804   AUBIN, ROBERT A.
"Behind Steele's Satire on Undertakers." PMLA 64 (1949):
1008-1026.

A brief history of the "modern trade of funeral undertaking" with an attempt "to explain the novelty, timeliness, justice, and development of Steele's satire on undertakers in
The Funeral and The Tatler."

2805   BETZ, SIEGMUND A. E.
"The Operatic Criticism of the Tatler and Spectator." Musical Quarterly 31 (1945): 318-330.

Suggests that "to the authors of the Spectator papers opera
was not, like the drama, a thing to be analyzed and discussed
according to a well-known, recognized tradition, but rather a
popular institution, a social phenomenon within the scope of
any intelligent gentleman's judgment and condemnation." Discusses the two major English objections to Italian opera, the
use of bizarre stage effects and the introduction of Italian
singers as well as the "Italianization" of the English; Addison
insists that the subject matter ought to be in the English lang
uage: "It is easy to see that underneath this criticism of
language and musical setting there lurks a general, almost
a primitive, fear of what is foreign."

2806   BLANCHARD, RAE.
"Steele and the SPCK." In [13], pp. 287-295.

Presents further insight into the relationship between Steele
and Henry Newman, Secretary of the SPCK, showing Newman's influence on Steele's benevolence as a religious and
social reformer.

2807   "Richard Steele's Maryland Story." Amer. Quart. 10 (1958):
78-82.

Story of an American Negro as an early specimen of primitivism [in The Lover, No. 36].

2808   "Steele, Charles King, and the Dunkirk Pamphlets." HLQ
        14 (1951): 423-429.

        Discusses the influence of a London merchant, Charles
        King, on Steele's views on foreign trade and the French port
        of Dunkirk as expressed in his Dunkirk pamphlets. Presents
        evidence to show that King was the source of technical data
        used by Steele.

2809   "The Songs in Steele's Plays." In [17], pp. 185-200.

        Considers briefly the fourteen songs in Steele's four plays:
        " ... their range and variety, the dramatic purposes they
        serve, their musical settings, the singers who sang them,
        and their fortune through the century as lyrics to be read
        and recited and songs to be sung." A marked characteristic
        was their variety in themes and forms, all possessing " ...
        conscious artistry, metrical precision, and quiet mien, hall-
        marks of eighteenth century light verse at its best...."

2810   "A Prologue and an Epilogue for Nicholas Rowe's Tamerlane
        by Richard Steele." PMLA 47 (1932): 772-776.

        Evidence shows that this prologue and epilogue were writ-
        ten by Steele for use at Dr. Newcome's School in Clapton,
        Hackney. This evidence is based on a small manuscript verse-
        book of poems collected by William Taylor.

2811   "Richard Steele and the Status of Women." SP 26 (1929):
        325-355.

        Attempts to examine Steele's views on women as expressed
        in his essays, periodicals, and plays from the Christian Hero
        to The Conscious Lovers and to interpret them in the light of
        contemporary thought on the subject; considers the reaction
        of three groups--the conservatives, the wits, and the reactions
        ers--to the main points of argument, attempting to place
        Steele among them and to evaluate his contribution to femin-
        ism. The article discusses four subjects: the nature of
        woman, her education, her status in marriage, and her role
        in society, and concludes that Steele's views did not coincide
        with those of any group of contemporary writers. "The con-
        servatism and the superficiality which Steele shared ... with
        the moralists and the wits make it impossible to identify him
        with the reformers ... his reforming intention ... was not in
        the confident spirit of the rationalistic group...."

2812   BOND, RICHMOND P.
        The Tatler: The Making of a Literary Journal.   Cambridge:
        Harvard Univ. Press, 1971.

Examines all aspects of the Tatler--of Steele himself and other writers, the business of production, the kinds of advertisements, the financial problems of the paper, the treatment of news, politics, and current topics, and a detailed analysis of the contents.

2813   ELLIOTT, ROBERT C.
"Swift's 'Little' Harrison, Poet and Continuator of the Tatler."
SP 46 (1949): 544-559.

Examines the literary work that gave Harrison his reputation in London and summarizes biographical information. Also discusses the publication of the Tatler after Steele gave it up in 1711, and Harrison's attempt to take over the role of Isaac Bickerstaff.

2814   GRAHAM, WALTER.
"Some Predecessors of the Tatler." JEGP 24 (1925): 548-554.

Shows relationship of the Tatler to earlier periodicals. Even though the Tatler and Spectator were superior, there is hardly a single trait that was not borrowed from their predecessors.

2815   GREEN, ELVENA M.
"Three Aspects of Richard Steele's Theory of Comedy." ETJ 20 (1968): 141-146.

Examines three aspects of Steele's theory: 1) the moral, didactic purpose of the theatre which was the heart of his theory, 2) his efforts to reform what he thought to be the licentiousness and moral degeneracy of the comedy of manners, and 3) the substitution of virtuous characters for wicked ones, and the replacement of the comedy of ridicule and laughter by a comedy of pity and tears.   Shows that Steele's theory is based primarily on morals rather than on aesthetics and that he fails to distinguish between comedy and tragedy.

2816   HAGSTRUM, JEAN H.
"Richard Steele." In [111], pp. 165-172.

Steele's emotions were strong and mature if we turn aside from The Conscious Lovers and examine the "elegant and moving vignettes of common life in The Tatler or the exquisite and sincere letters of devotion to his wife." In the letters to "Dear Prue" he exalted married love; the essays attempt to civilize a nation, reforming a society mainly interested in "love and wenching" (No. 3) by changing it to a Christian state governed by a civilized view of married love and domestic happiness.

2817   HOPKINS, ROBERT H.
"The Issue of Anonymity and the Beginning of the Steele-Swift Controversy of 1713-14: A New Interpretation. " ELN 2 (1964): 15-21.

When Steele signed his name to Guardian 53, it was an attempt to gain Notingham's patronage; he has been praised rather too highly for signing controversial works.

2818   KENNY, SHIRLEY S.
"Richard Steele and the 'Pattern of Genteel Comedy. ' " MP 70 (1972): 22-37.

An examination of Steele's four plays to show how he finally came up with a formula for sentimental comedy in The Conscious Lovers that was to influence generations of playwrights. In this formula " ... he combined devoted lovers, a melodramatic action, aphoristic speeches, and pathos in the main plot, and he put lively lovers, a comic action, witty and humorous dialogue, and laughter in the subplot. "

2819   KLINE, RICHARD B.
"Tory Prior and Whig Steele: A Measure of Respect?" SEL 9 (1969): 427-437.

Passages from the writings of Prior and Steele, plus other circumstantial evidence, are presented to support the thesis that the two men respected each other professionally in spite of their political differences and their occasional literary swipes at one another. This explains the " ... seeming paradox of the Scottish poet Allan Ramsay's having Steele among the mourners for Prior in his pastoral elegy marking the latter's death in 1721. "

2820   LOFTIS, JOHN.
Steele at Drury Lane. Berkeley: Univ. Calif. Press, 1952.

Examines " ... Steele's theatrical career in the context of early eighteenth-century stage and dramatic history--especially in the context of the dramatic reform movement in which Steele played such a prominent role. "

2821   "The Blenheim Papers and Steele's Journalism, 1715-1718. "
PMLA 66 (1951): 197-210.

Concerns several series of essays written between 1715 and

1718. Several arguments are given for Steele's authorship of Chit-Chat, and variants and cancelled passages in holographs of Town Talk are discussed.

2822   "Richard Steele and the Drury Lane Management." MLN 66 (1951): 7-11.

A request by Steele to John Dalrymple, second Earl of Stair, Minister Plenipotentiary to France, for two actors, then in France, shows not only his direct involvement in the internal management of Drury Lane but also his political influence.

2823   "Richard Steele's Censorium." HLQ 14 (1950): 43-66.

Traces Steele's efforts from about 1712 and 1722 or 1723 to establish a private theater, called the Censorium and located in York Buildings, which emphasized the arts--opera, poetry recited to music, scientific lectures, and dramatizations of ancient history.

2824   "Richard Steele, Drury Lane, and the Tories." MLQ 10 (1949): 72-80.

Discusses Steele's association with the Drury Lane theater and possible reasons why he turned down an interest in the theater in 1713 during the reign of Queen Anne; suggests that he was offered the governorship of Drury Lane by Lord Lansdowne partly because Lansdowne was a generous friend of poets and dramatists and partly because Harley, who would have had to approve the appointment, wished to continue pursuing a moderate policy toward the Whigs by maintaining friendly relations with Steele.

2825   MILIC, LOUIS T.
"Tone in Steele's Tatler." In [5], pp. 33-45.

Suggests that the tone of the Tatler implies a new attitude on the part of the Augustan gentleman toward life and politics: an attitude of moderation and tolerant amusement at life's eccentricities, a lack of enthusiasm for news and politics, even perhaps a contempt for the avid consumption of news; a belief that sensible people are interested in life, the world, people, in local affairs that have greater moral significance than foreign events beyond one's immediate community. The new gentleman had a different tone: "kindly, tolerant, wise yet witty, amused and ironic, never bitter or extreme...."

2826   MOORE, JOHN ROBERT.
        "Steele's Unassigned Tract Against the Earl of Oxford." PQ
        28 (1949): 413-418.

        Argues that the tract is a bitterly ironic attack on the Earl
        of Oxford, written about 1713, and sent to Lord Sunderland,
        a manager of Whig propaganda.

2827   NOVAK, MAXIMILLIAN E.
        "The Sentimentality of The Conscious Lovers Revisited and
        Reasserted." MLS 9, iii (1979): 48-59.

        Defends the use of the term "sentimental," especially as
        applied to Steele's comedies, and argues specifically that
        The Conscious Lovers is sentimental in three ways: "(1) The
        characters move in a world within which, by implication, the
        power of virtue will always overcome those forces ... oppos-
        ing it; (2) The focus on the family, from the servants up to
        the head of the household, invariably involves a series of emo-
        tional stereotypes; and (3) Love between men and women is
        taken directly from the sentiment and sensibility of contem-
        porary French romances and novels."

2828   STEPHENS, JOHN C., JR.
        "Steele and the Bishop of St. Asaph's Preface." PMLA 67
        (1952): 1011-1023.

        Although the Spectator was supposedly nonpartisan, No.
        384 carried a complete reprinting of Bishop Fleetwood's Pre-
        face to his Four Sermons, published in May 1712, which was
        powerful propaganda for the Whig party. With this publica-
        tion, Steele plunged directly " ... into one of the hottest po-
        litical arguments of Queen Anne's reign, the question of the
        Hanoverian Succession," showing that he was becoming restive
        under the nonpartisan restraint previously shown by the Spec-
        tator.

2829   WINTON, CALHOUN.
        "Richard Steele, Journalist--and Journalism." In [5], pp. 21-
        31.

        The influence of Steele on the rise of journalism, especially
        the nature of his achievement in developing "printing press
        journalism" and its responsiveness to the needs of both the
        reader and author/editor. Discusses literary and dramatic
        criticism in The Tatler and its influence on the development
        of fiction.

2830   Sir Richard Steele, M.P.: The Later Career. Baltimore:
        The Johns Hopkins Press, 1970.

Second volume of biography dealing with Steele's life from
the death of Queen Anne in 1714 to his own death in 1729.
Based on primary sources, it deals not only with his personal
life but also presents his activities in the theater and in Par-
liament and describes his dealings with the Duke of Newcastle,
his defense of Ormonde, his sympathy for the condemned Jacobite rebels, and his opposition to the Peerage Bill.   Steele
emerges as an individual in his own right not to be over-
shadowed by Addison.

2831   Captain Steele: The Early Career of Richard Steele.   Balti-
        more: The Johns Hopkins Press, 1964.

        Presents details of Steele's early life and career prior to
        the death of Queen Anne in 1714.   The book " ... is intended
        to serve as an introduction to [his] career ... and the starting
        point for further investigations."   Includes chapters on The
        Gazetteer, The Tatler, The Spectator, The Guardian, and The
        Englishman.   Presents all sides of Steele's early life--his
        careers in politics, literature, and the Army--and shows him
        " ... as he was known to his London friends and acquaintan-
        ces."

2832   "Steele and the Fall of Harley in 1714."   PQ 37 (1958):   440-
        447.

        Discusses Steele's journalistic attacks on Robert Harley--
        method and organization--which led to his removal as Lord
        Treasurer.

2833   "Steele, the Junto, and The Tatler, No. 4."   MLN 72 (1957):
        178-182.

        Discusses the political significance of the allegory in Tatler
        No. 4 which was a propaganda piece for the Whig Junto; shows
        the close relationship between literature and politics in the
        early eighteenth century.

See also: 189, 208, 223, 249, 2345

Collected Studies

2834 CASH, ARTHUR H. and J. M. STEDMOND, eds.
The Winged Skull: Papers from the Laurence Sterne Bicentenary Conference at the University of York. London: Methuen, 1971.

2835 HOWES, ALAN B. , ed.
Sterne: The Critical Heritage. London: Routledge & Kegan Paul, 1974.

2836 TRAUGOTT, JOHN, ed.
Laurence Sterne: A Collection of Critical Essays (Twentieth Century Views). Englewood Cliffs, N.J. : Prentice-Hall, 1968.

General Studies

2837 ALTER, ROBERT.
"Sterne and the Nostalgia for Reality." Far Western Forum 1 (1974): 1-21.

Concerned with the "paradox of evident artifice as seeming reality," suggesting that Sterne is extreme in his insistence on fictional self-consciousness: the zigzag movement of the narration is an accurate rendering of the mind's resistance to pattern and schematization, and at the same time is a declaration by the author of the "artful arbitrariness of all authorial decisions."

2838 ANDERSON, HOWARD.
"Sterne's Letters: Consciousness and Sympathy." In [1], pp. 130-147.

Analyzes Sterne's style in his letters and comments on difficulties and limitations of the text; discusses Journal to Eliza.

2839 BAKER, ERNEST A.

"Sterne." In The History of the English Novel, 10 vols. (London: H. F. & G. Witherby, 1924-39), vol. 4, pp. 240-277.

An historical account that examines such topics as Sterne's purpose and method, the characters in Tristram Shandy, the influence of Locke's theory of duration, Sterne's sentimentalism and emotionalism, the importance of the technique of impressionism, Sterne's plagiarism, and his alleged immorality.

2840   BRISSENDEN, R. F.
"Sterne and Painting." In [12], pp. 93-108.

Sterne's acquaintance with the theory and practice of art as revealed in his writings.

2841   CASH, ARTHUR H.
Laurence Sterne: the Early and Middle Years. London: Methuen, 1975.

The standard life, attempting to avoid the biases of Thackeray, Percy Fitzgerald, and Wilbur Cross, written for a generation that "does not expect a man to doff his libido when he dons his priestly robes, nor a writer of fiction to keep secret his personal life."

2842   COCKSHUT, A. O. J.
"Sterne." In Man and Woman: A Study of Love and the Novel 1740-1940 (New York: Oxford Univ. Press, 1978), pp. 46-53.

Attempts to answer the question: What exactly upset even contemporary readers of Sterne when they encountered passages of sexual innuendo? The answer would seem to be that Sterne refused to separate facts and styles of life; in the chapter entitled "The Rose" in A Sentimental Journey, "the lady's innocence and elegance are a titillating factor entirely absent from the crude passages of Fielding and Smollett.... What Sterne is seeking is the 'pleasing half guilty blush' which can only come from a mingling of guilt and innocence."

2843   CONNELY, WILLARD.
Laurence Sterne as Yorick. London: The Bodley Head, 1958.

Surveys the last nine years of Sterne's "writing life," emphasizing the close relationship between the books and the letters, between Sterne and Yorick; primarily biographical but useful for aiding in the understanding of Tristram Shandy.

2844   CROSS, WILBUR L.

The Life and Times of Laurence Sterne. New Haven: Yale
Univ. Press, 1925; 3rd. rev. ed., New Haven & London:
Yale Univ. Press, 1929.

Chiefly biographical, employing the direct method of "scrupulous narrative."

2845   "Sterne in the Twentieth Century." YR 15 (1926): 99-112.

Discusses Sterne's writing and reasons for his popularity.
"In an industrial age such as ours, that makes even pleasure
a sober business, we have an attitude in Sterne who took what
the world has to give--lightly, naturally, humorously."

2846   DAVIS, ROBERT GORHAM.
"Sterne and the Delineation of the Modern Novel." In [2834],
pp. 21-41.

Discusses the preoccupations of modern critics of the novel,
as well as three irreconcilable dualities which Sterne manipulates through the ambiguity of words: the "difference between
experiencing an event and telling about it, between an idea
and what it is an idea of, and between a sign and its signif-
ication."

2847   de FROE, A.
Laurence Sterne and His Novels Studied in the Light of Modern
Psychology. Groningen, Netherlands: P. Noordhoof, 1925.
Rpt. Norwood, Pa.: Norwood Editions, 1976.

Seeks neither to praise nor to damn in an attempt to understand Sterne's character and mental composition as a means
of understanding the works. Discusses such topics as the
sexual instinct, the working of the instincts on the imaginative
plane, Sterne's temper, Sterne and religion, the sentiments,
and his psyche as revealed in the novels.

2848   DILWORTH, ERNEST N.
The Unsentimental Journey of Laurence Sterne. New York:
King's Crown Press, 1948.

A close examination of passages in Tristram Shandy and
A Sentimental Journey to analyze Sterne's use of sentiment.
Calls "attention to Sterne's encounters with the feelings," considers "them critically in their context," and clarifies "both
their nature and the artist's intent."

2849   DOHERTY, FRANCIS.

"Sterne and Hume: A Bicentenary Essay."   E & S 22 (1969):
71-87.

Emphasizes Sterne's similarities to Hume and his divergences from Locke, especially in his dependence upon the
principle of the association of ideas.   Tristram Shandy demonstrates that reason has a limited effect on human actions.

2850   DONOVAN, ROBERT ALAN.
"Sterne and the Logos."   In The Shaping Vision: Imagination
in the English Novel from Defoe to Dickens (Ithaca, N. Y. :
Cornell Univ. Press, 1966), pp. 89-117.

Concerned primarily with Sterne's language--the "linguistic
surface,"--its nature and function, and the device by which
Sterne permits words to impinge on man's consciousness;
distinguishes between words as "exfoliations of mind" and as
substitutes for things, and their corresponding functions: language operates either as expression or as evocation, both of
which may be easily misunderstood.   "Tristram Shandy is in
fact an extraordinarily rich catalogue of the possibilities of
misunderstanding and confusion that are inherent in language....'
Sterne is interested in logos in another sense, as the rational
principle governing the universe; he is preoccupied with the
dangers of speculative thought--"hobby-horsical notions."

2851   DURRY, MARIE-JEANNE, ROBERT ELLRODT and MARIE-
THERESE JONES-DAVIES, eds.
De Shakespeare à T. S. Eliot: Mélanges offerts à Henri
Fluchère (Etudes Anglaises 63).   Paris: Didier, 1976.

Contains two essays on Sterne: "Le monde de Laurence
Sterne comme réalité et comme représentation," by Jean-
Jacques Mayoux, and "Sterne et les deux Ecoles du Regard
anglais," by C. Pons.

2852   FOSTER, JAMES R.
"Sterne," In The History of the Pre-Romantic Novel in England (New York: Modern Language Assoc. of America, 1949),
pp. 130-138.

Sees Sterne as part of the school of sentiment and sensibility.

2853   FREDMAN, ALICE GREEN.
"Diderot and Sterne.   New York: Columbia Univ. Press,
1955.

A study of the significant similarities and differences, con-

sidering such topics as humor, sensibility, fictional theories
and practices, and style.

2854   GOLDEN, MORRIS.
        "Sterne's Journeys and Sallies." <u>SBHT</u> 16 (1974): 47-62.

        Sterne "saw and created life as equivocal zigzags along a
        road from birth to death" and his metaphor of journey may
        be closer to the core of the world he sensed than his motifs
        of time and sex. His characters are always "sallying out"
        to seek something--some sort of fulfillment which takes on
        the essential qualities of life itself.

2855   HAGSTRUM, JEAN H.
        "Sterne." In [111], pp. 247-259.

        Sterne bestowed the term "sentimental" on that emotion
        represented by "sympathetic Tears," subsuming under it both
        the "sensible" and the "pathetic" and eliminating its intellec-
        tual and didactic content. Where "sentiment" had once stood
        for moral judgment and then, during its period of transition,
        for the combination of the head and the heart, it now referred
        primarily to feeling. Sterne raises the sentimental above the
        sensual; but especially in <u>Tristram Shandy</u>, sexual love and
        tender feeling cannot be isolated from one another. Sterne's
        eroticism is hardly ever present without its opposite quality,
        sentimental delicacy, also being present. Sterne, therefore,
        stands apart from the Men of Feeling by his unique combina-
        tion of "sexual nuance and tender sensibility."

2856   HAMMOND, LANSING VAN der HEYDEN.
        <u>Laurence Sterne's "Sermons of Mr. Yorick"</u> (Yale Studies in
        English, Vol. 108). New Haven: Yale Univ. Press, 1948.

        The extent of Sterne's indebtedness and his originality.

2857   HARTLEY, LODWICK.
        "Laurence Sterne and the Eighteenth-Century Stage." <u>PLL</u> 4
        (1968): 144-157.

        Though interested in the contemporary stage and in the
        acting technique of David Garrick, Sterne derived much of
        his dramatic qualities from other sources; describes unsatis-
        factory efforts to adapt his work for the stage after his death.

2858   <u>Laurence Sterne in the 20th Century: An Essay and a Bib-
        liography of Sternean Studies 1900-1965.</u> Chapel Hill: Univ.
        N.C. Press, 1966. Revised ed. 1900-1968, Chapel Hill,
        1968.

In addition to the annotated bibliography, contains an introduction discussing Sterne's life and works: the two novels,
biographical problems, the letters and sermons, the literary
reputation and influence, and a concluding chapter of general
comments.

2859   This is Lorence: A Narrative of the Reverend Laurence
        Sterne. Chapel Hill: Univ. N. C. Press, 1943.

        The author intends to write "not another biography of Sterne
        but an introduction to his life and works--a book light enough
        to do justice to the Shandaic mood and to be acceptable to the
        palate of the lay reader, yet accurate enough to be of value
        to the student of the eighteenth century and of the English
        novel."

2860   HNATKO, EUGENE.
        "Sterne's Conversational Style." In [2834], pp. 229-236.

        Analyzes Sterne's style and concludes that, although it has
        few of the qualities of everyday conversation and much of
        carefully and deliberately composed prose, it really does
        create an illusion of the speaking voice; Sterne, a master
        artist in prose style, has been able to fool the reader: "Sterne
        created the illusion of the speaking presence as perhaps no other
        writer has. Yet it is an illusion."

2861   HOLLAND, NORMAN N.
        "The Laughter of Laurence Sterne." HR 9 (1956): 422-430.

        Discusses the dual aspect of Sterne's humor and maintains
        that the "crux of his humor is the hobby-horse, which can be
        the ruling passion of a character, or a reader's preconceptions
        about relevancy, time-sequence, propriety, or sentiment, but
        in every case is both ludicrous and admirable."

2862   HOWES, ALAN B.
        Yorick and the Critics: Sterne's Reputation in England, 1760-
        1868 (Yale Studies in English, Vol. 139). New Haven: Yale
        Univ. Press, 1958.

        Sterne's critical reputation: in the eighteenth century, he
        stood out conspicuously among contemporary novelists, arous-
        ing much comment, especially because of his connection with
        sentimentalism.

2863   JEFFERSON, D. W.

Lawrence Sterne. (WTW) London: Longmans, 1954.

Short introduction to Sterne's life and works.

2864   KUIST, JAMES M.
        "New Light on Sterne: An Old Man's Recollections of the
        Young Vicar." PMLA 80 (1965): 549-553.

        Comments on and evaluation of notes on Sterne's life, now
        in the British Museum, taken by Joseph Hunter.

2865   LOCKRIDGE, ERNEST H.
        "A Vision of the Sentimental Absurd: Sterne and Camus."
        SR 72 (1964): 652-667.

        Applies Camus' philosophy of the Absurd as described in
        his The Myth of Sisyphus to Sterne's Tristram Shandy and
        A Sentimental Journey to show that the Absurd helps define
        Sterne's humor, his "whole vision, including his 'sentimental-
        ity' and his mocking even of those things which seem close
        to him, [and] his refusal to accept anything absolutely," and
        that "Sterne, in his own way, helps define and qualify the
        Absurd. "

2866   MCKILLOP, ALAN D.
        "The Reinterpretation of Laurence Sterne." EA 7 (1954):
        36-47.

        A survey of the qualities, method, and structure of Tris-
        tram Shandy, based on recent scholarship and criticism; but
        contains much original interpretation. Also considers Sterne
        in relation to his contemporaries; his achievement is that he
        shifts his claim to interpret life adequately to a comic level
        without destroying a meaningful universe.

2867   MOGLEN, HELENE.
        "Laurence Sterne and the Contemporary Vision." In [2834],
        pp. 59-75. Rpt. in [2965], pp. 145-162.

        Accepts Sterne's philosophical perspective as determining
        the modernity of his vision; his relation to Locke's epistemo-
        logical and linguistic theories anticipates the thought of Berg-
        son, James, and Freud.

2868   MUIR, EDWIN.
        "Laurence Sterne." AB 73 (1931): 1-5. Rpt. in Essays on
        Literature and Society (London: Hogarth Press, 1949), pp.
        49-56. Rpt. in enlarged & revised edition (London: Hogarth

Press, 1965; Cambridge: Harvard Univ. Press, 1967), pp. 50-57.

A general discussion of Sterne's achievement, commenting on such matters as style, persona, and method.

2869   NEW, MELVYN.
"Sterne and Swift: Sermons and Satire." MLQ 30 (1969): 198-211.

Examines the sermons to suggest that Swift and Sterne were both within the Latitudinarian tradition, that they shared a set of norms in the Anglican church that provided the moral basis for Augustan satire. They both shared a view of man in which reason is rendered imperfect by man's perverse tendency to evil; and the Augustan satiric vision is "accepted and upheld" in Tristram Shandy.

2870   OATES, J. C. T.
Shandyism and Sentiment, 1760-1800. Cambridge, England: Cambridge Bibliographical Society, 1968.

Surveys Sterne's popularity and the cult of Shandyism in England and abroad.

2871   PRICE, MARTIN.
"Sterne: Art and Nature." In [153], pp. 312-341; rpt. Garden City, N. Y.: Anchor Books, 1965, pp. 313-342.

Sterne is concerned with the theme of the "duality of man" in which he comically exaggerates the outside view of man as the victim of chance, a lonely product of a valueless material world; and he exaggerates the opposite view of man as a creature of feeling, creating the world in which he mainly lives by the energy of his own imagination.

2872   READ, HERBERT.
"Sterne." In The Sense of Glory (Cambridge: Cambridge Univ. Press, 1929; New York: Harcourt, Brace & Co., 1930), pp. 124-151. Rpt. in Collected Essays in Literary Criticism (London: Faber & Faber, Ltd., 1938; 2nd. ed. 1951), pp. 247-264.

An essay which deals with criticism of Sterne, his doctrine of sensibility, his humor, his mastery of English prose style and the art of narrative, and his approach to life as revealed in his Sermons.

2873   REID, B. L.

"Sterne and the Absurd Homunculus." VQR 43 (1967): 71-95. Rpt. in [154], pp. 100-127.

Discusses the purpose and method of comedy (madness) in the novel and concludes that the "serious mission of Sterne's gaudy work" is to build "a bridge to sustain us over the tragic gap between the real and the ideal as well as over the comic gap between the normal and the extravagant."

2874   "The Sad Hilarity of Sterne." VQR 32 (1956): 107-130.

Alternative readings of Sterne as a sly pornographer, a sentimentalist, a self-conscious writer, and a jester to substantiate thesis that "the emotional strength of Sterne's comedy comes from its hidden roots in tragedy."

2875   SHAW, MARGARET R. B.
Laurence Sterne: The Making of a Humorist, 1713-1762. London: Richards Press, 1957. Rpt. Norwood, Pa.: Norwood Editions, 1976.

Seeks primarily to "discover the true springs and origins of [Sterne's] genius" and to impose a coherent pattern on the various strands of his personality; and further seeks to refute, by reference to Sterne's own writings, Cross's condemnation of his moral values. Emphasizes the forces that went into the making of Sterne's humor.

2876   STEDMOND, JOHN M.
The Comic Art of Laurence Sterne: Convention and Innovation in "Tristram Shandy" and "A Sentimental Journey." Toronto: Univ. Toronto Press, 1967.

Sees Sterne as reviving conventions of the past and thus demonstrating their continuing usefulness to the novelist; as a comic writer, he examines critically the function of convention in artistic communication. A close reading of Sterne's "unconventional" writings reveals a great deal about the comic use of convention and the nature of comedy.

2877   STEWART, JACK F.
"Some Critical Metaphors for Shandean Style." CLAJ 13 (1969): 183-187.

"Three metaphorical terms have recurrently been applied to Sterne's rhythm, indicating its opposition to the rigid structure of the traditional novel: these are flow, whirl, and mosaic, all of which are meant to express a running or broken form."

2878 "Dramatic Theories of Humor Relating to Sterne." Personal-
ist 50 (1968): 459-473.

Studies the ideas of Coleridge, Hazlitt, Hunt, and Carlyle
about humor, especially in their relation to Sterne. These
critics do not systematize humor but appreciate it spontan-
eously for its "freedom."

2879 TUVESON, ERNEST.
"Locke and Sterne." In [39], pp. 255-277.

Seeks to determine what Locke meant for Sterne by trying
to see what was Locke's ultimate purpose in studying the
human mind; concludes that, for Sterne, Locke's Essay had
"wiped clean the window of the soul from the false ideas that
had hitherto obscured it."

2880 UPHAUS, ROBERT.
"Sentiment and Spleen: Travels with Sterne and Smollett."
Cent. Rev. 15 (1971): 406-421.

Argues that Sterne's attack on Smollett as "Smellfungus"
receives an implicit reply in Humphry Clinker, which is an
analysis of the limitations of the distinction between sentiment
and spleen. Discusses the issue between Sterne and Smollett, and concludes that both authors recognized that hobby-
horses--sentimental or splenetic--distort human experience.

2881 WATKINS, W. B. C.
"Yorick Revisited." In [182], pp. 99-156. Rpt. and abridged
in [2836], pp. 168-179.

An attempt to explore the meaning of Sterne's works through
an understanding of his personality.

2882 WHITE, F. EUGENE.
"Sterne's Quiet Journey of the Heart: Unphilosophic Projection
of Enlightened Benevolence." Enl. E. 2 (1971): 103-110.

Examines the entrance of sentiment into the restrained neo-
classical world, caused partly by Sterne's reading of Locke's
theories of sensation. White argues that Sterne had not strayed
beyond the eighteenth century's acceptance of and emphasis
on reason but had tried to find its limits and keep it in its
place; he notes that Sterne is one of those who revolted against
rationalism.

2883 YOSELOFF, THOMAS.
A Fellow of Infinite Jest. New York: Prentice-Hall, 1945.

A biographical portrait of Sterne--"an effort to recreate the man as he was known to the contemporary world, to his intimates and to himself."

See also: 452, 916, 2716

Tristram Shandy

2884   ALLENTUCK, MARCIA.
"In Defense of an Unfinished Tristram Shandy: Laurence Sterne and the Non Finito." In [2834], pp. 145-155.

Focuses upon the eighteenth-century aesthetic theory of "il non finito," suggesting that "Sterne may have known and related to it," and linking this "aspect to the problem of the ending of Tristram Shandy"; concludes therefore that Tristram Shandy is deliberately unfinished.

2885   ALTER, ROBERT.
"Tristram Shandy and the Game of Love." American Scholar 37 (1968): 316-323.

Wit is the means of communication, not Lockean judgment which sets up barriers between people. Wit is chiefly sexual for Sterne and is used as a rhetorical strategy to make the reader Sterne's accomplice; and by implicating the reader in sexual imaginings, Sterne demonstrates the power of imagination. Judgment is associated with artifice, wit with nature.

2885A ANDERSON, HOWARD, ed.
Tristram Shandy (Norton Critical Edition). New York: W. W. Norton & Co., 1980.

An authoritative text, backgrounds, sources, and criticism.

2886   "Tristram Shandy and the Reader's Imagination." PMLA 86 (1971): 966-973. Rpt. in [2885A], pp. 610-623.

Discusses ways in which Sterne makes the reader look at himself and leads him to understand that the causes of human events are richer and more complex than we typically assume. Tristram tests and teaches the reader and in the end our acceptance of Tristram becomes the sign of our acceptance of the world.

2887   "Associationism and Wit in Tristram Shandy." PQ 48 (1969): 27-41.

Argues that "Sterne's associationism, and the witty techniques in which it results, originate in such Renaissance
writers as Montaigne" and not so much with Locke's theories
as previously thought.

2888   "A Version of Pastoral: Class and Society in Tristram Shandy. "
SEL 7 (1967): 509-529.

Considers the use of pastoral elements in Tristram Shandy.
"The several kinds of aloofness which may seem to separate
the novel from social and moral concerns become methods of
reflecting on the contemporary world.... Among the old forms
which [Sterne] adapts to his purposes, the pastoral provides
a means of showing the new relevance of an ancient ideal of
brotherhood and responsibility" which social classes tend to
erode.

2889   BAIRD, THEODORE.
"The Time Scheme of Tristram Shandy and a Source. " PMLA
51 (1936): 803-820.

The time-scheme of Tristram Shandy proves that: 1) there
is a carefully planned and executed framework of calendar
time in what is usually considered a chaos of whimsicalities
and indecencies, and 2) Sterne used a particular source for
his dates, and for his allusions to, and details of, historical
events.   Argues that in spite of slight errors made by Sterne
there is a coherent and elaborate time-scheme.

2890   BAKER, VAN R.
"Sterne and Piganiol de la Force: The Making of Volume VII
of Tristram Shandy. " CLS 13 (1976): 5-14.

Sterne used Nouveau Voyage de France, by Jean Aimar
Piganiol de la Force, for some of the most interesting episodes of Volume VII; it provided the entire narrative framework for the volume, it gave him some travel writing to parody, and it furnished him with material for humorous and
sentimental episodes.

2891   BANERJEE, CHINMOY.
"Tristram Shandy and the Association of Ideas. " TSLL 15
(1974): 693-706.

Suggests that Sterne is better understood in the tradition
of Renaissance learning and contemporary thought than in the
light of Locke's Essay Concerning Human Understanding; concludes that "It is David Hume and his associationist followers
who provide the theoretical context for the truth of Tristram
Shandy. "

2892   BATTESTIN, MARTIN C.
        "Sterne: The Poetics of Sensibility." In [68], pp. 241-269.

        Suggests that Sterne is preoccupied with the theme of Chaos
        in Tristram Shandy, deliberately violating the formal rules of
        Augustan art in order to reveal their complete irrelevancy:
        in Tristram Shandy the "mind is presented as an autonomous,
        irrational mechanism preventing rather than promoting know-
        ledge of any objective reality.... The old ideals of Order
        and Right Reason ... have been replaced by the Hobby-horse,
        those private systems for survival that enable us to Shandy-
        it through life without succumbing completely to the muddle
        of things."

2893   BOOTH, WAYNE C.
        The Rhetoric of Fiction.   Chicago: Univ. Chicago Press,
        1962, pp. 221-240.

        Argues that Tristram supports Booth's theory that fiction
        is partly a design upon its readers.

2894   "The Self-Conscious Narrator in Comic Fiction before Tris-
        tram Shandy." PMLA 67 (1952): 163-185.

        Compares Tristram Shandy with other novels using an in-
        truding narrator and concludes that Sterne was more success-
        ful at using this kind of narrator to "impose unity, of how-
        ever 'loose' or unconventional a kind, on seemingly disparate
        materials," an achievement that made for the over-all excel-
        lence of Tristram Shandy.

2895   "Did Sterne Complete Tristram Shandy?" MP 48 (1951): 172-
        183.   Rpt. in [2885A], pp. 532-548.

        Argues that Sterne wrote Tristram Shandy according to a
        plan, however rough, that was in his mind from the begin-
        ning; he always had a fairly clear idea of what the final volume
        would contain: we have every reason to believe "not only that
        Sterne worked with some care to tie his major episodes to-
        gether but that, with his ninth volume, he completed the book
        as he had originally conceived it."

2896   BOWMAN, JOEL P.
        "Structural Values in Tristram Shandy." Re: Arts & Let-
        ters (Stephen Austin College) 6 (1973): 16-26.

        In choosing to imitate the structural form of the fugue in
        Tristram Shandy, Sterne chose "a form that would let him
        write as much or as little about any single event as he de-
        sired, a form that would permit an unending addition of epi-

sodes as long as they imitated the original theme of frustration of expectation, and a form that would allow him to rhapsodize on any subject at all."

2897   BOYS, RICHARD C.
        "Tristram Shandy and the Conventional Novel." PMASAL 27 (1951): 423-436.

        Presents diverse views about the nature and intention of Tristram Shandy and especially considers it as a protest against the conventional novel.

2898   BRADBURY, MALCOLM.
        "The Comic Novel in Sterne and Fielding." In [2834], pp. 124-131.

        Considers the structure and procedure that Tristram Shandy, a comic novel not in the species of social comedy, possesses as an anti-novel. The conflict between the farce of life and the comedy of ideas creates an irony of multiple presentation, so that Tristram Shandy is doubly ironic--a comedy of ideas which is also a comedy of misfortunes, a "novel which ironically distances its world and then ironizes again about the procedures by which this is done."

2899   BRADY, FRANK.
        "Tristram Shandy: Sexuality, Morality, and Sensibility." ECS 4 (1970): 41-56.

        Discusses the sexual jokes and especially the relationship of sexuality to composition and design. Sexuality and sentiment appear in a pure state, but often interpenetrate.

2900   BRIENZA, SUSAN D.
        "Volume VII of Tristram Shandy: A Dance of Life." UDR 10, No. 3 (1974): 59-62.

        Volume VII is thematically and imagistically a dance of life, one long affirmation of life and therefore the epitome of Tristram Shandy; it "celebrates the sexual aspect of life and serves as a fitting prologue to the story of Uncle Toby's amours."

2901   BRISSENDEN, R. F.
        "The Sentimental Comedy: Tristram Shandy." In Virtue in Distress: Studies in the Novel of Sentiment from Richardson to Sade (New York: Barnes & Noble; London: Macmillan, 1974), pp. 187-217.

Argues that "what transforms Tristram Shandy from an
exercise in learned satire or dramatic rhetoric or obscure
bawdry into a novel is primarily its sentimentalism"; it becomes a novel toward the end of Volume I when Toby and
Walter undergo a "transformation from Scriblerian humours
into living characters--and this transformation coincides ...
with the emergence of sentimentalism as a major theme."
Suggests that the theme of Tristram Shandy may be the comedy of human imperfection or limitations; that Sterne is mainly
concerned with the "attempts which every man must make,
first to discover a meaning in or to impose a meaning on
the apparently insensate and unordered universe of things into
which we are born, and next to communicate this meaning to
his fellow human creatures." Concludes that Tristram Shandy
is more than a literary joke because it combines successfully
"satiric wit and sentimentality--the recognition and evaluation
of feeling."

2902   " 'Trusting to Almighty God': Another Look at the Composition
        of Tristram Shandy." In [2834], pp. 258-269.

        Discusses the development of the character of Uncle Toby
        to support thesis that although Sterne may have had a fairly
        clear idea of the basic framework of the story, Tristram
        Shandy remains in detail and in origins a spontaneous and
        haphazard production. A close reading of Volume I suggests
        that Uncle Toby's story came to Sterne as he was writing.

2903   BROGAN, HOWARD O.
        "Fiction and Philosophy in the Education of Tom Jones, Tris-
        tram Shandy, and Richard Feverel." CE 14 (1952): 144-149.

        All three novels are "critiques of empirical educational
        theory": Fielding's and Sterne's ideas are derived from
        Locke, Meredith's especially from Herbert Spencer, but also
        from Fielding and Sterne. Compares the upbringing and edu-
        cation of the three heroes as influenced by educational philos-
        ophy of the time, and concludes that the three writers are
        rebelling from the "excesses of an oversystematized concept
        of education, too distrustful of nature and too confident in the
        powers of the rational intellect."

2904   BURCKHARDT, SIGURD.
        "Tristram Shandy's Law of Gravity." ELH 28 (1961): 70-
        88. Rpt. in [2885A], pp. 595-610.

        Argues that corporeal gravity orders Sterne's strange uni-
        verse; that we cannot understand the wit until we realize that
        substance and body out-wit "gravity by a far from ordinary
        obedience." Concludes that Tristram Shandy is a "universe

of language which reveals the nature of its medium by that medium's motions. "

2905   CASH, ARTHUR H.
       "The Birth of Tristram Shandy: Sterne and Dr. Burton. "
       In [10], pp. 133-154.

       Discusses the role Dr. John Burton played in Sterne's comedy as Dr. Slop. In Burton's theories and practices, "Sterne had discovered his profound comic vision of man's utter foolishness before the mysteries of life and death. "

2906   "The Sermon in Tristram Shandy. " ELH 31 (1964): 395-417.

       Considers Sterne's moral philosophy as reflected in The Abuses of Conscience Considered, and finds most of the ideas deriving from Locke. Sterne had absorbed the most liberal, enlightened Christian tradition.

2907   "The Lockean Psychology of Tristram Shandy. " ELH 22 (1955): 125-135.

       Argues that it is Locke's empiricism, not the association of ideas, that underlies Sterne's artistry in Tristram Shandy; that empiricism engendered the organic stream of consciousness that became the organizing principle of the novel.

2908   CHATTERJEE, AMBARNATH.
       "Dramatic Technique in Tristram Shandy. " Indian Jour. of English Studies 6 (1965): 33-43.

       Analyzes the relationship between dramatic production and Sterne's work; Sterne's dramatic technique, the dramatic presentation of ideas and feelings, and the physical gestures of the characters.

2909   COLUMBUS, THOMAS M.
       "Tristram's Dance with Death--Volume VII of Tristram Shandy. '
       UDR 8, ii (1971): 3-15.

       Analyzes the controlling metaphor of Volume VII, that of Tristram's dance with death, as an integral part of the novel' total pattern: Tristram's life and Tristram's book are journeys, and the short trip on the Continent becomes an emblem of the journey of a man's life.

2910   CONRAD, PETER.

Shandyism: The Character of Romantic Irony. New York:
Barnes & Noble, 1978.

Attempts to define the various contexts for Tristram Shandy
in the art of its period in order to suggest its romantic quality. Although Tristram Shandy remains a "sport," it is seen
as genuinely original, "not merely exhibitionistically new,"
when considered in relation to the history of romanticism.
Sterne's romantic originality consists in his rearrangement
of the Shakespearean relation of tragedy and comedy. From
the "similitude between tragedy and comedy comes irony, the
visionary composite expounded by Sterne's German critics."
Tristram Shandy is related to the aesthetic speculations of
Sterne's contemporaries: Hogarth's line of beauty, Burke's
sublimity, and Fuseli's introversion of pictorial genres.

2911   DAVIES, RICHARD A.
        "Tristram Shandy: Eccentric Public Orator." ESC 5 (1979):
        154-166.

        Presents the historical and biographical background to a
        popular form of entertainment in Sterne's day, the eccentric
        public oratory that constituted a significant influence on Tris-
        tram Shandy. Tristram's manner and behavior resemble that
        of the eccentric public orator, whose practice of lecturing
        "helped to give the age the public display of singularity it ad-
        mired and loved so much."

2912   DONALDSON, IAN.
        "The Clockwork Novel: Three Notes on an Eighteenth-Century
        Analogy." RES 21 (1970): 14-22.

        Discusses the representation of time in the novel, first by
        tracing "the philosophical background of two familiar eighteenth-
        century images of clocks" and, second, by looking at "the
        presentation of time in the eighteenth-century novel"--primarily
        Tristram Shandy.

2913   DONOGHUE, DENIS.
        "Sterne, Our Contemporary." In [2834], pp. 42-58.

        Discusses Lockean sensation and reflection, the relation
        between subject and object, the association of ideas, the na-
        ture of Tristram Shandy's plot, and the importance of feeling.

2914   DOWLING, WILLIAM C.
        "Tristram Shandy's Phantom Audience." Novel 13 (1980):
        284-295.

Argues that Tristram Shandy is a story without an audienc●
--or rather it possesses an internal or imaginary audience,
a conception that is intended to account for what happens when
we open a book and begin to read. The internal audience--
Sir and Madam, their "worships and reverences"--belong to
a plane of reality different from that inhabited by actual read●
ers; they are wholly imaginary presences in a double sense:
they correspond to no real body of readers, and they are
within the dramatic situation imagined by Tristram.

2915   DYSON, A. E.
       "Sterne: The Novelist as Jester." Crit. Quart. 4 (1962):
       309-320. Rpt. in The Crazy Fabric: Essays in Irony (Lon-
       don: Macmillan, 1965), pp. 33-48.

       Discusses Tristram Shandy's anti-Augustan qualities, the
       relationship of author to reader and to his characters, the
       nature of Sterne's irony, and the novel's psychological real-
       ism--"Psychological realism has entered the novel; and as it
       enters, it makes the satirist's sneers and exaggerations seem
       a little crude, a little unbalanced, a little untrue to the facts
       of human nature as they really are."

2916   EMERSON, EVERETT H.
       "An Apology for Tristram Shandy." Contributions to the Hu-
       manities, 1954 (Louisiana State Univ. Studies, Humanities
       Series 5). Baton Rouge: La. State Univ. Press, 1954, pp.
       1-10.

       Reevaluates the arguments as to whether Sterne was a de-
       stroyer or a master of the newly developed form of the novel
       and argues that he is best understood "as a lover of life and
       truth who saw the world as if it were put together without
       rhyme or reason, and, happily, regarded the result as hum-
       orous." Tristram Shandy is "humorous because humor is the●
       only healthy way to deal with the contradictoriness of life."

2917   ESKIN, STANLEY G.
       "Tristram Shandy and Oedipus Rex: Reflections on Comedy
       and Tragedy." CE 24 (1963): 271-277.

       Concerned with patterns of incongruity susceptible to either
       comic or tragic treatment; concludes that "The juxtaposition
       of Tristram Shandy and Oedipus Rex suggests that comedy and●
       tragedy may be different modes of dealing with similar prob-
       lems."

2918   FABRICANT, CAROLE.
       "Tristram Shandy and Moby-Dick: A Cock and Bull Story and
       a Tale of a Tub." JNT 7 (1977): 57-69.

In addition to the sexual allusiveness that connects Tristram Shandy and Moby-Dick, the two books are similar on a
more profound level: both novels are epistemological in that
they not only "examine the way in which each character sees
and interprets the world around him, but they also investigate
the fundamental grounds of such interpretation and the relationship of the artist's own consciousness to that of his characters. "

2919   FARRELL, WILLIAM J.
        "Nature Versus Art as a Comic Pattern in Tristram Shandy. "
        ELH 30 (1963):   16-35.

        "Not only on the level of style and action ... but even in
        the structure of the novel, Sterne creates a comic conflict
        of artifice and nature that mocks the fact-minded reader and
        the detail-bound writer as much as it does the naive corporal
        or the pedantic Shandys. " When Sterne has Tristram try to
        impose art on nature, he is emphasizing that a writer whose
        chief aim is fidelity to subject matter will produce chaos.

2920   FAUROT, RUTH MARIE.
        "Mrs. Shandy Observed. " SEL 10 (1970):   579-589.

        A reappraisal of Mrs. Shandy's role in the predominantly
        male Shandy household. She is seen as a many-faceted woman,
        not merely as phlegmatic or passive.

2921   FLUCHERE, HENRI.
        Laurence Sterne: From Tristram to Yorick: An Interpreta-
        tion of "Tristram Shandy. " Trans. & abridged by Barbara
        Bray.   London: Oxford Univ. Press, 1965.

        Translation of the French edition (Paris: Gallimard, 1961)
        with biographical section omitted. A thorough analysis of
        Tristram Shandy in terms of structure, themes, and style,
        together with a consideration of the problems of time and
        causality.

2922   FRANCIS, C. J.
        "Sterne: The Personal and the Real. " In [35], pp. 90-115.

        Insists upon the separation of author from narrator, Tris-
        tram being a fictional creation in his own right: "The real
        author, no longer to be thought of as a mere alter ego of the
        character, is a detached satirist, moralist and humorist whose
        ironies are not single but multiple, bearing criticism not only
        of the characters the narrator describes but of the speaker
        himself. " But argues that the separation of author from nar-

rator can be carried too far, since there is a connection between them that is both emotional and intellectual.

2923   FREEDMAN, WILLIAM.
       Laurence Sterne and the Origins of the Musical Novel. Athens:
       Univ. Georgia Press, 1978.

       This study of the role of music in Tristram Shandy sug-
       gests that music was influential in forming Sterne's prose
       style and that it "governed ... his choice of language, tone,
       rhythms, metaphors, [and] ... his sense of process and de-
       sign"; that the principles of order and rational structure in
       Tristram Shandy are similar to the principles and patterns
       of musical structure and design. Concludes that Sterne was
       "the first author to bring musical technique and patterns to
       fiction on a major scale...."

2924   "Tristram Shandy: The Art of Literary Counterpoint." MLQ
       32 (1971): 268-280.

       Music is everywhere in Tristram Shandy. By seeking to
       present an accurate picture of the mind, Sterne achieves si-
       multaneity by using several contrapuntal techniques.

2925   FURST, LILIAN R.
       "The Dual Face of the Grotesque in Sterne's Tristram Shandy
       and Lenz's Der Waldbruder." CLS 13 (1976): 15-21.

       Both works present the "ludicrously humorous face of the
       grotesque" in the preposterous plots and in the "style and
       narrative techniques which convey the unpredictability of exist-
       ence through the use of such devices as anti-climax, exaggera-
       tion and irony." The grotesque assumes either a comic or
       a horrendous guise: in both tendencies there is the same
       abrupt deviation from the norm, the same sense of inconguity,
       the same intention to shock.

2926   GOODIN, GEORGE.
       "The Comic as a Critique of Reason: Tristram Shandy."
       CE 29 (1967): 206; 211-223.

       Develops a theory of the comic that owes a great deal to
       Sterne: the author bases his theory on the laughter arising
       from emotional relief incident to a perception of an incongruity
       or disproportion; the comic arises from the conflict of satiric
       and sentimental frames of reference. It is critical of reason
       because reason is usually "single frame" thinking. Discusses
       the major episodes of Tristram Shandy.

2927   GRIFFIN, ROBERT J.
        "Tristram Shandy and Language." CE 23 (1961): 108-112.

        Considers one aspect of Locke's epistemological concern--
        the problem of language, of "human communication as re-
        flected in the uses, abuses, and imperfections of words."
        Sterne believed that rational control of language is practic-
        able.

2928   GROSSVOGEL, DAVID I.
        "Sterne: Tristram Shandy." In Limits of the Novel: Evolu-
        tions of a Form from Chaucer to Robbe-Grillet (Ithaca: Cor-
        nell Univ. Press, 1968), pp. 136-159.

        Examines the interaction between author and reader, and
        especially Sterne's central problem of not allowing his fiction
        to mask his own presence or to permit its phenomenal world
        to usurp his world.   Concludes that Sterne is too completely
        entangled with his writing: "Such entanglement is fatal: even
        as an alien book grows between Sterne and his reader ...
        [he] remains within the book from which he is crying out and
        is slowly, unavoidably fictionalized."

2929   HAFTER, RONALD.
        "Garrick and Tristram Shandy." SEL 7 (1967): 475-489.

        Suggests that Garrick had a profound influence on Sterne
        as he was composing Tristram Shandy; that "it was his adap-
        tation of Garrick's stage techniques to the purposes of prose
        fiction" that gives the novel much of its unique quality.   Dis-
        cusses the personal relationship of the two men, and describes
        Garrick's acting technique.

2930   HALL, JOAN JOFFE.
        "The Hobbyhorsical World of Tristram Shandy." MLQ 24
        (1963): 131-143.

        An examination of hobbyhorses--the obsessions that cause
        the comic failures of communication among the Shandy char-
        acters,--the relationship which the narrator enters into with
        the reader that defines Tristram's own hobbyhorse, and the
        relationships between this world and the world of impotence.

2931   HARTLEY, LODWICK.
        " 'Tis a Picture of Myself': The Author in Tristram Shandy."
        SHR 4 (1970): 301-313. Rpt. revised in [2834], pp. 159-169.

        Points out similarities between the novel and Sterne's per-

sonal life--the comedy and tragedy, the inability to triumph
over mortality, the need for an audience, and the way in
which Tristram was actually Sterne himself speaking. Tristram Shandy is Sterne's many frustrations, turned into literature.

2932   "Tristram and the Angels." CE 9 (1947): 62-69.

    Reviews the biographical and critical literature on Sterne
and discusses Sterne's role in his novels.

2933   HAY, JOHN A.
    "Rhetoric and Historiography: Tristram Shandy's First Nine
Kalendar Months." In [9], pp. 73-91.

    Considers the "nine months" problem: between Tristram's
conception (the first Sunday in March, 1718) and his birth
("the fifth day of November, 1718") only eight months had
elapsed, a curious fact that may suggest Tristram's illegiti-
macy; resolution of the problem is delayed until the end of
Volume IX, where the possibility of prematurity is allowed.

2934   HICKS, JOHN H.
    "The Critical History of Tristram Shandy." BUSE 2 (1956):
65-84.

    Traces development of criticism of the novel from the
eighteenth through the twentieth century showing how the reception of Tristram Shandy "is a record of criticism's awk-
ward assimilation of the unique."

2935   HNATKO, EUGENE.
    "Sterne's Whimsical Syntax: The Pseudo-Archaic Style."
Style 3 (1969): 168-181.

    Argues that much of Tristram Shandy is an attempt to imi-
tate the seventeenth century baroque or anti-Ciceronian style,
yet important differences remain: Sterne never forgoes the
Ciceronian love of balance and harmony.

2936   "Tristram Shandy's Wit." JEGP 65 (1966): 47-64.

    Concerned with four major principles of Sterne's wit: 1)
confounding of a conventional means of representing a mode
of reality with the reality itself, as in Sterne's handling of
"time"; 2) an extensive use of heterogeneous terms employed
in similitudes; 3) an irony growing out of an adopted "blind
spot"; and 4) a displacement of emphasis on some aspect of
discourse.

2937   HOLTZ, WILLIAM V.
        Image and Immortality: A Study of "Tristram Shandy." Prov-
        idence, R. I. : Brown Univ. Press, 1970.

        Analyzes the metaphor of painting as a principle of unity
        among Sterne's novel, his sensibility, and a tradition of liter-
        ary pictorialism, and argues that Sterne, in trying to replace
        the temporal structure of narrative with the spatial techniques
        of painting, discovers a "figure for the fundamental human
        philosophical problem of time and mortality." Tristram Shandy's
        structure reflects the conflict with death that is the central
        theme of the novel.

2938   "The Faces of Yorick." Queen's Quarterly 76 (1969): 379-
        391.

        Considers the problem of personal identities in Tristram
        Shandy--that of Tristram, of Yorick, and of Sterne himself;
        but "Sterne's life can be read as an extended exploration of
        the human relevance of fiction."

2939   "Time's Chariot and Tristram Shandy." Mich. Quart. Rev.
        5 (1966): 197-203.

        Sterne's fascination with time is transferred to his novel,
        which "is not like the conventional narrative; and its impor-
        tance in the history of fiction derives directly from this dif-
        ference in the conception of time governing the ordering of
        its materials." In reading the novel "we must hold in sus-
        pension a multitude of allusions and cross-references until
        we perceive the pattern of Tristram's life--not as what had
        happened in time, but as something that is, apart from time,
        in the mingled perception, speculation, and recollection of
        Tristram's mind."

2940   HUNTER, J. PAUL.
        "Response as Reformation: Tristram Shandy and the Art of
        Interruption." Novel 4 (1971): 132-146. Rpt. in [2885A],
        pp. 623-640.

        An analysis of the sermon episode (Vol. II, Chapter 17)
        as an example of Sterne's use of the "interpolated tale" for
        his moralizing. Discusses Sterne's didactic methods and as-
        serts that "if Sterne's artistic concerns are really with meth-
        odology more than with ideology, then the central problem of
        Tristram Shandy is to set up some positive possibilities for
        the rhetorician--possibilities that conform to the realities of
        human response."

2941   JACKSON, H. J.

"Sterne, Burton, and Ferriar: Allusions to the Anatomy of Melancholy in Volumes Five to Nine of Tristram Shandy." PQ 54 (1975): 457-470.

Supports view that Sterne copied from Burton but that his plagiarism was done in jest.

2942 JAMES, OVERTON PHILIP.
The Relation of "Tristram Shandy" to the Life of Sterne (Studies in English Literature, 22). The Hague: Mouton, 1966.

Argues that Tristram's life and opinions and Sterne's should not be regarded as identical and that Sterne created Yorick as a partial self-portrait to increase the distance between himself and his persona.

2943 JEFFERSON, D. W.
"Tristram Shandy and the Tradition of Learned Wit." EIC 1 (1951): 225-248. Amended version, "Tristram Shandy and its Tradition," in From Dryden to Johnson, ed. Boris Ford (Pelican Guide to English Literature, IV) (Harmondsworth: Penguin Books, 1957), pp. 333-345; original version rpt. in [2836], pp. 148-167; [2885A], pp. 502-521.

Argues that Tristram Shandy has form and thematic pattern in an established tradition of wit "essentially similar to that based on scholastic ideas," though Sterne also used ideas from Descartes and Locke which, when affected by the spirit of scholastic wit, became humorous: "the types of wit which come within our survey owe their character to intellectual habits belonging to the pre-Enlightenment world of thought." Article surveys main types of wit belonging to that tradition, and examines their use by Sterne.

2944 KARL, FREDERICK R.
"Tristram Shandy, the Sentimental Novel, and Sentimentalists." In [126], pp. 205-234.

Emphasizes the traditional and conventional in Tristram Shandy: it is "directly related to the picaresque narrative and ... relies upon literary ideas that were not at all unique in the 1760's ... Sterne's work ... is ... part of a dialectic of conflicting elements in which certain parts are thrown rathe violently against other parts, so that the resolution seems something very new, though the parts do not. Sterne ... established a unity or order upon disparate materials that was not anything substantially new but that appears new because every synthesis creates different shapes." Considers Sterne's use of the association of ideas, the importance of time, the relation of order and art, and the primitive thematic materials that constitute Tristram Shandy as a completed work of art.

2945   KETTLE, ARNOLD.
        [On Tristram Shandy.] In An Introduction to the English
        Novel, 2 vols. (London: Hutchinson's University Library,
        1951; New York: Harper Torchbooks, 1960), I, 81-87.

        Argues that there is in Tristram Shandy a "continuous and
        subtle tension between ... eighteenth-century common-sense
        enlightenment and the old scholastic tradition of the medieval
        world. "

2946   KHAZOUM, VIOLET.
        "The Inverted Comedy of Tristram Shandy." HUSL 7 (1979):
        139-160.

        Argues that "Tristram Shandy, though clearly a comedy,
        seems to defy the accepted categories, and to play out in
        comic terms the progress of the protagonist of tragedy to
        self-understanding ... it puts the conventional devices of com-
        edy into the service of a highly personal portrait of a mind
        coming to grips with itself through a process of self-examina-
        tion. " Progress toward that understanding provides the or-
        ganizing principle of the novel.

2947   KLEINSTUCK, JOHANNES.
        "Zur Form und Methode des Tristram Shandy." Archiv für
        das Studium der neueren Sprachen 194 (1957): 122-137.

        Discusses Sterne's role as author and the tactics he em-
        ploys to manipulate and control the narrative.

2948   KLOTMAN, PHYLLIS R.
        " 'Reconciliation of Contrasts' in Tristram Shandy. " CLAJ
        20 (1976): 48-56.

        The essence of Sterne's art is his ability to reconcile con-
        trasts through manipulating the time-scheme: "actual time
        with fictional time in Tristram's 'ironic dialogue' with reader,
        and ... 'subjective (personal) time with calendar time. ' "
        Whereas "Yorick reconciles the comic and the tragic ...
        Uncle Toby reconciles the contraries of humour and senti-
        ment. "

2949   KRIEGER, MURRAY.
        "Tristram Shandy." In The Classic Vision: The Retreat
        from Extremity in Modern Literature (Baltimore: Johns Hop-
        kins Univ. Press, 1971), pp. 269-285.

        A discussion of the Shandean system, of which Walter Shandy
        is the purest representation--he functions only through his use
        of language, which becomes the world for him; sees Tristram

Shandy as proving the "unmitigated joy" in defense of the
"human barnyard" and as showing that the "downward movement of the classic ... can regain its buoyancy in the delightful earthiness" of Sterne.   Concludes that the reconciliation of contrary motions is the heart of true Shandeism.

2950   KROEGER, FREDERICK P.
        "Uncle Toby's Pipe and Whistle." PMASAL 47 (1962): 669-
        685.

        A discussion of how Sterne brilliantly uses the devices of
        the Hobby Horse, the whistle, and the pipe to develop the
        character of Uncle Toby, and especially how he uses the pipe
        and Lillabullero in Toby's affair with the Widow Wadman:
        "It is the pipe and the whistle that convince us that simple
        descriptive words are truths about his [Toby's] character."

2951   LAMB, JONATHAN.
        " 'Uniting and Reconciling Everything': Book-Wit in Tristram
        Shandy." Southern Rev. (Adelaide) 7 (1974): 236-245.

        Examines Sterne's use of metaphorical ingenuities, puns,
        witty combinations; argues that his wit is that of Cervantes,
        Rabelais, Montaigne, and the English prose writers of the
        early seventeenth century, not that of Hobbes, Dryden, Locke,
        or Addison.   Discusses the effects of science on wit, and
        concludes that Sterne is "exploiting a more comprehensive
        vein of wit than any other eighteenth century writer."

2952   LANDA, LOUIS A.
        "The Shandean Homunculus: The Background of Sterne's
        'Little Gentleman.' " In [13], pp. 49-68; rpt. in [129], pp.
        140-159.

        Discusses the two schools of thought concerning human
        conception, the ovists and the animalculists, in an attempt
        to better understand the opening chapters of Tristram Shandy.

2953   LANHAM, RICHARD A.
        Tristram Shandy: The Games of Pleasure.   Berkeley: Univ.
        Calif. Press, 1973.

        Attempts a new definition of Sterne's seriousness, since
        too often an acceptance of comic pleasure seems to imply an
        end to significance; seeks to explain his kind of comedy with-
        out reducing it either to frivolity or to philosophical sobriety.
        Discusses Tristram Shandy in relation to the older tradition
        of classical, rhetorical, narrative forms, from which flows
        the definition of man and society and the kind of comedy that
        Sterne imitates.

2954   LEHMAN, B. H.
        "Of Time, Personality, and the Author: A Study of Tristram
        Shandy: Comedy." In Studies in the Comic (Univ. Calif.
        Publications in English, Vol. 8, No. 2, 1941), pp. 233-250.
        Rpt. Norwood, Pa.: Norwood Editions, 1975, pp. 83-100;
        rpt. in [2836], pp. 21-33.

        Sterne's achievement in the light of the later development
        of the novel. Discusses Sterne's world--the function of laugh-
        ter, the influence of Locke and Montaigne, the importance of
        Time, Tristram as narrator, and Sterne's characterization.
        Tristram's "fragment" has a unity--"the criteria being in the
        consciousness, not in the world of outer phenomena."

2955   LOUNSBERRY, BARBARA.
        "Sermons and Satire: Anti-Catholicism in Sterne." PQ 55
        (1976): 403-417.

        Sterne's anti-Catholic sentiments are much stronger in
        Tristram Shandy than in his sermons. In his novel, Sterne
        uses subtle devices to attack the church, such as creating
        the character of Dr. Slop, a Papist, who is continually held
        up to ridicule; equating the Catholic church with death and
        evil; extolling the virtues of Toby's Latitudinarian benevolence;
        and introducing a number of documents that present the church
        as being self-destructive.

2956   McCULLOUGH, BRUCE.
        "The Comic Novel: Laurence Sterne." In [133], pp. 69-83.

        Discusses Sterne's use of humor in Tristram Shandy to
        show how his "interest ... in the small, evanescent, personal
        aspects of life rather than in abstractly conceived problems
        ... made his fiction different from that of his contemporaries."

2957   McGLYNN, PAUL D.
        "Sterne's Maria: Madness and Sentimentality." ECLife 3,
        ii (1976): 39-43.

        Analyzes Maria's role in Tristram Shandy and A Sentimental
        Journey and Tristram's and Yorick's benevolence toward her.
        Maria's madness, her inability to communicate, and her sex-
        ual attractiveness, make her a vulnerable character--one who
        is thematically central to both novels. Discusses the tradi-
        tional role of women as the weaker sex, and the connection
        between sadism and pornography.

2958   McKILLOP, ALAN DUGALD.
        "Laurence Sterne." In [134], pp. 182-219. Rpt. in [2836],
        pp. 34-65.

A general appreciation: considers Sterne as a humorist,
the general plan of Tristram Shandy, the role of the narrator,
the importance of Locke, Sterne's method of linking by analogies and correspondences, his use of space and time, and
the history of the writing of the novel.

2959   McMASTER, JULIET.
"Experience to Expression: Thematic Character Contrasts
in Tristram Shandy." MLQ 32 (1971): 42-57.

An analysis of the pattern of contrasts between the four
main characters and their thematic relation to Sterne's subject of literary criticism reveals "a kind of allegory of the
relation between the physical and the conceptual worlds."

2960   MAYOUX, JEAN-JACQUES.
"Variations on the Time-sense in Tristram Shandy." In
[2834], pp. 3-18. Rpt. in [2885A], pp. 571-584.

Analyzes the time-structure of Tristram Shandy, especially
seeing My Uncle Toby and Tristram as microcosms with their
own time-dimension and their own structure, rhythm, and
flow.

2961   "Laurence Sterne parmi nous." Critique 18, No. 177 (1962):
99-120. Revised and rpt. as "Laurence Sterne" in [2836],
pp. 108-125.

Argues that Sterne's obscenity is not an "impish wish to
purge men of hypocrisy and lies," not a healthy search for
truth, but a sickly, morbid erotomania developing from non-
satisfaction of desire; we should admire him for turning his
misery into something of worth and genius. Also discusses
Sterne's sentimentalism, Tristram Shandy as parody, and the
theme of time.

2962   MELLOWN, ELGIN W.
"Narrative Technique in Tristram Shandy." PLL 9 (1973):
263-270.

An analysis of Sterne's narration of Tristram's birth to
illustrate how Sterne uses allusion to an event through symbolic representation and how this technique "is basic to the
telling of the story, to character exposition, and to the humour.... Realizing that story, character, and narration are
inseparable, he [Sterne] develops a narrative technique for
telling the story of Tristram which reveals, in itself, Tristram's character."

2963   MENDILOW, A. A.
        "Time, Structure and Tristram Shandy." In From Time and
        the Novel (London: Peter Nevill, Ltd. , 1952; New York:
        Humanities Press, Inc. , 1965), pp. 165-188. Rpt. in part
        as "The Revolt of Sterne," in [2836], pp. 90-107.

        Sterne's departure from the conventional novel, his use of
        digression and time-change, and his technique. "There is
        in Tristram Shandy a threefold development: the characters
        as they evolve; the author as he works out his conception;
        and the reader whom Sterne is educating to understand fiction
        aright. "

2964   MILIC, LOUIS T.
        "Information Theory and the Style of Tristram Shandy." In
        [2834], pp. 237-246.

        "The structure of Tristram Shandy, both on the narrative
        level and stylistic level ... is inevitably determined by the
        nature of information. Once Sterne had decided that origin-
        ality was to be the predominant characteristic of his book,
        he was committed to a pattern required to maintain informa-
        tion at a high level, i. e. , a constant shift in direction and
        a constant accumulation of stylistic devices to neutralize the
        contextualizing effect. "

2965   MOGLEN, HELENE.
        The Philosophical Irony of Laurence Sterne.   Gainesville:
        Univ. Fla. Press, 1975.

        Assuming that all experience is essentially ironic, the au-
        thor suggests that Sterne "impresses a new vision of reality
        which contains within itself a simplifying truth about the na-
        ture of man, who aspires despite his limitations, who per-
        sists despite his defeats, who, though locked in isolation, is
        still capable of loving. " Sees Tristram Shandy as an "elab-
        orately formed complex of interrelated ironic patterns"; con-
        siders the sources of Sterne's vision and its expression through
        the novel's forms, themes, and characters.

2966   NANNY, MAX.
        "Similarity and Contiguity in Tristram Shandy." ES 60 (1979):
        422-435.

        An investigation into the nature of Tristram Shandy in terms
        of Roman Jakobson's "fundamentals of language," the two great
        principles of which are similarity and contiguity. The essay
        analyzes the pervasive contrast between metaphoric and meto-
        nymic relations, i. e. , between similarity and contiguity. Ja-

kobson's dichotomy is especially appropriate for a study of Tristram Shandy because it can be traced back to the 17th- and 18th-century debate on the "association of ideas," and ultimately to Hobbes's and Locke's distinction between the similarity relation of "wit" and the dissimilarity relation of "judgment."

2967   NEW, MELVYN.
       "Sterne as Editor: The 'Abuses of Conscience' Sermon."
       Studies in 18th Cent. Culture 8 (1979):   243-251.

       Between the original version of 1750 and the text as it appears in Tristram Shandy, there are almost 90 substantive variants: "Together, they provide an indication of the subtlety of Sterne's prose, the care with which he sought the right word, the right phrase, even the right pointing.   In rewriting his sermon for Tristram Shandy, Sterne knew that the humor of his endeavor resided in his capacity to incorporate into his comic world a sermon actually preached from England's second most important pulpit; he could not resist, however, the opportunity to polish and refine his effort ten years after composition--to act, that is, as his own editor."

2968   "The Dunce Revisited: Colley Cibber and Tristram Shandy."
       SAQ 72 (1973):   547-559.

       Discusses the "relationship between 'disruptive ways' of prose style and the 'self-conscious Dunce' " in Cibber's Apology and how Sterne imitated this style making use of the "disruptive narrator" for his ironical comments upon the Shandean world.

2969   "Laurence Sterne and Henry Baker's The Microscope Made Easy."   SEL 10 (1970):   591-604.

       "For Sterne and Baker both, the new awareness of the relativity of size suggested the relativity of time....   This awareness in turn was used to remind man of his limited duration--a limit which Tristram refuses to acknowledge in the writing of Tristram Shandy."

2970   Laurence Sterne as Satirist: A Reading of "Tristram Shandy".
       Gainesville: Univ. Fla. Press, 1969.

       Provides a detailed reading of Tristram Shandy as a satire; argues that the novel can best be understood by placing it in the mainstream of the conservative, moralistic tradition and by emphasizing the intentions and conventions of the dominant literary form of that tradition--satire.   The satire moves from an opening in birth and creation to a conclusion in dissolution and death, and its fundamental point is that Sterne condemns Tristram's aesthetic and moral codes; the attack is ultimately against human pride.

2971   OLSHIN, TOBY A.
       "Genre and Tristram Shandy: The Novel of Quickness."
       Genre 4 (1971): 360-375. Rpt. in [2885A], pp. 521-532.

       Sees Tristram Shandy as a founder of a new genre, the "novel of quickness," in which the reader, through sympathy with the narrator, becomes persuaded of the need for sympathy with all of life; and argues that Tristram Shandy "derives its unity from the one living presence whose unity informs it, the writer himself."

2972   PARISH, CHARLES.
       "The Shandy Bull Vindicated." MLQ 31 (1970): 48-52.

       A word-by-word reading of the final chapter of Tristram Shandy shows the "cock and bull" story to be a joke which reinforces the seriousness of the chapter: "the similarity between man and beast is developed still further in a parable masquerading as a hilarious joke."

2973   "The Nature of Mr. Tristram Shandy, Author." BUSE 5 (1961): 74-90.

       Asserts that there are two worlds in Tristram Shandy-- the world of Shandy Hall and its environs and the world of Tristram's mind, infinite yet infinitesimal, "the mind in which the first world is seen, the mind of which the first world is only a part." Tristram has three functions: he is a minor character, he is the narrator, and he is the author, "who is concerned with the ideas of the second Tristram...."

2974   "A Table of Contents for Tristram Shandy." CE 22 (1960): 143-150. Rpt. in [2885A], pp. 640-648.

       Presents a skeleton of each of the nine books, enabling the student to locate a situation or theme at a glance; an aid in following the story. Seeks also to demonstrate the "consistency in the presence and role of the author-narrator Tristram."

2975   PARK, WILLIAM.
       "Tristram Shandy and the New 'Novel of Sensibility.'"
       Studies in the Novel 6 (1974): 268-279.

Suggests that in the 1760's and early 1770's, following the
example of Tristram Shandy, novels tended to adopt a new
set of conventions: rakes, rapes, brothels, London low life,
physical action, and country houses ceased to be the main
motifs, and were replaced by an emphasis on heroes and
heroines of exquisite sensibility, protagonists who lived with
their families, and heroes who became rash and melancholy;
states of mind became as important as physical actions, and
distresses became more emotional than physical.

2976   PETRIE, · GRAHAM.
"A Rhetorical Topic in Tristram Shandy." MLR 65 (1970):
261-266.

A discussion of Sterne's plagiarism, especially from Burton's Anatomy of Melancholy.   Argues that Sterne makes of
plagiarism an artistic device within the structure of the novel,
that borrowed phrases and sentences are worked together in
a rhetorical pattern which is Sterne's own, and that his re-
arranging was more work than if he had written something
original.

2977   "Rhetoric as Fictional Technique in Tristram Shandy." PQ
48 (1969):   479-494.

Analyzes ways in which Sterne uses the traditional devices
of rhetoric for his technique, theme, and characterization,
and how these rhetorical devices, to a very large extent, are
the basis of the unity of the novel.

2978   "Note on the Novel and the Film: Flashbacks in Tristram
Shandy and The Pawnbroker." WHR 21 (1967):   165-169.

Methods by which the transference through time takes place
are essentially the same in the novel as in the film.   Sterne
is continually using "flashbacks" and "flashforwards" and
"handles the shift from one chapter to the next in the same
way as a film editor handles the scissors."

2979   PIPER, WILLIAM BOWMAN.
Laurence Sterne.   New York: Twayne, 1965.

A study of Tristram Shandy and A Sentimental Journey
which is concerned with the narrator's efforts to make his
personal experiences effectively public.   Also looks at conversational style and ideology.

2980   "Tristram Shandy's Digressive Artistry." SEL 1, No. 3
(1961):   65-76.   Rpt. in [2885A], pp. 548-562.

Asserts that Tristram had artistic control over his digressions by having a "clear and comprehensible discursive intention" and by organizing them into "simple and publicly ex-
plicable patterns. " Tristram's digressions never digress from
his concern for his audience.

2981   "Tristram Shandy's Tragicomical Testimony. " Criticism 3
       (1961): 171-185.

A discussion of Tristram's life from birth to death as revealed by his testimony, "the equivocal nature of ... which
may be attributed to his problem of giving an acceptable mixed-
company utterance to a life whose crucial facts and events
are largely unmentionable [and which] leaves the truth of his
life snarled in terrible uncertainties. "

2982   PORTER, DENNIS.
       "Fictions of Art and Life: Tristram Shandy and Henry Bru-
       lard. " MLN 91 (1976): 1257-1266.

"In spite of important differences of emphasis, Tristram
Shandy and Henry Brulard are similar to the extent that they
are works of deconstruction situated in the confused border-
land between fiction and autobiography. " Sterne's real subject is not the "life of a man, but of a book. " It is an "elaborate shaggy-dog story ... in that it teases its reader to the
point of revolt in order to denaturalize the multiple masked
conventions of fiction. "

2983   POSNER, ROLAND.
       "Semiotic Paradoxes in Language Use, with Particular Ref-
       erence to Tristram Shandy. " ECent. 20 (1979): 148-163.
       From Zeichenprozesse: Semiotische Forschung in den Ein-
       zelwissenschaften, Roland Posner and Hans-Peter Reinecke,
       eds. , J. W. Kloesel, trans. (Wiesbaden: Athenaion, 1977),
       pp. 109-128.

Discusses the theory of semiotic language with examples
from Tristram Shandy which exhibit "inherent contradictions. "
Sterne's semiotic paradoxes are on four levels: "(1) the effect
of the representation corresponds to the effect of what is represented.   (2) The representation is part of what is represented,
and one corresponds to the other.   (3) The character of what
is represented influences the manner of representation.   (4)
The representation itself influences the character of what is
represented. "

2984   PRESTON, JOHN.
       "Tristram Shandy (i): The Reader as Author" and "Tristram
       Shandy (ii): The Author as Reader. " In [151], pp. 133-195.

I. Sees <u>Tristram Shandy</u> as a story that implicates the
reader in a situation in which he can know himself better--
a story, however, that is partly the story of its telling; the
reader must collaborate in the telling if he is to know himself better; the novel is therefore about the creative imagination. It is also a critique of rhetoric through parody, the
rhetoric itself urging the reader to be creative; the moral of
the book is that reading is a profoundly creative act, the discovery of meanings.

II. Argues that the writer is also a reader--the world
that he experiences is what he reads; what he has invented
is in some way what he knows already. <u>Tristram Shandy</u> is
made up of superimposed fictions, each one created by dis-
closing another: at each level the significant experience is
that of reading, including that of the last level where "Tristram and his readers are understood as a fiction by Sterne
and his readers"; the author therefore is able to read his own
novel. Finally, the author suggests that Sterne can do what
Tristram cannot do for himself: he can objectify himself in
the story; in "Yorick he can see himself as a fictional <u>char-
acter</u>, just as in Tristram he is a fictional <u>creator</u>."

2985   ROHRBERGER, MARY and SAMUEL H. WOODS, JR.
"Alchemy of the Word: Surrealism in <u>Tristram Shandy</u>."
<u>Interpretations</u> 11 (1979): 24-34.

Argues that, "if <u>Tristram Shandy</u> is a world where Ein-
stein and Alice-in-Wonderland and the man next door meet,
then the magic is that of dream, and the novel is governed
by dream logic, where distortions of form and perspective,
dislocations of space and time, condensations and displace-
ments dominate...." For both Sterne and the surrealists
the question is how to get out of the cage in which we pace
back and forth; "but where the surrealists went directly to the
dream to find time-space overlay, Sterne goes to time-space
overlay and in so doing suggests the timelessness of dream."

2986   ROSENBLUM, MICHAEL.
"The Sermon, the King of Bohemia, and the Art of Interpola-
tion in <u>Tristram Shandy</u>." <u>SP</u> 75 (1978): 472-491.

Whereas Sterne's digressions in the novel suggest continuity, his interpolations emphasize discontinuities. Although
"the main road of <u>Tristram Shandy</u> is the language of the
autobiographical narrative," the interpolations give us a variety of materials, such as the tale of the King of Bohemia,
the sermon "On the Abuses of Conscience," and Walter's
speech in response to Bobby's death. It is these interpolations that cause us to make our way along Sterne's "road"
much the same way as "Walter makes his way along his,
circumspectly, deliberately, and with surprise."

2987   "Shandean Geometry and the Challenge of Contingency." Novel
        10 (1977): 237-247.

        Tristram Shandy is one of the best novels for thinking about
        the nature of the novel as a form; the aspect of form that
        Rosenblum considers is "what may be called the logic of events
        in a narrative: why does what happens happen? To what ex-
        tent are the events predictable, to what extent are they ex-
        plainable? Does the sequence of events imply a character-
        istic way things have of happening, a set of laws for the fic-
        tional universe? ... Instead of playing variations on the mid-
        century theme of order threatened, Sterne develops a theme
        which ... is crucial to any novelist's continuing exploration
        of reality, the question of how men make their orders."

2988   ROTHSTEIN, ERIC. "Tristram Shandy." In Systems of Order
        and Inquiry in Later Eighteenth-Century Fiction. (Berkeley
        & Los Angeles: Univ. Calif. Press, 1975), pp. 62-108.

        Argues a thesis that several eighteenth-century novels em-
        ploy certain procedures that reflect formal and epistemological
        concerns that constitute a system historically peculiar to the
        eighteenth century; in the case of Tristram Shandy, two binary
        relationships--between Walter and Toby, and between Tristram
        and his elders--and the themes implicit in them (systems/
        authorship and brotherhood/family) construct the contents of
        the novel: the two familial relationships are developed by
        analogy and modification, which depend on associationist and
        epistemological principles. Considers formal structure: in
        episodes and volume Sterne maintains covert order that rein-
        forces the visible system of order Tristram provides, there-
        by achieving equilibrium within a set of unresolved forces;
        and concludes that Sterne retains "formal control, developing
        episodes with internal structures and rhythms, working with
        incremental repetition and fulcrums...."

2989   RUSSELL, H. K.
        "Tristram Shandy and the Technique of the Novel." SP 42
        (1945): 581-593. Also in Studies in Language & Literature
        (Univ. N. C. Sesquicentennial Publ.). Chapel Hill: Univ. N. C.
        Press, 1945.

        Examines characterization and plot structure of Tristram
        Shandy to show that Sterne "consciously examined the 'stand-
        ard' novel as represented by Fielding's work, critically ...
        indicated its shortcomings, and demonstrated what seemed to
        him preferable techniques."

2990   RYAN, MARJORIE.
        "Tristram Shandy and the Limits of Satire." Kansas Quart.
        1 (1969): 58-63.

By analyzing four sections of Tristram Shandy (the Sermon, II, 17; the Dinner, IV, 26-30; the reading of the Tristrapoedia, V, 30-43 and VI, 1-5; and Tristram's travels, VII), the author defends the satiric complexity of Sterne's technique, putting a formal theoretical document to the test of experience. The object of attack is men's attempts coldly to impose their systematized views on others.

2991 SALLE, JEAN-CLAUDE.
"A State of Warfare: Some Aspects of Time and Chance in Tristram Shandy." In [15], pp. 211-221.

Sterne's presentation of time is twofold: "the idea of the fragility of human existence is usually transposed into a humorous register, but the underlying pathetic note is also sounded by the narrator; in his shifts from self-pity to self-mockery appears the first stage of the attempt to turn an object of anxiety into one of laughter." Also suggests that "man's conflict with time and chance is dramatized both by Walter Shandy's attempts to make his son's life conform to a predetermined pattern and by the narrator's ... efforts to introduce order into his book."

2992 SEGAL, ORA.
"On the Difficulties of Novel-Writing: A Reading of Tristram Shandy." HUSL 1 (1973): 132-158.

Regards Tristram Shandy as a novel about novel-writing: tries to "show that Sterne's narrator is not only commenting on the problems facing him in his narrative situation but is also dramatizing those problems with a great show of paradoxical wit."

2993 SEIDEL, MICHAEL.
"Gravity's Inheritable Line: Sterne's Tristram Shandy." In [158], pp. 250-262.

The main narrative line in Tristram Shandy is the gravitational line: "From clay to dust: lighter spirits always risk being beaten down--the case, alas!, of poor Yorick, literally beaten to death by all too grave and serious fellows." Yorick, therefore, is Sterne's sacrifice to gravitational descent, and even in the Shandean household the line of comic continuity is weighed down by "satiric design and gravitational inheritance": gravity defeats all forms of systematic and organic continuity.

2994 SELTZER, ALVIN J.
"A Thousand Splinters: The Deliberately Distorted Narrative

of Tristram Shandy." In Chaos in the Novel, The Novel in
Chaos. (New York: Schocken Books, 1974), pp. 29-51.

"By considering Sterne's artistic devices ... along with
his vision ... we may find hope for the novel's future, and
a way into chaos which also leaves a way out of it.   Sterne
seems ... to have falsified neither his art nor his vision,
and the successful integration and assimilation of the two can
provide some important lessons for the modern practitioners
of the novel." Suggests the paradox that, though Sterne's
narrative technique seems so chaotic that it implies a lack of
aesthetic control, in fact the reader's experience has been
so ingeniously contrived and manipulated that the freedom is
seen to be an illusion.

2995   SHERBO, ARTHUR.
       "Some Not-So-Hidden Allusions in Tristram Shandy." In
       [160], pp. 128-135.

       Identifies "a number of Biblical and proverbial echoes and
       allusions" which, added to all the known borrowings, in large
       part give Sterne's style its unique texture.

2996   SHKLOVSKY, VIKTOR.
       "A Parodying Novel: Sterne's Tristram Shandy." In [2836],
       pp. 68-89. From O Teorii Prozy, trans. W. George Isaak
       (Moscow, 1929).

       Discusses structure of the novel and the "time-shift" de-
       vice used by Sterne.

2997   SHROFF, HOMAI J.
       " 'The Heart Rather than the Head.' " In [163], pp. 192-235.

       Deals with the characterization of My Uncle Toby in which
       Sterne "achieves an unusually subtle combination of idealism
       and irony, of sentiment and intellectual brilliance, of pathos
       and hilarity."

2998   SINGLETON, MARVIN K.
       "Deduced Knowledge as a Shandean Nub: Paracelsian Her-
       metic as Metaphoric Bridge in Tristram Shandy." ZAA 16
       (1968): 274-284.

       Argues that the most important single source for Tristram
       Shandy is the apocryphal Greek and Latin Trismegistic (or
       Hermetic) literature: seeks "to show the way a Paracelsian
       mediate hermetic idiom provides a crucial tie-in between ...
       the Trismegistic source and the novel's devil tropes."

2999   "Trismegistic Tenor and Vehicle in Sterne's Tristram Shandy."
        PLL 4 (1968): 158-169.

        A discussion of Hermetic literature and tradition as they
        influence the style and themes of Tristram Shandy. Mr.
        Shandy's own philosophy derives from Trismegistic literature,
        and he is an embodiment of the Egyptian Thoth figure.

3000   SKILTON, DAVID.
        "Sterne, Sentiment and its Opponents." In [165], pp. 45-58.

        Historical treatment of Sterne, the sentimentalists (Henry
        Brooke, The Fool of Quality; Henry Mackenzie, The Man of
        Feeling), and Fanny Burney, the latter refusing to exalt sen-
        timent over reason. Tristram Shandy is seen as an "anti-
        novel" which used sophisticated techniques to play with con-
        ventional novel-forms and cast doubt on the humanistic as-
        sumptions about the place of literature in western civilization.

3001   SMITTEN, JEFFREY R.
        "Tristram Shandy and Spatial Form." ArielE 8, iv (1977):
        43-59.

        Examines the dense interweaving of four motifs, 1) physi-
        cal destruction, 2) tyranny of circumstances, 3) sexuality,
        and 4) imprisonment of reason and sentiment in Volume III
        as they are developed in connection with Tristram's birth,
        hobby-horses, and opinions. This analysis uses the concept
        of spatial form to show how a network of images and events
        expresses the theme of impotence. This "total integration
        of all compositional elements, is one of the novel's most re-
        markable features and perhaps its greatest formal triumph."

3002   SOKOLYANSKY, MARK G.
        "The Rhythmical Pattern of Tristram Shandy." DUJ 73 (1980):
        23-26.

        Sterne's "cock and bull" story artistically uses a rhythmi-
        cal movement from lesser to greater to lesser irregularity.
        It often achieves a rhythm of regularity through repetition
        (e. g. , Uncle Toby's whistling "Lillabullero"), but three kinds
        of irregular rhythm predominate: unexpected digressions,
        sudden breaks in the narrative, and new associations. Three
        patterns of association interrupt the reader's expectation: an
        associative movement along a temporal axis, another one along
        a spatial axis, and a third movement interrupting philosophical
        meditations. The interaction of associative patterns underlies
        the plot of Tristram Shandy.

3003   SPACKS, PATRICIA MEYER.

"The Beautiful Oblique: Tristram Shandy." In [166], pp.
127-157.

Tristram Shandy, a fictional autobiographer, denies the
conceivability of telling a story; his history of himself intentionally imitates chaos.   In his roles as narrator and as
object of narration, Tristram faces the problem of pain,which
involves a series of conflicts over control: "between fictive
author and reader, between fictive author and characters,
between characters and their environment, animate and inanimate."   The author depicts a story-teller unable to understand the meaning of his story; he claims, in other words,
to imitate life, but insists that life displays no coherent pattern for him to imitate.

3004   SPECK, PAUL SURGI.
"Frustration, Curiosity and Rumor: Sterne's Use of Women
to Define Impotence in Tristram Shandy." PAPA 5, ii-iii
(1979): 30-35.

Shandean women possess three typifying traits: they are
keenly interested in physical sex, they are frustrated by a
life of virtual abstinence, and they are governed by an intense prurient curiosity.   The article discusses and explicates
a number of sexual allusions and double-entendres, and concludes that "ultimately, the frustration which typifies the Shandean female and the impotency and pride which mark the Shandean male are applicable, without regard to sex, to mankind
in general."

3005   STANZEL, FRANZ KARL.
"Tristram Shandy und die Klimatheorie." GRM 21 (1971):
16-28.

Sterne's characters illustrate the contemporary "climate
theory" of personality types.

3006   " 'Tom Jones' und 'Tristram Shandy.' Ein Vergleich als
Vorstudie zu einer Typologie des Romans." In Eng. Misc.
5 (1954): 107-148.

Compares the two novels in regard to narrative control,
medium, use of the narrator, and time structure.

3007   STEDMOND, J. M.
"Satire and Tristram Shandy." SEL 1, No. 3 (1961): 53-63.

Argues that Tristram Shandy belongs with Scriblerus, A
Tale of A Tub, and the Dunciad as engaged in the perpetual

war between wits and "dunces." But Sterne's attack is less bitter; he seeks to show up foolishness by playing the fool.

3008   "Sterne as Plagiarist." ES 41 (1960): 308-312.

Summary, with sources, of verbatim borrowings in Tristram Shandy and A Sentimental Journey; Sterne not as guilty of wholesale plagiarism as previously supposed.

3009   "Genre and Tristram Shandy." PQ 38 (1959): 37-51.

Sterne's relation to the tradition of "learned wit," "philosophic rhetoric," and "Menippean satire"; his relation to Rabelais, Burton, and Swift.

3010   "Style and Tristram Shandy." MLQ 20 (1959): 243-251.

"Sterne differs from most other eighteenth-century novelists ... in that his mind is fixed as much on the word as on the idea which he is seeking to express. Language is not merely raw material which he, as artist, must shape; it is also a problem to be analyzed and discussed."

3011   STEEVES, HARRISON R.
"A Fellow of Infinite Jest." In [169], pp. 171-192.

Defends Sterne against critics who have argued that his writings are full of sex and obscene language, that he plagiarizes from other writers, and that he is overly sentimental and frivolous. Also discusses his ability as an "artist" --his wit and his distaste for literary pretense.

3012   STEWART, JACK F.
"Sterne's Absurd Comedy." Univ. Windsor Rev. 5, No. 2 (1970): 81-95.

An attempt to compress the essence of Shandean comedy into the Absurd; concludes that "laughter is the passion and the drug is the Absurd. Shandean comedy exploits the element of absurdity in human relations to break down the illusion ... of a man-made world, controlled by reason...."

3013   STOBIE, MARGARET.
"Walter Shandy: Generative Grammarian." HAB 17 (1966): 13-19.

Argues that in the Tristrapoedia there emerges a "more

comprehensive foreshadowing of the generative theory than
the Transformationalists may be aware of"--the scientific
awareness, the idea of the machine, the terms, the role of
the child, the capacities of the native speaker, and the wealth
of examples.

3014   SWEARINGEN, JAMES E.
        Reflexivity in "Tristram Shandy": An Essay in Phenomeno-
        logical Criticism. New Haven: Yale Univ. Press, 1977.

        The purpose of this book is to apply the discipline of liter-
        ary criticism to Tristram Shandy as a means of "meditating"
        on the peculiar destiny of modern life, the need to "think
        ahead" by questioning and examining the assumptions and aims
        of the modern age. It uses Tristram Shandy as a "means of
        access to the esoteric reductions of Husserlian phenomenology";
        its thesis is "that Sterne's novel is an incipient phenomenology
        which clarifies the processes of human be-ing in the person
        of the protagonist...."

3015   TOWERS, A. R.
        "Sterne's Cock and Bull Story." ELH 24 (1957): 12-29.

        An examination of some sexual references in Tristram
        Shandy and their relation to major characters, themes, and
        style. Sex becomes the primary vehicle for suggesting the
        importance of incommunication, indirection, cross-purpose,
        and interruption in life. Discusses "the comedy of inade-
        quacy," "the comedy of displacement," and "the comedy of frus-
        tration" as aspects of the pervasive sexual comedy.

3016   TRACY, CLARENCE.
        "As Many Chapters as Steps." In [2834], pp. 97-111.

        Considers the ties that bind Tristram Shandy to its age;
        e.g., the relationship between the eighteenth-century novel,
        especially Sterne's, and eighteenth-century biography. Defines
        three motives for the use of anecdote--the scientific, the
        aesthetic, and the ethical--and discusses Sterne's use of them.

3017   TRAUGOTT, JOHN.
        "The Shandean Comic Vision of Locke." In [2836], pp. 126-
        147. From [3018], Chap. 1.

        Concerned with the philosophical content of Sterne's dra-
        matic rhetoric, and seeks to demonstrate his peculiar use
        of the formal elements of Locke's philosophy: "With Locke's
        hypotheses Sterne obviously has wrought something that is not
        Locke."

3018   Tristram Shandy's World: Sterne's Philosophical Rhetoric.
        Berkeley & Los Angeles: Univ. Calif. Press, 1954.

        An analysis of Sterne's rhetorical method: both action and
        characters are argumentative devices of the opinionative Tris-
        tram.   Concerned with Tristram Shandy's repetitious patterns,
        and argues that Sterne warped and subverted the philosophy
        of Locke, even undermining his rationalism by maintaining
        the importance of wit in communicating human motives.   Also
        examines the forms of Sterne's wit and his dialectical tech-
        niques.

3019   TYSON, GERALD P.
        "The Rococo Style of Tristram Shandy."   Bucknell Rev. 24,
        ii (1978): 38-55.

        Traces the relations between rococo style in the visual
        arts and the rococo style of Tristram Shandy in order to dis-
        cover a more complete knowledge of the novel's technique.
        Sterne was greatly influenced by Hogarth, whose serpentine
        "line of beauty" finds its counterpart in Sterne's many de-
        partures from conventional narrative and in the temporal and
        spatial experiments of the novel.

3020   UPHAUS, ROBERT W.
        "Sterne's Sixth Sense."   In [180], pp. 108-122.

        Argues that "Sterne, unlike Johnson, appeals to the reader's
        curiosity by transforming rationality, and its dependence on
        the world of the five senses, into a celebration of the world
        of the 'sixth sense' which obliterates the moral and cognitive
        distinctions so basic to Johnson's idea of 'equipoise.'"   Tris-
        tram Shandy is an elaborate reading paradigm intended to sub-
        vert the concept of the reader as detached observer; whereas
        readers usually observe human actions that are dependent on
        the five senses, readers of Tristram Shandy must rely on a
        principle of indeterminacy, which does not imply an absence
        of meaning but rather a plurality of meaning.

3021   VAN GHENT, DOROTHY.
        "On Tristram Shandy."   In The English Novel: Form and
        Function.   (New York: Rinehart, 1953; rpt. New York: Har-
        per Torchbook, 1961), pp. 83-98.

        Sees Sterne as precursor of Proust and Joyce and insists
        that the "unity of Tristram Shandy is the unity of Tristram's
        --the narrator's--consciousness."

3022   WAGONER, MARY S.

"Satire of the Reader in Tristram Shandy." TSLL 8 (1966): 337-344.

Sterne's attack on the reader's intellectual reliability based on his acceptance of Locke's epistemology. The four general types of errors found in Locke's theory are especially germane to Shandeanism and to the communications problem of Tristram and the reader.

3023   WALKER, ROBERT G.
"A Sign of the Satirist's Wit: The Nose in Tristram Shandy."
BSUF 19, ii (1978): 52-54.

Suggests "that Tristram's natal injury is meant to imply more than a subsequent lack of sexual potency" but also "an intellectual deficiency." The crushed nose suggests that "Tristram, aspiring to emulate his satiric masters Cervantes and Rabelais, is doomed to the failure reserved for 'the dull Jests and Stupidity of gross Clowns.' "

3024   WARNING, RANIER.
Illusion und Wirklichkeit in Tristram Shandy und Jacques le Fataliste (Theorie und Geschichte der Literatur und des schönen Kunste, Bd. 4). München: W. Fink Verlag, 1965.

A thorough academic investigation in the problematics of the two novels.

3025   WARREN, LELAND E.
"The Constant Speaker: Aspects of Conversation in Tristram Shandy." UTQ 46 (1976): 51-67.

By clarifying the nature and function of conversation, the author hopes to increase our understanding of the motives for writing suggested by Tristram Shandy. Tristram seems to engage his readers in conversation, in which two or more people exchange ideas or impressions, and which is free and open-ended. But Tristram's conversation may not be free and open. The question of conversation's relationship to the novel raises two issues that lie at the book's core: "the narrator's sincerity and the limitations of form." Sterne is interested in formulating rules for success in the art of conversation, as well as considering "how even in failure that art becomes meaningful to the artist."

3026   WATT, IAN.
"The Comic Syntax of Tristram Shandy." In [2], pp. 315-331.

Tristram Shandy has unity of style, and chapters as well

as paragraphs and sentences possess a structure "based on
the rhetorical patterns arising out of the complex tripartite
pattern of conversation between the narrator, his fictional
characters, and his auditors." The primary principle of
unity is Tristram's voice through which Sterne discovered a
principle of order residing in a kind of timeless consistency
of texture.

3027   WEALES, GERALD.
       "Tristram Shandy's Anti-Book." In Twelve Original Essays
       on Great English Novels, ed. Charles Shapiro (Detroit, Mich. :
       Wayne State Univ. Press, 1960), pp. 43-67.

       A defense of Tristram Shandy's digressive structure; ar-
       gues that the novel does have a pattern, one of attitude, and
       that it is an anti-book because Sterne makes fun of himself
       and the fact that he is writing a book by defying all conven-
       tions of the eighteenth-century novel--and even goes beyond
       that defiance.

3028   WRIGHT, ANDREW.
       "The Artifice of Failure in Tristram Shandy." Novel 2 (1969):
       212-220.

       Argues that the novel's structure is peripheral. "If the
       reader, and Sterne, are little nearer an understanding of the
       heart of the matter at the end of the novel than at the begin-
       ning, at least the ordinary mendacities by which men live
       have been discredited, and the magnitude of life's difficulties
       has been exposed to view. The testing of all hypotheses has
       ended in failure," which is the last word in the novel. But
       mirth attends failure and in this way the novel "offers true
       Shandean redemption."

See also: 725, 927, 1087, 1098, 1119, 1329, 1726, 2493, 2839,
     2843, 2848, 2849, 2850, 2855, 2865, 2866, 2869, 2876, 3008, 3227,
     3228, 3248

A Sentimental Journey

3029   ALVAREZ, A.
       "The Delinquent Aesthetic." HR 19 (1966): 590-600.

       The nature of Sterne's intention in A Sentimental Journey,
       of how he wrote from his nerve-ends to teach people how to
       feel with intensity. Sterne as a modernist, possessing the
       "art of controlled and detached delinquency," found more in
       films than in novels.

3030   BATTESTIN, MARTIN C.
        "A Sentimental Journey and the Syntax of Things." In [28],
        pp. 223-239.

        Argues in favor of the interdependence of theme and form
        in A Sentimental Journey; various themes are transmuted and
        softened by being apprehended through the "syntax of things,"
        which refers to the "logical process of grammatical predica-
        tion, by which subject is coupled with object or acts upon
        it" and to the "universal grammar of Nature herself...."
        These two senses of syntax, linguistic and metaphysical, help
        to clarify the ways in which Sterne's form implies his mean-
        ing: two movements--the journey of the heart in pursuit of
        Nature and the narrator's effort to achieve a closer relation-
        ship with the reader--have a "linguistic analogue in the para-
        digm of the sentence itself, in which the subject ... is linked
        through a copulative or transitive verb to an object beyond
        itself."

3031   BRISSENDEN, R. F.
        "The Sentimental Comedy: A Sentimental Journey." In Virtue
        in Distress: Studies in the Novel of Sentiment from Richard-
        son to Sade (New York: Barnes & Noble; London: Macmillan,
        1974), pp. 218-242.

        Argues that feeling is the essential and animating principle
        of A Sentimental Journey, and that, as in the episode with
        the lady at Calais, the real paradox is that Yorick's feeling
        of sexual desire for the lady leads to benevolence: insensibility
        and hardness of heart are the real evils in Sterne's world,
        not an occasional unchastity or a tendency to let the heart
        govern the head.   One of the main themes is that man must
        always keep alive in himself the capacity to feel, even though
        the exercise of that faculty may lead to a man's making a
        fool of himself.   The chapter is concerned with the relation-
        ship between the erotic and the moral connotations of "senti-
        mental," and emphasizes especially that our capacity for ben-
        evolence is intimately associated with our capacity for sexual
        responsiveness.

3032   CASH, ARTHUR HILL.
        Sterne's Comedy of Moral Sentiments: The Ethical Dimension
        of the Journey (Modern Humanities Research Assoc. Mono-
        graph: Duquesne Studies Philological Series, 6).   Pittsburgh,
        Pa.: Duquesne Univ. Press, 1966.

        A study of the Sentimental Journey, comparing it with
        Sterne's sermons, in order to define the nature of his senti-
        mentalism and to refute the thesis of Putney and Dilworth
        that the Journey was a hoax in which Sterne gave his readers
        the pathos they wanted to read.   Sterne is a humorist, de-

picting "comic man, trapped between his petty vileness and his noble ideals."

3033 CHADWICK, JOSEPH.
"Infinite Jest: Interpretation in Sterne's A Sentimental Journey." ECS 12 (1978-79): 190-205.

Sterne's ambiguous rhetoric and complicated narrative technique, which move "between moral, psychological, and epistemological polarities," provoke divergent readings by critics. Using these polarities, Chadwick attempts to show that "the ambiguous nature of the communication in and with A Sentimental Journey forms a recognition of a problematic element in the individual's interpretation of experience: the relation of thought and emotion to sense perception."

3034 DAVIDSON, ARNOLD E. and CATHY N. DAVIDSON.
"Yorick contra Hobbes: Comic Synthesis in Sterne's A Sentimental Journey." Cent. Rev. 21 (1977): 282-293.

The narrative method of A Sentimental Journey is to juxtapose contrasting images, themes, and scenes in order to create comic irony and ambiguity. Sterne's method has two other important functions: 1) it parallels Yorick's ambivalence about himself and his actions; and 2) " ... by mirroring the almost schizoid quality of his narrator's response to experience, Sterne also emphasizes, for comic and didactic purposes, the self-contradictions inherent in aspirations to a higher sensibility."

3035 DUSSINGER, JOHN A.
"A Sentimental Journey: 'A Sort of Knowingness.' " In [98], pp. 173-200.

Uncertainty in discourse is an "unlimited recourse for the imagination to play upon without guilt"; in A Sentimental Journey the hero possesses a "double awareness" that permits pathos and wit to coexist as the refinement of sensibility. The rhetorical technique of Sterne's wit ("a sort of knowingness") usually involves three persons--the agent, his accomplice, and their object of ridicule; especially important is Coleridge's recognition that the narrator is as "sinister toward his accomplice, the reader, as he is toward himself and others in the story."

3036 GARVY, JAMES W.
"Translation, Equivocation, and Reconciliation in Sterne's Sentimental Journey." SHR 12 (1978): 339-349.

Shows how Sterne's equivocation in A Sentimental Journey reinforces his "propensity for being in two places at once-- geographically, linguistically, emotionally, or morally--and for reconciling through wordplay perceptions conventionally considered antithetical." Suggests that "the equivocal lang- uage in which [Yorick's] travels are described is sometimes a measure of his failure to make the transition from context to context; but more often the carefully woven tissue of equi- vocations in language and situation confounds conventional no- tions of pure and impure, sacred and profane, as [he] achieves some sort of reconciliation among them."

3037   HARTLEY, LODWICK.
"Yorick's Sentimental Journey Continued: A Reconsideration of the Authorship." SAQ 70 (1971): 180-190.

A discussion of whether Hall-Stevenson did or did not com- plete A Sentimental Journey after Sterne's death.

3038   KOPPEL, GENE.
"Fulfillment Through Frustration: Some Aspects of Sterne's Art of the Incomplete in A Sentimental Journey." Studies in the Novel 2 (1970): 168-172.

Analyzes sexual frustration and incomplete desire in A Sentimental Journey as a source of human energy.

3039   LAMB, JONATHAN.
"Language and Hartleian Associationism in A Sentimental Jour- ney." ECS 13 (1980): 285-312.

A Sentimental Journey asks the "reader to consider the processes of getting and using words ... it is ... a journey of words in search of ideas, ideas in search of signs, and signs in search of contexts." Some of Sterne's words become key-words, and their evolution into figurative language is in- fluenced more by Hartley's Observations on Man than by Locke's Essay Concerning Human Understanding. Some of the words discussed include sentiment, hand, situation, rights, and con- science. Concludes that Sterne "approaches an eighteenth- century problem of naming in his novel, using Locke to de- fine it and Hartley to help solve it, and the solution is ... to find in literature and literary language a grammar for under- standing the world and a vocabulary for naming it."

3040   McGLYNN, PAUL D.
"Orthodoxy versus Anarchy in Sterne's Sentimental Journey." PLL 7 (1971): 242-251.

Argues that the protagonist of A Sentimental Journey violates Sterne's own values and beliefs by assuming that virtue
always accompanies sentiment; he accepts sentiment as a
pleasurable end in itself, so that his actions produce moral
anarchy uncontrolled by any force other than the momentary
impulse.   A Sentimental Journey "shows that benevolent in-
clinations not grounded in reason and religious principle are
morally meaningless."

3041   PARKS, A. FRANKLIN.
        "Yorick's Sympathy for the 'little': A Measure of his Senti-
        mentality in Sterne's Sentimental Journey." L & P 28 (1978):
        119-124.

        "Yorick's versions of his experiences ... often have double
        significances."   On one level his language relates sentimen-
        talized events, and on a lower level, it has meanings which
        reflect his sexual preoccupations and his true self.   Yorick's
        preoccupation with size is evident throughout the story and
        his persistent focus on the "small" has its roots in his sexual
        inadequacies.

3042   PUTNEY, RUFUS D. S.
        "Laurence Sterne, Apostle of Laughter." In [27], pp. 159-
        170. Rpt. in [18], pp. 274-284.

        Considers the Journey a "hoax," in which Sterne "persuade
        his contemporaries that the comedy he must write was the
        pathos they wished to read." Argues further that Sterne was
        not guilty of excessive sensibility, that he can be called a
        sentimentalist only if we "ignore the hard core of comic irony
        that made him critical of the emotional vagaries of his own
        life and of his imagined characters."

3043   "The Evolution of A Sentimental Journey." PQ 19 (1940):
        349-369.

        Discusses events in Sterne's life prior to and during his
        writing of A Sentimental Journey, especially his health, his
        affair with Eliza, and his literary fortunes, to show that the
        Journey "was a hoax by which Sterne persuaded his contem-
        poraries that the humor he wanted to write was the pathos
        they wished to read."

3044   SMITTEN, JEFFREY R.
        "Gesture and Expression in Eighteenth-Century Fiction: A
        Sentimental Journey." MLS 9, iii (1979): 85-97.

        The author develops a hypothesis about the function of ges-

ture and expression--a universal language which represents
the major contact between the reader's imagination and the
text.   When Diderot, for instance, reads Richardson, he tries
to visualize "character and scene completely; he becomes a
spectator, not a reader, of the action." This language, therefore, becomes the "major affective center of a novel, and the
way in which a novelist manipulates this language may well be
indispensable to his meaning and effect." The hypothesis is
illustrated by a close reading of A Sentimental Journey.

3045   "Spatial Form as Narrative Technique in A Sentimental Jour-
        ney." JNT 5 (1975): 208-218.

        Applies Frank's concept of spatial form to A Sentimental
        Journey in an effort to analyze Sterne's technique of juxtapos-
        ing contrasting images, themes, and tones to create "comic
        irony and perplexing ambiguity" and concludes that the signifi-
        cance of his technique is that the novel is not always ironic
        but is intended to reveal the "baffling complexity of the human
        moral situation."

3046   STOUT, GARDNER D. , JR.
        "Yorick's Sentimental Journey: A Comic 'Pilgrim's Progress'
        for the Man of Feeling." ELH 30 (1963): 395-412.

        Rejects the view that Sterne's real feelings are expressed
        in the comic aspects of the book and that the Sentimental
        Traveller is a self-deluded fool unwittingly exposed.   Rather,
        the "sentimental" and the "comic" aspects of the Journey are
        "complementary aspects of a unified, comic vision of human
        existence." Emphasizes the redeeming power of the comic
        spirit, so that by professing themselves fools men may be-
        come wise.

3047   THOMSON, J. E. P.
        "Contrasting Scenes and their Part in the Structure of A Sen-
        timental Journey." AUMLA 32 (1969): 206-213.

        Suggests that Sterne, whose chief aim is to record and
        analyze Yorick's changing thoughts and words, gains structural
        coherence by presenting brief and contrasting scenes which
        define his various states of mind.

3048   "The Morality of Sterne'e Yorick." AUMLA 27 (1967): 71-
        78.

        Compares Sterne's moral and religious principles in his
        sermons with those of Yorick in A Sentimental Journey, and
        concludes that Yorick seriously reflects Sterne's own views.

3049   WOOLF, VIRGINIA.
       "The 'Sentimental Journey.'" In The Second Common Reader
       (London: Hogarth Press, 1932), pp. 75-85; (New York: Har-
       court, Brace, 1932), pp. 80-88.

       Discusses Sterne's general qualities, his style and angle
       of vision, and suggests that A Sentimental Journey fails partly
       because we begin to doubt his tenderness of heart: "For we
       feel that Sterne is thinking not of the thing itself but of its
       effect upon our opinion of him."

See also: 885, 927, 2842, 2848, 2865, 2876, 2957, 2979, 3008

                              Sermons

3050   DOWNEY, JAMES.
       "The Sermons of Mr. Yorick: A Reassessment of Hammond."
       ESC 4 (1978): 193-211.

       Disputes Hammond's argument, in Laurence Sterne's Ser-
       mons of Mr. Yorick (New Haven 1948), that the sermons re-
       maining in manuscript at the time of Sterne's death were
       written earlier than the others published in Volumes I-IV, and
       that all but one of the 45 sermons had been written before
       1751. The conclusions are that Sterne continued to write ser-
       mons after 1750; that his sermons did not undergo a qualita-
       tive, methodological, or stylistic change in the mid-1740's or
       thereafter; that no evidence exists to support the assumption
       that the sermons published in 1769 (V-VII) were written be-
       fore those published by Sterne himself (I-IV); that the number
       of "dramatic" or "Shandean" sermons is small, comprising
       less than half the sermons in I-IV; and that we need a more
       precise statement than now exists of the variety of Sterne's
       homiletic styles and of the nature of his religious beliefs.

See also: 2856, 2869, 3032, 3048

Collected Studies

3051 DONOGHUE, DENIS, ed.
Jonathan Swift: A Critical Anthology (Penguin Critical Anthologies). Harmondsworth: Penguin, 1971.

3052 FISCHER, JOHN IRWIN and DONALD C. MELL, eds.
Contemporary Studies of Swift's Poetry. Newark, Del. : Univ.
Delaware Press; London & Toronto: Associated Presses,
1981.

3053 FRENCH, DAVID P. , et al.
Jonathan Swift: Tercentenary Essays (Univ. Tulsa Department
of English Monograph Series No. 3). Tulsa: Univ. Tulsa
Press, 1967.

3054 JEFFARES, A. NORMAN, ed.
Swift: Modern Judgements. London: Macmillan, 1968.

3055 Fair Liberty Was All His Cry: A Tercentenary Tribute to
Jonathan Swift, 1667-1745. London: Macmillan; New York:
St. Martin's Press, 1967.

3056 McHUGH, ROGER and PHILIP EDWARDS, eds.
Jonathan Swift 1667-1967: A Dublin Tercentenary Tribute.
Dublin: Dolmen Press, 1967.

3057 PROBYN, CLIVE T. , ed.
The Art of Jonathan Swift (Critical Studies). New York:
Barnes & Noble; London: Vision Press, 1978.

3058 RAWSON, C. J. , ed.
Focus: Swift. London: Sphere Books, 1971.

3059 TUVESON, ERNEST, ed.
Swift: A Collection of Critical Essays. Englewood Cliffs,
N. J. : Prentice-Hall, 1964.

3060 VICKERS, BRIAN, ed.
The World of Jonathan Swift: Essays for the Tercentenary.
Oxford: Blackwell; Cambridge: Harvard Univ. Press, 1968.

3061 WILLIAMS, KATHLEEN.

Swift: The Critical Heritage. London: Routledge & Kegan
Paul, 1970.

General Studies

3062   ADEN, JOHN M.
       "Swift, Pope, and 'the Sin of Wit.'" PBSA 62 (1968): 80-
       85.

       Attempts to link Swift's The Author Upon Himself, in which
the phrase "the Sin of Wit" occurs, to Pope's use of the phrase
in a well-known epigram of July 1715, and suggests that Swift
wrote his poem sometime between 31 May 1714 and 4-11 July
when he was visited by Pope and Parnell at Letcombe; Pope
possibly saw the poem or heard the expression at that time.

3063   ATKINS, G. DOUGLAS.
       "The Ancients, the moderns, and gnosticism." In Transac-
       tions of the Fourth International Congress on the Enlighten-
       ment (SVEC 151), Theodore Besterman, pub. (Oxford: Vol-
       taire Fndt., 1976), pp. 149-166.

       Considers the way in which the period 1660-1750 is related
to the idea of gnosticism as a pattern of thought; in particular, the author considers the distance of gnosticism from Augustan values, and by concentrating on Dryden, Swift, and
Pope, suggests that "there appears to be an important degree
to which these writers are not only safely distanced from
Gnostic contamination but perhaps directly confronting tendencies, aims, and desires that may best be viewed as Gnostic."

3064   BAKER, HARRY T.
       "Jonathan Swift." SR 34 (1926): 1-11.

       Sees Swift as an Arnoldian Liberal without illusions and
attempts to reconstruct the man as he lived; general and biographical, with little literary criticism.

3065   BALL, ALBERT.
       "Swift and the Animal Myth." Trans. Wisc. Acad. Sci.,
       Arts & Letters 48 (1959): 239-248.

       Discusses the history of the happy beast motif--its tradi-
tion and what Swift borrowed from it, and what he added to
it.   One of Swift's borrowings from the tradition is the fable
form itself, which he uses primarily to attack man's pride
and vanity.   When he adopts the theriophilistic argument, he
humanizes the animal and suggests that it is so rational that

it can outwit man at his own game: this technique is employed in the fourth voyage of Gulliver's Travels, where "theriophilism reaches its logical extreme: the beast becomes the master, man the servant.... The Houyhnhnms embody the ideal of the theriophilists to an outrageous degree, for they are neither bestial nor human." Swift synthesizes two opposing points of view, for or against the theriophilists, depending upon the satiric occasion.

3066   BARNETT, LOUISE K.
        " 'Saying the Thing That Is Not': Swift's Metalinguistic Satire." CP 12, i (1979): 21-27.

        Because Swift was concerned with the misuse of language, he focuses upon deceptive linguistic practices in a number of his poems; his "technique for satirizing reprehensible language is to exploit its own possibilities." He would "carry a metaphor to an extreme in order to expose its inherent foolishness," but he is still confident that language can be "a precise instrument of communication" and that through individual effort language can be simplified.

3067   BEAUMONT, CHARLES ALLEN.
        Swift's Use of the Bible: A Documentation and a Study in Allusion (University of Georgia Monographs, No. 14). Athens: Univ. Ga. Press, 1965.

        Discusses Swift's Biblical quotations chiefly from two points of view: 1) his use of a quotation to evoke a series of allusions that cannot be understood until the whole passage alluded to has been pondered; and 2) his habit of beginning with a simple quotation and gradually over several passages developing its content into a major metaphor. The study deals with the complete prose works, except the sermons. Concludes that the "incidence of Biblical quotations, especially their preponderance in certain works and their total absence or limited appearance in others, indicates that such quoting was not a habit of style or of the mind of Swift."

3068   Swift's Classical Rhetoric (University of Georgia Monographs, No. 8). Athens: Univ. Ga. Press, 1961.

        Seeks "to explore Swift's method in using the varied devices of classical rhetoric to create, sustain, and render plausible the ironic norms" of A Modest Proposal, An Argument Against Abolishing Christianity, A Vindication of Lord Carteret, and The Answer to the Craftsman; a detailed analysis according to the following major topics: the classical form of the essay; the ethical proof; Swift's use of the two major rhetorical devices, diminution and refining; and the less frequently used devices.

3069   BECKETT, J. C.
"Swift as an Ecclesiastical Statesman." In Essays in British
and Irish History in Honour of James Eadie Todd, eds. H. A.
Cronne, T. W. Moody, and D. B. Quinn. London: Muller,
1949, pp. 135-152. Rpt. in [3055], pp. 146-165.

Attempts to discover Swift's attitude toward the Anglican
Church as an organization, the part it played in his life, and
the connection between his life as a churchman and his life
as a politician and a man of letters.

3070   BLESCH, EDWIN J. , JR.
" 'A Species Hardly a Degree Above a Monkey': Jonathan
Swift's Concept of Woman." NR 3, iii (1977): 74-84.

Discusses Swift's pathological obsession with the excrement,
lust, filth, smell, stupidity, and deceit of women as they are
portrayed in his later poems and also in Gulliver's Travels
and A Modest Proposal. Swift is truly anti-feminist, and
"his perverse, unnatural, distorted depreciation of female
sexuality seems to imply a genital failure."

3071   BROWN, DANIEL R.
"Swift and the Limitations of Satire." Dublin Mag. 9, no. 4
(1972): 68-78.

Discusses the pros and cons of satirical writing and Swift's
role as a satirist.

3072   BROWN, JAMES.
"Swift as Moralist." PQ 33 (1954): 368-387.

A study of "Swift's metaphysics" of human nature. Examines Swift, considering "both satirist and Christian to be
manifestations--one in terms of a literary genre, the other
in terms of a religious or philosophical system of thought--
of the central, definitive unity which is Swift as moralist."
Compares Swift's views with those of Bishop Butler.

3073   BROWN, LLOYD W.
"The Person of Quality in the Eighteenth Century: Aspects
of Swift's Social Satire." DR 48 (1968): 171-184.

Demonstrates how Swift uses the person of quality simultaneously as "a realistic analyst of actual social evils and
the embodiment of many of these evils" and how "he combines
the satiric realism of the social critic with the inverted values
of the nominal moralist."

3074   BROWN, NORMAN O.
       "The Excremental Vision." From Life Against Death (Middle-
       town, Conn.: Wesleyan Univ. Press, 1959), pp. 179-201.
       Rpt. in [3059], 31-54; [3109], pp. 611-630.

       Deals with the psychoanalytical criticism of Swift and sug-
       gests that psychoanalysts condemn Swift for things that they
       are also guilty of. Points out that we should not try to "ex-
       plain away Swift's literary achievements as mere epiphenomena
       on his individual neurosis" but should instead "seek to appre-
       ciate his insight into the universal neurosis of mankind."

3075   BULLITT, JOHN M.
       Jonathan Swift and the Anatomy of Satire: A Study of Satiric
       Technique. Cambridge: Harvard Univ. Press, 1953.

       Investigates the "character, potentialities, and limitations
       of literary satire" by way of Swift's technical achievements;
       argues that his satiric devices evolve organically out of an
       intellectual perception of the disparity between expectation
       and reality, and therefore suggests that "those aspects of his
       satiric craftsmanship which most intimately join with and ex-
       press his intellectual attitudes and values" are of major im-
       portance.

3076   CARNOCHAN, W. B.
       "The Consolations of Satire." In [3057], pp. 19-42.

       The consolations that satire offered Swift for the pain and
       loss involved in living, for the disappointments that seemed
       to counterbalance his grand hopes, are detailed in this study:
       "His satire murdered--not only to dissect but, ironically, to
       heal the wound of life itself." Swift's most successful com-
       pensations are public, not private, in his art rather than in
       life. Discusses the poems, the Bickerstaff papers, A Modest
       Proposal, and Gulliver's Travels. "Gulliver's Travels does
       not finally cancel pain and loss; Gulliver has to go home.
       There is no 'great Happiness' in the outcome, no 'new Crea-
       tion.' "

3077   CARPENTER, ANDREW.
       The Irish Perspective of Jonathan Swift (Wuppertaler Hoch-
       schulreden 13). Wuppertal: Hammer, 1978.

       Attempts to demonstrate that "the circumstances of Swift's
       life, and above all the tone of ... A Tale of a Tub and Gul-
       liver's Travels, show that his roots were in Ireland" and that
       he did not hate everything Irish as is widely believed. Looks
       at Swift's political, personal, and literary relationship with
       Ireland which reveals that that country "was central to his

life and experience, and the Irish way of perceiving reality central to his work."

3078 COOK, RICHARD I.
"The Uses of Saeva Indignatio: Swift's Political Tracts (1710-1714) and His Sense of Audience." SEL 2 (1962): 287-307.

Traces "the bitter progression Swift ... [made] from the amused banter of A Tale of a Tub to the despairing gloom of Gulliver's Travels, the aroused moral earnestness of The Conduct of the Allies and the rest of the Tory tracts." This "transition toward the ultimate saeva indignatio ... impelled Swift to vex the world instead of diverting it."

3079 DAVIE, DONALD A.
"Irony and Conciseness in Berkeley and in Swift." Dublin Mag. 27 (Oct. -Dec. 1952): 20-29.

Argues that, if irony is characteristic of Swift's style, then it is less trenchant, and in that sense less concise, than is commonly supposed. Berkeley, on the other hand, is less ironic because as a moralist he is too straightforward and often too satirical.

3080 DAVIES, HUGH SYKES.
"Irony and the English Tongue." In [3060], pp. 129-153.

Discusses, first, Swift's theory and practice of language, and, second, how irony works on the linguistic level; suggests that, whereas in normal utterance there is a simple coincidence between message and set of signals transmitted, in ironic utterance the receiver must not only receive a set of signals, but also decode them, and thus reconstruct the uncoded version of what has never been uttered. This theory of irony is applied to A Modest Proposal.

3081 DAVIS, HERBERT.
"Swift's Character." In [3056], pp. 1-23.

Attempts to "discover what we can gather from some of [Swift's] self-portraits ... where at least he was pretending to tell us something about himself ... "; chiefly concerned with the poems, and concludes that "He had rather that his heart should be torn and his brain on fire with anger, than to have turned away unseeing and unmoved; and not to have attempted to make us see what he saw, and what he believed to be the truth of the human situation."

3082 "Swift's Use of Irony." In The Uses of Irony: Papers on

Defoe and Swift Read at a Clark Library Seminar, April 2, 1966 (Los Angeles: Clark Memorial Library, 1966), pp. 39-63. Rpt. in [43], pp. 221-243; [3060], pp. 154-170.

Discusses parody and irony in A Tale of a Tub and An Argument Against Abolishing Christianity, and attempts to interpret Swift's meaning and intentions in Gulliver's Travels, especially in Part IV: in the latter Gulliver does partly represent Swift's own views, and his intention is to "vex" mankind by ruthlessly exposing the vices and corruptions of man and society.

3083   Jonathan Swift, Essays on His Satire and Other Studies (Galaxy Books 106). New York: Oxford Univ. Press, 1964.

Reprints Stella, The Satire of Jonathan Swift, and seven essays.

3084   "Alecto's Whip. " REL 3 No. 3 (1962): 7-17. Rpt. in [3083], pp. 249-259.

Swift as satirist in his verse, assuming the role of Alecto and borrowing her whip of scorpions in order to "bring his adversaries before the bar of posterity, that all evil-doers might know that their crimes would be revealed for the instruction of future ages. "

3085   The Satire of Jonathan Swift.   New York: Macmillan, 1947. Rpt. with alterations and omissions in [3083], pp. 101-160.

Reprints of Davis's lectures at Smith College in 1946 on Swift's literary satire in A Tale of a Tub (pp. 9-43), his political satire in The Examiner and M. B. Drapier (pp. 45-75), and his moral satire in Gulliver's Travels (pp. 77-109).

3086   "The Conciseness of Swift. " In [54], pp. 15-32.   Rpt. in [18], pp. 84-101; [3083], pp. 216-235.

Argues that it is Swift's conciseness of style that sets him apart from his contemporaries and also that it is this conciseness which can be used to identify Swift's writings.

3087   Stella: A Gentlewoman of the Eighteenth Century.   New York: Macmillan, 1942.   Rpt. with alterations and omissions in [3083], pp. 31-97.

Reprints of the author's Alexander Lectures at the University of Toronto in 1942 on Swift's relationship to Stella and the qualities of his work and its relation to Stella--satire, comedy, and sentiment.

3088   "Swift and the Pedants." Oriel Rev. 1 (1942): 129-144. Rpt. in [3083], pp. 199-215.

Shows "Swift in the role of Bickerstaff, the wit and the humorist, at his work of exposing and making fun of quacks and shams ... " in opposition to that of madman as some of his contemporaries thought him to be.

3089   DOBREE, BONAMY.
"The Jocose Dean." In [3055], pp. 42-61. Rpt. in [3054], pp. 28-46.

Gives examples of Swift's humor to suggest that his " ... saeva indignatio was offset, even perhaps sustained, by his enormous gaiety. "

3090   DONOGHUE, DENIS.
Jonathan Swift: A Critical Introduction. Cambridge: Cambridge Univ. Press, 1969.

Not a systematic examination of Swift's works, but questions certain assumptions about his work dominant during the preceding twenty years: e. g. , that irony is the key to Swift, that Swift employs the persona as a reliable narrator.

3091   "Swift's Perspective." Studies 56 (1967): 248-265.

The influence of the pocket perspective on Swift's intellectual outlook; suggests that the characteristic modes of his satire are "perspective, pressure, irony, discontinuity, comparison, contrast, parody; one mode of being, and then (obliquely) another. "

3092   DOOLEY, D. J.
"Image and Point of View in Swift." PLL 6 (1970): 125-135.

Discusses various critics' readings of Swift and suggests that Swift's images "function as discriminators of meaning" giving force to the argument and establishing the point of view which the reader is expected to take toward the subject.

3093   EHRENPREIS, IRVIN.
"Jonathan Swift." Proc. of British Academy 54 (1968): 149-164. Rpt. London: Oxford Univ. Press, 1970.

Continuity and coherence in Swift's writings are provided
by "the belief that morality, religion, and politics are inseparable.... His scepticism and his comic imagination may
connect him with the Enlightenment, his intolerance opposes
it, his moral energy transcends it."

3094   "Swift and Comedy of Evil." In [3060], pp. 213-219.

Discusses the apparently contradictory relationship between
comedy and evil, as in the cases of Juvenal's Domitian, Mo-
lière's Tartuffe, and Brecht's Arturo Ui: their evil is not
lessened by the humor; but whereas the former three refuse
to accept responsibility for the triumph of evil, Swift creates
a persona who becomes intimately involved in evil: he does
not stand aloof like most satirists, and the reader is impli-
cated in the evil being satirized. "The greatness of Swift's
whole achievement as a satirist can be expressed in terms
of this comedy of impersonated evil, which forces us not
simply to grow indignant but also to admit we helped perpe-
trate the crime we deplore."

3095   Swift: The Man, His Works, and the Age. 2 vols. London:
        Methuen; Cambridge: Harvard Univ. Press, 1962-67. Vol.
        1: Mr. Swift and His Contemporaries. Vol. 2: Dr. Swift.

Vol. I: A definitive life that draws many parallels between
Swift and his contemporaries; seeks to suggest the connections and relationships that bind together a narrow, close-
knit society, and to indicate "how far intellectual traditions
and public events could ... endow Swift with principles which
might seem arbitrary to us." Includes a detailed analysis
of A Tale of a Tub.
Vol. II: Swift's life from 1699-1714, following his political
development: the emphasis is on the search for preferment
and the author hopes to modify the old story of his ambitions.
Contains detailed analysis of both prose and verse, including
a chapter on The Conduct of the Allies.

3096   The Personality of Jonathan Swift. London: Methuen; Cam-
        bridge: Harvard Univ. Press, 1958. Rpt. New York: Barnes
        & Noble; London: Methuen, 1969.

Attempts to show "how Swift's personality could enter into
his work," exploring the region where biography meets criticism; deals with Swift's treatment of women, the allegations
of obscenity and madness, politics and his philosophy of history, religion and Gulliver's Travels and the scatological
poems, and Swift's "Little Language" and his "Old Age."

3097   "Swift and Satire." CE 13 (1952): 309-312.

Defines some of Swift's ironic devices--simple irony, invective satire, personae--and shows relationship between them in Book IV of Gulliver's Travels.

3098   "Swift on Liberty." JHI 13 (1952): 131-146. Rpt. in [3054], pp. 59-73.

Swift's ideas on "liberty" or "freedom" as opposed to "slavery, tyranny, and oppression"; taken from a variety of Swift's writings.

3099   ELLIOTT, ROBERT C.
"Swift's Satire: Rules of the Game." ELH 41 (1974): 413-428.

"A major function of Swift's impersonations--as a mad Modern, an Irish projector, as Gulliver--is that they allowed him to think himself into the heart of evil, to traffic with the impermissible.... [His] feats of impersonations operate according to rules...." The most important rules have to do with the functioning of Swift's fictional spokesmen.

3100   "Swift's 'I.'" YR 62 (1973): 372-391.

Reviews the argument among critics over the "persona" in Swift's writings; attempts to show "a relation between the scuttling of the persona in Swift criticism--the easy collapse of distinctions between Swift and his spokesmen--and the appearance of the new romantic Swift...."

3101   EWALD, WILLIAM.
The Masks of Jonathan Swift. Cambridge: Harvard Univ. Press, 1954.

An account of Swift's personae in such works as A Tale of a Tub, the Bickerstaff papers, The Drapier's Letters, Gulliver's Travels, A Modest Proposal, and several other political and religious essays.

3102   FALLE, GEORGE.
"Divinity and Wit: Swift's Attempted Reconciliation." UTQ 46 (1976): 14-30.

" ... Swift uses his wit as a means of intensifying the complexity of the perennial problems that confront the Christian world, and this practice serves in turn to enhance the order of divine providence, to make us more fully aware of God's benevolence and grace." Swift felt that he had suc-

ceeded in reconciling wit with divinity, by which he meant
Christian doctrine as the church holds it.   Although he de-
plored the argument that man could "contribute to the honour
and glory of God," much of his work in "an ironic and perhaps 'witty' way" does just that.

3103   FERGUSON, OLIVER.
        Jonathan Swift and Ireland.   Urbana: Univ. Ill. Press,
        1962.

        A study of Swift's Irish writings and of his involvement in
        the cause of Ireland's liberty; attempts to justify his right to
        the title of "the Irish patriot" and to prove that Swift's "fierce
        indignation" in the end extended to the very people whom he
        championed: "he never forgave the nation for failing to re-
        spond adequately to his call."

3104   FRICKE, DONNA G.
        "Swift and the Tradition of Informal Satire."   In [3052], pp.
        36-45.

        Studies the background of English colloquial or informal
        satire, an influence that permitted Swift to reach a larger
        audience than Dryden and Pope wrote for; especially concerned
        with the early history of the octosyllabic form and its effect
        on Swift's own poetic expression.   Concludes that Swift "be-
        longs to a satiric tradition that differs from that of Dryden
        and Pope ... he deserves a place beside Dryden and Pope
        as the Augustan Archpoet, an Augustan English reviver of
        the medieval satiric tradition."

3105   FROST, WILLIAM.
        "The Irony of Swift and Gibbon."   EIC 17 (1967): 41-47.   In
        [3109], pp. 684-688.

        An answer to F. R. Leavis's essay on Swift [3127], in
        which Leavis presents a "portrait of an evil genius, a literary
        Satan whose creative energies are perverted to destruction be-
        cause his true nature is one of active malice."   Referring to
        the "woman flayed" passage in A Tale of a Tub, Frost sug-
        gests that Leavis overlooks the obvious fact that Swift alludes
        to the bloody backs of prostitutes whipped at the end of a
        cart on the way to the Fleet Prison.   Agrees with Leavis that
        Swift's irony is intended "to defeat habit, to intimidate, and to
        demoralize."

3106   GILBERT, JACK G.
        Jonathan Swift: Romantic and Cynic Moralist.   Austin: Univ.
        Texas Press, 1966. Rpt. New York: Haskell House, 1973.

Deals with Swift's ethical opinions--his attacks on human failings, his praise of human excellence, his devotion to a heroic or romantic ideal--and the ethical patterns of his satire in Gulliver's Travels. Attempts to "understand the ethical antitheses of each part [of the Travels] and to place these antitheses in the formal structure of the plot which Swift devised in each voyage."

3107   GOLDEN, MORRIS.
The Self Observed: Swift, Johnson, Wordsworth.   Baltimore: Johns Hopkins Press, 1972.

Contains a chapter on Swift's view of himself (his personae as projected in his writings), and his view of man in the world. As "master of the literary alter ego, Swift builds his visions of the world upon blown-up fragments of himself ... and his ironic writings usually convey meaning through the mutual illumination of two selves, a grotesquely acting persona and an implied general self who is the common ground shared with the decent, genteel, educated reader of all times and every place."

3108   GOLDGAR, BERTRAND A.
The Curse of Party: Swift's Relations with Addison and Steele. Lincoln: Univ. Nebr. Press, 1961.

The friendship of Swift, Addison, and Steele was destroyed by "this damned business of party"; the author's purpose, therefore, is to "examine in some detail the personal, political, and literary relations of these three men, and to set the known facts about their friendship and their quarrels against the background of party warfare and political journalism in the last six years of Queen Anne." The emphasis is on Swift, and much of his political writings are analyzed; and the Introduction provides a survey of contrasting intellectual traditions and literary assumptions as a background to the three men's personal difficulties.

3109   GREENBERG, ROBERT A. and WILLIAM B. PIPER, eds.
The Writings of Jonathan Swift (Norton Critical Edition).   New York: W. W. Norton & Co. , 1973.

An authoritative text; backgrounds, sources, and criticism; reprints, abridgments, and excerpts.

3110   GREENE, DONALD.
"Swift: Some Caveats. "   In [9], pp. 341-358.

Deals with Swift as the "archetypal right-winger--the reac-

tionary Tory, the extreme High Churchman, the hater of modern science and modern empiricism in general"; insists that
Swift was in his principles a Whig, in religion a moderate,
and in his attitude toward modern science on the side of Bacon
against Aristotelian and scholastic rationalism.

3111   HAGSTRUM, JEAN H.
        "Swift's Vanessa and Stella." In [111], pp. 145-159.

        Discusses Swift's opposition to marriage, not just to Ro-
        mantic love, and emphasizes that it derives from his physical
        repugnance to the union of the sexes. Yet he obviously felt
        "love" for Vanessa and Stella, a love "rational, sexless, spir-
        itual--based not on physical attraction ... but on wit, virtue,
        and charity...." Yet the Journal to Stella reveals that Swift's
        love, though not marital, sexual love, does go beyond normal
        friendship; that in fact psychosexual meaning exists in the
        language of the Journal.

3112   HOGAN, J. J.
        "Bicentenary of Jonathan Swift, 1667-1745." Studies 34 (1945):
        501-510. Rpt. in [3054], pp. 47-58.

        An essay about Swift, the man, and his grasp of the com-
        mon world and how this grasp is reflected in his writings.

3113   HOLLOWAY, JOHN.
        "The Well-Filled Dish: An Analysis of Swift's Satire." HR
        9 (1956): 20-37. Rpt. as "An Analysis of Swift's Satire"
        in The Charted Mirror: Literary and Critical Essays (Lon-
        don: Routledge & Kegan Paul, 1960; New York: Horizon
        Press, 1962), pp. 75-93.

        Comments on the various uses of satire and examines how
        successful Swift was in his use of satire to "expose and at-
        tack what is ridiculous or vicious." Looks at how "he or-
        ganizes his work so that its satirical indictment is created;
        and how much, in this or that given case, the indictment con-
        tains."

3114   HORSLEY, LEE SONSTENG.
        " 'Of all Fictions the Most Simple': Swift's Shared Imagery."
        YES 5 (1975): 98-108.

        An analysis of Swift's debasing images, many of which he
        shared with writers of political pamphlets and journals which
        were "laden with well-worn images of political corruption,
        baseness, deceit, fanaticism, and disruption.... Swift at times
        used such images just as casually, but, ... he vivified the

commonplaces of political discourse, building from them sustained and subtle fictions. "

3115 HUNTING, ROBERT.
Jonathan Swift. New York: Twayne, 1967.

An introduction to Swift's best prose and poetry; aims to present in roughly chronological order those writings that will always be contemporaneously relevant, and to indicate "what might be termed an area of interpretation, in and for our time, that a thoughtful reading invites. "

3116 JARRELL, MACKIE L.
" 'Jack and Dane': Swift Traditions in Ireland." Jour. Amer. Folklore 77 (1964): 99-117. Rpt. in [3055], pp. 311-341.

An examination of the oral traditions concerning Swift preserved by the Irish Folklore Commission; the material is largely literary in origin, deriving mainly from jestbooks. Many of the stories concern the hiring of a servant, but the most common pattern shows how the servant gets the better of his master, in repartee or in action. Concludes that Swift's impact on Ireland was considerable, and that many of the details preserved about him--his contempt for lawyers, his lame leg, his obsession with walking, etc. --seem to spring from actual knowledge.

3117 JEFFARES, A NORMAN.
Jonathan Swift. (WTW) London: Longman, 1976.

A brief survey of Swift's life and work: surveys the prose satires, political and historical writings, Irish anti-colonial writings, the poetry, and the correspondence, and also discusses Swift's prose style.

3118 JOHNSON, JAMES WILLIAM.
"Swift's Historical Outlook." Jour. of British Studies 4 (1965): 52-77. Rpt. in [3054], pp. 96-120.

Attempts to "explain in some detail Swift's ideas of history, where he got them, and how they affected his non-historiographical compositions"; lists four chief constituents of his historical outlook: his theory of Decline, his concept of Time, his emphasis on Climate, and his attitude toward Luxury.

3119 JONES, MYRDDIN.
"A Living Treasury of Knowledge and Wisdom: Some Com-

ments on Swift's Attitude to the Writing of History." DUJ
36 (1975): 180-188.

Swift's knowledge of history was enormous and influenced
almost everything he wrote, particularly Gulliver's Travels;
in Books II and III he expresses anger at the falsehoods of
historians, and "exploits the gap that had opened between the
pretence and the practice; between the eulogies of the benefits
of history and the bleak actuality of its partisanship." Swift
attacks historians' partiality, distortion, and pride, and suggests that they are similar to scientists in being victims of
the vanity of human wishes.

3120   KIERNAN, COLM.
        "Swift and Science." Historical Jour. 14 (1971): 709-722.

        A study of Swift's assault on Newtonian science, especially
        in Book III of Gulliver's Travels. Swift used the story of
        Laputa to condemn Newtonian science because of its inhuman-
        ity. He "was condemning not only the mechanist uniformitar-
        ian Newtonian science, but also its opposite, the extreme or-
        ganicist Paracelsian life science tradition.... It was his re-
        ligion that forced him to avoid the extremes of realism and
        subjectivism in science. In the process he subordinated his
        science to his religion."

3121   LAMONT, CLAIRE.
        "A Checklist of Critical and Biographical Writings on Jona-
        than Swift, 1945-1965." In [3055], pp. 356-391.

3122   LANDA, LOUIS A.
        Swift and the Church of Ireland. Oxford: Clarendon Press,
        1954.

        Concludes that Swift was pessimistic about the Irish Es-
        tablishment, primarily because he was aware of the Church's
        "general debility from historical despoliations, of its internal
        dissensions and vulnerability to external attack, and of the
        weakness of the Irish economy on which it depended."

3123   "Jonathan Swift." English Institute Essays, 1946 (1947): 20-
        40. Rpt. in [7], pp. 176-197; [3351], pp. 287-296; [129], pp.
        119-139.

        Comments on certain biographical considerations which
        have played an unhappy part in Swift criticism, and presents
        some biographical examples of value for literary criticism;
        concerned with Part IV of Gulliver's Travels and the attempt
        to explain its quality by reference to Swift's life.

3124   "Jonathan Swift and Charity." JEGP 44 (1945): 337-350.
        Rpt. in [129], pp. 49-62.

        Details Swift's attitude toward charity and toward wealth
        and his charitable activities.

3125   "Swift, the Mysteries, and Deism." In Studies in English,
        Department of English, University of Texas, 1944 (Austin:
        Univ. Texas Press, 1945), pp. 239-256. Rpt. in [129], pp.
        89-106.

        Defends Swift against the charge of irreligion by examining
        the sermon, "On the Trinity," in relation to contemporary
        religious ideas and controversies; it is an articulated defense
        of Christian mysteries and a reasoned opposition to the deists.
        Concludes that Swift's defense rests upon the reasonableness
        of faith.

3126   "Swift's Economic Views and Mercantilism." ELH 10 (1943):
        310-335. Rpt. in [3054], pp. 74-95.

        Examines Swift's ideas toward trade and mercantilism as
        expressed in The Drapier's Letters and the Irish tracts.

3127   LEAVIS, F. R.
        "The Irony of Swift." In Determinations, ed. F. R. Leavis
        (London: Chatto & Windus, 1934), pp. 79-108. Rpt. in The
        Common Pursuit (London: Chatto & Windus, 1952), pp. 73-
        87; in [3059], pp. 15-29; [3055], pp. 116-130; [3054], pp. 121-
        134.

        An analysis of Swift's irony, comparing it with Gibbon's
        and illustrating it with examples from Section IX of A Tale
        of a Tub; finding its most essential quality residing in a "pe-
        culiar emotional intensity" and concluding that it is "essentially
        a matter of surprise and negation; its function is to defeat
        habit, to intimidate, and to demoralize."

3128   LEE, JAE NUM.
        Swift and Scatological Satire.   Albuquerque: Univ. New Mex-
        ico Press, 1971.

        After surveying the history of Continental scatological writ-
        ings from Aristophanes to Rabelais and of English writings
        from Skelton to Pope, the author describes Swift's scatologi-
        cal poems and scatology in Gulliver's Travels; his purpose
        is to study scatology in Swift from a "literary point of view
        that analyzes its rhetorical functions and the thematic purposes
        it serves."

3129   McKENZIE, GORDON.
       "Swift: Reason and Some of its Consequences." In Five Stud-
       ies in English (Univ. Calif. Publications in English 8, No. 1).
       Berkeley: Univ. Calif. Press, 1940), pp. 101-129.

       Discusses Swift's use of the words "reason," "reasonable,"
       "rational," and "common sense"; suggests that he at times
       uses "reason" in a sense unfamiliar to modern ears, and that
       the meaning of the word undergoes fairly wide variations in
       different contexts. Swift uses the word frequently in the sen-
       ses of "right intuition" and of "common sense."

3130   MARESCA, THOMAS E.
       "Swift." In [137], pp. 135-178.

       A Tale of a Tub resembles The Rape of the Lock and The
       Dunciad: it resembles the former in its "radical disjunction
       of form and content," and the latter in its "employment of
       a pervasive materialism as a central metaphor." The spread
       of Dulness is summarized by the growth of ideas into words:
       ontogeny recapitulates phylogeny. The Discourse Concerning
       the Mechanical Operation of the Spirit is explicitly linked to
       A Tale of a Tub by imagery, metaphor, subject, and treat-
       ment and is mainly important as a mirroring of the attitudes
       and interests of the Tale. Gulliver's Travels, which exploits
       epic matter in a prose mock epic without the epic manner,
       explores the metaphoric and ontological world called into being
       by the Tale; it points the way, within the comic-parodic form,
       toward the "possible prose epic of our now prosaic world."

3131   MAXWELL, J. C.
       "Demigods & Pickpockets: the Augustan Myth in Swift and
       Rousseau." Scrutiny 11 (1942): 34-39.

       Parallels between Swift and Rousseau in their adaptation
       of classical antiquity to their own unorthodox purposes.

3132   MAYHEW, GEORGE P.
       Rage or Raillery: The Swift Manuscripts at the Huntington
       Library. San Marino, Calif.: Huntington, 1967.

       Chiefly bibliographical, these articles also throw light on
       Swift as writer and human being: "Notes for The History of
       the Four Last Years, Book IV" emphasizes how seriously he
       took his role as Tory historian, and "Swift's Letter to a Young
       Lady on Her Marriage" tells us a lot about Deborah Staunton
       and her husband, John Rockfort, and suggests that Swift him-
       self helped arrange the marriage. Since Miss Staunton was
       a beautiful and spoiled young lady Professor Mayhew sug-
       gests that the Letter is not simply evidence of Swift's mis-

ogyny and that it may have been intended as instruction to
Stella and Vanessa on the nature of women and marriage.

3133   "Jonathan Swift's Hoax of 1722 Upon Ebenezar Elliston. " Bull.
       of the John Rylands Library 44 (1962): 360-380. Rpt. in
       [3055], pp. 290-310.

       Seeks, through additional information from Dublin news-
       papers and records, "to trace more clearly Swift's motives
       in singling out Elliston as his victim, to evaluate with some
       precision the efficacy of Swift's method of satiric verisimili-
       tude, and, finally, to establish the significance of his hoax
       on Elliston within the wider scope and aims of Swift's satire
       between 1720 and 1727, during which time The Drapier's Let-
       ters and Gulliver's Travels were being written.... "

3134   MERCIER, VIVIAN.
       "Swift's Humour. " In [3056], pp. 116-136.   Rpt. in Tri-
       Quarterly 11 (1968): 125-143.

       Seeks to define Swift's humor, and suggests that much of
       his popular appeal may be ascribed to it; gives examples from
       his life and works, chiefly from the verse.   Suggests that he
       fused the two types of humor, being in fact himself at one
       and the same time a "humorist and a humour, a jester and
       a butt, a sane observer and an eccentric.... "

3135   "Swift and the Gaelic Tradition. " REL 3, No. 3 (1962): 69-
       79.   Rpt. in [3055], 279-289.

       Suggests that Swift fits into the Gaelic tradition in three
       distinct ways: 1) his wit and wilful eccentricity is similar
       to that of many Gaelic poets, 2) hints of the Gaelic tradition
       are found in Gulliver's Travels, and 3) two later Gaelic poets
       show indebtedness to Swift in their satiric poetry.

3136   MILIC, LOUIS T.
       A Quantitative Approach to the Style of Jonathan Swift (Studies
       in Literature 23).   The Hague: Mouton, 1967.

       A quantitative approach to an analysis of Swift's style, es-
       pecially of A Letter to a Young Poet which concludes that the
       "second half of the Letter is not statistically distinguishable
       from Swift's known writings, but the first half is. "

3137   MOORE, JOHN ROBERT.
       "Was Jonathan Swift a Moderate?" SAQ 53 (1954): 260-267.

Argues that Swift was not, on the basis of his writings, a moderate in religion and politics.

3138   "Swift as Historian." SP 49 (1952): 583-604.

Argues that Swift was not an accurate historian but that "the disappointment of [his] hopes as chronicler of Oxford's ministry bore fruit in many parts of Gulliver's Travels."

3139   MURRY, JOHN MIDDLETON.
Jonathan Swift: A Critical Biography.   London: Cape, 1954; New York: Noonday Press, 1955.

Both a life and a critical study of the works; controversial.

3140   NICHOL SMITH, DAVID.
"Jonathan Swift: Some Observations." Trans. Royal Soc. of Lit. 14 (1935): 29-48. Rpt. in [3055], pp. 1-14.

Considers Swift's fitness for religious orders, and the nature of his satire on religion and learning; comments on Book IV of Gulliver.

3141   NOKES, DAVID.
" 'Hack at Tom Poley's': Swift's Use of Puns." In [3057], pp. 43-56.

Swift's puns are not so much Joycean "epiphanies as incarnations, a constant process of words becoming flesh." Of particular concern, in the writings of both Swift and Pope, is the tendency of linking language and finance through the central concept of currency.   Both writers believed that the misuse of language would degrade that culture which depended on language for expression; that money, language, and science would permit unlimited freedom, which in turn would encourage debasement of language.   Swift and Pope wished to offer some restraints to the easy circulation of language and money: "The two currencies ... were too powerful to be independent of all controls save those of the market-place."

3142   "Swift and the Beggars." EIC 26 (1976): 218-235.

Compares Swift's attitude toward the poor as expressed in his satires and in his sermons, especially A Modest Proposal and Causes of the Wretched Condition of Ireland. In his satires he attacked the government for the wrongs against the poor, but in his sermons his humanitarian concern was far less; he actually looked upon "Economic ills, like all other hardships, [as a] part of the lot which fallen man must endure. "

3143 PEAKE, CHARLES.
"Swift and the Passions." MLR 55 (1960): 169-180. Rpt. in [3340], pp. 282-298.

Argues that interpretations that claim that Swift hated human passions distort his "views about mankind and [lead] to serious misinterpretation of his most important satirical work [Gulliver's Travels]." Maintains that "[Swift's] belief that the passions were the force behind all human actions necessarily led him to find the cause of all vice and folly in perverted or misdirected passions; but it is the evil of the perversion, not of the passion itself, which occasions the violence of Swift's attacks."

3144 PINKUS, PHILIP.
Swift's Vision of Evil: A Comparative Study of "A Tale of a Tub" and "Gulliver's Travels", 2 vols. (ELS 3, 4). Victoria, B.C.: Univ. Of Victoria, 1975. (Vol. I: Tale of a Tub; Vol. II: Gulliver's Travels).

The author suggests that the difference between the satire of fear and the satire of contempt is also the difference between A Tale of a Tub and Gulliver's Travels. His approach is essentially aesthetic: he emphasizes satiric imagery within the rhetorical structure in order to show how the satire functions in its context. He tries to "show how, in both the Tale and Gulliver, the various elements of the satire contribute to the imagery and help create ... a dominant image, Swift's vision of evil. The result should be two very different perceptions of evil derived from a very similar world, seen through the ironic prism of the two satires."

3145 "Sin and Satire in Swift." Bucknell Rev. 13, no. 2 (1965): 11-25. Rpt. in [3350], pp. 186-201.

Sees the purpose of satire as making the reader aware of evil in the world, not as diminishing the subject by ridicule; evil is not annihilated, but remains triumphant in satire. The article describes the dominant images in Swift's satires in order to present a fairly consistent view of life--Swift's satiric image of evil; seeks to explain the nature of his satire.

3146 "Swift and the Ancients-Moderns Controversy." UTQ 29 (1959): 46-58.

A criticism of Richard F. Jones's definition of the Ancient

vs. Modern controversy and of Swift's part in it: "Swift's attack on modernism ... is not the attack of the Ancient against the Modern. He is not the arch-conservative who can brook no change.... He is the gentleman and man of taste, the humanist and man of religion, the man of abundant sense who attacks whatever he considers to be a breach of his essentially moral and religious standard. Seeing in his own society tendencies which he felt would destroy the values giving dignity to man, he naturally focused his attack on his own society where it might serve some purpose--and this naturally suggested the term modern.... But essentially Swift's satire is a universal attack directed against a universal target.... To build ... a monolithic theory, such and R. F. Jones's description of the Ancients-Moderns controversy, and to expect this theory to apply to every allusion to the terms in the seventeenth and eighteenth centuries, is to ignore the facts of history."

3147   PONS, EMILE.
        Swift: Les Années de jeunesse et le "Conte du Tonneau."
        Strasbourg, France: Istra; London: Oxford Univ. Press,
        1925.

        Carries the life of Swift to his thirty-seventh year; deals with the development of Swift's character and his relationship with Sir William Temple, and defends the theory that Esther Johnson was a natural daughter of Temple. Almost half the book is devoted to an analysis and interpretation of A Tale of a Tub and The Battle of the Books.

3148   POTTER, GEORGE REUBEN.
        "Swift and Natural Science." PQ 20 (1941): 97-118.

        A look at Swift's knowledge and understanding of the sciences in an attempt to explain why his ridicule of human activities in the natural sciences in Book III of Gulliver's Travels was the least effective of all his satire in that work.

3149   PREU, JAMES.
        "Jonathan Swift and the Common Man." Fla. State Univ. Std.
        11 (1953): 19-24.

        Examines Swift's political writings to demonstrate that he possessed a firm confidence in the reasonableness of the common man.

3150   PRICE, MARTIN.
        Swift's Rhetorical Art: A Study in Structure and Meaning.

New Haven: Yale Univ. Press, 1953. Rpt. Hamden, Conn.:
Archon Books, 1963; Carbondale, Ill.: Southern Ill. Univ.
Press, 1973.

Primarily concerned with "structure in Swift's works as
it serves to create meaning--and particularly such meaning
as redirects attitudes," and with rhetoric, especially with
that aspect that deals with an author's typical designs that
facilitate the expression of meaning. The author also attempts
to define Swift's larger themes in his major works and in the
final chapter, "Patterns of Meaning: A Summary," he deals
with the work as a whole; concludes that Swift exemplifies
the "heroism of moderation," and that all of his versions of
inhumanity lead to the central metaphor--the relation of outside to inside. In the larger sense, Swift's patterns of meaning are concerned with a universal theme--how to unite the
timeless with the temporal.

3151   PROBYN, CLIVE T.
       Jonathan Swift: The Contemporary Background.   New York:
       Barnes & Noble, 1979.

       A selection of contemporary writing that illustrates the
       religious, the intellectual, the scientific, and the political
       contexts in which Swift's chief works had their origin; each
       of the seven sections has an introduction that relates Swift's
       work to the chosen passages.

3152   "Swift and the Human Predicament." In [3057], pp. 57-80.

       The influence of logic on Swift's life and thought. If we
       examine the sources of Swift's philosophical ideas, especially
       for the fourth voyage of Gulliver's Travels, we shall see that
       he transferred into literature "not only the terms but also
       some fundamental problems of contemporary epistemology."

3153   "Swift and the Physicians: Aspects of Satire and Status."
       Medical History 18 (1974): 249-261.

       Essentially a literary analysis dealing with Swift's attitude
       toward physicians.

3154   QUINLAN, MAURICE J.
       "Swift's Use of Literalization as a Rhetorical Device." PMLA
       82 (1967): 516-521.

       Examples of Swift's wordplay with the literal and metaphori-
       cal sense of terms and of his ability to make his style fit his
       thoughts.

3155   QUINTANA, RICARDO.
       Two Augustans: John Locke, Jonathan Swift. Madison: Univ.
       Wisc. Press, 1978.

       Quintana approaches Swift the writer from the point of view
       of his response to "successive situations of an intellectual--
       psychological character in which he found himself"; he con-
       siders Swift's satirical works, emphasizing in particular the
       structural irony, for instance, of the fourth voyage of Gul-
       liver's Travels: "Here Swift was drawing upon all of his
       past experience as a satiric ironist to fashion an absolutely
       unique statement concerning the human moral situation ...
       [Gulliver] errs in assuming that all Houyhnhnms are admir-
       able, and again in jumping to the conclusion that only Houyhn-
       hnms have been endowed with excellent qualitites."

3156   "A Modest Appraisal: Swift Scholarship and Criticism, 1945-
       65." In [3055], pp. 342-355.

       The survey is divided into two parts: 1) includes new edi-
       tions of Swift, bibliographical items, and the principal books
       of scholarship and criticism, and is "fairly comprehensive";
       and 2) is concerned with the more specialized essays and
       articles aimed at particular aspects of Swift and his work--a
       selective listing.

3157   Swift: An Introduction. London: Oxford Univ. Press, 1955.

       A general survey, including a chapter of condensed biog-
       raphy; after a chapter in which Swift is shown to exemplify
       four main aspects of Restoration and early eighteenth-century
       thought and literary tradition, the author devotes six chapters
       to A Tale of a Tub and Gulliver's Travels and to the major
       political and religious works done in the most important phases
       of his career.

3158   The Mind and Art of Jonathan Swift. London: Methuen; New
       York: Oxford Univ. Press, 1953. Revised from 1936 edition.

       A general study emphasizing the "intellectual intensity" of
       Swift's writing; projects Swift "against the background of his
       age to estimate the qualities of his mind and art."

3159   "Situational Satire: A Commentary on the Method of Swift."
       UTQ 17 (1948): 130-136. Rpt. in [3059], pp. 91-99; [7],
       pp. 258-265.

       Argues that Swift is not present in his work; "Swift's method
       is uniformly by way of dramatic satire. He creates a fully

realized character and a fully realized world for him to move in. " Swift's satire is an exhibited situation, and once that situation has been suggested it promply proceeds to grow and organize according to its own inherent principles.

3160   RAWSON, C. J.
        "Cannibalism and Fiction: Reflections on Narrative Form and 'Extreme' Situations. " Part I. Genre 10 (1977): 667-711.

        Deals with "fictional narrative and the way in which certain fictions present cannibal situations: with the play of sympathies and antipathies ... the ambiguities of attraction and repulsion ... its status as a supreme test of civilized man and of the validity of his moral codes, or as an image, literal or figurative or both, of vital authenticity, of physical, emotional and even political self-realization. " One of the three categories of fiction discussed called "radical satire," meaning "fundamental," or "dealing with the roots of human nature," is identified in the works of Jonathan Swift, especially Gulliver's Travels and A Modest Proposal.

3161   "The Character of Swift's Satire. " In [3058], pp. 17-75.

        For the specialist; concerned with the "radical restlessness" that Swift finds in man and with the parallels with Samuel Johnson's awareness of this "unceasing tension. "

3162   REDINGER, RUBY VIRGINIA.
        "Jonathan Swift, the Disenchanter. " American Scholar 15 (1946): 221-226.

        Deals with irony in Swift's writings, especially his attack on man's pride.

3163   ROGERS, KATHARINE M.
        " 'My Female Friends': The Misogyny of Jonathan Swift. " TSLL 1 (1959): 366-379.

        Surveys Swift's attitudes toward women, sex, and the excretory functions, placed in an historic context: his "degradation of the romantic ideal, disparagement of motherhood, and nauseating descriptions of the female body and sexual relations" suggests a "deep, unconscious revulsion against Woman as Animal. "

3164   ROGERS, PAT.
        "Swift and the Idea of Authority. " In [3060], pp. 25-37.

First, discusses Swift as defender of authority "in church
and state, in questions of style and linguistic usage, within
the commonwealth of writers, in the sphere of personal ethics,
in the regulation of domestic management, in learning and intellectual inquiry"; second, argues that Swift as satirist does
not offer us an ideal alternative of human behavior; that he
seems to prefer a profession of goodness, however hypocritical, to outright evil; and that he so often does not make his
own position clear that he compromises himself in order to
destroy his victim the more effectually.

3165   ROSENHEIM, EDWARD W. , JR.
        "Swift and the Atterbury Case." In [42], pp. 174-204.

Examines the main facts surrounding the prosecution of
Atterbury, in order to eliminate possible misconceptions, and
suggests that "the Bishop's prosecution and punishment are
reflected both more closely and more extensively in Gulliver's
Travels than has generally been recognized."

3166   Swift and the Satirist's Art.   Chicago: Univ. Chicago Press,
        1963.

Attempts to clarify the nature of Swift's achievement as a
satirist; has one chapter on the nature of satire in general,
followed by three in which close "analyses" are applied to
"The Argument Against Abolishing Christianity," "A Modest
Proposal," A Tale of a Tub, and Gulliver's Travels.

3167   ROSS, ANGUS.
        "The Hibernian Patriot's Apprenticeship." In [3057], pp. 83-
        107.

The author considers "some speculations on the possible
influence on a few prose texts written by Swift before 1714,
of his Irish birth, upbringing and connections," and concludes
that his Anglo-Irish heritage may be related to his theory of
style and his adventurous artistic practice.

3168   ROSS, JOHN F.
        Swift and Defoe: A Study in Relationship (Univ. Calif. Publi-
        cations in English, Vol. 11).   Berkeley & Los Angeles: Univ.
        Calif. Press, 1941.

The author's purpose is to "establish the more important
phases of the relationship of the two writers, and to attempt
to point out the chief significance of these phases in literary,
social, and human terms"; concludes that the attitudes of Swift

and Defoe toward each other are not mainly personal in nature but are influenced by the opposition of the two social groups to which they belong.

3169   SAMS, HENRY W.
        "An End to Writing About Swift." EIC 24 (1974): 275-285.

        A discussion of Swiftian scholarship and a consideration of why scholars are still frantically pursuing the study of Swift.

3170   "Swift's Satire of the Second Person." ELH 26 (1959): 36-44.

        Uses two examples of Swift's satire, Gulliver's behavior after his return to England at the end of the fourth Voyage and the "Digression on Madness" in A Tale of a Tub to illustrate his method of violating the alliance between author and reader. The "manner in which Swift circumvents the rhetorical alliance" is called by Sams the "satire of the second person."

3171   SCOTT-THOMAS, LOIS M.
        "The Vocabulary of Jonathan Swift." DR 25 (1946): 442-447.

        A discussion of Swift's objections to new, slang, and foreign words and his practice of unconsciously using words in a new sense and inventing or borrowing new words.

3172   SCRUGGS, CHARLES.
        " 'Sweetness and Light': The Basis of Swift's Views on Art and Criticism." TSL 18 (1973): 93-104.

        Uses the bee-spider episode to infer Swift's aesthetic principles; argues that he belongs to the tradition of Renaissance-Augustan humanism which believes that the purpose of all human learning is virtuous action. Art, represented by the bee, promotes such action because it delights as it instructs.

3173   "Swift's Views on Language: The Basis of His Attack on Poetic Diction." TSLL 13 (1972): 581-592.

        Summarizes Swift's views on language, emphasizing that he associated an incorrect use of words with a breach of moral conduct and that his desire to regulate the language did not mean he wanted it to stagnate: he only wished to expunge words that were dead when new, and he was willing to admit worthwhile words to the language. Discusses Cassinus and Peter, On Poetry: A Rapsody, The Progress of Beauty, The Lady's Dressing Room, and Phillis, or The Progress of Love.

3174   SELBY, HOPEWELL R.
        "The Cell and the Garret: Fictions of Confinement in Swift's
        Satires and Personal Writings." In [50], pp. 133-156.

        This study explores the relationship between the reader
        and Swift's satiric speakers "as it appears in [his] protean
        prisons" in an attempt to "clarify the relation between Swift's
        images of himself in the personal writings and their antitypes
        in the satires." Considers the behavior that occurs in Swift's
        "fictive prisons," explores some of the epistemological con-
        cerns, and examines "some ways in which their physical un-
        pleasantness offers both punishment and potential cure for
        the mind's omnivorous tendency to recreate the world in its
        image."

3175   SENA, JOHN F.
        "Swift as Moral Physician: Scatology and the Tradition of
        Love Melancholy." JEGP 76 (1977): 346-362.

        Critics have tended to relate Swift's scatological poems to
        a literary tradition of scatology and satires against women,
        whereas a non-literary tradition may also have been a de-
        cisive influence: "Medical works written to cure young men
        of love melancholy ... employ imagery, strategies, and an
        intensity of tone strikingly similar to Swift's. By placing
        "The Lady's Dressing-Room' and 'A Beautiful Young Nymph
        in the context of a medical tradition which began with Ovid
        and extended through the eighteenth century ... we may bet-
        ter understand those elements of the two poems ... which
        have offended so many readers, as well as the manner in
        which a great artist alters a tradition."

3176   SHEEHAN, DAVID.
        "Swift on High Pindaric Stilts." In [3052], pp. 25-35.

        An interpretation of Swift's early pindaric odes in the con-
        text of other seventeenth-century pindarics: argues specif-
        ically that "what some critics have seen as a struggle be-
        tween Swift's personal satiric awareness and the panegyrical
        intention of the pindaric form is in fact not such a struggle,
        but rather Swift's contribution to a development in the seven-
        teenth century that saw the pindaric turned to satiric as well
        as panegyric ends."

3177   "Swift, Voiture, and the Spectrum of Raillery." PLL 14
        (1978): 171-188.

        A study of Swift's complicated mode of raillery, especially
        in the poems to Stella; in those poems, Swift employs a sharp
        raillery in playing a social verse game. In the poems which
        "approach the fine line separating sharp from delicate raillery,

precariously balancing praise and blame," Swift illustrates an extraordinary control of language and tone. The writings of Vincent Voiture had a greater influence on Swift, and Voiture himself was a more accomplished railleur, than critics have commonly supposed. In the poems to Stella, Swift controls the whole spectrum of raillery, paralleled in the works of "his model," Voiture, which allowed him to express his awareness of the invariable mixture of frailties and virtues even in so perfect a person as Stella.

3178   SHERBURN, GEORGE.
       "Methods in Books About Swift." SP 35 (1938): 635-656.

       Analytical observations on books which have been written about Swift; urges more careful readings and interpretations.

3179   SIEBERT, DONALD T., JR.
       "Masks and Masquerades: The Animus of Swift's Satire." SAQ 74 (1975): 435-445.

       Deals with the argument as to whether Swift's writings do or do not have a persona and attempts to answer the question, Does the concept of persona do more to help or more to hinder our understanding of Swift the satirist? Concludes that Swift and his mask fuse together, and that to a large extent Swift is playing games with his readers; but he is not detached from the passions that the game generates: " ... disguise does not function to isolate or absolve the masker from responsibility as a moral agent, or to purify his intentions. ... "

3180   SMITH, FREDERIK N.
       "Swift's Correspondence: The 'Dramatic' Style and the Assumption of Roles." SEL 14 (1974): 357-371.

       Suggests that an analysis of Swift's prose style in his private correspondence will give us a "better understanding of his satiric techniques, and, ultimately, his meaning." Discusses Swift's syntactic elements.

3181   SMITH, ROLAND M.
       "Swift's Little Language and Nonsense Names." JEGP 53 (1954): 178-196. See also JEGP 56 (1957): 154-162.

       Considers Irish words in Lhuyd's Dictionary as a possible source for some of Swift's words in Gulliver's Travels.

3182   SODERLIND, JOHANNES.
       "Swift and Linguistics." ES 51 (1970): 137-143.

Brief discussion of Swift's "prescriptive" and "creative"
linguistics.

3183   SOUTHALL, RAYMOND.
        Literature, the Individual and Society: Critical Essays on
        the Eighteenth and Nineteenth Centuries.   London: Laurence
        & Wishart, 1977.

        Assuming that one effect of the rise of capitalism was the
        increasing importance of the individual and the consequent de-
        velopment of a sense of isolation and of conflict with society,
        Southall attempts "to explore the literary consequences in
        Swift and Smollett of the isolation of the individual" and to
        "consider the connection between the isolation of the individual
        and the conditions of life in town and country as those were
        envisioned in literature--in Gray, Goldsmith and Crabbe--and
        being transformed by the social movements of the times...."

3184   SPECK, W. A.
        Swift (Literature in Perspective).   London: Evans, 1969;
        New York: Arco Literary Critiques, 1970.

        A popular account of Swift, with chapters on the poetry
        (by Philip Roberts), A Tale of a Tub, and Gulliver's Travels.

3185   SPILLER, MICHAEL R. G.
        "The Idol of the Stove: The Background to Swift's Criticism
        of Descartes." RES 25 (1974): 15-24.

        Swift sees Descartes as an exemplar of the modern intel-
        lectual movement, finding him "mad, fanatical, and intro-
        verted"; Swift's views are influenced by those of critics liv-
        ing in the latter half of the 17th century, one such critic be-
        ing Meric Casaubon: the similarity of Casaubon's views to
        Swift's suggests that Casaubon represented an attitude wide-
        spread enough to be picked up by Swift in the last quarter of
        the century.

3186   STARKMAN, MIRIAM K.
        "Swift's Rhetoric: The 'overfraught pinnace.' " SAQ 68
        (1969): 188-197.

        Argues against attempts to turn Swift into a rhetorician
        but rather that he should be studied "as a satirist, a power-
        ful moral force, prolific in the satiric mode, and without
        rival in the genre of prose satire."

3187   STEELE, PETER.

<u>Jonathan Swift: Preacher and Jester.</u> Oxford: Clarendon
Press, 1978.

An attempt to suggest how different impulses are "fused
or counterposed" in Swift's work. Swift is, "famously, a
preacher in various causes, and in various spirits: but he
is, as crucially, a jester, and that over as wide an array
of events and moods. This study will undertake to show some
of the ways in which this impulse comes to realization, and
some of those in which it engages with the magisterial instinct in Swift." This book analyzes a number of dominant
motifs in Swift's writings, and sees how they are exemplified
in various contexts.

3188   STRANG, BARBARA.
       "Swift and the English Language: A Study in Principles and
       Practice." In <u>To Honor Roman Jakobson: Essays on the Oc-</u>
       <u>casion of His Seventieth Birthday, 11 October 1966</u> (Janua
       Linguarum, Ser. Maior 31). The Hague: Mouton, 1967,
       Vol. III, 1947-1959.

       A study of Swift's views on language, both his argument
       and practice; emphasizes that "Swift was facing a situation
       new in certain ways, that he faced it in, to say the least,
       a highly conservative manner, and that we must be very cau-
       tious of assuming that what he wrote was written <u>in propria</u>
       <u>persona.</u>"

3189   SUTHERLAND, JAMES.
       "Form and Methods in Swift's Satire." In [3056], pp. 61-77.

       Discusses various satirical methods used by Swift and rep-
       resentative works illustrating them: direct denunciation (sel-
       dom used), the process of diminution, detached and impersonal
       irony (<u>Short Character of ... Thomas, Earl of Wharton</u>), par-
       ody (the <u>Bickerstaff papers</u>), travesty and ridicule (<u>The Battle</u>
       <u>of the Books</u>).

3190   TIMPE, EUGENE F.
       "Swift as Railleur." <u>JEGP</u> 69 (1970): 41-49.

       Discusses how "this delicate irony by which seeming crit-
       icism turned to graceful praise, developed and flourished,
       once he had learned it from Voiture, under Swift's hand; in
       prose and verse, in public and private, in court and deanery,
       it served the master ironist when he chose to flatter with
       grace and criticize with impunity."

3191   TRAUGOTT, JOHN L.
       "The Professor as Nibelung." <u>ECS</u> 3 (1970): 532-541.

A criticism of modern literary critics who try to interpret such writers as Swift without imagining his artistic conception or reimagining the history he lived; suggests: "We do not seek to escape our own society and transport ourselves back to a past age ... but we criticize past thoughts by re-enacting them in ... our modern minds." Comments on why Swift's ideas do not appeal to today's students.

3192   "Swift, Our Contemporary." Univ. Rev. (Dublin) 4 (1967): 11-34. Rpt. in [3058], pp. 239-264.

Refutes Orwell's and Yeats's description of Swift as a fascist, and insists that he had no sympathy with Yeats's mystical nationalism; suggests further that Swift found a significant relation between individual psychology and history.

3193   TROWBRIDGE, HOYT.
"Swift and Socrates." In [178], pp. 81-123.

The allusions to Socrates and Plato suggest Swift's intellectual convictions on several subjects and help to elucidate particular works and passages whose meaning has often been disputed. They especially reveal his attitude toward the freethinker; his position on the place of reason in religion and morality; and the interpretation of Gulliver's Fourth Voyage.

3194   TYNE, JAMES L. , S. J.
" 'Only a Man of Rhimes': Swift's Bridled Pegasus." PLL 14 (1978): 189-204.

Swift all his life advocated literary correctness and opposed all instances of linguistic barbarism. In order to prevent any decline in literary standards even among poets themselves, Swift affirmed that poetry is little more than a matter of "Sense and Rhyme" by composing verses that illustrated his own definition of a good style as "proper words in proper places." Swift continually sought to endow his verse with the virtues of prose and regarded poetry as essentially an art or craft, though "sense" and the clarity and correctness of language are always of paramount importance.

3195   ULMAN, CRAIG H.
Satire and the Correspondence of Swift. Cambridge: Harvard Univ. Press, 1973.

Argues that a great many of Swift's letters resemble the prose satires, and that these "satirical" letters reveal much "about Swift's attitude toward letter-writing, about his relations with Pope, and about his stance as a satirist." Con-

cludes that the letters are not unstudied and unpolished, and
that many of them are calculated literary efforts.

3196   UPHAUS, ROBERT W.
       "Swift's Irony Reconsidered." In [3052], pp. 169-177.

       Using as his point of departure Leavis's suggestion [3127] that
       Swift's irony often lacks a positive model for the reader to
       hold on to, the author argues that "Swift's biographical pres-
       ence in his later poems replaced, even if it does not mediate,
       the ironic contrasts of his earlier prose works," and that the
       missing "positive" of which Leavis speaks performs in the
       poetry a personal rather than a thematic function; i. e., we
       are continually presented with Swift's personal convictions
       which we can accept or reject but which we cannot ignore.
       That "biographical presence," therefore, works against any
       New Criticism kind of critical approach to the poems.

3197   VICKERS, BRIAN.
       "Swift and the Baconian Idol." In [3060], pp. 87-128.

       Argues that Bacon, the "father-figure behind much
       seventeenth-century thought," represented many of the things
       Swift detested and that Swift expressed his scorn by mocking
       Bacon's opinions, attitudes, and style.

3198   VOIGHT, MILTON.
       Swift and the Twentieth Century.   Detroit, Mich.: Wayne
       State Univ. Press, 1964.

       Examines the major developments in the critical, biographi
       cal, and textual study of Swift; Chapter 1 presents the pre-
       vailing nineteenth-century images of Swift and his work and
       succeeding chapters analyze the most significant aspects of
       Swift studies--textual criticism, A Tale of a Tub, Gulliver's
       Travels, and Swift the man.

3199   WARD, DAVID.
       Jonathan Swift: an Introductory Essay.   London: Methuen,
       1973.

       Deals mainly with the satires and the verse; presents some
       background information, but seeks to avoid immersing the
       reader too deeply in a mass of historical facts--no attempt
       is made to provide detailed accounts of the topical issues to
       which Swift refers.   The biographical puzzles of Swift's life
       are also largely ignored.   The author considers the nature
       of satirical discourse, Swift's satirical idiom, and the rela-
       tion between satire and fantasy.

3200   WATKINS, W. B. C.
       "Absent Thee from Felicity." <u>Southern Rev.</u> 5 (1939): 346-
       365. In [182], pp. 1-24.

       Considers the resemblance between Swift and Shakespeare
       and how the line from Hamlet, "Absent thee from felicity
       awhile," may be called the essential purpose of all Swift's
       satire.

3201   "Vive La Bagatelle." In [182], pp. 25-48.

       An attempt to analyze Johnson's dislike of Swift, and a
       comparison of the two men.

3202   WATT, IAN.
       "The Ironic Tradition in Augustan Prose from Swift to John-
       son." In <u>Restoration and Augustan Prose.   Papers delivered
       by James R. Sutherland and Ian Watt at the Third Clark Li-
       brary Seminar, 14 July 1956</u> (William Andrews Clark Memor-
       ial Library, Univ. Calif. , Los Angeles, 1956), pp. 19-46.
       Rpt. in [43], pp. 161-188; [3058], pp. 216-238.

       Discusses essentials of irony dealing primarily with Swift
       as the originator of the ironic tradition in the eighteenth cen-
       tury and with Johnson whose position in the tradition of irony
       is opposite to that of Swift's.

3203   WEBSTER, CLARENCE M.
       "Swift and Some Earlier Satirists of Puritan Enthusiasm."
       <u>PMLA</u> 48 (1933): 1141-1153.

       Attempts to show "that many of the observations on enthu-
       siasm and zeal which are found in A Tale of a Tub and the
       Discourse on the Mechanical Operation of the Spirit were not
       new or original ... that Swift knew the principal satirists
       mentioned, ... and that [his] remarks on enthusiasm would
       have been understood by those Englishmen of the early eigh-
       teenth century who were thoroughly conversant with the earl-
       ier satires of enthusiasts. "

3204   WEST, PAUL.
       "Swift and Dry Religion." <u>Queen's Quarterly</u> 70 (1963): 431-
       440.

       Deals with Swift's attempt to reconcile religion with social
       discipline, to reconcile reason with orthodox Christianity.

3205   WILLIAMS, HAROLD.
       "Swift's Early Biographers." In [17], pp. 114-128.

Eighteenth-century biographers of Swift, with emphasis on
Johnson's "Life of Swift"; Swift fares better than the other
Augustan writers, being served by no less than five works
written by people who had known him in person: Mrs. Laeti-
tia Pilkington, Lord Orrery, Dr. Patrick Delany, Deane Swift,
and Thomas Sheridan.   Evaluations of these and other biographers are provided.

3206   WILLIAMS, KATHLEEN.
"Restoration Themes in the Major Satires of Swift." RES 16
(1965): 258-271.

Swift's ideas in The Battle of the Books, A Tale of a Tub,
and to some extent Gulliver's Travels are much easier understood in relation to problems concerning men during the Restoration than during the eighteenth century.

3207   Jonathan Swift and the Age of Compromise.   Lawrence: Univ.
Kansas Press, 1958.

Argues that Swift did not reject emotion in favor of any
rigid form of rational discipline but tried to maintain a compromise between Shaftesbury's emotionalism and the complete
condemnation of the passions represented by Mandeville; he
sought a via media between the extremes of accepting the total
corruption of human nature and the optimistic faith in man's
goodness and perfectibility.

3208   " 'Animal Rationis Capax': A Study of Certain Aspects of
Swift's Imagery." ELH 21 (1954): 193-207.   Rpt. in [3055],
pp. 131-145.

Swift's use of allegory and physical imagery to "sum up
his theme of the intermingling of man's intellectual powers
and spiritual aspirations with his senses and passions, and
... [to] suggest that though reason must be pre-eminent the
search for eternal and rational truth must not involve too
radical a weeding-out of the other parts of man's nature."

3209   WOLPER, ROY S.
"Swift's Enlightened Gulls." SVEC 58 (1967): 1915-1937.

Concerned with Swift's attack on rationalism, the archen-
emy being the natural scientist.

3210   YEATS, W. B.
The "Introduction" to Words Upon the Window-Pane.   Dublin:
Cuala Press, 1934.   Rpt. in [3055], pp. 186-199.

A great poet's personal appreciation of Swift.

See also: 659, 941, 967, 973, 1839, 1856, 1924, 1952, 2022, 2292, 2869, 3009

A Tale of a Tub
and
The Battle of the Books

3211   ADAMS, ROBERT M.
        "The Mood of the Church and A Tale of a Tub." In [55],
        pp. 71-99.

   Looks at the Tale as the work of a bitter young man who
had "attached himself to a hierarchy and to a set of values
... just as they were undergoing ferocious attack from outside, severe questioning from inside ..." giving him reason
"to doubt that there was going to be an eighteenth-century
establishment...." Relates "some extraordinary features of
the Tale to some extraordinary features of an extraordinary
historical era."

3212   "Jonathan Swift, Thomas Swift, and the Authorship of A Tale
        of a Tub." MP 64 (1967): 198-232.

   Reopens argument that parts of the Tale were written by
Swift's cousin, Thomas, and presents evidence to this effect.

3213   ANDREASEN, N. J. C.
        "Swift's Satire on the Occult in A Tale of a Tub." TSLL 5
        (1963): 410-421.

   Describes the philosophical aspects of occultism behind the
Tale, the influence of Thomas Vaughan and Henry More, and
the relationship between occultism and the central theme of
madness.

3214   ANSELMENT, RAYMOND A.
        "A Tale of a Tub." In "Betwixt Jest and Earnest": Marpre-
        late, Milton, Marvell, Swift & the Decorum of Religious Ridi-
        cule. Toronto: Univ. Toronto Press, 1979, pp. 126-162.

   A Tale of a Tub is concerned with the problem of church
polity, and especially with Swift's defense of late-seventeenth-
century Anglicanism. Specifically, the general attitudes of
the age toward religious ridicule provide a perspective from
which to view Swift as a religious satirist. Concludes that

"Swift dramatizes the precept that the satirist's manner does indeed determine the decorous use of religious ridicule"; that Swift sees, in the controversy over questions of church polity, much larger issues of human conduct central to the tradition of humanism; and that, by extending the literal decorum that governs earlier satirists' "preoccupation with the manner he gives further dimension to the principle of decorum personae and the emphasis on characterization."

3215   "A Tale of a Tub: Swift and the 'Men of Tast.'" HLQ 37 (1974): 265-282.

Swift's indebtedness to Andrew Marvell: "the question of taste implicit in his appreciation for Andrew Marvell is also central to the vision of A Tale of a Tub."

3216   BEAM, MARJORIE.
" 'The Reach and Wit of the Inventor': Swift's Tale of a Tub and Hamlet." UTQ 46 (1976): 1-13.

Both Swift's tale-teller and Hamlet reject literary convention out of spiritual pride and insist on the uniqueness of their own experience; they both emphasize their mastery of the forms and conventions even as they turn them inside out. But to abandon traditional form means abandoning the attempt to achieve order out of chaos, it means entering a world of intellectual relativism; the tale-teller, therefore, becomes what he deplores, and falls into the trap of the cabbalistic commentators whom he has attacked: "his tale, given its head, runs away with him; its digressions swallow him up; his own metaphors turn on him."

3217   BORKAT, ROBERTA F. SARFATT.
"The Spider and the Bee: Jonathan Swift's Reversal of Tradition in The Battle of the Books." ECLife 3 (1976): 44-46.

A discussion of how Swift reverses tradition in the use of insect imagery making The Battle of the Books "a unique work of literature in the Quarrel of the Ancients and the Moderns." In his fable of the spider and the bee, "Swift's implicit attack upon the 'Moderns' is greatly strengthened by his reversal of the traditional imagery." By turning the "Modern's" (the spider) own insect metaphors against them, Swift contrives that their accusations against the "Ancients" (the bee) return to strike them down.

3218   CALDERWOOD, JAMES L.
"Structural Parody in Swift's Fragment." MLQ 23 (1962): 243-253.

Minimizes the notion that Swift repudiated the Fragment--
"the repudiations are part of Swift's mask; they are intrinsic
to his technique, are more properly extensions than additions,
and are perfectly consistent with the persona Swift assumes
in the body of the work."

3219   CARNOCHAN, W. B.
"Notes on Swift's Proverb Lore." YES 6 (1976): 63-69.

Swift respected proverbs as a dying form and sought to
revivify them by collecting examples for perhaps thirty-six
years: "Looking at the Tale and The Battle of the Books ...
we discover still richer proverb lore than we had supposed."
Discusses the proverbial basis of the spider and the bee episode.

3220   "Swift's Tale: On Satire, Negation, and the Uses of Irony."
ECS 5 (1971): 122-144.

Discusses some of the satiric effects of the Tale; defines
satire and the link between satire and irony and concludes
that irony is the "indirection that converts criticism to satire
... that irony, Swift's especially, is the satirist's rhetorical
victory in the presence of self-defeat."

3221   CHIASSON, ELIAS J.
"Swift's Clothes Philosophy in the Tale and Hooker's Concept
of Law." SP 59 (1962): 64-82.

Purpose of article is "to show that, while Swift is in the
general tradition of Hooker, attention should be directed to
the close, if ironic, affinities between the philosophy of clothes,
which is central to Swift's religious allegory, and the concept
of law formulated in Hooker's Laws of Ecclesiastical Polity."

3222   CLARK, JOHN R.
Form and Frenzy in Swift's "Tale of a Tub." Ithaca, N. Y.:
Cornell Univ. Press, 1970.

The purpose of this study is "to explore A Tale of a Tub
as a work of mimetic art. Since mimetic masterpieces display a 'pattern' or 'rhythm' of action, a continuity of plot to
which characters, episodes, thought, diction, and scenes are
subservient ... we may expect ... to discover in Swift's Tale
of a Tub such a rhythm or plot, or its absence." Seeks to
determine whether the satire is a work of art, whether it is
mimetic, and whether it has a predominant single action.

3223   "Swift's Knaves and Fools in the Tradition: Rhetoric Versus
       Poetic in A Tale of A Tub, Sec. IX." SP 66 (1969): 777-
       796.

              Examines Sec. IX aesthetically and argues that Swift is
       not committed to the defense of credulity and to the tactics
       of rhetoric but that, as an artist, he "stands well aloof from
       the actions of the drama ... "; that "he has created and
       shaped the Modern persona as well as the contest between
       credulity and curiosity, like little tubs, and has embarked
       them upon their own sea of dramatic action."

3224   CLIFFORD, JAMES L.
       "Swift's 'Mechanical Operation of the Spirit.'" In [17], pp.
       135-146.

              An attempt to evaluate the "reactions of contemporary read-
       ers to the piece, and to make tentative suggestions concerning
       Swift's reasons for placing it at the end" of the 1704 edition
       of A Tale of a Tub.

3225   CRIDER, J. R.
       "Dissenting Sex: Swift's 'History of Fanaticism.'" SEL 18
       (1978): 491-508.

              An attempt to elucidate the recondite allusions in "History
       of Fanaticism," the climax of Mechanical Operation of the
       Spirit; presents the history of fanaticism as background, rang-
       ing from Eutychianism, Docetism, Gnostic dualism and liber-
       tinism to the fanatics of Reformation Germany, John of Ley-
       den, David George or Joris, and Adam Neuster, and conclud-
       ing with the nonconformists of seventeenth-century England.
       Concludes that Irenaeus was a major influence on Swift and
       that he admired particularly Irenaeus's support of a rational
       via media in religion.

3226   DAVIS, HERBERT.
       "Literary Satire--the Author of A Tale of a Tub." In [3085],
       pp. 9-43. Rpt. in [3083], pp. 106-125; in [3054], pp. 143-
       161, as "Literary Satire in A Tale of a Tub."

              Looks at Swift's preparedness to write the Tale and how
       he gathered so much of the spirit of the seventeenth century
       into it as part of the true line of wit. Shows that it is par-
       adoxical because it " ... is a product of the seventeenth cen-
       tury, entirely characteristic in form and manner, and at the
       same time a repudiation and criticism of all the most vigor-
       ous literary fashions of the previous sixty years."

3227   DePORTE, MICHAEL V.

Nightmares and Hobbyhorses: Swift, Sterne, and Augustan
Ideas of Madness.   San Marino, Calif.: Huntington, 1974.

A study of the theories of mental disorder and of the criteria for sanity established by philosophers and physicians in
the eighteenth century; compares Swift and Sterne in order to
suggest the changes in concepts of the mind that occurred dur-
ring the century and to show how their works can be illumin-
ated by a knowledge of eighteenth-century psychology.

3228   "Digressions and Madness in A Tale of a Tub and Tristram
Shandy."   HLQ 34 (1970):   43-57.

Compares the sinister overtones of madness in A Tale of
a Tub with the benign insanity of the Shandys.

3229   ELLIOTT, ROBERT C.
"Swift and Dr. Eachard."   PMLA 69 (1954):   1250-1257.

Traces similarities in tone and style between A Tale of a
Tub and writings by John Eachard.

3230   "Swift's Tale of a Tub: An Essay in Problems of Structure."
PMLA 66 (1951):   441-455.

Discusses the importance of the "point of view of the ingénu" as a structural principle which controls A Tale of a
Tub from beginning to end.

3231   FISHER, ALAN S.
"An End to the Renaissance: Erasmus, Hobbes, and A Tale
of a Tub."   HLQ 38 (1974):   1-20.

Attempts to define the quality of pleasure we derive from
A Tale of a Tub, and discusses the source of that pleasure--
the "false wit" of analogy-making; emphasizes the importance
for Swift of playful ingenuity and intellectual wit, and argues
that the "Tale is ... primarily a response, not an argument--
something Swift wants to say about the passing of ... the
Renaissance."

3232   FRENCH, DAVID P.
"Swift, Temple, and 'A Digression on Madness.' "   TSLL 5
(1963):   42-57.

Argues that Swift "combined with his fervent moral ardor
a strain of intellectual skepticism which at times contradicted
his humanistic leanings," and suggests that his aesthetic technique, when combined with his intellectual beliefs, brings about

a coalescence of form and content. "A Digression on Madness" contains elements of philosophical skepticism and political or religious conservatism.

3233 HARTH, PHILLIP.
Swift and Anglican Rationalism: The Religious Background of "A Tale of a Tub." Chicago: Univ. Chicago Press, 1961.

Analyzes the complex of ideas, assumptions, and attitudes that underlie the religious satire of A Tale of a Tub; seeks to show the probable sources of those materials in the immediate background of the satire and suggests the new and original uses to which Swift put them. Ignores the non-religious satire.

3234 HOPKINS, ROBERT H.
"The Personation of Hobbism in Swift's Tale of a Tub and Mechanical Operation of the Spirit." PQ 45 (1966): 372-378.

Examines A Tale and A Fragment for satiric allusions to Leviathan and suggests that Swift may have been satirizing Charles Blount.

3235 HUGHES, R. E.
"The Five Fools in A Tale of a Tub." L & P 11 (1961): 20-22.

Talks about the Socrates fool, the natural fool, the lunatic or monomaniac fool, the dangerous fool, and finally Swift himself as fool.

3236 JOHNSON, MAURICE.
"A Note on Swift's Meditation upon a Broomstick and A Tale of a Tub." Library Chronicle (Univ. Pa.) 37 (1971): 136-142.

Swift's "amusing little parody" of Robert Boyle displays a number of similarities in style and subject matter to A Tale of a Tub: "Both deal with the themes of Art-versus-Nature and of Rational-versus-Animal-Faculties" and both use sexual allusions for satirical purposes.

3237 JONES, RICHARD F.
Ancients and Moderns: A Study of the Background of the "Battle of the Books." St. Louis: Washington Univ. Studies in Lang. & Lit., n.s. 6, 1936. 2nd. ed., with minor revisions, 1961: Ancients and Moderns: A Study of the Rise of the Scientific Movement in Seventeenth-Century England (Rpt. Berkeley & Los Angeles: Univ. Calif. Press, 1965).

Concerned primarily with the controversy between the supporters of antiquity and those of modernity in the seventeenth century, but including material on the scientific movement generally. Interested more in what scientists say than in what they do, in their feelings and attitudes toward discoveries than in the discoveries themselves; and argues that Bacon was the leader of the movement, expressing and molding his age.

3238   KALLICH, MARTIN.
"Swift and the Archetypes of Hate: A Tale of a Tub." Studies in 18th Cent. Culture 4 (1975): 43-67.

Argues that Swift used typological discourse and several archetypal symbols and images to communicate meaning: e.g., he used archetypes of madness and sexual depravity, including the basic archetype, the image of clothes that conceal the real essence underneath: "of the two psychological themes in the Tale, madness, the result of a delusion that the outside is preferable to what lies beneath ... may be considered the central archetypal experience of the satire."

3239   KELLING, HAROLD D.
"Reason in Madness: A Tale of a Tub." PMLA 69 (1954): 198-222.

Argues against critics of the Tale and presents evidence to support theory that it is "perhaps the most skillful and important piece of rhetorical criticism in the English language." Suggests that the Tale is "an oration against [delusive] rhetoric and at the same time an example of good rhetoric" and that Swift's appeal to reason is hidden deep beneath the madness and is worth looking for.

3240   KINAHAN, FRANK.
"The Melancholy of Anatomy: Voice and Theme in A Tale of a Tub." JEGP 69 (1970): 278-291.

Argues that it is impossible to reduce the number of voices to any set number--the several voices do not exist in isolation: "The voices bounce off each other and back, and their interaction produces an echo which is a voice in its own right." The themes also shade off into each other; the themes constitute an indictment of the age, the most significant of which refers to the charge of solipsism.

3241   KOON, WILLIAM.
"Swift on Language: An Approach to A Tale of a Tub." Style 10 (1976): 28-40.

Cites examples of Swift's comments on language in his
other works to show that "the Tale's corrupt language [which]
marks corrupt religion and learning as well as the fallen nature of man" is a satire on corrupt language that is similar
to his other remarks on purifying the English tongue.   He
achieves this satire by using "a modern author who, in telling the story of the brothers, demonstrates his misunderstanding of language"; the modern author in abusing secular language as the brothers abuse Scripture demonstrates the connection of corrupt English to a lack of willingness to understand Divine Law, and to the pride that corrupts learning,
religion, and man in general.

3242   KOPPENFELS, WERNER V[on].
       "Swift's Tale of a Tub und die Tradition satirischer Meta-
       phorik. " DVLG 51 (1977):   27-54.

       Suggests that it is the imagery of aeolism and sartorism
       that gives unity to the Tale.

3243   KORKOWSKI, EUGENE BUD.
       "Swift's Tub: Traditional Emblem and Proverbial Enigma. "
       ECLife 4 (1978):   100-103.

       Looks at the various symbolisms of the tub and Swift's
       awareness of them.   The Puritan pulpit in Sections I and VIII
       is the only literal tub in the Tale; all the "other tubs are
       introduced figuratively, by way of analogy, metaphor, or in-
       cidental allusion, and these ... are heavily endowed with pro-
       verbial and traditional meanings, involving metonymy, allegory,
       iconography, and other figures beyond literalism. " Swift's
       play with the tub and its meanings is one of his "most in-
       trepid uses of the emblematic past. "

3244   "With an Eye to the Bunghole: Figures of Containment in
       A Tale of a Tub. " SEL 15 (1975):   391-408.

       Suggests that Swift's tub stands for all containment and
       that there is nothing the modern curioso will not pry into,
       trying to find the realness, the insides, the outsides, the es-
       sence, and the truth of things.   Argues that the tub "bears
       a very animated metaphorical relation to both curiosity and
       epistemology ... " and concludes that "nothing has been 'found
       out' except a very indirect lesson in ethics.   The figures of
       containment ... work to satirize unaided reason: the hack's
       brazen quest for physical (and metaphysical) certainty only
       serves the interest of the fideist Swift. "

3245   KORSHIN, PAUL J.

"Swift and Typological Narrative in A Tale of a Tub." Harvard English Studies 1 (1970): 67-91. Rpt. with alterations in [9], pp. 279-302.

Mainly concerned with Swift's use of biblical typology for satiric purposes, especially in Section VII which is seen as more than a rhetorically able attack on contemporary learning and scholarship; argues that it is central to the satiric purposes of the Tale and is closely involved with seventeenth-century religious and exegetical matters. Swift's devious misapplications of typological method are related to the undercurrents of Puritan dissent.

3246 LEVINE, JAY ARNOLD.
"The Design of A Tale of a Tub (with a Digression on a Mad Modern Critic)." ELH 33 (1966): 198-227.

A simple approach to the overall design (purpose and pattern) based on the "testimony of some of Swift's early readers" and "a willingness to grant that the Tale might be about what it says it is about." Attempts to "propose solutions to such fundamental problems as the relationship between the allegory and the digressions, the 'identity' of the author, and the 'occasion' or aim of the work."

3247 LINDERMAN, DEBORAH.
"Self-Transforming Ironies in Swift's Tale of a Tub." CLS 16 (1979): 69-78.

Focuses on Section VIII, the "Digression on Madness," and on "The Mechanical Operation of the Spirit" to show that "Swift bypasses moral prescriptions in his 'satire' because his writing does not always conform to the conventions of that genre, but to its own linguistic developments; and that his project is not so much to construct an ironic code, which can be naturalized to a straightforward one, as it is simply to grant the fullest possible scope to a play of formal and semantic ambiguities in his discourse."

3248 MARESCA, THOMAS E.
"Language and Body in Augustan Poetic." ELH 37 (1970): 374-388.

Argues that various ideas about language and body, as exemplified in MacFlecknoe, Absalom and Achitophel, The Rape of the Lock, A Tale of a Tub, and Tristram Shandy, were influenced by the premises and implications of the corpuscular theory, and that "Augustan poetic demands a poetry that weds word and body, thought and thing, in small as the Incarnation did in large."

3249   MECHANIC, LESLIE.
        "Food Imagery and Gluttony in A Tale of a Tub." ECLife
        5, iv (1979): 14-28.

            Food and medical imagery play an important role in Swift's
        writings, especially in the Tale of a Tub where he uses the
        sin of gluttony most effectively to satirize the corruptions in
        religion and learning.

3250   OLSON, R. C.
        "Swift's Use of the Philosophical Transactions in Section V
        of A Tale of a Tub." SP 49 (1952): 459-467.

            Presents evidence to show that Swift used material from
        the Philosophical Transactions for his ironic list of modern
        achievements of which Homer was ignorant: he certainly got
        material from reviews in the Transactions for Homer's "Dis-
        sertation upon Tea" and his "Method of Salivation without
        Mercury," and probably also material for an "Account of the
        Spleen" and an "Art of Political Wagering" from articles on
        the circulation of the blood and on political arithmetic.

3251   PAULSON, RONALD.
        Theme and Structure in Swift's "Tale of a Tub." New Haven:
        Yale Univ. Press, 1960. Rpt. Hamden, Conn.: Archon Books,
        1972.

            Argues that "one must try to come to terms with the Tale
        and determine what its particular kind of unity is.... To
        cope with Swift's Tale of a Tub the critic can neither ignore
        technical considerations of structure and satiric method nor
        reason away the religious accusations. The defender of Swift
        must accept the fact that ... the religious theme is the crucial
        one to an understanding of the Tale."

3252   PINKUS, PHILIP.
        "The Upside-down World of A Tale of a Tub." ES 44 (1963):
        161-175.

            An analysis of Swift's Tubbian World "to show what kind
        of a world [it] is and how it comes about." Views the Tale
        "as a sustained dramatic situation" in which "the various
        pieces do fit together."

3253   "A Tale of a Tub and the Rosy Cross." JEGP 59 (1960):
        669-679.

            Discusses the pervasiveness of Rosicrucianism and attempts
        to prove that the Dark Authors are all Rosicrucian.

3254   PULLEN, CHARLES.
       "The Role of the Reader of Eighteenth-Century Literature
       and Swift's A Tale of a Tub." ESC 1 (1975): 280-289.

       Concerns the reader's confrontation with the Tale and the
       character of the Grub Street writer, wherein lies the real
       greatness of the work: Swift both "uses" him as a satirical
       persona and allows him to live his own life as well; concludes
       that "the writer has been quite explicit about the tale; the
       writing is therapy, a way in which he makes purgative efforts
       at living outside the madhouse. It is this struggle which makes
       for much of the power of the book, its 'isness,' its 'artifact-
       ness' as a revelation of the writer's life...."

3255   QUINTANA, RICARDO.
       "Two Paragraphs in A Tale of a Tub, Section IX." MP 73
       (1975): 15-32.

       A close examination of the "Digression on Madness"; sum-
       marizes the theories, analyzes Swift's irony at work, and
       gives "concluding observations on Swiftian irony and what it
       can tell us about both Swift the satirist and Swift the man
       who controlled this satire."

3256   "Emile Pons and the Modern Study of Swift's Tale of a Tub."
       EA 18 (1965): 5-17.

       Reviews significant developments in scholarship and criti-
       cism of A Tale of a Tub (the entire tripartite work) since
       1920.

3257   RAWSON, CLAUDE.
       "Order and Cruelty: A Reading of Swift (with some comments
       on Pope and Johnson)." EIC 20 (1970): 24-56. Rpt. in
       [3350], pp. 223-247.

       Analyzes Swift's irony and argues that the interplay be-
       tween "deliberate attacking purposes (and tactics), and certain
       tense spontaneities of self-expression" results in Swift's char-
       acteristic style in Tale of a Tub, A Modest Proposal, and
       elsewhere. Discusses relationship between real and putative
       authors.

3258   REAL, HERMANN J.
       " 'That Malignant Diety': An Interpretation of Criticism in
       Swift's Battle of the Books." PQ 52 (1973): 760-766.

       Notes on the paragraph which describes the goddess,
       Criticism; interpretation of that patron deity of the Moderns

requires an awareness of two different ideas: the theory of
humors and the classical ideal of the vir bonus.   Criticism
becomes the incarnation of complete moral and intellectual
decay.

3259   ROGERS, PAT.
        "Form in A Tale of a Tub." EIC 22 (1972): 142-160.

        Proposes the thesis that in A Tale of a Tub "Swift is dram-
        atising, not formlessness ... but excess of form ... [that]
        the structure is one of inorganic, over-developed, useless
        'form,'" and that "its style, its comedy and its irony all pro-
        ceed from [a] pseudo-sophisticated approach, which is dram-
        atised by Swift."

3260   ROSCELLI, WILLIAM JOHN.
        "A Tale of a Tub and the 'Cavils of the Sour.'" JEGP 64
        (1965): 41-56.

        An attempt to determine whether or not the Tale was a
        blasphemous attack on religion, to show that Swift was unable
        to expose corrupt theological beliefs without undermining the
        foundations of Christian faith, and to reconcile the two anti-
        thetical concepts of faith--faith founded on reason and faith
        as a virtue to accept anything commanded by God.

3261   SCHAEFFER, NEIL.
        " 'Them that Speak, and Them That Hear': The Audience as
        Target in Swift's Tale of a Tub." Enl. E. 4 (1973): 25-35.

        Argues that "it is the audience, both as the object of Swift's
        satire in the Tale, and as the implied reader of the Tale, that
        connects the lesser themes into one broad and unified attack
        upon man's propensity for self-deception, and the great danger
        posed by this weakness."

3262   SCRUGGS, CHARLES.
        "Swift's Use of Lucretius in A Tale of a Tub." TSLL 15
        (1973): 39-49.

        Argues that, though Swift does attack De Rerum Natura,
        he uses it for "artistic purposes as it becomes one more
        patch on the crazy-quilt fabric of the Tale.   First, when
        Swift quotes Lucretius, he sometimes distorts De Rerum Na-
        tura, sometimes not, but in either case the narrator ... is
        revealed as an ardent and literal-minded admirer of both Lu-
        cretius and Epicurus....   His devotion to Lucretius makes
        him imitate the 'sublime' intentions, style, and stance of the
        Roman poet.   Secondly, echoes of De Rerum Natura give struc-

ture to a world where chaos and change are the primary realities. "

3263   SEIDEL, MICHAEL.
        "Fathers and Sons: Swift's A Tale of a Tub." In [158], pp.
        169-200.

        Interprets the Tale as a fable of misinheritance, in which
        the legacy carried by the allegory reveals the diminished
        mental integrity of the allegorist; the Tale is about "satirically
        weakened lines of descent: fathers to sons, ancients to moderns. " The putative subject is the failure to "transmit donated value across historical and generational boundaries. "

3264   SMITH, CURTIS C.
        "Metaphor Structure in Swift's Tale of a Tub." Thoth 5 (1964):
        22-41.

        Concerned with a certain kind of metaphor, that which expresses the relationship between what is "outer" and what is
        "inner"; the examination of this "inner versus outer metaphor
        structure" suggests that the Hack prefers the "outer," and
        that Swift is not completely committed to either "outer" or
        "inner," from which fact derives the point-of-view problem.
        Since the Hack can't remember all parts of the metaphor
        structure at once, he is sometimes inconsistent and the structure works against him.

3265   SMITH, FREDERIK N.
        Language and Reality in Swift's "A Tale of a Tub."   Columbus: Ohio State Univ. Press, 1979.

        Argues that in all of Swift's satire the one constant is
        his willingness to let style carry his message, that the main
        theme of the Tale is the relationship between language and
        reality, the basis of his unique style.   That theme was a subject of critical debate in the seventeenth century, and in the
        Tale Swift reflects and comments on that debate.   Assuming
        a connection between style and epistemology, the author suggests that the Tale's "configurations of style lead us back
        simultaneously to the Modern's and Swift's opposing epistemologies. "

3266   "The Epistemology of Fictional Failure: Swift's Tale of a
        Tub and Beckett's Watt." TSLL 15 (1974): 649-672.

        Argues that Beckett's Watt was greatly influenced by Swift's
        "amazingly modern fictional satire"; that A Tale of a Tub
        showed Beckett "how to use a fractured literary structure and

style in order to question the effects of literary form, the
relationship between form and experience, and beyond--the
very possibility of human knowledge. " For both writers, a
suspicion of speculative philosophy becomes the raison d'être
of an epistemological, pragmatic type of fiction.

3267   STARKMAN, MIRIAM KOSH.
       Swift's Satire on Learning in "A Tale of a Tub. "   Princeton,
       N. J. : Princeton Univ. Press, 1950.

       Argues that A Tale of a Tub assumes greater meaning and
       form when considered within the large context of the Ancients
       and Moderns controversy, and that it is a "self-consciously
       partisan" document in that controversy, not merely the ac-
       cidental by-product of it.   The author confines herself to the
       satire on abuses in learning and refers only incidentally to
       the religious allegory; nor does the study analyze the tech-
       nique of Swift's irony.   Her method consists of "the collation
       of the intellectual milieu of Swift ... with the text of A Tale
       of a Tub" in order to show that the satire is more meaning-
       ful and "formful" than previously supposed.

3268   STEPHENS, LAMARR.
       " 'A Digression in Praise of Digressions' as a Classical Ora-
       tion: Rhetorical Satire in Section VII of Swift's A Tale of a
       Tub. " TSE 13 (1963): 41-49.

       An analysis of Swift's digression to support the theory that
       "formfulness," not "formlessness" is Swift's tactic. "In-
       stead of being a parody, this digression is a satirical inver-
       sion of parody. " It is the work of the "persona" who "ap-
       pears to have fallen into the ways of righteousness despite
       himself. "

3269   STOUT, GARDNER D. , JR.
       "Satire and Self-Expression in Swift's Tale of a Tub. "   In
       [9], pp. 323-339.

       Argues that the "Tale can be experienced and understood
       most fully as a complex, enigmatic expression of Swift's per-
       sonality and state of being as its author and speaker"; and
       considers especially the obsessive elements in his art, his
       covert and largely unconscious complicity in the depravities
       of his satiric butts. Deals with Swift's buried life, his inner
       conflicts and paradoxes, the patterns of pain and pleasure as
       revealed in the Tale.

3270   "Speaker and Satiric Vision in Swift's Tale of a Tub. "   ECS
       3 (1969): 175-199.

Argues that Swift is the speaker in the Tale and that unless we read it that way we will not understand the complex shifting ironies and we will overlook "Swift's self-mocking and yet sympathetic probing of the satirist's character, aims, and achievements, especially of his own character and performance as author...." Sees the Tale as "a sort of glass wherein we may discover everybody's face, Swift's as well as our own."

3271   TRAUGOTT, JOHN.
"A Tale of a Tub." In [3058], pp. 76-120.

An essay on ultimate significance and implications of A Tale of a Tub; does not see Swift as an advocate of compromise or as the writer of meditative poetry. Analyzes the sexual imagery.

3272   TUVESON, ERNEST.
"Swift and the World Makers." JHI 11 (1950): 54-74.

Discusses Swift's role in the battle of the ancients and moderns and the conflict of religion and science in "the materialist, progressive era that Swift regarded as both imminent and degenerate."

3273   WEATHERS, WINSTON.
"A Technique of Irony in A Tale of a Tub." In [3053], pp. 53-60.

Identifies and analyzes a rhetorical technique that Swift employed to convey meaning ironically: Swift lets the persona (non-Swift) talk in denotative language, establishing a "norm of agreement," and then uses deviation (exaggeration, high diction, metaphor) to indicate his own involvement; having established that involvement, he uses "amelioration" to indicate disagreement with the persona, "pejoration" to indicate agreement.

3274   WEBSTER, CLARENCE M.
"Swift's Tale of a Tub Compared with Earlier Satires of the Puritans." PMLA 47 (1932): 171-178.

An "analysis of the various themes of the attack on the Puritans in the Tale of a Tub, and a comparison of the results with those obtained from a similar analysis of the more prominent earlier satires of the Puritans."

3275   WICKHAM, JOHN F.
"The Emergence of Swiftian Satire in The Battle of the Books."

In Trans. of the Samuel Johnson Society of the Northwest,
Vol. 6 (Calgary: Samuel Johnson Soc. of the N.W. , 1973),
pp. 82-90.

Swift's special kind of satire can be seen coming to birth
in the Battle, a theme of which is the bitterness of argument
of both sides; from the fable of the spider and the bee we
learn of Aesop's method of dealing with the problem, and
from "Pindar's style of attack we discover how Swift hopes
to strike hard blows at a shifting target. " Swift's own method
of attack is suggested in the fifth paragraph, where the persona of a modern historian is introduced.

See also: 3077, 3082, 3085, 3095, 3101, 3105, 3127, 3130, 3144, 3147,
   3157, 3166, 3170, 3184, 3189, 3198, 3203, 3206, 3312, 3374,
   3533

Bickerstaff Papers

3276   BOND, RICHMOND P.
   "Isaac Bickerstaff, Esq. " In [13], pp. 103-124.

   Describes how "Swift's original Bickerstaff caught the whim
   of the town, how other writers adopted his signature for their
   own use, and how he was transformed by Steele and Addison
   and their associates into the celebrated Censor of the Tatler. "

3277   EDDY, W. A.
   "Tom Brown and Partridge the Astrologer. " MP 28 (1930):
   163-168.

   A description of the character of Brown's parody of Partridge to show how important his influence was on Swift's
   treatment of the astrologer in the Bickerstaff papers.

3278   MAYHEW, GEORGE P.
   "Swift's Bickerstaff Hoax as an April Fools' Joke. " MP 61
   (1964): 270-280.

   Examines Bickerstaff's Predictions in detail to support argument that Swift's four-part hoax upon John Partridge was
   a carefully planned April Fools' joke.

3279   THOMAS, W. K.
   "The Bickerstaff Caper. " DR 49 (1969): 346-360.

   Describes Swift's satirical attack on John Partridge as a

threat to the established church as well as to the state of
learning.

See also: 3076, 3101, 3189

Journal to Stella

3280   EHRENPREIS, IRVIN.
        "Swift's 'Little Language' in the Journal to Stella."   SP 45
        (1948): 80-88.

        A further attempt to decipher Swift's code taken from let-
        ters 1, 41-53, 55-65 of the Journal.

3281   ENGLAND, A. B.
        "Private and Public Rhetoric in the Journal to Stella."   EIC
        22 (1972): 131-141.

        Argues that "a crucial feature of the Journal's meaning ...
        is dramatized by a contrast between the style of Pdfr and the
        style of the public man" and that Swift is not successful in
        "separating his public and his private self."

3282   PONS, EMILE.
        "Du Nouveau sur le 'Journal à Stella.' "   EA 1 (1937): 210-
        229.

        Contains some new interpretations of "the little language."

3283   SMITH, FREDERIK N.
        "Dramatic Elements in Swift's Journal to Stella."   ECS 1
        (1968): 332-351.

        Argues that the Journal ought not to be uncritically accepted
        as entirely self-revealing and reliable; that, in fact, the let-
        ters should be regarded as at least partly rhetorical in meth-
        od: "The most significant feature of Swift's 'private rhetoric'
        in the Journal to Stella is his intentional development of ele-
        ments that can be called dramatic."

3284   WHITLEY, E. M.
        "Contextual Analysis and Swift's Little Language of the Jour-
        nal to Stella." In In Memory of J. R. Firth, eds. C. E.
        Bazell, J. C. Catford, M. A. K. Halliday & R. H. Robins
        (London: Longmans, 1966), pp. 475-500.

Applies Professor Firth's contextual theory of meaning to the problem of Swift's "little language," considered under two main heads: 1) the nature of the "mystic letters," "cyphers," or "odd combinations of letters"; their identification with persons and the translation meanings given them by different editors; and 2) the nature of the little language as a whole, its place in the whole text and its function.

3285   WILLIAMS, SIR HAROLD.
        "Deane Swift, Hawkesworth, and the Journal to Stella." In [54], pp. 33-48.

The collection of letters written by Jonathan Swift to Esther Johnson and Rebecca Dingley in Ireland between September 1710 and June 1713 as published first by Deane Swift and later by John Hawkesworth.

3286   WOOLF, VIRGINIA.
        "Swift's Journal to Stella." In The Common Reader, Second Series (London: Hogarth Press, 1932), pp. 67-77. Rpt. in [3054], pp. 162-169; [3055], pp. 107-115.

Comments on the influence of Stella upon Swift, and Swift's influence upon Stella, through his letters to her.

See also: 3111

The Drapier's Letters

3287   COUGHLIN, MATTHEW N.
        " 'This Deluge of Brass': Rhetoric in the First and Fourth Drapier Letters." Eire 11, ii (1976): 77-91.

The Drapier's First and Fourth Letters differ in purpose: the First Letter opposes Wood's half pence on economic grounds, whereas the Fourth Letter appeals to Irish nationalism. Swift therefore employs different rhetorical techniques for the two letters: Letter One has the form of a classical oration, containing the Exordium; the Narration, which includes the Digressions; the Refutation; and the Peroratio. He uses half-truths, hypothetical examples, maxims, and innuendoes. In Letter Four, Swift begins with the Exordium, proceeds to the Refutation, and then, altering classical form, establishes the case for Irish freedom in three long digressions.

3288   EHRENPREIS, IRVIN.
        "Swift: The Examiner and the Drapier." In [99], pp. 51-82.

Swift supports the crown, the aristocracy, the gentry, the Church, and the Tories, and attacks the Whigs, the bankers, the stock jobbers, and other forces supposedly opposed to the crown.   But that explicit meaning is qualified by the implications that emerge from an analysis of his language.   Praise for the monarch is subtly undermined by an imaginative sensitivity to the vices and misdeeds of kings.   Swift employs irony to raise his treatment of the themes of the Examiner into powerful rhetoric; by creating a system of contraries, he can be ironic by praising the enemy for a quality he conspicuously lacks.

3289   GOODWIN, A.
"Wood's Halfpence." EHR 51 (1936): 647-674.

Historical background useful for understanding Swift's Drapier's Letters; attempts to "examine afresh the real nature of the Irish opposition to Wood's patent and to reassess the significance of the crisis in the history of Anglo-Irish relations."

3290   MACAREE, DAVID.
"Reason and Passion Harmonized: The Drapier's Letters and the Language of Political Protest." CJIS 2, ii (1976): 47-60.

Although Swift's Modest Proposal may have superior literary qualities, his Drapier Letters were more effective in uniting his countrymen in opposition to the British government's treatment of Ireland.   Although he was angry, he "tempered his feelings with reason and wit" and used all the tricks of rhetoric to achieve his intended effect.   His method of appealing to reason and not to violence was to be imitated by other protestors.   Swift saw it as "a function of his art to organize national protest based on sound constitutional precedents" rather than to use words to deliberately inflame passion.

3291   WOODRING, CARL R.
"The Aims, Audience, and Structure of the Drapier's Fourth Letter." MLQ 17 (1956): 50-59.

An analysis of "A Letter to the Whole People of Ireland" and the effect of "Swift's diverse aims and multifarious audience on [its] structure"; and an attempt to answer the question, Who were the Whole People of Ireland?

See also: 3085, 3101, 3126

Gulliver's Travels

3292   ALLISON, ALEXANDER W.
        "Concerning Houyhnhnm Reason." SR 76 (1968): 480-492.

        Looks at the two themes--that the Houyhnhnms "represent
        that faculty of mind which would rebuke our animal passions
        and our naked self-seeking" and also that they "represent
        both an absolute rationality which is incommensurate both
        with the sinfulness of man and with intimations of the divine
        in man"--to show that they are not incompatible and that Swift
        "endowed the perfectly rational Houyhnhnms with defects as
        well as with virtues, so that he might distinguish the futile
        or positively harmful uses of reason from the necessary and
        desirable uses."

3293   BARKER, ROSALIND ALLEN.
        "A Case for Religious Interpretation in Part III of Gulliver's
        Travels." In A Festschrift for Professor Marguerite Roberts,
        on the Occasion of Her Retirement from Westhampton College,
        University of Richmond, Virginia, Frieda Elaine Penniger, ed.
        (Richmond, Va.: Univ. Richmond Press, 1976), pp. 101-113.

        Seeks to discover what Swift found impious and "partial"
        about the new science by examining Part III against the back-
        ground of the sermons: Part III presents us with evidence
        of William Wotton's faith in human progress and its conse-
        quences, "showing us people who 'trusted in themselves for
        all things,' but lacked the wisdom of Christian revelation."
        Concludes that Swift's pessimism in Part III derives from
        his awareness of the inadequacy of human knowledge and moral
        conduct when not sustained by Christian revelation.

3294   BARROLL, J. LEEDS, III
        "Gulliver and the Struldbruggs." PMLA 73 (1958): 43-50.

        Considers "three aspects of the Struldbrugg episode: (1)
        old age and the fear of death as conventional subjects for
        moral reflection and satire; (2) a desire for immortality in
        the light of the homiletic tradition; and (3) the significance of
        Gulliver's conversations with his host."

3295   BENJAMIN, EDWIN B.
        "The King of Brobdingnag and Secrets of State." JHI 18
        (1957): 572-579.

        Establishes the background for Gulliver's suggestion of
        amoral statecraft as coming from commentaries on Tacitus
        and Machiavelli.

3296   BENTMAN, RAYMOND.
        "Satiric Structure and Tone in the Conclusion of Gulliver's
        Travels." SEL 11 (1971): 535-548.

        "Concerned both with the theories of the criticism of satire
        and with the application of these theories to the problems of
        Gulliver and the Houyhnhnms." Sees the last chapter as for-
        mal satire and that "Gulliver, like all narrators in good sat-
        ire, is unable to maintain his own ideals." The structure of
        the last two chapters is such that they yield a wide range of
        interpretations and contradictory conclusions depending upon
        one's theory of satire.

3297   BLOOM, ALLAN.
        "An Outline of Gulliver's Travels." In Ancients and Moderns,
        Joseph Cropsey, ed. (New York: Basic Books, 1964), pp.
        238-258. Rpt. in [3109], pp. 648-661; [3351], pp. 297-311.

        A general survey of the meaning and interpretation of each
        of Gulliver's four voyages, emphasizing in Book I modern
        political practice; in Book II ancient political practice, Brob-
        dingnag being a cross between Sparta and Republican Rome;
        in Book III, modern science in its effect on political practice
        and on life; and in Book IV, "ancient utopian politics used as
        a standard for judging man understood as the moderns wished
        to understand him." Concludes that Swift, one of the funniest
        men who ever lived, treats misanthropy as a joke: "it is
        the greatest folly in the world to attempt to improve human-
        ity.... Gulliver's Travels makes misanthropy ridiculous by
        showing us the complexity of our nature and thereby teaching
        us what we must accept."

3298   BORKAT, ROBERTA SARFATT.
        "Pride, Progress, and Swift's Struldbruggs." DUJ 37 (1976):
        126-134.

        Maintains that the Struldbruggs are "Swift's metaphorical
        attack on ... the religious and moral fallacies of the optim-
        istic Moderns." They are the "climax to the scientists and
        Moderns of Book III" and the "transition to the examination
        of aspects of the nature of man in the Yahoos and Houyhnhnms."
        Because Swift felt that too many "proud Moderns were relying
        upon unaided human reason to lead progressively toward per-
        fection," he used the Struldbruggs to show that " 'the univer-
        sal maturing man' is fallen, weak, dependent Man, who needs
        the help of religion and who cannot pridefully rely on his own
        constantly increasing wisdom and virtue to lead ever onward
        and upward to Progress."

3299   BRACHER, FREDERICK.
        "The Name 'Lemuel Gulliver.'" HLQ 12 (1949): 409-413.

Lemuel Gulliver, the pseudonymous author of the work
Swift usually referred to as "my Travels," was not born until his friends helped him to secure the publication of the
work by Benjamin Motte with the letter of "Richard Sympson"
sent to Motte on August 8, 1726; concludes that "it seems
most likely that [it] was a synthetic compound, like Isaac
Bickerstaff and Martin Scriblerus, with no meaning beyond
the hint conveyed in the first syllable of Gulliver, but carefully devised with regard to rhythm and euphony."

3300   BRADY, FRANK.
"Vexations and Diversions: Three Problems in Gulliver's
Travels." MP 75 (1978): 346-367.

Examines three problems of interpretation, each related
to a different aspect of Gulliver's Travels: 1) the use of
jokes, such as those involving matter-of-fact detail in Lilliput; 2) the theme of degeneration that appears in all four
parts; and 3) Swift's techniques in part 4, and what they imply about his attitudes.   Conflicting critical interpretations
are compared and evaluated on the basis of two principles:
to be valid, an interpretation must 1) explain "underlining,"
the use of repetition, contrast, or emphasis on a "fact"; 2)
must carefully consider any "seemingly irrelevant reference
or detail, though the critic has to remember that some details will remain inconsequential and that one man's pattern
is another's coincidence."

3301   BRADY, FRANK, ed.
Twentieth Century Interpretations of Gulliver's Travels: A
Collection of Critical Essays.   Englewood Cliffs, N.J.:
Prentice-Hall, 1968.

3302   BRINK, J. R.
"From the Utopians to the Yahoos: Thomas More and Jonathan Swift." JRUL 42 (1980): 59-66.

A comparison of Swift's and More's views on social reform and on dissent shows that Swift took a more pessimistic
view of human nature than did More.   Although More's pragmatism and social criticism are obvious in Gulliver's Travels,
it was his opposition to political tyranny which Swift admired
the most.   Swift's Yahoos are more like More's Utopians than
are the Houyhnhnms.

3303   BRYAN, MARGARET B.
"Swift's Use of the Looking-Glass in Gulliver's Travels."
Conn. Rev. 8 (1974): 90-94.

Uses four parallel scenes in which Gulliver views his reflection in a glass (or water) as a yardstick for measuring
his passage through the book and relates these scenes to Gulliver's "role as a static or changing character and his mental
state at the end."

3304   BUCKLEY, MARJORIE W.
"Key to the Language of the Houyhnhnms in Gulliver's Travels."
In [3055], pp. 270-278.

Arguing that Swift uses the behavior of both Houyhnhnms
and Yahoos as material for his indictment, especially attacking the absence of reason, emotion, and creativity in the
Houyhnhnms, the author suggests that the phonetic pronunciation of Yahoo is "Ye who," as in the sense of "Ye who behave thus," and that the pronunciation of Houyhnhnm is "Who
inhuman," as in the phrase "You who, inhuman, behave thus."
A phonetic key is provided to unlock the meaning of each
Houyhnhnm word.

3305   BYRD, MAX.
"Gulliver's Clothes: An Enlightenment Motif." Enl. E. 3,
No. 1 (1972): 41-46.

Discusses the role that Gulliver's clothes play in his experiences and suggests that his clothes, or lack of them,
"take us close to the heart of Swift's enlightened humanism."

3306   CANFIELD, J. DOUGLAS.
"Corruption and Degeneration in Gulliver's Travels." NDEJ
9 (1973): 15-22.

Surveys the themes of corruption and degeneration in all
four books of Gulliver's Travels, suggesting that the development of those themes in the first three books leads to Book
IV and "Gulliver's final acceptance of human corruption and
degeneration and his absurd reaction." Concludes that Swift
implies that a possible hope exists in man's very nature,
though Gulliver himself has degenerated from such humanity
in Part I to the point where he rejects his own family.

3307   CARNOCHAN, W. B.
Lemuel Gulliver's Mirror for Man.   Berkeley: Univ. Calif.
Press, 1968.

Offers a general theory of Augustan satire--what it is and
why it is excellent; then deals with the "Travels as an illustration of the theory; generically typical, a 'satire on man';

strategically typical, a satirist's apology for his art; an example of Swift's most characteristic methods; and a satire
that reflects his most personal and closely guarded feelings";
and finally argues that Swift may be satirizing Locke's epistemology.

3308   "Gulliver's Travels: An Essay on the Human Understanding?"
        MLQ 25 (1964): 5-21.

        Supports thesis that Gulliver's Travels is "an essay on
        human understanding--not only deriving from Locke's discus-
        sion of man's essential nature, but also stating some of the
        more general difficulties raised by his theory of knowledge."
        Relationship between Gulliver and Lockean man is also ex-
        plored.

3309   "Some Roles of Lemuel Gulliver." TSLL 5 (1964): 520-529.

        Argues that "Gulliver's change from innocent to misanthro-
        pic satirist ... is anticipated ... by some important and
        interlocking roles which he plays. Indeed Swift prepares for
        Gulliver's last role as a disillusioned reformer in ways that
        often deepen the ironies of his tale."

3310   "The Complexity of Swift: Gulliver's Fourth Voyage." SP
        60 (1963): 23-44.

        An attempt to reconcile the flaws in the characters of the
        Houyhnhnms with Swift's intention to portray them as an "ideal
        race." Swift's portrayal of Gulliver at the end of the Fourth
        Voyage is "both self-portrait and self-parody, the dramatized
        image of Swift's mixed feelings about his literary vocation
        and his reactions to the world."

3311   CASE, ARTHUR E.
        Four Essays on "Gulliver's Travels." Princeton, N.J.:
        Princeton Univ. Press, 1945; Gloucester, Mass.: Peter
        Smith, 1958.

        Includes essays on the text of Gulliver's Travels, on its
        geography and chronology, on personal and political satire,
        and on its significance. The Houyhnhnms are regarded as
        symbols of perfection: "Swift shows us at the end of the fourth
        voyage his conception of the effects which would be produced
        in the mind of an intelligent man who spent a long period in
        the company of creatures who were perfect in every way....
        Anything less than perfection would be adhorrent: degrees of
        imperfection would be imperceptible and irrelevant." The
        author insists that Gulliver's opinions are his own, not those
        of his creator.

3312   CASTLE, TERRY J.
        "Why the Houyhnhnms Don't Write: Swift, Satire and the Fear
        of the Text." ELWIU 7 (1980): 31-44.

            Considers Gulliver's Travels and A Tale of a Tub with
        reference to Grammaphobia, or fear of the written word.
        Suggests that Swift's "vision or hallucination of a fearful gap
        between speech and writing" compels the satire in A Tale of
        a Tub giving it "an anxious, obsessive force," and that the
        "themes Swift associates with writing--its fallen aspect, its
        hermeneutic indeterminacy, and physical and moral degeneracy
        --all reappear ... within the fictional context of Gulliver's
        Travels." Asks the question: Is the lack of writing a neces-
        sary feature of the Houyhnhnms' ideal community?

3313   CHAMPION, L. S.
        "Gulliver's Voyages: The Framing Events as a Guide to In-
        terpretation." TSLL 10 (1969): 529-536.

            Argues that the framing events at the beginning and end of
        each voyage, "depicting in sequence physical self-sufficiency,
        physical helplessness, spiritual certitude, and spiritual dis-
        location," were planned by Swift to serve as guideposts for
        the final episode when Gulliver rejects the human race.

3314   CLARK, PAUL ODELL.
        "A Gulliver Dictionary." SP 50 (1953): 592-624.

            Discusses Swift's use of language and provides the transla-
        tion of over one hundred words from the first three voyages
        plus an analysis of the different vocabulary of Houyhnhnmland.

3315   CLIFFORD, JAMES L.
        "Gulliver's Fourth Voyage: 'Hard' and 'Soft' Schools of Inter-
        pretation." In [15], pp. 33-50.

            A critical survey of modern criticism of the Fourth Voyage
        and a discussion of the various problems that center on the
        meaning of the Yahoos, the meaning of the Houyhnhnms, the
        significance of Captain Mendez, and the interpretation of the
        ending. Suggests in conclusion that "absolute standards are
        unattainable by fallen man.... All attempts at middle-ground
        solutions involve a certain amount of selfish retionalization
        and hypocrisy. This is man's predicament. He knows he
        can never attain perfection, yet his attempts to set up altern-
        ative solutions involve choices which he cannot wholly justify.
        And so he is caught in a great dilemma."

3316   CLUBB, MERREL D.
        "The Criticism of Gulliver's 'Voyage to the Houyhnhnms,'

1726-1914." In Stanford Studies in Language & Literature, ed. Hardin Craig (1941), pp. 203-232.

Does not attempt a reinterpretation of the fourth Voyage but traces the "most important or most effective pronouncements uttered between the publication of Gulliver and the beginning of the first World War...."

3317   COHAN, STEVEN M.
"Gulliver's Fiction." Studies in the Novel 6 (1974): 7-16.

Finds the appeal of Gulliver's Travels less in its satire than in its fictional structure: " ... underneath the entertaining, comic surface there is a fiction structuring for us a vision of man, by confronting his pretenses, fears, and desires"; the four voyages correspond to four stages of psychological progression that embody man's development from an "immature consciousness of self to a more mature consciousness of society and other men."

3318   COOK, TERRY.
" 'Dividing the swift mind': A reading of Gulliver's Travels." Crit. Quart. 22, iii (1980): 35-47.

A reading of Gulliver's Travels as "essentially the story of an individual's psychological and moral disintegration." Analyzes its structure to show that Gulliver's surrender to the Houyhnhnms' world view should come as no surprise to the reader; we have been prepared for it during his first three voyages. We must understand why Gulliver collapses and behaves as he does before we can react to his capitulation. This novelistic approach is compared with the view that Gulliver is not a personality but simply a device through which Swift can manipulate the responses of the reader. Both approaches can be reconciled.

3319   CORDER, JIM.
"Gulliver in England." CE 23 (1961): 98-103.

Discusses Swift's superb control of the point-of-view technique which is responsible for the "magnificent comedy" and the "double-edged satire" and enables him to give the illusion of travel while at the same time attacking England and mankind.

3320   CRANE, R. S.
"The Houyhnhnms, the Yahoos, and the History of Ideas." In [39], pp. 231-253. Rpt. in The Idea of the Humanities (Chicago: Univ. Chicago Press, 1967), II, pp. 261-282; in [3301], pp. 80-88 (abridged).

Examines the possible influence of the numerous logic texts still used in Trinity College, Dublin, including especially the Isagoge of Porphyry, on Swift's conception of man in the fourth Voyage; sees the central issue as primarily one of definition: Is man, or is he not, correctly defined as an "rational creature"?

3321   "The Rationale of the Fourth Voyage." In [3351], pp. 300-307; rpt. 1970, pp. 331-338.   Rpt. in [3350], pp. 148-156. Earlier version of [3320].

Concerned with three questions: 1) what is the satire of the fourth Voyage about?; 2) what is the method of the Voyage: is it allegorical or literal?; and 3) what is the form and purpose of its unifying argument?   Concludes that the argument is "broadly moral and psychological rather than specifically Christian ... worked out not allegorically but by means of a marvelous fable, and dependent, for its satirical point, on our taking Gulliver's misanthropy not as an error but as ... the natural and proper consequence of the experience he has had."

3322   DANCHIN, PIERRE.
        "The Text of Gulliver's Travels." TSLL 2 (1960): 233-250.

Supports Sir Harold Williams' conclusion that Faulkner's test of 1735 had the assistance and approval of Swift himself and should be the basis of all scholarly editions.

3323   DAVIS, HERBERT.
        "Moral Satire--Lemuel Gulliver." In [3085], pp. 77-109. Rpt. in [3083], pp. 143-160.

Considers "Gulliver's Travels as, both in form and in shape, wholly the product of the eighteenth century, while being at the same time the most violent satire of its hope and dreams and a repudiation of much that it most valued."

3324   DIRCKS, RICHARD J.
        "Gulliver's Tragic Rationalism." Criticism 2 (1960): 134-149.

An examination of Book IV of Gulliver's Travels and "an attempt to explore further the society of horses, not as a utopian society, but as an ironical portrait of the life of reason carried to excess."   Concludes that the life of perfect reason which Gulliver had led under the Houyhnhnms destroyed his last illusion and drove him insane.

3325   DOUGLAS, LLOYD.
       The Worlds of Lemuel Gulliver (Okla. State Univ. Monographs
       Humanities Series, No. 11).   1968.

       Approaches the problem of Gulliver's Travels, especially
       that of Book IV, through the character of Gulliver, who re-
       veals the continual presence of Swift, so that if we can see
       Gulliver entire, we can see Swift more adequately.   Argues
       that there are six Gulliver's but underneath all the changes
       is the same naive Gulliver who is at the mercy of his cur-
       rent experiences, and that Gulliver Six in Houyhnhnmland is
       mocking "any over-simplified world which is the product of
       presumption, of principles which are truly narrow and views
       which are truly short."

3326   DOWNIE, J. A.
       "Political Characterization in Gulliver's Travels."   YES 7
       (1977):   108-120.

       Argues against a strict political interpretation of Gulliver's
       Travels, which should be "emancipated from arguments over
       political content, for the sake of the wider social satire....
       It is the timeless quality of social, not political, satire that
       makes the work relevant to the modern reader ... this argu-
       ment assumes that Bolgolam, Reldresal, Munodi, even Flim-
       nap, become types, symbols, not actual personalities...."

3327   DYSON, A. E.
       "Swift: The Metamorphosis of Irony."   E & S 11 (1959):   53-
       67.   Rpt. in [3109], pp. 672-684; [3351], pp. 350-362; The
       Crazy Fabric (London: Macmillan, 1965), pp. 1-13; [3350],
       pp. 157-171.

       A discussion of Swift's use of irony as directed against
       people, against things which can be morally changed, and
       against states of mind which might or might not be altered.
       Considers Book IV of Gulliver in which "irony completes its
       transformation, and is turned upon human nature itself," and
       the relationship between Gulliver and Swift.

3328   EASTHOPE, ANTONY.
       "The Disappearance of Gulliver: Character and Persona at
       the End of the 'Travels.'"   Southern Rev. (Adelaide) 2 (1967):
       261-266.

       Suggests that two passages (in Chapters 11 and 12, Part
       IV) omitted from Faulkner's edition of 1735 confirm the in-
       terpretation that we have credited Gulliver with greater re-
       ality than he in fact possesses and that our habit of laughing
       at him came from taking too literally a character whose re-
       ality vanishes into a disembodied persona in the last chapter.

3329   EDDY, WILLIAM A.
        Gulliver's Travels: A Critical Study. Princeton, N. J. :
        Princeton Univ. Press, 1923; rpt. Gloucester, Mass. : Peter
        Smith, 1963.

        The aim is to "distinguish the philosophic types of Imagin-
        ary Voyage literature, and discuss briefly the most important
        of Gulliver's forerunners"; provides a detailed study of each
        of the voyages, each one being related to its own special tra-
        dition in fiction and satire; and describes the influence of
        Gulliver's Travels on the literature of the eighteenth century
        and its significance in the history of English literature.

3330   EHRENPREIS, IRVIN.
        "The Meaning of Gulliver's Last Voyage. "   REL 3, No. 3
        (1962): 18-38. Rpt. in [3059], pp. 123-142.

        Influence of John Locke's ideas on "the nature of man" on
        Swift's satire on mankind in Book IV of Gulliver's Travels.
        Here "Swift takes some fantastic examples of real or apparent
        humanity and has us test accepted definitions by them. "   At
        the close of Book IV, Swift addresses himself to anyone who
        "might not only regard the character of Houyhnhnm as admir-
        able but also treat it as an easy ideal for humanity...."

3331   "The Origins of Gulliver's Travels. "   PMLA 72 (1957):   880-
        899. Rpt. in [3055], pp. 200-225; [3096], pp. 83-116.

        Suggests "that Swift created much of Gulliver out of his
        own memories, experiences, and reflections from 1714 to
        1725" and attempts to identify various people that Swift was
        portraying in the Travels.

3332   ELLIOTT, ROBERT C.
        "Swift's Utopias. "   In The Shape of Utopia: Studies in a Liter-
        ary Genre (Chicago: Univ. Chicago Press, 1970), pp. 50-67.

        Deals with Swift's ideas of Utopia as expressed in Gulliver's
        Travels showing that "despite his own utopian predispositions,
        Swift was not of the Houyhnhnm party; he was not a designer
        of ideal societies which require the wholesale remaking of
        man ... he hoped that man could live in Brobdingnag. "

3333   "Gulliver's Travels. "   In The Power of Satire: Magic, Rit-
        ual, Art (Princeton, N. J. :   Princeton Univ. Press, 1960),
        pp. 184-222.

        An analysis of the "satirist-satirized" theme in Gulliver's
        Travels shows how Swift "created two dominant points of view

to control the materials of the Travels: that of his favorite
ingénu (the younger Gulliver) and that of the misanthrope."

3334   "Gulliver as Literary Artist." ELH 19 (1952):   49-63.

An examination of various passages relevant to Gulliver's
character from a double point of view: that of Gulliver as
author and Gulliver as character; also Gulliver as ingénu and
as critic.

3335   FINK, Z. S.
        "Political Theory in Gulliver's Travels." ELH 14 (1947):
        151-161.

Examines "the historical development of the view of govern
ment which Swift adopted ... to determine in what sense it
was a 'gothic' theory and ... to explain how Swift could advance such a concept and at the same time hold up classical
models as examples." Discusses elements of political deteri-
orationism in Gulliver's Travels.

3336   FIRTH, SIR CHARLES.
        "The Political Significance of 'Gulliver's Travels.'" Proc.
        of British Academy 9 (1920); rpt. in Essays Historical and
        Literary (Oxford: Clarendon Press, 1938; rpt. 1968), pp.
        210-241.

Shows relationship between the rebellion in Lindalino and
the Irish opposition to Wood's patent to coin currency in Ireland.   Concludes that "Gulliver's Travels show plainly that
when Swift began to write them England and English politics
filled his mind, and that when he completed them Ireland and
Irish affairs were his absorbing interest.   As he passed from
one subject to another his tone altered, his satire ceased to
be playful and became serious and bitter."

3337   FITZGERALD, ROBERT P.
        "The Structure of Gulliver's Travels." SP 71 (1974): 247-
        263.

A detailed examination of the Travels to support author's
theory that the book's popularity is due to its "vitality" which
is the "result of the use on Swift's part of a structure ...
which has been compellingly relevant to central concerns in
the lives of many generations of men," especially the "equivocal value of society: to survive the individual must live in
a society, must adapt to it, and yet the social order inevitabl
frustrates or disappoints him."

3338   "The Allegory of Luggnagg and the Struldbruggs in Gulliver's
        Travels." SP 65 (1968): 657-676.

        Maintains that Swift was attempting to show more than a
        general satire on the desire for eternal life in this allegory,
        that it represented the France of Louis XIV (Luggnagg) and
        the French Academy (Struldbruggs), an institution whose mem-
        bers are called "the Immortals."

3339   FORRESTER, KENT.
        "They Shoot Horses, Don't They? Gulliver and the Houyhn-
        hnms." KPAB 1974: 27-31.

        Supports the traditional view of the satire in Book IV--
        that the Houyhnhnm society was Swift's version of an ideal
        community--and offers reasons why recent critics who be-
        lieve that the satire is directed against the horses are mis-
        interpreting Swift. Recent interpretation is based on the cul-
        tural biases of our age where we are apt to view "the clas-
        sical ideals of stoicism, restraint, and moderation ... as
        negative traits." We need to interpret "Swift and his age on
        their own terms" and not "apologize for [his] philosophic views."

3340   FOSTER, MILTON P., ed.
        A Casebook on Gulliver Among the Houyhnhnms. New York:
        Crowell, 1961.

        Includes a "summary of the first three voyages of Gulliver,
        a complete reprinting of Gulliver's fourth voyage, and several
        works from the eighteenth, nineteenth, and twentieth centuries
        that attempt to evaluate or interpret it"; exhaustive bibliog-
        raphy.

3341   FRESE, JERRY.
        "Swift's Houyhnhnms and Utopian Law." HSL 9 (1977): 187-
        195.

        Book IV of Gulliver's Travels can tell us much about "the
        relationship that should exist between man and law in an ideal
        society." Swift falsely divides human nature into the ration-
        ale and the animal but omits man's value-creating capacity
        which is what forced him to invent law. By examining Gul-
        liver's mistaken view of the Houyhnhnms "we can better a-
        chieve an understanding of man's nature, his relationship to
        his fellow-man, and the role law must play in sustaining this
        relationship."

3342   FRYE, ROLAND M.

"Swift's Yahoo and the Christian Symbols for Sin." JHI 15 (1954): 201-217. Rpt. in [3340], pp. 208-226.

Examines the terminology, the symbols, and the typical phraseology of Christian anthropology and its relationship to the Yahoo which Swift created as "a filthy, depraved, and thoroughly repulsive figure." Shows how Swift appropriated ready-made symbols and a Christian rhetoric, embodying them in a fantasy and elevating them to the level of great art.

3343 FUSSELL, PAUL, JR.
"The Frailty of Lemuel Gulliver." In Essays in Literary History Presented to J. Milton French, eds. Rudolf Kirk & C. F. Main (New Brunswick, N. J.: Rutgers Univ. Press, 1960), pp. 113-125.

Finds in Gulliver's Travels an "important recurring motif of physical injury, damage, pain, and loss" that suggests the weakness and vulnerability of man; Swift's quasi-Christian theme concerns the "inadequacy of an unassisted self-esteem in redeeming Everyman from his own essential frailties."

3344 GEERING, R. G.
"Swift's Struldbruggs: The Critics Considered." AUMLA 7 (1957): 5-15.

Argues that the "essential point" of the Struldbrugg episode is "surely that Gulliver here sheds his last illusion and comes to terms with death." Accepts Middleton Murry's conclusion that the episode contributes to the process whereby Gulliver gains wisdom through self-discovery and self-annihilation, and rejects Arthur Case's argument that Chapter X is logically related to the purpose of Book III, a second description of bad government complementary to Book I.

3345 GILL, JAMES E.
"Man and Yahoo: Dialectic and Symbolism in Gulliver's 'Voyage to the Country of the Houyhnhnms.'" In The Dress of Words: Essays on Restoration and Eighteenth Century Literature in Honor of Richmond P. Bond, ed. Robert B. White, Jr. (Lawrence: Univ. Kansas Libraries [Library Series, 42], 1978), pp. 67-90.

An analysis of the complex dialectic of the first eight chapters of Part IV which "arises from the basic narrative situation--the confrontation of two fundamentally different worlds or points of view: the real but artificial world of Europe represented by Gulliver confronts the mythical but 'natural' world of the Houyhnhnms." Discusses the paradoxical development

of Gulliver as both inferior and superior to the Yahoos, the
ambiguous development of the symbolism, and the paradoxical
scheme of the theriophilic argument which shows civilized man
to be a Yahoo worse than the degenerate Yahoos of Houyhnhnmland.

3346   "Discovery and Alienation, Nature and Reason in Gulliver's
        Travels, Parts I-III." TSL 22 (1977): 85-104.

        Examines the first three parts of the Travels "for evidences
        of the theme of alienation and its relationship to the norms of
        nature and reason" to show how the last voyage is the culmin-
        ation of processes which began early in the work.   The terms
        "Nature" and "Reason," which are crucial points of inquiry
        in Part IV, seldom occur in Parts I, II, and III; however,
        there is a steadily mounting pressure throughout the first
        three voyages "toward the generation of a comprehensive treat-
        ment of the questions of men's physical and intellectual limi-
        tations"--a theme which becomes urgent and explicit in the
        natural world of the Houyhnhnms.

3347   "Beast Over Man: Theriophilic Paradox in Gulliver's 'Voy-
        age to the Country of the Houyhnhnms.'" SP 67 (1970): 532-
        549.

        Theriophilic forms of argument adapted to the narrative of
        the fourth Voyage give a "paradoxical conclusion, the aim of
        which is a recognition of the multiple incongruities of human
        thought and experience....   One might say that the fourth
        voyage does not state Swift's answer: it asks his question
        about the existential conjunction of good and evil, of reason
        and passion, and of pride and baseness in the human animal."

3348   GOLDGAR, BERTRAND A.
        "Gulliver's Travels and the Opposition to Walpole." In [42],
        pp. 155-173.   Rpt. in [106], pp. 49-63.

        Considers the question of how Gulliver's Travels was re-
        ceived in contemporary political circles; examines that reac-
        tion in political journals, "keys," newspapers, and pamphlets
        in the first five years following publication.   The book was
        received almost at once as a political document.

3349   GOULD, S. H.
        "Gulliver and the Moons of Mars." JHI 6 (1945): 91-101.

        Looks at Newton's Principia for information about where
        Swift got his idea about two moons around Mars, 150 years
        before they were discovered.   Concludes that Swift chose his
        numbers because they were easy to use in calculation.

3350   GRAVIL, RICHARD, ed.
        Swift, "Gulliver's Travels": A Casebook.   London: Mac-
        millan, 1974.

3351   GREENBERG, ROBERT A. , ed.
        Jonathan Swift: Gulliver's Travels (Norton Critical Edition).
        New York: W. W. Norton & Co. , 1961, 2nd. ed. , 1970.

        An authoritative text; The Correspondence of Swift; Pope's ver-
        ses on Gulliver's Travels; and criticism.

3352   GREENE, DONALD J.
        "The Education of Lemuel Gulliver. "   In [29], pp. 3-20.

        Gulliver seen as a dangerous, uncivilized man, comparable
        to Heinrich Himmler, whose main fault is a lack of feeling,
        a callous heart.   Interpretation of Part IV is given in Chris-
        tian terms--man should strive for the "imitation of Christ"
        in his own conduct.   Greene adopts a "hard" interpretation:
        human life is not a "compromise" between the Yahoos and
        the Houyhnhnms, for Swift's purpose is to "vex," not comfort
        us.

3353   "The Sin of Pride: A Sketch for a Literary Exploration. "
        New Mexico Quarterly 34 (1964):   8-30.

        Discusses pride as it is portrayed in literature, especially
        Gulliver's Travels, and points out that "it is an egregious er-
        ror of critical method to attempt to explicate ... classics of
        the Augustinian ethic ... without giving full weight to the mor-
        al and psychiatric doctrine on which they are constructed. "

3354   GRENNAN, MARGARET R.
        "Lilliput and Leprecan: Gulliver and the Irish Tradition. "
        ELH 12 (1945):   188-202.

        Establishes a parallel between two dominant themes in Irish
        Literature--the preoccupation with the very little and the very
        big--and suggests that Gulliver's adventures in Lilliput and
        Brobdingnag show that the Irish imagination had as much in-
        fluence on Swift as did Irish poverty.

3355   HALEWOOD, WILLIAM H.
        "Gulliver's Travels I, vi. "   ELH 33 (1966):   422-433.

        Suggests "that Swift in introducing the Utopian passage in
        Book I may have been following preacherly as well as satiric
        custom, patching up the argument for the virtue in order to

perfect the contrast with the vice, restoring symmetry to his
theme at the cost of coherence in his fiction." Draws a parallel between the Spartan ideal in Plutarch's "Life of Lycur-
gus" and Lilliputian utopia.

3356   HALEWOOD, WILLIAM H. and MARTIN LEVICH.
       "Houyhnhnm est Animal Rationale." JHI 26 (1965):   273-281.

       Takes the position that " ... Swift fully approved of the
       Houyhnhnm life of reason and conceived of it as fully as pos-
       sible for man--as, indeed, the only realistic standard by
       which to judge the adequacy of human conduct."

3357   HARLOW, BENJAMIN C.
       "Houyhnhnmland: A Utopian Satire." McNR 13 (1962):   44-
       58.

       Argues that Swift did not lose artistic control of Book IV,
       that the Houyhnhnms are intended as a satirical comment on
       utopian idealism.   Houyhnhnmland is not an ideal civilization.

3358   HART, JEFFREY.
       "The Ideologue as Artist: Some Notes on Gulliver's Travels."
       Criticism 2 (1960):   125-133.

       Concentrates primarily on the political and social content
       of the book.   Sees it as a defense of order, since, in each
       society Gulliver visits, "Swift carefully elucidates the relation-
       ship that exists in that society between the present and the
       past."

3359   HARTH, PHILLIP.
       "The Problem of Political Allegory in Gulliver's Travels."
       MP 73, iv, part 2 (1976): S40-S47.

       The attempt to interpret the Voyage to Lilliput as a con-
       sistent and systematic political allegory, in which each in-
       dividual and group found in Lilliput has its specific counter-
       part in the political history of England, is rejected as illogi-
       cal and not in accord with the actual political conditions of
       the age.   Two advantages result from abandoning allegorical
       interpretations in favor of reading the first book as a series
       of adventures: 1) Such a reading avoids looking upon the
       voyage as partisan satire, so that it becomes apparent that
       Swift portrays all parties as equally blameworthy; and 2) it
       permits us to "recognize the voyage to Lilliput for what it
       is: a devastating picture of man in his political dimension...."

3360   HASSALL, ANTHONY J.

"Discontinuities in <u>Gulliver's Travels</u>." <u>SSEng</u>. 5 (1979-80):
3-14.

Discusses the many discontinuities in the book and their
effect on the reader, and compares the reader to Gulliver in
that he is "cut off from familiar surroundings, disoriented,
and uncertain what to expect next." He is never allowed to
settle for long into an imagined world. Because the book is
"a disparate collection of episodes with discrete effects and
local strategies" instead of having consistent characters and
a unified theme, it is an uncomfortable book to read--but
challenging because we are asked to "defamiliarize our view
of ourselves, to see our human nature not as we have been
taught and have been accustomed to see it, but as it might
appear to an outsider, who viewed it afresh."

3361   HILL, JOHN M.
        "Corpuscular Fundament: Swift and the Mechanical Philosophy."
        <u>Enl. E</u>. 6 (1975): 37-49.

        Discusses Swift's attitude toward mechanical philosophy and
        examines several of his critiques on experimental projectors
        in Book III of <u>Gulliver's Travels</u>.

3362   HITT, RALPH E.
        "Antiperfectionism as a Unifying Theme in <u>Gulliver's Travels</u>.
        <u>Miss. Quart</u>. 15 (1963): 161-169.

        Suggests that Swift's negative philosophy of history--that
        the history of man shows goodness in building noble institu-
        tions and ideals which, however, become corrupted through
        man's pride and irrationality--provides a thematic unity to
        <u>Gulliver's Travels</u>. Physical degeneration is the main theme
        of Books I and II; intellectual or mental deterioration, of
        Book III; and moral disintegration is the main concern of
        Book IV.

3363   HOLLY, GRANT.
        "Travel and Translation: Textuality in <u>Gulliver's Travels</u>."
        <u>Criticism</u> 21 (1979): 134-152.

        Divided into two parts: "The first attempts to show the
        way in which Swift's text makes signifying its subject, by im-
        plying a vast textuality which incorporates the reader and
        which, therefore, he can participate in but is no longer free
        to comment on. As a way of avoiding the hypostasizing of
        signifying as the signified of the text, the second part of the
        essay attempts to indicate the problematic of differencing
        along which signifying plays without fear of falling into sense
        or significance."

3364   HORRELL, JOSEPH.
        "What Gulliver Knew." SR 51 (1943): 476-504. Rpt. in
        [3059], pp. 55-70.

        A study of Gulliver's Travels as a work of fiction, not
        satire, using a circle analogy to clarify its ironic structure.
        Argues that the fourth book is not a "distinct unit ... com-
        plete in itself" but rather forms the climax to the first three
        voyages by providing Gulliver with a choice between the world
        of men and the world of horses. Discusses some of the themes
        and motivations, or "fictional outlines," of the four books,
        and suggests that the "unifying fictional conception that in-
        forms" them is a series of "dominant themes about man ar-
        ranged by contrast, some of them supporting variations and
        each adding complexity to its predecessor."

3365   JARRETT, JAMES L.
        "A Yahoo versus Jonathan Swift." WHR 8 (1954): 195-200.

        Argues that "the misanthropy in The Voyage to the Houy-
        hnhnms is of an extremely morbid kind, destructive of the
        art," and that its ugliness spoils the whole book.

3366   JENKINS, CLAUSTON.
        "The Ford Changes and the Text of Gulliver's Travels."
        PBSA 62 (1968): 1-23.

        Argues that the "concentration on the editions of 1726 and
        1735 has caused editors to slight another body of important
        textual evidence--Charles Ford's holograph changes contained
        in a list and also in an interleaved copy of Gulliver's Travels."

3367   JOHNSON, MAURICE.
        "Remote Regions of Man's Mind: the Travels of Gulliver."
        UKCR 27 (1961): 299-303.

        The central matter of the book is Lemuel Gulliver's travels
        within his own mind; appreciation of Gulliver's Travels can
        only begin when the author is ruthlessly separated from pre-
        tended narrator.

3368   KALLICH, MARTIN.
        The Other End of the Egg: Religious Satire in "Gulliver's
        Travels." Bridgeport, Conn.: Conference on British Studies
        at the Univ. of Bridgeport, 1970.

        An analysis of Gulliver's four voyages for religious mean-
        ing establishes the Travels as a "profoundly religious satire
        ... and to underestimate the role of religion in the story,

results in serious distortions of meaning." Kallich finds
Swift's Anglican theology crucially different from the thinking
of the Houyhnhnms and maintains that "the horses do not represent ideal man any more than the Yahoos do."

3369   "Three Ways of Looking at a Horse; Jonathan Swift's 'Voyage
to the Houyhnhnms' Again." Criticism 2 (1960): 107-124.

An analysis of "the horses in the light of the generally accepted ideals and values of contemporary western civilization."
Maintains that Gulliver's eulogy was meant by Swift as an
ironical attack on the deists whom he disliked; Swift suggests
that the ethical rationalism and naturalism of the Houyhnhnms
approximated that of the deists.

3370   KEESEY, DONALD.
"The Distorted Image: Swift's Yahoos and the Critics." PLL
15 (1979): 320-32.

A review of recent literature on the fourth book of Gulliver. Concludes that it is no longer accurate or useful to
refer to man's "middle state" or to see the Yahoos as representing "fallen man" or "depraved man"--it is mankind who
represents depravity and sin; the Yahoos are not men, but a
satiric weapon with which Swift attacks man's exorbitant pride.

3371   KELLING, H[arold] D.
" 'Gulliver's Travels' IV, Once More." Scholia Satyrica 2,
ii (1976): 3-12.

Attempts to show that the problem of Part IV, the significance of the Houyhnhnms, has a fairly simple solution; namely,
that Swift intended not to impart a "message" but to create a
satire, using a kind of irony that permits the reader's interpretation to depend on his own beliefs. Houyhnhnms (and
Yahoos) are imaginary creations, known only as metaphors
that suggest the nature of man, but do not represent some
individual or group of Swift's age: "If we are to read Part
IV accurately, we have to see that the Yahoos and Houyhnhnms are terms in metaphors and that the Houyhnhnm psychology is important, not their physiology." Concludes that
the main reason for misunderstanding Part IV is the "failure
of Gulliver, of the Houyhnhnms, and of the Houyhnhnm language to represent man's nature accurately."

3372   "Gulliver's Travels: A Comedy of Humours." UTQ 21 (1952):
362-375.

Concerned with Gulliver's function as a humourist in the

structure of the book. "If we see Gulliver ... as a Don
Quixote, a humourist, Gulliver's Travels is in the tradition
of a great comedy, offering hope for man's situation rather
than offering heroic despair because man cannot achieve perfection." Gulliver provides the human point of view in the
four societies, consciously or unconsciously relating them to
reality; however, "his humour prevents him from coming to
common-sense conclusions, with the result that he draws a
ridiculous picture of human vice and folly."

3373   "Some Significant Names in Gulliver's Travels." SP 48 (1951):
        761-778.

        Offers some suggestions as to the origin and significance
        of some of the exotic nouns in the Trildrogdribian and Houy-
        hnhnm languages.

3374   KELLY, ANN CLINE.
        "After Eden: Gulliver's (Linguistic) Travels." ELH 45 (1978):
        33-54.

        The psychological impact of the Civil War provoked the as-
        sumption that a unified and purified language was necessary
        for a unified and purified country. Swift's views on linguistic
        speculation are contained, in addition to those of A Tale of a
        Tub and Polite Conversation, in Gulliver's Travels where he
        describes the process of Gulliver's acquisition of language and
        the nature of his host's language, as well as the political sys-
        tem of each country Gulliver visits. Gulliver especially pro-
        vides details of an important Swiftian theme, the association
        of language and governance, a theme popular also with many
        contemporary commentators and linguistic reformers.

3375   "Swift's Explorations of Slavery in Houyhnhnmland and Ire-
        land." PMLA 91 (1976): 846-855.

        Since slavery is at the center of Book IV, perhaps Swift
        is showing parallels between the Yahoos and Ireland, the Houy-
        hnhnms and England. Swift is intrigued by "the subtle re-
        lationships between external slavery and internal debasement,
        between nurture and nature"; if we apply "the premises and
        observations [which he] gleaned from conditions in Ireland to
        Gulliver's Travels, conditions in Houyhnhnmland appear in
        a new and surprising light."

3376   KELSALL, M. M.
        "Iterum Houyhnhnms: Swift's Sextumvirate and the Horses."
        EIC 19 (1969): 35-45. Rpt. in [3350], pp. 212-222.

Draws a parallel between the society of the Houyhnhnms and the ideals of the sextumvirate Swift refers to (III, vii), Brutus, Junius, Socrates, Epaminondas, Cato the Younger, and Sir Thomas More, to determine whether Swift was serious when he had Gulliver propose the horses as a model fit for imitation. Concludes that "the thing [the society of horses] is utterly ridiculous."

3377   KENNER, HUGH.
"The Gulliver Game." Spectrum 8 (1966): 114-128.

The object of the "Gulliver Game" is to see what we can tell about a man if we think he may be an artifact; Gulliver is a "casually programmed talking machine," our spokesman and ambassador, and the author seeks to describe both the Gulliver we see and the Gulliver the beings in the book see. Compares Gulliver to a computer.

3378   KLIGER, SAMUEL.
"The Unity of Gulliver's Travels." MLQ 6 (1945): 401-415. Rpt. in [3340], pp. 148-165.

Discusses the relationship and order among the parts of the novel as they are achieved through balance and contrast. If we do not regard the novel as an ordered form we "overlook the expository devices of balance and contrast ... [and] fail to appreciate the paradoxical solution which Swift offers to the problem of human folly from his double viewpoint: anti-perfectionism and skepticism of abstract reasoning." Discusses the "happy beast" theme.

3379   KORSHIN, PAUL J.
"The Intellectual Context of Swift's Flying Island." PQ 50 (1971): 630-646.

Considers several sources for the Flying Island to give us a clearer understanding of Swift's satiric intentions in Part III of Gulliver's Travels; concludes that Swift is satirizing not only the errors of experimental and applied science but also the vanities of speculative pseudo-science.

3380   LaCASCE, STEWARD.
"The Fall of Gulliver's Master." EIC 20 (1970): 327-333.

Argues that the Master Houyhnhnm, having learned from Gulliver the difference between good and evil and changing his attitude toward the Yahoos, "demonstrates in a comic manner the moral inefficacy of any strictly secular ideal of reason," an interpretation which "differs profoundly from that of the hard-core critics."

3381   Gulliver's Fourth Voyage: A New Look at the Critical De-
        bate." SNL 8 (1970): 5-7.

        Suggests "that two categories of criticism be established,
        one based on philosophic assumptions concerning the nature
        of man, the other based on theological assumptions concerning
        the nature of man," and that an attempt should be made to
        differentiate sharply between them.

3382   "Swift on Medical Extremism." JHI 31 (1970): 599-606.

        Medical theory as discussed in Chapter IV of Gulliver's
        Travels reveals Swift's attitude toward certain medical ex-
        tremists of the day and helps provide a better insight into
        the character of Gulliver who was trained in medicine and
        supported the classical approach to medicine and the ancient
        theory of contraries.

3383   LANDA, LOUIS A.
        "The Dismal Science in Houyhnhnmland." Novel 13 (1979):
        38-49.

        An examination of Part IV of Gulliver's Travels to see
        "how Swift has assimilated certain economic ideas into his
        work, and to place these ideas in the context of the prevail-
        ing thought of his time, mainly--but not entirely--economic
        thought, that amorphous body of economic ideas and assump-
        tion called mercantilism." Part IV uses traditional motifs,
        conventions, and imagery derived from Golden Age, Pastoral,
        and Utopian economics in order to present Swift's reaction to
        the dogmas of the mercantile philosophy. Houyhnhnmland rep-
        resents Swift's rejection of a basic assumption of the mer-
        cantile philosophy, the belief that a society organized to satisfy
        man's materialistic and acquisitive instincts will provide a
        satisfactory and rewarding way of life for a people.

3384   LAWLIS, MERRITT.
        "Swift's Use of Narrative: The Third Chapter of the Voyage
        to Lilliput." JEGP 72 (1973): 1-16.

        Discusses different ways in which Swift combines four qual-
        ities--diversity, inconsistency, playfulness, and ambiguity--
        into the first three chapters, with emphasis on Chapter 3,
        in an attempt "to see these early chapters in relation to the
        work as a whole."

3385   LAWLOR, JOHN.
        "The Evolution of Gulliver's Character." In [3351], pp. 372-
        376. Excerpted from "Radical Satire and the Realistic Novel."
        E & S 8 (1955): 58-75.

An analysis of the development of Gulliver's character so that, in order to break down the reader's "defensive reaction," Gulliver himself, the "observer and reporter, shall win respect for his candour and objectivity." Concludes that, in Part IV, Gulliver must leave the land of the Houyhnhnms: he is supremely lonely, for, falling infinitely short of the perfection of his masters, he is yet superior to the Yahoos in possessing "some rudiments of reason"; therefore "Swift's satiric genius has penetrated to the final truth that when man falls, he falls below the level of the brute creation": partial reason combined with the "natural pravity" of the Yahoos presents incalculable possibilities for evil.

3386   LAWRY, JON S.
       "Dr. Lemuel Gulliver and 'the Thing Which Was Not.'"
       JEGP 67 (1968): 212-234.

       An analysis of three "faces" of Gulliverian character: 1) that of Gulliver who gulls others, 2) that of Gulliver who is gulled by others, and 3) that of Gulliver who gulls himself, to reveal his vision and veracity. Stresses patterns of recurrence across the entire work and the basic continuity which is found in narrator and style. Adopts "middle ground" approach in the controversy between "hard" and "soft" interpretations.

3387   LEYBURN, ELLEN DOUGLASS.
       "Gulliver's Clothes." SNL 1 (1964): 35-40.

       The structural and thematic function of the clothes imagery: "Not only are the clothes used from the first to convey part of the essence of Gulliver's relation to the country he is in at the moment; but from book to book the complexity of the implications in the treatment of clothes increases, in keeping with Gulliver's own progress toward the derangement of Book IV."

3388   Satiric Allegory: Mirror of Man. (Yale Studies in English, 130). Yale Univ. Press, 1956.

       Based on the belief that satires in allegorical form must be considered as allegories; analyzes Gulliver's Travels as the model of one type of fantastic satire, that of the fantastic journey: "it is by means of [Gulliver's] travels that his creator projects both the allegory and the satire: the satire through the allegory."

3389   "Certain Problems of Allegorical Satire in Gulliver's Travels."
       HLQ 13 (1950): 161-189.

Considers Swift's handling of the problem of allegorical
satire in four ways: 1) the relation of Gulliver to the genre
of the voyage, 2) Swift's establishment of his allegorical intent, 3) the degree of allegorical meaning in Gulliver, and
4) some particular points connected with the separate voyages.

3390   LOCK, F. P.
        The Politics of "Gulliver's Travels." Oxford: Clarendon Press,
        1980.

Since Swift didn't want his proposals for reform to be tied
to any political platform, he emphasized general issues--the
character of an ideal ruler and the evils of factions, for instance. This book is the first attempt at a "comprehensive
study of [Gulliver's] politics, embracing personalities, issues,
and philosophies"; the author's particular aim is "to devote
more attention than is usual to the general political background ... to give fuller treatment of the knowledge of political thought and European history that went into the making"
of the book; and to largely ignore the accumulated mass of
personal and particular allusions that modern criticism has
discovered.

3391   MACK, MAYNARD.
        "Gulliver's Travels." From Introduction to English Master-
        pieces, V, The Augustans, 2nd. ed. (Englewood Cliffs, N.J.,
        Prentice-Hall, 1961), pp. 14-16. Rpt. in [3059], pp. 111-
        114.

Suggests that one of Swift's aims in Gulliver is to show
that human nature is instinctively good except when corrupted
by civilization. Each of Gulliver's voyages deals with a different aspect of the human situation and it is through Gulliver
that "Swift is able to deliver the most powerful indictment of
man's inhumanity ever written in prose, and at the same time
to distinguish his own realistic view of man's nature from the
misanthropy of which he has sometimes been accused."

3392   McMAMMON, JOHN J.
        "The Problem of a Religious Interpretation of Gulliver's Fourth
        Voyage." JHI 27 (1966): 59-72.

Maintains that "there is no internal evidence in Gulliver
IV that its author was either a clergyman or a Christian"
and therefore attempts by critics to root it in Christian doctrine and morality lead to errors in interpretation.

3393   MERTON, ROBERT C.
        "The 'Motionless' Motion of Swift's Flying Island." JHI 27
        (1966): 275-277.

Considers several interpretations of Gulliver's explanation
of how the island could float motionless and concludes that
Swift was being satiric. "If, indeed, the Laputans were unable to put a house together, they might also have failed at
their specialty of making islands fly. And as for Swift, what
better joke could he play on his abstract scientists than to
suggest that the very theories that set their island afloat would
also bring it crashing down."

3394   MEZCIEMS, JENNY.
       "Gulliver and Other Heroes." In [3057], pp. 189-208.

The author discusses the problem of Swift's use of allusion, "so indirect where Pope's is direct, taking his attitude
and method of reference to the concept of the hero as an example on which to focus." Swift, like Pope, always places
a central figure within a formal literary context or a genre
that has a relationship to society, and the satire explores that
relationship, using allusion all the time to emphasize "risible
incompatibilities": Swift generally weaves borrowed material
silently into his narrative without comment, so that the reader
has to do the work himself, drawing from his own literary
experience, without help from Swift, the models by which the
satiric objects are to be judged.

3395   "The Unity of Swift's 'Voyage to Laputa': Structure as Mean-
       ing in Utopian Fiction." MLR 72 (1977): 1-21.

The author's aim is to show "that the Voyage to Laputa is
as carefully structured as any other Voyage, that its placing
is part of a pattern essential to the whole work, and that
particular effects are achieved by particular methods which
can be recognized if we examine the procedures of certain
literary genres and especially the genre of utopian fiction."

3396   MONK, SAMUEL H.
       "The Pride of Lemuel Gulliver." SR 63 (1955): 48-71. Rpt.
       in [3109], pp. 631-647; [3351], pp. 312-330; [3301], pp. 70-
       79; [3340], pp. 227-245; [18], pp. 112-129.

An analysis of Gulliver's four voyages to show his progression from simplicity to sophistication to madness. Illustrates
how Swift forces the reader to "gaze into the stupid, evil,
brutal heart of humanity" and to understand that even if "the
surface of the book is comic, at its center is tragedy,
transformed through style and tone into icy irony." Shows
how Gulliver's experiences are in reality a parody on man
and on society in England.

3397   MOORE, JOHN BROOKS.

"The Rôle of Gulliver." MP 25 (1928): 469-480. Rpt. in [3340], 95-107.

Argues that Gulliver's role is progressively to attain ultimate wisdom and knowledge and to arrive at total disillusionment--the "inevitable, imminent wisdom of misanthrophy"; the final revelation in Gulliver's education is to avoid all human contact. Gulliver is not Swift in disguise.

3398   MOORE, JOHN R.
        "The Geography of Gulliver's Travels." JEGP 40 (1941): 214-228.

Maintains that the "geography of the book is so incredible that we must assume (1) that Swift intended an extravagant burlesque on voyages, or (2) that he was ignorant of geography, or (3) that he intended a burlesque and knew too little geography to carry it out accurately."

3399   MORRIS, JOHN N.
        "Wishes as Horses: A Word for the Houyhnhnms." YR 62 (1973): 355-371.

Concerned with "the various things that generations of readers have said that it [Gulliver's Travels] means"--a look in the mirror at "invisible faces that the glass of satire reflects." Maintains that Swift's object is to excite the reader and force him to examine some of his own assumptions about himself and that his utopian Houyhnhnmland is "one version of that object of almost universal human desire, an unconflicted life, a civilization without discontents."

3400   MORRISSEY, L. J.
        Gulliver's Progress. Hamden, Conn.: Archon Books, 1978.

In seeking a pattern that will corroborate our sense of Gulliver's wholeness and aesthetic significance, the author argues that Swift is a religious moralist who embedded in the text a hidden pattern based on the lectionary of the Church of England: "The lectionary dates offer such a satisfyingly coherent pattern of allusion, such as aesthetic wholeness, for Gulliver's Travels. They also form a basic Christian trope for this moral book which elucidates its larger ironies." The lectionary readings provide a persuasive commentary on the action of Gulliver's Travels, and offer invariably a Christian solution to every problem or dilemma that Gulliver confronts.

3401   MOSS, WILLIAM M.
        "Mounting Evidence in Book IV." SHR 8 (1974): 191-194.

Relates the meaning of Book IV to "one of the most crucial, and least understood, periods of [Swift's] life"; suggests that the Yahoos represent the church, and the Houyhnhnms Esther Vanhomrigh, presenting Swift with the dilemma of abandoning the beauteous Miss Vanhomrigh in order to return to the church that had denied him recognition, or of deserting the church in order to "uxoriously deposit himself in the lap of his Vanessa. "

3402 MUNRO, JOHN H.
"Book III of Gulliver's Travels Once More. " ES 49 (1968): 429-436.

Gives arguments pro and con on organization of Gulliver's Travels and supports the argument that Book III not only fits into the narrative scheme of the book but that it plays an "integral part in the total design: the presentation of Man seen both at his worst and as the kind of creature he might be, in the opposing conditions of humanity and disembodied reason. "

3403 NATH, VISHWANADHA HARI HARA.
"The Wisdom of the Ancients Is the Folly of the Moderns: A Reading of Gulliver's Travels, Book III. " PAPA 6, ii (1980): 61-76.

Disagrees with other critics about the unity of Book III and analyzes it to show that it possesses unity of theme as well as unity of character. Because of its internal unity and coherence, Book III plays a pivotal role in the transition from Book II to Book IV. Its two major themes, "the satire on corruption in learning and in politics are synthesized by the larger confrontation between the Ancients and the Moderns. "

3404 NICOLSON, MARJORIE and NORA M. MOHLER.
"The Scientific Background of Swift's Voyage to Laputa. " Annals of Science 2 (1937): 299-334. Rpt. in Science and Imagination (Ithaca, N. Y.: Cornell Univ. Press, 1956), pp. 110-154; [3055], pp. 226-269; [3054], pp. 210-246.

Presents evidence that Swift borrowed heavily from contemporary scientists, especially from the "Philosophical Transactions of the Royal Society" for his scientific details in the Voyage to Laputa. Shows parallels between the Transactions and the projectors of the Grand Academy, the Flying Island, the mathematicians, and the theories of the Laputans and the Balnibarians.

3405 "Swift's 'Flying Island' in the Voyage to Laputa. " Annals of Science 2 (1937): 405-430.

Argues that the "Flying Island" was not a "creation of
fancy" but that "every detail of its structure and mechanism
was drawn carefully and thoughtfully from contemporary science," and that it represents "one of the most remarkable
pseudo-scientific passages in the literature of the eighteenth
century." Demonstrates how "the Laputans had learned--
as Swift's generation had learned--both the greatness and the
ironic limitations of man's supposed conquest of nature."

3406   ORWELL, GEORGE.
"Politics vs. Literature: An Examination of Gulliver's Travels." In Shooting an Elephant and Other Essays (New York:
Harcourt Brace, 1945), pp. 53-76. Rpt. in [3055], pp. 166-
185; [3054], pp. 192-209.

An overall discussion of Gulliver's view of the world, as
expressed in his various voyages, which Orwell finds barely
sane, while still maintaining that if only six books could be
preserved, he would put Gulliver's Travels among them. A
largely political interpretation, Orwell even declaring that the
Houyhnhnms had "reached ... the highest stage of totalitarian
organization, the stage when conformity has become so general
that there is no need for a police force."

3407   PAPAJEWSKI, HELMUT.
"Swift and Berkeley." Anglia 77 (1959): 29-53.

Analyzes the ideas of relativity and perception in Gulliver's
Travels; suggests that Berkeley's influence is small.

3408   PATTERSON, ANNE E.
"Swift's Irony and Cartesian Man." Midwest Quart. 15 (1974):
338-351.

Argues that Swift in Book III attacks certain dangerous
tendencies of the new science, especially Cartesian science
which mathematicized and mechanized both man and nature.

3409   PEAKE, CHARLES.
"The Coherence of Gulliver's Travels." In [3058], pp. 171-
196.

Insists that Gulliver's Travels is not a modern novel and
that Lemuel Gulliver is a satiric device manipulated by Swift;
therefore, he cannot go mad. Attempts to explain the organization of the work, especially as an ordered attack on man's
pride.

3410   PETERSON, LELAND D.

"On the Keen Appetite for Perpetuity of Life." ELN 1 (1964):
265-267.

Suggests that the Struldbrugg episode reflects contemporary
interest in prolonging life, and gives Robert Samber's Long
Livers as an example, though not as a source, of the kind of
interest satirized in Book III of Gulliver's Travels.

3411   PHILMUS, ROBERT M.
        "The Language of Utopia." Std. in Lit. Imag. 6, No. 2
        (1973): 61-78.

        A comparison of Book IV of Gulliver's Travels and Orwell's
        1984 to show the differences between the utopias of Houyhnhnm-
        land and Oceania: " ... both provide precisely defined con-
        texts for testing the limiting conditions of language as a func-
        tion of political order [and] both are hypothetical models of
        societies in which language can do no more than reflect, and
        thus guarantees, the nature of the social order. ... Gulliver's
        exclusion and Winston Smith's inclusion define the nature of
        the two different social orders."

3412   "Swift, Gulliver, and 'The Thing Which Was Not.'" ELH
        38 (1971): 62-79.

        Makes a distinction between Swift and Gulliver, seeing
        Gulliver as "the type of the satirist devoid of ironic self-
        regard," Swift is possessed of an ironic self-perception which
        removes his delusions about himself. The idea of Gulliver
        as this type of satirist helps interpret three textual puzzles:
        1) the quotation from the Aeneid which Gulliver applies to
        himself, 2) the meaning of "I said the thing which was not,"
        and 3) the expulsion of Gulliver from Houyhnhnmland.

3413   PIERRE, GERALD J.
        "Gulliver's Voyage to China and Moor Park: The Influence
        of Sir William Temple Upon Gulliver's Travels." TSLL 17
        (1975): 428-437.

        Swift's mental journey back to Temple's library at Moor
        Park influenced his writing of Gulliver's Travels: "Temple's
        essays and life partially explain the significance of the Houy-
        hnhnms and the Yahoos and the meaning of Gulliver's final
        stance."

3414   PULLEN, CHARLES H.
        "Gulliver: Student of Nature." DR 51 (1971): 77-89.

        Argues that Gulliver, when he arrives in the land of the

Houyhnhnms, has been so brainwashed that he can no longer choose effectively between the Yahoos and the Houyhnhnms: "The Yahoos stand for the surface of life, the horror of humanity at its worst, the Houyhnhnms for the enthusiast's obsession with the ideal. The answer is in neither, but in the via media as exemplified in the actions of the Portuguese captain on the social level and the King of Brobdingnag on the political level."

3415   QUINLAN, MAURICE J.
"Treason in Lilliput and in England." TSLL 11 (1970): 1317-1332.

Examines the political allegory of Book I of Gulliver's Travels, especially the satire on the charge of treason against Gulliver; compares the government of Lilliput with that of England, analyzes the nature and application of the treason laws, and their use by the Whigs to gain revenge on Swift's Tory friends, and describes the particular objects of Swift's satire.

3416   QUINTANA, RICARDO.
"Gulliver's Travels: The Satiric Intent and Execution." In [3056], pp. 78-93.

Presents the known facts about Gulliver's Travels and Swift's intentions, including the background of ideas, principles, and convictions that lie behind the Travels: "Certain things concerning Swift's satiric intent ... and his satiric execution are apparent; they are already known, being matters of historical fact...." Also discusses Swift's "rhetoric of realism," and finds as the central design of the work the "comedy of exclusion" that unites three of the four parts.

3417   RADNER, JOHN B.
"The Struldbruggs, the Houyhnhnms, and the Good Life." SEL 17 (1977): 419-433.

Suggests that Swift wrote Book III about Gulliver's decision to stay with the Struldbruggs to illuminate his later decision to stay with the Houyhnhnms and to help guide readers through the final voyage. The chapter shows that not only is Gulliver wholly unaware of what virtue is but that he is only a nominal Christian whose vision is secular, never thinking of the Fall or the Resurrection but only of earthly immortality. In the end Gulliver is no wiser about the degenerate nature of man than he was in Book III; to him the Houyhnhnms are truly virtuous, and he ignores religion as he begins "to instruct the Yahoos of my own Family as far as I find them docile Animals."

3418   RAWSON, CLAUDE J.
        Gulliver and the Gentle Reader: Studies in Swift and Our
        Time.   London: Routledge & Kegan Paul, 1973.

        Like Rawson's other book, Henry Fielding and the Augustan
        Ideal Under Stress, this book is primarily concerned with style
        and authorial temperament which reflect a "tension between
        Augustan ideals of correctness and 'polite' civilization on the
        one hand, and inner and outer forces of misrule on the other."
        Another major theme is that "Swift's satire reveals itself not
        primarily as a Satire on Man in some impersonal or third-
        person sense which leaves the reader and the author out, but
        some of its most powerful energies attack the reader (or
        'second person') and finally implicate the author himself (or
        'first person') in various ways, 'official' and 'unofficial.' "

3419   "Gulliver and the Gentle Reader."   In [36], pp. 51-90.

        Suggests that in Swift's relations with his reader there is
        something that can be "described approximately in terms of
        the edgy intimacy of a personal quarrel that does not quite
        come out into the open, with gratuitous-seeming sarcasms on
        one side and a defensive embarrassment on the other."   Be-
        hind the masks, indirections, and ironies can be felt a central
        Swiftian personality.

3420   REICHARD, HUGO M.
        "Satiric Snobbery: The Houyhnhnms' Man."   SNL 4 (1967):
        51-57.

        Argues that among the Houyhnhnms Gulliver is a snob, and
        that the "Houyhnhnms and their admirer succeed in casting
        discredit upon no men except for a very evil, very reprehen-
        sible few....   Swift is using his snob to perpetrate a hoax,
        to produce irony, and to accomplish social satire."

3421   "Gulliver the Pretender."   PLL 1 (1965):   316-326.

        Argues that Gulliver's account of the Houyhnhnms is colored
        by charming deceit in the first seven chapters of Part IV: "It
        is by being of the Houyhnhnms' party without showing it to us
        that he contrives to legitimate or conceal the distortions in
        his account of Western civilization, and it is later by telling
        us of the attachment without correcting the account that he
        enables his interrogator to equate men and Yahoos."

3422   REICHERT, JOHN F.
        "Plato, Swift, and the Houyhnhnms."   PQ 47 (1968):   179-192.

Explores in detail similarities between Book IV and The Republic and uses the "Platonic qualities of both the content and style of Book IV ... to define ... what Swift's intentions were, and what they were not."

3423   REISS, EDMUND.
"The Importance of Swift's Glubbdubdrib Episode." JEGP 59 (1960): 223-228.

Maintains that Gulliver's experiences with the dead in Glubbdubdrib are the pivotal point of the Travels in terms of his psychological development, that this episode is a direct link between parts II and IV.

3424   RENAKER, DAVID.
"Swift's Laputians as a Caricature of the Cartesians." PMLA 94 (1979): 936-944.

Attempts to refute the idea advanced by Nicolson [3404] that both the Laputa and Balnibari episodes in Book III of Gulliver's Travels satirize the Royal Society by showing that the traits of the Laputians represent the traits of the Cartesians. The unity of Gulliver's Travels is "greatly enhanced" by interpreting "the Laputians as Cartesians, Laputa as France, and Balnibarbi as England," although the fact that "the Laputians' fear of being incinerated by the tail of a comet ... is alien to Descartes's Principles" is a weakness in this interpretation.

3425   ROGERS, J. P. W.
"Swift, Walpole, and the Rope-Dancers." PLL 8 (1972): 159-171.

An analysis of the rope-dancing scene in Book I, Chapter 3, as political satire. Indicates ways in which the passage ministers "to the deepest and most inward workings of the satire as a whole" and the ways in which the allegory resembles the techniques of Scriblerian farce.

3426   ROGERS, PAT.
"Gulliver's Glasses." In [3057], pp. 179-188.

Gulliver associates his glasses, which he concealed from the Lilliputians, with secrecy, privacy, ownership, and identity. Rogers argues "that this is connected with the mixed feelings about sight which Swift reveals, and that such a concern lies at the centre of the Travels." The argument consists of three stages: a brief discussion of the psychology

of spectacles; an analysis of various attitudes to the faculty
of vision in the Augustan Age; and then an application of these
ideas to Gulliver's Travels. Gulliver's quasi-objectivity as
Spectator represents the intrusive intellect, which scrutinizes
what is better left unexamined because it causes pain when
pried into by the empiricist. Gulliver wants to peep, and
his glasses are the emblem of his meddling and inquisitive
nature; he stands for idle curiosity as opposed to purposeful,
spiritualized living.

3427   "Gulliver and the Engineers." MLR 70 (1975): 260-270.

        The "Southern" journey to which Gulliver refers is perhaps
an allusion to the great South Sea Bubble of 1720. Argues
that Part III of Gulliver's Travels is based on "the doings of
speculators, engineers, inventors, and company promoters ...
[that it is] a lively engagement in contemporary life, and a
ready exposure to the popular news-stories of the day."

3428   ROSENHEIM, EDWARD, JR.
        "The Fifth Voyage of Lemuel Gulliver: A Footnote." MP
        60 (1962): 103-119.

        A "tongue-in-cheek" commentary on Gulliver's Fifth Voyage
in the "Land of the Critics." A critical survey of diverse
interpretations of Gulliver's Travels and an assertion that perhaps "we avoid the essential character of Swift's masterpiece
largely because it is an attack, directed ... against ourselves."

3429   ROSS, ANGUS.
        "The Social Circumstances of Several Remote Nations of the
        World." In [3060], pp. 220-232.

        Analyzes the social circumstances of the various groups
which come before Gulliver in the course of his voyages, including such matters as politics, social and civic institutions,
economics, and class structure; concerned with them as revealing Swift's own assumptions about society or as objects
of satire.

3430   Swift: "Gulliver's Travels" (Studies in English Literature).
        London: Edward Arnold, 1968.

        A general survey of the book emphasizing the variety and
diversity of meanings and satirical approaches: the conduct
of the satire is complex, yet possesses a unity.

3431   ROSS, JOHN F.

"The Final Comedy of Lemuel Gulliver." In Studies in the
Comic, eds. J. M. Cline, B. H. Bronson, C. D. Chrétien.
Univ. Calif. Publ. in English, vol. 8, No. 2 (Berkeley &
Los Angeles, 1941), pp. 175-196. Rpt. Norwood Editions,
1975, pp. 25-46. Rpt. in [3059], pp. 71-89; [3350], 100-119;
[3340], pp. 121-138.

Sees Gulliver as a comic figure, and the entire work as
a complex satire. A defense of Voyage IV, the essay argues
that Gulliver in Book IV is not Swift, and that Swift superadds
to his corrosive satire a large amount of comic satire. In
Chapters 10-12, Swift shows us the insufficiency of Gulliver's
attitude toward the Yahoos. It is Gulliver, not mankind, who
is satirized.

3432   RYLEY, ROBERT M.
        "Gulliver, Flimnap's Wife, and the Critics." Std. in Lit.
        Imag. 5, No. 2 (1972): 53-63.

Using Gulliver's defense of Flimnap's wife and critical commentary on it, the author argues that the critics often err in
interpreting the work as a Jamesian novel and that consequently
Gulliver should be treated not as a character but as a voice.

3433   SACKETT, S. J.
        "Gulliver Four: Here We Go Again." RMMLA Bull. 27 (1973):
        212-218.

Interprets Gulliver Four from standpoint of psychology of
personality. Theorizes that it presents "a view of man which
shows that he has two sides to his nature, symbolized by the
Yahoos and the Houyhnhnms; and that although it does not specifically establish that there is also a third element in the
human personality, it does show that Gulliver's lack of such
an element mediating between the other two and unifying his
personality leads him to an absurd misapprehension of reality."

3434   SAUERS, PHILIP.
        "Wisdom is a Nut; or, the Idols of Jonathan Swift." In If By
        Your Art, Testament to Percival Hunt, ed. Agnes Lynch Star-
        rett (Pittsburgh: Univ. Pittsburgh Press, 1948), pp. 71-95.

An interpretation of Book III of Gulliver's Travels. Finds that
Amorphy is the disease of Human Nature dealt with in Part III.

3435   SAVAGE, D. S.
        "Swift." Western Rev. 15 (1950): 25-36.

Considers the nature of Swift's irony, finding its crowning
achievement in the fourth book of the Travels, and sees Swift

as essentially a political writer, devoid of imagination, in
whom Reason and Nature were in conflict. Suggests that
Parts I and II depict Swift's remembered childish situation
and his adult effort to return to its state of innocence, Part
III portrays the specific problems of the adult consciousness,
while Part IV describes the final descent to nihilism which
is Swift's only solution to the dilemma of his life.

3436   SCHUSTER, SISTER M. FAITH, O. S. B.
       "Clothes Philosophy in Gulliver's Travels." American Bene-
       dictine Rev 15 (1964): 316-326.

       A Christian interpretation of Gulliver's Travels, arguing
       that the clothing imagery supports the main theme of the
       work--"man's moral degeneracy from the ideal which he should
       achieve and which it is possible for him to achieve."

3437   SCRONSY, CECIL C.
       "Sir Politic Would-Be in Laputa." ELN 1 (1963): 17-24.

       Presents evidence of Jonson's influence on Swift in Sir
       Politic Would-Be's political and "scientific" activities as re-
       flected in Book III of Gulliver's Travels.

3438   SEELYE, JOHN D.
       "Hobbes' Leviathan and the Giantism Complex in the First
       Book of Gulliver's Travels." JEGP 60 (1961): 228-239.

       Suggests that "below the superstructure of the satire upon
       faction in politics ... there are at least three layers of al-
       lusion and meaning in the first book.... (1) the three-phase
       political cycle--concerned with the 'fundamental human vitali-
       ties' of social endeavour.... (2) the giantism complex, a
       satire upon Hobbes' Leviathan and the paradox of absolutism,"
       and (3) the problem of Ireland.

3439   SEIDEL, MICHAEL.
       "Strange Dispositions: Swift's Gulliver's Travels." In [158],
       pp. 201-225.

       Swift presents a vision of degeneration that involves both
       historical and political decline; the fact that Gulliver is absent
       intermittently from England between 1699 and 1715 is signifi-
       cant because it suggests that Swift's scheme of degeneration
       applies to the historical and cultural events of that period
       and the Walpole era: "In Lilliput Gulliver practices state-
       craft; in Brobdingnag he defends it; in Laputa he hears of its
       abuses; in Houyhnhnmland he attacks it."

3440   SENA, JOHN F.
       "Swift, the Yahoos and 'the English Malady.'" PLL 7 (1971):
       300-303.

           Brief discussion of the relationship between the Yahoos'
       disease of the spleen and that of Englishmen. By having the
       Yahoos suffer from a typically English disease, Swift not only
       demonstrates his medical knowledge but also draws a closer
       relationship between the Yahoos and man.

3441   SHERBO, ARTHUR.
       "Swift and Travel Literature." MLS 9, iii (1979): 114-127.

           Describes various possible sources for Gulliver's Travels
       in contemporary travel literature, emphasizing in particular
       that "Swift occasionally parodies travel literature or is other-
       wise satiric at its expense ... and, even more important,
       that he everywhere uses the language, conventions, and the
       very details of travel literature as the vehicle for his satire
       of man and his institutions."

3442   SHERBURN, GEORGE.
       "Errors Concerning the Houyhnhnms." MP 56 (1958): 92-
       97. Rpt. in [3340], pp. 258-266.

           Disagrees with Ehrenpreis's [3331] interpretation of the
       Houyhnhnms and argues that to Swift, the Houyhnhnms repre-
       sented "perfection of nature"--a perfection to which Gulliver
       could not attain.

3443   SMITH, RAYMOND J., JR.
       "The 'Character' of Lemuel Gulliver." TSL 10 (1965): 133-
       140.

           Argues that Gulliver ought not to be studied as a fictional
       character that changes and develops, since "Swift's basic in-
       tent is to manipulate him as an instrument, a construct prop-
       erly shorn of all novelistic ego--a creature in relationship
       to which notions of development, or consistency, are irrele-
       vant."

3444   STONE, EDWARD.
       "Swift and the Horses: Misanthropy or Comedy?" MLQ 10
       (1949): 367-376. Rpt. in [3340], pp. 180-192.

           Attempts to "question the justice of the over-all verdict
       that Part IV of the Travels was an unprovoked outburst of
       misanthropy, that its chief merit was the doubtful one of not

having succeeded in damaging the comic success of Parts I
and II." Considers "(1) the intent of the author; (2) the significance of the Beast-Fable tradition, and Swift's use of it;
(3) the characterization of Gulliver"; and (4) the reception of
Part IV by its first readers.

3445   STURM, NORBERT A.
        "Gulliver: The Benevolent Linguist." UDR 4 No. 3 (1967):
        43-54.

        Argues that Swift puts Gulliver, an insane castaway, on an
        island with animals and then has him people this real world
        with fantastic creatures he has created from the material facts
        of his existence and the current ideas of eighteenth-century
        England: "the tribulations of Gulliver's journey explain how
        he became insane; the Yahoos and the Houyhnhnms serve as
        vehicles of satire against English society, Gulliver's pride,
        and the pretended reason of the reader; and Pedro de Mendez
        enables the reader to see through the fantasy of Gulliver's
        world and to recognize in Gulliver a viciousness disguised as
        extreme respect for truth, virtue, and benevolence."

3446   SUITS, CONRAD.
        "The Rôle of the Horses in 'A Voyage to the Houyhnhnms.'"
        UTQ 34 (1965): 118-132.

        Argues that Gulliver is not mad and therefore not a comic
        figure, and that the Houyhnhnms are to be admired; suggests
        that the "whole point of inverting the normal man-animal re-
        lation is not to elevate animals at the cost of humanity ...
        but to deflate man's notion of himself by stripping him of his
        proudest possession"--his rationality. The horses are not
        models of a superior kind of existence.

3447   SUTHERLAND, JOHN H.
        "A Reconsideration of Gulliver's Third Voyage." SP 54
        (1957): 45-52.

        Presents arguments "that Part III as a whole is very nec-
        essary to both the satiric and the fictional structure of Gul-
        liver's Travels."

3448   SWAIM, KATHLEEN M.
        A Reading of "Gulliver's Travels." The Hague: Mouton,
        1972.

        The author analyzes the imagery of each voyage: Voyage
        I is an exploration of man's physical nature; Voyage II ex-

plores his emotions; Voyage III analyzes his intellectual nature; and Voyage IV describes his moral nature.

3449   TAKASE, FUMIKO.
       "The Houyhnhnms and the Eighteenth-Century Goût Chinois."
       ES 61 (1980):   408-417.

           Suggests that "the eighteenth-century interest in China and
       Japan, especially the goût chinois stimulated by the knowledge
       of China governed by a philosopher king under the dictates
       of Confucianism, not yet enlightened by Christianity, might
       have some part in Swift's constructing the theme and struc-
       ture of Gulliver's Travels and might also help clarify some
       of the controversies over the import of the rational Horses
       and Gulliver's fourth voyage."

3450   TALLMAN, WARREN.
       "Swift's Fool: A Comment Upon Satire in Gulliver's Travels."
       DR 40 (1961):   470-478.

           Points out that Gulliver is portrayed as a fool because
       throughout all his troubles he never once asks for divine
       guidance, and in the end his "forgetfulness of God carries
       him to madness."   Gulliver's journey is a testimonial to
       "Christian truth in which Swift is saying to the fool: lift up
       thine eyes," and forgo a life based exclusively on bodily and
       human values.

3451   TAYLOR, ALINE MACKENZIE.
       "Sights and Monsters and Gulliver's Voyage to Brobdingnag."
       TSE 7 (1957):   29-82.

           Provides a historical background to Book II of Gulliver's
       Travels--the universal craze for "monsters" and curiosities
       in the popular shows of the day.   In particular, the episode
       of Gulliver's public exhibition is analyzed with emphasis on
       five motifs--animal, infant, toy, the "gladiator," and the box.

3452   TAYLOR, DICK, Jr.
       "Gulliver's Pleasing Vision: Self-Deception as a Major Theme
       in Gulliver's Travels."   TSE 12 (1962):   7-61.

           An analysis of the theme of self-deception suggests that it
       is the major theme of the Travels, "that it is the focus of
       the whole work, the controlling idea, the unifying image, and
       subsumes all other themes and motifs."   Even Gulliver's blast
       at Pride shows that he is "deceiving himself here, as he has
       been ... through the voyages, and he well demonstrates the
       difficulty of knowing oneself."

3453   TAYLOR, SHEILA.
"The 'Secret Pocket': Private Vision and Communal Identity
in Gulliver's Travels." StHum. 6, ii (1978): 5-11.

Describes the relationship between the novelistic and the
satiric aims of Gulliver's Travels. Focuses on the pocket
scene in Part I as emblematic of Swift's concern with the
theme of identity and touches briefly on the other three parts
to show that the work "is an exploration of the delicate relationship between individual and society, as well as a warning
against capitulation." Contends that the book "which began as
a satire against literary form concludes as an endorsement
of novelistic values."

3454   TILTON, JOHN W.
"Gulliver's Travels as a Work of Art." Bucknell Rev. 7
(1959): 246-259.

Argues that Gulliver's Travels is an artistic unity, with
consistent development of character brought about by Gulliver's
"experiences on his voyages, which are so artistically ordered
that no one can be omitted or rearranged without destroying
the development of Gulliver and by consequence destroying the
theme which is embodied in the change Gulliver undergoes."

3455   TINTNER, ADELINE R.
"Lady into Horse: James's 'Lady Barberina' and Gulliver's
Travels, Part IV." JNT 8 (1978): 79-96.

First part of the essay attempts "to document the pervasive
though implicit metaphor by which a social group is presented
in terms of the horse;" the second part discusses the even
more pervasive and explicit metaphor used by Swift in contrasting horses with human beings. James has given his characters "names, activities, accoutrements and a behavior pattern which are suggestive of the world of horses." Several
details in Lady Barberina suggest that Gulliver's Travels was
a model for James.

3456   TODD, DENNIS.
"Laputa, the Whore of Babylon, and the Idols of Science."
SP 75 (1978): 93-120.

Argues that science is not the "background" to Laputa, but
rather the "foreground" and that it is through his description
of the loadstone that Swift organizes and gives substance to
the entire episode. "The organization of the episodes--Laputa
and Balnibarbi, the calling up of the ghosts of the dead, the
eternal Struldbruggs--parodies the course of divine history:
the coming of the Whore, the resurrection of the dead, and

the life-everlasting." Swift's theme is one of "hopelessness" because "man confirms himself in his weakness when he worships the idols of his own powers instead of that one Power which will help him transcend his limitations."

3457   TORCHIANA, DONALD T.
"Jonathan Swift, the Irish, and the Yahoos: the Case Reconsidered." PQ 54 (1975): 195-212.

Reexamines Sir Charles Firth's interpretation of Gulliver's Travels as being a picture of Ireland, and presents comparisons of "Swift's depiction of the Yahoos with the account of the Irish usually reported by English travellers." Supports thesis that Book IV contains much of Swift's hatred of the Irish.

3458   TRACY, CLARENCE.
"The Unity of Gulliver's Travels." Queen's Quarterly 68 (1961-62): 597-609.

Argues that 1) "the structural principle of Gulliver's Travels is a series of contrasts, echoes, and anticipations--intersecting links that hold the work together ... "; 2) that unity in the third voyage is based on inductive reason; 3) that a "similar antithetical relationship [exists] between voyages one and two," and 4) that "the balancing of ... two great themes-- thought and action--forms the main structural principle" in Gulliver's Travels.

3459   TRALDI, ILA DAWSON.
"Gulliver the 'Educated Fool': Unity in the Voyage to Laputa." PLL 4 (1968): 35-50.

Deals with a double theme in Book III: "man, because of his inordinate pride, refuses to recognize the limits of nature, particularly of human nature; and at the same time, man ignores the possibilities inherent in, and unique to, his nature." Contends that "Gulliver is treated ironically in the third voyage, just as he is in the others," and that he does not "comprehend either his limitations or his potentialities as a human being, and therefore falls prey to his own misconceptions when he reaches the land of the Houyhnhnms."

3460   TRAUGOTT, JOHN.
"Swift's Allegory: The Yahoo and the Man-of-Mode." UTQ 33 (1963): 1-18.

Finds the discovery of "grotesque fantasies" in everyday life as characteristic of Swift's satire; equally fundamental is

the "association of modishness and hideous degeneracy." The
overwhelming power of that satire is attributed to the inevitability with which the realistic surface of life changes into
a "grotesque" reality.

3461   "A Voyage to Nowhere with Thomas More and Jonathan Swift:
        Utopia and The Voyage to the Houyhnhnms." SR 69 (1961):
        534-565. Rpt. in [3059], pp. 143-169.

        Compares the irony of Swift and More. Both books "are
        discoveries of the moral and spiritual reality of Utopia in
        our everyday lives, and to this end employ as a satiric de-
        vice a voyager who is maddened by a glimpse of the reality
        of the Good in a fantastic land and of the unreality of every-
        day life in real England." More and Swift propose a third
        choice in life--"one can live in the world by playing the fool
        and not being one, by keeping Utopia a city of the mind...."

3462   TREADWELL, J. M.
        "Jonathan Swift: The Satirist as Projector." TSLL 17 (1975)
        439-460.

        Argues the importance of the third voyage in Gulliver's
        Travels; Swift regarded the notion of the projector as appli-
        cable to himself, making himself both as individual and as
        satirist an important target for the satire of the third and
        fourth books.

3463   TRIMMER, JOSEPH F.
        "A Note on Gulliver and the Four Captains." BSUF 12, No.
        2 (1971): 39-43.

        Considers the thematic and structural importance of the
        captain in each book, and concludes that two of the captains,
        Mr. Wilcocks and Don Pedro, not only bring Gulliver back
        to England, but also attempt to bring him back to reality.

3464   TUVESON, ERNEST.
        "Swift: The View from Within the Satire." In [30], pp. 55-
        85.

        Analyzes Swift's rhetoric in Gulliver's Travels, his satiric
        intentions, and his success in carrying those intentions out.
        Notes that Swift's ability to control his audience is what makes
        him great.

3465   "Swift: the Dean as Satirist." UTQ 22 (1953): 368-375.
        Rpt. in [3059], pp. 101-114.

Discusses the satire in Gulliver's Travels attempting to reconcile Swift the satirist and Swift the Dean. By understanding Swift's attitude towards Christian doctrine, especially that of original sin, we can better place men, Yahoos, and Houyhnhnms in proper perspective.

3466   TYNE, JAMES L., S. J.
"Gulliver's Maker and Gullibility." Criticism 7 (1965): 151-167.

A comparison of Book IV of Gulliver's Travels with Swift's anti-romantic poems shows that they share a common theme: "an initially unrealistic and exalted view of human nature in due course terminates in an equally unrealistic and debased view of that same nature." Gulliver's gullibility about the Houyhnhnms is the same as that of the lovers in the poems, and both illustrate the differences between things as they really are and as they are conceived to be.

3467   UPHAUS, ROBERT W.
"Gulliver's Travels, A Modest Proposal, and the Problematical Nature of Meaning." PLL 10 (1974): 268-278. Rpt. in [180], pp. 9-27.

Discusses how Swift uses "manifest fictions as a device for exposing, analyzing, and often undercutting the latent fictions of ordinary human life," and how Swift forces the reader "to establish contexts within which he may apprehend some discernible meaning even if it is not ... within the text.... These meanings are ... a set of experiences ... varying with each reader, which grow out of the interaction between the reader's expectations and assumptions and the various 'events'--including single words and sentences--which Swift places in the texts of Gulliver's Travels and A Modest Proposal."

3468   VANCE, JOHN A.
"The Odious Vermin: Gulliver's Progression Towards Misanthropy." Enl. E. 10 (1979): 65-73.

Traces Gulliver's references to the word odious until he finally accepts the fact that he is the same as the odious Yahoos and comes to equate the human race with them. When Gulliver finally "accepts such a revolting portrait of himself and his fellow man then his misanthropy may be judged total and irreversible."

3469   VAN TINE, JAMES
"The Risks of Swiftian Sanity." Univ. Rev. 32 (1966): 235-240; 275-281.

Relates Gulliver's experiences in Houyhnhnmland, especiall
with the Yahoos, to Swift's satiric indictment of England and
its degeneration. "Gulliver's maniacal hatred becomes complete when he unequivocally identifies himself and all fellow-
Europeans with the lazy, quarreling, unteachable beast whose
resemblance to human kind he has spent so much thought and
energy trying to deny." Gulliver's "portrayal of self-nausea
is Swift's most violent attack on the standards, restrictions,
and corruptions that shackle man and warp his attempts to
live."

3470   VICKERS, BRIAN.
"The Satiric Structure of Gulliver's Travels and More's Utopia." In [3060], pp. 233-257.

Focuses on the satiric targets and techniques common to
Swift and More: "The findings do not merely argue that Swift
used Utopia more than has so far been supposed, and refined
on its irony, but also try to illuminate the way both writers
apply the naive and ignorant partner in a dialogue to create
fundamental objections to the ethics of human society."

3471   WALTON, J. K.
"The Unity of the Travels." Hermathena 104 (1967): 5-50.

Argues for the unity of the four Parts: Part III, in form
and content, is a logical development of Parts I and II, and
is in no way inferior to them. Part II represents a reversall
of Part I, and Part III of Part II and also of Part I; in Part
IV, Swift continues his technique of reversal.

3472   WEDEL, T. O.
"On the Philosophical Background of Gulliver's Travels." SP
23 (1926): 434-450. Rpt. in [3350], pp. 83-99.

The philosophical and religious background of Gulliver's
Travels, emphasizing the ethical revolution in Swift's age:
the change from the pessimism of Pascal to the optimism of
Leibnitz; discusses the seventeenth-century misanthropic view
of man and the role of Stoicism and Cartesianism.

3473   WHITE, DOUGLAS H.
"Swift and the Definition of Man." MP 73, No. 4, Part 2
(1976): S48-S55.

Background material on attempts to discredit the growing
enthusiasm for natural religion and the subsequent attacks on
man as animal rationale, to help in interpreting Gulliver's
Travels.

3474   WHITE, JOHN H.
       "Swift's Trojan Horses: 'Reasoning but to Err.'" ELN 3
       (1966): 185-194.

          Suggests that the Houyhnhnms do not represent a perfect
       ideal, but rather one of "Swift's three principal targets in
       Voyage IV, the other two being ... Gulliver and the Yahoos."
       The Houyhnhnms' mode of thought is typically human, and they
       do not hesitate to conceal the truth.

3475   WILDING, MICHAEL.
       "The Politics of Gulliver's Travels." In [9], pp. 303-322.

          Uses Gulliver's Travels to emphasize the non-naturalistic
       tradition of English political fiction, and suggests that it con-
       tains many of the standard approaches and themes of that tra-
       dition; Swift's final conclusion in Book IV is that all societies
       are political and that "all political societies are corrupt or
       exploitive or both."

3476   WILLIAMS, HAROLD.
       The Text of "Gulliver's Travels" (Sanders Lectures in Bib-
       liography, 1950). Cambridge: At the University Press,
       1952.

          Argues that Swift worked closely with Faulkner, and that
       where the 1735 edition alters the sense of a word, expres-
       sion, or passage, the author himself was probably responsible.
       The Faulkner edition of 1735, therefore, takes precedence
       over the Motte edition of 1726 and the Motte fifth edition of
       1727.

3477   WILLIAMS, KATHLEEN M.
       "Gulliver's Voyage to the Houyhnhnms." ELH 18 (1951):
       275-286. Rpt. in [3350], pp. 136-147; [3340], pp. 193-203;
       [3054], pp. 247-257.

          Deals with the ambiguity of the Fourth Voyage: Swift's
       portrayal of the Houyhnhnms as an ideal society in spite of
       the fact that they were often presented as unadmirable beings.
       Suggests that Swift's satirical method was deliberate, that
       "the Houyhnhnms, far from being a model of perfection, are
       intended to show the inadequacy of the life of reason."

3478   WILSON, JAMES R.
       "Swift, the Psalmist, and the Horse." TSL 3 (1958): 17-
       23.

          Suggests that the Houyhnhnms are not wholly ideal or utopian

creatures and that Gulliver is inferior to and distinct from
Swift; discusses the role of the Houyhnhnms, and finds in
the Bible the origin of Swift's choice of the horse in "six
references which are pertinent to [his] message regarding
the Houyhnhnms: the danger of putting trust in the horse
rather than in God. "

3479   "Swift's Alazon. " Studia Neophilologica 30 (1958): 153-164.

Except for his pride, Gulliver is entirely different at the
end of his travels from what he was at the beginning: "From
the naive optimist he has become the naive pessimist; throughout the Travels he has remained a comic figure, the not-
unsympathetic Alazon or imposter.... "

3480   WINTON, CALHOUN.
        "Conversion on the Road to Houyhnhnmland. " SR 68 (1960):
        20-33. Rpt. in [3340], pp. 270-281.

Presents Gulliver's Travels as a "satiric presentation of
what Swift regarded as the new, 'enlightened' religion [i. e. ,
deism] ... and a defense, couched in Swiftian irony, of Au-
gustinian Christianity. " Gulliver is presented as a "pilgrim"
who starts from a position of complete religious ignorance
and ends up "converted" to the "reasonable" faith of the Houyhnhnms, only to return to man's world and find that his new
religion will not work.

3481   YEOMAN, W. E.
        "The Houyhnhnm as Menippean Horse. " CE 27 (1966): 449-
        454.. Rpt. in [3350], pp. 202-211; [3054], pp. 258-266.

Argues for the study of Book IV as Menippean satire which
shows that "the Houyhnhnms are sometimes solemn models of
the good life, sometimes vehicles for satiric burlesque attack,
and sometimes a combination of both. "

3482   ZIMANSKY, CURT A.
        "Gulliver, Yahoos, and Critics. " CE 27 (1965): 45-49.

A historical approach to the criticism of Book IV based
on the formula that "Swift's readers believed that man is distinguished from animals by his gift of reason, and is no better than a beast unless he uses that reason. "

3483   ZIMMERMAN, EVERETT.
        "Gulliver the Preacher. " PMLA 89 (1974): 1024-1032.

Analyzes Gulliver's actions in each of the voyages and concludes that Gulliver's Travels is both a satire and a psychological analysis of Gulliver as satirist. Swift "shows us the
immoral intentions of Gulliver; although Gulliver pretends he
wants to reform us, his pretense is a strategy for disguis-
ing his own evil from us and from himself. The satiric attack ... becomes double; Gulliver satirizes man, and Swift
satirizes the motives for Gulliver's satire."

3484   ZIMMERMAN, LESTER F.
        "Lemuel Gulliver." In [3053], pp. 61-73.

        Analyzes the narrative structure and the role of Gulliver
        to emphasize the unity of the whole work: the author argues
        that a controlling motif through the various voyages is that
        of "man as the measure," and since we cannot accept Gul-
        liver as a norm in Voyage Four, we also reject him in Voy-
        age Three, where he is a humanist without humane values.

3485   ZIRKER, HERBERT.
        "Lemuel Gulliver's Yahoos und Swift's Satire." Anglia 87
        (1969): 39-63.

        Argues that Yahoo comes from Yahu, an older form of
        Jahve (Jehovah); this is related rather questionably to Shaftes-
        bury's deism and the Houyhnhnm-Yahoo contrast.

See also: 949, 1724, 2170, 3065, 3070, 3076, 3077, 3082, 3085,
    3097, 3101, 3106, 3119, 3120, 3123, 3128, 3130, 3135, 3138,
    3143, 3144, 3148, 3152, 3155, 3157, 3160, 3165, 3166, 3170, 3181,
    3184, 3193, 3198, 3206, 3497, 3533

A Modest Proposal

3486   BEAUMONT, CHARLES.
        "Swift's Classical Rhetoric in 'A Modest Proposal.'" Georgia
        Rev. 14 (1960): 307-317.

        Suggests that the irony of "A Modest Proposal" is "built
        by and sustained by the devices of classical rhetoric, even
        to its very structure, which Swift modeled on the five-part
        classical oration," and that the classical form is itself an
        important part of Swift's irony.

3487   BROWN, THOMAS.
        "Ellipsis in 'The Modest Proposal.'" CEA 38, i (1975): 14-
        16.

Brief analysis of how Swift uses the classical rhetorical
scheme of ellipsis to achieve terror by implying violence with
out directly stating it.

3488   EHRENPREIS, IRVIN.
        "Personae. " In [13], pp. 25-37.

Discusses the use of a persona by writers, especially Pope
in An Epistle to Dr. Arbuthnot and Swift in A Modest Proposal.   Suggests that the use of a persona is a rhetorical
pose inseparable from all language and communication: in
A Modest Proposal, on the other hand, Swift employs an
"ironical persona," a form of art intended to convey attitudes
unacceptable to the reader by creating a "disguise that is intended to be seen through, a mask that the reader at first
supposes to be genuine but at last sees removed. " Suggests
that "A Modest Proposal makes sense only if we treat the
voice as the author's throughout. "

3489   FERGUSON, OLIVER W.
        "Swift's Saeva Indignatio and A Modest Proposal. " PQ 38
        (1959): 473-479.

Purpose of the study is "to show that Swift's anger in the
Modest Proposal was directed towards Ireland, not England,"
and that it was an indictment against every class of Irish
life, Swift's view of the Irish being that of "the defeated mora
reformer."

3490   GREANY, H. T.
        "Satiric Masks: Swift and Pope. " SNL 3 (1966): 154-159.

An analysis of Pope's "masks" in the Epistle to Dr. Arbuthnot in comparison with Swift's differing technique in A Modest
Proposal and An Argument for the Abolishing of Christianity:
"With Pope the technique of mask demands verbal and argu-
mentative skill in sustaining the appropriate tone of the poet's
'second voice. ' In An Argument ... and A Modest Proposal,
Swift is at pains to establish a more specific personality for his
persona....   Employing a reverse technique to that used by
Pope in which the latter's sane outlook and arguments make
his opponent's principles appear venal, Swift through his im-
perturbably naive persona is seemingly on the side of his opponents."

3491   JACOBS, EDWARD CRANEY.
        "Echoes of Micah in Swift's Modest Proposal. " Eire 13, iii
        (1978): 49-53.

There are many similarities between Swift's proposal to
the Irish and that of the prophet Micah in his Proposal to the
Hebrews (c. 714-700 B. C.); e. g. , Micah's metaphor of butch-
ery and cannibalism, his prophecy of God's retribution against
the rich who have used their power against the poor, and the
existing evil situations that can't be corrected because men
"seem incorrigibly bent to evil ways." Beneath "the benevolent, rational tone of Swift's narrator" there are many references to the "impassioned speech" of the prophet.

3492   JOHNSON, MAURICE.
        "The Structural Impact of A Modest Proposal." Bucknell Rev.
        7 (1958): 234-240.

        An analysis of the essay's structure, compared to that of
        a contemporary sermon by Swift: "A Modest Proposal is in-
        directly expressed through dramatic fiction, with Swift acting
        in character and addressing a fictional audience. Swift's re-
        lationship with his reader is indirect throughout; his relation-
        ship with his created persona ... is almost ... antithetical."

3493   LANDA, LOUIS A.
        "A Modest Proposal and Populousness." MP 40 (1942): 161-
        170. Rpt. in [18], pp. 102-111; [129], pp. 39-48.

        As seen against the economic thought of the age, A Modest
        Proposal is interpreted as "another protest, in Swift's unique
        manner, against the unqualified maxim that people are the
        riches of a nation."

3494   LOCKWOOD, THOMAS.
        "Swift's Modest Proposal: an Interpretation." PLL 10 (1974):
        254-267.

        Argues against interpretations dealing with the "projector"
        idea in "favor of the less artificial proposition that Swift simply
        speaks to the reader ironically ... speaking as if he had
        matter-of-factly accepted the public attitude of indifference
        to what he ... had for so long taken to be the main issues"
        and that "he does speak ironically in the obvious sense that
        he does not mean what he says when he recommends his pro-
        posal."

3495   MACEY, SAMUEL L.
        "The Persona in A Modest Proposal." Lock Haven Rev. 10
        (1968): 17-24.

        Concerns "itself with the persona in A Modest Proposal,

firstly as a satire against projectors, secondly as a vehicle
for a satire against ourselves, and lastly as a vehicle for
the positive proposals of the puppet master who stands behind him. "

3496   PATTERSON, EMILY H.
        "Swift, Voltaire, and the Cannibals." Enl. E. 6, ii (1975):
        3-12.

        Speculates that Swift in A Modest Proposal and Voltaire
   in Candide defend the practice of cannibalism because of their
   belief that men do not behave rationally, and both authors
   "out of desperation and frustration, create speakers who support inhuman programs as 'reasonable' expedients. Their
   appeals to reason are but a mockery, yet each author for a
   moment steps forward as himself to speak the searing truth,
   hoping to shock mankind into a compulsion to act, by showing
   the practices of 'civilized' nations to be the practices of sav-
   ages and no less abhorrent. "

3497   PULLEN, CHARLES.
        "Eighteenth-Century Madness: Swift and A Modest Proposal. "
        DR 58 (1978): 53-62.

        The projector in the Proposal is Swift's most lethal char-
   acter because he hides his insanity "behind blandly profes-
   sional competence, his step-by-step reasonableness, his good
   intentions...." The division of the century in attitude toward
   madness as suggested by Professor Max Byrd in Visits to
   Bedlam, Madness and Literature in the Eighteenth Century--
   that the first half was fearful and unsympathetic--does not
   hold true for Gulliver's Travels and A Modest Proposal. For
   Swift there are different kinds of madness: the Grub Street
   writer, rather feckless and harmless; the projectors in the
   third book of Gulliver; and Gulliver himself, more of a tragic
   figure at the end of the story than a madman. A Modest
   Proposal is a peculiar case: the projector's horrifying proposal meets no rebuttal from the satirist Swift.

3498   RAWSON, C. J.
        "A Reading of A Modest Proposal." In [28], pp. 29-50.

        Swift was not speaking ironically when he referred, in the
   title to A Modest Proposal, to the children of the poor "Being
   a Burthen to their Parents, or the Country"; he was extremely
   hostile to beggars, and we should realize that "ridding society
   of its beggarly 'burdens' was not a notion which Swift identified exlusively with the cant of the profiteering and the in-
   humane." Another suggestion is that Swift, even when feeling
   compassion for the Papist poor, is partly also exposing to

derision the modest proposer's sentimental expression of tenderness where it is not justified; he is partly exposing the
hypocrisy of do-gooders and partly attacking "lazy-minded
(and mainly Whiggish) benevolism, given to indiscriminate
tolerance [and] misguided charities...."

3499   TILTON, JOHN W.
        "The Two 'Modest Proposals': A Dual Approach to Swift's
        Irony." Bucknell Rev. 14 (1966): 78-88.

        Argues that the confusion among critics, concerning the
        possible failure of consistency in Swift's use of a persona,
        may be resolved by accepting two ways of reading the "Modest
        Proposal": it can be read as an anonymous utilitarian essay
        of 1729, entirely the work of the persona, and it can be read
        as a well-known work of satire by Jonathan Swift.   The am-
        bivalent reading of the essay derives from our confusing the
        two approaches.

3500   WILLSON, ROBERT F., JR.
        "A Modest Proposal: Swift's Persona as Absentee." BSUF
        17, iv (1976): 3-11.

        Suggests that Swift is using satiric characterization in the
        Proposal and that the persona "is clearly intended to stand
        as an archetypal absentee landlord." Through his "powerful
        ad hominem technique, in which the careful manipulation of
        puns and euphemisms points up the anti-human nature of the
        speaker," Swift hopes to convince his audience that their real
        enemy is the absentee landlord who is intent on totally de-
        stroying them.   A careful look at Swift's diction provides the
        clues to this interpretation.

3501   WITTKOWSKY, GEORGE.
        "Swift's Modest Proposal: The Biography of An Early Georgian
        Pamphlet." JHI 4 (1943): 75-104.

        Considers the Modest Proposal as a superb work of art
        highly saturated with economic theory.   Relates Swift's satire
        to such economic problems as projects concerning population,
        "political arithmetic," regarding children as commodities, and
        the impotent poor, and considers it as a burlesque on projects
        and on political arithmetic.

See also: 874, 3068, 3070, 3076, 3080, 3101, 3142, 3160, 3166,
      3257, 3290, 3467

Poems

3502   ADEN, JOHN M.
"Those Gaudy Tulips: Swift's 'Unprintables.'" In [15], pp.
15-32.

A very close reading of "The Progress of Beauty," "The
Lady's Dressing Room," "A Beautiful Young Nymph Going to
Bed," "Strephon and Chloe," and "Cassinus and Peter." They
are bound together by the theme of appearance and reality,
and all undertake to "strip down some delusion to the reality
it masquerades for."

3503   "Corinna and the Sterner Muse of Swift." ELN 4 (1966):
23-31.

Argues in defense of the poetic qualities of "A Beautiful
Young Nymph Going to Bed" that it possesses a double perspective, tragic and comic, or ridiculous and pathetic (in the
Aristotelian sense); that Swift's poem is not "inhuman," but
an ultimately pathetic image of failure, ugly, sordid, and
comic.

3504   ANDERSON, PHILLIP B.
"Transformations of 'Swift' and the Development of Swift's
Satiric Vision in Verses on the Death of Dr. Swift." PAPA
6, i (1980): 19-32.

An examination of the structure and characteristic techniques of the poem as a whole shows that the "panegyric"
emerges "as the last in a series of transformations of the
fictive 'Swift' and as a final, complexly ironic condemnation
of mankind." It also shows that Swift's "transformations"
of his fictive self "move from a concrete and credible speaking voice, to an ailing man, to a dead man, and then to a
man as represented in his literary works."

3505   BALL, F. ELRINGTON.
Swift's Verse, an Essay.   London: John Murray, 1929.

A historical and biographical survey of Swift's poetic career.

3506   BARNETT, LOUISE K.
"Fictive Self-Portraiture in Swift's Poetry." In [3052], pp.
101-111.

Argues that "Swift's depiction of self lacks the dichotomized
presentation of good opposing bad that is essential to the sa-

tiric speaker. The self is both exalted and ridiculed within
a full spectrum of character possibilities that includes the
satirist--hero at one extreme and the unscrupulous opportunist
at the other." Concludes that Swift's poetry of fictive self-
portraiture develops the "closest and most intractable of ma-
terials--the poet's own experience and psyche, the most available and compelling example of that problematical entity,
human nature."

3507   "The Mysterious Narrator: Another Look at 'The Lady's
        Dressing Room.'" CP 9, ii (1976): 29-32.

        The narrator is not Swift, and he creates distance between
        himself and Strephon by his condescending tone; he revels in
        unsavory details, every one of which he finds worthy of em-
        phatic comment: his "extravagant relish" of the facts of Cel-
        ia's bodily functions contrasts with Strephon's disgust. Swift
        pleads for order and cleanliness, and seems to suggest that
        the "body must neither be celebrated (the narrator) nor loathed
        (Strephon) nor covered with misleading adornment (Celia)."
        He dramatizes through the narrator's fascination with an ex-
        cremental vision the attraction it has for our imagination.

3508   BORKAT, ROBERTA F. S.
        "Swift, Shaw, and the Idealistic Swain." ES 61 (1980): 498-
        506.

        In Arms and the Man, Shaw's character (Major Saranoff)
        undergoes the same kind of disillusionment that Swift's Cas-
        sinus and Strephon do. Both authors use the idealistic swain
        to "examine not only the subject of romantic love but also
        the nature of mankind; the masks and extreme illusions which
        man employs to deny his mixture of the godlike and the bes-
        tial; and the role of the satirical unmasker, the author him-
        self."

3509   CLARK, JOHN R.
        "Embodiment in Literature: Swift's Blasted Pocky Muse of
        Poetry." Thalia 2, iii (1979): 23-33.

        An evaluation of three recent books on Swift's poetry (Jaffe:
        The Poet Swift; Fischer: On Swift's Poetry; and Schakel:
        The Poetry of Jonathan Swift) and a brief examination of some
        outstanding passages for the purpose "of isolating some key
        strategies that permit him to generate both urgency and potency
        in his poetry." Points out the "features of tension, contradic-
        tion, and damnable bedevilment" in his public and private
        verse, and "the taut figures of perversion, corruption, dis-
        ease, and damnation" in his political verse; suggests that "the
        electric quality of [Swift's] images and lines ... tend[s] to be

pressured in the extreme, to burst into seminal topics be-
setting the human condition: disgrace, overwhelming foetor,
ravishment, mortification, decay, and damnation. "

3510   DAVIS, HERBERT.
        "A Modest Defence of 'The Lady's Dressing Room. ' "   In
        [13], pp. 39-48.

        Discusses Swift's parody and humor in 'The Defence' and
        some of his other poems maintaining that "it was [his] inten-
        tion ... to make every sense revolt with disgust ... because
        of all the bestialities hidden beneath the surface of polite so-
        ciety, and because of his constant shock, as a moralist, at
        the insane pride of these miserable vermin, crawling about
        the face of the earth. "

3511   "The Poetry of Jonathan Swift. "   CE 2 (1940):   102-115.

        A general discussion of Swift's poetry, chronologically pre-
        sented, to show that for a complete understanding of Swift we
        need to look at his poetry as well as his prose.

3512   "Swift's View of Poetry. "   In Studies in English by Members
        of University College, Toronto, ed. Malcolm W. Wallace
        (Toronto: Univ. Toronto Press, 1931), pp. 9-58. Rpt. in
        [3083], pp. 163-198; [3055], pp. 62-97.

        A detailed survey of Swift's poetic career, with numerous
        analyses of individual poems and quotations from letters to
        illustrate his essentially antiromantic and witty poetic nature
        in a world in which there is no room for the sublime and the
        pathetic, "there is nothing left to do but to rail, or simply
        to amuse oneself and one's friends. "   Includes a defense of
        the scatological poems.

3513   ENGLAND, A. B.
        Energy and Order in the Poetry of Swift.   Lewisburg, Pa. :
        Bucknell Univ. Press; London & Toronto: Associated Univ.
        Presses, 1980.

        Concerned with two contrasting types of stylistic tendencies
        in Swift's poetry: 1) "energy," or the ways in which Swift
        departs from certain orderly forms of discourse usually as-
        sociated with Augustan literature; 2) an opposing tendency that
        subjects details to "alignments that are noticeably ordered
        and much more consistent with some traditional assumptions
        about the forms that Augustan literature tends to take. "   Con-
        cludes that the relationship between subject and structure in-
        volves conscious irony that apparently questions the adequacy
        of the structure itself.

3514   "Rhetorical Order and Emotional Turbulence in 'Cadenus and
        Vanessa.'" <u>PLL</u> 14 (1978): 116-123. Rpt. in [3052], pp. 69-
        78.

        Argues that in Swift's poems orderly rhetorical systems
        often appear to be subverted or challenged by contrasting ele-
        ments within the poetry: "Although there is a noticeable and
        persistent rhetorical ordering of the central experience [in
        "Cadenus and Vanessa"], Swift constantly implies the presence
        in that experience of unruly forces that are not adequately con-
        tained by the several frameworks imposed on them."

3515   "The Subversion of Logic in Some Poems by Swift." <u>SEL</u> 15
        (1975): 409-418.

        Shows how Swift shows disrespect for rigid argumentative
        procedures and formal, consecutive logic in "The Description
        of a Salamander," "The Fable of Midas," "The Virtues of
        Sid Hamet the Magician's Rod," and "A Serious Poem Upon
        William Wood," and how these poems are examples of Swift's
        "irresponsible attacks upon individuals."

3516   "World Without Order: Some Thoughts on the Poetry of Swift."
        <u>EIC</u> 16 (1966): 32-43.

        An examination of some of Swift's most familiar poems for
        "satiric apprehension of disunity." These poems, "pictorially
        and sometimes structurally indecisive, are in a sense images
        that illustrate one of Swift's reactions to his world."

3517   FABRICANT, CAROLE.
        "The Garden as City: Swift's Landscape of Alienation." <u>ELH</u>
        42 (1975): 531-555.

        Examines the imagery in Swift's verses upon the houses
        and estates of his friends from Swift's "angle of vision" to
        show the relationship between landscape and human behavior.
        "Swift's observations of the Irish countryside and its houses
        produce images of prevailing corruption as well as approaching
        doom"; whereas Pope creates idyllic landscape settings, Swift
        creates settings of decadence and disintegration.

3518   FISCHER, JOHN IRWIN.
        "Faith, Hope, and Charity in Swift's Poems to Stella." <u>PLL</u>
        14 (1978): 123-129. Rpt. in [3052], pp. 79-86.

        The Stella poems exist within a recognizable tradition of
        consolatory philosophy, partly Stoic but more essentially Chris-
        tian: they "are comic and imaginative attempts to reconcile
        Stella to mortality."

3519   On Swift's Poetry.   Gainesville: Univ. Presses of Florida,
        1978.

        Seeks to trace the ways in which Swift tries to "temper
        his hubristic indignation with the world into a morally respon-
        sible reaction to it...."; argues that that attempt, in his verse
        at least, is Swift's most significant human lesson.

3520   "The Dean contra Heathens: Swift's The Day of Judgement."
        Revue des Langues Vivantes 43 (1977): 592-597.

        A reading of the poem which attempts to reconcile its force
        with "its purposive absurdity" and suggests that although it is
        an involuted poem, it may be simply read.   Concludes that
        Swift's depiction of Jove is in its absurdity "significantly am-
        bivalent."

3521   "Apparent Contraries: A Reading of Swift's 'A Description
        of a City Shower.'"   TSL 19 (1974): 21-34.

        Sees poem as intentionally ambivalent; considers it in con-
        text of great flood legends of western literature as teaching
        the limits of our capabilities.   By recapturing the grace im-
        plicit in legend of Noah's flood, poem demonstrates that our
        worth as "living beings is consistent with an admission that
        life possesses a power and an integrity independent of us."

3522   "How to Die: Verses on the Death of Dr. Swift."   RES 21
        (1970): 422-441.

        A study of Swift's meditations on death; the relationship
        between the panegyric with which the poem ends and the maxim
        of La Rochefoucauld, "In the Adversity of our best Friends,
        we find something that doth not displease us."   An analysis
        of the Verses shows that "the poem's three-part structure is
        controlled ... by the three traditional topics of the meditation
        on death....   Beginning with a painfully clear vision of that
        sinful and worldly nature he shares with every man, Swift
        ends with a demonstration of what can be made of it."

3523   "The Uses of Virtue: Swift's Last Poem to Stella."   In Es-
        says in Honor of Esmond Linworth Marilla, eds. Thomas
        Austin Kirby and William John Olive (Baton Rouge: La. State
        Univ. Press, 1970), pp. 201-209.

        Reads the poem as dealing with Swift's view of the "ad-
        vantages, nature, and purposes of a virtuous life."

3524   FISHER, ALAN S.

"Swift's Verse Portraits: A Study of His Originality as an Augustan Satirist." SEL 14 (1974): 343-356.

Discusses the ethics of perception in Swift's satire and defines the imaginative qualities which his verse portraits have in common. Believes that Swift's verse portraits are worth studying because they give an insight into Swift's pessimistic view of the world.

3525   FOX, JEFFREY R.
"Swift's 'Scatological' Poems: The Hidden Norm." Thoth 15, iii (1975): 3-13.

Swift's scatological poems should be studied in relation to his other poetry because they too are satires which attack certain human vices and follies and defend the qualities of virtue and wisdom. Once the subjects of his censure have been isolated, it becomes possible to identify the norm of behavior which Swift defends. The scatological poems are compared with his other love poems, especially the "Stella" poems which show "a love built on precisely those qualities ... absent from the fictional love relationships in [his] satires." Examines "The Lady's Dressing Room," "Strephon and Chloe," and "Cassinus and Peter" as well as several of the "Stella" poems.

3526   FRICKE, DONNA G.
"Jonathan Swift's Early Odes and the Conversion to Satire." Enl. E 5, No. 2 (1974): 3-17.

Divides Swift's poetic career into three parts, 1690-93, 1698-26, and 1727-37; "examine[s] the juvenalia and speculate[s] on his conversion to the satiric poetic mode in which he was so successful in the latter two periods."

3527   GILMORE, THOMAS B., JR.
"Freud and Swift: A Psychological Reading of Strephon and Chloe." PLL 14 (1978): 147-151; rpt. as "Freud, Swift, and Narcissism: A Psychological Reading of Strephon and Chloe" in [3052], pp. 159-168, with additions.

Argues that Strephon and Chloe's wedding night changes them, as they move from "polymorphous perversity to anal fixation--from the innocence of children to the neurosis of immature adults." In the poem, Swift faces his own horror of anality, and he recommends the civilizing virtue of friendship.

3528   "The Comedy of Swift's Scatological Poems." PMLA 91 (1976): 33-43. "Swift's Scatological Poems," rejoinders by

Donald Greene, Peter J. Schakel, and Thomas B. Gilmore,
Jr. , PMLA 91 (1976): 464-467.

An analysis of Swift's scatological artistry in A Beautiful
Young Nymph Going to Bed, The Lady's Dressing Room, Strephon and Chloe, Cassinus and Peter, and A Panegyreck which
considers his solutions or resolutions of the satiric-comic
situations in which the characters find themselves.   Swift
skillfully exploits "the incongruities between lofty expectations
and ugly realizations, misleading appearances and squalid
actualities, pretentious language and raw facts" for the comic
effects which most critics fail to see because of their emphasis on the scatology.

3529   GREENE, DONALD J.
        "On Swift's Scatological Poems. " SR 75 (1967):   672-689.

        Discusses "The Lady's Dressing Room," "Strephon and
        Chloe," and "Cassinus and Peter," pointing out that "Swift's
        concept of the relationship between men and women is that
        neither of a romantic nor of a Freudian, nor, above all, of
        a neurotic, but simply the view of an orthodox Christian moral-
        ist. "

3530   HARRIS, KATHRYN M.
        " 'Occasions so few': Satire as a Strategy of Praise in
        Swift's Early Odes. "   MLQ 31 (1970):   22-37.

        Discusses Swift's "panegyrical strategy" in his early odes,
        written between 1691 and 1693, and shows how his satiric
        vision and "fundamental distrust of praise are the primary
        links between these early odes and his mature work in both
        prose and verse. "

3531   HILL, GEOFFREY.
        "Jonathan Swift: The Poetry of 'Reaction. ' " In [3060], pp.
        195-212.

        Surveys the themes and attitudes of Swift's poems, em-
        phasizing his capacity to be both resistant and reciprocal;
        argues that as a moral artist Swift transfigures his patterns
        of acceptance and rejection.   Discusses the early Pindarics,
        the comic verse, the political satire, and the scatological
        verse.

3532   HORNE, C[OLIN] J.
        "Swift's Comic Poetry. " In [28], pp. 51-67.

        In Swift's "poetry there are abundant instances of his love

of fun and nonsense, of jokes and amusing trifling, never wholly nonsensical, for it is always charged with intellectual acuity as well as verbal wit, and mostly has some moral concern in view." Horne seeks to take a corrective view to the popular conception of Swift as "the gloomy Dean," and thinks that the bawdy and scatological poems have been taken too seriously by modern readers: they should be read as Swift's contemporaries largely read them--as matter for a hearty laugh. His comic skill consists of the art of exposure by transformation and reversal.

3533   " 'From a Fable form a Truth': A Consideration of the Fable in Swift's Poetry." In [10], pp. 193-204.

Argues that Swift was not ridiculing L'Estrange's doctrine about fables in A Tale of a Tub but that Swift himself was indebted to Aesop and Ovid for such fables as those of the "Spider and the Bee" in The Battle of the Books, "The Beasts Confession," "The Fable of Midas," and several other instances.

3534   IRWIN, W. R.
"Swift the Verse Man." PQ 54 (1975): 222-238.

Considers the nature of light verse in general and the specific characteristics of Swift's verse.

3535   JAFFE, NORA CROW.
"Swift and the Agreeable Young Lady, but Extremely Lean." PLL 14 (1978): 129-137. Rpt. [3052], pp. 149-158.

In an effort to explain various difficulties and obscurities in "Death and Daphne," the author argues that Death represents Swift himself and that the poem describes his tutorial relationship with Lady Acheson. The poem evokes Swift's wish that his pupil be made over into an image of himself, while the story of Pluto and Proserpina that Swift weaves into the poem implies possible sexual feelings for Lady Acheson.

3536   The Poet Swift. Hanover, N. H.: Univ. Press of New England, 1977.

A close reading of the whole body of Swift's poetry, providing an "overview" that has hitherto, according to the author, been lacking among Swift's critics. She sees Swift as looking to poetry as an outlet for the energy of his feelings and the pressures of his psychological life. His most effective tool is his own forceful personality, shaped and controlled by his art.

3537   JEFFERSON, D. W.
       "The Poetry of Age." In [3058], pp. 121-137.

       A general survey of Swift's poetry primarily written during
       his late period--his mythological, personal, and comic verse;
       concludes that, though he often writes with a modest Augus-
       tan directness, "both in imagery and in dialectic, and in their
       interplay, he has the agility and inventiveness of the writers
       of a century before."

3538   JOHNSON, MAURICE.
       "Swift's Poetry Reconsidered." In [40], pp. 233-248.

       Structural patterns in Swift's poems, his voice and bio-
       graphical presence, his visualized depictions of himself as
       he ages.

3539   "Text and Possible Occasion for Swift's 'Day of Judgement.'"
       PMLA 86 (1971): 210-217.

       Argues that the specific occasion for the poem was the at-
       tempt of dissenters in 1732-33 to repeal the Sacramental Test
       Act in Ireland, and that for contemporary readers the poem's
       "timeless and wide-ranging relevance" was less apparent than
       its immediate intention of condemning dissenters.

3540   The Sin of Wit: Jonathan Swift as a Poet.   Syracuse, N.Y.:
       Syracuse Univ. Press, 1950.

       A consideration of the wit and humor of Swift's poetry and
       an attempt to interpret his moral, intellectual, and artistic
       aims.   Examines Swift as a conscious craftsman in his use
       of verse rhythms, alliteration, and phonetic echo.

3541   JOHNSTON, OSWALD.
       "Swift and the Common Reader." In [11], pp. 174-190.

       On Swift's poetic technique--"Contrary to our normal ex-
       pectations, he does not allow us to settle upon a recognizable
       poetic style as a means of judgment--as a fixed standard
       whose values we share and against which we can measure
       divergences."

3542   JONES, GARETH.
       "Swift's Cadenus and Vanessa: A Question of 'Positives.'"
       EIC 20 (1970): 424-440.

       Takes issue with F. R. Leavis (Revaluation, Ch. 4) commenting about Swift's "positives." Argues that "Cadenus and Vanessa is a masterpiece of satiric counterpointing; and that Swift is far from resting on his positives with the immovable firmness which has been urged." A close reading of the poem.

3543   KLEIN, JULIE B.
"The Art of Apology: 'An Epistle to Dr. Arbuthnot' and 'Verses on the Death of Dr. Swift.'" Costerus 8 (1973): 77-88.

Examines the two poems for similarities to Roman models and concludes that "like many of the Neoclassicists, Pope and Swift have captured the spirit and temper of the original works rather than observe the demands of structure."

3544   KULISHECK, CLARENCE L.
"Swift's Octosyllabics and the Hudibrastic Tradition." JEGP 53 (1954): 361-368.

Traces the extent and the limitations of the Hudibrastic influence in Swift's poetry; emphasizes striking similarities in tone and in controlling ideas.

3545   MELL, DONALD C., JR.
"Imagination and Satiric Mimesis in Swift's Poetry: An Exploratory Discussion." In [3052], pp. 123-135.

An assessment of Swift's attitude toward language and poetic art. Argues that Swift is aware of the capacities and limits of the satiric imagination to render moral truths and aesthetic ideals, and that his suspicion of the imagination is not so much anti-poetic as "pro-poetic" in that it expresses indirectly a belief in art's moral force: "Through the satirical imagination life is converted into art, which in turn reflects life, and such mimetic action emphasizes processes of creation and criticism, satiric method and purpose."

3546   "Elegiac Design and Satiric Intention in 'Verses on the Death of Dr. Swift.'" CP 6, No. 2 (1973): 15-24.

Approaches the poem by analyzing the interplay between "satirical effects and the elegiac sentiments and design, especially as related to the familiar tensions inherent in the idea of the imagination as a defense against time and mortality, and to the more fundamental opposition between art and time at the heart of the Augustan elegiac mode."

3547   NUSSBAUM, FELICITY.

"Juvenal, Swift, and The Folly of Love." ECS 9 (1976): 540-552.

Juvenal's Sixth Satire, Ovid's Remedia Amoris, and Richard Ames's The Folly of Love provide "a context of commonplaces and set scenes" which influenced Swift's "A Beautiful Young Lady Going to Bed," and gave him "classical precedent for presenting shocking scenes from a woman's private closet." Swift's message is that, when stripped of its feminine mystique, "the boudoir offers a check on lust, a restraint on the madness of passion, and a possibility of rescuing man from his own irrational fancies."

3548 O HEHIR, BRENDAN.
"Meaning of Swift's 'Description of a City Shower.'" ELH 27 (1960): 194-207.

A study of the poem and its commentary as "an urbanized Georgic" shows its impact "to lie within its own terms, and to be primarily an oblique denunciation of cathartic doom upon the corruption of the city."

3549 OHLIN, PETER.
" 'Cadenus and Vanessa': Reason and Passion." SEL 4 (1964): 485-496.

A close study of the poem reveals it as: "A delicately executed dialogue between reason and passion, utilizing the conflict between those two principles as the controlling device." The poem is cool to romantic love and "sets out to discuss the possibility of human love in terms of reason and passion"; it "becomes ... one long metaphor for the fall of man, leading into a presentation of the only love possible in the human situation."

3550 PARKIN, REBECCA PRICE.
"Swift's 'Baucis and Philemon': A Sermon in the Burlesque Mode." SNL 7 (1970): 109-114.

Swift's imitation of Ovid applies burlesque techniques to a concept presented seriously in the original: the metamorphosis no longer directly serves either theology or ethics; as a sermon in verse, the poem preaches against imprudent hospitality, a superstitious belief in miracles, accepting external signs for internal graces, sentimentalism, and against a low opinion of sainthood, parsonhood, and "parson's-wifehood."

3551 PAULSON, RONALD.
"Swift, Stella, and Permanence." ELH 27 (1960): 298-314.

The relationship between body and soul in Swift's poems, especially "Verses on the Death of Dr. Swift," his poems to Stella, and "The Lady's Dressing Room," and Swift's role in this relationship.

3552   PEAKE, CHARLES.
"Swift's 'Satirical Elegy on a Late Famous General.'"   REL 3, No. 3 (1962): 80-89.

An analysis of the poem showing that it has "great emotional power controlled by taut and precise language and by firm poetic organization."

3553   PROBYN, CLIVE T.
"Realism and Raillery: Augustan Conversation and the Poetry of Swift."   DUJ 39 (1977): 1-14.

The dominant tone of Swift's poetry derives from his awareness that life is a drama "of proper places requiring the appropriate public postures" and that the ordinary human voice, expressing with ease and informality the materials of common experience, is the essential ingredient of a dramatic representation of life.   His moral satire uses the idiom and rhythm of conversation to achieve its aims, while at the same time its conversational ease is disrupted by discontinuities and tensions: Swift's poetry is full of talk in conflict with forms and conventions imposed from without.

3554   RAWSON, C. J.
"The Nightmares of Strephon: Nymphs of the City in the Poems of Swift, Baudelaire, Eliot."   In [44], pp. 57-99.

Explores certain aspects of Swift's treatment of cities, and of two inhabitants of the city, the whore and the lady, by comparing those Swiftian features with similar or different features in Baudelaire and Eliot.   Suggests that Swift's employment of parody and Hudibrastic verse in his city poems serves as a visible "dress of thought" to cover or distance the "unsettling nakedness of fact" that revolted him in the life of his age.   Another form of poetic deflation occurs in the parodies of conventional love poetry, in which excremental imagery is played off against erotic idealism.   Swift insists, however, that decency and civilization require that cloacal truth be kept firmly out of sight.   The scatological poems are directed less at the human bodily functions than against the complacency, shoddy idealism, and self-deception of the reader.

3555   " 'Tis only infinite below': Speculations on Swift, Wallace Stevens, R. D. Laing and Others."   EIC 22 (1972): 161-181.

Studies the infinite/circular "chain of rapacity," the life-death cycle, in various poems including Swift's "On Poetry: A Rapsody." Deals with cannibalistic fantasies and the "infinity" of the flea-biting chain as applied to poetry.

3556   REES, CHRISTINE.
"Gay, Swift, and the Nymphs of Drury Lane." EIC 23 (1973): 1-21.

Examines the relation between truth and fiction in the work of Gay and Swift, especially the fiction of the " 'nymph' whose beauty is satirically defined by the conflicting principles of art and nature." Both " ... make original poetry out of the nymph fiction because they have the wit to see how, in conjunction with the concepts of art and nature, this convention can relate to ultimately serious themes."

3557   REICHARD, HUGO M.
"The Self-Praise Abounding in Swift's Verses." TSL 18 (1973): 105-112.

Defends the self-praise in "Verses on the Death of Dr. Swift" as hard to dislike; justified partly by shifts in methods and emphasis within and between the three sections, partly by comic uses of dramatic, rhetorical, and logical forms.

3558   RODINO, RICHARD H.
"Notes on the Developing Motives and Structures of Swift's Poetry." In [3052], pp. 87-99.

Surveying Swift's entire poetic career, Rodino suggests that it divides into four periods: 1) the earliest period, up to 1698, is characterized by verse structures that are inclusive and conciliatory, and in which idealism and honesty contend so strenuously that the poet often failed to reconcile them; 2) the next phase, 1698-1714, contains poems that work defensively, by exclusion and rejection; 3) in the third phase, 1714-1730, Swift employs a structure organized serially, in which independent observations are controlled by spatial form; and 4) in the final period he seems unconcerned about deceiving the reader, at first affirming the existence of "a normative position, a way of understanding the world in moral terms," and then sweeping that position out from under him.

3559   "Blasphemy or Blessing?   Swift's 'Scatological Poems.' "
PLL 14 (1978): 152-170.

From 1730 to 1733, when most of the scatological verse was written, Swift's formal strategy underwent a change: the "vexatious" mode forces the reader to make a seemingly impossible choice between "fraudulent alternatives," such as that between blasphemy and delusive "blessing," in which both alternatives are equally horrible. The scatological poems treat vexatiously the sexual relations of men and women by describing plausible but deceptive speakers who seek the reader's agreement and then trap him into a moral position he cannot accept; the "misanthropic" satirist seems detached from sympathy with the human predicament and "refuses to be identified with a definable moral solution."

3560   "The Private Sense of Cadenus and Vanessa." CP 11, ii (1978): 41-47.

Emphasizes that Cadenus and Vanessa was a private poem, written not for publication but solely for the eyes of Swift and Esther Vanhomrigh. Its motive was not public instruction or public vexation but private assessment of an intimate relationship--"a private experience of physical consummation, together with a more rational 'Delight,' intelligible only to Swift and Vanessa." The poem insists upon the private, personal nature of true love, and emphasizes that the extremes of reason and passion are inadequate to sustain love relationships in the real world.

3561   ROSENHEIM, EDWARD W., JR.
"Swift's Ode to Sancroft: Another Look." MP 73, iv, part 2 (1976): S24-S39.

Presents the writing and publishing history of the ode and argues for greater respect for it than it has hitherto received. The Ode is both a partisan and a polemical document in which Swift appears unable to continue focusing on the "saintly victim" in the presence of his evil oppressors. Satiric artifice is also reflected in the Ode: Swift dramatizes the pose of a satirist "as, time after time, the speaker appears to be forced from his professed panegyric task into helpless rage at the enormities which surround him."

3562   ROTHSTEIN, ERIC.
"Jonathan Swift as Jupiter: 'Baucis and Philemon.'" In [42], pp. 205-224.

Considers the reasons for Swift's revisions, with Addison's assistance, when the original version has more verve than the later one.

3563   ROWSE, A. L.
"Swift as Poet." In The English Spirit: Essays in History

and Literature (London: Macmillan, 1945), pp. 182-192.
Rpt. in [3054], pp. 135-142; [3055], pp. 98-106.

Briefly looks into " ... the background to Swift's thought,
the various elements that entered into it from other thinkers,
where they came from and how they affected him...." A
review of Sir Harold Williams's edition of Swift's poems, the
article insists that "in force, range, persistence, he is a
great poet.   Swift expressed himself more fully and more
continuously in his verse than in his prose. "

3564   San Juan, E. , Jr.
       "The Anti-Poetry of Jonathan Swift. "   PQ 44 (1965):   387-396.

       Analyzes the anti-poetic elements in some of Swift's poetry
       to show that they are manifested "in the intense awareness
       of a unifying sensibility" and that they embodied his "sense
       of proportion between justice and reality. "

3565   SAVAGE, ROGER.
       "Swift's Fallen City: A Description of the Morning. "   In
       [3060], pp. 171-194.

       Sees the poem as basically a mock-descriptio, a comic
       imitation of the classical ideal, reading almost like a parody
       of the dawn-scene in Bysshe's British Parnassus; unless we
       are aware of the Augustan stock-responses to Swift's title,
       we are not likely to gain more than a partial reading of the
       poem.   It is not a piece of uncomplicated realism.

3566   SCHAKEL, PETER J.
       The Poetry of Jonathan Swift: Allusion and the Development
       of a Poetic Style.   Madison: Univ. Wisc. Press, 1978.

       Swift frequently used allusions to "introduce a set of con-
       ventions or a structural framework, to clarify or reinforce
       his themes, and to establish or strengthen his tones. "   Since
       the purpose of allusions is more important than their discovery,
       the author analyzes explicit or repeated allusions, not refer-
       ences to classical figures or literary quotations used in pas-
       sing as decoration or as a means of expression.   Concludes
       that the personal element appears most effectively in the al-
       lusions and that they are indispensable for an understanding
       of Swift as both man and artist.

3567   "Swift's Remedy for Love: The 'Scatological' Poems. "   PLL
       14 (1978):   137-147; rpt. [3052], pp. 136-148; [3566], pp.
       106-120.

Swift intended in the "scatological" poems to suggest his own remedies for romantic and erotic love, the kind of love disparaged in the Stella poems; these remedies were to be comic poems, with an underlying seriousness. Too often, however, the scatological poems fail in whole or part as comedy: Swift was not in total control of his material since he also is offended in some degree by those natural functions of women that he satirizes his characters for being offended at.

3568   "Swift's 'dapper Clerk' and the Matrix of Allusions in 'Cadenus and Vanessa.'" Criticism 17 (1975): 246-261. Rpt. in [3566], pp. 82-96.

A close reading of the poem shows "that Swift achieves control, complexity, and comprehensiveness by his use of a matrix of allusions to 'The Art of Love' and the 'Aeneid.'"

3569   "The Politics of Opposition in 'Verses on the Death of Dr. Swift.'" MLQ 35 (1974): 246-256. Rpt. in [3566] with alterations, pp. 141-146.

Asks the questions: 1) who was the eulogist and what was his relation to Swift the poet and the Swift of the poem? 2) why did Swift select the topics for the eulogist that he did? and 3) what is the relationship of the eulogy to the opening lines of the poem?

3570   "Virgil and the Dean: Christian and Classical Allusion in The Legion Club." SP 70 (1973): 427-438. Rpt. in [3566], pp. 167-177.

"By his selective use of Virgil and the Bible, Swift gains authority for his venomous attack on men who were, in his eyes, guilty of impiety and injustice." By brilliantly fusing "madness with damnation and the classical with the Christian [he made] The Legion Club his finest political satire in verse."

3571   SCOUTEN, ARTHUR H.
"Swift's Poetry and the Gentle Reader." In [3052], pp. 46-55.

Argues that Swift, though his poems were intended for the "gentle reader," always distinguished between public and private poems: he always thought in terms of the intended audience. Scouten warns us of the danger that awaits critics who praise "minor, playful" pieces for their artistic merit or who attempt to interpret light humorous verse when in fact it was intended as an "in-joke," intelligible only to a particular group or family.

3572   SCOUTEN, ARTHUR H. and ROBERT D. HUME.
"Pope and Swift: Text and Interpretation of Swift's Verses
on His Death. "   PQ 52 (1973): 205-231.

Traces and compares four versions of the poem to show
its final basic structural coherence.

3573   SHINAGEL, MICHAEL.
A Concordance to the Poems of Jonathan Swift.   Ithaca, N. Y. :
Cornell Univ. Press, 1972.

3574   SLEPIAN, BARRY.
"The Ironic Intention of Swift's Verses on His Own Death. "
RES 14 (1963): 249-256.

An analysis of the style and structure of the poem and its
ironic attack upon vanity to show that Swift was not really
taking himself seriously.   Refutes John Middleton Murry's
statement that the latter part of the poem is not good.

3575   SOLOMON, HARRY M.
" 'Difficult Beauty': Tom D'Urfey and the Context of Swift's
'The Lady's Dressing Room. ' "   SEL 19 (1979):   431-444.

Gives evidence to show that the situation, the diction and
the imagery of Swift's poem derives either from early Augustan pastoral or from Restoration scatological satire, and shows
an especially close similarity to D'Urfey's "Paid for Peep-
ing. "   Specifically applies the image of the nymph to the poem
in which the pastoral goddess, Celia, has been "shifted of
her divinity. "

3576   SOLOMON, MILLER.
" 'To Steal a Hint was never known': The Sodom Apple Motif
and Swift's 'A Beautiful Young Nymph Going to Bed. ' "   TSL
22 (1977): 105-116.

Suggests that Swift's poem was not original but that he was
deeply indebted to Restoration anti-feminist poems such as
"The Folly of Love" and "A Satire Against Wooing," and that
he was especially influenced by Matthew Prior's 1718 Works.

3577   STEENSMA, ROBERT C.
"Swift's Apologia: 'Verses on the Death of Dr. Swift. ' "
PUASAL 42 (1965): 23-28.

Intends "to show how the 'Verses on the Death of Dr. Swift'
reviews the course of Swift's career as a Churchman, a polit-

ical propagandist, and a literary man; and how the poem defends his view and use of the satiric mode."

3578   TYNE, JAMES L., S. J.
       "Swift and Stella: The Love Poems." TSL 19 (1974): 35-
       47.

       Discusses eleven poems Swift addressed to Esther Johnson;
       argues that he compliments her less on her physical attributes
       than on her psychological character, seeing her above all as
       a person of "masculine" good sense and good humor. Swift
       celebrates amor benevolentiae, not amor concupiscientiae.

3579   "Swift's Mock Panegyrics in 'On Poetry: A Rapsody.'" PLL
       10 (1974): 279-286.

       Swift's parody serves a serious satiric purpose, "almost
       every phrase has a double allusion, and the marvelous skill
       of the workmanship is only appreciated when the irony is
       thoroughly understood." Swift imitates both the stylistic char-
       acteristics and sycophantic position of the laureates, Eusden
       and Cibber, to parody their poetic ineptitude, while at the
       same time he incorporates into his lines verbal echoes from
       the verses that Horace and Virgil directed to Augustus and
       Maecenas.

3580   "Vanessa and the Houyhnhnms: A reading of 'Cadenus and
       Vanessa.'" SEL 11 (1971): 517-534.

       Considers the problem of "determining exactly how much
       moral integrity can be expected of finite and conditioned human
       beings in an imperfect world" and concludes that Vanessa is
       more Houyhnhnm than human, that the poem has the same
       meaning as Gulliver's Travels: if one seeks complete perfec-
       tion, rationality, and moral goodness one cannot find such
       absolutes in our finite world.

3581   UPHAUS, ROBERT W.
       "Swift's 'Whole Character': The Delaney Poems and 'Verses
       on the Death of Dr. Swift.'" MLQ 34 (1973): 406-416.

       "Verses on the Death of Dr. Swift" has been misread be-
       cause its connection with the Delaney poems has been ignored;
       yet both the Delaney poems and the "Verses" reveal a shift
       in Swift's literary method from irony to autobiography, for
       it is not an abstract principle but Swift himself who is the
       poem's most obvious model.

3582   "Swift's Poetry: The Making of Meaning." ECS 5 (1972): 569-586.

     Argues that Swift is not "anti-poetic," but that he writes poetry by "projecting his own vision of reality--a simultaneous opposition to the visionary imagination and a firm commitment to the material world as the primary source of human knowledge--within certain traditional literary conventions."

3583   "From Panegyric to Satire: Swift's Early Odes and A Tale of a Tub." TSLL 13 (1971): 55-70.

     Suggests that a relationship exists between the disunity of the odes and Swift's use of satire in A Tale of a Tub, and that the "persona of A Tale is, to a large extent, a satiric representation of Swift's own Pindaric self, and the early odes may well be precursors of the 'Artificial Mediums, false Lights, refracted Angles, Varnish, and Tinsel' that Swift satirizes in A Tale of a Tub."

3584   VANCE, JOHN A.
     "As Much for Swift as They Are for Stella." GyS 5 (1978): 87-95.

     A study of the six "Birthday" poems which Swift wrote to Stella to "bring into focus a strong and somber personal theme which reflects [his] concern for his advancing age and inevitable demise," and to show that these poems should be read as much for what they can tell us about Swift's character as for what they say about Stella.

3585   VIETH, DAVID M.
     "Metaphors and Metamorphoses: Basic Techniques in the Middle Period of Swift's Poetry, 1698-1719." In [3052], pp. 56-68.

     Suggests that many of the poems that Swift wrote between 1698 and 1719 can be understood as "transforming metaphors or metaphorical metamorphoses"; or that they depict mock-Ovidian metamorphoses or mock-Christian miracles--mock in that the metamorphoses change nothing essential. Each technique "involves, in intention at least, a eucharistic transformation of the bread and wine of life into the body and blood of art, which may be triumphantly successful on the part of the poet, or hilariously unsuccessful on the part of his subjects, or--ideally --both at once."

3586   "The Mystery of Personal Identity: Swift's Verses on His Own Death." In [38], pp. 245-262.

Adopts an "affective" approach to <u>Verses on the Death of</u>
<u>Dr. Swift</u>, an approach less in terms of intrinsic meaning
than in terms of reader response, and attempts to analyze
the multiplication of identities, several of which can be called
"Jonathan Swift." Concludes that the <u>Verses</u> are another example of "Swift's uncanny skill in perpetrating hoaxes, as
with the Bickerstaff Papers and the Drapier's Letters," in
which Swift creates a fantasy that not only competes with
reality but pushes it aside and takes its place.

3587 "Fiat Lux: Logos versus Chaos in Swift's 'A Description of
the Morning.'" <u>PLL</u> 8 (1972): 302-307.

A reading of the poem "as a parody of Creation, as depicting a postlapsarian world of disorder and imperfection...."

3588 WAINGROW, MARSHALL.
"Verses on the Death of Dr. Swift." <u>SEL</u> 5 (1965): 513-518.

Argues that the "eulogy is neither unqualified, nor is it
qualified by a totally negating irony.... The poem shows that
[Swift's] vanity is knowledgeable, that it doesn't disguise his
kinship with other men, and that upon such knowledge virtue
may be built." Concludes that the poem's expanding moral
is that "that private end which is death can indeed have its
public uses."

3589 WALLER, CHARLES T.
"Swift's <u>Apologia Pro Satura Sua</u>." <u>SNL</u> 10 (1973): 19-25.

Argues that "An Epistle to a Lady, Who Desired the Author
to Make Verses on Her in the Heroic Style" is an important
poem in Swift's poetic canon; that it is a "complete and successful adaptation of the traditional <u>apologia pro satura sua</u>."

3590 WILLIAMS, AUBREY.
"Swift and the Poetry of Allusion: 'The Journal.'" In <u>Liter-</u>
<u>ary Theory and Structure: Essays in Honor of William K.</u>
<u>Wimsatt</u>. Eds. Frank Brady, John Palmer, and Martin Price
(New Haven & London: Yale Univ. Press, 1973), pp. 227-
243.

A close reading of the poem (later "The Country Life")
seen as a "humorous yet telling illustration of the way in
which the quite humdrum, and quite autobiographical, events
of a manorial day may be turned into an artful and canny
comment on the inherent dissatisfactions of mortal life...."

3591   WIMSATT, WILLIAM K.
       "Rhetoric and Poems: The Example of Swift." In [38], pp.
       229-244.

           Attempts to "show some of the main ways in which the
       short couplet, rather than the long, emerged as [Swift's] ap-
       pointed expressive instrument."

3592   WOOLLEY, JAMES.
       "Autobiography in Swift's Verses on His Death." In [3052],
       pp. 112-121.

           Analyzes a specific instance of Swift's self-characterization
       in order to resolve the conflict between what Swift said and
       what he meant or intended; concerned, in other words, with the
       relationship between what Swift says to what he believed about
       himself.   The author, therefore, compares statements in
       "Verses on the Death of Dr. Swift" with other statements
       mainly drawn from the letters in order to gain a view of Swift
       that he himself took seriously.   Concludes that the "eulogy
       as a whole is far closer to a serious representation of Swift
       than is sometimes supposed."

3593   "Friends and Enemies in Verses on the Death of Dr. Swift."
       Studies in 18th Cent. Culture 8 (1979):   205-232.

           The poem's intended meaning can be more fully revealed
       by emphasizing the themes of friendship and enmity: "To
       that end, I seek to show how the poem emphasizes friendship
       of a particular kind; then, to illuminate a crucial context of
       the poem in the details of Swift's actual friendship and enmity
       with Queen Caroline and Mrs.   Howard; and finally, to discuss
       some implications of this subject for the poem's most vexed
       critical problem, which is the interpretation of the concluding
       eulogy on Swift."

See also: 3070, 3076, 3111, 3173, 3175, 3177, 3184

Miscellaneous Works

3594   BACKSCHEIDER, PAULA R.
       "The First Blow Is Half the Battle: Swift's 'Conduct of the
       Allies.'"   In [5], pp. 47-55.

           Examines The Conduct of the Allies as literature, as more
       satire than essay; the success of The Conduct was caused by
       Swift's disguising his pamphlet as a political essay, thereby
       disarming the defenses of those who know they are reading

satire.   Analyzes the various rhetorical devices by which
Swift effectively satirizes the folly of the English people and
suggests that The Conduct is unanswerable because of its fictional elements.

3595   COOK, RICHARD I.
        Jonathan Swift as a Tory Pamphleteer.   Seattle: Univ. Wash.
        Press, 1967.

        Analyzes specific rhetorical techniques and approaches in
        Swift's Tory tracts; provides a biographical context and sur-
        veys Swift's more important works written prior to 1710 and
        after 1714 in order to clarify the significance of the pamphlets
        in his artistic career.

3596   "Swift's Polemical Characters."   Discourse 6 (1962-63): 30-
        38, 43-48.

        Discusses Swift's technique of "detachment" in his satiric
        portrayal of character in his Tory tracts.

3597   "The 'Several Ways ... of Abusing One Another':   Jonathan
        Swift's Political Journalism."   Speech Monographs 29 (1962):
        260-273.

        Swift's range of stylistic and rhetorical techniques in his
        Tory tracts.   "Much of [his] effectiveness is attributable to
        the skill with which [he] ... manipulated such specific rhetori-
        cal devices as imagery, anecdote, analogy, historical example,
        allegory, insinuation...."

3598   "Swift as a Tory Rhetorician."   TSLL 4 (1962): 72-86.

        Discusses Swift's persuasive devices (ethical, pathetic, and
        logical appeals) in the Examiner papers, the Conduct of the
        Allies, and the History of the Four Last Years of the Queen;
        the character Swift presents to his readers is essentially his
        own, and, despite his self-declared moderation, he was "above
        all an aggressive polemicist much more interested in attacking
        his enemies than in proselytizing them."

3599   DOWNIE, J. A.
        "The Conduct of the Allies: The Question of Influence."   In
        [3057], pp. 108-128.

        An account of the origin, characteristics, themes, and
        historical occasion of Swift's Conduct of the Allies.   Suggests
        that the art of the pamphlet lies "not in the use of more ex-

pected Swiftian rhetorical devices such as irony and satire, but in the manner in which Swift impresses himself on his audience as a plain speaker, frank, ingenuous, when in fact he is quite the opposite."

3600 EHRENPREIS, IRVIN.
"Letters of Advice to Young Spinsters." In [43], pp. 245-266.

Discusses letters between Swift and Esther Johnson and Swift and Esther Vanhomrigh to determine "how deeply his genius as an author is connected with, or derived from, his attitude toward women."

3601 "Swift's Letters." In [3058], pp. 197-215.

The letters as literature; discusses the form of the eighteenth-century "spontaneous" epistle and Swift's variations within that form.

3602 "The Literary Side of a Satirist's Work." Minn. Rev. 2 (1962): 179-197.

Using Swift's "An Argument Against Abolishing Christianity," the author discusses the source of a reader's pleasure in reading satire: it is not in discovering the author's purpose but in appreciating a situation in which "one man, the reader, is listening with pleasure to the abuse or ridicule which a second man, the author, is dropping upon a third man, the object of satire." Also analyzes Swift's "disconcerting propositions" and attempts to resolve his paradoxes.

3603 EVANS, JAMES E.
"Swift's Partisan Pen: The Example of Lord Wharton." Enl. E. 6 (1975): 13-21.

Swift's satires against Wharton in the Examiner and A Short Character "still usefully remind us that greatness and goodness are not synonymous and help us anatomize the disguises of artful politicians"; they also "remain remarkably vigorous performances, displaying the nicest touches of Swift's partisan pen."

3604 FERGUSON, OLIVER W.
" 'Nature and Friendship': The Personal Letters of Jonathan Swift." In [1], pp. 14-33.

Excerpts from some of Swift's letters show that they were

spontaneous and natural but also that Swift considered the
writing of letters a literary art.

3605   HAMILTON, DAVID.
        "Swift, Wagstaff, and the Composition of Polite Conversation."
        HLQ 30 (1967): 281-295.

        Correlates George Mayhew's interpretations [3614] of Polite
        Conversations with an analysis of the Introduction, and refutes
        Mackie Jarrell's conclusions [3607] that Swift took his mater-
        ials for Polite Conversations from printed collections of prov-
        erbs; argues that "the literary merit of the Introduction
        arises from its carefully controlled dramatic irony."

3606   HARTH, PHILLIP and LELAND D. PETERSON.
        "Swift's Project: Tract or Travesty?" PMLA 84 (1969):
        336-343.

        A series of critical exchanges between Harth and Peterson
        regarding Peterson's interpretation of Swift's Project for the
        Advancement of Religion and the Reformation of Manners [3615].
        Harth takes exception to Peterson's ironic and satirical read-
        ing of the Project.

3607   JARRELL, MACKIE L.
        "The Proverbs in Swift's Polite Conversation." HLQ 20 (1956):
        15-38.

        Traces proverbs to written material rather than oral.

3608   JOHNSON, MAURICE.
        "Swift and 'the Greatest Epitaph in History.'" PMLA 68
        (1953): 814-827.

        Considers Swift's epitaph to himself as "a conscious work
        of art, composed from the materials of [his] experience" and
        discusses the various epitaphs of the period, many of which
        he wrote.

3609   JONES, MYRDDIN.
        "Further Thoughts on Religion: Swift's Relationship to Filmer
        and Locke." RES 9 (1958): 284-286.

        Argues that Swift's fragment, Further Thoughts on Religion,
        is refutation of Sir Robert Filmer's statement of the doctrine
        of the Divine Right of Kings in Patriarcha, and that it follows
        the argument previously laid down by Locke.

3610   KAY, JOHN.
        "The Hypocrisy of Jonathan Swift: Swift's Project Recon-
        sidered. " UTQ 44 (1975): 213-223.

            Argues that the Project is not a satire exposing the hy-
        pocrisy of the Societies for the Reformation of Manners, for
        Swift was serious in advocating hypocrisy as an acceptable
        social norm. Argues also against the existence of a persona,
        for Swift speaks in his own voice, and suggests that the Proj-
        ect is an attack on the anti-clerical policies of the Whigs.

3611   KELLY, ANN CLINE.
        "Swift's Polite Conversation: An Eschatological Vision. " SP
        73 (1976): 204-224.

            Paper is divided into two parts: a discussion of the human-
        ist concern with conversation and Swift's affinity with its basic
        tenets, and his familiarity with the conversation cookbooks
        which he parodies in Polite Conversation: "The function of
        the parody is to highlight the irrationality Swift thought this
        genre embodied--irrationality, which left unchecked, could
        destroy ... society.... " Polite Conversation is, in a sense,
        "an eschatological vision in which civilization perishes by
        boring itself to death. "

3612   LEIN, CLAYTON D.
        "Rhetoric and Allegory in Swift's Examiner 14. " SEL 17
        (1977): 407-417.

            An examination of Examiner 14, on political lying, reveals
        that Swift's views on the Tory's assumption of power were
        more "complex and colored" than previously supposed and
        provides new insights into Swift's polemical techniques.   The
        principal rhetorical pattern consists of the polarization im-
        plicit in a vision of warring demonic and heavenly forces;
        the essential structure of the essay may be found in the defin-
        ition of things sacred and profane. Equally important is Swift's
        secret allegory concerning "Truth, who is said to lie in a
        Well, " but who eventually prevails with the triumph of the
        Tory opposition.

3613   McKENZIE, ALAN T.
        "Proper Words in Proper Places: Syntax and Substance in
        The Conduct of the Allies. " ECS 1 (1968): 253-260.

            Discusses effectiveness of the pamphlet by analyzing Swift's
        use of words: "His own style ... relies heavily on nouns....
        Swift has too long been credited with skill with res, when he
        was also a master of verba. "

3614   MAYHEW, GEORGE P.
        "Swift's Anglo-Latin Games and a Fragment of Polite Conversation in Manuscript." HLQ 17 (1954): 133-159.

        Analysis of Huntington Library Manuscript (HM14341) which consists of Swift's Anglo-Latin games with language written between 1734 and 1736, some used in Polite Conversation, showing Swift's use of puns.

3615   PETERSON, LELAND D.
        "Swift's Project: A Religious and Political Satire." PMLA 82 (1967): 54-63.

        Traces the attitude toward hypocrisy at the time the Project for the Advancement of Religion and the Reformation of Manners was written and the reasons behind Swift's advocacy of hypocrisy, primarily his desire to embarrass the Whig ministry. [See 3606]

3616   PHILMUS, ROBERT M.
        "Swift's 'Lost' Answer to Tindal." TSLL 22 (1980): 369-393.

        The suggestion that the Argument Against Abolishing Christianity represents Swift's "lost" answer to Matthew Tindal's The Rights of the Christian Church (1706) helps to account for the apparent hyperbole of Swift's satiric fiction and also "discloses an irony sufficiently complex to accommodate all of the other suggested victims of the satire." The governing logical paradox is that "nominal Christianity" must be preserved; therefore the Argument's final irony is simply that it must be upheld for the sake of "real" Christianity.

3617   QUINLAN, MAURICE J.
        "Swift's Project for the Advancement of Religion and the Reformation of Manners." PMLA 71 (1956): 201-212.

        Considers the influences that led Swift to write the Project, the emphasis in the essay, and his position at the time he composed it.

3618   ROBERTSON, MARY F.
        "Swift's Argument: The Fact and the Fiction of Fighting with Beasts." MP 74 (1976): 124-141.

        The controversy over the Argument resolves itself into three questions: 1) was Swift in any way capable of defending nominal Christianity for any purpose? 2) who is the speaker

of the Argument? and 3) who or what is the satiric target?
The speaker both does and does not defend nominal Christianity, depending on which of his aspects he assumes at any
given moment; assuming that hypocritical freethinkers are
vicious, the speaker uses nominal Christianity to keep them
fighting so that real Christianity will not be abolished. The
conclusion is that we should not despise the "edifier" for not
speaking in defense of real Christianity or for subjecting nominal Christianity to scorn.

3619   ROSENHEIM, EDWARD, JR.
       "Swift and the Martyred Monarch." PQ 54 (1975): 178-194.

       Argues that Swift's "Sermon Upon the Martyrdom of King
       Charles I" merits more attention than it has received, and
       that it demonstrates Swift's characteristics both as a preacher
       and as a polemicist.

3620   SAMS, HENRY W.
       "Jonathan Swift's Proposal Concerning the English Language:
       A Reconsideration." In [47], pp. 76-87.

       Speculates on Swift's purpose in writing the Proposal and
       its political overtones, and provides evidence that Swift wrote
       his imitation of part of the Seventh Epistle of the First Book
       of Horace because of his discontent at being appointed Dean
       of St. Patrick's.

3621   VAN METER, JAN R. and LELAND D. PETERSON.
       "On Peterson on Swift." PMLA 86 (1971): 1017-1025.

       Criticizes the view of Leland D. Peterson in "Swift's Proj-
       ect: A Religious and Political Satire" [3615] that the Project
       for the Advancement of Religion and the Reformation of Man-
       ners (1709) is a satire; with Peterson's reply.

3622   WEITZMAN, ARTHUR J.
       "A Spider's Poison: Wit in Swift's 'Letter of Advice to a
       Young Poet.'" ArielE 4, No. 1 (1973): 24-34.

       Suggests Swift's "stylistic ideal: simple, bare, direct ex-
       pression undisfigured by the clichéd wit of the age"; A Letter
       deflates the popular homage to wit, and also confesses Swift's
       "sin of wit" in his own career--such self-revelation confirms
       Swift's authorship.

See also: 3068, 3082, 3095, 3132, 3166, 3189, 3236, 3374, 3490

General Studies

3623 ADAMS, PERCY G.
"James Thomson's Luxuriant Language." In [61], pp. 118-135.

An analysis of how the consonant and vowel echoes affect the quality of Thomson's "luxurious language" in The Four Seasons. His constant revision of the poem over a twenty-year period shows the development of his art and technique.

3624 ADEN, JOHN M.
"Scriptural Parody in Canto I of The Castle of Indolence." MLN 71 (1956): 574-577.

Suggests that Thomson seeks to ensnare the innocent and virtuous by clothing his appeal in phrases and tones reminiscent of Holy Scripture. The action of the first canto parodies the biblical account of the Fall: "The Scriptural parody frames the more obvious Spenserian core of the canto, which begins with an allusion to the curse placed upon fallen man by God and a mock dramatization of the temptation, and ends with a scene ... suggestive of hell."

3625 CAMERON, MARGARET M.
L'Influence des Saisons de Thomson sur la Poésie Descriptive en France, 1759-1810. Paris: H. Champion, 1927.

Cameron traces the fortunes of "des Saisons en France" naming French writers influenced by Thomson. Chapters on the philosophical and narrative elements and on the theory of descriptive poetry.

3626 CAMPBELL, HILBERT H.
James Thomson. Boston: Twayne, 1979.

Aims to "provide a critical account of the poetic and dramatic career" of Thomson; incorporates material that has become available since G. C. Macaulay's life in 1908. Rejects the view that Thomson was a complete anomaly in his own period, and urges that the "nature and significance of not only [his] accomplishments but also his failures can be grasped only by placing him squarely in the context of his backgrounds, ambitions, and purposes as an Augustan writer."

3627   "Thomson's Seasons, the Countess of Hertford, and Elizabeth Young: A Footnote to The Unfolding of the Seasons." TSLL 14 (1972): 435-444.

Agrees with and supports Ralph Cohen in The Unfolding of the Seasons, that Thomson wrote about personal feelings and incidents more often than critics have supposed; gives as an extended example the "tortured lover" passage in Spring (ll. 1004-73), which was written while Thomson was deeply in love with the Countess of Hertford. That passage can be linked to Thomson's love for the Countess.

3628   CHALKER, JOHN.
"Thomson's Seasons and Virgil's Georgics: The Problem of Primitivism and Progress." Studia Neophilologica 35 (1963): 41-56. Rpt. in part in [87], pp. 90-140.

A consideration of the meaning and function of Thomson's patriotic and moral passages and why he mixed description and morality the way he did. Discusses the Georgic influence on the Seasons, especially the contrast between the Golden and the Iron age and the theme of patriotic exaltation.

3629   COHEN, RALPH.
The Unfolding of "The Seasons": A Study of James Thomson's Poem. Baltimore: The Johns Hopkins Press, 1970; London: Routledge & Kegan Paul, 1971.

A full-length study of The Seasons analyzing Thomson's adaptations of language to convey his vision of the world. Tries to show "unity" in The Seasons by pointing out how patterns of repetition of images, themes, and words are used to "connect" parts of each season and of the poem as a whole.

3630   "Spring: The Love Song of James Thomson." TSLL 11 (1969): 1107-1182. Rpt. in [3629], Chap. I.

A comprehensive analysis arguing the artistic validity of the poem. Cohen discusses rhetorical techniques of harmony and disharmony in lines 1-233; illusive allusion and themes of harmony in lines 234-571; and the contrary contexts of language and love in lines 867-1176. Spring is a "witty, comic, pathetic, sometimes even sublime song that moves between the actual and the ideal, between life as it is or can be and life as it was in the Golden Age."

3631   "An Introduction to The Seasons." Southern Rev. (Adelaide)
        3 (1968): 56-66.

        Primarily an examination of Thomson's language and style--
        his use of periphrasis, images, metaphors, participles (to
        convey a sense of process), adjectives, and hyphenated words;
        also discusses the characters in the poem (the two chief ones
        being the narrator and God), and the relation between man,
        nature, and God: "Thomson develops the relation ... by mov-
        ing from particulars to prospects to infinity."

3632   "Thomson's Poetry of Space and Time." In [2], pp. 176-192.

        Although Thomson's poetry dealing with changes of nature
        in time and space was based on georgic conventions, he fre-
        quently experimented with new expressions for space and time.
        The essay analyzes these experiments and their artistic ef-
        fects.   Discusses Thomson's view of nature and his innovation
        of combining personification and natural description.

3633   The Art of Discrimination: Thomson's "The Seasons" and
        the Language of Criticism.   Berkeley: Univ. Calif. Press,
        1964.

        "This is a book about criticism: it explores the principles
        and practice of criticism applied to a single poem, James
        Thomson's The Seasons (1730-46).... This book analyses
        claims and comments that English critics have made about
        The Seasons" between 1750 and 1960. "It is not an explica-
        tion of the poem ... but of interpretations of the poem."
        Appendix includes checklist of editions of The Seasons.

3634   "Literary Criticism and Artistic Interpretation: Eighteenth-
        Century English Illustrations of The Seasons." In [39], pp.
        279-306.

        Notes that illustrations at their best are not merely decor-
        ations but, as the original meaning shows, "explanation" or
        "spiritual enlightenment"--a comment on the text. "Illustra-
        tion plays an extremely important part in the criticism of the
        Seasons because for more than one hundred and fifty years it
        was the most illustrated poem in the English language." The
        illustrations need to be "read" with the text. Interpretive
        shifts are shown by the changes in illustrations in succeeding
        editions.

3635   COOKE, ARTHUR L.
        "James Thomson and William Hinchcliffe." JEGP 57 (1958):
        755-761.

Refutes earlier statements by C. A. Moore and Alan D. McKillop that Thomson was not influenced by a four-poem sequence of Hinchcliffe, entitled "The Seasons," which appeared in 1718. Cooke finds more resemblances than the earlier critics did and nominates Hinchcliffe to the list of Thomson's sources.

3636   CRONK, GERTRUDE GREENE.
        "Lucretius and Thomson's Autumnal Fogs." Amer. Jour. of
        Philology 51 (1930): 233-242.

        "Thomson's description of autumnal fogs represents his generalized observation permeated with Lucretian theory and principle, and often expressed in language derived from Lucretius, or from Lucretius as adapted by Milton."

3637   DAS, P. K.
        "James Thomson's Appreciation of Mountain Scenery." Englische Studien 64 (1929): 65-70.

        Identifies Thomson as being by common critical consent "the first original figure of considerable importance in the dawn of Naturalism in English poetry." Marshals the evidence to prove that his love of nature is not as limited as other critics would have it, but that his appreciation of the awesome, savage, stark, and terrible in mountain scenery was strongly felt and effectively expressed.

3638   DOUGHTY, W. LAMPLOUGH.
        "The Place of James Thomson in the Poetry of Nature."
        London Quart. & Holborn Rev. 174 (1949): 154-158, 249-254.

        Thomson's picture of nature in The Seasons shows that he was a literary photographer of great skill but not an artist, that he taught others to see, and that he had a great influence on other poets.

3639   DRENNON, HERBERT.
        "James Thomson and John Norris." PMLA 53 (1938): 1094-1101.

        Explores and details Thomson's indebtedness, in "Upon Happiness," to John Norris who was one of the early influences to which he was exposed. Doctrines of "The Moral Gravity of the Soul" and Norris's recipes for the achievement of happiness are discussed for their effect on Thomson.

3640   "Newtonianism in James Thomson's Poetry." Englische Studien 70 (1936): 358-372.

Thomson was attracted to the scientists because they were interpreting the world in which he lived. Newton as philosopher-scientist, with Boyle, Bacon, and others, gave him the beautifully logical world of scientific rationalism. Thomson's Newtonianism is illustrated with quotations from his works.

3641   "James Thomson's Ethical Theory and Scientific Rationalism." PQ 14 (1935): 70-82; also see 175-176.

Thomson's ethical theory studied against the background of his times is seen to be that of an ethical rationalist. Through Nature he comes to the doctrine of "moral gravitation" or the law of benevolence.

3642   "James Thomson's Contact with Newtonianism and His Interest in Natural Philosophy." PMLA 49 (1934): 71-80.

Analyzes Thomson's education at the University of Edinburgh between 1715 and 1725 to trace the beginnings of his attitudes in religion and philosophy. His writings are shown to bear witness to thorough grounding in the natural philosophy of the times.

3643   "Scientific Rationalism and James Thomson's Poetic Art." SP 31 (1934): 453-471.

Traces the relation between the scientific movement of the period and Thomson's choice of nature as a poetic theme and his theory of poetic art which was dominated by scientific rationalism.

3644   GRANT, DOUGLAS.
James Thomson: Poet of "The Seasons." London: Cresset Press, 1951.

Tells only the story of Thomson's life, and neither criticizes the poetry in detail nor writes a history of his philosophical ideas. Prints for the first time Thomson's letters to Miss Elizabeth Young.

3645   GREENE, DONALD.
"From Accidie to Neurosis: The Castle of Idolence Revisited." In [44], pp. 131-156.

Considers the poem in its moral and psychiatric context in an effort to prove that it should be taken seriously; concludes that The Castle of Indolence is a "discussion of a personal psychological or psychiatric--in the end, theological--problem of Jemmy Thomson himself, and at the same time of a universal one of the fallen human condition of all ages."

3646   HAGSTRUM, JEAN H.
        "James Thomson." In [112], pp. 241-267.

        Attempts to "separate Thomson from the forerunners of
        romanticism and place him firmly among his neoclassical
        contemporaries." Discusses his iconic idealization; his re-
        lationship with seventeenth-century landscape as a whole; and
        his personfication of nature, which was his "chief instrument
        in creating the pictorial image."

3647   HAMILTON, HORACE E.
        "James Thomson's 'Seasons': Shifts in the Treatment of Pop-
        ular Subject Matter." ELH 15 (1948): 110-121.

        Follows the Seasons from its youthful author's first version
        through revisions which show more and more influences from
        Harris's Travels, Defoe's Robinson Crusoe, and other ac-
        counts from geographers and adventurers, added for authen-
        ticity and wider interest. Many of these elements were omit-
        ted in the final version of 1744 or substantiated with scien-
        tific evidence.

3648   HAVENS, RAYMOND DEXTER.
        "Primitivism and the Idea of Progress in Thomson." SP 29
        (1932): 41-52.

        There is a dichotomy in Thomson's writings showing "his
        enthusiasm for progress and likewise for pastoral simplicity."
        This "dichotomy was not superficial but profound; it sprang
        from a cleavage in his life and led to one in his work, in
        his taste, and in his sense of values."

3649   "Thomson." In The Influence of Milton on English Poetry
        (Cambridge: Harvard Univ. Press, 1922; rpt. New York:
        Russell & Russell, 1961), pp. 123-148.

        Sees the main significance of The Seasons as lying in its
        popularity: for it showed how real nature could be dealt with
        effectively in poetry, and how blank verse could be used in
        writing about everyday things--two accomplishments that could
        not have occurred had Thomson not been popular. Discusses
        Thomson's kinship with Milton, as in his love for the grand
        style; and especially emphasizes the nature of Thomson's dic-
        tion.

3650   HUGHES, HELEN SARD.

"Thomson and the Countess of Hertford." MP 25 (1928):
439-468; 28 (1931): 468-470.

Evidence, gleaned from the Percy manuscripts at Alnwick
Castle, seems to demonstrate the friendly intercourse with
the Countess--despite Dr. Johnson's statement to the contrary.

3651   HUNT, JOHN DIXON.
"The Ingenious and Descriptive Thomson." In [121], pp. 105-
144.

Argues that "once poets had acquired certain habits of
looking and thinking inside a garden they found them equally
serviceable beyond the ha-ha." Also emphasizes the increased
role of landscape gardens in the revised versions of The Seasons as Thomson came to realize that they were a useful
means of formulating and shaping his thoughts among natural
scenery. Thomson tried to link the "internal territory of his
mind" with the external world by replacing traditionsl emblems
and iconographical language with expressive images found in
the early English landscape garden.

3652   JOHNSON, WALTER GILBERT.
James Thomson's Influence on Swedish Literature in the Eighteenth Century. Univ. Ill. Std. in Lang. & Lit., Vol. 19
(1936), Nos. 3-4.

Traces the influence of Thomson on some ten Swedish poets
of the eighteenth century; concludes that his influence was twofold: he was more influential in the development of nature
poetry than any other poet, and he contributed greatly to the
development of patriotic verse in Sweden.

3653   KERN, JEAN B.
"James Thomson's Revisions of Agamemnon." PQ 45 (1966):
289-303.

Primarily concerned with the revisions made between January 14, 1738, when the manuscript was submitted for approval of the licenser, and April 24, 1738, when the first
edition was printed. But this is more than a textual analysis
of the manuscript; it contains a lively recital of the assistance
of other writers, the involvement of the manager of Drury
Lane theater, of Mrs. Cibber, and others.

3654   "The Fate of James Thomson's 'Edward and Eleanora.'"
MLN 52 (1937): 500-502.

Refutes Addison's statement that this play was unreasonably
banned in 1739. The ban reflected the quarrel between the

king and his son, the Prince of Wales, who was Thomson's patron; by eighteenth-century political standards, the ban was reasonable.

3655   McKILLOP, ALAN D.
        "The Early History of Alfred." PQ 41 (1962): 311-324.

        Provides not only a history of the masque's production and its relation to the musical career of Thomas Arne, but also emphasizes its original political intentions and discusses its content and its imperfect fusion of the pastoral and the patriotic themes.

3656   "Thomson and the Licensers of the Stage." PQ 37 (1958): 448-453.

        Follows Thomson's problems with the government Licensers from 1737 to about 1741. Thomson's writings often carried a thinly disguised political message, which was the ultimate cause of his difficulty.

3657   The Background of Thomson's "Liberty" (Rice Inst. Pamphlet: monograph in English, Vol. 38, No. 2). Houston: Rice Institute, 1951.

        It is not the intention of the present study to "rehearse the early external and textual history of the poem ... but rather to offer some account of the ideas and patterns"; describes the poem's political-historical themes in their contemporary contexts, and specifically Thomson's political intentions.

3658   "The Early History of Thomson's Liberty." MLQ 11 (1950): 307-316.

        Considers the date of composition, the printing history of the several editions, and provides textual variations.

3659   "Thomson and the Jail Committee." SP 47 (1950): 62-71.

        Thomson's lines in Winter (ll. 340-361) in praise of the Committee headed by General Oglethorpe to inquire into the state of the prisons are considered in relation to some other contemporary references to the Committee.

3660   "Ethics and Political History in Thomson's Liberty." In [17], pp. 215-229.

"Whig liberty" is celebrated by Thomson after his trip to Italy, where the English gentleman customarily mourned over the once-great Rome, whose mantle of liberty has fallen to England. His anti-Walpole politics and beliefs as seen in Liberty are discussed. The influence of the Craftsman is emphasized.

3661   The Background of Thomson's "Seasons." Minneapolis: Univ. Minn. Press, 1942; rpt. Hamden, Conn.: Archon Books, 1961.

Mainly concerned with the general philosophical and literary conditions in which Thomson worked; deals specifically with his use of natural science and of the literature of travel and geography.

3662   MARSH, ROBERT.
"The Seasons of Discrimination." MP 64 (1967): 238-252.

A comprehensive review of Ralph Cohen's The Art of Discrimination: Thomson's "The Seasons" and the Language of Criticism [3633]. Contains Marsh's own interpretations and analyses of the critical tradition of The Seasons.

3663   MIRZA, TAQI ALI.
"Deism in Thomson's 'The Seasons.'" Osmania Jour. of English Std. 2 (1962): 55-60.

Although the first version of Winter (1726) is largely free of deistic thought, the second edition (1730) has included so many references to deism that they cannot be considered extraneous to the basic scheme.

3664   NICHOL SMITH, DAVID.
"Thomson and Burns." In [141], pp. 56-80; rpt. in [18], pp. 180-193.

Discusses Thomson and Burns as representative poets of the eighteenth century. "Both of them were Scots, and neither could have written as he did had he not been a Scot." Thomson, as a nature poet, "meditates the book of Nature. His interests are partly intellectual, partly moral, and ... what he says comes 'warm from the heart'." Burns, the national poet of Scotland " ... kept to the old subjects, the old measures, and the old manner [but] was original in the mastery with which he used them."

3665   POTTER, G. R.

"James Thomson and the Evolution of Spirits." Englische
Studien 61 (1926): 57-65.

Treats of the changes from the earlier to the later versions
of the Seasons to show the change and growth in Thomson's
philosophical thinking, particularly in his theory of spirit-
evolution. Potter reconstructs Thomson's thought processes
on which such concepts as "chain of being" and the doctrine
of Pythagoras were influential.

3666 PRICE, MARTIN.
"The Theater of Nature: James Thomson." In [153], pp.
351-361.

A discussion of Thomson's images and of the basic pattern
or design of The Seasons: " ... there is a double movement
--the descent of God in plentitude and ascent of man's mind
in recognition of order. Between the two stands the challenge
that lies at the outward edge of plentitude before the ascent
can begin: the threat of the ambiguous or the meaningless."

3667 ROGERS, PAT.
"James Thomson and the Correspondence of the Seasons."
Revue des Langues Vivantes 42 (1976): 64-81.

Discusses the pattern of seasonal correspondences which
influenced Thomson--the pattern that links together abstract
concepts, physical and psychological characteristics, meteoro-
logical phenomena and the standard "elements," all related
to the signs of the Zodiac. This broad scheme affected The
Seasons on several levels, ranging from diction and imagery
to theme and narrative; the author concentrates on the significance of that relationship for verbal texture.

3668 SPACKS, PATRICIA M.
"James Thomson: The Retreat from Vision." In [167], pp.
46-65.

Argues that The Castle of Indolence does not rely on visual
imagery, and that the sense of hearing becomes increasingly
important; "Thomson elevates the technique of negative suggestion ... into a vital structural principle." His images
are frequently impressionistic.

3669 "Vision and Meaning in James Thomson." SIR 4 (1965): 206-
219; rpt. as "James Thomson: The Dominance of Meaning"
in [167], pp. 13-45.

Defends Thomson in The Seasons against the charge that

he possesses a clear physical vision but lacks the gift of
transforming imaginative vision; raises the question about the
poetic value of Thomsonian descriptions; and argues that much
of Thomson's description is not visual at all but reveals a
preoccupation with emotional and intellectual significances
rather than with visual appearances: "In Thomson's imagery,
meaning does not really inhere in the landscape; it is felt as
the product of human imagination or intelligence contemplating
the natural scene." Defends Thomson's style and concludes
that its "special diction and syntax ... derive from his constant, almost obsessive effort to reveal the patterns he perceives as he 'sees' the world."

3670   The Varied God: A Critical Study of Thomson's "The Sea-
        sons" (Univ. Calif. English Studies No. 21).   Berkeley &
        Los Angeles: Univ. Calif. Press, 1959.

        Deals with the "relation between Thomson's ideas about
        man and nature and his poetic techniques and achievements,"
        and approaches the poem "as both an aesthetic and a sociologi-
        cal phenomenon." Considers four main aspects of poem: em-
        phasis on cosmic order, descriptive technique, use of scien-
        tific material, and treatment of human morality; discusses
        the achievement and the weakness of the poem.

3671   SPENCER, JEFFRY B.
        "James Thomson and Ideal Landscape: The Triumph of Pic-
        torialism." In Heroic Nature: Ideal Landscape in English
        Poetry from Marvel to Thomson.   (Evanston: Northwestern
        Univ. Press, 1973), pp. 253-295.

        Regards Thomson as the "culmination of the heroic tradition
        in landscape and an anticipation of the later fully developed
        picturesque ... the nature of his landscapes and the sources
        from which they derive link him closely to the other Augus-
        tans and beyond them to poets of the previous century like
        Milton and Dryden."

3672   TODD, WILLIAM B.
        "The Text of 'The Castle of Indolence.'"   ES 34 (1953): 117-
        121.

        Compares the first three editions or printings of The Castle
        of Indolence in an attempt to identify the definitive edition.

3673   WELLS, JOHN EDWIN.
        "Thomson's Seasons 'Corrected and Amended.'"   JEGP 42
        (1943): 104-114.

"Deals with verbal changes in The Seasons that appear in
the issues of 1750, 1752, 1757, and 1762." Indicates that
Lyttleton made extensive changes which were protested by
Murdoch.

3674   "Thomson's Britannia: Issues, Attribution, Date, Variants."
        MP 40 (1942): 43-56.

        Describes the complicated printing history of Britannia,
        listing nine issues appearing between 1729 and 1744 and re-
        cording the variants among those issues as well as the var-
        iants in the Aldine and Oxford texts. Suggests that the poem
        was probably written in December 1728 or January 1729.

3675   WILLIAMS, CHARLES A.
        "James Thomson's 'Summer' and Three of Goethe's Poems."
        JEGP 47 (1948): 1-13.

        Directs attention to "Goethe's use of lines from 'Summer'
        in three of his best-known poems composed within a period
        of little more than a decade from 1773 on. A few parallels
        from other parts of The Seasons and from Liberty [are] in-
        cluded."

3676   WILLIAMS, GEORGE G.
        "Did Thomson Write the Poem To The Memory of Mr. Con-
        greve?" PMLA 45 (1930): 1010-1013.

        Analyzes the style and structure of the poem; finds evidenc
        favoring Thomson's authorship.

3677   WILLIAMS, RALPH M.
        "Thomson's 'Ode on the Winter Solstice.'" MLN 70 (1955):
        256-257.

        Gives complete text of this manuscript poem, unpublished
        at least until the date of this article. Offers speculation as
        to why it was never published.

3678   "Thomson and Dyer: Poet and Painter." In [27], pp. 209-
        216.

        Accounts for the change in style from Winter (1726), in
        which passages of description consist mainly of single details,
        to Summer, in which the pictorial elements consist of "land-
        scape" and "prospect," to Thomson's friendship with John Dyer.

See also: 143, 503, 1490, 2035, 2093

General Studies

3679   BAILEY, MARGERY.
"Edward Young." In [27], pp. 197-207.

A general survey of Young's life and career, emphasizing in particular the new note in poetry that he represents: " ... his characteristic work shows a vigorous individual straining at the bonds of correctness and regularity, and often breaking through them to assert himself."

3680   BIRLEY, ROBERT.
"Edward Young: 'Night Thoughts.'" In Sunk Without a Trace (London: Rupert Hart-Davis; New York: Harcourt, Brace & World, 1962), pp. 76-109.

Although Young "uses a completely conventional form, that of the poetry of Melancholy and Night, to treat a completely conventional subject, the defence of the revealed Christian religion against infidelity," his manner of writing was original and the poem deserves to be read more today that it is. Its strength comes from the fact that Young was compelled to write the poem because of the deaths of three people close to him; his purpose was to destroy infidelity.

3681   BLISS, ISABEL ST. JOHN.
"Young's Night Thoughts in Relation to Contemporary Christian Apologetics." PMLA 49 (1934): 37-70.

Takes the position that Young's aim was to follow the outstanding defenders of religion and that Night Thoughts should be classified as religious apologetics.

3682   Edward Young. New York: Twayne, 1969.

A biography from today's perspective, correcting many widespread misconceptions concerning the man and his writings. Includes an "overview" of each of his writings.

3683   BROWN, WALLACE C.

"Young and Cowper: The Neo-Classicist Malgré Lui." In
[81], pp. 120-141.

Analyzes Young's use of the heroic couplet in Love of Fame,
The Universal Passion and the two epistles to Pope, and Cowper's group of eight satires and didactic poems. Although
neither was a master of the heroic couplet, their poems illustrate the persuasive power of this poetic form.

3684 CLARK, HARRY HAYDEN.
"The Romanticism of Edward Young." Trans. Wisc. Acad.
Sci., Arts & Letters 24 (1929): 1-45.

Emphasizes Young's kinship with the Romantic movement
by seeking to "discover which of his doctrines he held in common with those later nineteenth century writers generally referred to as romanticists"; discusses such characteristics as
Young's dissatisfaction with actual life, his love of solitude,
his conception of the imagination, his revolt against the rules,
his preference for spontaneity and the teachings of nature in
place of learning and logic, and his attitude toward nature.
Finally, the author seeks to define the results of Young's romanticism, especially as it seems to cause his melancholy;
concludes that a large part of the cause for that melancholy
much be located in Young's romantic philosophy of life: he
failed to maintain a balance between extremes, emphasizing
romantic imagination, solitude, escape from the world, and
the teaching of nature.

3685 "A Study of Melancholy in Edward Young." MLN 39 (1924):
129-136, 193-202.

Young is regarded as especially qualified to be studied as
an index to the changing literary taste of his times because
he is a mixed or linking poet, partly of the past, partly of
the future. His brand of melancholy is examined for the
growing sentimentalism of the day and for its causes in his
personal life and his philosophy. In Part II, the connection
between melancholy and solitude is discussed. Young's religious convictions as part of his attitude toward the world,
his tendency to go to extremes, and other aspects of his personality are explored as causes of his melancholy.

3686 GOLDSTEIN, LAURENCE.
"Graveyard Literature: The Politics of Melancholy." In
[107], pp. 73-94.

The Christian writings of the graveyard school represent,
among other things, a stringent criticism of worldliness, an
antipastoral mode, and a systematic attack on pagan pleasure.

They deemphasize man's physical body in order to exalt his
spiritual body soon to be gained, and similarly devalue the
natural world for the same reason. No writer in that tradition enjoyed apocalyptic scenes more than Edward Young: his
imagination takes fire when he "dramatizes acts of annihilation or the casualties of terrific force and power." As the
century progressed, poets turned to childhood experiences
and events for anticipations of a happy existence to come; of
this tendency, Cowper is the best example, especially of the
relation between nostalgia and the ruin sentiment. The past
became a refuge from an unhappy present, but his memories
of childhood produced pain as well as pleasure.

3687   HALL, MARY S.
        "On Light in Young's Night Thoughts." PQ 48 (1969): 452-
        463.

        Young's Night Thoughts, now considered outmoded largely
        because of its oppressive melancholy, has more to offer when
        read as a reasoned yet emotional philosophic statement about
        the nature of man. Hall's reading equates its lugubrious be-
        ginning with the first part of an evangelical sermon which in-
        duces melancholy or "conviction of sin"; the latter part, like
        the joyful hymns after a candidate has been saved, is intended
        to shed light. Thus the final effect should be positive since
        the poem seeks to prove that man has a divine nature by pro-
        gressing from darkness to light. Without a belief in immor-
        tality man experiences only melancholy darkness; Young uses
        rational proofs of revelation drawn from the Cambridge Pla-
        tonists, Newtonian science, and Physico-theology.

3688   KELLY, RICHARD M.
        "Imitation of Nature: Edward Young's Attack upon Alexander
        Pope." XUS 4 (1965): 168-176.

        Argues that Young's theories concerning imitation are very
        similar to Pope's; that Pope, like Young in the Conjectures,
        stressed the importance of originality over imitation, and that
        their views on the rules of composition are similar--they
        should not restrict the poet's invention.

3689   McKILLOP, ALAN D.
        "Richardson, Young, and the Conjectures." MP 22 (1925):
        391-404.

        Provides new evidence for an account of the Conjectures
        by discussing Young's letters to the Monthly Magazine for
        1813-19; these letters "help to explain the intrusion of the
        story of Addison's death."

3690   MUTSCHMANN, H.
        "The Origin and Meaning of Young's Night Thoughts" (Acta
        et Commentationes Universitatis Tartuensis, B, XLIII. 5).
        Tartu, Estonia: 1939.

            Suggests that it was Young's illness that occasioned the
        poem, and that Philander represented the poet's ideal self,
        Lorenzo his real self.

3691   ODELL, DANIEL W.
        "Young's Night Thoughts as an Answer to Pope's Essay on
        Man." SEL 12 (1972): 481-501.

            A close look at Night Thoughts reveals that "Young regards
        the Essay as a misleading argument on the insufficient basis
        of reason alone that man's complaints about his condition in
        this world not only question God's providence but reveal as
        mere pride and vanity the belief God created all things for
        man." Examines the way in which "Night Thoughts confronts
        two of the most significant contemporary problems, man's
        nature and place in the chain of being, and the problem of
        evil."

3692   "Young's Night Thoughts and the Tradition of Divine Poetry."
        BSUF 12 (1971): 3-13.

            Argues that the personal, subjective note in Young is best
        explained in terms of the Renaissance-Christian tradition of
        divine poetry; he allied himself, in other words, with a tra-
        ditional conception of poetry by emphasizing genius and in-
        dividuality and by supporting a belief in the high purpose of
        poetry that has been made sublime by Christian themes.

3693   "Locke, Cudworth and Young's Night Thoughts." ELN 4 (1967):
        188-193.

            "Night VI reveals ... influence of Locke but also an epis-
        temology opposed to Locke's and formulated in terms strik-
        ingly similar to those of ... Cudworth, who believed that
        knowledge is made possible by innate ideas, not ... by the
        senses."

3694   PETTIT, HENRY.
        "The Making of Croft's Life of Young for Johnson's Lives of
        the Poets." PQ 54 (1975): 333-341.

            An account of the origin and reception of Sir Herbert Croft's
        Life of Young written at the request of Johnson for inclusion
        in the Lives; especially the reception of Croft's "subtle derog-

ation of Young's character" by the Temple family, and Boswell's activities in the affair.

3695   "The Occasion of Young's Night Thoughts." ES 50 (1969):
Anglo-Amer. Suppl.: xi-xx.

Poses the question, what really occasioned this poem?
Postulates that the cause was Young's close brush with death
in 1740 which moved him to a long undertaking in self-portrayal,
taking several years to complete.

3696   "The English Rejection of Young's Night Thoughts." Univ.
Colo. Studies in Lang. & Lit. 6 (1957): 23-38.

Traces the rejection of the poem, on both moral and aesthetic grounds, from the beginning to the middle of the nineteenth century. George Eliot uncompromisingly rejected it because of its false emotion.

3697   "Preface to a Bibliography of Young's Night Thoughts." In
Elizabethan Studies and Other Essays in Honor of George F.
Reynolds (Univ. Colo. Studies, Series B, Stds. in the Humanities, vol. 2, No. 4). Boulder: Univ. Colo. Press (1945):
215-222.

Intends not so much to consider the conditions of printing
and the traditions both linguistic and social that surrounded
the printing of Night Thoughts as "to describe the more striking details of the special pattern of circumstances peculiar"
to its publication.

3698   SITTER, JOHN E.
"Theodicy at Mid-Century: Young, Akenside, and Hume."
ECS 12 (1978): 90-106.

A comparison of the similarities between Night Thoughts
and The Pleasures of the Imagination and then their differences
from Pope's An Essay on Man show that the two poems have
more in common with each other than they do with Pope's
essay. Also speculates that "the poetic world of Pope and
the blanker universe of Young and Akenside" are "analogous
to the distance separating the philosophic procedures of Locke
and Hume...." Both poets, like Hume, "dramatize individual
isolation and inescapable egocentricity."

3699   STEVENS, IRMA NED.
"Beckett's Texts for Nothing: An Inversion of Young's Night
Thoughts." Std. in Short Fiction 11 (1974): 131-139.

Suggests that, in Beckett's Texts for Nothing, the narrator's preoccupation with death is a theme that seems to go back to the eighteenth-century school of graveyard poets who emphasized the physical aspects of death; a hint of influence is supplied in Text VIII in an allusion to the title of Young's poem: "nights' young thoughts." The Texts resemble Night Thoughts in setting, imagery, characterization of the elderly, and treatment of the theme of time. Concludes that " ... Beckett consistently employs motifs associated with the graveyard tradition for ends quite unlike those of Young. Throughout the Texts, echoes of the imagery and themes of Night Thoughts suggest that Beckett has Young in mind and is consciously referring to Young's poem for an ironic purpose. In essence Beckett is not following but inverting the graveyard tradition."

3700   WHITBURN, MERRILL D.
"The Rhetoric of Otherworldiness in Night Thoughts." ELWIU 5 (1978): 163-174.

Whereas analyses of Night Thoughts usually either deal with the narrative aspects--Young's reaction to the death of his friends--or with the argument--his attempt to convince Lorenzo and the reader to forego earthly pursuits for "Otherworldliness"--this study attempts to "resolve the dichotomy" between the two approaches. It suggests a central coherence in which both narrative and argument are functional. Young's appeal becomes rational, emotional, and ethical when viewed as "a rhetorical attempt to discourage secularism and encourage otherworldliness."

3701   WICKER, C. V.
Edward Young and the Fear of Death: A Study in Romantic Melancholy (Univ. N.M. Publ. in Lang. & Lit. no. 10). Albuquerque: Univ. N.M. Press (1952), pp. 7-100.

Studies in what way Young contributed significantly to the development of melancholy as a recurrent and dominant theme of nineteenth-century romanticism; considers such topics as his relation to the Graveyard School, the causes of his melancholy, evidences of his fear of death from both Night Thoughts and the minor works, his influence and literary fate.

See also: 503, 1921, 2232